Crime and Justice

Crime and Justice
A Review of Research
Edited by Michael Tonry

VOLUME 39

The University of Chicago Press, Chicago and London

The University of Chicago Press, Chicago 60637
The University of Chicago Press, Ltd., London

ISSN: 0192-3234

ISBN: 978-0-226-80881-9

LCN: 80-642217

Contents

Preface

When *Crime and Justice* was created in 1977, Norval Morris and I would never have believed or predicted that it would be alive and thriving a third of a century later. In many prefaces we noted, usually with a sense of wonderment, that the series was publishing its tenth or twentieth or thirtieth volume or had been in business for lengthening periods of years. That sense persists.

The people who have written for *Crime and Justice* are the key to such success as the series has had. Review, rewriting, and editing processes have been unusually exacting from the outset. To a remarkable degree writers have put up with them with equanimity. Many have been willing to write more than once. The recidivists this time are Philip J. Cook and Peter Reuter, whose first—now classic and still-cited—essays in the series, on deterrence and the economics of drug control, respectively, were published in the 1980s, and Kathy Daly and John Laub, whose first appeared a little later. The other writers in this volume are a healthy mix of distinguished senior scholars and rising stars.

Inevitably in a series that specializes in review essays on contemporary research and policy subjects, the contents of most volumes reflect current policy preoccupations. Volume 39 is no exception. Police innovation and punishment policy have been the primary subjects of institutional change in recent decades; this volume has two fine essays on policing (vol. 38 contained a sizable number on punishment policies and their effects). The primary targets of police and punishment initiatives have been drug offenses and violent and sexual crimes; one essay in this volume concerns the effectiveness of drug policies, and three concern violence and sex crimes. The others concern the effects of community characteristics and changes on crime, the underlying causes of racial disparities in imprisonment, and national and international approaches for monitoring conditions inside prisons.

Many of the essays in this volume are sequels to earlier ones that proved particularly influential. Research on crime and the criminal justice system came of age in the 1980s and 1990s. Much more is known now than in earlier times. David Kirk and John Laub's essay on community crime careers builds on and updates many of the essays in volume 8, *Communities and Crime* (1986), which Albert J. Reiss Jr. and I edited. Jonathan Caulkins and Peter Reuter's essay nearly a quarter century later updates and expands on Reuter's "Risks and Prices: An Economic Analysis of Drug Enforcement" (vol. 7). Stephen Mastrosfki and James Willis's on police organization succeeds Al Reiss's influential essay on "Police Organization in the Twentieth Century" (vol. 15), and Michael Reisig's on problem-oriented and community policing is a worthy successor to Mark Moore's "Problem-Solving and Community Policing" (also vol. 15). Keith Soothill's essay on child sexual abuse, Philip J. Cook, Denise Gottfredson, and Chongmin Na's on school violence, Dirk van Zyl Smit's on prison conditions, and mine on racial disparities in prison build on worthy predecessors. Only the essay by Kathy Daly and Brigitte Bouhours on attrition in the processing of rape cases covers largely new ground.

Crime and Justice essays involve much work by many people: the writers and their assistants; people who served, in some cases more than once, as referees (Philip J. Cook, Anthony Doob, John Eck, Jeffrey Fagan, Marie Gottschalk, Richard Harding, Candace Kruttschnitt, Roxanne Lieb, Daniel Nagin, Kevin Reitz, Wesley Skogan, Cassia Spohn, Ralph Taylor, James Q. Wilson, and Franklin E. Zimring); staff of the University of Chicago Press, especially Tess Mullen and Sarah Ibis and the copy editors who work with her; and not least Su Smallen and Adepeju Solarin, who oversee every detail of the preparation of the essays and the production of the volumes. I am grateful to them all. Readers will decide for themselves whether the final product justifies all that effort.

Michael Tonry
Deer Isle, Maine, September 2010

Michael D. Reisig

Community and Problem-Oriented Policing

ABSTRACT

Community and problem-oriented policing have shaped the debate over the role of the American police for three decades. In the 1990s, the federal government provided billions of dollars via the COPS program to promote police reform. During this time, community and problem-solving practices became more common. Research focusing specifically on whether COPS grants directly resulted in reductions in crime remains mixed. Two archetypes of community policing can be identified, each rooted in a different neighborhood theory of crime: broken windows theory and social disorganization theory. Problem-oriented policing draws on theories of criminal opportunity, such as routine activity and rational choice theory, to direct interventions aimed at altering environmental conditions to reduce crime and disorder. The weight of the empirical evidence is that community and problem-oriented policing can reduce crime and disorder. Many important questions require systematic investigation.

Over the past 30 years, debate in the United States over the role of the police has largely focused on community and problem-oriented policing. In practice, these two strategies are highly compatible and are often employed simultaneously. However, they are conceptually distinct and should be understood as such. Community policing includes a variety of philosophical and operational elements that are geared toward developing police-community partnerships to address neighborhood conditions that give rise to public safety concerns, including crime, disorder, and fear of crime. Problem-oriented policing provides an analytic framework (the scanning, analysis, response, and assessment [SARA] model) used by police to identify and solve problems that result in repeated calls for service. Such concerns may transcend neigh-

Michael D. Reisig is professor of criminology and criminal justice at Arizona State University.

borhood boundaries or be contained to a single street corner and may be directly related to crime or not. Police responses may vary from one problem to the next.

Following a period in American police history marked by corruption, inefficiency, and discrimination, municipal policing agencies during the early part of the twentieth century became bureaucratized, and the police mandate was narrowed to crime suppression. In the 1960s, however, the crime control model was viewed by many as too abrasive, contributing to high levels of disaffection with local police, especially among African Americans. Several high-profile studies, published in the 1970s, called into question the effectiveness of crime control policing strategies (e.g., routine motorized patrols), and departments began experimenting with alternatives to the status quo. In the late 1970s and early 1980s, community and problem-oriented policing emerged. Problem-oriented policing changes the prime focus of the police away from incidents toward identifying, understanding, and solving problems. Community policing redefines the role of the public. Instead of playing a passive role, citizens are invited to partner with the police to improve neighborhood conditions. In these ways, both reforms are historically distinct.

The move toward community and problem-oriented policing received considerable financial backing from the federal government in the 1990s. From 1995 to 2008, the Community Oriented Policing Services (COPS) program awarded more than $13 billion in grants to local police agencies to hire community policing officers and foster police-community problem solving, among other things. During this time, tens of thousands of community policing officers were hired, and policing agencies of all shapes and sizes reported greater involvement in community policing and problem-solving activities. To date, however, the research evidence addressing whether COPS grants reduced crime rates is inconclusive.

Two distinct models of community policing can be identified, both of which employ a variety of common practices and tactics to improve neighborhood quality of life. One, rooted in broken windows theory, emphasizes the use of disorder reduction police strategies (e.g., misdemeanor arrests, situational prevention, and citizen involvement) to reduce neighborhood crime. Studies focusing on departmentwide broken windows strategies across precincts typically operationalize order maintenance policing very narrowly (i.e., misdemeanor arrests; see, e.g., Kelling and Sousa 2001). Studies evaluating the effects of broken windows policing interventions targeted at specific locations have been able to focus on a more complete set of police practices and tactics (see, e.g., Braga and Bond 2008). Overall, the research shows that broken windows policing reduces crime and disorder.

A number of studies have also tested key hypotheses derived from broken windows theory. Perhaps most important are the assessments of the crime-disorder nexus. While some studies find support for the contention that disorder causes crime (Skogan 1990), other researchers report that the effect of disorder on crime is spurious once neighborhood-level structural characteristics and social processes are accounted for (Sampson and Raudenbush 1999). The disorder-crime link remains a topic of controversy.

A second approach to community policing is rooted in the basic tenets of social disorganization theory and focuses on bolstering local community social processes that mediate the adverse effects of structural constraints (e.g., poverty) on crime, disorder, and analogous outcomes. Ethnographic research has described how formal social control agents can work with community members to improve neighborhood conditions (Carr 2005). For example, problem-solving training and beat meetings are among the mechanisms that the police can provide to boost the effectiveness of informal social controls. Although this variety of community policing appears promising, quantitative research on the effects of formal-informal social control linkages on crime and crime-related outcomes is limited. Available research does indicate, however, that police-community collaboration mediates the adverse effect of structural disadvantage on neighborhood quality of life.

Environmental criminologists view problem-oriented policing as a method of preventing and controlling crime (Wortley and Mazerolle 2008). A primary objective of police officials during the problem-solving process is to determine how environmental conditions can be manipulated to reduce opportunities for crime. Rational choice and routine activity theory provide guidance in this respect. Overall, the research literature shows that problem-oriented policing interventions are quite effective at dealing with crime, although the magnitude of the effect generally varies with the methodological rigor of the study (i.e., weaker studies show stronger effects). Research has also examined problem-oriented policing in practice, revealing that the standards specified by the SARA model are rarely met by police officers on the beat.

Despite the growing number of important empirical contributions to the community and problem-oriented policing literatures, gaps and limitations remain. Research is needed that develops more precise measures of order maintenance policing, evaluates the potential intervening role of social processes (e.g., collective efficacy) on the effect of misdemeanor arrests on violent crime, and assesses whether community policing practices (e.g., beat meetings) promote levels of collective efficacy.

This essay is divided into five sections. Section I provides an overview of community and problem-oriented policing, highlighting the key elements of both. Section II discusses the history of the American police, with an aim to place community and problem-oriented policing in historical context. In Section III, the extent and nature of the federal government's involvement in community and problem-oriented policing via the COPS program are described, and the research assessing the effects of the program on crime rates is reviewed. Section IV focuses on the theoretical frameworks that guide community and problem-oriented policing interventions. This section also reviews the relevant research and identifies lingering theoretical and research issues. Section V concludes by specifying priorities for future research.

I. An Overview

Community and problem-oriented policing are conceptualized as "organizational strategies." Moore (1992), for example, argues that both concepts represent strategic attempts to redefine the traditional functions of the police; to modify key programs, tactics, and technologies on which the police rely; and to redefine sources of police legitimacy. If properly implemented, community and problem-oriented policing entail changing the way in which police work was conducted for much of the twentieth century.

A. Community Policing

Community policing is sometimes framed as an amorphous philosophy that permeates every aspect of a police department. While this conceptualization may be partly correct, individuals have used this view to label traditional law enforcement tactics, such as exploratory traffic stops, erroneously as community policing. Others view community policing as limited to specific police activities, such as school-based drug prevention programs and foot patrols. In practice, community policing often includes specific operational programs and tactics, but it encompasses much more.

Community policing is a multidimensional concept. Cordner (1999) groups the many elements of community policing into four key dimensions: philosophical, strategic, tactical, and organizational. The *philosophical dimension* includes the core ideas and beliefs about what the police should do. For example, community policing values and promotes the active solicitation of input from neighborhood residents and civic organizations, especially with regard to decisions and policies that affect local residents. Citizens often want the police to address a variety of problems, such as maintaining social order and providing nonemergency assistance to area citizens, which go beyond the traditional police mandate (Trojanowicz and Bucqueroux 1990). Community policing also involves the adoption of a personal service orientation to police work, which requires that local norms and values are taken into consideration, along with organizational, professional, and legal factors, during decision making at all levels of the police organization.

When the philosophical elements of community policing are translated into police action, Cordner (1999) contends, the focus shifts to the *strategic dimension*. From an operational standpoint, community policing requires police officers regularly to seek out face-to-face interactions with the general public. Two strategic elements aid officers in this endeavor. First, police officers spend less time in their squad cars by adopting alternative patrol strategies (e.g., foot and bike patrol). Second, police officers are assigned to specific beats for extended periods. These two elements not only help officers develop positive relationships with local residents but also familiarize them with neighborhood concerns (Skogan 2008*b*). Breaking down the social distance between the police and public can pay off in the form of increased levels of public trust and support.

Specific police practices and behaviors are included in the *tactical dimension* (Cordner 1999). One of the key tactical elements of community policing is problem solving. Following the four-step problem-solving process established by Goldstein (1979, 1990; discussed below), police officers are encouraged to investigate and develop an understanding of local problems and tailor community-specific solutions to address them (Goldstein 1987). Police-community partnerships to solve local problems lie at the heart of community policing. The ability of police officers to build meaningful partnerships with local residents hinges to a great extent on how officers conduct themselves during everyday, routine interactions with the public. Officers who treat citizens respectfully, take time to listen to their concerns, and inquire about local problems on a regular basis are better able to cultivate active participation among residents in collaborative problem-solving projects, which also helps to ensure that police services are consistent with citizens' expectations.

The *organizational dimension* concerns altering traditional structural arrangements within police departments to support community policing activities (Cordner 1999). The paramilitary organizational structure that dominated American policing during the mid-twentieth century is not conducive to collaborative problem-solving practices (Greene 2000). Instead, community policing requires flattening the organizational hierarchy (i.e., reducing the number of ranks) and increasing the formal authority and responsibility of low-ranking officers (Trojanowicz and Bucqueroux 1990). Rules and supervisory practices are loosened to allow beat officers to use their creativity to solve local problems (Kelling and Moore 1988). Finally, community policing requires police departments to be systematic information seekers. Programs are evaluated, crime patterns are analyzed, and information is shared within the organization, with other municipal agencies, and with the community. In this way, police departments become catalysts for community change.

Over the past two decades, American police departments have adopted and implemented different community policing elements. The result has been a hodgepodge of organizational arrangements, strategies, and tactics that varies from one city to the next. Different forms of community policing can also be observed within cities across beats. This is to be expected. After all, neighborhood problems and resources (both financial and social) vary both qualitatively and quantitatively between and within cities (Skogan 2008*b*). Despite widespread variation in the practice of community policing, an overarching conceptual definition has been advanced: "Community policing is a philosophy that promotes organizational strategies, which support the systematic use of partnerships and problem-solving techniques, to proactively address the immediate conditions that give rise to public safety issues such as crime, social disorder, and fear of crime" (U.S. Department of Justice 2009*a*, p. 3).

B. *Problem-Oriented Policing*

Problem-oriented policing entails identifying, understanding, and solving the array of troubles that prompt citizens repeatedly to call on the police for service and assistance. In an influential article, Herman Goldstein (1979) provided the basic structure of problem-oriented policing. Since that time, advocates have used the SARA acronym to market the problem-solving process outlined by Goldstein (Eck and Spelman 1987).

During the *scanning* stage, the police work to define a problem. To accomplish this task successfully, the police should avoid broad classifications based on criminal codes (e.g., auto theft, assault, and burglary). Broad labels, according to Goldstein, are problematic because they are too heterogeneous. Instead, Goldstein insists that the police develop highly nuanced and precise problem definitions (e.g., joyriding, bar fights, and burglaries of college dorms). The geographic scope of problems that police identify may vary widely. For example, the police may focus on problems that occur in contained spaces, such as street corners and alleyways. Other problems may take place throughout large portions of a city, such as a rash of convenience store robberies.

The second stage involves *analysis*. Here, the police work to understand the magnitude and nature of the problem. Doing so is critical for identifying the underlying factors that are responsible for causing problems. Successful analysis requires information. According to Goldstein, the police should not simply rely on traditional information sources (e.g., crime records) but should take advantage of the information that is available from other agencies and community residents, among other sources. Bynum (2001, p. 8) recommends that police departments form "analysis teams" composed of individuals, such as patrol officers, crime analysts, and external researchers, with relevant knowledge and skills to develop a thorough understanding of problems.

Next, the police need to search for possible solutions. During the *response* stage, Goldstein (1979, p. 250) advises the police to engage in an "uninhibited search for alternative responses that might be an improvement over what is currently being done." The response may focus primarily on the time and location of crime events and involve traditional law enforcement tactics (e.g., directed patrols and crackdowns; termed "enforcement problem-oriented policing"), or it may call for mobilizing local residents and city agencies to collaborate with police in a developing situational response (termed "situational problem-oriented policing"; Braga and Weisburd 2006, p. 146). The chief criterion used when selecting the preferred response should be which tactics provide the greatest likelihood of eliminating the problem at hand.

Finally, the police need to conduct a rigorous *assessment* to determine whether their solution worked and identify ways in which responses can be altered to improve future interventions. Sherman (1991) urges police officials to employ basic principles of evaluation research when assessing the results of problem-solving activities (e.g., testing and instrumentation). However, the use of social science methodologies to evaluate interventions falls outside the scope of traditional police work. Accordingly, police departments committed to problem-oriented policing are encouraged not only to develop internal evaluation capabilities but also to form partnerships with external evaluators (Scott et al. 2008).

As an analytic framework, problem-oriented policing is quite versatile. So it is not surprising that problem-oriented policing has taken many forms in police departments in the United States, United Kingdom, and elsewhere. When problem-oriented policing is implemented in a manner that closely conforms to Goldstein's conception, operations are usually based in centralized units. Doing so allows analysts to examine problems and dispense advice to police officers directly involved in planning responses and provide technical assistance to assess intervention outcomes (Eck 2006). In recent years, however, it has become much more common for frontline officers to engage in problem-solving endeavors, often with little or no support from departmental crime analysis units. The problems handled by these officers are usually less ambitious and problem-solving processes less rigorous than those Goldstein originally called for (Cordner 1998).

C. Conclusion

Community and problem-oriented policing are often used in tandem. For example, some departments that have adopted both strategies encourage community policing officers, who are responsible for specific geographic areas, to implement problem-oriented policing techniques (Scott et al. 2008). It is argued that community policing officers' familiarity with their beats provides them with firsthand knowledge that helps facilitate the problem-solving process (Leigh, Reed, and Tilley 1996). It is also worth noting that officers who have dedicated considerable efforts to establishing ties with the community likely have significant reserves of local support to draw on as they work collectively to solve neighborhood problems.

Although the two strategies may work well in concert, community and problem-oriented policing are distinct concepts, and differences must be duly noted. For example, while community policing considers citizen involvement a necessity, it is not a requisite in problem-oriented policing. Under the latter strategy, the process of solving problems may entail the police working with local residents, but it may also be that the responsibility of enacting and carrying out problem-solving measures falls squarely on the shoulders of the police. What is more, problem-oriented policing allows the police to identify problems on their own or consider problems nominated by community members. And unlike community policing, problem-oriented policing does not emphasize the use of specific tactics (e.g., alternative patrol strategies) or significant alterations to existing organizational arrangements (e.g., reducing the number of ranks). In short, while community policing promotes building collaborative police-citizen partnerships to address neighborhood problems, problem-oriented policing seeks to identify and develop a sophisticated understanding of the underlying factors causing problems, design effective police responses, and assess the effect of police interventions.

The history of American policing is littered with strategies and tactics that initially were received with great enthusiasm but eventually fell out of favor. The cycle of adopting and replacing policing models has continued for more than a century. It was through this evolutionary development of American policing that community and problem-oriented policing emerged onto the scene.

II. Historical Development

Policing scholars regularly frame the historical development of the American police as a three-stage process: early uniformed police, bureaucratic policing, and community and problem-oriented policing (see, e.g., Kelling and Moore 1988). Although such a conceptualization of police history mistakenly implies that police reform in the United States is revolutionary in nature, it nevertheless provides the means (albeit imperfect) to organize historical developments. It is more accurate to view the transition between successive stages as gradual, thus reflecting a more evolutionary development.

A. First Stage: Early Uniformed Police

Early policing in the United States was greatly influenced by the English experience. The first modern police force, the London Metropolitan Police, was established in 1829. The home secretary, Sir Robert Peel, and his commissioners sought to establish a police force that did not resemble a standing army and in which officers (or "bobbies") maintained a healthy level of social distance from community members (Monkkonen 1981). This was thought to contribute to an impartial, impersonal police image rooted not in community norms and values, but rather in the English Constitution (Miller 1977). To help achieve this objective, officials regularly recruited new officers from rural areas outside of London. Peel's commissioners insisted that their officers exercise restraint and display a polite demeanor while on patrol (Lane 1980). Such interpersonal treatment, it was believed, helped "compensate for distance from local residents" and would even "win respect" among area residents (Miller 1977, p. 38). The legitimacy of the London police was based on the rule of law, which was thought to translate into more consistent, less discretionary policing across locales. London officers were closely monitored, and those who abused their authority were reprimanded by supervisors (Lane 1980).

The establishment of formal, unified police departments in New York, Chicago, and other major American cities was motivated by two factors. First, there were growing concerns that informal neighborhood social controls were rapidly deteriorating as urban populations grew larger and as more affluent citizens self-segregated into local communities away from the lower classes (Miller 1977). At the time, collective disorders (e.g., food riots and wage protests), crime, and disorder were increasingly disruptive (Uchida 2005). The introduction of more effective and efficient formal social controls, such as uniformed police forces, was viewed as one way to help alleviate the social problems in urban areas. Second, the spread of formal, semibureaucratic police organizations in the United States occurred during a time when a broader movement to establish rational municipal governmental services was taking place (e.g., fire, health, and sewerage; Monkkonen 1981).

Some early police reformers in the United States regarded the London model as an exemplar. Individuals holding this view argued that adopting the London model would be a significant improvement over the traditional constable-watch system, which was increasingly viewed as ineffective at dealing with and preventing urban crime and disorder. Opponents argued, however, that the London model encroached on civil liberties, would prove too costly, and resembled a military presence (Monkkonen 1981). Throughout the mid-1800s many American cities established new police departments (Haller 1975). Like their English counterparts, the American police donned uniforms (albeit reluctantly in many cases). On the whole, however, reformers selectively adopted certain aspects of the London model. What emerged in practice was a style of policing that was uniquely American.

The primary objective of the new American police was the prevention of crime and disorder (Miller 1977). Lane (1980) notes, however, that American foot patrol officers went about their jobs differently than their London counterparts. Because of public concerns of government tyranny, American police officers were granted less formal legal authority. Instead, police officers exercised broad discretionary powers. Officers were expected to use their discretion in a manner consistent with informal community expectations, norms, and values, as opposed to bureaucratic ideals and the rule of law (Miller 1977). Extralegal methods, such as physical force and verbal intimidation, were commonly employed. Indeed, foot patrol officers were expected to dominate their beats physically and use violence as opposed to arrest to handle disorderly individuals and petty criminals (Haller 1975). Individualized street justice was largely condoned by police supervisors (unless directed at respectable citizens) and by members of the community, especially among middle- and upper-class residents who expected the police to control members of the "dangerous class" (i.e., tramps, foreign-born, out-of-towners, unemployed young men), who were thought to be more prone to criminal and disorderly behavior (Haller 1975; Miller 1977; Lane 1980). But the police did not rely on only coercive tactics to achieve class control. A number of social service mechanisms were also used, such as providing indigents with night lodging (Monkkonen 1981).

Policing scholars sometimes refer to this period as the "political era" because of the intimate connection that existed between the police and political actors (Kelling and Moore 1988). Local political agents exerted tremendous power. They appointed police captains in their districts and used the force to provide patronage jobs to party loyalists (Haller 1975; Lane 1980). The police were also used to influence the outcomes of local elections (e.g., ballot rigging and voter intimidation) and to regulate vice (e.g., gambling and liquor). For example, local political concerns influenced how existing liquor laws were enforced. In some police districts liquor laws were enforced strictly, in others loosely, in still others not at all (Lane 1980). The regulation of vice provided the police opportunities to receive bribes, collect protection money, and engage in extortive practices. Along with a portion of their salaries, officers regularly "contributed" shares of their ill-gotten gains to dominant political parties (Monkkonen 1981).

B. Second Stage: Bureaucratic Policing

As the nineteenth century drew to a close, many municipal agencies, not just the police, were criticized by Progressive Era reformers as inefficient, corrupt, and discriminatory. Political influences were viewed as a primary culprit. Progressive Era reformers argued that politics should set the objectives for administration and administration should carry out the policies in the absence of political meandering (Wilson 1887; Goodnow 1900; White 1926). This view is often referred to as the "politics-administration dichotomy" model. Applied to municipal government, the model holds that local politicians should stay out of the administrative affairs of local agencies (e.g., hiring and firing decisions in local police departments), agency managers should not get involved in shaping government policies, and the role of the agency manager is that of a politically neutral expert who strives to carry out the policies developed through political processes effectively and efficiently (Svara 1998). One result of this reform movement was the enactment of civil service laws that helped insulate municipal agencies from local political influences, especially with regard to employee selection and promotion. Such changes did not occur overnight, but rather took several decades. The extent to which such laws influenced police officer behavior on the beat was probably modest (Haller 1975).

Progressive Era reformers also called on public agencies to employ management practices consistent with classical organization theory, which at the time were quite popular in the private sector (see, e.g.,

Taylor 1911; Fayol [1916] 1949). The basic themes included the following: organizations and members behave rationally, organizations strive to be efficient, efficiency is achieved through specialization and the division of labor, and efficiency is maximized through scientific inquiry (Shafritz and Ott 1996, pp. 29–31). The ideas espoused by Progressive activists were closely aligned with the objectives of several early police reformers (see, e.g., Fosdick [1915] 1969; Vollmer [1936] 1971; Smith 1940; Wilson 1950). August Vollmer, for example, advocated for a professional police force that was "an efficient, nonpartisan agency committed to the highest standards of public service" (Walker 1980, p. 134). This new approach to policing, which came to be known as the "professional model," featured a narrowing of the police mandate: the police no longer employed a variety of tactics to control the dangerous class, but instead focused specifically on crime control. Applying the basic themes from classical organization theory, the professional police department was characterized by a centralization of command and standardization of procedure, division of labor and task specialization, improved standards of recruiting and training, and the use of scientific methods to investigate crimes (Goldstein 1990, pp. 6–8). Other reforms and innovations, including preventive motorized patrols, rapid response, systematic recording of crime data, and the use of two-way radios, were geared toward accomplishing three objectives: enhancing organizational efficiency, reducing crime, and increasing control over patrol officers.

The professional model was the dominant organizational design in American policing for much of the mid-twentieth century. Police officers in large cities maintained a presence through motorized patrols, racing from one call to the next. The image they portrayed was that of a crime fighter. Over time, however, the professional model began to falter. In the 1960s, for example, crime was on the rise, and the inability of the police to reverse crime trends called into question their crime fighter image. Several televised civil rights marches showed African American demonstrators being beaten and water-hosed by police and attacked by dogs. In some cities, such as Detroit and Newark, police actions (e.g., raids and shootings) were perceived as the cause of urban riots. An investigation by the National Advisory Commission on Civil Disorders (1968) concluded that the police represent "white power, white racism, and white repression" (p. 5) among black ghetto dwellers. Among other things, the commission recommended that the police "eliminate abrasive practices" in inner-city neighborhoods and implement "innovative programs to ensure widespread community support for law enforcement" (p. 8).

A number of research studies conducted in the 1970s challenged key aspects of the professional model. For example, the Kansas City Preventive Patrol Experiment showed that routine motorized patrols not only fail to deter crime but also have little effect on citizens' fear of crime (Kelling et al. 1974). Another influential study, conducted by researchers at the Rand Corporation, reported that variation in investigative training, staff, workload, and procedures had no meaningful effect on crime, arrest, and clearance rates. In addition, the Rand researchers found that over one-half of serious felonies (e.g., homicide and rape) reported to the police received only "superficial attention" by investigative staff (Greenwood and Petersilia 1975, p. vii). Finally, a study conducted by researchers at the Police Executive Research Forum (PERF) found that efforts to reduce police response time had no effect on arrest rates. PERF researchers discovered that other factors, such as citizen-reporting time, played a more important role (Spelman and Brown 1984).

C. Third Stage: Community and Problem-Oriented Policing

During the 1970s and 1980s, various attempts to improve policing practices were under way (see Moore 1992, pp. 131–38). One example, community crime prevention, sought to build collaborative partnerships between criminal justice agencies and community organizations to address crime and related problems. This approach rested on the assumption that crime-ridden, disorderly neighborhoods lacked the informal social controls necessary to regulate the behavior of residents and visitors (Hope 1995). Many crime prevention programs attempted to address the problem by organizing community members. Residents were encouraged not only to harden their domiciles to prevent break-ins but also to work collectively by communicating suspicious activity to neighbors, form civilian patrols to roam the neighborhood, call on and assist the police when crime happens, and engage in other collective anticrime activities. However, participation in such programs proved difficult to sustain (Rosenbaum 1988). On the basis of a comprehensive review of the research literature, Skogan (1988) noted that community organizations were much more likely to arise and flourish in more affluent cities and that program awareness and participation tended to be dominated by residents from higher socioeconomic backgrounds (also see Rosenbaum, Lurigio, and Davis 1998, pp. 22–27).

Team policing was another attempt to move beyond the professional model. This police innovation called for establishing teams of officers in various beats throughout cities and holding them accountable for local conditions (Bloch and Specht 1973). Traditional car patrols remained in use, but routine calls for service were first given to team officers in the area in which they originated. Evaluation research studies generally reported positive findings (see, e.g., Sherman, Milton, and Kelly 1973). However, the ability to strike a proper balance between a traditional crime-fighting force and a second patrol force consisting of area teams that were more responsive to local community needs proved difficult. Team officers were expected to respond to calls for service and foster community involvement. The more citizen involvement officers were able to stimulate, the less time they were available to respond to calls. Given the traditional crime fighter values that dominated police organizations, it was only a matter of time before team officers morphed back into traditional patrol officers (Sparrow, Moore, and Kennedy 1990).

A third set of reforms involved the reemergence of foot patrols in a number of American cities (e.g., Houston, Boston, and Baltimore). Initiated because of growing concerns about the effectiveness of car patrols, investigators sought to determine whether foot patrols could reduce levels of perceived disorder (e.g., loitering and drug use), reduce perceived crime, improve perceptions of safety and citizen evaluations of police service, and reduce actual crime and victimization (Pate 1986). In Flint, Michigan, Trojanowicz (1986) found that citizens residing in foot patrol areas reported higher levels of satisfaction with police services and that they felt safer. Crime rates also went down in the study areas, except for robbery and burglary. Trojanowicz noted, however, that rates for these serious crimes were considerably higher in other areas of the city that did not receive foot patrols (also see Trojanowicz 1982). A second study, conducted in Newark, New Jersey, reported positive findings of foot patrols in influencing individual perceptions of safety, perceptions of crime problems, perceptions of disorder problems, and ratings of police service. However, the researchers in Newark did not find any effect of foot patrols on reported crimes levels (Pate 1986). Many police reformers interpreted these findings as showing that foot patrols could have positive effects.

Police reform in the United States gained momentum after the publication of two influential articles by prominent policing scholars. The first, Wilson and Kelling's (1982) "Broken Windows" article, used the Newark foot patrol experiments as a point of departure to support their reform agenda. The authors noted that Newark foot patrol officers became intimately familiar with their beats and were quite effective at upholding local community standards, such as making sure "disreputable regulars" kept their alcoholic beverages in paper bags and did not lie down for sidewalk naps. Sometimes the police used their powers of arrest to remove disorderly people from the streets; at other times less formal (even extralegal) tactics were used. The authors likened this form of policing to the style observed in earlier periods of American history. Wilson and Kelling cautioned that some informal tactics employed by officers "probably would not withstand legal challenge" (p. 31) and that they are not "easily reconciled with any conception of due process or fair treatment" (p. 35). But, the authors argued, the rules were well understood by area residents who condoned informal and extralegal police tactics. According to Wilson and Kelling, citizens were pleased that the police were doing something about disorderly behavior.

Wilson and Kelling's paper sparked considerable debate. Focusing specifically on Wilson and Kelling's work, Walker (1984) rejected the notion that the police in the nineteenth century enjoyed high levels of legitimacy. As evidence, Walker pointed to the many political battles over the enforcement of drinking laws that undermined public support. Walker also claimed that Wilson and Kelling portrayed a highly romanticized view of early American policing. In actuality, Walker argued, early foot patrols were plagued by corruption and were terribly inefficient. Others focused their criticisms on the methodological limitations of the foot patrol experiments cited by Wilson and Kelling. For example, Greene and Taylor (1988) pointed out that none of the foot patrol experiments at the time, including the Newark study, actually used "ecologically valid neighborhood units" (p. 217). Failing to do so meant that foot patrol officers toured several local communities, which made it incredibly difficult (if not impossible) to learn the specific local norms.

Other critics took aim at the order maintenance function of policing more generally. Manning (1988, p. 44) argued, for example, that the police cannot "coerce, enforce, punish, and maintain formal social control" and expect to maintain high levels of support in all segments of the general population. But not everyone objected to the notion of police officers sometimes resorting to aggressive forms of order maintenance. Sykes (1986) argued that maintaining order was not inherently repressive, but instead actually provided protection and regulation that are necessary for a free, well-functioning community. Mastrofski (1988, p. 60) pointed out, however, that relaxing bureaucratic and legal constraints on police behavior can potentially increase "police misbehavior, abuse of authority, and bad judgment."

The second important article, by Goldstein (1979), also directed criticism toward the professional model of policing. Goldstein argued that police professionals in the United States suffered from the "means over ends syndrome" (p. 238). Put simply, too much emphasis had been placed on formalizing police processes. Goldstein conceded that the establishment of businesslike procedures was appropriate when Progressive Era reformers began their work. After all, at that time the police were horribly inefficient and poorly trained, and supervision was lax. But improvements to police efficiency came at a significant cost: police officials no longer concerned themselves with the objectives of preventing and controlling crime and related problems. Goldstein advocated that the police focus their attention on the problems that result in calls for service as opposed to the calls themselves.

Much of the early research in support of problem-oriented policing relied on case study methodologies, which provided detailed contextual assessment of problem-oriented policing interventions in departments throughout the United States. In his highly acclaimed book *Problem-Oriented Policing*, Goldstein (1990) presents a case study that he says is a classic example of problem-oriented policing at work. The case involved an increase in convenience store robberies in Gainesville, Florida. After carefully studying the problem, which included an independent assessment conducted by a university-based researcher, the police concluded that the robbers were targeting stores staffed by a single clerk during the night shift. At the urging of the police, the city council passed an ordinance requiring convenience stores to have two clerks on duty at specific times. Shortly after the ordinance passed, convenience store robberies dropped by 65 percent.

Although the Gainesville case is straightforward and, at first glance, appears to demonstrate the merits of problem-oriented policing, some observers argue that the findings are largely anecdotal. For example,

Sherman (1991, pp. 700–701) asks the following questions: Did the number of convenience stores decline after the new ordinance passed requiring that more clerks be employed? Were known convenience store robbers apprehended about the same time the new law went into effect? In addition, Sherman notes that clerks who worked alone at night could simply have pocketed money from the cash register and reported to the police that they were robbed to cover up the embezzlement. Once a second clerk was placed in the store, the scheme would require a coconspirator, potentially making reported robberies less common. The Gainesville case study did not address these questions, nor did it adequately rule out potential rival explanations. Much as with the criticisms directed at the early foot patrol experiments, police scholars in the early years of problem-oriented policing called for more systematic and exhaustive assessments of policing interventions that employed more scientifically rigorous methodologies, such as experimental and quasi-experimental designs, to evaluate the effect of police interventions.

D. Conclusion

This brief review of the history of police reform shows that the emergence of community and problem-oriented policing was initiated by a confluence of factors. These were the accusation that overly aggressive police practices in black ghettos were contributing to racial strife in American cities and to the estrangement of African Americans from the police. The broader social context was characterized by rising crime rates, which tarnished the crime fighter police image. In academic circles, a series of systematic studies reported findings that shined an unflattering light on the professional model of policing. And within the field of policing, departments throughout the United States were experimenting with innovative practices (e.g., team policing, community crime prevention, and foot patrols), suggesting that the profession was becoming increasingly open to change.

Both community and problem-oriented policing include among their component parts previously established police tactics and practices. Community policing, for example, resurrected foot patrols, order maintenance, and long-term beat assignments from the early uniformed police era. It also called for police officers to display a polite demeanor when interacting with citizens, a practice consistent with Sir Robert Peel's edict issued over 175 years ago. Problem-oriented polic-

ing, especially the enforcement variety, makes use of traditional policing practices, such as directed patrol and crackdowns. On the surface,
then, these two reforms may appear to some casual observers as nothing more than "old wine in new bottles."

But as organizational strategies, community and problem-oriented
policing are historically distinct. Problem-oriented policing changes
the focal point of police work, away from incidents and toward recurrent problems. The problem-solving process espoused by Goldstein
(1979, 1990) entails activities (e.g., problem formulation and systematic
assessment) that clearly fall outside the traditional scope of police practice. Community policing redefines the relationship between the public
and the police. Instead of merely responding to calls for service, police
work with citizens to improve neighborhood quality of life by identifying problems, maintaining surveillance, and helping to prevent crime.
Various community policing practices, such as beat meetings and problem-solving training, can be used to build these cooperative relationships and empower citizens. Accounts suggesting that police-community relations during the early uniformed policing era resembled
contemporary community policing expectations are misleading. Policing during this earlier period was frequently coercive and fraught with
favoritism and corruption. To sum up, although community and problem-oriented policing entail the use of established tactics, as organizational strategies both models of policing are, in a historical sense,
unique.

As the 1980s drew to a close, few could have predicted the rate at
which the police reform movement would sweep across the country.
Interest in community and problem-oriented policing among law enforcement agencies in big cities, rural counties, affluent suburban communities, college towns, and elsewhere grew by leaps and bounds in
the 1990s. At about the same time, approximately 2 years after William
Jefferson Clinton was elected president, the federal government enacted legislation providing unprecedented levels of financial support to
help police departments develop community and problem-oriented policing.

III. The COPS Program

In the 1990s, the federal government became involved in the police
reform movement with the passage of the Violent Crime Control and

Law Enforcement Act of 1994 (Crime Act). Between fiscal years 1995 and 2000, the Crime Act authorized appropriation of $8.8 billion in grants to support local law enforcement agencies' community policing efforts. The Community Oriented Policing Services program was established by the Department of Justice to award a variety of different grants to law enforcement agencies to accomplish four goals: increase the number of police officers, foster police-community interaction and problem solving, encourage police innovation, and develop new police technologies to reduce crime (Roth and Ryan 2000). In 2005, the COPS program was reauthorized by Congress.

By 2000, the COPS program reportedly funded more than 100,000 police officers.[1] This was accomplished through the use of three-year hiring grants that paid up to 75 percent of the cost of hiring new officers. Agencies receiving these awards were required to hire police officers who would engage in community policing activities (Roth and Ryan 2000). COPS grants were also used to acquire crime-fighting technology, fund innovative police programs, establish a nationwide network of Regional Community Policing Institutes (RCPI), and to support the establishment and operation of the Center for Problem-Oriented Policing (POP Center). The RCPI network was set up to provide training and technical assistance to law enforcement agencies (U.S. Department of Justice 2006). As of midyear 2009, the RCPIs had trained more than 600,000 police officers, government officials, and community members (U.S. Department of Justice 2009b). The POP Center is dedicated to advancing the concept and practice of problem-oriented policing. Among other things, the POP Center provides publications designed to help guide problem-solving efforts to police officials and others concerned with crime and disorder.

The amount of money appropriated to the COPS program from 1995 to 2008 was substantial (approximately $13.6 billion in nominal dollars). As shown in figure 1, a large percentage of the appropriations to the COPS program between 1995 and 1999 (approximately 86.7 percent) went to hiring programs. Federal appropriations remained fairly stable from 1995 to 1999 (about $1.4 billion per year) but declined thereafter. In 2000, appropriations were reduced by 57.5 percent

---

[1] The number of new police officers hired using COPS grants is disputed (see, e.g., Davis et al. 2000). A study published by the Urban Institute estimates that COPS funding resulted in the hiring of between 69,100 and 92,200 police officers (Koper, Moore, and Roth 2002).

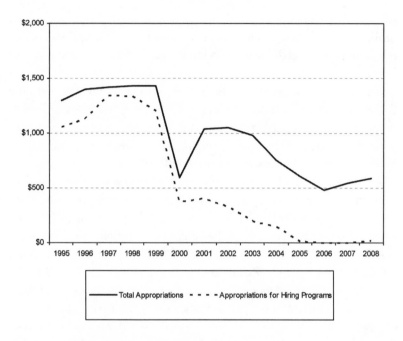

FIG. 1.—Funding requests and appropriations for the COPS program, 1995–2008 (in millions of nominal dollars). Source: James (2008, p. 11).

(an $835 million reduction). Appropriations then increased for several years, even exceeding funding requests by the Bush administration. In 2008, the COPS program was appropriated $587 billion (James 2008).

A. COPS and Community Policing

The adoption of community and problem-oriented policing practices expanded following the passage of the Crime Act of 1994. Using multiple waves of survey data collected in 1996, 1998, and 2000 and site visits to police agencies, Roth, Roehl, and Johnson (2004) tracked the adoption of four police reforms—tactics for building partnerships, problem solving, crime prevention, and supportive organizational changes—from 1995 to 2000. Roth and his colleagues found that the implementation of partnership-building tactics, such as working with citizens to prevent crime and reduce disorder and holding regular community meetings, increased significantly between 1995 and 1998 among large agencies (i.e., departments serving populations of 50,000 or more). No change was observed between 1998 and 2000. From their site visits, Roth et al. found that partnerships usually took two forms: problem-solving partnerships formed with other service providers and community partnerships with neighborhood residents, groups, and businesses.

The adoption of problem-solving (e.g., activities consistent with the SARA model) and crime prevention tactics (e.g., police/youth programs and graffiti eradication programs) among large agencies followed patterns similar to partnership building—significantly increasing from 1995 to 1998 and holding steady between 1998 and 2000. The authors, however, uncovered concerns with crime prevention efforts. They report that police officials usually pointed to existing programs (e.g., DARE and Neighborhood Watch) as successful programs and seldom were able to "articulate any philosophy of prevention, logical productions of collaboration with communities and problem solving focused on underlying causes" (Roth, Roehl, and Johnson 2004, p. 16). By comparison, the most modest community policing reforms adopted by large police departments were in the area of supportive organizational changes. When the specific elements were assessed separately, the findings showed that nearly 80 percent of large police departments reportedly established neighborhood patrol boundaries by 1998.

Roth et al. also tracked adoption patterns for small agencies. Among departments policing populations less than 50,000, the adoption of partnership building and supportive organizational changes grew steadily over the three time periods. Increases in problem-solving and crime prevention tactics were more pronounced over the latter two observation periods. Despite the increase in the adoption of community policing tactics among small agencies, in 2000 a much greater percentage of large agencies had adopted the four types of community policing tactics relative to small agencies.

Roth and his associates were able to demonstrate that the implementation of community policing tactics grew steadily following the passage of the Crime Act of 1994. Some caution must be exercised when interpreting the authors' survey results because data like these tell us little (if anything) about the extent to which agencies actually practiced community policing activities (see Maguire and Mastrofski 2000). However, the authors' site visits helped overcome this data limitation, revealing that some of the involvement in community policing, such as the use of crime prevention tactics, was rather limited.

B. COPS and Crime Research

Research investigating the effect of COPS grants on crime has been the subject of a fair amount of controversy. Some of it stems from the numerous methodological challenges confronting researchers who attempt to tackle the question (see Worrall 2010, pp. 42–44), and some is probably associated with deep-seated political views regarding the proper role of the federal government. Zhao, Scheider, and Thurman (2002) were the first to evaluate the effect of COPS funding on crime rates. Using panel data (1995–99) from 6,100 cities, Zhao and his associates showed that two COPS programs (i.e., hiring and innovative grants) significantly reduced violent and property crime rates in cities with populations exceeding 10,000. Although they did not find similar effects in smaller cities and towns, Zhao et al. concluded that COPS grants appeared to be an effective way to reduce crime in the United States (also see Zhao, Scheider, and Thurman 2003).

The Zhao, Scheider, and Thurman (2002) study was the focus of considerable criticism. For example, Muhlhausen (2002, p. 8) argued that the study was "critically flawed" because it failed to account for a variety of factors known to influence crime rates and to control for local law enforcement efforts, among other shortcomings. Muhlhausen (2001) attempted to replicate Zhao et al.'s findings using panel data (1995–98) from 752 counties. Muhlhausen found that hiring grants and grants for purchasing new technology had no appreciable effect on violent crime.

Three additional studies soon followed. The Government Accountability Office (GAO) attempted to address criticisms of the Zhao et al. study, such as the variable omission bias. For example, the GAO study included controls for other types of federal funding. On the basis of their analysis, the GAO concluded that "COPS grant expenditures did reduce crime during the 1990s" (2005, p. 17). Evans and Owens (2007) used panel data (1990–2001) from 2,074 cities and towns to assess the effect of COPS funding. They found that four types of crime (i.e., auto theft, burglary, robbery, and aggravated assault) dropped in the years following the receipt of COPS hiring grants. That same year, however, a second study was published that arrived at a different conclusion. Worrall and Kovandzic (2007) assessed panel data (1990–2000) from 189 large cities. The authors included non-COPS police expenditures in their analysis, thus addressing criticism directed at the Zhao et al. study. After evaluating the effect of COPS funding on seven types of serious crime, the authors concluded that "COPS grants had no discernible effect on serious crime during the period covered by our analysis" (p. 170).

The research evidence addressing whether the COPS program has reduced crime is thus mixed. While some observers conclude that investments made in policing to expand the number of police officers contributed to the crime drop in the 1990s (see, e.g., Levitt 2004), others remain steadfast in their position that COPS hiring grants failed to reduce crime (Muhlhausen and Walsh 2008).

IV. Theory and Research

A variety of theoretical frameworks undergird community and problem-oriented policing research and practice. For example, two neighborhood theories of crime—broken windows and social disorganization theory—identify key neighborhood-level factors that community policing practitioners can target to reduce and prevent crime and disorder. Criminal opportunity theories, such as routine activity and rational choice theory, which fall under the environmental criminology heading, can be used to guide problem-oriented policing processes (e.g., analyzing problems and designing responses).

A. Broken Windows Theory

Broken windows theory posits that neighborhood disorder indirectly causes crime through a cascading sequence of events (see fig. 2). Disorder is typically conceptualized as a two-dimensional concept. One dimension, social disorder, is defined as "boorish and threatening behavior" that disrupts urban life (Kelling and Coles 1996, p. 16). Examples include aggressive panhandling, street prostitution, public drinking and drug use, and urinating in public spaces. Albert J. Reiss Jr. (1985) referred to these behaviors as "soft crimes"; while technically crimes (usually misdemeanors or petty offenses), such behaviors are traditionally not a high police priority. The second dimension, physical disorder, refers to "visual signs of negligence and unchecked decay" in neighborhood settings (Skogan 1990, p. 4). Broken streetlights and windows, vacant lots filled with garbage, abandoned or burned-out buildings and cars, and gang graffiti are common examples of physical disorder. Importantly, broken windows theory posits that observable signs of disorder (or "incivilities"), when left unchecked, elevate levels

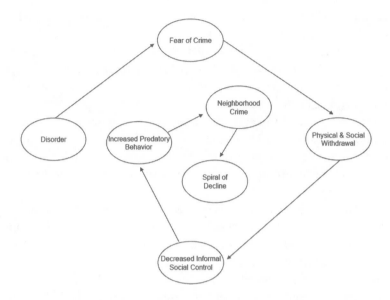

FIG. 2.—The broken windows theory of neighborhood crime. Source: Adapted from Kelling and Bratton (1998, p. 1219).

of fear among area residents (Wilson and Kelling 1982). Fearful citizens take steps to reduce their perceived victimization risk. For example, some residents move to less disorderly (and presumably safer) neighborhoods. Those unable to relocate minimize their potential exposure to victimization by altering their daily routines (e.g., avoiding local markets, finding alternatives to public transportation, and spending more time indoors).

Fear-induced physical and social withdrawal has detrimental effects on the ability of local communities to regulate the behavior of residents and visitors. Citizens are more reluctant to intervene on behalf of the public (e.g., break up fights between teenagers), are less willing to participate in local civic organizations, and neglect their social ties with neighbors. In short, informal social controls break down as social isolation sets in (Kelling and Coles 1996, p. 20). In the absence of effective social controls, neighborhood conditions become increasingly criminogenic, and disorder becomes more pervasive and intense (e.g., panhandlers are more menacing, rowdy teens are emboldened, and gang graffiti accumulates), all of which signals miscreants that "no one cares" and that the neighborhood is ripe for "criminal invasion" (Wilson and

Kelling 1982, pp. 31–32). In turn, open-air drug markets become larger and busier, street prostitutes increase in number, muggings become more frequent, and other forms of street violence happen with greater regularity. Over time, neighborhoods that reach the bottom of the spiraling cycle of decline "may no longer be recognized as neighborhoods" (Skogan 1990, p. 14).

Broken windows theory has received a fair amount of empirical attention. Harcourt and Ludwig (2006) group broken windows research studies into two categories: those that assess the effect of broken windows policing and those that test hypotheses derived from broken windows theory.

1. *Research on the Effect of Broken Windows Policing.*   Broken windows theory is widely considered the guiding force behind order maintenance policing (also termed "broken windows policing"). The idea is pretty straightforward: given the series of harmful effects that flow from neighborhood disorder, order maintenance policing requires police officers to address disorder problems on a routine basis. Two important questions arise. First, when do disorder-related problems warrant police intervention? Kelling and Coles (1996) contend that police officers must determine the seriousness of the offense in context. For example, a group of intoxicated men consuming alcohol on a busy street corner during the day necessitates intervention more than a single person drinking a beer in a paper sack in an alleyway at night. A teenager urinating on a car in a busy parking lot in broad daylight requires police intervention more than a teen doing the same thing behind a dumpster after midnight. Police officers, according to Kelling and Coles, must also evaluate the harm done to the victim or the effect on the community. The group of male drunkards will adversely affect the ability of nearby shop owners to conduct business. An elderly neighborhood resident walking by the parking lot will be disturbed by the sight of a teenager urinating in plain sight. In situations in which the seriousness and harm of disorderly acts are not so clear-cut, the police must rely on their training and departmental policy to determine whether intervention is warranted.

The second question concerns how police officers should handle encounters with disorderly individuals. In theory, order maintenance policing calls on the police to exhaust nonarrest approaches, such as persuasion, counseling, and ordering, to resolve the disorder problems they encounter. If such attempts fail, then making an arrest for a misdemeanor offense is appropriate (Kelling and Coles 1996, p. 23). Research addressing the effect of broken windows policing has adopted two different strategies: assessments of departmentwide order maintenance strategies across police precincts and targeted interventions focusing on specific urban locations.

A growing body of research has attempted to determine the effect broken windows policing had (if any) on the declining crime rate in New York City (NYC). The NYC crime drop has attracted the attention of researchers for several reasons. NYC experienced dramatic decreases in rates of violent and property crime during the 1990s (56 percent and 65 percent, respectively). What is more, during the 1990s NYC officials, including Mayor Rudolph Giuliani and Police Commissioner William Bratton, implemented their version of order maintenance policing, which resulted in an explosion of misdemeanor arrests. Reflecting on the NYC crime drop, Kelling and Bratton (1998, p. 1217) commented that the "police played an important, even central, role in getting people to stop committing crime in New York City." Some observers, however, contend that the effects of policing strategies on NYC's declining crime rates are "exaggerated" (Levitt 2004, p. 173).

Kelling and Sousa's (2001) study was one of the first sophisticated attempts to investigate the effects of order maintenance policing on NYC crime rates in the 1990s. Using police precincts as their unit of analysis, Kelling and Sousa operationalized order maintenance policing as arrests for misdemeanor offenses. After regressing violent crime (murder, rape, robbery, and felonious assault) onto misdemeanor arrests and statistical control variables, the authors observed that order maintenance policing contributed to the NYC crime drop. Specifically, Kelling and Sousa reported that for every 28 misdemeanor arrests, one violent crime was prevented. The authors estimated that from 1989 to 1998, over 60,000 violent crimes were prevented, which corresponds to a 5 percent reduction in violent crime (Kelling and Sousa 2001, p. 10).

A second study that used monthly time-series data over a 25-year period (1974–99) arrived at a similar conclusion (Corman and Mocan 2005). Like Kelling and Sousa, the authors operationalized order maintenance policing as misdemeanor arrests. However, Corman and Mocan assess the effect of misdemeanor arrests on specific types of crime (e.g., murder, robbery, motor vehicle theft, and grand larceny), net of statistical controls. Evidence in support of broken windows policing was observed: a 10 percent increase in misdemeanor arrests was associated with a 2.5–3.2 percent decline in robbery, a 1.6–2.1 percent decrease in motor vehicle theft, and a 0.5–0.6 percent decline in grand larceny (p. 255). The authors report, however, that the effect of order maintenance policing on the other types of crimes included in the study was null.

The Kelling and Sousa and Corman and Mocan studies were not met with universal praise. Harcourt and Ludwig (2006) took issue with several technical aspects of these two studies. For example, the Kelling and Sousa study, according to Harcourt and Ludwig, failed to account for a variety of important control variables and to adjust their multivariate models to account for "mean reversion." Harcourt and Ludwig argued that NYC precincts that received the most intense order maintenance policing also experienced the largest increases in crime during the 1980s. The authors contend that areas where crime rates go up the most are usually the places where they decline the most. Their reassessment of the effects of misdemeanor arrests on violent crime, which included measures of police manpower, age composition, and structural disadvantage, showed that misdemeanor arrests had no significant effect on violent crime in NYC between 1989 and 1999 (also see Harcourt and Ludwig 2007).

Other recent studies throw additional light on the effects of broken windows policing in NYC. Rosenfeld, Fornango, and Rengifo (2007) assessed the effect of order maintenance policing (operationalized as misdemeanor and ordinance violation arrests) on two types of violent crime—robbery and homicide—at the precinct level from 1988 to 2001. After controlling for a variety of factors hypothesized to influence violent crime rates (e.g., felony arrests and drug markets), Rosenfeld et al. found that order maintenance policing resulted in declines in both robbery (a 1–5 percent decline) and homicide (a 7–12 percent decline) during the 1990s (p. 377). Adopting a slightly different focus, Messner et al. (2007) assessed the effect of misdemeanor arrests on three measures of homicide (gun-related, non-gun-related, and total homicides) and robbery across NYC precincts from 1990 to 1999. Like Rosenfeld et al., Messner and colleagues' analysis controlled for other factors hypothesized to influence aggregate crime rates, such as felony arrest rates, cocaine use, and neighborhood characteristics. Their findings revealed that misdemeanor arrests were associated with reductions in robbery, gun-related homicide, and total homicide. Messner et al. estimate that an increase of 833 misdemeanor arrests resulted in one fewer homicide for a precinct of 100,000 population (p. 400; also see Cerdá et al. 2009).

On balance, the research on the effect of policing strategies on the NYC crime drop indicates that order maintenance policing had a modest effect on certain types of crime, especially robbery and gun-related homicide. Although informative, these studies employ a narrow operational definition of order maintenance policing (e.g., misdemeanor arrests). As Thacher (2004, p. 393) notes, "simply equating order maintenance policing with misdemeanor arrests is clearly too simple" (also see Braga and Bond 2008, p. 581). Whether more nuanced order maintenance measures that capture instances of police dealing with disorderly behavior by way of persuasion, warnings, and reminders in the absence of formal sanction also affected crime rates across NYC precincts during the 1990s remains an open empirical question.

While a number of studies have sought to assess the effect of broken windows policing strategies and tactics on specific urban locations, three other well-crafted studies are discussed here. Perhaps the most sustained, comprehensive, and methodologically rigorous evaluation of community policing is Wesley Skogan's work on the Chicago Alternative Policing Strategy (CAPS). Chicago-style community policing is based on broken windows theory. However, unlike the approach adopted in NYC, CAPS does not address "community problems by making tens of thousands of arrests for minor offenses." In Chicago the "solution for broken windows is to fix them" (Skogan 2006, p. 179). The CAPS program incorporated several community policing characteristics, including officers assigned to specific beats, officers trained in problem solving, emphasis placed on community involvement, and crime analysis. When comparing research beats (i.e., those targeted for CAPS interventions) to comparison beats, Skogan and Hartnett (1997) found that citizens residing in disadvantaged areas reported that neighborhood conditions, such as drug sales and abandoned buildings, improved significantly following police intervention. In more affluent areas, however, improvements were also observed, but it was not clear whether they were attributable to police interventions (i.e., conditions in comparison beats also improved). In short, Chicago's broken windows approach to community policing produced positive outcomes in distressed residential settings, but in areas where neighborhood problems were low to begin with, gains following police intervention were comparatively modest.

Operation Restoration, a policing program in Chandler, Arizona, emphasized order maintenance and zoning ordinance enforcement to address disorder problems (Katz, Webb, and Schaefer 2001). The police department targeted four intervention zones. At the beginning stages of the program, Chandler police actively sought community input by conducting community surveys and holding meetings with local residents and stakeholders. Citizen input showed that disorder-related problems were prevalent in a number of different residential communities. After selecting specific areas for intervention, the police held community meetings to educate residents about the operation and ask them to tell others about Operation Restoration. Katz and his colleagues tracked the number of calls for service over a 1,245-day period (from pre- to postintervention). Their analyses revealed that the number of calls for service pertaining to public morals offenses, such as street prostitution and public drinking, decreased significantly. Operation Restoration proved successful in reducing community-nominated problems.

More recently, Braga and Bond (2008) evaluated the effect of broken windows policing on a variety of outcomes, such as citizen calls for service and pre- and postintervention levels of physical and social disorder. The authors employed a randomized block field experiment design. The police intervention involved various broken windows policing tactics, including situational prevention, social service, and misdemeanor arrest. Braga and Bond found that the total number of calls, robbery and nondomestic assault calls, and disorder and burglary calls were all significantly reduced in the treatment areas. The authors were able to determine which police strategies had the largest effect on calls for service. The number of different situational prevention strategies proved most salient, followed by misdemeanor arrests. The effect of social service strategies on calls for service was null. Regarding pre- and postintervention levels of disorder, Braga and Bond report that social (e.g., loiterers, public drinkers, and the homeless) and physical disorder (trash, graffiti, and abandoned cars) were significantly reduced in the treatment areas. Summing up the implications of their study, the authors note that "a sole commitment to increasing misdemeanor arrests is not the most powerful approach" (p. 600).

Broken windows policing is the subject of considerable debate. Critics argue that narrowly conceived order maintenance strategies that focus solely on making misdemeanor arrests walk a fine line between keeping streets safer and harassing local citizens (see Kubrin 2008). A focus of aggressively cracking down on public order offenses by making a high number of arrests is referred to as "zero tolerance policing" (Cordner 1998; Greene 2000). Some claim that the broken widows policing strategy developed in NYC under Police Commissioner William Bratton was more closely aligned with zero tolerance policing than a community collaboration approach (Greene 1999; Skogan 2006, p. 179; cf. Kelling and Coles 1996, p. 160). Arguably, zero tolerance policing can result in both positive and negative outcomes.

Conventional wisdom states that police-community collaboration is exceedingly difficult to nurture and sustain in high-crime, minority neighborhoods where informal social controls are deteriorating and trust among neighbors is lacking. Police are viewed negatively, and social institutions are weak. Some might conclude that adopting a community policing approach that relies on citizen input to identify neighborhood problems and citizen involvement in crime reduction and prevention strategies will be doomed to failure. Under such conditions, the argument follows, a zero tolerance policing approach geared toward eradicating crime in the short run will give local communities an opportunity to organize and develop the social controls necessary to regulate the behavior of residents and visitors, thus preventing crime in the long run (see Meares 1998).

Opponents of zero tolerance policing take issue with this position. Neighborhood policing research consistently shows that police officers exercise a higher level of coercive authority in poverty-stricken, socially distressed residential settings (Smith 1986; Fagan and Davies 2000; Mastrofski, Reisig, and McCluskey 2002; Terrill and Reisig 2003; Ingram 2007); that more inhabitants of these neighborhoods perceive the police to be abusive (Weitzer 1999); and that disadvantaged citizens are not terribly receptive to such police tactics (Skogan 1990; Piquero et al. 2000; Stoutland 2001). Implementing police crackdowns on public order offenses in these communities can further alienate residents who already distrust and question the legitimacy of the police (Meares 1998; Greene 2000; Thacher 2001a).

2. *Research Testing Broken Windows Hypotheses.*   Several studies have tested hypotheses derived from broken windows theory. The preponderance of research in this particular area has focused on two relation-

ships: the disorder and crime nexus and the connection between disorder and fear of crime.

Establishing the empirical relationship between disorder and crime is a salient undertaking for order maintenance policing advocates. If it exists, it provides support for policing disorder. Skogan's (1990) early work appeared promising. After combing data from several research sites, Skogan assessed the effect of disorder on neighborhood robbery rates. He found that neighborhood characteristics (poverty and instability) and racial composition influenced crime rates, but he argued that the empirical link between neighborhood features and robbery was largely mediated by disorder. Kelling and Coles (1996, pp. 25–26) interpreted Skogan's finding as providing "empirical proof to confirm Wilson and Kelling's hypothesis."

Harcourt's (1998) reassessment of Skogan's data casts doubt on the disorder-crime link. Evaluating the scope of the connection between disorder and crime, Harcourt found that neighborhood disorder was not significantly related to two types of crime (i.e., purse snatching and sexual assault) and that the relationship between disorder and two other crime types (i.e., physical assault and burglary) was attenuated when poverty, stability, and racial composition were accounted for. Harcourt also found that the effect of disorder on robbery appeared to be highly situational. He found that the relationship reported by Skogan was dependent on a select group of neighborhoods from a single research site (Newark).[2] Taylor's (2001) study also called into question the disorder-crime connection. His evaluation focused on the effects of three different neighborhood disorder measures on changes in homicide, rape, robbery, and aggravated assault using longitudinal data. The results from his analyses failed to support the argument that disorder causes crime.

In 1999, an article published in the *American Journal of Sociology* challenged broken windows theory by proposing and testing an alternative explanation for the understanding of disorder and crime. Sampson and Raudenbush (1999) argued that disorder and crime reflect opposite ends of a seriousness continuum and share the same structural and social origins. At the bivariate level, Sampson and Raudenbush observed a significant correlation between disorder and three types of crime (i.e., homicide, robbery, and burglary). However, when more

---

[2] Various technical aspects of Harcourt's replication have been criticized (see Xu, Fiedler, and Flaming 2005).

stringent tests were conducted, which controlled for concentrated disadvantage (a measure of racially segregated, economic deprivation), collective efficacy (a measure reflecting levels of trust among neighbors and informal social controls), and prior crime rates, the effect of disorder on crime was null. These results supported the authors' theoretical argument.[3] As for police policy and practice, Sampson and Raudenbush concluded that attacking disorder by means of aggressive tactics represented a "weak strategy" because it fails to address the common origins of disorder and crime (p. 638).

Some of the controversy surrounding research on the disorder-crime nexus focuses on the measurement of disorder. Systematic social observation (SSO) measures and neighborhood residents' subjective assessments each have strengths and weaknesses. SSO measures are constructed using physical and social inventory data collected by trained researchers, which may be viewed as more objective relative to perceptual indicators. However, observations may be restricted to daytime hours, which some argue overlooks "bar closings, early-morning drug sales, prostitution, and other forms of disorder that take place between dusk and dawn" (Bratton and Kelling 2006, p. 2). Subjective disorder measures reflect local residents' perceptions. Comparing SSO to citizens' assessments, Skogan (2008a, p. 197) notes, "I am not sure why we should think that pairs of students who come in for an hour or so are more accurate raters of local conditions than many pairs of people who live there." Not all subjective measures are created equal, however. Thacher (2004, p. 396) argues that subjective measures that reflect context-specific forms of disorder, such as "lying down on public steps" and "flagrant public urination in a highly visible location" are preferred over broadly worded items (e.g., "panhandling" and "youth parties").[4] It is doubtful that the debate over SSO versus perceptual disorder measures will be resolved any time soon. For now, it may be sufficient to note that the evidence shows that measures derived from both sources are strongly correlated with one another at the neighborhood level (Raudenbush and Sampson 1999, p. 31; Sampson and Raudenbush 1999, p. 625).

Evidence from recently conducted field experiments in the Neth-

---

[3] Research conducted in nonmetropolitan communities has also shown that the relationship between disorder and crime is mediated by aggregate-level social processes (Reisig and Cancino 2004).

[4] For a list of disorder measures that have been used previously, see Ross and Mirowsky (1999, pp. 427–29).

erlands provides empirical support for the disorder-crime link (Keizer, Lindenberg, and Steg 2008). Keizer et al. constructed six controlled experiments in which participants were exposed to various manipulations (i.e., the presence of different forms of disorder) and provided with staged opportunities to violate the law (e.g., litter, trespass, and commit theft). The control groups were provided with the same crime opportunities but in orderly settings. Guided by broken windows theory, the authors argued that the presence of disorder weakens social norms on appropriate conduct (termed the "cross-norm inhibition effect"). It was hypothesized that participants exposed to the disorder condition would violate the law more frequently relative to control group members. The results from all six experiments conformed to the authors' expectations. For example, when researchers placed paper flyers from a fictitious business on the handlebars of bicycles parked in a public bike rack, individuals who retrieved their bikes under the disorder condition (i.e., the wall adjacent to the rack was covered in graffiti) were significantly more likely to discard the flyer improperly (69 percent) relative to the control group (33 percent). Although the results from the experiments are intriguing, cynics are likely to point out that the criminal behaviors observed in the study do not represent serious predatory offenses.

Research on the empirical connection between neighborhood disorder and fear of crime has been frustrated by a lack of theoretical clarity and measurement ambiguity. Regarding the latter, fear of crime is measured in a variety of ways. Some researchers use survey-based measures that reflect cognitive judgments of victimization risk and safety. Others prefer survey measures that reflect affective emotions tapping into the anxiety about crime and crime-related symbols (Ferraro 1995). At the individual level, these different fear variables are empirically distinct. When aggregated to the neighborhood level, however, these items are highly correlated and tend to behave similarly with regard to their relationship with other known correlates of fear (see Markowitz et al. 2001).

Three rigorous neighborhood-level studies show consistent findings. Reisig and Parks (2004) found that their neighborhood incivilities measure was significantly correlated with cognitive judgments of safety across 59 neighborhoods in Indianapolis and St. Petersburg, Florida. Rountree and Land (1996) observed that neighborhood incivilities were associated with perceptions of crime or victimization risk (or cognitive judgments of safety) and burglary-specific fear (a measure reflecting affective emotions). Both of these studies are limited by their reliance on cross-sectional designs. Using information from three waves of the British Crime Survey, Markowitz et al. (2001) found support for the causal connection between disorder and fear (a composite measure consisting of both cognitive judgments and affective emotions). Which type of fear is most consistent with broken windows theory? A clear explanation remains elusive. To some observers, this represents a theoretical shortcoming in that those evaluating whether community policing can decrease fear among citizens fail to articulate whether effects should vary from one dimension of fear to the next or whether the effects should be uniform (Greene and Taylor 1988, pp. 205–6).

B. Social Disorganization Theory

Community policing can be conceptualized using variant forms of social disorganization theory. The use of social disorganization theory in the field of policing can be traced back to the community crime prevention movement. During this time it was argued that the police should work with community organizations to alter neighborhood-level social conditions that give rise to crime (Hope 1995; Greene 2000). This view was influenced greatly by the pioneering work of the Chicago school of sociology, especially that of Shaw and McKay (1942). Early disorganization theorists posited that impoverished neighborhoods inhabited by racially and ethnically heterogeneous populations that experience high levels of residential instability were less likely to exhibit high levels of social organization. Socially disorganized local communities share two common characteristics: a lack of value consensus among residents and an inability to maintain effective social controls (Kornhauser 1978). According to this perspective, disorganized neighborhoods will experience higher rates of crime and delinquency. Although highly influential in criminology, Shaw and McKay's theory is relatively limited in providing insights into how the police can improve criminogenic neighborhood conditions.

A more meaningful approach to situating the police within a social disorganization framework is provided by the systemic model, which focuses on the effects of social controls exerted from relational and social networks said to mediate the adverse effects of structural constraints (e.g., concentrated poverty and residential instability; see fig.

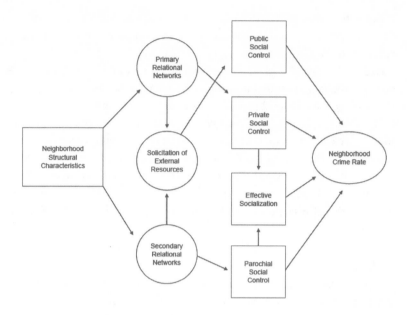

FIG. 3.—The systemic model of neighborhood crime. Source: Adapted from Bursik and Grasmick (1993, p. 39).

3). Such networks vary both qualitatively and in terms of their ability to regulate the behavior of local residents and visitors. Hunter (1985) identified three social orders, listed here in descending order of affect: private (e.g., close friends and family), parochial (neighbors and civic organizations), and public (e.g., the police; also see Bursik and Grasmick 1993, pp. 24–59). Since the informal social controls that flow from private and parochial networks have been shown to reduce neighborhood crime (see, e.g., Sampson and Groves 1989), scholars argue that the police should work with residents to develop stronger regulative mechanisms (Kubrin and Weitzer 2003). Hunter (1985), for example, notes that parochial networks are effective at surveillance, a facet of social control that the police are inadequately staffed to provide via patrol. By reaching out to neighborhood organizations and working with community residents, the argument follows, the police can help shore up informal social controls and, in turn, reduce neighborhood crime and improve residents' quality of life (e.g., increase perceptions of safety, reduce visible signs of disorder, and develop trust among neighbors).

A recent ethnographic study conducted in a middle-class Chicago neighborhood (Beltway) provides a look at how neighborhood residents and formal social control agents can work together to reduce crime and disorder. Carr (2005) notes that in Beltway traditional informal social controls were breaking down: large numbers of children of working parents were left unsupervised (private controls), and area residents were reluctant to discipline neighborhood children who engaged in wrongdoing (parochial controls). Following two local gang-related shootings, community members attempted to organize. One of the groups worked with community organizers and police officials through the CAPS program. CAPS officials provided problem-solving training, helping the community group identify local problems and develop action plans. Once this had taken place, CAPS officials withdrew from the process but remained available to provide services and assistance when called on. The community group successfully solved the targeted problems (e.g., closing down a local tavern and removing gang graffiti). Carr argues that this type of police-community collaboration reflects a hybrid form of social control, which he terms "the new parochialism" (p. 7). Put simply, in neighborhoods where traditional private and parochial social controls are weak, the police and other formal social control agents can put mechanisms in place to bolster the ability of community groups to exert informal social controls (e.g., problem-solving training) and obtain services from public agencies. The other community groups that formed after the shootings that did not partner with public agencies, Carr notes, dissolved within a year.

Quantitative studies on the effects of formal-informal social control linkages on crime and crime-related outcomes at the neighborhood level are scant. Reisig and Park's (2004) multilevel study of the effect of community policing on neighborhood quality of life sheds some light on the topic. Using data from the Project on Policing Neighborhoods, Reisig and Parks tested whether their measure of community policing—"police-community collaboration" (operationalized using information from citizen and police surveys aggregated to the neighborhood level)—mediated the effect of concentrated disadvantage on perceived incivility (visible signs of physical and social disorder) and perceived safety (cognitive judgments), net of violent crime rates and a host of individual-level statistical controls. Consistent with their expectations, Reisig and Parks found that police-community collaboration fully mediated the adverse effects of structural disadvantage, lead-ing them to conclude that the "police should work to address crime and disorder by establishing mutual levels of trust, building working relationships with citizens, and strengthening both informal and formal social controls" (pp. 163–64).

Yet another branch of social disorganization theory, one that features the concept of collective efficacy, has also been used in discussions of community policing. Collective efficacy is conceptualized as consisting of two key elements—social cohesion and informal social control. Ac-cording to this perspective, neighborhood social controls are most ef-fective when trust among area residents is high (Sampson 2004). Re-search has shown that collective efficacy is a strong predictor of neighborhood crime (Sampson, Raudenbush, and Earls 1997), delin-quency (Simons et al. 2005), and disorder (Sampson and Raudenbush 1999; Reisig and Cancino 2004). However, collective efficacy is not restricted to indigenous neighborhood resources but also draws on ser-vices and assistance from public agencies, such as the police, to achieve and maintain social order. As Skogan (2008b, p. 48) recently noted, however, the direct effects of community policing on collective efficacy are "undocumented."

How can community policing promote neighborhood collective ef-ficacy? Broadly speaking, the police need to employ innovative strat-egies that enhance their legitimacy and promote procedurally just part-nerships, which in turn encourage residents to take responsibility for public spaces and activate local social controls (Sampson 2004). Per-haps the most useful community policing tactic for achieving this ob-jective is the beat meeting. Bringing residents together in a forum that encourages interaction and dialogue and the facilitation of collaborative efforts to improve neighborhood conditions (e.g., reduce disorder) may enhance levels of collective efficacy and reduce crime in the long run (Sampson and Raudenbush 2001; Sampson 2004).

Stimulating healthy levels of beat meeting participation can be a daunting task for the police. Whether residents decide to get involved is influenced by a number of factors. Local citizens may get involved because they are concerned about neighborhood conditions and want to do their part to improve things. However, participants may distrust their neighbors and get involved only to maintain a watchful eye on the interests that are being advanced (St. Jean 2007). Known justifi-cations for nonparticipation are numerous, including fear of retaliation from individuals who become police targets, concern that friends and family will become targets of the police, a high level of distrust in the police, and a lack of free time. All these factors shape beat meeting attendance, which is rarely representative of the community. In Chicago beat meetings, Skogan (2004) found evidence of a middle-class participation bias. Homeowners and individuals with higher levels of education were significantly more likely to turn out. Minority citizens, especially Latinos, were much less likely to get involved. Skogan found that participants' concerns with disorder-related problems (drugs, gangs, and physical decay) were generally reflective of the concerns expressed by the broader community; however, their views on crime problems, such as burglary, were less representative. The potential problem that emerges is that police responsiveness to the concerns expressed during beat meetings may conflict with the equally important value of equity, which necessitates that police services be provided fairly across all segments of the community (Thacher 2001b). For beat meetings to be successful, Thacher notes, the police must not simply be reactive to concerns expressed by involved citizens, but rather engage participants in problem-solving activities that are consistent with the well-being of the community as a whole. Doing so may require that the police provide evidence (e.g., crime statistics, calls for service data, and results from officer investigations) to dispel local myths, correct misperceptions, and educate participants about legal constraints.

On the basis of his fieldwork, Thacher (2001a) cautions that value conflicts often surface when the police work to develop community partnerships. One area of contention concerns the goal of public safety. Thacher observed that residents who attended beat meetings were primarily concerned with disorder problems, whereas the police tended to focus on more serious crimes. Interestingly, broken windows theory helped provide common ground. Citizens' disorder concerns were addressed by the police, who believed that doing so would reduce more serious crime. The second type of conflict, according to Thacher, concerns the proper use of legal authority. He argues that sustaining community partnerships requires "greater attention to parsimonious and fair use of authority" (p. 788). Research supports Thacher's observations. Residents who perceive that police exercise their authority in a procedurally just manner are more likely to view the police as legitimate, cooperate with the police, and express a willingness to participate in police programs (Sunshine and Tyler 2003; Tyler 2003; Reisig 2007; Reisig, Bratton, and Gertz 2007).

C. Problem-Oriented Policing: Theory and Research

The problem-oriented policing process can be demanding. As Goldstein (1987) envisioned it, problem-oriented policing entails intensive scanning for recurring problems, the careful analysis of data from a variety of sources to better understand the underlying causes of problems, the development of creative responses to solve problems, and the rigorous assessment of interventions to gauge effectiveness. As an analytic tool, however, problem-oriented policing is quite flexible. The SARA model can be applied to a variety of crime- and non-crime-related problems (Eck and Spelman 1987). The manner in which the police respond to crime and disorder problems can take diverse forms, including the use of traditional law enforcement tactics (e.g., directed patrol and crackdowns) and even zero tolerance policing if the problem calls for taking back sidewalks from street criminals, such as drug dealers, prostitutes, and gangs (Cordner 1998). Community policing tactics (e.g., neighborhood clean-up programs) can also be used when deemed appropriate.

Problem-oriented policing can be conceptualized as a method of preventing and controlling crime that is consistent with the teachings of the environmental criminology school of thought (Eck 2006; Scott et al. 2008). Environmental criminologists posit that criminogenic environmental elements give rise to criminal and disorderly behavior (Wortley and Mazerolle 2008). In environmental criminology, opportunity is viewed as a key aspect in every type of crime, and opportunity-blocking measures represent the best approach to reducing crime (Clarke 2008). The opportunity reduction approach to problem-oriented policing, which involves reducing opportunities for crime by manipulating local environments, is similar to the concept of situational crime prevention (Clarke 1992). Braga (2008, p. 4) notes that the police "are best positioned to prevent crimes by focusing on the situational opportunities for offenders rather than to manipulate socioeconomic conditions that are the subjects of much criminological theory."

Two theories offer guidance with regard to limiting criminal opportunity. Rational choice theory views criminal behavior as a purposeful and deliberate attempt to benefit the offender. When contemplating the commission of a crime, the theory holds, offenders weigh the potential risks, rewards, and effort involved. In terms of crime prevention, rational choice theory suggests that the parties involved in such efforts should work to change environmental conditions by elevating risks, reducing rewards, and curtailing provocations and temptations (Cornish and Clarke 2008). A host of police tactics can be used to accomplish this goal. For example, police officials may opt for traditional law enforcement tactics, such as directed patrols, crackdowns, and stop and frisk interrogations, to elevate the risk of apprehension.

A second approach, routine activity theory, posits that criminal incidents occur when three elements are present: suitable targets, absence of capable guardians, and motivated offenders (Cohen and Felson 1979; Felson 2008). Police officials who adopt this perspective are aided by an important tool, the "crime triangle" (Hough and Tilley 1998; Eck 2003). The crime triangle consists of three elements (i.e., victim, offender, and location). Assuming that all three elements are necessary for crime to occur, during the analysis stage of the problem-solving process the police collect information on the three sides of the triangle and work to determine which element is most vulnerable to police intervention (Read and Tilley 2000; Scott et al. 2008). During the response stage, the police work to develop a strategy for reducing the influence of the target element. For example, the police may determine that criminal opportunities need to be reduced at a particular location and work to change site features by asking other government agencies to add streetlights and board up abandoned buildings (Braga 2008, p. 63).

Few police innovations have enjoyed as much empirical attention as problem-oriented policing (see Scott [2000] for a review). One line of research has focused on the effectiveness of problem-oriented policing in combating crime and disorder. The scientific rigor of research in this area varies widely, however. A recent meta-analysis, conducted by David Weisburd and his colleagues (2008), identified only 10 studies (published and unpublished) that evaluated the effects of problem-oriented policing on crime and disorder using either experimental or quasi-experimental designs (with comparison groups). Of the 10 studies, eight reported favorable results. When the studies were grouped together, however, the magnitude of the treatment effect (i.e., problem-oriented policing interventions) was fairly modest (Cohen's $d = .125$; Weisburd et al. 2008, p. 25). The authors also looked at less methodologically rigorous studies (i.e., pre/posttests). Among this grouping, the reported outcomes were overwhelmingly positive (43 of the 45 studies reported a decline in disorder or crime). Overall, the research literature is generally supportive of problem-oriented policing interventions, though the level of support appears to vary inversely with the level of scientific rigor characterizing the research designs employed.

A second empirical question has to do with how problem-oriented policing is actually practiced on the streets. Cordner and Biebel's (2005) study of the San Diego Police Department (SDPD) addressed this question. The SDPD is well known for its strong commitment to problem-oriented policing. Using the SARA model to guide their assessment, the authors found that officers were fairly passive in the scanning stage. Personal observations and complaints were most frequently used to initiate the process. The analysis stage was largely informal. Officers generally depended on their own observations to frame problems. This is not atypical. Bynum (2001, p. 18) notes that police officers often view the analysis stage as "requiring too much time and too many resources." Cordner and Biebel found that traditional police tactics, such as targeted enforcement, directed patrol, and the like, were among the most common responses. Finally, the assessment stage was usually limited in scope, restricted largely to officers' personal observations. Limited assessments of intervention outcomes are not unique to the SDPD. In their review of problem-solving initiatives in England and Wales, Read and Tilley (2000, p. vii) concluded that "high quality, dependable outcomes evaluations were rare." To some observers, these findings may simply reflect the use of problem-oriented policing jargon to legitimize traditional policing tactics. But Cordner and Biebel were encouraged that the officers they observed were regularly involved in problem-solving activities. There may be reason for optimism. Some researchers believe that the brand of problem-oriented policing practiced by the SDPD, sometimes referred to as "shallow problem solving," can be effective at alleviating crime and disorder problems (Braga and Weisburd 2006).

V. What Next?
Community and problem-oriented policing have probably done more to shape the debate over the role of the American police than anything

since the introduction of the patrol car and two-way radio. Many police departments nationwide have implemented community and problem-oriented policing tactics to reduce crime and disorder and improve citizens' quality of life. However, the extent to which such reforms have been adopted is uneven. Only time will tell whether community and problem-oriented policing will continue to influence debate over the proper role of the police.

The research on community and problem-oriented policing is encouraging. Not only are such studies becoming increasingly sophisticated in terms of theoretical application and methodological rigor, but many of the questions regarding the usefulness of community and problem-oriented policing appear to have been answered. For example, the weight of the evidence suggests that community and problem-solving policing tactics can reduce crime, albeit modestly, and improve citizens' perceptions of neighborhood conditions. Echoing this conclusion, Harcourt and Ludwig (2006, pp. 314–15) recently noted that "outside of perhaps a few remaining university sociology departments and some Berkeley coffee shops, the notion that 'police matter' is (or at least should be) widely accepted." Yet, many gaps in the understanding of police strategies and tactics remain unanswered. Accordingly, three areas are ripe for empirical investigation.

Much of the broken windows–based policing research has assessed the effect of misdemeanor arrests on precinct-level crime rates. While informative, some observers have noted that focusing solely on misdemeanor arrests is only part of the picture. Future research that employs more complete order maintenance variables, including a variety of tactics, would certainly be viewed as an important contribution. However, achieving such a feat could prove difficult. As Thacher (2004, p. 391) has noted, "one of the most serious gaps" in the policing literature is studies detailing "what exactly order maintenance policing activities involve—what behaviors they target in which contexts, and what actions police take to control them." Book-length ethnographic studies of policing were once quite common but are now rarely published. Qualitative accounts that describe the ways in which police officers familiarize themselves with local norms and customs, the tactics they use to resolve encounters with disorderly individuals on the streets, and the ways in which the use of order maintenance tactics varies across urban neighborhoods would prove valuable in designing more precise tests of order maintenance policing.

To date, studies of the effects of policing strategies on aggregated crime rates have neglected the potential influence of social processes, such as collective efficacy. Accordingly, the possibility of omitted variable bias cannot be ruled out. Cerdá et al. (2009, p. 540) identify two potential effects of collective efficacy. First, collective efficacy may mediate the effect of misdemeanor arrests on crime because residents in neighborhoods with higher levels of collective agency experience greater success at securing police services. Second, it may be that the effect of misdemeanor policing on crime operates through collective efficacy. In other words, misdemeanor arrests increase the collective capacity of neighborhood residents to work together toward the common good. At this point, however, neither hypothesized effect has been subjected to empirical scrutiny.

Another question in need of investigation is what effect (if any) community policing practices, such as beat meetings and other social organizing activities, have on collective efficacy and whether observed changes in levels of neighborhood social conditions influence crime and disorder. Sampson (2004) has posited that beat meetings may promote collective efficacy. Unfortunately, very little is known about this causal connection (Skogan 2008b). A variety of research designs could be employed to address this issue. For example, studies employing pre- and posttests (with matched comparison groups) could help determine whether community policing interventions facilitate collective engagement among residents and, in turn, improve neighborhood conditions.

Not only has community and problem-oriented policing transformed the ongoing debate on police policy and practice, but the two models have also been the impetus for a series of important research projects that have produced some of the most scientifically rigorous studies published in the social sciences (see, e.g., Skogan 2006; Braga and Bond 2008). Contemporary policing scholars have successfully moved the field forward. Continued scientific advancement is contingent on the ability of future researchers to construct informative theoretical frameworks to guide their work, construct valid and reliable measures, and design thoughtful experiments, systematic social observational studies, and longitudinal assessments using multiple data sources.

REFERENCES

Bloch, Peter B., and David Specht. 1973. *Neighborhood Team Policing: Prescriptive Package*. Washington, DC: U.S. Department of Justice, Law Enforcement Assistance Administration, National Institute of Law Enforcement and Criminal Justice.

Braga, Anthony A. 2008. *Problem-Oriented Policing and Crime Prevention*. 2nd ed. Monsey, NY: Criminal Justice Press.

Braga, Anthony A., and Brenda J. Bond. 2008. "Policing Crime and Disorder Hot Spots: A Randomized Controlled Trial." *Criminology* 46:577–607.

Braga, Anthony A., and David Weisburd. 2006. "Problem-Oriented Policing: The Disconnect between Principles and Practice." In *Police Innovation: Contrasting Perspectives*, edited by David Weisburd and Anthony A. Braga. Cambridge: Cambridge University Press.

Bratton, William, and George Kelling. 2006. "There Are No Cracks in the Broken Windows." *National Review* (February 28), http://www.national review.com/comment/bratton_kelling200602281015.asp.

Bursik, Robert J., Jr., and Harold G. Grasmick. 1993. *Neighborhoods and Crime: The Dimensions of Effective Community Control*. Lanham, MD: Lexington.

Bynum, Timothy S. 2001. *Using Analysis for Problem-Solving: A Guidebook for Law Enforcement*. Washington, DC: U.S. Department of Justice, Office of Community Oriented Policing Services.

Carr, Patrick J. 2005. *Clean Streets: Controlling Crime, Maintaining Order, and Building Community Activism*. New York: New York University Press.

Cerdá, Magdalena, Melissa Tracy, Steven F. Messner, David Vlahov, Kenneth Tardiff, and Sandro Galea. 2009. "Misdemeanor Policing, Physical Disorder, and Gun-Related Homicide: A Spatial Analytic Test of 'Broken-Windows' Theory." *Epidemiology* 20:533–41.

Clarke, Ronald V. 1992. *Situational Crime Prevention: Successful Case Studies*. Albany, NY: Harrow and Heston.

———. 2008. "Situation Crime Prevention." In *Environmental Criminology and Crime Analysis*, edited by Richard Wortley and Lorraine Mazerolle. Devon, UK: Willan.

Cohen, Lawrence E., and Marcus Felson. 1979. "Social Change and Crime Rate Trends: A Routine Activity Approach." *American Sociological Review* 44: 588–608.

Cordner, Gary. 1998. "Problem-Oriented Policing vs. Zero Tolerance." In *Problem-Oriented Policing: Crime-Specific Problems, Critical Issues and Making POP Work*, edited by Tara O'Connor Shelley and Anne C. Grant. Washington, DC: Police Executive Research Forum.

———. 1999. "Elements of Community Policing." In *Policing Perspectives: An Anthology*, edited by Larry K. Gaines and Gary W. Cordner. Los Angeles: Roxbury.

Cordner, Gary, and Elizabeth Perkins Biebel. 2005. "Problem-Oriented Policing in Practice." *Criminology and Public Policy* 4:155–80.

Corman, Hope, and Naci Mocan. 2005. "Carrots, Sticks, and Broken Windows." *Journal of Law and Economics* 48:235–66.

Cornish, Derek B., and Ronald V. Clarke. 2008. "The Rational Choice Perspective." In *Environmental Criminology and Crime Analysis*, edited by Richard Wortley and Lorraine Mazerolle. Devon, UK: Willan.

Davis, Gareth, David B. Muhlhausen, Dexter Ingram, and Ralph A. Rector. 2000. *The Facts about COPS: A Performance Overview of the Community Oriented Policing Services Program*. Report no. 00-10. Washington, DC: Heritage Foundation, Center for Data Analysis.

Eck, John E. 2003. "Police Problems: The Complexity of Problem Theory, Research and Evaluation." *Crime Prevention Studies* 15:79–113.

———. 2006. "Science, Values, and Problem-Oriented Policing: Why Problem-Oriented Policing?" In *Police Innovation: Contrasting Perspectives*, edited by David Weisburd and Anthony A. Braga. Cambridge: Cambridge University Press.

Eck, John E., and William Spelman. 1987. *Problem-Solving: Problem-Oriented Policing in Newport News*. Washington, DC: Police Executive Research Forum.

Evans, William N., and Emily G. Owens. 2007. "COPS and Crime." *Journal of Public Economics* 91:181–201.

Fagan, Jeffrey A., and Garth Davies. 2000. "Street Stops and Broken Windows: *Terry*, Race, and Disorder in New York City." *Fordham Urban Law Journal* 28:457–504.

Fayol, Henri. 1949. *General and Industrial Management*. London: Pitman. (Originally published in 1916.)

Felson, Marcus. 2008. "Routine Activity Approach." In *Environmental Criminology and Crime Analysis*, edited by Richard Wortley and Lorraine Mazerolle. Devon, UK: Willan.

Ferraro, Kenneth F. 1995. *Fear of Crime: Interpreting Victimization Risk*. Albany: SUNY Press.

Fosdick, Raymond B. 1969. *European Police Systems*. Montclair, NJ: Patterson Smith. (Originally published in 1915.)

GAO (Government Accountability Office). 2005. *Community Policing Grants: COPS Grants Were a Modest Contributor to Declines in Crime in the 1990s*. GAO-06-104. Washington, DC: Government Accountability Office.

Goldstein, Herman. 1979. "Improving Policing: A Problem-Solving Approach." *Crime and Delinquency* 25:236–58.

———. 1987. "Toward Community-Oriented Policing: Potential, Basic Requirements, and Threshold Questions." *Crime and Delinquency* 33:6–30.

———. 1990. *Problem-Oriented Policing*. New York: McGraw-Hill.

Goodnow, Frank J. 1900. *Politics and Administration: A Study in Government*. New York: Russell & Russell.

Greene, Jack R. 2000. "Community Policing in America: Changing the Nature, Structure, and Function of the Police." In *Criminal Justice 2000*, vol. 3, edited by Julie Horney. Washington, DC: U.S. Department of Justice, National Institute of Justice.

Greene, Jack R., and Ralph B. Taylor. 1988. "Community-Based Policing and Foot Patrol: Issues in Theory and Evaluation." In *Community Policing: Rhet-*

oric or Reality, edited by Jack R. Greene and Stephen D. Mastrofski. New York: Praeger.

Greene, Judith A. 1999. "Zero Tolerance: A Case Study of Police Policies and Practices in New York City." *Crime and Delinquency* 45:171–87.

Greenwood, Peter W., and Joan Petersilia. 1975. *The Criminal Investigation Process*. Vol. 1, *Summary and Policy Implications*. Santa Monica, CA: Rand.

Haller, Mark H. 1975. "Historical Roots of Police Behavior: Chicago, 1890–1925." *Law and Society Review* 10:303–23.

Harcourt, Bernard E. 1998. "Reflecting on the Subject: A Critique of the Social Influence Conception of Deterrence, the Broken Windows Theory, and Order-Maintenance Policing New York Style." *Michigan Law Review* 97: 291–389.

Harcourt, Bernard E., and Jens Ludwig. 2006. "Broken Windows: New Evidence from New York City and a Five-City Social Experiment." *University of Chicago Law Review* 73:271–320.

———. 2007. "Reefer Madness: Broken Windows Policing and Misdemeanor Marijuana Arrests in New York City, 1989–2000." *Criminology and Public Policy* 6:165–81.

Hope, Tim. 1995. "Community Crime Prevention." In *Building a Safer Society: Strategic Approaches to Crime Prevention*, edited by Michael Tonry and David P. Farrington. Vol. 19 of *Crime and Justice: A Review of Research*, edited by Michael Tonry. Chicago: University of Chicago Press.

Hough, Michael, and Nick Tilley. 1998. *Getting the Grease to Squeak: Research Lessons for Crime Prevention*. Crime Detection and Prevention Series, no. 85. London: Home Office.

Hunter, Albert. 1985. "Private, Parochial, and Public Social Orders: The Problem of Crime and Incivility in Urban Communities." In *The Challenge of Social Control: Citizenship and Institution Building*, edited by Gerald D. Suttles and Mayer N. Zald. Norwood, NJ: Ablex.

Ingram, Jason R. 2007. "The Effect of Neighborhood Characteristics on Traffic Citation Practices of the Police." *Police Quarterly* 10:371–93.

James, Nathan. 2008. *Community Oriented Policing Services (COPS): Background, Legislation, and Issues*. Report for Congress. Washington, DC: Congressional Research Service.

Katz, Charles M., Vincent J. Webb, and David R. Schaefer. 2001. "An Assessment of the Impact of Quality-of-Life Policing on Crime and Disorder." *Justice Quarterly* 18:825–76.

Keizer, Kees, Siegwart Lindenberg, and Linda Steg. 2008. "The Spreading of Disorder." *Science* 322:1681–85.

Kelling, George L., and William J. Bratton. 1998. "Declining Crime Rates: Insiders' Views of the New York City Story." *Journal of Criminal Law and Criminology* 88:1217–31.

Kelling, George L., and Catherine M. Coles. 1996. *Fixing Broken Windows: Restoring Order and Reducing Crime in Our Communities*. New York: Free Press.

Kelling, George L., and Mark H. Moore. 1988. "From Political to Reform to

Community: The Evolving Strategy of Police." In *Community Policing: Rhetoric or Reality*, edited by Jack R. Greene and Stephen Mastrofski. New York: Praeger.

Kelling, George L., Tony Pate, Duane Dieckman, and Charles E. Brown. 1974. *The Kansas City Preventive Patrol Experiment: A Summary Report*. Washington, DC: Police Foundation.

Kelling, George L., and William H. Sousa Jr. 2001. *Do Police Matter? An Analysis of the Impact of New York City's Police Reforms*. New York: Center for Civic Innovation, Manhattan Institute.

Koper, Chris S., Gretchen E. Moore, and Jeffrey A. Roth. 2002. *Putting 100,000 Officers on the Street: A Survey-Based Assessment of the Federal COPS Program*. Washington, DC: Urban Institute.

Kornhauser, Ruth R. 1978. *Social Sources of Delinquency: An Appraisal of Analytic Models*. Chicago: University of Chicago Press.

Kubrin, Charis E. 2008. "Making Order of Disorder: A Call for Conceptual Clarity." *Criminology and Public Policy* 7:203–14.

Kubrin, Charis E., and Ronald Weitzer. 2003. "New Directions in Social Disorganization Theory." *Journal of Research in Crime and Delinquency* 40: 374–402.

Lane, Roger. 1980. "Urban Police and Crime in Nineteenth-Century America." In *Crime and Justice: An Annual Review of Research*, vol. 2, edited by Norval Morris and Michael Tonry. Chicago: University of Chicago Press.

Leigh, Adrian, Tim Reed, and Nick Tilley. 1996. *Problem-Oriented Policing: Brit Pop*. Crime Detection and Prevention Series, Paper no. 75. London: Home Office.

Levitt, Steven D. 2004. "Understanding Why Crime Fell in the 1990s: Four Factors That Explain the Decline and Six That Do Not." *Journal of Economic Perspectives* 18:163–90.

Maguire, Edward R., and Stephen D. Mastrofski. 2000. "Patterns of Community Policing in the United States." *Police Quarterly* 3:4–45.

Manning, Peter K. 1988. "Community Policing as a Drama of Control." In *Community Policing: Rhetoric or Reality*, edited by Jack R. Greene and Stephen D. Mastrofski. New York: Praeger.

Markowitz, Fred E., Paul E. Bellair, Allen E. Liska, and Jianhong Liu. 2001. "Extending Social Disorganization Theory: Modeling the Relationships between Cohesion, Disorder, and Fear." *Criminology* 39:293–320.

Mastrofski, Stephen D. 1988. "Community Policing as Reform: A Cautionary Tale." In *Community Policing: Rhetoric or Reality*, edited by Jack R. Greene and Stephen D. Mastrofski. New York: Praeger.

Mastrofski, Stephen D., Michael D. Reisig, and John D. McCluskey. 2002. "Police Disrespect toward the Public: An Encounter-Based Analysis." *Criminology* 40:519–51.

Meares, Tracey L. 1998. "Place and Crime." *Chicago Kent Law Review* 73: 669–705.

Messner, Steven F., Sandro Galea, Kenneth J. Tardiff, Melissa Tracy, Angela Bucciarelli, Tinka Markham Piper, Victoria Frye, and David Vlahov. 2007.

"Policing, Drugs, and the Homicide Decline in New York City in the 1990s." *Criminology* 45:385–414.

Miller, Wilbur R. 1977. *Cops and Bobbies: Police Authority in New York and London, 1830–1870*. Chicago: University of Chicago Press.

Monkkonen, Eric H. 1981. *Police in Urban America, 1860–1920*. Cambridge: Cambridge University Press.

Moore, Mark H. 1992. "Problem-Solving and Community Policing." In *Modern Policing*, edited by Michael Tonry and Norval Morris. Vol. 15 of *Crime and Justice: A Review of Research*, edited by Michael Tonry. Chicago: University of Chicago Press.

Muhlhausen, David B. 2001. *Do Community Oriented Policing Services Grants Affect Violent Crime Rates?* Report no. CDA01-05. Washington, DC: Heritage Foundation, Center for Data Analysis.

———. 2002. *Research Challenges Claim of COPS Effectiveness*. Report no. CDA02-02. Washington, DC: Heritage Foundation, Center for Data Analysis.

Muhlhausen, David B., and Brian W. Walsh. 2008. "COPS Reform: Why Congress Can't Make the COPS Program Work." Backgrounder, Executive Summary no. 2188. Washington, DC: Heritage Foundation.

National Advisory Commission on Civil Disorders. 1968. *Report of the National Advisory Commission on Civil Disorders*. Washington, DC: U.S. Government Printing Office.

Pate, Anthony M. 1986. "Experimenting with Foot Patrol: The Newark Experience." In *Community Crime Prevention: Does It Work?* edited by Dennis Rosenbaum. Beverly Hills, CA: Sage.

Piquero, Alex, Jack Greene, James Fyfe, Robert J. Kane, and Patricia Collins. 2000. "Implementing Community Policing in Public Housing Developments in Philadelphia: Some Early Results." In *Community Policing: Contemporary Readings*, 2nd ed., edited by Geoffrey P. Alpert and Alex Piquero. Prospect Heights, IL: Waveland.

Raudenbush, Stephen W., and Robert J. Sampson. 1999. "Ecometrics: Toward a Science of Assessing Ecological Settings, with Application to the Systematic Social Observation of Neighborhoods." *Sociological Methodology* 29:1–41.

Read, Tim, and Nick Tilley. 2000. *Not Rocket Science? Problem-Solving and Crime Reduction*. Crime Reduction Research Series, Paper no. 6. London: Home Office.

Reisig, Michael D. 2007. "Procedural Justice and Community Policing: What Shapes Residents' Willingness to Participate in Crime Prevention Programs?" *Policing: A Journal of Policy and Practice* 1:356–69.

Reisig, Michael D., Jason Bratton, and Marc Gertz. 2007. "The Construct Validity and Refinement of Process-Based Policing Measures." *Criminal Justice and Behavior* 34:1005–28.

Reisig, Michael D., and Jeffrey Michael Cancino. 2004. "Incivilities in Nonmetropolitan Communities: The Effects of Structural Constraints, Social Conditions, and Crime." *Journal of Criminal Justice* 32:15–29.

Reisig, Michael D., and Roger B. Parks. 2004. "Can Community Policing Help the Truly Disadvantaged?" *Crime and Delinquency* 50:139–67.

Reiss, Albert J., Jr. 1985. *Policing a City's Central District: The Oakland Story.* Washington, DC: U.S. Department of Justice, National Institute of Justice.

Rosenbaum, Dennis P. 1988. "Community Crime Prevention: A Review and Synthesis of the Literature." *Justice Quarterly* 5:323–95.

Rosenbaum, Dennis P., Arthur J. Lurigio, and Robert C. Davis. 1998. *The Prevention of Crime: Social and Situation Strategies.* Belmont, CA: Wadsworth.

Rosenfeld, Richard, Robert Fornango, and Andres F. Rengifo. 2007. "The Impact of Order-Maintenance Policing on New York City Homicide and Robbery Rates: 1988–2001." *Criminology* 45:355–84.

Ross, Catherine E., and John Mirowsky. 1999. "Disorder and Decay: The Concept and Measurement of Perceived Neighborhood Disorder." *Urban Affairs Quarterly* 34:412–32.

Roth, Jeffrey A., Jan Roehl, and Calvin C. Johnson. 2004. "Trends in the Adoption of Community Policing." In *Community Policing: Can It Work?* edited by Wesley G. Skogan. Belmont, CA: Wadsworth.

Roth, Jeffrey A., and Joseph F. Ryan. 2000. *The COPS Program after 4 Years: National Evaluation.* Washington, DC: National Institute of Justice.

Rountree, Pamela Wilcox, and Kenneth C. Land. 1996. "Perceived Risk versus Fear of Crime: Empirical Evidence of Conceptually Distinct Reactions in Survey Data." *Social Forces* 74:1353–76.

Sampson, Robert. 2004. "Neighborhood and Community: Collective Efficacy and Community Safety." *New Economy* 11:106–13.

Sampson, Robert J., and W. Byron Groves. 1989. "Community Structure and Crime: Testing Social-Disorganization Theory." *American Journal of Sociology* 94:774–802.

Sampson, Robert J., and Stephen W. Raudenbush. 1999. "Systematic Social Observation of Public Spaces: A New Look at Disorder in Urban Neighborhoods." *American Journal of Sociology* 105:603–51.

———. 2001. *Disorder in Urban Neighborhoods: Does It Lead to Crime?* Research in Brief. Washington, DC: U.S. Department of Justice, National Institute of Justice.

Sampson, Robert J., Stephen W. Raudenbush, and Felton Earls. 1997. "Neighborhoods and Violent Crime: A Multilevel Study of Collective Efficacy." *Science* 277:918–24.

Scott, Michael S. 2000. *Problem-Oriented Policing: Reflections on the First 20 Years.* Washington, DC: U.S. Department of Justice, Office of Community Oriented Policing Services.

Scott, Michael, John Eck, Johannes Knutsson, and Herman Goldstein. 2008. "Problem-Oriented Policing and Environmental Criminology." In *Environmental Criminology and Crime Analysis,* edited by Richard Wortley and Lorraine Mazerolle. Devon, UK: Willan.

Shafritz, Jay M., and J. Steven Ott. 1996. *Classics of Organization Theory.* 4th ed. Fort Worth, TX: Harcourt Brace.

Shaw, Clifford R., and Henry D. McKay. 1942. *Juvenile Delinquency and Urban Crime*. Chicago: University of Chicago Press.

Sherman, Lawrence W. 1991. "Problem-Oriented Policing by Herman Goldstein." *Journal of Criminal Law and Criminology* 82:690–707.

Sherman, Lawrence W., Catherine H. Milton, and Thomas V. Kelly. 1973. *Team Policing: Seven Case Studies*. Washington, DC: Police Foundation.

Simons, Ronald L., Leslie Simons, Callie Burt, Gene Brody, and Carolyn Cutrona. 2005. "Collective Efficacy, Authoritative Parenting and Delinquency: A Longitudinal Test of a Model Integrating Community- and Family-Level Processes." *Criminology* 43:989–1029.

Skogan, Wesley G. 1988. "Community Organizations and Crime." In *Crime and Justice: A Review of Research*, vol. 10, edited by Michael Tonry and Norval Morris. Chicago: University of Chicago Press.

———. 1990. *Disorder and Decline: Crime and the Spiral Decay in American Neighborhoods*. Berkeley: University of California Press.

———. 2004. "Representing the Community in Community Policing." In *Community Policing: Can It Work?* edited by Wesley G. Skogan. Belmont, CA: Wadsworth.

———. 2006. *Police and Community in Chicago: A Tale of Three Cities*. New York: Oxford University Press.

———. 2008a. "Broken Windows: Why—and How—We Should Take Them Seriously." *Criminology and Public Policy* 7:195–202.

———. 2008b. "An Overview of Community Policing: Origins, Concepts and Implementation." In *The Handbook of Knowledge-Based Policing: Current Concepts and Future Directions*, edited by Tom Williamson. New York: Wiley.

Skogan, Wesley G., and Susan M. Hartnett. 1997. *Community Policing, Chicago Style*. New York: Oxford University Press.

Smith, Bruce. 1940. *Police Systems in the United States*. New York: Harper & Row.

Smith, Douglas A. 1986. "The Neighborhood Context of Police Behavior." In *Communities and Crime*, edited by Albert J. Reiss Jr. and Michael Tonry. Vol. 8 of *Crime and Justice: A Review of Research*, edited by Michael Tonry and Norval Morris. Chicago: University of Chicago Press.

Sparrow, Malcolm K., Mark H. Moore, and David M. Kennedy. 1990. *Beyond 911: A New Era for Policing*. New York: Basic Books.

Spelman, William, and Dale K. Brown. 1984. *Calling the Police: Citizen Reporting of Serious Crime*. Washington, DC: U.S. Government Printing Office.

St. Jean, Peter K. B. 2007. *Pockets of Crime: Broken Windows, Collective Efficacy, and the Criminal Point of View*. Chicago: University of Chicago Press.

Stoutland, Sara E. 2001. "The Multiple Dimensions of Trust in Resident/Police Relations in Boston." *Journal of Research in Crime and Delinquency* 38: 226–56.

Sunshine, Jason, and Tom R. Tyler. 2003. "The Role of Procedural Justice and Legitimacy in Shaping Public Support for the Police." *Law and Society Review* 37:513–48.

Svara, James H. 1998. "The Politics-Administration Dichotomy Model as Aberration." *Public Administration Review* 58:51–58.

Sykes, Gary W. 1986. "Street Justice: A Moral Defense of Order Maintenance Policing." *Justice Quarterly* 3:497–512.

Taylor, Frederick W. 1911. *The Principles of Scientific Management*. New York: Norton.

Taylor, Ralph B. 2001. *Breaking Away from Broken Windows: Baltimore Neighborhoods and the Nationwide Fight against Crime, Grime, Fear, and Decline*. Boulder, CO: Westview.

Terrill, William, and Michael D. Reisig. 2003. "Neighborhood Context and Police Use of Force." *Journal of Research in Crime and Delinquency* 40: 291–321.

Thacher, David. 2001a. "Conflicting Values in Community Policing." *Law and Society Review* 35:765–98.

———. 2001b. "Equity and Community Policing: A New View of Community Partnerships." *Criminal Justice Ethics* 20:3–16.

———. 2004. "Order Maintenance Reconsidered: Moving beyond Strong Causal Reasoning." *Journal of Criminal Law and Criminology* 94:381–414.

Trojanowicz, Robert. 1982. *An Evaluation of the Neighborhood Foot Patrol Program in Flint, Michigan*. East Lansing: National Neighborhood Foot Patrol Center, Michigan State University.

———. 1986. "Evaluating a Neighborhood Foot Patrol Program: The Flint, Michigan, Project." In *Community Crime Prevention: Does It Work?* edited by Dennis Rosenbaum. Beverly Hills, CA: Sage.

Trojanowicz, Robert, and Bonnie Bucqueroux. 1990. *Community Policing: A Contemporary Perspective*. Cincinnati: Anderson.

Tyler, Tom R. 2003. "Procedural Justice, Legitimacy, and the Effective Rule of Law." In *Crime and Justice: A Review of Research*, vol. 30, edited by Michael Tonry. Chicago: University of Chicago Press.

Uchida, Craig D. 2005. "The Development of the American Police: An Historical Overview." In *Critical Issues in Policing: Contemporary Readings*, 5th ed., edited by Roger G. Dunham and Geoffrey P. Alpert. Long Grove, IL: Waveland.

U.S. Department of Justice. 2006. *Regional Community Policing Institutes: Training Network*. Washington, DC: U.S. Department of Justice.

———. 2009a. *Community Policing Defined*. Washington, DC: U.S. Department of Justice, Office of Community Oriented Policing Services.

———. 2009b. "Regional Community Policing Institutes." http://www.cops.usdoj.gov/Default.asp?Item=115.

Vollmer, August. 1971. *The Police in Modern Society*. Monclair, NJ: Patterson Smith. (Originally published in 1936.)

Walker, Samuel. 1980. *Popular Justice: A History of American Criminal Justice*. New York: Oxford University Press.

———. 1984. "Broken Windows and Fractured History: The Use and Misuse of History in Recent Police Patrol Analysis." *Justice Quarterly* 1:75–90.

Weisburd, David, Cody W. Telep, Joshua C. Hinkle, and John E. Eck. 2008.

The Effects of Problem-Oriented Policing on Crime and Disorder. Campbell Systematic Reviews, no. 2008-14. Oslo: Campbell Collaboration.

Weitzer, Ronald. 1999. "Citizens' Perceptions of Police Misconduct: Race and Neighborhood Context." *Justice Quarterly* 16:819–46.

White, Leonard D. 1926. *Introduction to the Study of Public Administration*. New York: Macmillan.

Wilson, James Q., and George L. Kelling. 1982. "Broken Windows: The Police and Neighborhood Safety." *Atlantic Monthly* 249(March):29–38.

Wilson, O. W. 1950. *Police Administration*. New York: McGraw-Hill.

Wilson, Woodrow. 1887. "The Study of Administration." *Political Science Quarterly* 2:197–222.

Worrall, John L. 2010. "The Effects of Policing on Crime: What Have We Learned?" In *Critical Issues in Policing: Contemporary Readings*, 6th ed., edited by Roger G. Dunham and Geoffrey P. Alpert. Long Grove, IL: Waveland.

Worrall, John L., and Tomislav V. Kovandzic. 2007. "COPS Grants and Crime Revisited." *Criminology* 45:159–90.

Wortley, Richard, and Lorraine Mazerolle. 2008. "Environmental Criminology and Crime Analysis: Situating the Theory, Analytic Approach and Application." In *Environmental Criminology and Crime Analysis*, edited by Richard Wortley and Lorraine Mazerolle. Devon, UK: Willan.

Xu, Yili, Mora L. Fiedler, and Karl H. Flaming. 2005. "Discovering the Impact of Community Policing: The Broken Windows Thesis, Collective Efficacy, and Citizens' Judgment." *Journal of Research in Crime and Delinquency* 42: 147–86.

Zhao, Jihong, Matthew C. Scheider, and Quint Thurman. 2002. "Funding Community Policing to Reduce Crime: Have COPS Grants Made a Difference?" *Criminology and Public Policy* 2:7–32.

———. 2003. "A National Evaluation of the Effect of COPS Grants on Police Productivity (Arrests) 1995–1999." *Police Quarterly* 6:387–409.

Stephen D. Mastrofski and James J. Willis

Police Organization Continuity and Change: Into the Twenty-first Century

ABSTRACT

American policing demonstrates both continuity and change. A high degree of decentralization persists, as do bureaucratic structures of larger police agencies. The structures and practices of the nation's numerous small agencies remain underexamined. The potential growth of professional structures inside and outside the police organization is largely unexplored. The core police patrol technology has remained essentially unchanged for decades, and early police adaptations to information technology have not yet profoundly altered policing structures and processes in easily observable ways. The demography and education levels of police workers are changing, but the consequences are not obvious. Police culture has long been under siege. Current reforms attempt to reduce the occupation's isolation from the communities it serves and the scientific community that presumably serves it. Mechanisms and styles for governing police retain considerable variation, but the growing role of grassroots community groups and police professional associations remains underexplored. The complexity of the dynamics of change manifests itself in the reaction of American police organizations to two consequential reform movements: community policing and terrorist-oriented policing. American police agencies have shown a remarkable capacity to absorb these reforms while buffering core structures and practices from change.

Police organizations change. Whether we find that remarkable depends

Stephen D. Mastrofski is university professor and director of the Center for Justice Leadership and Management, and James J. Willis is assistant professor, both in the Department of Criminology, Law and Society at George Mason University. They are grateful to Roger B. Parks, who made many useful comments on an earlier draft.

on how much and how quickly we expect them to change. In his insightful essay nearly two decades ago, Albert Reiss (1992) tracked the major features of American police organization continuity and change in the twentieth century, indicating that some aspects of policing had changed little whereas others had changed considerably. He noted that the public police industry in America had resisted pressures to consolidate, remaining a highly decentralized system embedded in the many thousands of local governments across the nation. However, he noted that how police organizations are commanded, how their patrol officers are mobilized, how patrol work is carried out, and how information is accessed and used changed considerably during the twentieth century. American police departments became more bureaucratized, but this process was far from total, still leaving considerable discretion to the rank and file and only partially effective accountability systems still vulnerable to corruption. He observed that as a result of changes in demography, political governance, and technology, the twentieth century witnessed the transformation of the police from the minions of local political patrons to greater independence as they became attached to legalistic and technocratic sources of power and legitimacy. He noted the as-yet unresolved tension between the structures and cultures of bureaucracy versus those of nascent professionalism, some of which were playing out in the emergence of community and problem-oriented policing. These reforms were designed to counter some of the pathologies of the growing strength of a bureaucratic system of internal organization that by the restive 1970s was experiencing a crisis in legitimacy in urban America, due in part to its perceived isolation from, and unresponsiveness to, neighborhood and community concerns.

A decade into the twenty-first century is an appropriate time to reflect on what has become of American police organizations—their structure, technologies, and culture and the forces that shape them. Although this essay focuses on America's local police organizations, we take occasion to compare America to other nations to more fully appreciate the implications of the American context for the patterns observed. Throughout the essay we note opportunities for future research. Our arguments and conclusions are briefly summarized below.

American policing demonstrates both continuity and change as it completes the first decade of the twenty-first century. A high degree of industry decentralization persists, despite periodic calls to consolidate service delivery. A growing private security sector adds to the multiplicity of service providers. Although there are ways in which the nation's system is less fragmented than a mere count of policing providers indicates, the endurance of this system may be attributable to both its technical performance and the ease with which a more fragmented system provides responsiveness to local preferences.

Bureaucratic structures of larger police agencies also persist, despite recent reform movements launched to de-bureaucratize them. The impact of structural variation on organizational innovation and success is not well established empirically, and the structures and practices of the nation's numerous small agencies remain underexamined. The potential strengthening of professional structures inside and outside the police organization is largely unexplored.

The core police patrol technology has remained essentially unchanged for decades, and early police adaptations to the information technology revolution have not yet profoundly altered policing structures and processes in easily observable ways. Yet the increasing centrality of police as "information workers" bears close watching. New information technologies have the potential to transform how police relate to their task environment and how they regulate themselves internally. While much past research indicates that technological innovations frequently fail to produce the expected benefits, a long-term approach may be required to perceive the impact on structures and practices.

The demography and education levels of police workers are changing, with racial minorities and females constituting increasing proportions of the nation's sworn force. However, the consequences are not yet obvious and will require a careful assessment of the processes by which changes in culture and practice are expected to occur.

Police culture is a term used to distinguish policing as an occupation, to distinguish police organizations, and to distinguish individual police officers. The extent to which these constructs actually account for police practices is not well established empirically. Nonetheless, police culture has been under siege since the 1960s. Currently popular reforms attempt to reduce the occupation's isolation from the communities police serve and the scientific community that presumably serves them, but it is not at all clear how successful these reforms will be.

Mechanisms and styles for governing police retain considerable variation, but the research literature on how governance is accomplished is thin, relying mostly on national surveys of agencies with data of limited theoretical utility or in-depth case studies. The growing role of grassroots community groups and police professional associations remains underexplored.

The complexity of the dynamics of change manifests itself in the reaction of American police organizations to the two most consequential reform movements of the twenty-first century thus far: community policing and terrorist-oriented policing. American police agencies have shown a remarkable capacity to absorb these reforms while buffering core structures and practices from change. However, profound changes may take more time than a couple of decades, so observers should take care to attend to incremental change over longer time periods.

The essay is organized as follows: Section I, the structure of the American policing industry; Section II, the internal structure of American police agencies; Section III, police technology; Section IV, the people serving in police organizations; Section V, organizational culture of police; Section VI, external governance of police; Section VII, forces of stability and change for American policing; and Section VIII, conclusion.

I. The Structure of America's Policing Industry

To understand police organizations, there is value in first considering how they are structured as a public service "industry" (Ostrom, Tiebout, and Warren 1961; Ostrom and Ostrom 1965). In that respect, "American policing is local policing" (Manning 2006, p. 99). Among police scholars America is regarded as the most fragmented and complex system for delivering public policing services in the industrialized world (Bayley 1985, 1992; Klinger 2004; Skogan and Frydl 2004, p. 48). A National Research Council panel of American policing scholars suggested that at the end of the twentieth century there were approximately 19,000–21,000 federal, state, and local police agencies, of which the Bureau of Justice Statistics estimated 13,500 were attached to local governments. A few years later, a 2004 census showed 12,766 local police agencies, 3,067 sheriff's departments, and 1,481 special jurisdiction agencies (Bureau of Justice Statistics 2007, p. 2). No other nation matches the United States in the number of agencies embedded in different levels of government and the complexity of interagency arrangements, such as mutual aid agreements and interjurisdictional task forces (Bayley 1992; Mawby 1999; Skogan and Frydl 2004, p. 48). This degree of fragmentation, or multiplicity, may be the most distinguishing feature of America's policing system and also the most consequential.

A. Character of Industry Fragmentation

Several things are worth noting about American policing fragmentation. First, it appears to be associated with a fondness for decentralized democratic governance (Geller and Morris 1992, p. 233). Some attribute this to the absence of sustained violent threats to a national government, which in the presence of such threats would find a need to form and retain a national police service (Bayley 1992, p. 534). It is unclear whether the democratic predilections of Americans fostered a fragmented structure of policing or whether the latter made the former possible. Regardless of the direction of causality, this association is not unique to the United States but is noted in other English-speaking democracies.

Second, the degree of fragmentation may be declining, albeit at a glacial pace. Reliable national counts of local police agencies over long time periods are not available (Maguire et al. 1998), but a detailed study of Ohio departments from the 1970s through the 1990s shows a net loss of 100 agencies, an 11 percent reduction (Maguire and King 2007, p. 340). The research also found a net increase in the number of agencies in Arizona and Nevada, two states with the highest population growth in the 1990s. There is uncertainty about this trend at the national level, but if defragmentation were to continue at the above rate for the first half of the twenty-first century, the number of Ohio agencies would decline from 801 to 654, which would still leave many more police agencies than most nations currently have. The safe bet is that the high level of police industry organizational multiplicity in the United States will be sustained far into the future, barring violent threats to the stability of the national government (Bayley 1992, pp. 533–35).

But counts of police agencies do not show the complete picture about the nature and extent of industry fragmentation (Klinger 2004, p. 121). The 2004 census of state and local law enforcement agencies showed that the largest 6 percent of state and local agencies (100 or more full-time sworn officers) accounted for 64 percent of all sworn personnel, whereas the 74 percent of the nation's departments with fewer than 25 officers accounted for only 14 percent of the nation's state and local sworn force (Reaves 2007, p. 2). Although these statistics reflect a still impressive level of multiplicity within the police industry, it shows that most Americans receive service from fewer and larger police agencies. That is, America's policing industry is more concentrated than a mere tally of agencies suggests.

Further, the high degree of police service fragmentation in America is concentrated in patrol services. The provision of many specialized services (including criminal investigations, detention, communications, training, and crime labs) is more centralized, often provided under contract, or by law, to smaller departments by nearby larger municipal, county, or state agencies or regional facilities (Ostrom, Whitaker, and Parks 1978; Fyfe 1983; Parks 2009). Even basic patrol services in small departments may involve special arrangements with other agencies to provide service in certain areas or at certain times of the day. In addition, mutual support and backup agreements often exist between proximate police agencies (Parks 2009). Observers often suggest that the American system is rife with overlapping jurisdictions and sporadic coordination of agencies (President's Commission 1967, p. 301; Reiss 1992, p. 65; Manning 2006, p. 118), but there is some evidence that the overlap (though real) is managed, does not merely rely on evanescent personal relationships, and rarely produces confusion, inefficient duplication, and conflict in the actual delivery of local service (McDavid 1977; Ostrom, Parks, and Whitaker 1978, pp. 301–16; Parks 2009). The reason is that for the most part the web of arrangements is cooperative and institutionalized. And there is not systematic evidence showing that the degree of integration of units within police agencies (especially large ones) is any greater than the degree of integration between them (especially small ones). It may be easier for Andy of Mayberry to coordinate police operations with the neighboring counties than it is for the commissioner of the New York Police Department to coordinate the various components of his massive organization.

B. Police Consolidation Movement

The desire to consolidate small American police agencies first surfaced as good government reform in the 1930s and then again as part of a movement in the late 1960s and 1970s, with the support of a number of national commissions and police leaders (Altshuler 1970, p.

38; Douthit 1975; Murphy and Plate 1977; Walker 1977, pp. 141–46; Parks 2009). It never gathered much steam and has remained mostly low visibility except for the rare occasion when large agencies are joined, such as the merger of New York City's housing, school, and transit police with the municipal force in the 1990s (Maguire and King 2007, p. 341).

The principal objective of the consolidation advocates has been to merge the nation's many small agencies into much larger entities. The typical arguments for consolidation of these small agencies are as follows: new police technologies cost more than most small departments can afford, large departments make cost-efficient the hiring of specialist experts that small departments cannot afford, small communities cannot afford to deal with the increasing litigation or threat of litigation against the police, larger departments can afford to hire better-qualified personnel and give them more training, larger departments can provide more and better service by achieving economies of scale, and larger agencies are better equipped to adapt to the changing nature of crime (e.g., cybercrime; Tully 2002).

The ability of so many "Lilliputs" of policing (Ostrom and Smith 1976) to withstand these criticisms comes from several sources. First, there are the explanations that derive from technical performance—the "rational" evidence, so to speak. Small agencies have dealt with many of the challenges of cost-efficiency and economies of scale by seeking consolidated assistance for the specialist functions expected of contemporary police, while continuing to deliver more basic patrol service, widely regarded as the "backbone" of police work. This patrol efficiency appears especially easy for small agencies to achieve because as agencies grow in size, they seem to require disproportionately more administrative, supervisory, and support staff (Ostrom, Whitaker, and Parks 1978, pp. 85–91; but cf. Langworthy and Hindelang 1983; Scott 1998; Klinger 2004, p. 132). Other sources of small-department efficiency undoubtedly derive from the characteristically lower salary and benefits offered (especially in rural areas) and lower investment in training (Weisheit and Hawkins 1997; Weisheit 2005).[1] If the cost of policing is directly related to its quality,

---

[1] Although small agencies may not match their larger counterparts in material incentives and training, they have been forced to upgrade minimum hiring and training requirements by state mandates that proliferated in the latter part of the twentieth century, thus closing some of the professional gap that may have previously existed in the formal indicators of professional quality.

smaller and rural departments should be in trouble, but at least one standard indicator of performance suggests that they tend to outperform large agencies in clearance rates for major offenses (Cordner 1989; Falcone, Wells, and Weisheit 2002).[2]

Second, the people served by small departments may place a special premium on certain things that small departments deliver with greater ease but that large departments struggle to produce: accessibility and interpersonal familiarity with the community, less "red tape," more time on patrol, and law enforcement that is customized to the preferences of a smaller, more homogeneous community (Wilson 1968, pp. 211–15; Crank and Wells 1991; Mastrofski and Ritti 1996; Weisheit and Wells 1999; Maguire 2003; Schafer, Burruss, and Giblin 2009). This may be reflected in the often higher levels of satisfaction with police reported by residents of smaller communities, which, while not always showing a clear superiority of small-town over big-city policing (Lovrich 1985), does undermine the consolidationists' claims that big-city police service is necessarily better than that of small towns in metropolitan America (Mastrofski 1981, chap. 3; Skogan and Frydl 2004, pp. 171–73; Parks 2009).

Finally, there is an array of political and historical forces at work (Reiss 1992, pp. 63–68): the enduring custom, noted by Alexis de Toqueville ([1835] 1990), of Americans' fondness for using local government to deliver key services; the legal constraints placed on central cities to incorporate outlying areas, thus creating an environment conducive to the explosive growth of suburbs ringing the metropolitan area; and the absence of a cohesive constituency to support consolidation and the absence of widespread police leadership interest in consolidation—all in the face of a persistent desire among community leaders for local control of the police (Mastrofski 1989). If "autopsies" were routinely held for disestablished small police organizations (King 2000, p. 228), a useful hypothesis would be that the more frequent cause of death was failure to find financial subsistence, not public dissatisfaction with performance.

---

[2] Some research that actually focuses on the effects of variation in industry structure across metropolitan areas finds mixed effects (Parks 2009, p. 196). Greater multiplicity of patrol service providers in a metro area is associated with greater patrol deployment, but greater multiplicity in criminal investigations is associated with lower crime clearance levels.

C. Private Security

The efflorescence of private security and private policing in the United States adds to the fragmentation of the policing industry (Cunningham, Strauchs, and Van Meter 1991; Reiss 1992, p. 65; Shearing 1992; Bayley and Shearing 1996; Jones and Newburn 1998; Loader 1999). To the extent that public police and private police compete in the same market place, it seems clear that in the latter half of the twentieth century, private policing considerably expanded its share of the market, private security officers outnumbering sworn public officers by a factor of four by 1995 (Maguire and King 2004, p. 20; Forst 2005, p. 363). Yet, except in rare cases, it is not clear that private security is moving American police out of their traditional niche; rather it may be expanding much more aggressively into rapidly growing sectors of the marketplace for policing services, for example, mass private space (Shearing and Stenning 1981), a pattern noted in the United Kingdom (Crawford 2003, p. 149). Indeed, the public side of the American policing industry increased employment in the 1990s and early 2000s,[3] a time when crime was declining nationally (Blumstein and Wallman 2006). What may have changed is the appetite for public policing services desired by communities and their ability to pay for them in an expanding national economy. A significant stimulus to the increase in local police may have been fueled by the public's growing desire for a more community-oriented brand of policing (Mastrofski 2006a, p. 45) coupled with the emergence in 1994 of an effectively marketed federal program with the stated purpose of adding 100,000 officers to America's police industry to engage in this practice (Roth 2000).

The implications of private policing's growing presence in the marketplace may not be obvious. First, off-duty public police are one source of labor for private policing (Reiss 1988). Second, there are at least two alternatives to a zero-sum competitive market model that have been noted abroad (Crawford 2003, p. 157): one in which the public police serve in a "steering capacity" to accredit and govern private policing and another in which public and private police are coordinated in a loose network rather than in a hierarchical relationship.

---

[3] Between the 1996 and 2004 census of law enforcement agencies, the number of full-time sworn employees in local police and sheriffs' departments grew by 58,000, representing an impressive increase of over 10 percent in an 8-year time span (Reaves 2007). This trend in overall growth is consistent with that in other nations (Maguire and Schulte-Murray 2001).

Adding to this complexity is the late-twentieth-century decline in the monopolization of police authorization and governance by the state, with many other authorizing entities arising (private corporations and not-for-profit groups, e.g.; Shearing 1992). It remains unclear as to who governs the domains of private policing and to what effect. A useful line of research would attempt to establish more clearly the presence of each model and its implications for the practice of policing.

D. Attenuators of Fragmentation's Effects

The tenacity of this American cultural phenomenon notwithstanding, other forces are afoot in the United States that may do more to unify police practices across the nation than organizational consolidation. Professional police associations (e.g., the Police Executive Research Forum and the Commission on Accreditation of Law Enforcement Agencies) appear to be exerting a growing influence on police organization practice, especially in the interest of identifying and promoting "best practices." They are abetted by a federal government that has worked with them in developing policies that guide federal support (especially financial) to promote community policing and other au courant reforms (Mastrofski, Willis, and Kochel 2007). And add to this the pressures from the federal government to get state and local agencies to collaborate with federal agencies and adhere to their operational preferences in combating the threat of terrorism (Thacher 2005; Greene and Herzog 2009; Maguire and King, forthcoming). Thus, the pressure to reduce variability among America's numerous local police agencies necessarily takes a more subtle, but perhaps no less consequential, form. Indeed, it is the pressure for orthodoxy in structures, forms, and practices continuously emanating from wave after wave of American police reform since the mid-nineteenth century that should make us cautious about the claim that the fragmentation of America's police industry sustains "independent entities with their own unique structures, cultures, policies, and procedures" (Maguire 2003, p. 3). Like reforms in other types of organizations, police reform has a "viral" or "copycat" quality (DiMaggio and Powell 1983), perhaps making police departments (especially in the same size range) as much alike as different. The multiplicity of American police agencies nowadays may well belie a much higher degree of conformity than scholars, police, and politicians commonly allow. The consequence of an industry with many organizational entities is not necessarily a commensurate degree of diversity.

E. Accounting for the Persistence of Fragmentation

We consider two theoretical approaches for accounting for the American persistence with the fragmentation and complexity of the public policing industry (Mastrofski and Ritti 2000; Maguire and King 2007; Willis, Mastrofski, and Weisburd 2007). One is a technical/ rational, or contingency, theory that organizations strive to succeed in their environments by a rational process of adopting the structures and practices that evidence shows are best suited to achieving their ostensible (technical) objectives, such as community safety. Here organizations (or their leaders) survive and thrive or wither (or depart) according to their ability to compete with others in the marketplace for providing the relevant technical results. Another approach is institutional theory, which emphasizes that organizations respond, not to the technical aspects of their environment, but rather to cultural features (beliefs) about how organizations should be structured and operate— beliefs and systems that operate independently of what the technical environment may require. Organizational legitimacy depends then on adhering to the beliefs and preferences of powerful entities in the environment, stakeholders of consequence for police organizations— sometimes called "sovereigns." In what ways are each of these theories useful?

One can make a straightforward argument that an industry populated with many smaller departments persists because this arrangement works well in a technical/rational sense. The preponderance of evidence reviewed above suggests that most smaller communities are not convinced that larger agencies are in general more effective in keeping their communities safe, but rather that they are often less efficient and usually less responsive in serving their more diverse stakeholders than their smaller, generally less diverse counterparts.

Or it may be that a more complex technical/rational argument applies. Perhaps smaller communities, especially those with lower levels of crime and disorder than their big-city counterparts, place a higher priority on other aspects of police service than the assurance of public safety. Perhaps in less crime-threatened environments, citizens place a higher premium on being able to govern their police than they would in a more threatened environment and are therefore reluctant to consolidate, even when consolidation might be the more efficient route in terms of technical performance (Mastrofski 1989). If this were so, then rapidly rising crime rates in the smaller communities should be associated with a subsequent increase in the likelihood that police service would be consolidated into a larger agency. We are unaware of any tests of this hypothesis. Some cross-sectional studies have attempted to compare the impact of large versus small departments by matching the character of neighborhoods, but such studies are limited in what they can tell us about the consequences of greater consolidation or fragmentation for a given community.

What is more challenging for rational/technical theory is explaining the persistence of the many fewer large police organizations in the face of their efforts to acquire the responsiveness of the smaller agencies. Here it may be that the availability of more resources for these agencies makes it possible to acquire the trappings of legitimacy that institutional theory predicts will be adopted because of the acceptance of those structures and practices by powerful sovereigns as the "right" way to organize a police department. The adoption of community policing and Compstat reforms has been understood in this way (Crank 1994; Mastrofski 2006a; Willis, Mastrofski, and Weisburd 2007).

The consequences of America's nationwide system of fragmentation are not conclusively established because determining that requires cross-national comparisons, which are few and are often more impressionistic than rigorous. It is not established that a fragmented national industry structure is necessarily more or less effective in coping with crime and public safety; nor is it well established that a fragmented system is more or less efficient or equitable or more or less observant of human rights. According to some, this can be explained by a highly unitary national police system compensating for being highly decentralized in its internal command structure, thereby affording the sort of local flexibility that many have felt is the key to a police organization's survival (Bayley 1992, pp. 540–41). Submitted in evidence are the Japanese *koban* system and certain decentralized community consultation features of large Australian state agencies.

Explaining the persistence of extensive organizational multiplicity in local policing in the United States is made more challenging when the American experience is compared to that of nations with a somewhat similar legal historical background, the United Kingdom, Canada, and Australia. All of these nations have consolidated police service into many fewer and larger agencies, with state and regional forces taking a more pervasive role (Bayley 1992). Reiss (1992, p. 67) attributed the difference, at least in the United Kingdom, to financial incentives supplied by Parliament, noting that Americans were loath to forfeit control to a central federal government, a preference that we note was reinforced by constitutional limitations on the restructuring of local government in the United States.

F. Implications of Fragmentation for Police Innovation

In addition to receiving good public service from their police, vital societies have an interest in stimulating innovation. What are the implications of a fragmented system structure for the innovativeness and adaptability of police organizations in that system? Not much is empirically established, but the general literature on organizational innovativeness offers an interesting possibility: system fragmentation could facilitate more experimentation and testing, while impeding the widespread adoption of organizational innovations.

It has not been empirically established that highly consolidated policing systems are more innovative or adaptive; they may in fact be less so, precisely because the risks, challenges, and visibility of change increase with the size and complexity of the (more consolidated) organization and the entrenched influence of stakeholders. The highly decentralized structure of the American policing industry would appear to provide a nurturing environment for the percolation and testing of new ideas. Some innovation will occur, and police departments throughout the industry can benefit from knowledge gained from these novel efforts. Yet observers note the challenges of accomplishing widespread diffusion of local police innovation, since change must be accomplished on a "city by city, county by county, and state by state basis" (Walker and Macdonald 2009, p. 486). This frustrates many American police reformers because major changes tend to take a long time to diffuse widely, or as they diffuse, they are diluted or substantially modified, so much so that departments will claim to have implemented the same reform but be performing it quite differently (Mastrofski 2006a). Thus, in America's fragmented system, even when an innovation has matured and achieved widespread adoption, we should expect considerably more variation in the execution of that innovation among American police than in a system in which policing is more consolidated.

Addressing this issue with more than theoretical speculation calls for cross-national comparisons of systems with different degrees of system fragmentation. Such comparisons must be made carefully, since there are other system-level factors that may influence the susceptibility of a law enforcement system to innovation, such as the commitment to research to develop and assess innovations, conducted largely by people working outside of police agencies (Bayley 2008, p. 15). With this in mind, it might be fruitful to assess the impact of profoundly different levels of system structure in the United States and Israel, which has a highly centralized policing system. Israel might be expected to show greater resistance to adopting innovations but to implement them rapidly and comprehensively once the decision is made to adopt them.[4]

There are many challenges in learning broader lessons about industry structure from cross-national comparisons, due to so many other features of nations and their policing systems that may influence outcomes. However, America's policing industry itself is sufficiently diverse to make possible the observation of effects of within-nation variation at the metropolitan level. A 1977 survey of 85 metropolitan areas in the United States found that the number of agencies providing patrol service ranged from as few as one (complete consolidation) to as many as 91 (highly fragmented) per area (Parks 2009, p. 191). Researchers should consider updating and assessing the implications of such inter–metropolitan area variation.

II. The Internal Structure of American Police Organizations

Organizational structure is the "internal differentiation and patterning of relationships among an organization's components" (Thompson 1967, p. 51). We attend to a police organization's structure because of the commonly held belief that structure plays an important role in its effectiveness, whether defined as mission accomplishment or regime survival. Presumably, some structures are better than others in mediating between an organization's technologies and its task environment, which is characterized as those parts of an organization's surroundings

---

[4] Here we draw on Bayley's (1985, p. 54) careful distinction of two dimensions of policing structure: the number of commands (agencies) in a system and the extent to which operational direction is commanded from a single center of control. Israel represents a highly unified system (one command and one center of control), whereas the United States represents a highly fragmented system with many thousand independent commands that are neither hierarchically organized nor coordinated (as in France; p. 59).

or context that are "relevant or potentially relevant to goal setting and goal attainment" (Dill 1958; quoted in Thompson 1967, p. 27).

A. An Overview of Historical Trends

The dominant structural trend in American police agencies from the late nineteenth to the late twentieth century was what is popularly termed "bureaucratization" (Reiss 1992, p. 69): more hierarchy, specialization, and formalization (specific rules/policies and documentation of adherence to them).[5] Police organizations were hardly unique in this regard, as this trend dominated both the American public and private sectors generally (Wilson 1989). The social, economic, and cultural forces driving this trend were manifested in various police reform waves (Fogelson 1977; Walker 1977) that appeared almost as soon as American policing shifted from avocational/entrepreneurial modes to vocational ones embedded in municipal and county organizations, a process taking many years (Klockars 1985, chaps. 2–3). Historical analysis suggests that both the law and the military served as models for reform (Fogelson 1977; Klockars 1988), first creating "politicized bureaucracies" and later weakening political influences with the introduction of civil service reforms that based selection and career advancement on merit, rather than the influence of weakened urban political party machines (Reiss 1992, pp. 69–72). The consequences for the structure of American police organizations, especially visible among medium-size and large departments, were much greater relevance of internal decision processes, as political penetration declined; the elaboration of an internal command and control hierarchy designed to centralize the power of top department officials (visible in the growth of supervisory and management ranks); and increased complexity in the form of the division of labor among growing numbers of specialist units.

At the end of the first decade of the twenty-first century, American police organizations are still well characterized as bureaucratic in structure, although perhaps more for larger than for smaller ones, since most of what we know about police organization structure comes from studying departments with 100 or more officers (Langworthy 1986; cf. Mastrofski, Ritti, and Hoffmaster 1987; Hassell, Zhao, and Maguire 2003; Maguire 2003; Maguire et al. 2003). Whether and in what way

---

[5] Bureaucracy and bureaucratization can have a variety of meanings. The concept is multidimensional, and its elements are not necessarily tightly linked (Wilson 1989).

the many smaller municipal agencies are becoming more bureaucratized is unknown, although there are clear limits for truly small departments. Another shortcoming of our knowledge is that police researchers have tracked only police agencies over time; we know little about how bureaucratic police departments are compared to other organizations, such as armies, schools, hospitals, courts, churches, private security firms, and manufacturing firms. While there are reasons to suspect that public organizations tend to be more bureaucratic than private ones (because of the inclination of government to place more constraints on public than on private organizations, and this is becoming increasingly so for police; Wilson 1989; Boyne 2002), we lack a body of empirical research that compares the nature and extent of police bureaucracy to bureaucracy in other types of organizations.

B. Measuring Dimensions of Organizational Structure and Structural Change

Police organization researchers, drawing on Blau (1970) and others, have identified many dimensions of organizational structure relevant to police that subsume the three described above (Langworthy 1985; Maguire et al. 2003; Wilson 2003, 2006). One group of characteristics pertains to the ways in which the organization's work can be divided: functionally (across different department units, such as patrol, investigations, and communications), occupationally (using persons from different occupations), vertically (the degree of hierarchical differentiation), and spatially (geographical dispersion, such as dispersing police work among precincts and patrol beats). In addition, there are structural elements associated with control and coordination of the organization's work: centralization (the extent to which decision making is concentrated), formalization (the amount of emphasis on specific rules and procedures), and administrative intensity (the degree to which organization resources are committed to administration or support instead of operational matters).

Two questions arise about the internal structure of policing: how much do American police agencies vary structurally, and how, if at all, is this pattern changing? Students of American police typically characterize the structure of local agencies in the United States as highly variable in a way that is virtually taken for granted. Yet it is not so clear just how much structural variation there is, in large part because of the difficulties in acquiring comparable data for a fully representative sample of local police agencies. What is available typically focuses on agencies with 100 or more sworn personnel. Focusing only on larger agencies undoubtedly reduces a great deal of the variation, but even within this large group, the pattern of structural variability does not exactly conform to expectations. One study of 401 large departments based on 1997 data sets showed impressive levels of variation on spatial differentiation (number of stations and beats in the jurisdiction; Wilson 2003, p. 283). For example, the average number of beats for the agencies surveyed was 11 with a standard deviation of 29. However, such variation is undoubtedly driven in large part by covariation with the population of the jurisdiction served, so that a mere count of beats is as much a reflection of the jurisdiction's size as of the degree to which it spatially subdivides its patrol work. In the same study comparatively modest variation was found on many other structural indicators reflecting other forms of differentiation and structural control. For example, formalization was measured as the number of issues covered by policy directives (up to 15). The average for the departments was 12, but the standard deviation was only 2, suggesting that there was not a lot of variation on this dimension. One might expect even less variation among smaller agencies, especially the many with fewer than 25 officers, because of the constraints placed by small size on the number of beats, hierarchy, functional specialization, and administrative staff (Falcone, Wells, and Weisheit 2002, p. 374).

How much the internal structure of police organizations has changed depends, of course, on the time frame. Reiss (1992) suggested that police departments had made tremendous changes toward greater bureaucratization by the end of the twentieth century. These claims are based largely on records from departments' archives and historians' accounts. Recently researchers have attempted to track longitudinal structural change from surveys of large numbers of police agencies conducted at more or less regular intervals. One analysis tracked structural change in 236 police departments of 100 or more officers between 1987 and 1993, finding that functional differentiation significantly increased and organizational height (the extent to which the top department salary differs from the bottom one) significantly decreased, but formalization, administrative density (persons assigned to administrative jobs), and occupational differentiation (civilians employed) showed no significant change (Maguire 1997). A follow-up study tracked a slightly later and longer time period (1990–98), showing statistically significant declines in centralization and administrative intensity and significant increases in occupational differentiation (civilianization) and organizational height, but no change in segmentation (number of command levels), formalization, and perhaps functional differentiation. The spatial differentiation increased in some ways (number of stations and ministations), but there was no change in the number of beats (Maguire et al. 2003).

Given the mixed nature of effects over just a few years, it is difficult to generalize about their meaning; but perhaps most significantly, the researchers noted that where it occurred, the magnitude of change was "quite small" (Maguire et al. 2003, p. 271). Further, the reliability of some measures was a concern to them; perhaps even more telling, one can worry about the validity of measures derived from institutional surveys requiring the respondent to make broad generalizations about such things as the extent of centralized decision making or spatial dispersion (Weiss 1997; Maguire and Mastrofski 2000; Wilson 2006).[6] Worries about measurement reliability and validity aside, what we may take from these studies appears to be that in the 1990s there was no dramatic trend toward or away from the forms of bureaucratic structure noted by Reiss early in the decade.

The absence of evidence of dramatic structural change among American police agencies during the late twentieth and early twenty-first century, though perhaps not surprising, is counter to the hopes of many progressive reformers whose advocacy of a less bureaucratic, more flexible, and community-oriented policing began to surface in the turmoil of the 1970s and achieved federal financial support and widespread acceptance among police leaders by the first half of the 1990s. Tapping into many of the organizational prescriptions popular in the private sector, community policing advocates encouraged departments to deformalize, reduce hierarchy, decentralize, and functionally despecialize, while increasing geographic specialization (Skolnick and Bayley 1986; Kelling and Moore 1988; Goldstein 1990; Reiss 1992; Mastrofski 1998; Mastrofski and Ritti 2000; Maguire 2003; Skogan 2006c). National surveys of police departments repeatedly have shown that community po-

---

[6] And sometimes the proxy measures available, even when accurately reported, are of questionable validity for the constructs they are intended to represent, such as using the number of beats or officers on patrol as an indicator of spatial dispersion. Given the vicissitudes of police staffing and dispatching habits, the designation of beat boundaries is not necessarily a reliable indicator of how patrol officers are actually dispersed (Mastrofski 1981; Skogan 2006b, p. 61).

licing programs (community partnership, problem solving, crime prevention) and easy-to-implement organizational changes (revising mission statements, creation of joint task forces) have been widely popular as a way to implement the reform (Maguire and Mastrofski 2000; Roth 2000; Roth, Roehl, and Johnson 2004), but these changes appear to have been appended to the organization without much altering the underlying structure (Mastrofski 2006a). As early as 1993 nearly all respondents to a large national survey of police executives felt that community policing should be pursued, but fewer than half said that the meaning of community policing was clear, and only 27 percent felt that it would require extensive reorganization of police agencies (Wycoff 1994). That is not to say that there is no evidence of any change made under the rubric of community policing. Some in-depth, on-site studies of individual departments have suggested that structural changes have taken place, especially in decentralization and territorial specialization, but there are also many such studies that fail to find basic structural changes (Mastrofski 2006a, p. 49).

C. Implications of Structure for Police Innovativeness

Just as the structure of America's policing industry has implications for its innovativeness, so too does the internal structure of a given police organization. Some of the innovation diffusion research indicates that several structural features may promote innovativeness, such as decentralization, complexity (measured as the range of occupational specialties employed and their level of professionalism as reflected in formal training), formalization, and organizational slack (the availability of uncommitted resources; Rogers 2003, p. 412). However, no structural features have emerged that distinguish more from less innovative organizations (Wolfe 1994, p. 409). The adoption of community policing as an innovation lends itself to a study of this sort, and some have examined this issue, finding only weak or modest effects for most structural features on the adoption of community policing elements and not necessarily consistent with expectations (Zhao 1996; Wilson 2006). Perhaps the most consistent finding is that police department size (presumably a proxy measure of organizational slack) is significantly related to the adoption and implementation of community policing.

Two points are noteworthy for researchers desiring to explore police structure-innovation linkages. First, innovation researchers have found that structures that may encourage experimenting with or adopting an innovation may later impede the scope, intensiveness, or quality of its actual implementation (Zaltman, Duncan, and Holbek 1973; Hage 1980, pp. 209–10; Damanpour 1991; Wolfe 1994; Rogers 2003, chap. 10). Thus, researchers should be careful to distinguish the initial acceptance/adoption of a police reform from its actual implementation. Second, over the life course of an innovation in a police agency, there is clearly reciprocal causation between the structure of the organization (decentralization) and the practice of the innovation (partnering with community groups), a feature that is made quite explicit in the reform doctrine of community policing, which lumps structural changes with a host of programs and officer practices (Wilson 2006). Failure to model this feedback loop could cause researchers to overstate the effects of many structural variables on the implementation of the reform.

D. Consequences of Structure for Organization Success

We care about the structure of police organizations insofar as it has consequence for their success. Here we face many challenges, largely unmet, in learning the influence of structure on police organization performance. First is the challenge of measuring success (Moore and Braga 2004). According to a National Research Council committee's report, the most frequently used measures of police organization success focus on crime and disorder control and law enforcement (Skogan and Frydl 2004, chaps. 5–6). Also used are general measures of citizen satisfaction or assessments of police competence (Gallagher et al. 2001). Less frequently measured are police use-of-force measures and complaints against police. Rarely used are indicators of how police use their authority informally (which is far more frequent than formal applications), the quantity and quality of assistance rendered to citizens in need, and the fairness and effectiveness of police processes. Even less studied is police organization success in community building (Mastrofski 2006a, p. 58). Although there is a growing literature on many of these outputs and outcomes in assessing the practices of individual officers (Skogan and Frydl 2004, chap. 4), there is much less of this research at the organization level, attempting to learn the impact of organizational features. These lacunae are due in part to the priority given by police, policy makers, and researchers on crime control and law enforcement as central police missions, which has translated into a reduced priority for gathering other sorts of information (Willis,

Mastrofski, and Kochel 2010). Changing performance monitoring systems is a major task, and that may not be the highest priority of even those police leaders who see merit in it (Mastrofski 2003). The gaps in performance measurement are also due to a disinclination of social scientists to develop measures that distinguish good from less good performance, for example, rather than predicting arrests, predicting the best resolution of an incident, which in many cases might be something other than arrest (Mastrofski 2004, p. 109). Finally, there is a dearth of studies of the extent to which different organizational structures contribute to the short- and long-term success of the organization as an entity—resource growth, "market share," prestige, regime tenure, and so on. These outcomes may not seem as compelling for the purposes of program evaluation, but they are very much on the minds of local police and the officials responsible for them and thus figure largely in a reform's prospects.

Second, the research that attempts to estimate the effects of police organization structure is often captive to the limitations of readily available data sets (often large surveys and censuses of American police departments and the communities they serve), which means that the empirical analysis is impoverished by its limited capacity to test interesting theoretical propositions. For example, a long list of contemporary police experts (Bittner 1970, 1983; Muir 1977; Goldstein 1990; Klockars 1995; Kelling 1999) and two of the most popular and radical proposals to change police organizations in recent decades—problem-oriented and community policing—have embraced the adoption of a model of true professionalism (e.g., requiring knowledge and skill in a special body of expertise, commitment to an ethical code of how to practice, and a significant degree of autonomy from those outside the profession) for discretion control, rather than that associated with being a "snappy, low-level, soldier-bureaucrat" (Bittner 1990, p. 260). Wilson (1968) identified a department's professionalism, along with its degree of bureaucratization, as the source of differences in policing styles. Reiss (1971, pp. 121–24) illuminated the tension between police as professionals and bureaucrats, particularly because the expectations of professionalism call for them to exercise their well-informed, autonomous judgment independent of commands from the organization's hierarchy. Much of his book was devoted to appreciating how the low-ranking patrol officer negotiated the conflicting requirements of professionalism and bureaucracy. Many of the most popular contemporary reforms call for a strengthening of professionalism, and it may be ascending as a means of securing organizational legitimacy.

Yet with few exceptions (e.g., Smith 1984) researchers have done little to examine whether there has been a commensurate strengthening of structures that promote professionalism and trace their consequences. Instead, structural studies focus almost exclusively on the classic elements that define the extent to which the police organization is bureaucratized. The presence of professionalism cannot be assumed by the degree to which bureaucracy is absent. Organizational indicators of professionalism might include, for example, policies, units, and procedures designed to screen for and develop certain aspects of moral character and technical skill among police officers. They would also include organizational structures designed to promote the development and institutionalization of a professional body of police knowledge (Bayley and Bittner 1984). And they could include organizational elements that provide for a professional (as opposed to bureaucratic) review of the degree to which police practice conforms to professional standards. One indicator of professional influence is the extent to which police organizations accept lateral transfers between organizations of officers of mid and upper ranks. Undoubtedly, many police professional structures are only weakly developed in most police organizations, yet the absence of research that looks for this starkly illustrates the limited scope of research on police organizational structures.

At the intersection of both bureaucratic and professional structures rests the office of the first-line police supervisor, usually holding the rank of sergeant. Despite the widely held view among police and scholars of the critical nature of the sergeant's boundary-spanning role between management and line worker (Rubinstein 1973; Muir 1977, 2008; Van Maanen 1983, 1984; Werder 1996), remarkably little empirical research has been done to consider how the requirements of bureaucracy and professionalism are advanced through this office, how organizational structures influence supervisory styles, and with what consequence for the work unit's performance. The best available empirical work is mostly ethnographic and dated, occurring in the 1970s, although a small body of quantitative observational work has appeared in recent years. Much of the older work emphasizes how sergeants negotiate the tensions arising between the often conflicting expectations of the hierarchy and subordinates. More recent work, drawn from a single observational study, examines different supervisory styles that emerge and their consequences for behavior (Engel 2000, 2001, 2002). One study found that subordinate officers' choices about how to spend their time were influenced by their perception of their supervisors' personal priorities more than their own, although subordinates often misperceived the values of their supervisors (Engel and Worden 2003). This suggests the dominance of a somewhat clumsy bureaucratic model over a professional one. Future research would benefit from distinguishing the supervisors' priorities from their methods of leadership so that we might better understand the role they play regarding bureaucratic and professional models of policing.

Another limitation of the research on organizational structures is the concentration on comparing police organization structures at a given time. Longitudinal data, where available to support quantitative analysis, cover only a few years (typically less than a decade). While it may be a valuable exercise to track short-term structural changes and their consequences, the expectations of politicians and entrepreneurial police leaders notwithstanding, it is hardly realistic to expect most trends to be distinguishable except over much longer time periods. Neither Rome nor most contemporary police structural reforms were built in a day. Cross-sectional data sets make causal inference challenging, and it is very difficult to gather reliable, theoretically useful data across large numbers of agencies, not only on performance measures but also to control for other influences that might mask or reveal as spurious the effects of structure on performance.

For example, researchers often wish to take into account the nature of the police organization's environment in estimating the effects of organization structure; yet those who try to do this with large samples of departments find that available measures are typically limited to a narrow range of demographic and socioeconomic indicators routinely collected by the Census Bureau rather than the sorts of environmental forces that produce more direct and consequential influences. Not uncommonly, data on the most interesting and policy-relevant environmental features are not readily available, and so researchers are unable to say much of use about how police organization structure interacts with those parts of environment that truly matter. One of the most obvious omissions in this literature is variations and changes in the legal environment—legislation and judicial decisions (Reiss and Bordua 1967; Klinger 2004). Another is the nature and extent of other organizations and leaders who try to influence police policies, practice, and performance (Skogan and Frydl 2004, pp. 196–202). We might well expect that there are important interaction effects between a police department's structures and these features of its environment that determine how it will respond. And not infrequently, measuring these effects requires a degree of subtlety and ability to distinguish variation in police practice within a jurisdiction (Mastrofski and Ritti 1996). That is why the most cited studies often rely on in-depth comparisons of small numbers of departments, such as the eight agencies in Wilson's classic *Varieties of Police Behavior* (1968). These small comparative studies also have their challenges, such as their limited capacity to generalize from small, nonrepresentative samples.

In the face of all these hurdles, it is unsurprising that the National Research Council panel on police policy and practices (Skogan and Frydl 2004, pp. 173–85) and others (Klinger 2004) concluded that relatively little can be said about the influence of police organization structure on actual police practice. They found that there was insufficient research to draw conclusions about the impact of decentralized police structures on meeting the needs of jurisdictions. The panel noted that there were few studies assessing the impact of occupational and functional specialization, and the results are mixed. The committee found inadequate evidence to make any conclusion about the effects of hierarchy on police practices. The committee further concluded that there was some evidence that spatially focusing police work (e.g., stable beat assignments and efforts to have officers spend time in those beats) did increase officer knowledge of and commitment to the neighborhood, but that these effects were sustained only when organizations employed other structures to reinforce this behavior. Finally, the committee found that the limited evidence available was suggestive that formalizing policies can produce desired effects. The supporting research came from case studies of efforts to increase the formality and constraints on specific policies, usually studied in one or a few organizations. The results were encouraging for restrictions on the use of lethal force (especially when following an organizational crisis), but other policy areas failed to produce similar results (handling public drunks, dealing with pornography, and implementing domestic violence policies; Klinger 2004, p. 128). Perhaps formal policies more easily extinguish undesired behaviors than stimulate desired ones. And of course, because the committee did not conduct a full systematic review of the entire body of research, it is likely that many studies failing to show a formalization effect were not published, thus perhaps overstating the effects of formalization. This led to a qualified conclusion, making obvious the need to know more about the aspects of formalization and other features of the policy's context that may influence its success.

Finally, with rare exception American police research has avoided studying rural and small-town policing, despite what on the face appear to be profound differences from larger departments in terms of structure. The nation's major engines of police reform gear their recommendations to larger agencies, yet there is very little evidence of the value of these reforms (such as community policing structures) for smaller departments. In the absence of such research, we are left to ask what works for the distinctly less bureaucratic departments that are small and rural.

III. Police Technology

The structure of police organizations is widely thought to be influenced by and to influence technologies that police may adopt. "A *technology* is a design for instrumental action that reduces the uncertainty in the cause-effect relationships involved in achieving a desired outcome" (Rogers 2003, pp. 13–14) or, in more practical terms, it is "the means by which raw materials are converted into processed outputs" (Manning 1992, p. 353). Technologies can have a number of components: material (physical), logical (processes that presumably transform inputs into work products), and social (who does what and in what manner; Manning 1992, 2005; Mastrofski and Ritti 2000). Technologies can vary on a number of features, an important one being their "determinacy," the reliability of the technology in producing the desired result (Hasenfeld and English 1974, p. 13). Some policing technologies are thought to have high determinacy, such as DNA analysis; some are thought to be much lower, such as fingerprint analysis; and some are virtually discredited, such as bite mark analysis (Committee on Identifying the Needs of the Forensics Science Community 2009).

Technologies employed by the police are numerous and support diverse functions (Manning 1992, p. 351), such as coercion (weapons and martial arts), mobility (transportation vehicles), detection (forensics methods, such as DNA analysis), surveillance (closed-circuit television

[CCTV], digital imaging for facial recognition, and remote sensing devices), and analysis (data mining software). Clusters of technologies may coalesce to perform some function (Rogers 2003, p. 14), such as those involved in crime prevention and problem solving (Eck 2006) or information gathering, processing, and communication (Manning 2003). Moreover, some technologies have been slow to change. Despite the remarkable growth of information technology available to patrol officers in the last few decades (mobile digital terminals connected to vast databases, portable radios, video cameras, and cellular phones; see Manning 2003, chap. 5), the basic elements of police motor patrol have remained little changed since its ascendancy in the 1930s and thus far have not been significantly displaced by new and competing patrol technologies, such as hot-spots policing (Manning 2003, chap. 5; Mastrofski 2005*b*; Mastrofski, Weisburd, and Braga 2009). It leaves low-ranking officers the discretion to patrol where and how they choose when they are not otherwise assigned to respond to calls for service or administrative duties. However, communications and surveillance technologies have changed considerably, "trickling down" from technology developments in the military (Haggerty and Ericson 1999). These changes have vastly increased the accessibility of information to law enforcement officials.

The array of technologies police employ is vast and diverse; generalizing across them is risky. We focus our discussion of police technologies on the above two (patrol and information) because they afford opportunities for insights into technologies' stability and changeability. Patrol still consumes the lion's share of resources in most local police agencies and for that reason alone warrants consideration. There are three reasons that we have elected also to discuss technologies designed for information gathering and processing. First, "The *core technology* of police organizations is the *production and processing of information*" (Reiss 1992, p. 82; see also Manning 1992, p. 352). Second, many contemporary organizational innovations rely heavily on transforming past police information technologies for their success: community policing, problem-oriented policing, hot-spots policing, Compstat, evidence-based policing, and predictive policing (Weisburd and Braga 2006; Bratton, Morgan, and Malinowski 2009). Third, there is a small but significant body of research that assesses the consequences of contemporary developments of information technologies in police departments. In the case of police patrol, we consider reasons for its remarkable stability as a core technology. In the case of information technology, we consider its impact on police organization, culture, and practice.

A. Police Patrol Technology

Preventive patrol has been used by police as early as thirteenth-century Hangchow (Kelling et al. 1974) and was one of Sir Robert Peel's innovations introduced with the London Metropolitan Police in 1829. Before technological advancements of the automobile, telephone, and two-way radio were incorporated, police patrol was not too mobile (limited largely to walking beats), and decision making was highly decentralized and little supervised (Kelling and Moore 1988; Reiss 1992, p. 83). By midcentury the rising star among police progressives, O. W. Wilson, was trumpeting motorized preventive patrol as a way to avert crime (Kelling and Moore 1988, p. 13). For at least 70 years it has been the most visible, most common, and most resource-consuming crime control strategy that American police employ. The technology consists of making uniformed police as visible as possible (e.g., using uniforms and marked vehicles on "random" patrol) on the streets and in other public areas to create a sense of police presence sufficient to deter potential wrongdoers from committing offenses and disturbances and to enable police to respond quickly to developing problems and crimes in progress.

The boon companion of preventive patrol is "reactive patrol," which requires the patrol officer to interrupt preventive patrol to respond to requests for intervention. Presumably a rapid response enables the police to deal with problems before they can escalate further, catch criminals, or at least gather information and evidence that will facilitate apprehension of the offender (Spelman and Brown 1981). Together these techniques have been enabled by the automobile (mobility), the telephone (allowing the community to easily summon the police), and the two-way radio (giving administrators the capacity to direct and monitor operations; Reiss 1992, p. 83). They have been termed the "standard" model of police crime and disorder control because they rely heavily on interventions that are reactive and one-size-fits-all, as opposed to targeted and customized (Skogan and Frydl 2004, p. 223).

Research conducted in the 1970s and 1980s helped discredit these standard model technologies by failing to find crime control effects (Kelling et al. 1974; Spelman and Brown 1981). Although some of this research has since been faulted methodologically, their conclusions have been widely publicized among police and scholars and become part of the received wisdom of criminologists and a growing body of progressive police leaders: standard approaches to crime control are regarded as ineffective and inefficient (Sherman et al. 1997; Skogan and Frydl 2004, chap. 6; Weisburd and Eck 2004). In the wake of these revelations, other patrol techniques have been developed and tested: disorder (broken windows) policing, police crackdowns, hot-spots policing, repeat offenders policing, and community and problem-oriented policing (Bayley 2008). The evaluations of most of these approaches to patrol have produced small or no effects, have mixed results, have been subject to few tests, or have used weak evaluation designs. The striking exception is hot-spots policing, which has repeatedly yielded positive results using rigorous evaluation designs (Skogan and Frydl 2004, p. 240; Braga and Weisburd, forthcoming).

Thus far, community and problem-oriented policing have probably had the greatest impact in challenging American departments' commitment to the standard approach to police patrol. These methods require unhitching officers from the yoke of 911 reactive policing and using their time instead to work in partnership with community groups to solve the problems to which citizens give high priority. Instead of spending so much time dealing with citizens' requests and preventive patrol, officers mobilize by attending community group meetings and working with them and other organizations to focus proactively and creatively on problems (Skogan 2006*b*).

We do not have studies drawing on a representative cross section of departments that tell us the extent to which the standard patrol model has been displaced by community and problem-oriented policing. However, some case studies of a few progressive agencies committed to these reforms suggest that departments implementing these reforms worked hard to maintain their commitment to standard patrol technology while developing small groups of patrol officers who were given time to engage in community and problem-oriented policing. Chicago's storied Chicago Alternative Policing Strategy program kept 75 percent of its patrol force engaged only in the standard model, but the remainder were assigned to "beat teams" and were given a lighter standard patrol workload to find time to engage in community policing (Skogan 2006*b*, pp. 59–64, and personal communication). The department clearly maintained a major commitment to sustaining the model of standard policing, but the size of the resource commitment to the alternative strategy was considerable. Unfortunately, neither the department nor the researchers were able to gather much information about the extent to which beat officers used their spare time to engage in the new methods. Systematic observation of similar efforts in other cities has shown, however, that although community policing specialists do spend significantly more time on nontraditional methods, traditional patrol and engaging the public in face-to-face service contacts tend to dominate the work of community policing specialists, as well as traditional patrol officers (Parks et al. 1999; Smith, Novak, and Frank 2001). Thus, while the last two to three decades have witnessed an increasing willingness of American police to experiment with new methods for patrol officers, they do not appear to have supplanted the resource commitment of American police to continue standard preventive/reactive patrol in the traditional fashion (Lum 2009).

What could account for the persistence of a largely discredited patrol technology while other alternatives are available? One possibility is that American police are simply too invested in the structures and practices of the standard patrol technology, even if the scientific community considers it ineffective. For decades, police staffing levels have been justified to meet calls for service demand and to having adequate slack time for preventive patrol. That strategy has endured in bad economic times as well as good, when crime was rising and falling, and whether public confidence in police was ascendant or declining (Gallagher et al. 2001). Thus, although the main features of the now standard technology were adopted over the course of only a couple of decades (following the rapid expansion of mass availability of motor vehicle ownership beginning in the 1920s), since then there may be insufficient environmental pressure to stimulate a similarly rapid change from that technology to something else. Or it could be that transforming such a massive and fundamental technology just takes more time. American police organizations may still be in the early stages of testing and experimenting with alternative technologies, such as hot-spots policing,[7] but they may be on the road to meaningful change. If some early adopters develop and successfully implement an alternative technology

[7] A survey of a sample of departments with 100 or more sworn officers found that in 2001 about two in five local agencies claimed to have developed computerized crime mapping to support hot-spots policing (Weisburd and Lum 2005, p. 428), but the nature and extent of hot-spots policing implementation were not measured.

on a radical scale, then that may encourage others to follow (Rogers 2003). In the interim, police departments may be keeping the new, alternative technologies at the periphery of the organization's service delivery system, allowing them to learn by experimentation, while receiving credit from relevant stakeholders and peers for being innovative.

A second possibility is that scientific evaluations of the standard model have not measured the performance indicators that exert the greatest influence on police policies and practices. Police visibility and responsiveness increase citizens' perceptions of crime-fighting effectiveness and satisfaction with police service (Dukes, Portillos, and Miles 2009), and one of the most frequent complaints police administrators receive is that a neighborhood is not getting enough police patrol or timely police responses to calls for service.[8]

The importance of the police-citizen encounter has been emphasized in a great deal of ethnographic and quantitative research on police service delivery. The standard model gives priority to citizens' requests for service, and in-person encounters serve as the principal medium by which the public is able to experience and assess police service (Reiss 1971). With fairly high consistency researchers have found that what the police do in these encounters powerfully sways the public's confidence in and satisfaction with the police (Skogan 2005), and the aspects that seem to be especially powerful are not displays of crime-fighting prowess but rather process-oriented actions that demonstrate fairness and concern toward the public (Tyler and Huo 2002; Skogan and Frydl 2004, chap. 8; Skogan 2006a). Ironically, good police performance in these contacts with the public does not appear to improve significantly the public's confidence in police, but bad performance has a strong negative effect (Skogan 2006a). This may reflect what Bittner (1970) noted about the public's ambivalence about the police as a sort of necessary evil (using tainted methods to accomplish worthy ends), but it in no way diminishes the public's desire to have the police at their beck and call, which is the hallmark of democratic policing (Jones, Newburn, and Smith 1994, pp. 185–86; Bayley 2006, p. 20).

One of the drawbacks of the most promising focused technologies

---

[8] Greater police visibility often appears to have little or no effect on criminal offending; some studies indicate that it reduces fear of crime, but others indicate that it may increase it, especially if the changes are substantial, targeted, and unexpected by the public (Kelling 1981; Brown and Wycoff 1987; Torres and Vogel 2001; Scheider, Rowell, and Bezdikian 2003; Hinkle and Weisburd 2008).

is presumably what makes them effective—their strategic nature. Being strategic means being far more selective about who or what gets targeted, which increases the sensitivity of various segments of the community about getting their fair share of police protection and service (Thacher 2001; Mastrofski, Weisburd, and Braga 2009). If we think of police resource allocation as a poker game, the new strategic alternatives require police to place fewer bets (e.g., on hot spots) at much higher stakes and with greater uncertainty as to outcome, whereas the standard policing technology (e.g., a reactive calls for service system) allows police to make many bets (e.g., whether to respond to each of a host of individual calls) with much lower stakes per bet, but with a more certain outcome. Few responses result in unhappy service requesters, and research suggests that contemporary urban police agencies distribute service according to this mechanism with a high degree of equity according to need (Skogan and Frydl 2004, p. 315). Strategic redistributions of police resources make very transparent any inequality in the distribution of effort, which subjects police to greater pressure from any constituency feeling ignored. Thus, despite the crisis mentality that not uncommonly arises among police administrators faced with limited resources that cannot keep pace with rising calls for service workloads, police departments have not drastically revised this long-standing feature of their organizations.

The standard patrol technology may have remained robust over many decades because it (and the accompanying organizational structures it requires) is best designed to serve, not as a means of crime and disorder control, but rather as a way to distribute fairly equitably a wide range of services on which the public places high value. Although community policing promises this too to some extent, it has remained at the periphery of policing's technical core, a "spice" that flavors the "main course" of traditional police patrol. Police and their governing overseers may simply not be willing to cut substantially a standard strategy that distributes without much controversy what the public perceives as highly tangible benefits (Mastrofski 1999; Manning 2003, p. 246).

It is worth comparing the American experience with patrol technology to that of other nations that have had profoundly different ones. Societies that emerged from colonial status in the twentieth century are a good example. Generalizing about the nature of their colonial and postcolonial experiences is risky, but as one review concluded,

"Post-colonial policing is still generally concerned with law enforcement and the maintenance of internal security. Other similarly important areas of police work like police welfare roles and community policing are yet to emerge as significant features of policing in many post-colonial countries in the developing world" (Cole 1999, p. 99). Many, though by no means all, of the current police forces in post-colonial developing democracies remain strongly influenced by their former colonial paramilitary functions, designed to suppress disorder and insurrection that threatened colonizers' economic interests. In some cases, this has resulted in the persistence of an entirely different approach to serving the public. For example, in Trinidad and Tobago officers remained "barracked" in police stations, performing patrols much less frequently and with the primary purpose of suppressing offenses and enforcing laws rather than responding to citizens' requests for service. Efforts to move toward the service-oriented model now standard in America are highly challenged, even though there is a strong public desire for such a transformation (Mastrofski and Lum 2008). Those challenges are many and vary with the society. They certainly include resource limitations and the inertia of a deeply ingrained police culture, but perhaps the most significant is a reluctance of authoritarian governments to relinquish the use of police as instruments of their political will (Cole 1999, p. 101). There are rich research opportunities here for understanding the adoption and implementation of policing technologies in the very different environments of these postcolonial states.

B. Information Technology

We focus our discussion of information technology (IT) on whether innovations in IT alter police structures and practices or whether their uses and usefulness are determined by existing structures and practices. Optimists look for and find that technological advances improve efficiency and performance and that they require and stimulate changes in the structures, culture, and practices of policing. Skeptics find that new technologies have little impact on these aspects of the organization or that they have perverse, unanticipated consequences (Chan 2003).

Police departments were using large mainframe computers in the 1970s primarily for administrative tasks; by the early 1980s, the use of computers was fairly widespread among larger American police agencies (Allen et al. 1983). The adoption of personal computers for use by operational personnel skyrocketed, jumping from 5 percent to 56 percent between 1990 and 2003, with 83 percent of police nationwide employed in departments for in-field use (Hickman and Reaves 2006). By 2003 the vast majority (80–90 percent) of the nation's police agencies used computerized data systems to monitor the activities of their officers (arrests, citations, calls for service, etc.); as many as one in four of departments serving a million or more population used computer files to track illegal attempts to purchase firearms (Hickman and Reaves 2006), and these files are growing massively in size and in some cases accessibility across jurisdictions (Haggerty and Ericson 1999). By 2003 the vast majority of departments serving more than 25,000 made a wide variety of enforcement-relevant information readily accessible to officers in the field (Hickman and Reaves 2006). New approaches to surveillance grew rapidly as well. Between just 2000 and 2003 the number of departments regularly using video cameras in patrol cars jumped from 37 to 55 percent. About half of the nation's officers worked in departments using thermal imagers. And finally, it appears that increasing numbers of departments have been analyzing patterns in their data sets to detect actionable patterns of crime. A 1993 survey of large departments found that 13 percent of departments required most patrol officers to conduct crime analysis for their assigned area (Maguire 2003, p. 126), and a more recent survey found that crime analysis technologies were concentrated in typically small special units overwhelmingly staffed by civilians, where the average ratio (including those with no one assigned to crime analysis) in 2000 was one full-time crime analyst per 143 sworn personnel (O'Shea and Nicholls 2003). Although these findings suggest that crime analysis is far from fully used by patrol officers, this example illustrates the potential of innovations in information gathering, storage, retrieval, and processing.

The impact of these ITs is variable by type of technology and police organization or system. Although IT has not supplanted human police entirely, certain uses seem to have reduced the need for police to perform some traditional patroling techniques. For example, the widespread use of surveillance devices in the United Kingdom (Goold 2004), especially the CCTV on motorway hot spots and other locations, presumably frees officers from preventive patrol and reactive enforcement to perform other duties.[9] Evidence of CCTV's crime con-

---

[9] Although CCTV can also be labor intensive (monitoring the transmitted images), these tasks can be performed by civilians at remote locations, and new technologies are

trol effectiveness is mixed though in general deemed to be positive, but heavily contingent on the type of offense and spatial context in which the technology is used (Ratcliffe 2006, p. 20).

A view of the effects of new IT as more pervasive is represented by Ericson and Haggerty (1997), who see the proliferation of these devices as a key element in facilitating the growth of police work as "information work." They and others (Chan et al. 2001) note that much of the patrol officer's time is spent acquiring, recording, and using information from records and that this far exceeds the amount of time consumed in law enforcement activities that are the grist for popular mass media portrayals of the police. Their framework gives the new IT in policing a prominent role in the growing "risk society" network of information exchange, in which the police provide other government and private-sector risk-managing institutions huge amounts of information, as well as drawing from those institutions (insurance companies, financial institutions, retail establishments, departments of transportation and health, etc.) The important issue is how and how much the new IT has altered what police do and how they do it. It is difficult to know how much time was spent on these activities at various points before the IT revolution, but we can be fairly confident about some things. Police now appear to rely more heavily on certain IT-based forms of surveillance—"database policing"—where officers use computers to "patrol" massive data files (e.g., wanted lists) looking for "hits" on information they possess on suspects (Haggerty and Ericson 1999, p. 240; Meehan and Ponder 2002; Chan 2003, p. 659). And while such surveillance-based policing is made more efficient, timely, and accurate, it may be less useful for other purposes that require an analytic capacity to detect patterns in events that illuminate the utility of possible interventions (Nunn and Quinet 2002).

How much individual officers have become dependent on IT to do their everyday work, and how much it has supplanted traditional methods of acquiring and sharing information, has not been systematically documented, but the qualitative contrast between the "old-time beat cops" depicted by Joseph Wambaugh's "blue knight" (1973) and the IT-savvy twenty-first-century cop is striking. The former specialized in developing a highly personalized storehouse of information about

---

being developed that enable machines to digitally monitor and detect actionable events (Ratcliffe 2006).

people and places on his beat, derived mostly from personal contacts and observation that yielded information rarely recorded or accessible to other officers. The officer zealously guarded this information—an unsurprising reaction given the considerable skills and effort it took to acquire (Rubinstein 1973). From his ethnographic work, Bittner (1967) considered an officer's capacity to garner intimate knowledge as essential to good patrol work, but this practical knowledge based on experience now operates in a workplace where occupational status is becoming more tied to IT proficiency (Chan 2003, p. 664) and where the creation of a network of interpersonal contacts has become increasingly difficult to nourish because officers rarely stay assigned to the same beat long enough to develop the personal networks and knowledge base that sustained officers from the late nineteenth to the mid to late twentieth century (Mastrofski 1981). Indeed, elements of "turf-oriented" community policing have been designed to support the old patrol officer knowledge technology, but doing so requires heroic efforts that have not stemmed the erosion of the old individual-based street knowledge technology (Skogan 2006b, pp. 58–65). Over time systematic observation of police can tell us the extent to which street-level officers, like the general public, are investing more time in their computer screens and less in face-to-face contact with people. Perhaps more important, these studies can tell us how such a trend is affecting the way the police and public conceive the police mission and how decision making is altered.

Another way in which the new IT may be altering police work is the way in which the reporting requirements (increased amount of information required for documentation, more intensive monitoring of officer decision making, proposal of decision protocols) may actually structure how officers make what were previously seen as their highly discretionary decisions in the field (Ericson and Haggerty 1997). For example, the mandatory electronic report form for a routine burglary investigation walks the responding officer through the key steps of the process, thus standardizing the sorts of questions the officer asks, the sorts of evidence looked for, and hence the nature of the entire inquiry. Computerized systems can police the inquiry by requiring that certain data entry fields be completed before the officer may proceed to complete other fields, and the range of acceptable responses can be controlled as well. The transparency of the officer's work is facilitated by the ready availability of this information to supervisors and even the public (Chan 2001, 2003). The profound difference this can make is observable by comparing the IT-intensive report forms of America and the United Kingdom to those in a developing nation, where such technology either is not available or is simply ignored (Mastrofski and Lum 2008, p. 8), and hence the quality of the investigation depends much more on the skill and motivation of the individual officer.

Some of the rapidly developing surveillance technologies adapted from the military and health occupations show potential for making tremendous changes to how the police organize, supervise, and review decisions that have long been visible to the organization's hierarchy only after the fact. For example, automated vehicle locators, tracking the position of police vehicles, appeared on the scene in the 1970s but experienced many flaws and were easily disabled or fooled by police officers who did not want their locations tracked (Larson and Simon 1978). However, advances in global positioning systems may deliver a much more robust technology (Groff, Weisburd, and Jones 2008).

Even more impressive are the devices worn on the headgear of some emergency medical responders. These minidevices transmit to a remote site the image and sound of what the responder is seeing and hearing. It is a form of highly portable CCTV. Police are already experimenting with a Bluetooth-sized version that records the officer's encounters with the public digitally to be downloaded and reviewed at the end of the shift (Noguchi 2009). If the technology to transmit the data in real time to a remote site were made affordable for distribution to street officers, its widespread implementation could radically alter the supervision of the traditionally nonroutine, high-discretion work of the rank-and-file patrol officer. It would enable supervisors at remote sites to monitor, command, and evaluate the on-site activities of police in real time. For example, whether and how an officer should interrogate and search a suspect could be monitored and directed by a legal expert at headquarters. Such a system, now imaginable, would undoubtedly be treated with hostility by the rank and file, and possibly also by supervisors, who might be held much more accountable for the outcome of events that they now serve to judge only after the fact. And these data would probably serve as evidence in court and administrative hearings, creating a level of transparency in street-level policing heretofore unknown. How this would alter police practices and whether it would constitute an improvement would certainly be matters for research.

From a skeptic's perspective, the tremendous potential impact of new IT technology on the police organization and police work has not been realized. Much of the available evidence suggests that early experiences with technological advancements have had modest effects, have been perverted or undermined by police users, or have had unanticipated and undesirable consequences. Peter Manning (1992, 2003, 2005), one of the most prolific articulators of this perspective, has argued that police departments, especially the rank-and-file workers, resist using or actively undermine many of the innovative information technologies. When used, they tend to be employed in support of traditional practices and structures (see also Weisburd et al. 2003; Willis, Mastrofski, and Weisburd 2007), or these technologies may be poorly adapted to police uses. Furthermore, police often have inadequate technical sophistication and appreciation for what some technologies could actually do for them. On the basis of his own research and that of others, he concluded, "There is little evidence thirty years of funding technological innovations has produced much change in police practice or effectiveness" (Manning 2003, p. 136) and that the principal function of most of the new police IT was to serve as "icons of science" that legitimate the police (Manning 2005, p. 243). Yet he was more optimistic about the future prospects of techniques of rational crime prevention (e.g., crime analysis, crime mapping, rational resource allocation) to modify police practice (Manning 2003, p. 249)

Manning was not clear on the causes for this optimism, but we can think of several reasons to expect that the effects of police IT innovations in the first 30 years would be substantially less than what we can anticipate in the next 30. First, technological innovations, most of them originating for use in other industries (Haggerty and Ericson 1999), require time to be adapted and proven for police use. Second, many technologies require major changes in the skill set and culture of the police, changes that can be realized only over the course of a generation or two of police workers. In comparison to the private sector, personnel turnover in police organizations proceeds at a slow pace, making short-term change especially challenging (Sklansky 2006). And third, the organizational theory and empirical research notwithstanding (Maguire 2003, pp. 22–26), it takes time and energy to know what structures work best for a given technology and then to adjust those well-embedded structures (many of which have committed stakeholders who are more interested in how the technology affects their interests than whether it is successful in meeting its ostensible objectives). Some of these new technologies may eventually have profound effects on police, but those who expect them early and without the fits and starts that come with trial and error will often be disappointed.

Widespread acceptance and implementation of new technologies may take considerable time, but the creation of new technologies continues apace. As we write, progressive police leaders and the U.S. Department of Justice are launching a campaign to develop and test a cluster of IT technologies under the rubric of "predictive policing" (Beck and McCue 2009; Bratton, Morgan, and Malinowski 2009). Currently in the development and evaluation stages, "Predictive policing includes strategies and tactics that improve the situational awareness of law enforcement concerning individuals or locations before criminal activity occurs" (National Institute of Justice 2009, p. 3). Its elements include closely integrated information systems that offer a broad range of data about crime; discerning broad patterns in events, people, and places involved in crime; the use of "cutting-edge" technologies for information gathering and data analysis; continuing evaluation of system performance against expectations; and careful integration of information products with operations people and processes for effective interventions (Bratton, Morgan, and Malinowski 2009). Drawing heavily from business analytics that forecast market conditions and industry trends, predictive policing will link data gathered by a wide range of technologies to a variety of methods of analysis, including some sophisticated quantitative methods: "dynamic systems modeling and forecasting such as algorithmic methods, machine or statistical learning, or ensemble methods" (National Institute of Justice 2009, p. 5). It will also draw on methods of qualitative intelligence gathering and analysis. These methods have already been used to anticipate and reduce random gunfire and to evaluate the usefulness of DNA collection criteria used in convicted felon DNA databases (Beck and McCue 2009). Predictive policing is seen by advocates as the extension of a trend in database police analytics, moving from crime analysis to Compstat (more timely analysis) to Compstat "plus" (real-time analysis) into predicting the future (Bratton and Malinowski 2008).

Predictive policing is then a forward-looking crime diagnostic system designed to help police identify where and how their interventions can be most effective in preventing future crime. Its proponents envision a system that can focus narrowly (predicting future offenses of a serial killer) or large scale (predicting homicide patterns of an entire city), short term (predicting crime occurrences in hot spots over the next few days) or long term (predicting how city development plans will affect police resource allocations for many years; Bratton, Morgan, and Malinowski 2009). Proponents suggest that it will make police forces more agile, able to accomplish more with fewer resources. There are already early-adopting departments around the nation reporting encouraging results with the application of predictive analytics (Perlman 2008), and some are making substantial investments in IT hardware and data sharing.

The emergence of predictive policing offers a rich set of research opportunities to follow the genesis of what could be a major IT innovation. One set of questions concerns where and how it will be adopted and how intensively it will be implemented. Another concerns the performance of the technology: not only whether it will prove effective in reducing crime but also how it scores on other criteria, such as efficiency, equity, and accountability to law and principles of just punishment. It is largely untested as a crime prevention tool, and there may be some understandable skepticism about the utility of such predictive analytics for police in light of concerns raised about the role of probabilistic forecasting models in the recent economic downturn (*Economist* 2010, p. 5). Yet another set of questions ask how the technology will influence the internal distribution of power, the nature of the organizational "game," and the organizational and occupational culture in policing (Chan 2003, pp. 663–68). Independent of these effects, researchers should also attend to consequences of adopting this cluster of technological innovations for the legitimacy and support police enjoy from external stakeholders. While these await empirical examination, a treatise has already surfaced that argues against the adoption of such "actuarial innovations." Harcourt (2007) argues that such a system will likely "profile" certain types of people, but if that group's response is inelastic to the threat of getting caught and punished, then the overall amount of crime may actually increase. He also argues that such an approach may also incur unacceptable, disproportionate social costs for certain groups of people who are targeted for incarceration. And finally, he is concerned that such a system will target the greatest policing and punishment effort on those groups that are predicted to cause the greatest criminal harm in the future, basing state-invoked punishment not on past practice but on future risk, a path of justice that may trouble many.

IV. The People Doing Policing

It seems plausible that the nature of the people brought into police organizations will influence how police work is done and how successfully. American police organizations have changed over their history in whom they have accepted and rejected as workers. From the mid-nineteenth century until well into the twentieth century, American police drew heavily on certain European immigrant groups that found police work to be a ladder for upward mobility. But other groups, such as women and blacks, were largely excluded until civil rights reforms began to take hold in the latter part of the twentieth century (Fogelson 1977; Walker 1977; Skogan and Frydl 2004, p. 312). The representation of previously excluded racial minorities has continued to increase into the twenty-first century, although in most jurisdictions it still has not achieved parity with their presence in the community (Williams and Murphy 1990; Sklansky 2006). The same can be said for women in policing (Sklansky 2006). Those brought into policing have received more formal education, and once they have become police officers, departments are giving them more training than ever before (Reaves and Hickman 2002, p. 3; Mastrofski 2005a).

The changes in the demographic profile of American police agencies are attributable to equal employment and affirmative action changes in hiring laws and court and administrative rulings stimulated by the civil rights and women's rights movements and litigation (Skogan and Frydl 2004, pp. 79–81; Sklansky 2006; Zhao, He, and Lovrich 2006). The increasing presence of more formal education and training[10] emerges from a more diffuse set of forces but was undoubtedly given focus since the 1970s by reformers, police leaders, and professional associations wishing to raise policing's occupational status and improve performance (Skogan and Frydl 2004, pp. 139–42). So in these important ways the profile of American police is changing, but the key question is, With what consequence?

---

[10] A recent nationally representative sample of police officers showed that 33 percent held a 4-year college degree, 19 percent held a 2-year degree, and an additional 33 percent had taken at least some college, leaving those with only a high school diploma or less in the distinct minority (Weisburd et al. 2001, p. 11).

The answer is that there is not sufficient evidence available to answer with confidence, and much of what does exist is contradictory (Sklansky 2006). Although a number of studies document a difference between black and white officers' beliefs and attitudes, most studies of actual behavior fail to find a difference in such things as arrest, use of force, demeanor, methods of restoring order, and engaging in community policing (Skogan and Frydl 2004, pp. 148–49). These studies are usually based on systematic field observations of individual police officers. The National Academy of Sciences panel on police policy and practices concluded that the small body of available research provided "no credible evidence that officers of different racial or ethnic backgrounds perform differently during interactions with citizens simply because of race or ethnicity" (Skogan and Frydl 2004, p. 148). When considering the effects of the officer's sex on police behavior, they found the amount of research too small and results too variable to offer conclusions (p. 151). Similarly, this panel also judged the evidence to be insufficient to offer conclusions on the impact of increased formal (college) education and training on police practice (pp. 139–47). A notable deficiency in much of the research is its capacity to test whether the effects of the officer's race, sex, and education/training vary in specific contexts, especially according to the race, sex, and education of the citizen (Mastrofski 2006*b*).

Some suspect that the changing demography of American police organizations is profoundly affecting organizational dynamics—that by officers having to work closely with persons of a different race, sex, or sexual orientation, the culture of policing is changing (Sklansky 2006, pp. 1229–34). Evidence here is scant, although the emergence of "rival trade groups" of minority officers who are willing to challenge the traditional perspective of other traditional police fraternal and bargaining units raises the possibility that these new groups encourage and sustain a more fragmented culture. We address the evidence on fragmentation of the police culture in the following section. Here we suggest that it would be useful to learn the effects of different levels of minority presence on police forces by comparing the culture and practices of police in departments with low, moderate, and high levels of minority presence.[11]

---

[11] A review of minority staffing levels in large departments in 2000 shows that it exceeded 60 percent in only two of 10 departments, but that four had achieved 40–50 percent (Sklansky 2006, p. 1214).

Despite the lack of evidence on the consequences of the trend toward more demographic diversity and education/training in American police agencies, there is considerable public approval of these change trajectories, but less so on how they should be achieved and used. For example, overwhelming majorities of the American public support the principle that a community's police force should reflect the racial composition of the city. Half or more (depending on race) say that more minority officers should serve more minority neighborhoods (Weitzer and Tuch 2006, pp. 139–44). Where consensus breaks down most strikingly is in whether this diversity should be achieved with racially preferential hiring practices; minority citizens approve at more than twice the rate of whites. The high support for the abstract principle of police force diversification undoubtedly derives from the general support in the American populace for the desirability of representative democracy (Krislov and Rosenbloom 1981).

V. Police Culture

The discussion to this point has illuminated numerous ways in which police and police organizations in America have changed or may be changing. But what changes, if any, have occurred in the things that police believe and value—the culture of the police? For many contemporary reformers, changing the culture of police is the key to changing police practices and organizational performance. Culture is the term we use for the set of understandings and interpretations that are shared by a group, that create meanings for the significant events and challenges the group experiences, that guide how members of the group deal with each other and those outside the group, that assist them in managing the strains of their shared tasks, and that distinguish the group and its members from outsiders (Skogan and Frydl 2004, p. 131).

A. Types of Police Culture

Before we address the question of changes in police culture, we must first acknowledge the different ways in which the quality of "culture" has been ascribed to police. Researchers have used three characterizations of culture (Paoline 2001, chap. 1). First, *occupational* culture has been used to capture those value and belief orientations that are presumed to differentiate police as an occupation from all others and the general public. Second, the notion of *organizational* culture applied to police has made possible the observation that culture may vary from one police organization to another. Third, *subculture* has introduced the proposition that across the occupation and within organizations, it is possible to distinguish distinctly different beliefs, values, and perceptions that police employ in their daily work. We summarize the literature on each of these approaches before turning to changes in police culture, drawing on Paoline's (2001) review of this literature in characterizing each.

When social scientists began ethnographic studies of police, they looked for and found a number of features of contemporary police work that illuminated a monolithic occupational culture. The physical danger that might emerge, even from seemingly innocuous situations, coupled closely with the unique authority of the police to coerce and control, serves to isolate police from the rest of society inasmuch as society does not fully appreciate the requirements of dealing effectively with danger and using coercive authority effectively (Skolnick 1966; Westley 1970). Consequently, officers share a deep suspicion of situations and people's motives, and they feel constant pressure to be alert for signs of danger and anything that undermines their authority. Police work is also laden with uncertainty. Officers routinely find themselves called on to figure out what is really going on under circumstances in which the quality of information is untested and the pressure for timely diagnosis is great (Bittner 1967; Muir 1977, chap. 10). Further, there may be uncertainty about what the organization hierarchy will, after the fact, judge to be the order of priorities (e.g., catching criminals vs. not violating their procedural rights; Reuss-Ianni and Ianni 1983). And additional uncertainty is introduced by the asymmetry of consequences for outcomes. Most police actions may produce no visible consequences, but of those that do, officers perceive that the greater likelihood is that undesired events and outcomes are more likely to be noticed and punished than desired ones are to be recognized and rewarded. The pervasive threats issuing from within the organization encourage a "minimax," lay-low-and-play-it-safe attitude toward unnecessary risk, while clinging to the ideal of the crime fighter image and being perpetually alert to opportunities to validate it.

Police isolation derives also from the widespread belief that the most valuable skills in police work do not come from the public and its democratic institutions, from professional sources, or from the bureaucracy (Bayley and Bittner 1984). The public is viewed as largely clueless as to what constitutes good policing and how to get it. Formal fonts of knowledge, especially when based on science, are distrusted as invalid, too general to be of use in the field, or contrary to the interests of the rank and file (Thacher 2008). Even when results from controlled experiments indicate the most effective crime control response, officers are reluctant to change their behavior (Sherman 1984, p. 75). Laws, department rules, and policies may establish a rationale for consequences ex post facto when things go awry, but they are of little use in selecting the best course of action in the field. Thus, the skills of the police officer are acquired by learning to piece together the minutiae of situations on a case-by-case basis in which no two circumstances are necessarily the same. So, what police officers know, they must learn from personal experience acquired over time on a case-by-case basis, supplemented by on-the-job guidance from those most experienced in the craft (Bittner 1967). Only those who have experienced this reality-based, practical training-by-doing can be entrusted to judge the work of others, and even here, there is a reluctance to judge the work of others unless one was on the scene to observe all aspects of the situation.

So the hazards of the job incline police to social isolation from those who are not police, and another, related consequence is loyalty to the members of the police group. Cultural expectations are that an officer will protect other police, not only when physically threatened but when threatened with citizen complaints or management scrutiny. Whistle-blowing, such as that of the legendary Frank Serpico in New York City, is a major transgression of the police "code of silence" regarding corrupt and abusive practices of one's peers (Skolnick 2002).

This view of policing as a more or less uniform and distinct occupation defined by these features has had a powerful influence on scholars, public policy makers, and the police themselves. Indeed, reformers and scholars widely regard the principal challenge of achieving community policing reforms to be that of transforming the police culture to be less isolated, more willing to take the risks that innovation requires, and more accommodative of a diverse and complex role identity (Skolnick and Bayley 1986; Sparrow, Moore, and Kennedy 1990; Rosenbaum and Wilkinson 2004). Despite its widespread appeal, the evidence on the explanatory power of police culture as a determinant of police practice is virtually nonexistent (Skogan and Frydl 2004, p. 130). First, researchers have not demonstrated the extent to which these (or any) features of the police culture distinguish it from other occupational groups. Indeed, social isolation is a primary feature of the military and certain clergy, whereas group loyalty would seem pervasive among a host of other occupations as well, such as lawyers, physicians, and accountants. If the concept of police occupational culture is to have utility, the ability of its key features to distinguish its practitioners from those of other occupations seems essential. Second, the ubiquity of these cultural values is undercut by research of the last four decades that shows considerable variation among police in the extent to which they adhere to a common set of values or perspectives.

Wilson's *Varieties of Police Behavior* (1968) articulated the view that officers' policing styles are patterned by features of police organizations (especially the chief's priorities and methods), which in turn are shaped by the political culture of their communities. His much-cited depiction of watchman, legalistic, and service style departments sought validation in field research coupled with an examination of patterns in arrest rates for various offenses. Since then a number of studies have explored the variation in police culture that may be attributable to police organization characteristics. For example, Klockars and colleagues used surveys of officers to measure the orientations of police to hold and enforce integrity standards (regarding corruption and abuse). They found significant variation among police organizations in their support of integrity and attributed that variation to certain key features of the organization and its leadership (Klockars et al. 2000; Klockars, Ivkovic, and Haberfeld 2004, 2006). Other cross-jurisdictional studies have linked department size and other features to the inclination of officers to make arrests for certain offenses (Brown 1981; Mastrofski, Ritti, and Hoffmaster 1987). However, most of these studies focus on central tendencies of officer attitude responses; while some find statistically significant differences across departments, little attention is paid to the size of those effects relative to other influences. Stated another way, what is the scope of variation within departments? One study looked at officers' orientations to aggressive enforcement and community partnership in two departments seeking to promote different styles of community policing and found that although there was a small and significant difference on one measure (a 4 percent higher approval score on community partnership), the level of variation in both departments on all measures was quite modest (Terrill and Mastrofski 2004). The issue raised is whether there is enough cultural coherence *within* police organizations to speak meaningfully about differences in culture *between* departments. Researchers have simply not explored this issue in enough places to offer a rigorous test of this proposition.

The most examined aspect of police culture has been how much it may be fragmented into subcultures within police departments. A number of studies have identified different styles of policing, some looking for distinct differences between management and street officers (Reuss-Ianni and Ianni 1983; Paoline 2001), but most focus on the rank and file only (Broderick 1972; Muir 1977; Brown 1981; Paoline 2001; Mastrofski, Willis, and Snipes 2002; Wood, Davis, and Rouse 2004). Most of these studies highlight to what degree officers within the same department exhibit different cultural orientations toward a wide range of issues.[12] One should note that although there are some similarities among some of the studies in the sorts of attitudes, beliefs, and perceptions that are measured, there are also important differences. Measures and methods of observation vary considerably, especially between the studies that explore each of the three general approaches to defining police culture. Thus, while it is tempting to accept these findings as undermining the occupational and organizational cultural theses, they constitute at best a fuzzy test. Careful attention to using common measures and methods across multiple jurisdictions would enable researchers to say more conclusively whether and how culture varies at all three levels.

B. Changes in Police Culture

We now turn to the question of whether police culture has changed or is changing. The answer depends on what type of culture we are considering. If there are some aspects of police culture that bridge all American police, then by virtue of the size and diversity of the American policing industry, this would be the slowest to change and the most difficult to detect. One might do so by tracking representative samples of American police officers, conducting a survey every several years. This has not been done, but the Police Foundation conducted a single such national survey (Weisburd et al. 2001). The authors found that certain police attitudes differed substantially from the traditional

---

[12] Paoline (2001) found fairly high consensus among officers in two departments favoring the police role as law enforcement and aggressive patrolling tactics, but he found significant differences among officers on many other dimensions.

characterization of the occupational culture as isolated, defensive, and hostile to legal constraints.

We may also draw on case studies of police organizations that track the change in police attitudes over time. An interesting study used a variety of measures to assess whether the police culture changed in two Illinois police departments that were trying to implement community policing and get officers to embrace its values and practices (Rosenbaum and Wilkinson 2004). The virtue of this research is that five survey waves were conducted between 1991 and 1997, an impressive effort by conventional social science standards. Although some changes were observed, even here there was backsliding over time, causing the researchers to conclude that the officers' orientations had not changed for the most part. One might attribute some of this to failures and limitations in the departments' efforts, but we think that it more likely represents a much broader challenge. Police organizations try to control the transmission of culture through formal mechanisms, such as selection, training, supervision, and exhortation by top leaders (Muir 1977, chap. 12), but police agencies, like many other organizations, transmit their culture largely through informal mechanisms over which police leaders simply have little direct control, at least for the short run. Changing fundamental police values and beliefs rarely happens as a Pentecost (Buerger 1998), but rather can be expected to evolve only as the "old hands" depart, leaving more of the new ones, who may have been selected with a particular orientation or at least may be more open to accepting new ways. It is especially difficult to anticipate reforming the values of officers who have developed their skill set under one cultural system. To the extent that values follow skills and habits, the longer officers are invested in the skill inventory they possess, the harder it is to get them to be positive about investing in a radically different set. Hence, we should be surprised and skeptical if police leaders or researchers report that in a few or even over the course of several years, they have transformed the culture of their department.

This is not to say that short-term behavioral change is impossible. There are a variety of ways to structure work to achieve compliance with expectations, which was one of the principal virtues of bureaucracy according to Weber ([1922] 1978, p. 223). Commissioner William Bratton (1998) reported "turning around" the New York City Police Department, moving it away from its lassitude about enforcing minor quality-of-life violations in the city, but we doubt that much of the impressive increase achieved in levels of enforcement (citations and arrests) was accomplished by changing the police culture. Rather, it was by changing the supervisory and incentive/disincentive systems that harnessed existing cultural values to the leader's goals. But we hypothesize that achieving widespread internalization of a remarkably different set of beliefs and priorities from those dearly and long held simply takes sustained effort over the course of at least a couple of generations of workers to accomplish.

C. Sources of Cultural Change

So what forces might work to transform police culture? The answer depends of course on which aspects of culture we consider. We have selected three types of cultural change that have been the object of reformers during the last several decades: reducing police alienation and isolation from the communities they serve (community policing), shifting greater reliance from craft to science values (problem-oriented policing), and increasing commitment to integrity over group loyalty (corruption reduction).

Accomplishing a profound shift toward less police isolation from the community and stronger police-community bonds will require structural changes that go well beyond leadership's exhortation and the creation of special community-oriented units and programs (Reiss 1992, pp. 91–94). Structural changes one might hypothesize would promote and reinforce such a cultural shift include recruiting police from populations that more closely match the populations served in terms of their cultural heritage (particularly important in minority and low-income areas that receive police attention disproportionate to their numbers), maintaining stable assignments of officers to specific areas over long time periods (years rather than months), and rationalizing the system of skills and motivation by giving officers useful training and measuring individual and unit performance in terms of meeting community needs and expectations and rewarding accordingly. The first facilitates the development of a better knowledge base, greater symbolic representation (Lim 2006), and more amicable relations between the police and the public (Sklansky 2006). The second makes it possible to sustain and use that knowledge and the closer police-public relations presumed to result (Mastrofski 1981). And the third reinforces desired practices by enabling officers to engage in desired practices, monitoring, and rewarding them (Willis, Mastrofski, and Kochel 2010).

The brief history of community policing, however, shows little evidence of American police organizations being willing or able to implement these changes. If anything, the pressure for requiring a college education, the difficulty of recruiting qualified minorities to a police career, and officers' desire for having the opportunity for a wide range of career-enhancing job assignments have made it difficult to bring people onto the force who bring with them familiarity with the cultures of the specific communities they will police. Instead, police organizations have relied heavily on "training" to fill in the knowledge gaps, training of untested value in altering the officer's cultural orientation to the communities to which they are assigned (Skogan and Frydl 2004, p. 141). Some departments have attempted to stabilize officers' beat assignments, but the competing pressures of meeting the demands for timely response to a burgeoning load of calls for service, the constraints of personnel procedures that facilitate frequent changes in job assignments, and the constraints of labor contracts have made it extremely difficult to achieve these goals, even in departments that made impressive efforts to do so (Skogan 2006b, 2008). And as best as one can tell without a systematic study, American police agencies have not radically transformed the way they evaluate and reward officer and unit performance. Reinforcing a community-oriented culture would, for example, place a much higher value on advancing the careers of those officers who had accumulated extensive knowledge of, contacts in, and influence in the neighborhoods they were assigned to police. Compare what a promotion test of this sort would require to what typically appears on police promotion exams. Especially with the concurrent growth in Compstat's popularity in the last 15 years, most departments continue to focus on enforcement and crime-focused measures to assess and reward performance (Willis, Mastrofski, and Kochel 2010). Even the most progressive departments concentrate on general community policing principles, not the particular knowledge needed to apply them. Without such structural changes, it is difficult to see how a substantial and enduring cultural shift toward community partnerships can be accomplished. And it is not necessarily due to a lack of will among police leaders. Such structural changes would mean making complicated and profound changes in some of the basic ways of doing police business in America, changes that would require the collaboration and support of a wide variety of institutions and authorities, many of which might be hostile to such proposals.

The second cultural shift we consider is the movement of police toward an ethos receptive to a problem-oriented approach—one that shifts from a craft-based culture to one that gives much greater weight to science (Bayley and Bittner 1984). Reiss (1992, p. 92) outlined problem-oriented policing as one direction that police organizations were poised to pursue in the late twentieth century. Two visions of the integration of science into police culture have been advanced. One views a bifurcation of the process into scientists as generators of useful knowledge and of police as adept users of that knowledge (Bayley and Bittner 1984; Reiss 1992). A more radical conception is of police in full partnership with the scientific community, engaged in a highly integrated system, such as systems employed in several health professions, where the organizational lines separating knowledge-generating enterprises (universities) and users of that knowledge (medical practitioners, pharmacists) are blurred or eliminated (Wood and Bradley 2009; Weisburd and Neyroud, forthcoming). This approach may be more advanced in other countries, such as the United Kingdom and Australia, at least in attempting to close the gap between the worlds of research and practice.

Changes within and outside the police organization are necessary to effect changes of either sort in the cultural orientation of police. First, the science of policing must be sufficiently advanced to offer the police knowledge they can use reliably to solve problems. The explosion of scientific research that assesses police tactics and strategies in the last two decades has done much to move beyond the negative findings of the 1970s and 1980s regarding responding rapidly to calls for service, engaging in preventive patrol, and investing in criminal investigation specialists. Attempts to evaluate empirical tests of other strategies have led to encouraging conclusions about what does or may work well (Sherman et al. 1997; Skogan and Frydl 2004, chap. 6; Weisburd and Eck 2004). Some leaders are turning to scientific evidence to help design and select strategies to solve problems (Weisburd and Neyroud, forthcoming), and others are trying to use a combination of scientific and intelligence analysis to engage in real-time decisions in the field to predict the occurrence of problems (Bratton and Malinowski 2008).

The question arises as to whether the state of scientific knowledge about crime, disorder, and other problems police face is sufficient to bolster the faith of police in its use. Here the state of scientific knowledge might be judged by comparison to other human service industries (health and education) to be still in the early stages and not well developed to guide the selection of most common police practices, much less establish the effectiveness of new ones. On the basis of a National Academy of Sciences review of evaluations of police crime, disorder, and fear-reduction strategies, two of the panel's members concluded that "many policing practices applied broadly throughout the United States either have not been the subject of systematic research or have been examined in the context of research designs that do not allow practitioners or policy makers to draw very strong conclusions" (Weisburd and Eck 2004, p. 42). The panel of criminologists did find cause for optimism in the growing body of studies employing stronger research methods. These studies yield with considerable consistency support for more focused and specific policing strategies, especially if they are customized to deal with the specific problem at hand. Hot-spots policing is arguably the strategy whose promise is most well documented (Braga and Weisburd, forthcoming), but even here there is a great deal that is unknown about the circumstances under which this approach will be most successful and least likely to generate undesirable side effects (Mastrofski, Weisburd, and Braga 2009). The course of action falls mainly to the police organization's environment—the research industry that supports the potency of the "technical core" of police (Mastrofski and Uchida 1993; Scott 1998). In turn, this will also require more financial support to bolster the modest funding for such research than it currently receives—$10 million per year in an industry that annually expends $43 billion (Weisburd and Neyroud, forthcoming).

An even bigger challenge in shifting from the traditional craft-based cultural norms to ones that elevate scientific validation as a basis for strategic and operational decision making is convincing police themselves that, first, it will work better and, second, it will not expose them and their organizations to unacceptable risks. Greater rigor and transparency in the evaluation of what works may be perceived as increasing the likelihood that failures will be widely publicized, resulting in loss of one's job, resources, or legitimacy. This is not an insignificant risk since many innovations fail, especially early in their development (Rogers 2003). Even those researchers and police leaders most committed to achieving this transformation acknowledge that science is not now a central part of the culture of police, and it will be a major uphill slog to make it so (Weisburd and Neyroud, forthcoming). Others have argued that the policing environment is characterized not just by a desire to reduce crime but by multiple, conflicting, and ambiguous values, including equity, due process, and just deserts. Experimental research may illuminate the best means to a given end, in this case crime prevention, but it cannot resolve how trade-offs between these values should best be made (Thacher 2001).

Assessments of police innovation diffusion suggest that police are strongly inclined to rely not on outside experts in deciding to adopt an innovative path, but rather on what they learn from the experience of their professional peers (Weiss 1997; Sherman 1998; Bayley 2008). Hence, diffusion of this approach at the top levels of the organization will undoubtedly require persuading high-status police leaders to engage in and promote this approach and to mobilize the occupational and professional organizations that disseminate information about what is new and in vogue. Some have argued that the best path to accomplishing this would be developing close relations between universities and police departments, just as has been done to structure a vital science-based arrangement in health care professions and the military (Bradley, Nixon, and Marks 2006; Weisburd and Neyroud, forthcoming). Aside from whatever technical benefits may derive from such a close collaboration, it surely will not go unobserved by many chiefs that an ongoing close association with high-status research institutions can offer a significant degree of legitimacy to the police, regardless of the technical results.

Ensuring that a science-based approach to problem solving permeates to the street-level officers will undoubtedly take more time and involve an array of structural changes in recruitment and selection of officers (more with a science-based college education); protection for those who seek to override bureaucratic, craft, or political pressures when science suggests another pathway; and a set of incentive structures that reward active involvement in and success with applications of scientific knowledge. It may be that successful integration of a science-accepting culture will not require police officers who do science so much as ones who accept its legitimacy. The military may serve as a model here, where science-based technologies and strategies are devised by specialists (usually civilians).

The third domain we explore is changing the police culture from one that prizes group loyalty to one that gives greater weight to professional standards of integrity. This requires that police develop an intolerance of corruption and abuse of authority among their members. It requires a dramatic shift from the "code of silence" thought to permeate the ranks of the police (Skolnick 2002). This means not only that officers apply those standards personally but that they are committed to applying them to their peers, which would include whistleblowing and informal expressions of disapproval when they become aware of corruption and abuse.[13] Internalizing these norms requires at least two things of the police organization: clearly stated standards of behavior that are viewed as reasonable and appropriate and a system of discipline that is predictable, fair, and corrective—as opposed to being solely punitive (Klockars 1995; Tyler, Callahan, and Frost 2007). In the first case, it has been argued (with the support of some evidence), that strong leadership at the very top of the organization is essential for emphasizing the importance of police integrity as an organizational priority and convincing officers that they should adopt it as their priority (Muir 1977; Klockars, Ivkovic, and Haberfeld 2006). In the second, the willingness of officers to subject their peers to a disciplinary process requires that they invest it with good faith, or what some call legitimacy (Tyler, Callahan, and Frost 2007), which comes from a system that is seen to attempt to correct problem behaviors, is fair and meticulous in observing officers' procedural rights, and delivers punishments that are proportionate to offenses.

Although some analysts view it as a system independent of the self-regulatory culture of integrity, also influencing the culture of integrity is the bureaucratic system of "command and control." This attempts to manipulate organizationally controlled incentives and disincentives to act in accordance with integrity standards, assuming that officers are motivated instrumentally, to maximize their personal outcomes (Tyler, Callahan, and Frost 2007, p. 462). The command and control approach presumably does not need to change the officers' culture, just their behavior, by applying incentives and disincentives that workers most care about (e.g., continued employment and career prospects). Even if intended to deter misbehavior and promote actions that express intol-

[13] Having a culture of high integrity, one that is intolerant of corrupt and abusive practices, is not synonymous with having little or no corruption, but is rather one that is thought to bring to bear what an organization can do to prevent corrupt and abusive practices (Klockars, Ivkovic, and Haberfeld 2006).

erance of misbehavior in others (such as whistle-blowing), the specifics of how such a system operates cannot but convey to officers the organization's expectations, as well as its commitment to enforcing them.

What is not particularly clear from the limited empirical research is how police organizations can be designed and led to activate either system of control so that it will promote stronger systems of integrity with some reliability. One researcher found that when agencies became more authoritarian and bureaucratized, they increased their capacity to limit corruption, through such specific practices as holding supervisors accountable for their officers' practices, using closer surveillance, implementing covert integrity tests, and ending quotas for units specializing in vice arrests (hence reducing perjury about evidence that is difficult to acquire; Sherman 1978). Whether and how that operated only through the command and control path of instrumental variation or whether that also produced value changes among officers is unknown.

Another perspective on changing the culture of integrity is offered by Klockars and colleagues in a series of studies of police and police organizations, based on surveys of officers in a variety of American departments (Klockars, Ivkovich, and Haberfeld 2004) and 13 other countries and an in-depth study of three American agencies (Klockars, Ivkovich, and Haberfeld 2006). To measure the cultural environment of integrity the researchers asked samples of officers to respond to a number of scenarios representing varying degrees of integrity lapses. The culture of integrity was estimated in terms of how serious the misconduct was judged to be, the seriousness of the discipline expected, and the willingness of the respondent to report the misconduct. Researchers found substantial variation among 30 American agencies in their level of integrity and selected three that scored as "high integrity" for the collection of detailed information about the processes producing integrity in these agencies. From the survey of officers, the researchers found strong correlations between the officers' judgments of the seriousness of the misconduct, the severity of the likely discipline, and the likelihood of reporting it. They speculated that the driving force behind high integrity scores was not the values officers brought with them when they became police or the ethical persuasiveness of training, but rather the signals given by the organization's leadership in its disciplinary practices, for example, the certainty, celerity, severity, and fairness of punishment given for misconduct, a pattern they also perceive in 14 other nations (Klockars, Ivkovich, and Haberfeld 2004, chaps. 1, 15). Recommendations to foster an environment that breaks down the code of silence were offered from the three case studies: making it a punishable offense to fail to report knowledge of misconduct, dismissing officers for lying when questioned by authorities about alleged misconduct, rewarding officers who report misconduct, and facilitating anonymous and confidential reporting of misconduct. These researchers argued that these command and control practices will, when provided with consistency, produce cultural changes that are ultimately manifested in behavior.

However, these recommendations await rigorous empirical testing. Such research would benefit from two features. First, it would be important to avoid the many risks of common-method bias by ensuring that measures of the department's policies relevant to integrity are independent of the surveys used to measure the culture of integrity in a department (Podsakoff et al. 2003). Second, the sample of agencies evaluated should not be restricted solely to those that are high integrity. To learn the consequences of the recommended strategies, one must allow the criterion measure to vary naturally in either a cross-sectional or longitudinal fashion.

VI. Governance of the Police

American democratic principles prescribe that the police are subject to the governance of other institutions in all three branches of government. At the local level this means the executive (the mayor or city or county manager), the legislative branch (the city or county council), and the court system. Sheriffs, as directly elected county officials, have a somewhat different relationship to the executive and legislative branches than appointed police chiefs do (Falcone and Wells 1995, pp. 125–30). But in all instances, the police are expected not to be a self-governing entity but rather to receive direction or oversight from all three branches. The key issues here are what forms this governance takes, how much direction and oversight they impose, and with what consequence for police practice.

A. Historical Trends in Police Governance

Historians have chronicled the change in local police structures and practices from the nineteenth to the twentieth century, some of which have already been noted. American police governance began as a system in which police were at the center of partisan politics during the heyday of local political machines. As a consequence, party bosses and elected officials routinely had a hand in shaping daily and mundane police practices (Fogelson 1977; Walker 1977; Kelling and Moore 1988; Reiss 1992). However, good government and professional reform waves of the first quarter of the twentieth century set in motion a series of changes. These changes promoted many police forces that by midcentury were highly buffered from local politicians' ability to manipulate the particulars of policing, relegating their influence primarily to selecting the chief, approving the police budget, and passing local ordinances for police to enforce.

Wilson (1968) traced a relationship between the political structure of a city (traditional, unreformed at one extreme and reformed at the other), its structures and modes of operation, and ultimately the style of policing its officers tended to employ. The local political culture influenced police operations by establishing the boundaries within which the police could operate without concern for external interference. The key mechanism by which this occurred was the determination of who would be the police chief, not direct issue-specific intervention by elected officials. This is not inconsequential, of course, since the selection or removal of a chief can powerfully signal to his or her successor the consequences of pleasing or failing to please officials with responsibility for police governance (Reiss and Bordua 1967).

Nonetheless, these earlier reforms had clearly given police chiefs and their departments considerable freedom from everyday political intervention, but by the late 1960s the police underwent intense public scrutiny and criticism for having become too removed from the community they served, especially those ethnic minorities and the poor who lacked political power in city hall. The emergence of community policing in the 1980s and its 1970s precursors (e.g., team policing) is directly attributable to a desire among reformers to rebuild police legitimacy and strengthen effectiveness by reestablishing a bond with the community, one that had strong elements of participatory and deliberative democracy. This is captured by the popular characterization of the reformers' desired relationship between police and community as a "partnership" (Fung 2001; Sklansky 2008).

Of course, police governance practices have proven not to conform so readily to sweeping historical generalizations. In the late 1970s, a time by which the political era of policing was thought to be long defunct, research showed that among a sample of 24 municipalities and counties, American communities still displayed considerable variety in the structures and practices of governance, some exhibiting the sort of police autonomy expected but others retaining the artifacts of the "political" era—an active level of involvement in directing policing by local elected officials (Mastrofski 1988). A review of extant research on police governance showed that little research had been conducted: "based mostly on a few case studies, the available evidence suggests that when local officials, such as the mayor, exercise influence over the department, they tend to do so most potently through executive appointment, job review, and the threat of removal from office" (Skogan and Frydl 2004, p. 196). Some of the studies suggested the involvement of political officials in policing matters as safely within the bounds of democratic accountability, but others found evidence of inappropriate or negative interventions (pp. 198–202).

Besides these case studies, most of the scholarship that concerns itself with the effects of governing structures on policing examines cross-sectional variation in the structures, not processes, of governance in large numbers of communities. Hence, beginning with Wilson's seminal work, a few researchers have used cross-sectional data to assess the effects of reformed versus unreformed local political systems[14] on such things as staffing levels, internal organization structure, and patterns of law enforcement, but they have by and large failed to replicate his findings, at least with regard to explaining variation in internal organization structure (Liederbach 2008). But, considering a broader historical perspective, this line of research may be barking up the wrong governance tree by focusing on less relevant features of police organization structure and practice. The general effect of decades of professional reform may well have been to move formal governing officials in many cities further to the periphery of police governance, but other entities may be filling the void. We consider two possibilities: local community organizations and professional associations that create a national market for police administration and leadership. Finally, we consider a traditional source of governing certain aspects of police practice, the courts.

---

[14] They typically consider the elective or appointive nature of the government's chief executive, district vs. at-large elections, and whether elections are partisan or nonpartisan (Stucky 2005, p. 39).

B. Grassroots Governance

Inasmuch as community policing has been the most visible banner of recent progressive reform and law enforcement innovation, it may be especially important to know to what extent the participatory and deliberative democracy goals for the governance of America's local police have been realized. Community policing promises to reestablish a link between the police and members of the community, but one that focuses not on promoting the political prospects of partisan interests, but rather on improving the quality of life in neighborhoods. By encouraging neighborhood residents and businesses to participate in associations that frequently and actively engage the police in face-to-face public meetings, the police themselves become directly involved with them in a grassroots politics of municipal service delivery. It displaces or augments, at least to some extent, the principal bureaucratic mechanism for determining how and where police are mobilized: the calls for service response system that developed during the "professional" reform era as a way of delivering police services efficiently and equitably. However, it does not give local elected politicians a significant role in the decision making about what police do and how their services are distributed (Mastrofski 2006a, p. 59). In theory, the direct engagement of police and public in grassroots politics should have profound consequences for who gets what from the police (Thacher 2001).

Much of what we know about the community-building and community partnership aspects of community policing comes from two in-depth studies of the implementation of community partnership programs, one in Chicago and another in Seattle. The difference between the two is striking. At its powerful mayor's insistence, Chicago developed a robust and vibrant citywide program promoting citizen participation in community groups that work with the police to identify and solve neighborhood problems (Skogan 2006b, chaps. 4, 5). Through trial and error and considerable effort sustained over many years, the Chicago neighborhoods showed impressive attendance at monthly neighborhood organization meetings with police, where issues were debated and discussed, plans for action made, and results assessed. These meetings were designed to resemble town hall meetings of New England. Remarkably, involvement in these meetings was highest in places that most needed police help: neighborhoods afflicted with violent crime, disorder, and a range of structural disadvantage in economic and social conditions. The meetings involved more community griping and less problem solving than the department's planners desired, but they were rich sources of feedback to the police on neighborhood preferences and assessments of how things were going. And although the participants in these meetings tended to draw more heavily on the better-off and more established denizens of the neighborhoods, those people's concerns were likely to reflect the concerns of their less advantaged neighbors. And most important, research shows that the police and an array of other municipal services were responsive to the residents' priorities and meeting attendance rates (Skogan 2006b, p. 208). Although other political considerations were not without consequence in affecting the level of service delivery a neighborhood received (e.g., the precinct's support for the incumbent mayor), it suggests that Chicago's grassroots structure had become a significant element in determining who gets what.

Seattle's experience with police-neighborhood partnerships in the 1990s produced a result very different from Chicago's (Lyons 1999). There the impetus for community involvement originated among community groups, not the department. Some early advances in participatory and deliberative democracy were achieved (in terms of police-public engagement, problem solving, and accountability), but these withered over time, leaving the researcher to judge that they had become less a two-way communications mechanism than a means to garner community acquiescence to police priorities and acceptance of police-generated programs.

The experiences of two large police agencies hardly constitute a sufficient sample from which to generalize across America's law enforcement industry. But the striking difference in experience between these two cities suggests that those wishing to understand the governance of police and its consequences during the community policing era would do well to pay at least as much attention to variations within jurisdictions as to variations between them. Where police have established vital grassroots linkages, there may well be developing a form of governance that renders even less relevant the traditional electoral mechanisms for influencing who gets what in the community.

C. Police Professional Associations

In contrast to the political implications of police involvement in grassroots organizing, recent decades have also witnessed a growth in the activity of national police professional associations, and this may affect the governance of the police by influencing the career prospects of persons seeking advancement to top police leadership positions (Hassell, Zhao, and Maguire 2003, p. 245; Skogan and Frydl 2004, p. 309; Mastrofski 2006*b*; Teodoro 2009). While it was once commonplace for police chiefs to be selected from within department ranks, that is now less common, especially for large and medium-sized departments, where the market is becoming regionalized and nationalized, providing less assurance of the in-house candidate's selection (Mastrofski 2006*b*). There is a growing reliance on executive search firms to define and screen the pool of candidates. Even more important, police professional associations have prospered and over the last three decades have engaged in high-visibility marketing of the "best" and "most promising" ways to do policing, in effect creating a much stronger professional environment than existed before. Their members and former members are often called on to provide the "professional" element in the selection of the top police executive. Up-and-coming chiefs who are not thoroughly familiar with cutting-edge ideas and programs touted by these professional associations place their career prospects at risk. And not only do these associations influence standards, they themselves provide a nationally visible arena in which reputations are established (Teodoro 2009). They are actively engaged in efforts to advance their positions, not only among police leaders but also with policy makers at all levels of government (especially mayors, city managers, federal legislators, and agencies). Even when these associations play no direct part in the selection of chiefs, they constitute an "invisible hand" in establishing what candidates for the chief's job must support and do to succeed.

Of course, the professionalization of governance generally has been going on since the Progressive Era (Finegold 1995), but it may well have accelerated substantially in recent years and be achieving even more influence as the demand for identifying with legitimating standards of performance intensifies (DiMaggio and Powell 1983). A fruitful line of research would be to explore how much police leaders' involvement in and ties to occupational professional associations, and how much they embrace the received wisdom of those groups, predicts their success in the marketplace of top executive positions, as well as the policies and practices they seek to adopt once selected. It would be interesting to learn how local political agendas interact with professional dynamics.

D. Courts

Courts oversee a range of police practices: personnel and administrative matters, as well as practices in the field. Here we concentrate on their role in overseeing the criminal process, although they play other important roles in adjudicating civil suits concerning internal administration of police organizations (Sklansky 2006). Local courts oversee police adherence to the law by monitoring the criminal cases police bring, and appellate courts establish, clarify, and change standards of acceptable criminal procedure. One important question is the nature and extent of the courts' influence on police practice in its case-by-case oversight function. Another is the extent to which police follow the operant legal requirements.

Estimating the influence of local courts on police practices requires two challenging tasks: measuring variations in how courts and police operate. As students of court processes have noted, it is not easy to capture the complexity of court processes since they are the product of the interactions of independent decision makers such as prosecutors, defense attorneys, and judges (Eisenstein and Jacob 1977; Eisenstein, Flemming, and Nardulli 1988). Imagine, though, that one could find ways to capture variations in the degree to which police procedures are exposed to rigorous scrutiny and the courts act on them. One might then offer predictions about how closely police conform to legal expectations, the extent to which they seek ways to "get around" the law (Sutton 1986), and the degree to which other activities or priorities are affected (such as police stop, search, and arrest frequencies). One might expect to observe considerable variation across American criminal courts at any time and changes over time. To our knowledge, such studies are not available.

Police compliance with criminal procedure standards has been studied since the "due process revolution" of the 1960s. Most of it has been descriptive, merely attempting to establish how much police deviate from applicable legal standards (Skogan and Frydl 2004, pp. 255–67). The results are quite variable. Police compliance with some standards (e.g., *Miranda* on police interrogation) was spotty initially but eventually did achieve a high rate (96 percent in one study), albeit performed in a rather perfunctory manner designed to undermine the defendant's inclination to invoke his or her rights. Or in compensation, the police increased their use of noncustodial interviews to avoid *Miranda*'s requirements. Similarly, some studies have observed either no appreciable change in police practices in response to restrictive court rulings or a host of strategies to circumvent Fourth Amendment protections (sometimes with the cooperation of magistrates; Sutton 1986; Uchida and Bynum 1991). However, some research has reported high, though variable, rates of police noncompliance with the rule of law in such areas as the use of less-than-lethal force (38–84 percent; Terrill and Mastrofski 2004) and warrantless searches (30 percent; Gould and Mastrofski 2004).

What emerges from this pattern is the obvious point that appellate court decisions are not self-enforcing and that the consequences of a given ruling for street-level practice are highly conditioned by what the police organization and other local legal institutions do about it. For example, researchers have found instances in which departments have coupled a variety of administrative actions with a restrictive ruling on use of deadly force to reduce the frequency of its use (Fyfe 1979; Sherman 1983; Tennenbaum 1994). The situation-contingent nature of the consequence of appellate court governance is part of a larger pattern noted in research on the effects of appellate court cases involving the practices of local government agents (Becker 1973).

VII. Stability and Change in American Policing

A leitmotif of this essay has been the tension between the temptation to overstate the capacity of American police to resist change (Guyot 1979; Manning 2006, p. 104) and the temptation to overstate their susceptibility to change (Zhao 1996). These temptations arise in part from the American habit of valuing change (De Tocqueville [1835] 1990) and, depending on our perspective, being frustrated by failing to observe change that meets our expectations or being inclined to find indicators that our police are fulfilling them.

Resistance to change arises from a variety of ranks and units, from unions, from other organizations that have business with the police, from politicians, and from the public (Guyot 1979; Skogan 2008; Greene and Herzog 2009). The very difficulties of leading police organizations today, especially large ones, make it challenging to provoke, guide, manage, and sustain change, even when there is no lack of will to do so (Mastrofski 2002). Yet we must be careful not to mischaracterize police organizations as "especially" intransigent, for it is not at all clear that they as a group are any more resistant to change than other organizations, such as schools, armies, hospitals, churches, and, in recent years, American automobile manufacturers. Some have argued that police organizations were remarkably susceptible to pressures to change in the nineteenth and twentieth centuries, albeit largely symbolic ones that preserved the legitimacy of the core functions of the police (Klockars 1988). And some have argued that the last three decades have been a period of intense ferment and real change for American police as well (Bayley and Shearing 1996; Braga and Weisburd 2006, forthcoming; Weisburd and Braga 2006; Bayley 2008). All this is to say that generalization about police organization change is hazardous.

In this section we consider two movements for change that are "big reforms" (Bayley 2008): community policing and terrorist-oriented policing. The former had precursors in the 1970s and surfaced in the 1980s; the latter emerged in the wake of the September 11, 2001, terrorist attacks on New York and Washington. We attempt to understand how these reform movements have transformed American policing. We recognize that they represent broad and complicated innovations and do not represent all movements for change, but for their scope alone, they deserve attention. In both cases we note that the forces at work over the life course of each reform movement are dynamic and that how innovations such as these are initially conceptualized and how they are institutionalized tend to differ. In both cases, pressure for change was initiated outside of police agencies, but as is often the case (Weisburd and Braga 2006; Bayley 2008), the scope and direction of change that actually occurred were heavily influenced by police efforts to protect the core service-oriented structures and operations that have long sustained American police. To the extent that these preservationist efforts reflect conscious leadership choices, we suspect that the motivation is primarily one of not putting at risk what the public values most in the current environment.

A. Community Policing

The key elements of change introduced by community policing are that the public should be much more engaged in policy making and service delivery; that the police should engage in problem-oriented policing, which requires a focus on outcomes, experimentation, and empirical evaluation and a commitment to customizing the selection of a policing approach to the particular problem at hand; and that decision making should be decentralized in the organization to middle managers and the rank and file (Skogan 2006c). It has not been conclusively established nor is there agreement on just how far American police agencies as a group have progressed on these change dimensions or whether these changes are accomplishing their goals,[15] but it is widely acknowledged that many agencies are challenged to go beyond superficial implementation and that the changes that have been accomplished are still fragile and vulnerable to fluctuations in federal funding and competition from other reforms with competing priorities (such as Compstat; Roth, Roehl, and Johnson 2004; Braga and Weisburd 2006; Eck 2006; Mastrofski 2006a; Skogan 2006c; Reisig, in this volume). Despite the indeterminate evidence on its implementation and success, community policing remains a popular idea among police and community leaders and the public.

To better appreciate this state of affairs, it is useful to consider the trajectory of the community policing reform. Crisis or strong external pressure often makes organizations more susceptible to trying something new by creating an acute sense of a "performance gap," which can set off the innovation process (Rogers 2003, p. 422). It is now standard among police scholars to describe crisis-inducing events and trends of the late 1960s and 1970s as the motivating force behind what eventually developed as the community policing movement (Fogelson 1977; Walker 1977; Kelling and Moore 1988). Skyrocketing crime rates, riots, accusations of racism and brutality, corruption, inefficiency, studies discrediting the effectiveness of standard policing technologies, and middle-class cynicism about government generally and the police in particular came together in ways that placed American police in a defensive posture. That stimulated blue-ribbon panels, experts, and some progressive police leaders to propose alternatives to alleviate this pressure. While precursors of community policing surfaced in the 1970s (team policing and community relations units), community policing began to emerge as a distinct entity in the 1980s and achieved widespread acceptance within a few years of the federal government's promotion of it by the creation of the Community Oriented Policing

---

[15] Two 2004 reviews of the evaluation research on community policing found a lack of strong support for its crime control effectiveness (Skogan and Frydl 2004, p. 232; Weisburd and Eck 2004, p. 52), but a very recent review that included several newer studies concluded that although the evidence is mixed, the weight of the body of research "indicates that community and problem-oriented policing can reduce crime and disorder" (Reisig, in this volume).

Services (COPS) Office in 1994.[16] Interestingly, just about the time the COPS program was launched, urban departments around the nation began to experience a decline in crime, especially violent crime (Eck and Maguire 2000), a trend that has continued, largely unabated, to the present.

One might argue that the "big-ticket" crime-focused pressure for change had begun to dissipate, at least at the national level, although there was certainly continuing local community pressure for greater involvement and more responsiveness to neighborhood needs in some cities. Public confidence in police has remained high, and while local law enforcement staffing growth rates are now slowing in a troubled economy, the industry is not (yet) in crisis.[17] There is, in fact, little reason to risk the demanding changes called for by the more structurally disruptive elements of the reform, especially those that require altering a host of difficult-to-change structures and practices: creating permanent beat assignments, maintaining high levels of beat integrity, freeing up large amounts of time from answering calls for service to work with community groups on neighborhood problems, giving community members a say in how their neighborhoods are policed, and training officers to do problem-oriented policing. And unless some compelling force (such as a powerful mayor) pressures police organizations to attend to these things, a good working hypothesis is that it will be difficult for police agencies to create or sustain momentum to make such changes. One might argue that merely "building a better mousetrap" is enough to have the nation beat a path to the reform and follow suit, but Chicago's impressive effort of more than a decade to build and institutionalize neighborhood-oriented community partnerships into its structures and practices has not been widely emulated, or at least not validated empirically. Thus, while it may no longer be fair to write community policing off as a mere "circumlocution" (Klockars 1988), it appears not to have done a great deal to transform long-

[16] By 1998, on average, large agencies reported that they had implemented 80 percent of eight partnership-building tactics (Roth, Roehl, and Johnson 2004). By 2006 a national survey of departments with 100 or more officers found that 97 percent reported having adopted community policing; 59 percent reported its scope as major, 32 percent as moderate, and 6 percent as minor (Mastrofski, Willis, and Kochel 2007).

[17] Some police leaders and professional associations have argued that in the midst of a nationally declining crime trend, some communities are experiencing alarming increases in violent crime (Police Executive Research Forum 2006), but thus far this has not proven an effective cause for mobilizing a large influx in (especially federal) resources that advocates argue are needed to counter these selective trends.

established structures and operations of the vast majority of American police agencies. Drawing on the innovation diffusion literature, Braga and Weisburd (forthcoming) suggest that police innovations will be adopted to the extent that they are compatible with existing values and ways of doing things. Given the smorgasbord of community policing innovations available, it is not surprising that changes are modest. Making truly radical changes requires unsettling often well-ensconced and powerful interests, and this may be accomplished only if a sense of pressing need pervades this phase of the innovation process.

B. Terrorist-Oriented Policing as Innovation

If one is struck by the attenuation of a crisis mentality to energize the implementation of community policing in that reform's third decade, one must certainly acknowledge the crisis atmosphere that propels the movement to involve state and local police in countering terrorism in the United States in the first decade following the terrorist attacks of September 11, 2001. These events reshaped national policy and also focused attention on the role of local police in combating the threat of terrorism (Greene, forthcoming; Maguire and King, forthcoming). Unlike community policing reform, few local police themselves have been in the vanguard of this movement, which arguably has been led by national leaders who have urged on federal law enforcement and homeland security agencies the task of recruiting local law enforcement into this role.

Given the far greater number of state and local police officers compared to federal law enforcement agents, it stands to reason that a substantial counterterrorism role is envisioned for local agencies, but many other nations with subnational, decentralized police services also expect substantial involvement in counterterrorism by those agencies (Bayley and Weisburd 2009, p. 85). In addition to the response and recovery operations so visibly provided by local police in the wake of the 9/11 attacks, local police are expected to be on the lookout for likely suspects or people with useful information about terrorism (based in part on information provided by federal agencies), to pass potentially useful information along to federal agencies, to investigate terrorists on their own and by collaborating with other agencies in special multiagency Joint Terrorism Task Forces, to participate in the interrogation of suspects and witnesses, to collaborate in the disruption of terrorist plans, to perform risk analyses and target hardening recommendations, and to mobilize the community for prevention and detection (Kelling and Bratton 2006; Bayley and Weisburd 2009, p. 87; Greene and Herzog 2009; Maguire and King, forthcoming). Local police are encouraged to acquire and use special technologies to combat terrorism, to acquire special training in the use of these technologies and intelligence gathering, and to increase security and surveillance efforts (Lum et al. 2009).

Given the range and diversity of changes called for by the movement toward terrorist-oriented policing, it represents the confluence of a large number of innovations brought to bear on local departments. Organizational focus runs the gamut from highly technical (the application of security and surveillance technologies) to administrative (extensive interagency collaboration and information sharing). It is expected to alter what all police officers look for and report in the way of suspicious persons and activities, so some of its features are central and pervasive. Yet the need for limiting the dissemination of sensitive information also demands isolating information to a few people, driving certain activities to the organization's peripheral, specialized units. Some demands of counterterrorism require radical changes in policing strategies (giving priority to gathering intelligence over gathering and acting on criminal evidence), but others require little or no change (making routine traffic stops and reporting them, responding to large-scale emergencies, and implementing various security strategies designed to deter or incapacitate terrorist attacks). And to the extent that reformers call for local involvement in intelligence gathering and clandestine terrorism disruption measures (called "high policing"), one can anticipate both police and public resistance to a method that is incompatible with the historical preference for a more visible, transparent, and reassuring approach (Brodeur 1983; Bayley and Weisburd 2009). Thus, even more than with community policing, we might expect to see a very mixed pattern in the willingness of local police to adopt and implement certain features of counterterrorism.

Some dramatic changes have been reported in agencies that responded to the 9/11 attacks (Holden et al. 2009), but the limited evidence available suggests that most American police agencies have been slow to adopt many of the new structures and practices of terrorist-oriented policing. One tentative conclusion drawn from impressionistic evidence was that in a 14-nation sample, general policing has been least changed by the counterterrorism movement in the United States (Bayley and Weisburd 2009). America's local policing industry remains fragmented and focused on the delivery of crime control, order maintenance, and routine service provision. Although a few (mostly) larger departments, such as in New York City and Los Angeles, have committed significant resources to the development of terrorism intelligence units with full-time personnel (some even deployed overseas), the vast majority had not done so by 2003 (Lum et al. 2009, p. 107). A recent national survey of small and large departments found that the "on-the-ground" counterterrorism tactics and technologies requiring the use of resources (such as surveillance and general deterrence) were rare, as were community-based activities that might draw on police-community relationships strengthened by community policing (Lum et al. 2009, pp. 112–22; see also Schafer, Burruss, and Giblin 2009). The most commonly employed measures were strengthening interagency coordination and undertaking general preparedness planning, which do little to disrupt core, routine service delivery operations. Here federally sponsored programs figured prominently: Joint Terrorism Task Forces, fusion centers,[18] and preparedness exercises. For example, 80 percent of large departments had received hazardous materials training, 76 percent had purchased protective clothing, and 65 percent had received terrorism-related information from the federal government. But only 57 percent had received training in intelligence gathering, and only 39 percent used federal watch lists. Only 11 percent reported increasing the number of personnel assigned to counterterrorism duties. And less than 10 percent reported engaging in high-visibility security strategies, such as enforcing illegal immigration laws, randomly searching public places, and setting up random traffic checkpoints. Covert surveillance was even less frequently reported (Lum et al. 2009).

Thus, in the decade following the 9/11 attacks, local American police, even in most large organizations, appear to have assigned counterterrorism to the periphery of their operations, at least those parts that they are willing to report to researchers. Why that might be the case offers an interesting contrast to the experience with community policing. American communities appear to be content with modest community policing reforms that do not disrupt a traditional police role, namely, a strong service delivery orientation that developed over

---

[18] Fusion centers facilitate the assembly, analysis, and sharing of information among state and federal jurisdictions, as well as involving private organizations (Bureau of Justice Assistance 2006).

many prior decades. While local law enforcement agency leaders clearly are concerned about the threat of terrorism, as judged by actions taken by agencies to plan for dealing with future attacks following 9/11 (Davis et al. 2004; International Association of Chiefs of Police 2005; Bureau of Justice Statistics 2006), there appears to be considerable ambivalence about what the role of local law enforcement should be. Most American police leaders appear reluctant to reallocate substantial resources used to deal with the "ordinary" crime, disorder, and service needs of their communities. Some have expressed concern that assigning personnel to terrorist-oriented policing inhibits departments' capacity to engage in community policing (Kerlikowske 2004; Oliver 2004). The high-policing aspects of counterterrorist policing are neither visible nor tangible in the ways that routine police activities are, thus undermining a powerful source of community legitimacy and support, especially important among the segments of society most at risk for police counterterrorist attention (Bayley and Weisburd 2009, p. 94).

While communities may be accepting of local police efforts to promote *their* safety from terrorists and respond to terrorist-initiated emergencies, many are not so convinced of the benefits of the high-policing strategies that federal agencies have encouraged them to perform (Thacher 2005). Involvement in these activities increases the risk of human rights violations that eventually surface in the form of bad publicity and expensive lawsuits. Although public concern for such violations might abate when fear of terrorism is high, it tends to reappear when the crisis mentality passes. Between 1970 and 2004, Latin America, the region most vulnerable to terror attacks, experienced more than 20 times the number of attacks as North America, by far the least vulnerable region (LaFree and Dugan 2009, p. 60). Of course, repeated terrorist attacks on U.S. soil, whether foiled or completed, could alter the public's willingness to accept or even insist on greater local police involvement in counterterrorism strategies. But failing a sustained crisis, there simply does not appear to be sufficient incentive for most local communities and their police leaders to resort to a radical reorientation of their mission.

Just because counterterrorism appears not to have significantly displaced routine policing structures and practices of the local police, it does not mean that new developments are insignificant. For example, the increase in intensive interagency coordination (among local police agencies, between police and other emergency services, between the police and federal law enforcement and homeland security agencies) marks a distinct departure from a long history of loosely coordinated interagency activity between local and federal agencies, not infrequently fraught with misunderstanding, jealousies, suspicions, and reluctance to collaborate fully (Geller and Morris 1992; Skogan and Frydl 2004, p. 211). Although these challenges have not disappeared as a consequence of heightened efforts to coordinate and collaborate (Maguire and King, forthcoming), only a few years after 9/11, there appeared to be a growing consensus among local, state, and federal officials that substantial progress had been made and would continue (Davies and Plotkin 2005). Indeed, with regard to information sharing, local law enforcement leaders have expressed a desire to become "full partners" in information networks run by the federal government—to find ways for street-level officers to contribute more information on a timely basis to federal data bases; but they also want to receive more usable information from federal sources on threats to their locales (chap. 5). And they support an "all-crimes" approach to information sharing that includes not only terrorist-based threats but other crimes and disorders that might threaten communities. Thus, one predictable consequence of the movement toward involving local police in counterterrorism efforts is an industry that is a bit less loosely coupled, where once-impermeable information membranes between local and federal agencies (Geller and Morris 1992) are increasingly permeable. Networks designed for one purpose may be exploited for others, so America's complex industry structure may be becoming more tightly connected by "information highways" created to combat terrorism. However, we are not seeing a systemwide centralization of policing structures to accommodate the war on terror that several observers have associated with an increased focus on combating terror on domestic soil (Bayley and Weisburd 2009; Feucht et al. 2009; Greene and Herzog 2009).

Thus, 9 years after concern about the nation's vulnerability to terrorism reached a fever pitch, and even while the threat of terrorism remains a daily news topic, American police remain heavily focused on the same local problems, using essentially the same structures and systems that preceded 9/11. This is not to dismiss the peripheral changes (especially in specialist units) that have developed, but to note that they operate largely independent from the core policing operation. Of course, this could change if the United States were to be subjected to a much greater frequency of terrorist attacks, such as those experienced by Israel.

VIII. Conclusion

We addressed several aspects of police organization in the twenty-first century. The American policing industry remains highly decentralized and has strong prospects for continuing to do so. This has many powerful implications for how and how well American police practice their work and with what success, but it is difficult to test propositions without meaningful cross-national comparisons to systems less fragmented than the American case.

Studies of the internal structure of American police confirm the persistence of its bureaucratic character as we move into the twenty-first century, finding little change over short time periods. However, most of this research ignores the effects of professional structures and hence is unable to tell us how much competing frameworks for organizational control may be developing. The need for long-term studies of structural change and better insight into the actual change processes has been noted.

Some policing technologies, such as standard patrol, have changed little over many decades, whereas recent years have observed a large number of important changes in others, such as information technology. There are a number of rational explanations for the persistence of standard patrol technologies in the face of scientific evidence that discredits their effectiveness. Although the capacity of police organizations to resist and pervert the use of new information technologies is great in the short run, there is evidence to suggest that profound long-term effects into the future are possible.

There are distinct trends in *who* does police work, as the numbers of members of racial minorities, women, and college-educated and better-trained personnel continue to grow. Although there are theories that predict that these personnel trends will have profound consequences for the practice of policing, thus far the evidence has been modest and mixed.

Police culture can assume several meanings. There is not much evidence available to test the notion that policing is culturally distinct from other occupations. Relatively few studies exist that demonstrate how police organizational culture differs and with what effects. And although a growing body of studies finds diversity in the outlook of police on a number of dimensions, it is not yet obvious how influential that diversity is for the actual practice of policing. Traditional scholarship has characterized the police occupational culture as highly resistant to change, but there are many contemporary pressures to reduce the alienation, isolation, and defensiveness that have been used to describe it in the past: community policing and efforts to weaken the "blue code of silence" on matters of police integrity. Less well developed, but potentially no less consequential, is the movement to change the dominant culture of policing from that of a craft to a science-based occupation.

Despite the importance of external governance to the preservation of democratic policing, this topic remains underdeveloped as an area of study. Even many decades after the triumph of good-government reform, America's local governments appear to exhibit considerable variation in the ways they govern their police. Case studies have tended to focus on the role of political officials. Largely unexamined are the roles of grassroots community organizations and police professional associations, although there is reason to expect that they may be having increasing influence on policies and practices of local agencies.

Although the experiences of police agencies with innovation surely vary with the nature of the innovation, experience with the two "big" innovations—community policing and terrorist-oriented policing— shows how police organizations manage to adopt and absorb pressures for change while minimizing threats to the stability of the core features of the organization. This was the case for community policing, now about three decades old, and also for terrorist-oriented policing, which is not yet a decade old.

American police agencies today, as in the nineteenth century, are targets of change, often from forces outside their boundaries (Bayley 2008), but we should not underestimate the capacity of those who are members of the organization to resist (Skogan 2008) but also to channel these pressures to change. Indeed, what we may have witnessed in the last few decades of the twentieth century was an increasing capacity of police leaders to appropriate and engineer reforms that were originally powered by external pressure. Community policing, problem-oriented policing, broken-windows policing, and pulling-levers policing (Weisburd and Braga 2006) can all be understood in that way, whereas Compstat and the just-emerged predictive policing are the progeny of the police themselves. That does not mean that police leaders are becoming masters of the industry's destiny, but it does suggest that in our efforts to discern and predict the trajectory of police organization stability and change, we need to attend closely to the inclinations and capacities of the police themselves to shape it.

Throughout this essay we have suggested opportunities for future research. We do not restate suggestions about *what* to study here but conclude with some recommendations on *how* to study police organizations. First, scholars and policy makers would benefit from expanding the study of police organizations to include more cross-national comparisons. It not only places the American situation in a larger context but also provides insights into alternative ways of organizing the delivery of policing. This sort of research is costly, and funding sources in America have rarely supported such comparisons, perhaps because they appear more academic than practical. Nonetheless, a recent U.S. government–funded foray into this sort of project has yielded useful policy as well as theoretical insights from cross-national comparisons (Weisburd et al. 2009). We encourage the U.S. government to explore the possibility of developing a well-supported, cross-national research and evaluation program so that developed and developing nations can learn from each other's experiences.

Most police researchers are hampered by their ability to track the changes in police organizations over long time periods. At best, some can invest in tracking a single agency, producing the occasional useful but limited case study. But we could learn more from the history of police if there were a systematic effort to track a large number of police organizations over long time periods. The U.S. Department of Justice has funded a small, pilot version of such a project, the National Police Research Platform (Rosenbaum and Hartnett 2010). The project is developing instruments and methods to study the life course of police organizations, as well as longitudinal changes of individual police officers and supervisors.

Most of the research on police organizations is based on mail surveys of large numbers of police organizations or on-site case studies of one or a few organizations. Both are useful, but each has severe limitations. Although they enable researchers to draw large, more or less representative samples of American police agencies, they are limited in the validity and reliability of the data they gather, and they also afford poor opportunities to learn much about the structures, processes, and outcomes that are of greatest interest. The case studies afford an opportunity for greater validity and reliability of observations, but their representativeness is always questionable, and their small number limits the capacity to compare and control for a variety of possible influences on whatever is being studied. Two alternatives seem valuable, but both are costly. One is to develop a consortium of police researchers around the nation who agree to use a common set of methods and instruments to observe key aspects of police organizations. The second is for research funding agencies to support more midrange studies that permit researchers to conduct in-depth on-site observation of police organizations in a substantial number of departments. A model for this is the Police Services Study, which in 1977 conducted on-site observation in 24 police agencies and 60 urban neighborhoods over the course of 3 months (ICPSR 2010).

Studies of police organization are at least as valuable to policy makers as studies that evaluate the effects of police interventions. Police strategies and tactics are relevant only to the extent that they are implemented, and implementation is determined in large part by the capacity of police organizations to manage, guide, and structure the operations of their people and organizational components (Fernandez and Rainey 2006). Those who fund rigorous studies to test the effects of police interventions should commit as much funding to help police learn how to implement and sustain the changes that these innovations require.

REFERENCES

Allen, David N., Robert P. McGowan, and Stephen D. Mastrofski. 1983. "Analytic Reports and Computerized Information Processing in Medium and Large Police Agencies." *Computers, Environment, and Urban Systems* 8(3): 175–86.
Altshuler, Alan A. 1970. *Community Control*. New York: Bobbs-Merrill.
Bayley, David H. 1985. *Patterns of Policing: A Comparative Analysis*. New Brunswick, NJ: Rutgers University Press.
———. 1992. "Comparative Organization of the Police in English-Speaking Countries." In *Modern Policing*, edited by Michael Tonry and Norval Morris. Vol. 15 of *Crime and Justice: A Review of Research*, edited by Michael Tonry. Chicago: University of Chicago Press.

———. 2006. *Changing the Guard: Developing Democratic Police Abroad*. Oxford: Oxford University Press.

———. 2008. "Police Reform: Who Done It?" *Policing and Society* 18(1):7–17.

Bayley, David H., and Egon Bittner. 1984. "Learning the Skills of Policing." *Law and Contemporary Problems* 47:35–59.

Bayley, David H., and Clifford D. Shearing. 1996. "The Future of Policing." *Law and Society Review* 30(3):585–606.

Bayley, David H., and David Weisburd. 2009. "Cops and Spooks: The Role of the Police in Counterterrorism." In *To Protect and to Serve: Policing in an Age of Terrorism*, edited by David Weisburd, Thomas E. Feucht, Idit Hakimi, Lois Felson Mock, and Simon Perry. New York: Springer.

Beck, Charlie, and Colleen McCue. 2009. "Predictive Policing: What Can We Learn from WalMart and Amazon about Fighting Crime in a Recession?" *Police Chief* (November), 18–24.

Becker, Theodore Lewis. 1973. *The Impact of Supreme Court Decisions*. New York: Oxford University Press.

Bittner, Egon. 1967. "The Police on Skid-Row: A Study of Peace Keeping." *American Sociological Review* 32:699–715.

———. 1970. *The Functions of the Police in Modern Society*. Washington, DC: National Institute of Mental Health.

———. 1983. "Legality and Workmanship: Introduction to Control in the Police Organization." In *Control in the Police Organization*, edited by Maurice Punch. Cambridge, MA: MIT Press.

———. 1990. "Florence Nightingale in Pursuit of Willie Sutton: A Theory of Police." In *Aspects of Police Work*. Boston: Northeastern University Press.

Blau, Peter M. 1970. "A Formal Theory of Differentiation in Organizations." *American Sociological Review* 35:201–18.

Blumstein, Alfred, and Joel Wallman, eds. 2006. *The Crime Drop in America*. Cambridge: Cambridge University Press.

Boyne, George. 2002. "Public and Private Management: What's the Difference?" *Journal of Management Studies* 39(1):97–122.

Bradley, David, Christine Nixon, and Monique Marks. 2006. "What Works, What Doesn't, and What Looks Promising on Police Research Networks." In *Fighting Crime Together: The Challenges of Policing and Security Networks*, edited by Jenny Fleming and Jennifer Wood. Sydney: University of New South Wales Press.

Braga, Anthony A., and David Weisburd. 2006. "Problem-Oriented Policing: The Disconnect between Principles and Practice." In *Police Innovation: Contrasting Perspectives*, edited by David Weisburd and Anthony A. Braga. New York: Cambridge University Press.

———. Forthcoming. *Policing Problem Places: Crime Hot Spots and Effective Prevention*. New York: Oxford University Press.

Bratton, William J., with Peter Knobler. 1998. *Turnaround: How America's Top Cop Reversed the Crime Epidemic*. New York: Random House.

Bratton, William J., and Sean W. Malinowski. 2008. "Police Performance

Management in Practice: Taking Compstat to the Next Level." *Policing: A Journal of Policy and Practice* 2(3):259–65.

Bratton, William J., John Morgan, and Sean Malinowski. 2009. "Fighting Crime in the Information Age: The Promise of Predictive Policing." Paper presented at the annual meeting of the American Society of Criminology, Philadelphia, November 6.

Broderick, John J. 1972. *Police in a Time of Change.* Morristown, NJ: General Learning Press.

Brodeur, Jean-Paul. 1983. "High and Low Policing: Remarks about the Policing of Political Activities." *Social Problems* 39(5):507–20.

Brown, Lee P., and Mary A. Wycoff. 1987. "Policing Houston: Reducing Fear and Improving Service." *Crime and Delinquency* 33:71–89.

Brown, Michael K. 1981. *Working the Street: Police Discretion and the Dilemmas of Reform.* New York: Russell Sage Foundation.

Buerger, Michael. 1998. "Police Training as a Pentecost: Using Tools Singularly Ill-Suited to the Purpose of Reform." *Police Quarterly* 1:27–63.

Bureau of Justice Assistance. 2006. *Fusion Center Guidelines: Developing and Sharing Information and Intelligence in a New Era.* Washington, DC: U.S. Department of Justice. http://www.iir.com/global/products/fusion_center _guidelines_law_enforcement.pdf.

Bureau of Justice Statistics. 2006. *Law Enforcement Management and Administrative Statistics LEMAS: 2003 Sample Survey of Law Enforcement Agencies.* Washington, DC: U.S. Department of Justice.

———. 2007. *Census of State and Local Law Enforcement Agencies, 2004.* Bulletin NCJ 212749. Washington, DC: U.S. Department of Justice.

Chan, Janet. 2001. "The Technological Game: How Information Technology Is Transforming Police Practice." *Criminal Justice* 1(2):139–59.

———. 2003. "Police and New Technologies." In *Handbook of Policing,* edited by Tim Newburn. Portland, OR: Willan.

Chan, Janet, D. Brereton, M. Legosz, and S. Doran. 2001. *E-Policing: The Impact of Information Technology on Police Practices.* Brisbane: Criminal Justice Commission.

Cole, Bankole A. 1999. "Post-colonial Systems." In *Policing across the World: Issues for the Twenty-first Century,* edited by R. I. Mawby. London: UCL Press.

Committee on Identifying the Needs of the Forensics Science Community. 2009. *Strengthening Forensic Science in the United States: A Path Forward.* Washington, DC: National Research Council.

Cordner, Gary W. 1989. "Police Agency Size and Investigative Effectiveness." *Journal of Criminal Justice* 17(3):145–55.

Crank, John P. 1994. "Watchman and Community: Myth and Institutionalization in Policing." *Law and Society Review* 28:325–51.

Crank, John P., and L. E. Wells. 1991. "The Effects of Size and Urbanism on Structure among Illinois Police Departments." *Justice Quarterly* 8:169–82.

Crawford, Adam. 2003. "The Pattern of Policing in the UK: Policing beyond the Police." In *Handbook of Policing*, edited by Tim Newburn. Portland, OR: Willan.

Cunningham, W. C., J. Strauchs, and C. Van Meter. 1991. *Private Security: Patterns and Trends*. Washington, DC: National Institute of Justice.

Damanpour, F. 1991. "Organizational Innovation: A Meta-analysis of Effects of Determinants and Moderators." *Academy of Management Review* 34: 555–90.

Davies, Heather, and Martha R. Plotkin. 2005. *Protecting Your Community from Terrorism: Strategies for Local Law Enforcement*. Vol. 5, *Partnerships to Promote Homeland Security*. Washington, DC: Police Executive Research Forum.

Davis, Lois M., Jack K. Riley, Greg Ridgeway, J. E. Pace, S. K. Cotton, P. Steinberg, K. Damphousse, and B. L. Smith. 2004. *When Terrorism Hits Home: How Prepared Are State and Local Law Enforcement?* Santa Monica, CA: RAND Corporation.

De Tocqueville, Alexis. 1990. *Democracy in America*. 2 vols. Introduction by Daniel Boorstin. New York: Vintage Books. (Originally published 1835.)

Dill, William R. 1958. "Environment as an Influence on Managerial Autonomy." *Administrative Science Quarterly* 2:409–43.

DiMaggio, Paul J., and Walter W. Powell. 1983. "The Iron Cage Revisited: Institutional Isomorphism and Collective Rationality in Organizational Fields." *American Sociological Review* 48:147–60.

Douthit, Nathan. 1975. "August Vollmer, Berkeley's First Chief of Police, and the Emergence of Police Professionalism." *California Historical Quarterly* 54(Spring):101–24.

Dukes, Richard L., Edwardo Portillos, and Molly Miles. 2009. "Models of Satisfaction with Police Service." *Policing: An International Journal of Police Strategy and Management* 32(2):297–318.

Eck, John E. 2006. "Science, Values, and Problem-Oriented Policing: Why Problem-Oriented Policing?" In *Police Innovation: Contrasting Perspectives*, edited by David Weisburd and Anthony A. Braga. New York: Cambridge University Press.

Eck, John E., and Edward Maguire. 2000. "Have Changes in Policing Reduced Violent Crime? An Assessment of the Evidence." In *The Crime Drop in America*, edited by Alfred Blumstein and Joel Wallman. New York: Cambridge University Press.

Economist. 2010. "Number-Crunchers Crunched: The Uses and Abuses of Mathematical Models." February 13–19, 5–8.

Eisenstein, James, Roy Flemming, and Peter Nardulli. 1988. *The Contours of Justice: Communities and Their Courts*. Boston: Little, Brown.

Eisenstein, James, and Herbert Jacob. 1977. *Felony Justice: An Organizational Analysis of Criminal Courts*. Boston: Little, Brown.

Engel, Robin S. 2000. "The Effects of Supervisory Styles on Patrol Officer Behavior." *Police Quarterly* 3(3):262–93.

———. 2001. "Supervisory Styles of Patrol Sergeants and Lieutenants." *Journal of Criminal Justice* 29:341–55.

————. 2002. "Patrol Officer Supervision in the Community-Policing Era." *Journal of Criminal Justice* 30(1):51–64.

Engel, Robin S., and Robert E. Worden. 2003. "Police Officers' Attitudes, Behavior, and Supervisory Influences: An Analysis of Problem-Solving." *Criminology* 41:131–66.

Ericson, Richard V., and Kevin D. Haggerty. 1997. *Policing the Risk Society.* Toronto: University of Toronto Press.

Falcone, David N., and L. Edward Wells. 1995. "The County Sheriff as a Distinctive Policing Modality." *American Journal of Police* 14(3–4):123–49.

Falcone, David N., L. Edward Wells, and Ralph A. Weisheit. 2002. "The Small-Town Police Department." *Policing: An International Journal of Police Strategies and Management* 25(2):371–84.

Fernandez, Sergio, and Hal G. Rainey. 2006. "Managing Successful Organizational Change in the Public Sector: An Agenda for Research and Practice." *Public Administration Review* 66(2):1–25.

Feucht, Thomas E., David Weisburd, Simon Perry, Lois Felson Mock, and Idit Hakimi. 2009. "Policing, Terrorism, and Beyond." In *To Protect and to Serve: Policing in an Age of Terrorism,* edited by David Weisburd, Thomas E. Feucht, Idit Hakimi, Lois Felson Mock, and Simon Perry. New York: Springer.

Finegold, Kenneth. 1995. *Experts and Politicians.* Princeton, NJ: Princeton University Press.

Fogelson, Robert M. 1977. *Big City Police.* Cambridge, MA: Harvard University Press.

Forst, Brian. 2005. "Private Policing." In *Encyclopedia of Law Enforcement,* vol. 1, *State and Local,* edited by Larry E. Sullivan and Marie Simonetti Rosen. Thousand Oaks, CA: Sage.

Fung, Archon. 2001. "Accountable Autonomy: Toward Empowered Deliberation in Chicago Schools and Policing." *Politics and Society* 29(1):73–103.

Fyfe, James J. 1979. "Administrative Interventions on Police Shooting Discretion: An Empirical Examination." *Journal of Criminal Justice* 7:309–23.

————. 1983. *Police Personnel Practices, Baseline Data Reports.* Vol. 15, no. 1. Washington, DC: International City Management Association.

Gallagher, Catherine, Edward Maguire, Stephen D. Mastrofski, and Michael Reisig. 2001. *The Public Image of the Police: Final Report to the International Association of Chiefs of Police.* Manassas, VA: George Mason University, Administration of Justice Program. http://marcpi.jhu.edu/marcpi/Ethics/ethics_toolkit/public_image.htm.

Geller, William A., and Norval Morris. 1992. "Relations between Federal and Local Police." In *Modern Policing,* edited by Michael Tonry and Norval Morris. Vol. 15 of *Crime and Justice: A Review of Research,* edited by Michael Tonry. Chicago: University of Chicago Press.

Goldstein, Herman. 1990. *Problem-Oriented Policing.* New York: McGraw-Hill.

Goold, Benjamin. 2004. *CCTV and Policing: Public Area Surveillance and Police Practices in Britain.* Oxford: Oxford University Press.

Gould, Jon, and Stephen D. Mastrofski. 2004. "Suspect Searches: Assessing

Police Behavior under the U.S. Constitution." *Criminology and Public Policy* 3(3):315–62.

Greene, Jack R. Forthcoming. "Community Policing and Terrorism: Problems and Prospects for Local Community Security." In *Criminologists on Terrorism and Homeland Security*, edited by Brian Forst, Jack Greene, and James Lynch. Cambridge: Cambridge University Press.

Greene, Jack R., and Sergio Herzog. 2009. "The Implications of Terrorism on the Formal and Social Organization of Policing in the US and Israel: Some Concerns and Opportunities." In *To Protect and to Serve: Policing in an Age of Terrorism*, edited by David Weisburd, Thomas E. Feucht, Idit Hakimi, Lois Felson Mock, and Simon Perry. New York: Springer.

Groff, Elizabeth, David Weisburd, and Greg Jones. 2008. "What Does Automated Vehicle Locator Data Measure about Police Presence?" Paper presented at the annual meeting of the American Society of Criminology, St. Louis Adam's Mark, St. Louis, November 12. http://www.allacademic.com/meta/p269426_index.html.

Guyot, Dorothy. 1979. "Bending Granite: Attempts to Change the Rank Structure of American Police Departments." *Journal of Police Science and Administration* 7(3):253–84.

Hage, Jerald. 1980. *Theories of Organizations*. New York: Wiley.

Haggerty, Kevin D., and Richard V. Ericson. 1999. "The Militarization of Policing in the Information Age." *Journal of Political and Military Sociology* 27(2):233–55.

Harcourt, Bernard E. 2007. *Against Prediction: Profiling, Policing, and Punishing in an Actuarial Age*. Chicago: University of Chicago Press.

Hasenfeld, Yeheskel, and Richard A. English. 1974. "Human Service Organizations: A Conceptual Overview." In *Human Service Organizations: A Book of Readings*, edited by Yeheskel Hasenfeld and Richard A. English. Ann Arbor: University of Michigan Press.

Hassell, Kimberly D., Jihong "Solomon" Zhao, and Edward R. Maguire. 2003. "Structural Arrangements in Large Municipal Police Organizations: Revisiting Wilson's Theory of Local Political Culture." *Policing: An International Journal of Police Strategies and Management* 26(2):231–50.

Hickman, Matthew J., and Brian A. Reaves. 2006. *Local Police Departments, 2003*. Washington, DC: Bureau of Justice Statistics.

Hinkle, Joshua, and David Weisburd. 2008. "The Irony of Broken Windows Policing: A Micro-Place Study of the Relationship between Disorder, Focused Police Crackdowns, and Fear of Crime." *Journal of Criminal Justice* 36:503–12.

Holden, Gwen, Gerard Murphy, Corina Solé Brito, and Joshua Ederheimer. 2009. *Learning from 9/11: Organizational Change in the New York City and Arlington County, VA, Police Departments*. NCJ 2273456. Washington, DC: National Institute of Justice.

ICPSR (Inter-University Consortium for Political and Social Research). 2010. "Description and Citation: Study no. 8605—Police Services Study, Phase II.

1977: Rochester, St. Louis, and St. Petersburg." http://www.icpsr.umich.edu/icpsrweb/ICPSR/studies/8605?q=Police+Services+Study.

International Association of Chiefs of Police. 2005. *Post 9-11 Policing: The Crime-Control–Homeland Security Paradigm—Taking Command of New Realities*. Alexandria, VA: International Association of Chiefs of Police.

Jones, Trevor, and Timothy Newburn. 1998. *Private Security and Public Policing*. Oxford: Clarendon.

Jones, Trevor, Tim Newburn, and David J. Smith. 1994. "Policing and the Idea of Democracy." *British Journal of Criminology* 36(2):182–98.

Kelling, George L. 1981. *Conclusions: The Newark Foot Patrol Experiment*. Washington, DC: Police Foundation.

———. 1999. *"Broken Windows" and Police Discretion*. NCJ 178259. Washington, DC: National Institute of Justice. http://www.ncjrs.gov/pdffiles1/nij/178259.pdf.

Kelling, George L., and William J. Bratton. 2006. *Policing Terrorism*. New York: Manhattan Institute. http://www.manhattan-institute.org/html/cb_43.htm.

Kelling, George L., and Mark H. Moore. 1988. "From Political to Reform to Community: The Evolving Strategy of Police." In *Community Policing: Rhetoric or Reality*, edited by Jack R. Greene and Stephen D. Mastrofski. New York: Praeger.

Kelling, George L., Tony Pate, Duane Dieckman, and Charles E. Brown. 1974. *The Kansas City Preventive Patrol Experiment: A Summary Report*. Washington, DC: Police Foundation.

Kerlikowske, Gil. 2004. "The End of Community Policing: Remembering the Lessons Learned." *FBI Bulletin* 73(4):6–10.

King, William R. 2000. "Measuring Police Innovation: Issues and Measurement." *Policing: An International Journal of Police Strategies and Management* 23(3):303–17.

Klinger, David A. 2004. "Environment and Organization: Reviving a Perspective on the Police." *Annals of the American Academy of Political and Social Science* 593(May):119–36.

Klockars, Carl B. 1985. *The Idea of Police*. Beverly Hills, CA: Sage.

———. 1988. "The Rhetoric of Community Policing." In *Community Policing: Rhetoric or Reality*, edited by Jack R. Greene and Stephen D. Mastrofski. New York: Praeger.

———. 1995. "A Theory of Excessive Force and Its Control." In *And Justice for All: Understanding and Controlling Police Abuse of Force*, edited by William A. Geller and Hans Toch. Washington, DC: Police Executive Research Forum.

Klockars, Carl B., Sanja Kutnjak Ivkovic, and Maria R. Haberfeld. 2004. *The Contours of Police Integrity*. Thousand Oaks, CA: Sage.

———. 2006. *Enhancing Police Integrity*. Dordrecht, Netherlands: Springer.

Klockars, Carl B., Sanja Kutnjak Ivkovich, William E. Harver, and Maria R. Haberfeld. 2000. *The Measurement of Police Integrity*. Research in Brief. Washington, DC: National Institute of Justice.

Krislov, Samuel, and David H. Rosenbloom. 1981. *Representative Bureaucracy and the American Political System*. New York: Praeger.

LaFree, Gary, and Laura Dugan. 2009. "Tracking Global Terrorism Trends, 1970–2004." In *To Protect and to Serve: Policing in an Age of Terrorism*, edited by David Weisburd, Thomas E. Feucht, Idit Hakimi, Lois Felson Mock, and Simon Perry. New York: Springer.

Langworthy, Robert H. 1985. "Police Department Size and Agency Structure." *Journal of Criminal Justice* 13:15–27.

———. 1986. *The Structure of Police Organizations*. Westport, CT: Praeger.

Langworthy, Robert H., and Michael J. Hindelang. 1983. "Effects of Police Agency Size on the Use of Police Employees: A Reexamination of Ostrom, Parks, and Whitaker." *Police Studies* 5:11–19.

Larson, G. C., and J. W. Simon. 1978. *St. Louis MO—Police AVM Automatic Vehicle Monitoring System—Phase 2 City-wide Implementation, Evaluation*. NCJ 064852. Washington, DC: National Institute of Law Enforcement and Criminal Justice.

Liederbach, John. 2008. "Wilson Redux: Another Look at Varieties of Police Behavior." *Police Quarterly* 11(4):447–67.

Lim, Hong-Hai. 2006. "Representative Bureaucracy: Rethinking Substantive Effects and Active Representation." *Public Administration Review* 66(March/April):193–204.

Loader, Ian. 1999. "Consumer Culture and the Commodification of Policing and Security." *Sociology* 33(2):373–92.

Lovrich, Nicholas, Jr. 1985. "Scale and Performance in Governmental Operations: An Empirical Assessment of Public Choice Prescriptions." *Public Administration Quarterly* 9(Summer):163–95.

Lum, Cynthia. 2009. *Translating Police Research into Practice*. Ideas in American Policing. Washington, DC: Police Foundation

Lum, Cynthia, Maria Maki Haberfeld, George Fachner, and Charles Lieberman. 2009. "Police Activities to Counter Terrorism: What We Know and What We Need to Know." In *To Protect and to Serve: Policing in an Age of Terrorism*, edited by David Weisburd, Thomas E. Feucht, Idit Hakimi, Lois Felson Mock, and Simon Perry. New York: Springer.

Lyons, William. 1999. *The Politics of Community Policing: Rearranging the Power to Punish*. Ann Arbor: University of Michigan Press.

Maguire, Edward R. 1997. "Structural Change in Large Municipal Police Organizations during the Community Policing Era." *Justice Quarterly* 14(3):547–76.

———. 2003. *Organizational Structure in American Police Agencies: Context, Complexity, and Control*. Albany: State University of New York Press.

Maguire, Edward R., and William R. King. 2004. "Trends in the Policing Industry." *Annals of the American Academy of Political and Social Science* 593:15–41.

———. 2007. "The Changing Landscape of American Police Organizations." In *Policing 2020: Exploring the Future of Crime, Communities, and Policing,* edited by Joseph A. Schafer. Washington, DC: Federal Bureau of Investigation.

———. Forthcoming. "Federal-Local Coordination in Homeland Security." In *Criminologists on Terrorism and Homeland Security*, edited by Brian Forst, Jack Greene, and James Lynch. Cambridge: Cambridge University Press.

Maguire, Edward R., and Stephen D. Mastrofski. 2000. "Patterns of Community Policing in the United States." *Police Quarterly* 3(1):4–45.

Maguire, Edward R., and Rebecca Schulte-Murray. 2001. "Issues and Patterns in the Comparative International Study of Police Strength." *International Journal of Comparative Sociology* 42(1–2):75–100.

Maguire, Edward R., Yeunhee Shin, Jihong "Solomon" Zhao, and Kimberly D. Hassell. 2003. "Structural Change in Large Police Agencies during the 1990s." *Policing: An International Journal of Police Strategies and Management* 26(2):251–75.

Maguire, Edward R., Jeffrey B. Snipes, Craig D. Uchida, and Margaret Townsend. 1998. "Counting Cops: Estimating the Number of Police Departments and Police Officers in the USA." *Policing: An International Journal of Police Strategies and Management* 21(1):97–120.

Manning, Peter K. 1992. "Information Technologies and the Police." In *Modern Policing*, edited by Michael Tonry and Norval Morris. Vol. 15 of *Crime and Justice: A Review of Research*, edited by Michael Tonry. Chicago: University of Chicago Press.

———. 2003. *Policing Contingencies*. Chicago: University of Chicago Press.

———. 2005. "Information Technologies." In *Encyclopedia of Law Enforcement*, vol. 1, edited by Larry E. Sullivan and Marie Simonetti. Thousand Oaks, CA: Sage.

———. 2006. "The United States of America." In *Plural Policing: A Comparative Perspective*, edited by Trevor Jones and Tim Newburn. London: Routledge.

Mastrofski, Stephen D. 1981. "Reforming Police: The Impact of Patrol Assignment Patterns on Officer Behavior in Urban Residential Neighborhoods." PhD dissertation, University of North Carolina, Chapel Hill.

———. 1988. "Varieties of Police Governance in Metropolitan America." *Politics and Policy* 8:12–31.

———. 1989. "Police Agency Consolidation: Lessons from a Case Study." In *Police Management Today*, edited by James J. Fyfe. Washington, DC: International City Management Association.

———. 1998. "Community Policing and Police Organization Structure." In *Community Policing and the Evaluation of Police Service Delivery*, edited by Jean-Paul Brodeur. Thousand Oaks, CA: Sage.

———. 1999. "Policing for People." In *Ideas in American Policing*. Washington, DC: Police Foundation.

———. 2002. "The Romance of Police Leadership." In *Theoretical Advances in Criminology: Crime and Social Organization*, edited by Elin Waring, David Weisburd, and Lawrence W. Sherman. New Brunswick, NJ: Transaction.

———. 2003. "Personnel and Agency Performance Appraisal." In *Local Gov-

ernment Police Management, edited by William A. Geller. Washington, DC: International City Management Association.

——. 2004. "Controlling Street-Level Police Discretion." *Annals of the American Academy of Political and Social Science* 593(May):100–118.

——. 2005*a*. "Education of Police." In *Encyclopedia of Law Enforcement*, vol. 1, *State and Local*, edited by Larry E. Sullivan and Marie Simonetti Rosen. Thousand Oaks, CA: Sage.

——. 2005*b*. "Patrol Work." In *Encyclopedia of Law Enforcement*, vol. 1, *State and Local*, edited by Larry E. Sullivan and Marie Simonetti Rosen. Thousand Oaks, CA: Sage.

——. 2006*a*. "Community Policing: A Skeptical View." In *Police Innovation: Contrasting Perspectives*, edited by David Weisburd and Anthony A. Braga. New York: Cambridge University Press.

——. 2006*b*. "Police Organization and Management Issues for the Next Decade." Report to the National Institute of Justice. http://www.ncjrs.gov/pdffiles1/nij/grants/218584.pdf.

Mastrofski, Stephen D., and Cynthia Lum. 2008. "Meeting the Challenges of Police Governance in Trinidad and Tobago." *Policing: A Journal of Policy and Practice* 2(4):481–96. doi:10.1093/police/pan051.

Mastrofski, Stephen D., and R. Richard Ritti. 1996. "Police Training and the Effects of Organization on Drunk Driving Enforcement." *Justice Quarterly* 13:291–320.

——. 2000. "Making Sense of Community Policing: A Theoretical Perspective." *Police Practice and Research Journal* 1(2):183–210.

Mastrofski, Stephen D., R. Richard Ritti, and Debra Hoffmaster. 1987. "Organizational Determinants of Police Discretion: The Case of Drinking-Driving." *Journal of Criminal Justice* 15:387–402.

Mastrofski, Stephen D., and Craig D. Uchida. 1993. "Transforming the Police." *Journal of Research in Crime and Delinquency* 30:330–58.

Mastrofski, Stephen D., David Weisburd, and Anthony A. Braga. 2009. "Rethinking Policing: The Policy Implications of Hot Spots of Crime." In *Contemporary Issues in Criminal Justice Policy: Policy Proposals from the American Society of Criminology Conference*, edited by Todd R. Clear, Natasha A. Frost, and J. D. Freilich. Florence, KY: Cengage Learning.

Mastrofski, Stephen D., James J. Willis, and Tammy R. Kochel. 2007. "The Challenges of Implementing Community Policing in the United States." *Policing: A Journal of Policy and Practice* 1(2):223–34.

Mastrofski, Stephen D., James J. Willis, and Jeffrey B. Snipes. 2002. "Styles of Patrol in a Community Policing Context." In *The Move to Community Policing: Making Change Happen*, edited by Merry Morash and J. K. Ford. Thousand Oaks, CA: Sage.

Mawby, Robert, ed. 1999. *Policing across the World: Issues for the Twenty-first Century*. London: Routledge.

McDavid, James. 1977. "The Effects of Interjurisdictional Cooperation on Police Performance in the St. Louis Metropolitan Area." *Publius* 7(2):3–30.

Meehan, Albert J., and Michael Ponder. 2002. "Race and Place: The Ecology of Racial Profiling African American Motorists." *Justice Quarterly* 19(3): 401–32.

Moore, Mark, and Anthony Braga. 2004. "Police Performance Measurement: A Normative Framework." *Criminal Justice Ethics* 23:3–19.

Muir, William Ker, Jr. 1977. *Police: Streetcorner Politicians*. Chicago: University of Chicago Press.

———. 2008. "Police and Social Democracy." *Policing and Society* 18(1):18–22.

Murphy, Patrick, and Thomas Plate. 1977. *Commissioner: A View from the Top*. New York: Simon & Schuster.

National Institute of Justice. 2009. "Solicitation: Predictive Policing Analytic and Evaluation Research Support." Washington, DC: National Institute of Justice. http://www.ncjrs.gov/pdffiles1/nij/sl000879.pdf.

Noguchi, Sharon. 2009. "San Jose Police Test Head-Mounted Cameras for Officers." *Mercury News*, December 21. http://www.infowars.com/san-jose-police-test-head-mounted-cameras-for-officers/.

Nunn, Sam, and Kenna Quinet. 2002. "Evaluating the Effects of Information Technology on Problem-Oriented Policing: If It Doesn't Fit, Must We Quit?" *Evaluation Review* 26(1):81–108.

Oliver, W. 2004. "The Homeland Security Juggernaut: The End of the Community Policing Era?" *Crime and Justice International* 20:4–11.

O'Shea, Timothy C., and Keith Nicholls. 2003. "Police Crime Analysis: A Survey of US Police Departments with 100 or More Sworn Personnel." *Police Practice and Research* 4(3):233–50.

Ostrom, Elinor, Roger B. Parks, and Gordon P. Whitaker. 1978. *Patterns of Metropolitan Policing*. Cambridge, MA: Ballinger.

Ostrom, Elinor, and Dennis C. Smith. 1976. "On the Fate of 'Lilliputs' in Metropolitan Policing." *Public Administration Review* 36(2):192–200.

Ostrom, Elinor, Gordon P. Whitaker, and Roger B. Parks. 1978. "Policing: Is There a System?" In *The Policy Cycle*, edited by Judith May and Aaron Wildavsky. New York: Russell Sage Foundation.

Ostrom, Vincent, and Elinor Ostrom. 1965. "A Behavioral Approach to the Study of Intergovernmental Relations." *Annals of the American Academy of Political and Social Science* 359(May):137–46.

Ostrom, Vincent, Charles M. Tiebout, and Robert Warren. 1961. "The Organization of Governments in Metropolitan Areas." *American Political Science Review* 55:831–42.

Paoline, Eugene A., III. 2001. *Rethinking Police Culture: Officers' Occupational Attitudes*. New York: LFB Scholarly Publishing.

Parks, Roger B. 2009. "Metropolitan Organization and Police." In *The Practice of Constitutional Development*, edited by Filippo Sabetti, Barbara Allen, and Mark Sproule-Jones. Lanham, MD: Lexington.

Parks, Roger B., Stephen D. Mastrofski, Christina DeJong, and M. Kevin Gray. 1999. "How Officers Spend Their Time with the Community." *Justice Quarterly* 16:483–518.

Perlman, Ellen. 2008. "Policing by the Odds." *Governing* (December 1). http://www.governing.com/article/policing-odds.

Podsakoff, Philip M., Scott B. MacKenzie, Jeong-Yeon Lee, and Nathan P. Podsakoff. 2003. "Common Method Biases in Behavioral Research: A Critical Review of the Literature and Recommended Remedies." *Journal of Applied Psychology* 88(5):879–903.

Police Executive Research Forum. 2006. *Police Chief Concerns: A Gathering Storm—Violent Crime in America.* Washington, DC: Police Executive Research Forum.

President's Commission on Law Enforcement and Administration of Justice. 1967. *The Challenge of Crime in a Free Society.* Washington, DC: U.S. Government Printing Office.

Ratcliffe, Jerry. 2006. *Video Surveillance of Public Places.* Washington, DC: Office of Community Oriented Policing Services.

Reaves, Brian A. 2007. *Census of State and Local Law Enforcement Agencies, 2004.* Washington, DC: Bureau of Justice Statistics.

Reaves, Brian A., and Matthew J. Hickman. 2002. *Police Departments in Large Cities, 1990–2000.* Washington, DC: Bureau of Justice Statistics.

Reisig, Michael D. In this volume. "Community and Problem-Oriented Policing."

Reiss, Albert J., Jr. 1971. *The Police and the Public.* New Haven, CT: Yale University Press.

———. 1988. *Private Employment of Public Police.* Washington, DC: National Institute of Justice.

———. 1992. "Police Organization in the Twentieth Century." In *Modern Policing,* edited by Michael Tonry and Norval Morris. Vol. 15 of *Crime and Justice: A Review of Research,* edited by Michael Tonry. Chicago: University of Chicago Press.

Reiss, Albert J., Jr., and David J. Bordua. 1967. "Environment and Organization: A Perspective on the Police." In *The Police: Six Sociological Essays,* edited by David J. Bordua. New York: Wiley.

Reuss-Ianni, Elizabeth, and Francis A. J. Ianni. 1983. "Street Cops and Management Cops: The Two Cultures of Policing." In *Control in the Police Organization,* edited by Maurice Punch. Cambridge, MA: MIT Press.

Rogers, Everett. 2003. *Diffusion of Innovations.* 5th ed. New York: Free Press.

Rosenbaum, Dennis P., and Susan Hartnett. 2010. *The National Police Research Platform.* Chicago: Center for Research in Law and Justice, University of Illinois at Chicago.

Rosenbaum, Dennis P., and Deanna L. Wilkinson. 2004. "Can Police Adapt? Tracking the Effects of Organizational Reform over Six Years." In *Community Policing: Can It Work?* edited by Wesley G. Skogan. Belmont, CA: Wadsworth.

Roth, Jeffrey A., ed. 2000. *National Evaluation of the COPS Program—Title I of the 1994 Crime Act.* Washington, DC: National Institute of Justice.

Roth, Jeffrey A., Jan Roehl, and Calvin C. Johnson. 2004. "Trends in Community Policing." In *Community Policing: Can It Work?* edited by Wesley G. Skogan. Belmont, CA: Wadsworth.

Rubinstein, Jonathan. 1973. *City Police.* New York: Farrar, Straus and Giroux.

Schafer, Joseph A., George W. Burruss Jr., and Matthew J. Giblin. 2009. "Measuring Homeland Security Innovation in Small Municipal Agencies: Policing in a Post-9/11 World." *Police Quarterly* 12(3):263–88.

Scheider, Matthew C., Tawnadra Rowell, and Veh Bezdikian. 2003. "The Impact of Citizen Perceptions of Community Policing on Fear of Crime: Findings from 12 Cities." *Police Quarterly* 6(4):363–86.

Scott, W. Richard. 1998. *Organizations: Rational, Natural, and Open Systems.* 4th ed. Upper Saddle River, NJ: Prentice Hall.

Shearing, Clifford D. 1992. "The Relation between Public and Private Policing." In *Modern Policing*, edited by Michael Tonry and Norval Morris. Vol. 15 of *Crime and Justice: A Review of Research*, edited by Michael Tonry. Chicago: University of Chicago Press.

Shearing, Clifford D., and Philip C. Stenning. 1981. "Modern Private Security: Its Growth and Implications." In *Crime and Justice: An Annual Review of Research*, vol. 3, edited by Michael Tonry and Norval Morris. Chicago: University of Chicago Press.

Sherman, Lawrence W. 1978. *Scandal and Reform: Controlling Police Corruption.* Berkeley: University of California Press.

———. 1983. "Reducing Police Gun Use: Critical Events, Administrative Policy, and Organizational Change." In *Control in the Police Organization*, edited by Maurice Punch. Cambridge, MA: MIT Press.

———. 1984. "Experiments in Police Discretion: Scientific Boon or Dangerous Knowledge?" *Law and Contemporary Problems* 47:61–81.

———. 1998. *Evidence-Based Policing.* Ideas in American Policing. Washington, DC: Police Foundation.

Sherman, Lawrence, Denise Gottfredson, Doris Mackenzie, John Eck, Peter Reuter, and Shawn Bushway. 1997. *Preventing Crime: What Works, What Doesn't, What's Promising.* Washington, DC: National Institute of Justice, U.S. Department of Justice.

Sklansky, David Alan. 2006. "Not Your Father's Police Department: Making Sense of the New Demographics of Law Enforcement." *Journal of Criminal Law and Criminology* 96(3):1209–44.

———. 2008. *Democracy and the Police.* Stanford, CA: Stanford University Press.

Skogan, Wesley G. 2005. "Citizen Satisfaction with Police Encounters." *Police Quarterly* 8(3):298–301.

———. 2006a. "Asymmetry in the Impact of Encounters with Police." *Policing and Society* 16(2):99–126.

———. 2006b. *Police and Community in Chicago: A Tale of Three Cities.* New York: Oxford University Press.

———. 2006c. "The Promise of Community Policing." In *Police Innovation: Contrasting Perspectives*, edited by David Weisburd and Anthony A. Braga. New York: Cambridge University Press.

———. 2008. "Why Reforms Fail." *Policing and Society* 18(1):23–34.

Skogan, Wesley G., and Kathleen Frydl, eds. 2004. *Fairness and Effectiveness in Policing: The Evidence.* Washington, DC: National Academies Press.

Skolnick, Jerome H. 1966. *Justice without Trial: Law Enforcement in Democratic Society*. New York: Wiley.

———. 2002. "Corruption and the Blue Code of Silence." *Police Practice and Research* 3:7–19.

Skolnick, Jerome H., and David H. Bayley. 1986. *The New Blue Line: Police Innovation in Six American Cities*. New York: Free Press.

Smith, Brad W., Kenneth J. Novak, and James Frank. 2001. "Community Policing and the Work Routines of Street-Level Officers." *Criminal Justice Review* 26(1):17–37.

Smith, Douglas. 1984. "The Organizational Context of Legal Control." *Criminology* 22:19–38.

Sparrow, Malcolm K., Mark H. Moore, and David M. Kennedy. 1990. *Beyond 911: A New Era for Policing*. New York: Basic Books.

Spelman, William G., and Dale K. Brown. 1981. *Calling the Police: A Replication of the Citizen Reporting Component of the Kansas City Response Time Analysis*. Washington, DC: Police Executive Research Forum.

Stucky, Thomas D. 2005. *Urban Politics, Crime Rates, and Police Strength*. New York: LFB Scholarly Publishing.

Sutton, L. Paul. 1986. "The Fourth Amendment in Action: An Empirical View of the Search Warrant Process." *Criminal Law Bulletin* 22(5):405–29.

Tennenbaum, Abraham N. 1994. "The Influence of the Garner Decision on Police Use of Deadly Force." *Journal of Criminal Law and Criminology* 85(1): 241–60.

Teodoro, Manuel P. 2009. "Ambition and Professionalism: Executive Mobility and Law Enforcement Agency Accreditation." Unpublished manuscript. Hamilton, NY: Colgate University, Department of Political Science.

Terrill, William, and Stephen D. Mastrofski. 2004. "Toward a Better Understanding of Police Use of Nonlethal Force." In *Police Integrity and Ethics*, edited by Alex Piquero, Matthew Hickman, and Jack R. Greene. Belmont, CA: Wadsworth.

Thacher, David. 2001. "Equity and Community Policing: A New View of Community Partnerships." *Criminal Justice Ethics* 20(Winter/Spring):3–16.

———. 2005. "The Local Role in Homeland Security." *Law and Society Review* 39(3):635–76.

———. 2008. "Research for the Front Lines." *Policing and Society* 18(1):46–59.

Thompson, James D. 1967. *Organizations in Action: Social Science Bases of Administrative Theory*. New York: McGraw-Hill.

Torres, Sam, and Ronald E. Vogel. 2001. "Pre and Post-test Differences between Vietnamese and Latino Residents Involved in a Community Policing Experiment: Reducing Fear of Crime and Improving Attitudes toward the Police." *Policing: An International Journal of Police Strategies and Management* 24:40–55.

Tully, Edward J. 2002. "Regionalization or Consolidation of Law Enforcement Services in the United States." National Executive Institute Associates, Major Chiefs Association and Major County Sheriff's Association. http://www.neiassociates.org/regionalization.htm.

Tyler, Tom R., Patrick E. Callahan, and Jeffrey Frost. 2007. "Armed, and Dangerous? Motivating Rule Adherence among Agents of Social Control." *Law and Society Review* 41:457–92.

Tyler, Tom R., and Yuen J. Huo. 2002. *Trust in the Law: Encouraging Public Cooperation with the Police and Courts.* New York: Russell Sage Foundation.

Uchida, Craig D., and Timothy S. Bynum. 1991. "Search Warrants, Motions to Suppress and 'Lost Cases': The Effects of the Exclusionary Rule in Seven Jurisdictions." *Journal of Criminal Law and Criminology* 81(4):1034–66.

Van Maanen, John. 1983. "The Boss: First-Line Supervision in an American Police Agency." In *Control in the Police Organization,* edited by Maurice Punch. Cambridge, MA: MIT Press.

———. 1984. "Making Rank: Becoming an American Police Sergeant." *Urban Life* 13:155–76.

Walker, Samuel. 1977. *A Critical History of Police Reform: The Emergence of Professionalism.* Lexington, MA: Heath.

Walker, Samuel, and Morgan Macdonald. 2009. "An Alternative Remedy for Police Misconduct: A Model State Pattern or Practice Statute." *Civil Rights Law Journal* 19(3):479–552.

Wambaugh, Joseph. 1973. *The Blue Knight.* Boston: Little, Brown.

Weber, Max. 1978. *Economy and Society.* 2 vols. Edited by Guenther Roth and Claus Wittich. Berkeley: University of California Press. (Originally published 1922.)

Weisburd, David, and Anthony A. Braga. 2006. "Introduction: Understanding Police Innovation." In *Police Innovation: Contrasting Perspectives,* edited by David Weisburd and Anthony A. Braga. New York: Cambridge University Press.

Weisburd, David, and John E. Eck. 2004. "What Can Police Do to Reduce Crime, Disorder, and Fear?" *Annals of the American Academy of Political and Social Science* 593(May):42–65.

Weisburd, David, Thomas E. Feucht, Idit Hakimi, Lois Felson Mock, and Simon Perry, eds. 2009. *To Protect and to Serve: Policing in an Age of Terrorism.* New York: Springer.

Weisburd, David, Rosann Greenspan, Edwin E. Hamilton, Kellie A. Bryant, and Hubert Williams. 2001. *The Abuse of Police Authority: A National Study of Police Officers' Attitudes.* Washington, DC: Police Foundation.

Weisburd, David, and Cynthia Lum. 2005. "The Diffusion of Computerized Crime Mapping in Policing: Linking Research and Practice." *Police Practice and Research* 6(5):419–34.

Weisburd, David, Stephen D. Mastrofski, Anne-Marie McNally, Rosann Greenspan, and James J. Willis. 2003. "Reforming to Preserve: Compstat and Strategic Problem-Solving in American Policing." *Criminology and Public Policy* 2:421–56.

Weisburd, David, and Peter Neyroud. Forthcoming. "Police Science: Toward a New Paradigm." In *New Perspectives in Policing.* Washington, DC: National Institute of Justice, U.S. Department of Justice; Cambridge, MA: Program in Criminal Justice Policy and Management, John F. Kennedy School of Government, Harvard University.

Weisheit, Ralph A. 2005. "Rural Police." In *Encyclopedia of Law Enforcement*, vol. 1, *State and Local*, edited by Larry E. Sullivan and Marie Simonetti Rosen. Thousand Oaks, CA: Sage.

Weisheit, Ralph A., and Carl W. Hawkins Jr. 1997. "The State of Community Policing in Small Towns and Rural Areas." In *Community Policing in a Rural Setting*, edited by Quint C. Thurman and Edmund F. McGarrell. Cincinnati: Anderson Publishing.

Weisheit, Ralph A., and L. E. Wells. 1999. *Crime and Policing in Rural and Small-Town America*. 2nd ed. Prospect Heights, IL: Waveland.

Weiss, Alexander. 1997. "The Communication of Innovation in American Policing." *Policing: An International Journal of Police Strategies and Management* 29(2):292–310.

Weitzer, Ronald, and Steven A. Tuch. 2006. *Race and Policing in America: Conflict and Reform* New York: Cambridge University Press.

Werder, Edward J. 1996. "The Great Sergeant!" National Executive Institute Associates, Major Cities Chiefs Association and Major County Sheriff's Association. http://www.neiassociates.org/sergeant.htm.

Westley, William A. 1970. *Violence and the Police: A Sociological Study of Law, Custom, and Morality*. Cambridge, MA: MIT Press.

Williams, Hubert, and Patrick Murphy. 1990. "Evolving Strategy of Police: A Minority View." Report to the National Institute of Justice. Washington, DC: National Institute of Justice.

Willis, James, Stephen D. Mastrofski, and Tammy Kochel. 2010. "Recommendations for Integrating Compstat and Community Policing." *Policing: A Journal of Policy and Practice* 4(2):182–93.

Willis, James J., Stephen D. Mastrofski, and David Weisburd. 2007. "Making Sense of Compstat: A Theory-Based Analysis of Organizational Change in Three Police Departments." *Law and Society Review* 41:147–88.

Wilson, James Q. 1968. *Varieties of Police Behavior: The Management of Law and Order in Eight Communities*. Cambridge, MA: Harvard University Press.

———. 1989. *Bureaucracy: What Government Agencies Do and Why They Do It*. New York: Basic Books.

Wilson, Jeremy M. 2003. "Measurement and Association in the Structure of Municipal Police Organizations." *Policing: An International Journal of Police Strategies and Management* 26(2):276–97.

———. 2006. *Community Policing in America*. New York: Routledge.

Wolfe, Richard A. 1994. "Organizational Innovation: Review, Critique and Suggested Research Directions." *Journal of Management Studies* 31(3):405–31.

Wood, Jennifer, and David Bradley. 2009. "Embedding Partnership Policing: What We've Learned from the Nexus Project." *Police Practice and Research* 10:133–44.

Wood, Richard L., Mariah Davis, and Amelia Rouse. 2004. "Diving into Quicksand: Program Implementation and Police Subcultures." In *Commu-*

nity Policing: Can It Work? edited by Wesley G. Skogan. Belmont, CA: Wadsworth.

Wycoff, Mary Ann. 1994. "Community Policing Strategies." Unpublished report. Washington, DC: Police Foundation.

Zaltman, Gerald, Robert Duncan, and Jonny Holbek. 1973. *Innovations and Organizations*. New York: Wiley-Interscience.

Zhao, Jihong. 1996. *Why Police Organizations Change: A Study of Community-Oriented Policing*. Washington, DC: Police Executive Research Forum.

Zhao, Jihong "Solomon," Ni He, and Nicholas P. Lovrich. 2006. "Pursuing Gender Diversity in Police Organizations in the 1990s: A Longitudinal Analysis of Factors Associated with the Hiring of Female Officers." *Police Quarterly* 9:463–85.

Keith Soothill

Sex Offender Recidivism

ABSTRACT

There have been major shifts in the perception of sex offender recidivism over the past 30 years and increased interest in public and professional spheres. However, the discourses of the public and the professionals are becoming increasingly discrepant. The media are pivotal in demonizing all sex offenders and focusing on punitiveness. Media myths have developed that mask professional advances. A paradigm shift is needed from the current emphasis on behavioral science research toward a fuller recognition of system changes and processual questions. History instructs that only a minority of sex offenders are really dangerous. Nevertheless, sex offending is a pervasive problem, and criminal justice solutions alone will not be enough. Indeed, current policies to prevent or address sexual offending have largely failed. Social justice solutions with compassion as an ingredient need to be brought more to the fore.

The founders of one of the first big hedge funds, Long-Term Capital Management, which crashed in the late 1990s, both won Nobel Prizes for economics and for a time made annual gains of more than 40 percent (Wilby 2008). They had come up with a mathematical formula that supposedly took account of the volatility of shares. They calculated that events to cause the loss of all their capital could happen less than once in the lifetime of the known universe.

However, the data they used to factor in market volatility went back only 5 years, and therefore, they failed to take account of such historical events even as recent as the 1987 crash, never mind the 1929 crash or the Russian debt default of 1918. In fact, the Russian debt default of 1998 took them by surprise and led to Long-Term's collapse. Niall

Keith Soothill is emeritus professor of social research at Lancaster University. This work was partly supported by the Economic and Social Research Council under its National Centre for Research Methods initiative (grant RES-576-25-0019). I much appreciate the assistance of my colleague, Brian Francis, for his help and support. Finally, I wish to thank Michael Tonry and three anonymous reviewers for some important comments that helped considerably in the revision of this essay.

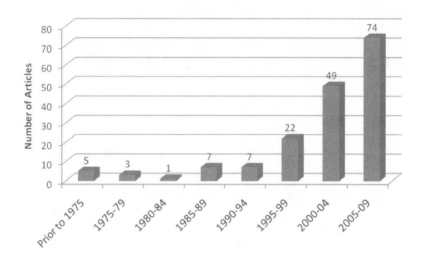

FIG. 1.—Articles published on sex offender recidivism. Source: Adapted from ISI Web of Knowledge database (see n. 1).

Ferguson, in a book focusing on a financial history of the world concludes, "The Nobel prize-winners had known plenty of mathematics, but not enough history" (2009, p. 330).

This is a cautionary tale that reminds us of the dangers of building a theoretical edifice on shaky methodological foundations. Is it a warning sign that is applicable to the topical issue of sex offender recidivism? Quite simply, the public wants the issue to be "solved." However, as the focus on sexual offender recidivism gets more mathematically precise, is there a bigger picture that we are overlooking? While it may perhaps seem unlikely, nevertheless it is an inquiry that seems worthwhile exploring.

Forty years ago few academics were interested in sex crime research and few members of the public were concerned about sex offender recidivism. Today the situation is very different. Using the search facilities of the Web of Knowledge,[1] figure 1 shows that 168 articles with titles including the terms sex recidivism or reconviction or reoffending were identified, and the numbers have steadily increased over the years.

[1] The Institute for Scientific Knowledge (ISI) Web of Knowledge Service for UK Education provides a single route of access to various databases, including Web of Science, ISI Proceedings, Journal Citation Reports, Current Contents Connect, and many others.

TABLE 1

Most-Cited Articles on Sex Offender Recidivism

Article	Times Cited
Hanson and Bussiere (1998)	421
Furby, Weinrott, and Blackshaw (1989)	237
Quinsey, Rice, and Harris (1995)	171
Hall (1995)	162
Hanson and Harris (2000)	123
Rice, Quinsey, and Harris (1991)	119
Seto and Barbaree (1999)	107
Gretton et al. (2001)	94
Marques et al. (1994)	88
Hanson and Morton-Bourgon (2005)	79
Smith and Monastersky (1986)	57
Soothill and Gibbens (1978)	47
Worling and Curwen (2000)	47

SOURCE.—Adapted from ISI Web of Knowledge database (see n. 1).

NOTE.—In addition, there is an article by Miller et al. (1978) that is cited 92 times, but their primary focus is about sex assault victims and is outside the scope of the present review.

Prior to the mid-1970s there were only five such titles, but this may, of course, reflect the limitations of the Web of Knowledge in those early years. Nevertheless, the interest began to rise from the mid-1990s and seems to be continuing on an upward trajectory. The last column of the histogram, representing the years 2005–9, shows 74 relevant articles identified, clearly towering over earlier 5-year groupings.

However, there is another story to grasp. Most articles probably have a low readership and certainly attract few subsequent citations. Citations enable articles to continue to live. Of the 168 articles revealed in the search, 70 have not been subsequently cited, and another 51 are cited elsewhere on fewer than 10 occasions. So only 47 (or 28 percent) pick up any sort of momentum with 10 or more citations. Being cited takes time, and there is about a 3-year time lag before an article becomes more widely noticed and cited, as table 1 indicates.

One can make several observations about table 1, which lists the most cited articles identified in the Web of Knowledge search. There are several kinds of articles that are widely cited: important reviews or meta-analyses (e.g., Furby, Weinrott, and Blackshaw [1989], which presented a comprehensive review of empirical studies of sex offender recidivism; Hall [1995], which focused on a meta-analysis of recent treatment studies; Hanson and Bussière [1998], in which a meta-analysis tried to identify the factors most strongly related to recidivism among sexual offenders; and Hanson and Morton-Bourgon [2005], in which a meta-analysis focused on the characteristics of persistent sexual offenders), which appear about every decade or so; a focus on predictors (Quinsey, Rice, ánd Harris 1995; Hanson and Harris 2000) and treatment issues (Marques et al. 1994; Seto and Barbaree 1999), which emerged in the mid- to late 1990s; and articles on particular types of offender (e.g., child molesters [Rice, Quinsey, and Harris 1991] and adolescent sex offenders [Smith and Monastersky 1986; Worling and Curwen 2000; Gretton et al. 2001]).

My own article (Soothill and Gibbens 1978) does not fit easily into this classification. I was challenging the then-current orthodoxy that sexual offending had a low recidivism rate by reconsidering the methodological basis on which this claim seemed to rest (Christiansen et al. 1965). Our main concern was that recidivism studies needed to take into account the time at risk when offenders have opportunities to commit offenses. Long prison sentences effectively remove offenders from the community and thus reduce their potential to reoffend. While most sex offenders are not incarcerated, it seemed probable that those most likely to recidivate would be. The need to import statistical techniques, such as survival analyses, which were already routine in medicine, was considered to be imperative. In a similar spirit, I think it is important to reopen the fundamental debate about current orthodoxies.

This essay is essentially a narrative review focusing on primary studies, but the discussion takes a qualitative rather than a quantitative approach. However, meta-analyses, systematic reviews, and the like are now considered the gold standard in this field. Certainly some commentators suggest that systematic reviews are superseding narrative reviews. But this probably reflects a failure to recognize that systematic and narrative reviews are attempting different things (Collins and Fauser 2005).

As Davies and Crombie (1998, p. 1) suggest, "High-quality systematic reviews take great care to find all relevant studies published and unpublished, assess each study, synthesize the findings from individual studies in an unbiased way and present a balanced and impartial summary of the findings with due consideration of any flaws in the evidence." Proponents of systematic reviews are very much taken up with the idea of being unbiased and impartial. However, this can be only at the individual level, for such reviews are necessarily rather caught up in discussing whatever is available in the form of individual studies, and these may sometimes just reflect current "flavors of the month." Hence, in an important sense, such reviews are biased in relation to what is available and, thus, may present only a partial picture.

While there is the same danger of narrative reviews simply being caught up with the enthusiasms of the moment, the narrative review has more potential to take a step back and consider the issues more widely. Hence, although such an essay could appear to be more biased and partial (in the sense of representing the passions of the author), there is perhaps more scope in such an approach to be challenging and thought-provoking. In short, while there are strict rules for a systematic review, the narrative review has more individuality and flexibility, not following rules about the search for evidence but, nevertheless, respecting the demands of validity and relevance. So within this kind of framework, I now focus on whether there has been the development of a paradigm in the consideration of sex offender recidivism over the past 30 or so years.

Kuhn's *Structure of Scientific Revolutions* (1962) is widely regarded as the most influential book in modern philosophy of science. Essentially Kuhn argues that scientists work within and against the background of an unquestioned theory or set of beliefs. This is what he characterizes as a "paradigm." Sometimes the paradigm no longer seems helpful and it is necessary that a new one be provided.

Theorizing is the motor of a discipline. The notion of a "criminological career" is an attempt to recognize that theoretical concepts used within criminology may be captured and perhaps change over time (Soothill 2005), that is, something akin to a paradigm shift. Or put in a more Kuhnian way, what is the set of unquestioned beliefs within which current practitioners and researchers operate? My contention is that it is certainly very different from around 40 years ago when sexual offending was generally regarded as a minor problem with little public interest. In short, while there were early attempts to treat sex offenders, thinking about sex offending was rather fragmented, and what was articulated could not be considered as a rounded paradigm. However, over the past few decades there has been a movement toward developing a paradigm, that is, a coherent way of thinking about sex offending.

On the basis of knowledge acquired over the last four decades, I contend that this new way of looking at sex offender recidivism in particular can be summarized in four main sections:

- Focus on recidivism rates (Sec. I)
- Question of prediction and risk factors (Sec. II)
- Focus on the effectiveness of clinical treatment and other interventions (Sec. III)
- Consideration of policy (Sec. IV)

However, this is not a detective novel, and the dénouement will be revealed at the outset. While great progress has been made within the area of understanding sex offender recidivism, there are still challenges ahead. There are two major issues to confront. First, there is currently a widening gap between the public reaction to sex crime and the approach of much of professional orthodoxy. Second, the current paradigm may be constraining developments, and the possibility of a paradigm shift needs to be addressed.

Before focusing on the specific areas of recidivism rates, prediction and risk factors, treatment and other interventions, and policy issues, one needs, however, to probe more generally about developments over the past 40 years. While they are strongly interrelated, one can make an analytical distinction between the public and professional spheres.

The reasons for a shift in public interest are complex. Certainly the new wave of the women's movement in the late 1960s and early 1970s began to embrace the crime of rape as a focus of concern and helped to develop an appreciation and understanding of the immense harm and trauma caused by sexual violence. Hence, sexual crime began to capture public interest and concern more widely as the serious nature of the offense of rape began to be recognized. However, the gradual discovery of child sexual abuse, which began in the 1960s, accelerated in the 1980s with the recognition of child sex abuse in the family culminating in the United Kingdom, for example, in "the Cleveland affair" that produced the challenge of widespread incest and sexual abuse within families (Soothill and Francis 2002).

Since the 1990s the focus has shifted from the family to "stranger-danger" with a series of high-profile cases of sexual murders involving children. In the United States, these included 12-year-old Polly Klaas in 1993 (later, proponents of "three strikes and you're out"—proposed as a solution to the problem of violence—claimed that it would have prevented Polly's murder) and 7-year-old Megan Kanka in 1994 (whose death led to laws being enacted—informally known as Megan's Law—to make information available to the public regarding registered sex offenders). Similarly, in the United Kingdom, high-profile cases included the murder of 8-year-old Sarah Payne in 2000 (Sarah's murder led directly to a campaign—spearheaded by the tabloid *News of the World*—for a Sarah's Law to allow controlled access to the Sex Offenders Register, so parents with young children could know whether a child sex offender was living in their area; the campaign had only limited success) and the murder in Soham in 2002 of two 10-year-old schoolgirls, Holly Wells and Jessica Chapman (this case led to the Bichaud Inquiry, which recommended a registration scheme for people working with children and vulnerable adults and, ultimately, to the foundation of the Independent Safeguarding Authority in 2009). These quite recent cases have aroused public interest and have led to definite policy changes.

However, from the 1970s sex crime has increasingly been used to sell newspapers (Soothill and Walby 1991). Hence, the darker side of an increasing interest in child sex murder has been the media seeing much potential in exploiting the topic for marketing purposes. Recently, Monckton-Smith (forthcoming) has argued that the analytically distinct crimes of homicide and rape are dangerously linked, particularly in media (mis)representations. The ready conflation by the media of sex crime with murder means that readers are getting an increasingly distorted view of sex offending. Public attitudes are molded in part by media representation. Media interest, in turn, partly explains the current discrepancy between public and professional perceptions of sex offending.

However, there are also dangers in stressing the comparative recency of an increasing public concern about certain kinds of sex crime. Freedman (1987, p. 105) points to how "from the 1930s through the 1950s, the sexual psychopath provided the focus for public discussions of sexual normality and abnormality, while the state played an increasingly important role in defining sexual deviance and in prescribing psychiatric treatment." The sex crime panics described by Freedman began in the mid-1930s but declined during World War II. He notes that "although arrest rates for sexual offenses in general rose throughout the period, the vast majority of arrests were for minor offenses, rather than for the violent acts portrayed in the media" (p. 84). Freedman makes the strong claim that "the new image of aggressive male sexual deviance that emerged from the psychiatric and political response to sex crimes provided a focus for a complex redefinition of sexual boundaries in modern America" (p. 84). The sex crime panic of the past two decades awaits a similar analysis.

Have the statistics of sex crime over the past two decades shown patterns similar to the earlier sex crime panic starting in the 1930s? Analyzing crime trends is a complex task. While categories of sex crime—for example, rape, indecent assault, exhibitionism—seem fairly static and, thus, comparable, the *meaning* of sex crimes changes quite markedly over time. Higher arrest or conviction rates may simply mean that certain behavior is now taken more seriously rather than necessarily signifying any behavioral change in the activity within the community. Reporting of rape and child sexual abuse may simply reflect greater public awareness of these crimes. Certainly the sensitivity of reporting sexual offenses tends to result in the underreporting of these offenses to the police, so the routine warning is that "trends in sexual offenses should be treated with caution" (Roe, Coleman, and Kaiza 2008–9, sec. 3.8).

The British Crime Survey (which reports on England and Wales) indicates that—on the basis of the 2008/9 self-completion module— "approximately three per cent of women aged 16 to 59 and less than one per cent of men (of the same age) had experienced a sexual assault (including attempts) in the previous 12 months. The majority of these are accounted for by less serious sexual assaults" (Roe, Coleman, and Kaiza 2008–9, sec. 3.8). There were 51,488 sexual offenses recorded by the police in 2008/9, 4 percent fewer than in the previous year. There is evidence that violent incidents have fallen in England and Wales following a peak in 1995. In terms of violence, rather than specifically sexual violence, the British Crime Survey suggests that "there have been large and statistically significant falls in domestic and acquaintance violence, but stranger violence has remained relatively stable over the past fifteen years" (sec. 3.9).

In contrast, *recorded* sexual crime by the police—although difficult to interpret because of changing recording practices—seems to have risen quite considerably over this period. This perhaps suggests that members of the public are increasingly more willing to report.

In the United States, FBI figures suggest that, following a forcible rape rate peak of 42.8 per 100,000 inhabitants in 1992, the comparable rate has fallen to 29.3 in 2008 (*Crime in the United States* 2008). In 2008, the estimated number of forcible rapes (89,000) is noted as the lowest figure in the last 20 years. The violent crime rate has similarly fallen from 757.7 per 100,000 inhabitants in 1992 to 454.5 in 2008.

A variability in public reporting helps to explain why police statistics and victim surveys sometimes seem to tell different stories. Against a media backdrop of often misleading concern about rising crime rates, there is some apparently more reassuring but still somewhat conflicting evidence. So, for example, in terms of various forms of child maltreatment and child victimization, Finkelhor and Jones (2006, p. 685) have claimed that they "declined as much as 40–70 percent from 1993 until 2004, including sexual abuse, physical abuse, sexual assault, homicide, aggravated assault, robbery and larceny." More specifically, they assert that "sexual abuse started to decline in the early 1990s, after at least 15 years of steady increases. From 1990 through 2004, sexual abuse substantiations were down 49 percent" (p. 685). The apparent decline is remarkable, and these authors review a wide variety of possible explanations for these changes. They think it is unlikely that there is one particular explanation that will account for all of the declines and, thus, multiple factors probably contributed. Nevertheless, economic prosperity, increasing agents of social intervention, and psychiatric pharmacology emerge as their principal candidates in accounting for the breadth and timing of the improvements. All this, however, is in complete contrast to the doom-laden messages of most contemporary media sources regarding sex crime.

As a response to the increasing public concern that became more pervasive from the 1970s onward, there seemed initially to be few experts around. There were psychiatrists who had traditionally been called on to furnish psychiatric reports to the court, but sex offenders were just a small part of their portfolio. Forensic psychiatry was establishing itself as a subdiscipline (see Rogers and Soothill 2008), but psychiatrists largely lost the opportunity, in the United Kingdom at least, to capture sex offending as an area of special interest. In this respect, there are perhaps differences between the United Kingdom and the United States. Certainly in the United Kingdom psychologists embraced this opportunity to develop their skills and identified sex offending as providing scope for their developing expertise. However, while there may be differences in the influences of the two disciplines between, say, the United Kingdom and the United States, there is no doubt that psychologists have become major players in the area of sex offending. So what has been their impact?

Essentially the arrival of psychology as the pivotal discipline has sharpened up the questions in the specific field of sex offender recidivism. With a focus on behavior and much more emphasis on research and empirical evidence, this approach has essentially narrowed the questions to two issues that are identified as of interest in relation to sex crime recidivism: first, can one predict who will continue with illegal sexual behavior, and, second, can one successfully intervene in preventing such unacceptable sexual behavior in the future?

Blanton and Jaccard (2006, p. 27), among others, insist that "measurement is a cornerstone of psychological research and practice," and Saelens and Glanz (2009, p. S166) widen it to science: "Accurate measurement is a cornerstone of science, with improvements in knowledge intricately dependent on solid instrumentation that is reliable (consistent and repeatable); valid (measuring what it purports to measure); and sensitive to meaningful change." Certainly the arrival of psychology in the specific field of sex offender recidivism has attempted to meet these demands. So, for example, the scientific focus on measurement underpinned a noticeable shift in considering sex offender recidivism from an almost sole reliance on clinical intuition to the use of actuarial measures in predicting risk.

Nevertheless, while there are some fundamental differences in approach, I contend that these disciplines are essentially similar, for psychiatrists and psychologists both tend to individualize social problems. They look for the cause of aggression, for example, within the individual and tend to regard the source of the problems for the individual as often wrapped in some form of psychopathology that certainly cannot explain why there are significant variations in rates of sex offending over time and between societies. In failing to consider broader societal questions, I believe that their approach produces a rather tunneled vision about sex offender recidivism that is shared by both psychiatrists and psychologists. In short, both disciplines focus almost exclusively on behavior, and in that sense, there is no difference between the two disciplines. They make a contribution but without recognizing fundamental changes over time and differences between societies.

However, there are essentially two elements to understanding social activity—in this case, sexual offender recidivism—namely, behavior and systems. Psychiatrists and psychologists tend to focus on the former, whereas sociologists and anthropologists, for instance, focus more on the latter. Systems are, in fact, embedded in a *societal* response to behavior. Societal response can be considered at the informal and formal levels of control. Informal levels of social control operate largely at the familial level, and usually only the more serious forms of deviance are reported to public bodies, such as the police who, among others, operate the more formal levels of social control.

We do not really know the behavior of persons in terms of measuring their social deviance or, in the present case, their sexual offending. We rely on the responses mediated by public bodies as a surrogate measure of a person's social behavior. In various societies there can be very different relationships between behavior and social response from behavior being almost totally hidden by a failure of any sort of social response to behavior being almost totally visible by high social reporting. Not only are there differences between societies but particular societies may vary tremendously over time. Currently, in the search for a gold standard to measure sex offender recidivism, the relevance and importance of a varying social response over both time and place have not been fully recognized. In other words, there are historical trends to understand and different locations to consider. In short, we are now perhaps at a juncture when another significant paradigmatic shift needs to take place.

First, however, we need to review the progress (or lack of progress) over the past 30 years. As table 1 indicated, there has been a vast amount of material published over recent years. Another observation that can be made about table 1 is that five of the 13 papers (i.e., disregarding the Miller et al. [1978] paper on victims) come from two teams: Quinsey and his colleagues, on the one hand, and Hanson and his on the other. These two teams also work together (e.g., Hanson, Gordon, Harris, Marques, Murphy, Quinsey, and Seto 2002), although a set of authors contributing to an article may not necessarily be uniform regarding a full endorsement of any conclusions. Nevertheless, perhaps together these widely cited scholars can be said to represent the current orthodoxy. Their 2002 paper has an optimistic tone following their meta-analysis examining the effectiveness of psychological treatment for sex offenders: "averaged across all studies, the sexual offense recidivism rate was lower for the treatment groups (12.3 percent) than the comparison groups (16.8 percent, 38 studies, unweighted average)" (p. 169). The authors go on to say that "older forms of treatment (operating prior to 1980) appeared to have little effect" (p. 169). In short, the picture currently being offered is different from the prevailing orthodoxy of the late 1970s. In broad terms, in the late 1970s, sex offender recidivism was seen as a relatively minor problem, and criminologists, if pushed—under the prevailing shadow of the Martinson (1974) dictum that "nothing works"—would not offer much hope in terms of avoiding future danger. Today, sex offender recidivism is seen as a major public issue, and following the thrust of the 1990s under the quest of "what works?" (McGuire 1995), there is a modest optimism that change is possible. One needs to explore this shift, which has developed into the prevailing paradigm.

Each decade seems to have a major review specifically on sex offender recidivism (e.g., Furby, Weinrott, and Blackshaw 1989; Hanson and Bussière 1998; Hanson and Morton-Bourgon 2005). The Furby, Weinrott, and Blackshaw review is an important benchmark for it not only summarizes the material to that date but also raises some issues to be considered. The authors conclude their pioneering narrative review with the words, "despite the relatively large number of studies on sex offender recidivism, we know very little about it" (p. 27).

Nevertheless, despite their claim of a paucity of knowledge, Furby, Weinrott, and Blackshaw (1989, p. 27) identified three suggestive trends: "(a) The longer the follow-up period is, the greater is the percentage of men who will have committed another crime (though not necessarily a sex offense). (b) There is as yet no evidence that clinical treatment reduces rates of sex reoffenses in general and no appropriate data for assessing whether it may be differentially effective for different types of offenders. (c) There is some evidence that recidivism rates may be different for different types of offenders."

Furby, Weinrott, and Blackshaw stress that these trends must all be viewed as only tentative conclusions. So what has happened with respect to these "suggestive trends"? In fact, issues *a* and *c* relate to recidivism rates in general and then, more specifically, to whether recidivism rates may be different for different types of offenders. Issue *b* relates to the effectiveness of clinical treatment.

I. Recidivism Rates of Sex Offenders
In the last 20 years the technical competence of researchers (aided by the power of technology) has improved quite remarkably: the designs

TABLE 2

Cumulative Failure Rates for Sexual Offenses over Nine Time Gates

| | Rate at a Given Time Gate | | | | | | | | |
Disposition	1 Year	2 Years	3 Years	4 Years	5 Years	10 Years	15 Years	20 Years	25 Years
Rapists:									
Charge	.09	.12	.15	.17	.19	.26	.31	.36	.39
Conviction	.04	.06	.08	.09	.11	.16	.20	.23	.24
Prison	.04	.06	.07	.08	.10	.14	.17	.19	.19
Child molesters:									
Charge	.06	.10	.14	.17	.19	.30	.39	.46	.52
Conviction	.04	.07	.10	.12	.14	.23	.31	.37	.41
Prison	.04	.07	.09	.11	.13	.21	.28	.33	.37

SOURCE.—Prentky et al. (1997, p. 653).

and the analyses are now often, perhaps usually, sound. However, while the importance of long-term follow-up studies has certainly been recognized in theory, it has not often been matched in practice. Both large numbers and a long-term follow-up are thought to be crucial in the quest for a definitive study about recidivism rates. Although systematic reviews suggest that the observed sexual recidivism rates are only 10–15 percent after 5 years (Hanson and Bussière 1998), the rates continue to increase gradually with extended follow-up periods. The study by Prentky et al. (1997), using a follow-up to 25 years from a treatment center, demonstrated that if they had restricted the follow-up to less than 24 months, they would have missed up to 45 percent of new charges. Even with a 5-year follow-up period, they would still miss 30 percent of the charges they finally identified. In fact, they examined the cumulative failure rates for new charges for sexual offenses only and for new charges of any offense. They used nine time gates, broken down by charge, conviction, and imprisonment. Table 2 shows the recidivism rate for new *sexual* charges.

As table 2 shows, the conviction rates after 1, 5, 10, and 25 years were 4 percent, 11 percent, 16 percent, and 24 percent for rapists; the comparable figures for child molesters were 4 percent, 14 percent, 23 percent, and 41 percent. The work of Prentky and his colleagues provides a very clear case in demonstrating the importance of long-term follow-ups.

However, the results from long-term follow-ups can be contentious. Recently a study by Langevin et al. (2004, p. 550) reported a recidivism rate of 88.3 percent for sex offenders. These investigators considered a total of 351 men (320 sex offenders and 31 violent nonsex offenders) referred for psychiatric assessment or treatment by the court, police, probation and parole services, defense lawyers, or other mental health professionals between 1966 and 1974. They considered the two groups retrospectively on recidivism rates to 1999, that is, over a minimum of 25 years. It is important to understand the measures: "The first arrest, charge or conviction was used as the index marker event, and all subsequent charges or convictions were considered instances of recidivism" (p. 538). A result of an 88.3 percent recidivism rate could well attract considerable media publicity since it seems to confirm popular prejudices about the high recidivism rates of sex offenders.

However, critics of the study have had concerns. For example, Webster, Gartner, and Doob (2006, p. 79), completing a detailed analysis of the study, suggested that "this unusually high level is *uninterpretable* because the offenders whose criminal careers were followed are unlikely to be representative of sex offenders in general." Essentially there is a serious sample selection bias in the study: sex offenders referred for psychiatric assessment or treatment cannot be considered as representative of all sex offenders. Webster, Gartner, and Doob also point to the danger of "pre-selecting a sample of which a substantial proportion were already recidivists" (p. 89). Going back to the sample's *first* conviction does not overcome this problem, for the selection process has simply artificially inflated the reoffending rates.

In a spirited response, Langevin, Curnoe, and Federoff (2006, p. 115) argued that they "have presented one of the few long-term follow-up studies in the world literature," while also acknowledging that "ours is one study from one setting in one country in one time period." Sadly, the response does not meet the fatal flaw of the selection bias. In attempting to identify the recidivism rates of the population (rather than a biased sample) of sex offenders, one must recognize long-term follow-ups as a necessary but not sufficient condition.

Although the challenges of Webster, Gartner, and Doob (2006) are cogent and appropriate on scientific grounds, the claims of Langevin, Curnoe, and Federoff (2006) should not be readily dismissed. It is important to recognize the need to widen outcome measures beyond the traditional one of reconviction and that their emphasis on the *relative* nature of their results highlights that the search for a definitive study on sex offender recidivism is a chimera.

Broadening the outcome measures is a crucial, but also sensitive, task. Because of the low base rate of sexual reconviction for sexual offenders, the appeal for new outcome measures to supplement reconviction rates is now widespread among commentators (e.g., Friendship and Thornton 2001). In their major review, Hanson and Bussière (1998) note that reconviction was used as a criterion in 84 percent of the studies, arrests in 54 percent, parole violations in 16 percent, and self-report only in 25 percent. Not unexpectedly, Falshaw et al. (2003), whose sample consisted of 173 sexual offenders who had completed a sex offender treatment program, display results that show that broadening the outcome measures produces a higher level of offense-related sexual behavior than is reflected by reconviction data. Using reconviction rates calculated from the Offenders Index (which is currently the most common outcome measure used by treatment evaluators in the United Kingdom), they reported a sexual reconviction rate of 3 percent. When they used the Police National Computer (an operational database available only to restricted Home Office personnel), the sexual reconviction rate rose to 9 percent. With unofficial sexual recidivism evidence from other sources, the rate increased to 21 percent. In the United States, Rice et al. (2006, p. 525) have similarly demonstrated that different sources provide different information, and their results, for example, indicated that "police rapsheets (and data based on them) underestimated the number and severity of sexually motivated violent offenses for which sex offenders were actually apprehended." Assessing sources is tedious but essential work in interpreting recidivism rates.

Definitional issues are also crucial. Falshaw et al. (2003, p. 201) usefully distinguish sexual reconviction, sexual reoffending, and sexual recidivism as follows:

Sexual reconviction	A subsequent conviction for a sexual offense
Sexual reoffending	The perpetration of another illegal sexual act (whether caught or not)
Sexual recidivism	The commission of an offense-related behavior, legal or illegal, with a clear sexual motivation

The main concern is about the use of the term "recidivism." These authors note that "there is little consistency in the way this term is used and the specific behavior it refers to" (Falshaw et al. 2003, p. 209).

They remind us that Maltz (1984) noted the use of nine different indicators of recidivism across a total of 90 studies in the United States (i.e., absconding, arrest, incarceration, parole violation, parole suspension, parole revocation, reoffense, reconviction, and probation violation). Maltz was not specifically focusing on sexual recidivism, but outcome measures are even more difficult to interpret in this area.

First, though, I need to highlight a matter of increasing concern in discussing reoffending and recidivism. There is a tendency, particularly in the United States, to accept, for example, arrest figures as a valid measure of sexual offending. Rearrest is a hazard for known sex offenders and is likely to happen on much less evidence than for other members of the population. Without the scrutiny of the court, there is the danger of recidivism rates being inflated by police simply acting on the stereotype of the repeat sex offender.

Trying to measure *sexual* recidivism also produces issues. Normally, legal statutes that categorize sexual offenses (e.g., rape, indecent assault, exhibitionism, etc.) are used. However, some might regard "bigamy," for instance, as more of a deception than a sexual offense, whereas other offenses captured under a "theft" rubric (e.g., stealing ladies' underclothes from an outdoor clothesline) could be regarded as more indicative of a sexual than an acquisitive motivation but are unlikely to be included. Such definitional borderline disputes are legion and well recognized. Less well recognized is that most reconviction studies are based on the principal offense committed. Hence, someone convicted of both murder and rape, for example, is recorded for murder as the principal offense, and the offense of rape is masked.

While there are always methodological issues to confront, the patterns of recidivism rates of sex offenders are becoming evident. In contrast, the picture is less clear about the notion that recidivism rates, however defined, may be different for different types of offenders. This is particularly the case for adults, but there have been some modest developments. Earlier work had already hinted that some types of sex offenders were more likely to commit new sexual crimes than others. Grunfeld and Noreik (1986, p. 102) suggested that "rapists [had] the highest tendency to commit new sexual crimes," while noting that "acts like incest were least likely to be repeated." More recently, Serin, Mailloux, and Malcolm (2001, p. 242) have confirmed that recidivism rates are higher for rapists than for child molesters. Hanson (2002, p. 1046) notes that "rapists were younger than child molesters, and the recidivism risk of rapists steadily decreased with age." Thus, there has certainly been work, mainly in the 1990s, on patterns of recidivism and the type of sexual offender (e.g., Rice, Harris, and Quinsey 1990; Quinsey, Rice, and Harris 1995; Motiuk and Brown 1996; Rice and Harris 1997). Also differences within the same kind of sex offense have been noted: for example, pedophiliac versus nonpedophiliac child molesters (i.e., those with an erotic attachment to children vs. those without an erotic attachment but who may, e.g., be aroused by violence; Hanson and Morton-Bourgon 2005).

In a comparison of the criminal records of the 6,097 males convicted in 1973 in England and Wales of one of four offense categories—indecent assault against a female, indecent assault against a male, indecency between males, and unlawful sexual intercourse (USI) with a girl under 13—over a 32-year observation period, very different patterns emerged. This study (Soothill et al. 2000) showed that each offense group had very different criminality patterns in terms of their likelihood of being convicted of any offense on another occasion—ranging from 37 percent for those convicted of indecency between males to 76 percent for those convicted of USI under 16. These sex offenders were shown to differ greatly in terms of general offending behavior: a *higher* proportion of those committing *heterosexual* offenses (i.e., indecent assault on a female or USI with a girl under 16) tend to be convicted for violence against the person, property offenses, and criminal damage compared with the other two groups; however, a *lower* proportion of these offenders commit *sexual* offenses on other occasions. In contrast, those committing *homosexual* offenses (i.e., indecent assault on a male or indecency between males) are the mirror image. They are much less likely, compared with other sex offenders, to be convicted of violence or property offenses, whereas those committing indecent assault on a male are much more likely to be convicted of sexual offenses on other occasions.

A rather neglected but important topic regarding recidivism is the likelihood of sexual offenders going on to be convicted of homicide, the most serious type of reconviction. Focusing on the 7,442 persons convicted of an indictable sexual offense in England and Wales in 1973, Francis and Soothill (2000) consider subsequent homicides (murder or manslaughter) over a 21-year follow-up period. There were 19 persons who were so convicted—or about one of every 400 sex offenders. Importantly, this contrasts with an estimate of about one person in 3,000 for males in the general population. While differences between various types of sex offenders are considered, the numbers are small. More recently, Sample (2006) similarly considered the popular assumption that sex offenders often kill their victims. In fact, her findings from Illinois data indicated that sex offenders do not frequently commit murder and, more importantly, their homicide rate is no higher than that for other types of offenders.

Since the Furby, Weinrott, and Blackshaw (1989) review, there have been three notable advances in considering recidivism rates. First, there is the recognition that there are female as well as male sex offenders; second, the age variable has begun to be considered in a more sophisticated manner; and, third, it is only in the last decade and a half that there has been a significant focus on sexually abusive juveniles or adolescents.

The prevalence of female sex offending is a moot point. In 1973, for example, of the 7,442 offenders convicted of an indictable sexual offense in England and Wales, only 41 (or 0.006 percent) were females, with these seemingly involved females mostly assisting males (e.g., aiding and abetting rape). More recently the picture has changed with a greater perception that females may, indeed, commit sexual offenses. However, prevalence rates are still hard to come by. Speculation is rife. For example, a recent case attracting widespread media coverage in Britain of a female nursery school teacher convicted of child sex abuse provoked David Findlater, the director of research and development at the child protection charity Lucy Faithfull Foundation, to suggest that "up to 20 percent of a conservative estimate of 320,000 suspected UK paedophiles were women" (*Observer*, October 4, 2009). The newspaper headline announced "Up to 64,000 Women in UK 'Are Child-Sex Offenders.'" Freeman and Sandler (2008, p. 1410) note how the rate of known female perpetrated sexual offenses in the United States increased dramatically from 1994 to 1997. Using statistics from the Center for Sex Offender Management (2000), they report that "female sex offenders accounted for only 1 percent of all rape and sexual assault arrests in 1994, whereas this rate increased to 8 percent in 1997." A more recent report notes that in the United States, "of all adults who come to the attention of the authorities for sex crimes, females account for less than 10 percent of these cases (FBI 2006)" (Center for Sex Offender Management 2007, p. 1).

Freeman and Sandler (2008) rightly note that few studies have empirically validated the widespread belief that female and male sex offenders are vastly different. However, it appears that this assertion is partly true. From a matched series of 780 female and male sex offenders in New York State, their results demonstrated that male sex offenders were significantly more likely than female sex offenders to be rearrested for both sexual and nonsexual offenses. In contrast, however, only limited differences in terms of risk factors between female and male offenders were found. This work usefully builds on some earlier work that had shown some differences between sexes (e.g., Allen 1991; Mathews, Hunter, and Vuz 1997; Miccio-Fonseca 2000; Kubik, Hecker, and Righthand 2002).

Freeman and Sandler's work illustrates the importance of more sophisticated statistical analyses. While the initial binary results suggested numerous differences between female and male sex offenders in terms of offender demographics and offense characteristics, most of these differences disappeared when other risk factors were statistically controlled for. In fact, "only the victim's gender and the type of sexual contact distinguished the two groups of offenders on risk for nonsexual arrest, with these variables being more important for male sex offender general recidivism than for female sex offender general recidivism" (Freeman and Sandler 2008, p. 1409). Consistent with the findings for nonsexual offense rearrest, no significant differences between female and male sex offenders were found for the hazard rate of rearrest for a sexual offense. However, the low base rate of sexual recidivism—only six female offenders were rearrested for a sexual offense—militates against this being a totally convincing finding. Nevertheless, the four variables that emerged as significant predictors of sexual offense rearrest are discussed later.

Moving on and focusing on age has both practical and theoretical implications, and there has been some useful recent work on the age variable. Practical issues have meant that this variable has attracted much attention in the United States. So, for example, there has been much court activity regarding which persons confined as sexually violent predators are safe to be released. Thus, for persons convicted of rape, the age variable is argued by the defense as an important reason that the person is ready to be released. Many of the individuals who have conducted research on this topic have been hired as expert witnesses. So some of the recent focus on age has a particular practical origin.

However, the age variable is also theoretically very relevant, particularly in relation to developmental psychology. For instance, Hanson (2002) identifies three broad factors relevant to sexual offending—deviant sexual interests (motivation), opportunity, and low self-control—and uses these to help explain the variation in the recidivism rates of various offenses. So, he maintains that, for rapists, all three factors should decline with age: "self-control should increase in young adulthood, deviant sexual drives should decrease in late adulthood, and opportunities should gradually decline throughout the life span" (p. 1058). Consequently, Hanson is not surprised that most rapists are young and that their recidivism rate steadily decreases with age. In contrast, in explaining that child molesters are generally older than rapists, he points to competing factors influencing recidivism risk during early to middle adulthood, with, for instance, self-control probably improving, but the opportunities for child molesting may well be increasing.

Thornton (2006, p. 123) has noted that "sexual offenders released at a younger age tended to be more general criminals while those released at an older age tended to be sexual specialists." But Barbaree, Blanchard, and Langton (2003, p. 59), focusing more specifically on sexual recidivism, produce an extra twist. They argue that "if libido [seen as one of the important determinants of sexual aggression] decreases with aging, then it follows that sexual aggression should show similar aging effects." Certainly their results suggested that "offenders released at an older age were less likely to recommit sexual offenses and that sexual recidivism decreased as a linear function of age-at-release" (p. 59).

Following reviews and meta-analyses, the understanding is that there is an inverse relationship between sexual offenders' age at the time of their release from incarceration and their sexual recidivism risk (Hanson and Bussière 1998; Hanson 2002). However, Doren (2006, p. 137) notes some recent challenges to this "iron law": he found a series of "study-specific conclusions . . . that were often mutually exclusive." Reanalysis of existing data showed numerous potential interacting variables, such as participation in treatment, type of risk measure used, type of sexual offender, jurisdiction, and even a different measure of offender age. In other words, to explain the wide disparity of findings among the studies he reviewed, there were perhaps confounding variables in all of the reviewed research. While the age variable is now definitely on the agenda, Doren concludes that "we have a lot of work to do before we can say we understand how to consider offender age in sexual recidivism assessments" (p. 156).

In law and policy the age divide between juveniles and adults is particularly crucial. As with offending by females, the activity of juvenile sex offending has only comparatively recently attracted attention and interest. However, over the past decade or so, sexually abusive juveniles or adolescents have increasingly been distinguished from adult offenders. Worling and Långström (2003) provide a useful and detailed narrative review of studies indicating criminal recidivism risk with adolescents who have offended sexually. I return to this analysis in the next section. However, the amount of material available contrasts markedly with the extensive data for adults.

An important counterweight to a possible concern that juvenile sex offenders are likely to be particularly dangerous is provided by Caldwell (2007). He compared 249 juvenile sex offenders and 1,780 nonsexual-offending delinquents who were released from secured custody and contrasted the sexual recidivism figures for juvenile sexual offenders and nonsexual offenders and found nonsignificant differences—6.8 percent compared to 5.7 percent after a 5-year follow-up. This result has important implications for policy concerns. Quite simply, most juvenile sex offenders may not be the future threat that many might have expected.

The low rates of sexual recidivism among juveniles and adolescents are certainly noteworthy. Vandiver (2006) confirms how nonsexual offenses predominate in recidivism among juvenile sex offenders. She focuses on 300 registered male sex offenders who were juveniles at the time of their initial arrest for a sex offense. The offenders are followed through for 3–6 years after they reached adulthood, and while more than half of them are arrested at least once for a nonsexual offense during this adult period, only 13 (or 4 percent) were rearrested for a sex offense. Similar results are portrayed in Nisbet, Wilson, and Smallbone (2004), showing relatively low rates of detected adult sexual recidivism but high rates of detected nonsexual recidivism among young men who committed sexual offenses as adolescents. Hence, one is identifying relatively stable patterns of general antisocial conduct in adolescent sex offenders, but continuing aberrant *sexual* behavior is not much in evidence. Curiously, with this study, while age at assessment was found to predict sexual recidivism, rather counterintuitively, it was an older age at assessment that predicted adult sexual offense charges:

"the likelihood of being charged with sexual offenses as an adult increased by 60 percent with each year increase in age at assessment" (p. 230). This is an important finding since it confirms that very early sexual crime is generally unlikely to be a precursor to persistent sexual offending in adult life.

To suggest that gender and age issues are all that has advanced in considering recidivism rates would be misleading. There are also other familiar debates that are ongoing. Specialization is one such issue and is a puzzle in criminal careers research (for a recent review, see Soothill, Fitzpatrick, and Francis [2009, chap. 6]). From fictional representations of criminals that we see in films or television or read about in books, we perhaps come to expect criminals to specialize. However, the research evidence on the topic is much more ambivalent. The specialization/versatility debate is currently undergoing a transformation in criminology. What plagues criminology in relation to the specialization debate is the insistence that offenders either specialize or are versatile. Soothill et al. (2000) suggested that they can do both. This becomes understandable when one appreciates that in relation to sex offending (and the argument can be extended to any kind of offending), there are essentially two levels of analysis: analysis of offenders' participation in crime in general and, within their sexual offending career, the analysis of specific kinds of sex offending. At one level, therefore, offenders may or may not specialize within their general criminal career, whereas at a more specific level, they may or may not specialize in specific kinds of sex offending within their sexual criminal career. These two levels may act quite independently: an offender could be a specialist at one level and a generalist at another.

Two examples may help. An offender may be convicted of a wide range of offenses as well as sex offending and so can be regarded as a "generalist" at the more global level. But when he is involved in sexual offending, it is always related to committing indecent assaults against males. In this more specific level he can be regarded as a "specialist" in terms of the type of sexual offending he commits. The opposite may also happen. An offender who commits only sexual offenses can be regarded as a "specialist" in sexual offending at the more global level, but in relation to his sexual offending, he may be involved in a variety of sexual offenses and so can be regarded as a "generalist" at the more specific level.

Only two other possibilities remain. Thus, a person who is convicted only of rape with no evidence of any other types of offenses can be regarded as a "specialist" at both levels, whereas an offender who is involved in two or more types of crime (robbery, sexual offending, fraud, etc.) and also involved in various types of sexual offending can be regarded as a "generalist" at both levels (Soothill, Fitzpatrick, and Francis 2009, p. 117).

Another way of reconciling apparently discrepant findings about specialization and versatility of offending is suggested by McGloin, Sullivan, and Piquero (2009). They propose that offenders may favor certain offense types during the short term, largely because of opportunity structures, but that because of changing situations and contexts over the life course, their offending profiles aggregate to versatility over their criminal career as a whole. There is some modest support for the idea from their own evidence, but the notion has not been considered specifically for sex offending. However, it seems possible that offenders may well have particular sex crime preferences in relatively narrow time periods and then transition to other kinds of behavior over time. It is certainly an idea that needs to be examined.

Interpreting recidivism rates of sex offenders correctly is crucial in understanding the general risk to the public. While there has been much progress in the last 30 years, the intricacies and complexities of the issue have not been grasped by the media that provide a distorted perception of recidivism based on a few sensational cases. In contrast, academic progress has been based on more appropriate methodology. Failing to take into account "time at risk," among other limitations, led to an earlier view that sexual recidivism was comparatively low. This view has been substantially modified, but still there are dangers that flawed designs—based on unrepresentative samples—may exaggerate the risk of sexual recidivism. However, to get the full story, long-term follow-ups remain crucial. Gender and age are variables that are beginning to be understood more fully with the recognition that neither gender nor age is a barrier to committing sex offenses. However, male sex offenders are significantly more likely than female sex offenders to be rearrested for both sexual and nonsexual offenses. The comparatively low rates of sexual recidivism among juveniles and adolescents have perhaps been a surprise, but there are still serious issues to confront. The need for the identification of those most at risk of reoffending—among both juveniles and adults—has created a new criminological industry, which is next discussed.

II. Prediction and Risk Factors

Twenty years after Furby, Weinrott, and Blackshaw (1989), with many more studies completed, is the same refrain of "we know very little" appropriate? Certainly the methodological difficulties have not changed, and with increased ethical constraints and the political imperative for immediate results becoming more demanding, perhaps the problems of producing sound empirical work in this area have multiplied. Nevertheless, the knowledge base has certainly increased. The most notable development has been the focus on prediction and risk factors. Mostly using official records, much progress has been made in trying to predict who is likely to recidivate and in identifying the appropriate risk factors. Already studies have been mentioned that consider these topics, but there still needs to be a separate section to emphasize its importance and to review the progress made. Interestingly, developments in this area have been especially telling in identifying changes of focus over the past few decades. Increasingly, it has been recognized that findings relating to prediction and risk have implications for policy. However, critics would argue that these have been largely atheoretical developments in which attempts to understand social processes have been cast aside. While perhaps harsh, criticisms have perhaps made the proponents of identifying risk factors keener more recently to try to work within a theoretical framework (see, e.g., Farrington 2003).

The references are legion. Nearly one-third of the studies identified in the original search of articles are especially focused on this topic. However, the similarities in the conclusions are somewhat reassuring. In broad terms, it is evident that one can identify that some groups are more likely to recidivate in terms of sexual crime than others. At the individual level, however, there are no certainties and one is trading in uncertainties or, in statistical language, probabilities. It is perhaps in this area that the dangers of trying to become more mathematically precise while overlooking the bigger picture are most evident.

The focus on risk factors and subsequent sex offense recidivism is part of a development in criminology that can be summarized as "Developmental Criminology and Risk-Focused Prevention."[2] Farrington has emerged as a pivotal player in risk-focused prevention on both sides

---

[2] This is, in fact, the title of David Farrington's chapter in the authoritative *Oxford Handbook of Criminology*, which usefully summarizes the body of knowledge in the area of risk-focused prevention (Farrington 2002).

of the Atlantic. His coedited volume (Farrington and Coid 2003) use-fully reviews important childhood risk and protective factors for a range of crime and other antisocial behavior, but sex offender recidi-vism is absent from the index. Criminologists have tended to focus on high-frequency and low-seriousness crimes, and there has been much less focus on serious and rarer crime (i.e., low-frequency and high-seriousness crimes), which can, indeed, be very threatening to the vic-tim. Hence, an important question is whether much of the material on more general risk factors is, in fact, relevant to the particular focus of sex offending.

While theorists have pointed to a variety of factors that are associ-ated with the *development* of sexual offending (Ward and Siegert 2002; Knight and Sims-Knight 2003; Malamuth 2003), *persistence* in sexual offending may be a different matter. So, while, as Hanson and Morton-Bourgon (2005, p. 1158) point out, negative family backgrounds and internalization of psychological problems are common among sexual offenders (Smallbone and Dadds 1998; Raymond et al. 1999; Lee et al. 2002), these factors are unrelated to sexual recidivism. Further, as Hanson and Bussière (1998) indicate in their earlier review, sexual of-fenders are more likely to reoffend with a nonsexual offense than with a sexual offense. As Freeman and Sandler (2008, p. 1404) show in their carefully analyzed study comparing recidivism patterns and risk factors for female and male sex offenders, only four variables emerged as sig-nificant predictors of time to rearrest for a *nonsexual* offense: number of prior drug offenses, number of prior violent felony offense arrests, number of prior incarceration terms, and offender's age at the time of the registerable sex offense arrest. There is nothing surprising about any of these variables, and with minor variations, similar risk factors for a subsequent nonsexual offense are likely to emerge for any group of offenders. The crucial question in relation to considering persistence is whether "the predictors of sexual recidivism are substantially differ-ent from the predictors of nonsexual recidivism" (p. 1155).

Hanson and Morton-Bourgon (2005), following a meta-analysis of 82 recidivism studies, identified deviant sexual preferences and anti-social orientation/lifestyle instability as the major predictors of sexual recidivism for both adult and adolescent sexual offenders. Not sur-prisingly, following mainstream work on risk factors, antisocial orien-tation (which refers to antisocial personality, antisocial traits—such as impulsivity, substance abuse, unemployment—and a history of rule violation) was the major predictor of violent recidivism and general (i.e., any) recidivism. In contrast, deviant sexual preferences refer to "enduring attractions to sexual acts that are illegal (e.g. sex with children, rape) or highly unusual (e.g. fetishism, autoerotic asphyxia)" (p. 1154). In brief, sexual deviancy was related to sexual recidivism but unrelated to nonsexual recidivism. However, in operationalizing the variables related to sexual recidivism, there was some considerable variability, and Hanson and Morton-Bourgon note that "such variability suggests that further research is needed to uncover those aspects of attitudes and social functioning most associated with persistent sexual offending" (p. 1158). While these authors greatly extend the range of variables that need to be considered, they also make the prudent call that "the predictive accuracy of most of the characteristics was small" (p. 1159). They also remind us that the task of combining risk factors into a useful overall evaluation remains an active topic of scientific debate (Berlin et al. 2003; Hanson, Morton, and Harris 2003).

Increasingly, authors distinguish between static historical factors (e.g., offense history), which cannot be changed, and dynamic risk factors, which can be changed. Hanson and Morton-Bourgon (2005, p. 1155) note that the latter are also called "criminogenic needs" (Andrews and Bonta 2003), "stable dynamic risk factors" (Hanson and Harris 2000), or "causal psychological risk factors" (Beech and Ward 2004). Hanson and Harris usefully distinguish between stable dynamic factors and acute dynamic factors: "stable dynamic risk factors are expected to remain unchanged for months or years (e.g. alcoholism). . . . In contrast, acute dynamic factors, such as alcohol intoxication or negative mood, change rapidly (days, hours, and even minutes)" (2000, p. 7). Cortoni (2009) has recently produced a useful review of static and dynamic factors, but the review applies only to adult male sex offenders.

The shift of interest toward dynamic factors usefully provides a link with treatment or intervention that should be associated with change in some form. Hanson and Harris (2000) suggest that interventions aimed at creating enduring improvements need to target *stable* dynamic factors, whereas *acute* dynamic risk factors are simply related to the timing of reoffending and so, they contend, may have little relationship to long-term risk potential. In contrast, static risk factors simply indicate what one is up against and tend to encourage pessimism rather than optimism. To use another analogy, someone born in poverty (a static factor that cannot be changed) seems unlikely to be a promising candidate to become a wealthy capitalist, and to labor the point, this fact is hardly encouraging for the candidate. However, to point to more dynamic factors in his or her situation—that is, things that can be changed, such as providing the opportunity for education—seems to chart a more promising journey. A current debate that is relevant to sex offending is the question of genetic and environmental factors.

Genetic factors are essentially historical risk factors that cannot—at least with the current state of genetic technology—be changed after birth, but environmental factors can. Most commentators nowadays recognize that many behavioral characteristics are the outcome of the interaction of genetic and environmental factors. Certainly the crucial ingredient for future trouble seems to be—for example, in relation to conduct disorder—the combination of a genetic predisposition and a high-risk environment (Viding, Larsson, and Jones 2008). Understanding the possible interaction effects is important. In terms of conduct disorder, what seems to be emerging is that a low-risk environment may well moderate an adverse genetic predisposition. This point is highly relevant to the notion of change. While to date one cannot do much about changing the genetic component, the environmental component is open to change. In other words, genetic risk can be effectively moderated by environmental intervention and leads to such prescriptions as proposing that "at-risk families should be monitored and helped regardless of the child's or parent's genotype" (Viding, Larsson, and Jones 2008, p. 2524). None of this evidence to date has been related to sex offending, but the reasoning is important to grasp. The possibility of an interaction between historical factors (which cannot be changed) and dynamic factors (which can) needs to be probed.

The distinction between static and dynamic factors is not new to criminology, and to support the contention of the potential importance of dynamic factors, one can point to empirical work on nonsexual criminals, which suggests that dynamic risk factors predict recidivism as well as or better than static, historical variables (Gendreau, Little, and Goggin 1996; Zamble and Quinsey 1997). Gerhold, Browne, and Beckett (2007) point to some static or historical risk variables that could be found to be linked to sexual recidivism in adolescents, such as previous offending and multiple or stranger victims. However, they found that there is much less documented evidence relating to dynamic variables, possibly owing to a lack of appropriate psychometric tools to measure such variables. Sensibly and cautiously, Hanson and Harris (2000) recognize that "the dynamic risk factors that predict general criminal recidivism may not predict sexual offense recidivism" (p. 7). Nevertheless, this is a promising avenue to explore. Certainly the notion that sexual recidivism is predicted by unique factors unrelated to general (nonsexual) reoffending becomes important when deciding on the nature of clinical treatment.

In focusing on the use of static versus dynamic factors, Beech and Ford (2006) showed that it was generally men who were rated as a high level of dynamic risk that were reconvicted for a sexual offense (13 percent vs. 5 percent over a 2-year period; 44 percent vs. 10 percent over a 5-year period).

The case for some risk factors is more convincing than for others. Worling and Långström (2003), identifying which risk factors for sexual offending are supported by the evidence, go on to present other risk factors as promising candidates, possible factors, and, finally, unlikely ones. Their focus is on the assessment of criminal recidivism risk among adolescents who have offended sexually, and some examples will illustrate the different levels of acceptance of these various risk factors. Thus, supported risk factors for sexual reoffending include deviant sexual interests, prior criminal sanctions for sexual assault, past sexual offenses against two or more victims, and so on. Promising candidates include problematic parent-adolescent relationships or parental rejection and attitudes supportive of sexual offending. Possible risk factors for sex offending include a high-stress environment, obsessive sexual interests or preoccupation, impulsivity, a selection of a male victim, and, among many others, negative peer associations and influences. Finally, among unlikely risk factors for sexual reoffending, Worling and Långström cite denial of the sexual offense, lack of victim empathy, a history of nonsexual crimes, and penetrative sexual assaults. Certainly the article provides an important challenge to some available checklists and guidelines where the varying empirical support for risk factors is not discussed.

There are some surprises. So, for instance, listing the selection of a male victim as only a *possible* risk factor for sexual reoffending merits discussion. Worling and Långström (2003) argue that "although the research supporting the use of this factor with adults is clear . . . , the findings for adolescents are mixed" (p. 349). This leads to the recognition that predictors for adolescents may differ somewhat from those found for adults. Miner (2002) points specifically to an increased risk for reoffense among juveniles being associated with impulsivity, involvement with significantly younger children, and a younger age at first offense, whereas decreased risk for reoffense was associated with having a male victim, having been a sexual abuse victim, and suffering multiple paraphilias. As a consequence, Miner (2002) suggests his data indicate that risk prediction methods used for adult sex offenders are not appropriate for adolescent populations. However, there are also risk factors that are similar. For example, Gretton et al. (2001) found that psychopathy may have much the same implications for the criminal justice system in adolescent offenders as it does in adult offenders.

As with adult offenders, some scholars have stressed the importance of identifying subgroups among juvenile sex offenders. Worling (2001) produced a four-group typology based solely on personality functioning—antisocial/impulsive, unusual/isolated, overcontrolled/reserved, and confident/aggressive—which is suggestive of differential etiological pathways and treatment needs and so usefully demonstrates that adolescent sexual offenders are not a homogeneous group. However, Worling reports that "although there were no significant differences between groups with respect to sexual assault recidivism specifically, the two relatively more pathological groups, Antisocial/Impulsive and Unusual/Isolated offenders, were most likely to have been charged with a subsequent violent (sexual or nonsexual) or non-violent offense after a mean follow-up period of 6 years" (p. 161).

While the earlier claim that the focus has been largely on outcome rather than process can be sustained, the study of process certainly emerges in Ward and Hudson's (1998, 2000) and Webster's (2005) work when they consider the former's self-regulation model of relapse in sexual offenders, which classifies offenders into one of four pathways. As Webster stresses, "the offence-specific nature of the model is a clear strength, allowing clinicians to tailor offenders' treatment targets to their specific pathways" (p. 1192). While the interview data did not always elicit a predominant pathway, the use of more qualitative material is a welcome approach.

More and more potential risk factors are being brought into play. Soothill, Francis, and Liu (2010), for example, stress the importance of co-convictions in making predictions. Co-convictions are, for these authors, multiple offenses resulting in convictions at the same court appearance. Taking the two serious crimes of blackmail and kidnapping, they show that co-convictions provided extra explanatory power in predicting the risk of a subsequent sexual or violent offense for both of these offenses. They conclude that co-convictions are a useful measure of short-term specialization and are potentially important additional predictors of serious recidivism.

There are other important topics that are very much part of the criminal careers literature but seem rarely to have been addressed in relation to sex offending. One such is the notion of escalation—defined as "a measure of how an offender's criminal career increases in seriousness" (Soothill, Fitzpatrick, and Francis 2009, p. 5)—and has obvious importance in terms of policy initiatives in which the focus should perhaps be directed toward offenders who are likely to escalate into serious sexual offending. MacPherson (2003) has usefully focused on this issue in attempting to provide the clinician with a structured clinical assessment procedure that offers the potential for early detection of noncontact sex offenders whose offending behavior may escalate toward sexual violence. His study suggests that a progressive pattern of sex offending from noncontact sex offending to contact sex offending seems to be reliably associated with a combination of risk factors. These factors are primarily historical in nature, reflecting fixed or relatively stable characteristics. Certainly there seems scope in both replicating this study and probing further in terms of its implications.

While more and more risk factors come into play, some that have had an interest and a momentum in the past have not necessarily retained a high profile more recently. Psychiatric diagnosis is one example that partly reflects the decline of psychiatrists and the rise of psychologists as the main players in this area. Among psychiatrists, psychiatric diagnoses would routinely be regarded as important. Such an interest is less evident now. Indeed, in the United States the laws have intentionally omitted diagnosis as a concept of merit. Nevertheless, Långström, Sjostedt, and Grann (2004) present a large study, which in itself is unusual, from Sweden, which involved all adult male sexual offenders released from Swedish prisons in 1993–97. Essentially, their findings endorse the meta-analysis of Hanson and Bussière (1998) in that an increased risk of sexual recidivism in sexual offenders diagnosed with psychosis was suggested. However, in their study, alcohol use disorder and personality disorder were both associated with risk for sexual as well as violent nonsexual recidivism. Certainly, this study suggested a much more important role for alcohol use disorder in predicting recidivism. However, this may be the outcome of a hospital admission sample that, thus, identified subjects with severe substance misuse. Nevertheless, perhaps the most important feature of this study is a reminder of the comparatively low rates of psychiatric morbidity among sexual offenders: "substance use disorders, personality disorders, and psychoses diagnosed during admission to hospital up to 10 years before the onset of registered sexual offending, were found among 1.4–7.8 percent in an unselected cohort of sexual offenders sentenced to imprisonment" (Långström, Sjostedt, and Grann 2004, p. 148).

The importance of psychiatry continues to be challenged in another way and emerges in work on the familiar old chestnut—the accuracy of clinical evaluations and risk assessment instruments. The comparison is essentially between clinical judgments and actuarial risk measures. Actuarial measures use summary measures of criminal career data on a large set of offenders together with other information about the age, gender, and circumstances of the offender to produce a risk score. The offenders are followed up for the required period of time, and each offender is then identified as a recidivist or not. The risk score estimate is made through the application of statistical modeling methods such as logistic regression or other score-building models (Soothill, Fitzpatrick, and Francis 2009, p. 126). Clinical risk assessment, however, takes the judgment of professionals, such as psychiatrists or probation officers, to make a relatively informal judgment on the likelihood of an offender to reoffend. Although these professionals will have access to the same information on past criminal history, they may also take into account a whole set of personal factors such as the degree of remorse, demeanor, family support, and so forth to determine risk (Milner and Campbell 1995).

There has been much debate as to which of these approaches gives better predictions. An important study by Grove and Meehl (1996) seemed largely to resolve the dilemma. They took 136 separate studies (not necessarily relating to sex offending)—a mix of clinical and actuarial studies. In general, the clinical studies had a great deal more information available than the actuarial studies. Their study showed that there was little agreement between practitioners and that, despite using less information, the actuarial studies were either equal or superior to clinical risk assessment.

However, more recently, there have been some criticisms of the actuarial approach (e.g., Quinsey et al. 1998, chap. 9). In brief, while actuarial risk measures can categorize whole groups of individuals into various risk categories, the knowledge of personal circumstances can, for instance, mean that an apparently low-risk individual should, for a while at least, be in a higher risk category. Also actuarial risk measures focus on the individual to the exclusion of other causes of crime, notably economic and social deprivation (Young 1999). Actuarial measures do provide a fairly robust and reliable estimate of risk and are increasingly used in daily criminal practice. However, Woods and Lasiuk (2008) suggest that for dangerous offenders, current practice relies increasingly on some combination of a structured clinical judgment and actuarial measures. This is also the conclusion of Craig, Beech, and Harkins (2009), who report on the accuracy of various risk frameworks.

Much is now known about the predictive efficacy of various risk factors, but some say that "the state of the art of risk assessment for sex offenders is still in its infancy" (Veysey and Zgoba 2009, p. 3). There is still much more to do in terms of clarifying whether risk factors hold in different places and at different times. Prediction scores need to be continually revalidated; new variables may need to be considered and old variables reevaluated. Veysey and Zgoba have developed an interesting study comparing sex offenders released before and after the implementation of Megan's Law. While many criminal history variables successfully predicted sexual recidivism for both pre– and post–Megan's Law samples, they found that the two samples each had a unique set of predictors as well: "predictors of pre–Megan's Law recidivists revolved around relationship/employment variables, whereas predictors of post–Megan's Law recidivists were commonly related to behavioral health issues" (2010, p. 594). Identifying that there are some changes in risk variables over time is an important first step; understanding why there are such changes is ultimately the more crucial issue theoretically, but this has not yet been fully addressed.

To conclude this section, one can say unequivocally that there has been considerable progress in identifying potential risk among sex offenders. The importance of gender and age is being more fully understood. Other risk factors have been usefully evaluated. Hanson and Morton-Bourgon's (2005) authoritative review notes that "there was substantial consistency within many of the categories of predictors" (p. 1159), but there is still a sense that the work is dealing with a higher level of generality than is appropriate. In other words, the meta-analyses largely focus on a mixed group of sexual offenders, and there is little effort to identify specific predictors for subgroups, such as rapists or exhibitionists. Of course, there is no theoretical objection to doing so, but meta-analyses need studies to analyze. Currently the cupboard seems fairly bare in relation to this level of specialization.

While the prediction industry in sex crime research has produced a rich seam of results, rich seams will eventually be exhausted. Some researchers will continue to seek the philosopher's stone of trying to iron out uncertainties into certainties. In fact, at best, the group of "certainties" about who will commit sexual crime in the future will be very small, and for most offenders, the uncertainties will remain. While there will always be sufficient work to do to keep a core set of researchers busy in this area of research, the crucial question for the future is in identifying where the main area of investment needs to be.

One can, for instance, usefully recognize that there is a link between identifying risk factors and moving toward effective intervention. As Hanson and Harris (2000, p. 6) stress, effective intervention with sexual offenders requires the targeting of appropriate risk factors. The effectiveness of treatment and other interventions is the next major issue to be addressed.

III. The Effectiveness of Clinical Treatment and Other Interventions

As Brooks-Gordon and Bilby (2006), among others, have stressed, there is enormous political and institutional pressure to prove that treatment works. Yet, as Scalora and Garbin (2003, p. 309) note, the impact of treatment involvement and subsequent recidivism is given limited attention in comparison to other forensic mental health issues. Of course, in trying to answer such a question, there is a need for a consideration of what treatment might involve and to decide what is an appropriate measure of effectiveness. For the latter it is important to build on the earlier discussion of an understanding of recidivism rates. The familiar approach is to focus on reconviction rates. If so, what type(s) of reconviction should be considered? Broadhurst and Maller (1992) maintain that "the evaluation of interventions should proceed on the estimates of violent rather than repeat offending" (p. 54). Widening the range of outcome measures is certainly relevant in terms of considering effectiveness.

Nevertheless, whatever the measure, the pessimism of "no evidence" of clinical treatment effectiveness in the 1970s has, as already stated, moved to a guarded optimism of "some evidence." So what is the basis of this revised claim? Certainly there are more studies, but the evidence for a strong claim, either for or against, is not always compelling.

First, however, a comment about the phrase "the effectiveness of clinical treatment," for this issue is a subset of the broader question of whether one can successfully intervene in any way. In thinking about interventions, one needs to have a fuller conception in recognizing that some form of intervention usually occurs when an inappropriate sexual act comes to notice. The reaction can range from no response to bringing the behavior to public notice.

More usually, the focus has been on the most serious outcome when inappropriate sexual behavior comes to *public* notice, namely, incarceration. Incarceration is often touted by the media as the most appropriate response. What difference, if any, does such an imposition make in the long term? Nunes et al. (2007, pp. 305–6) come out strongly that "sentencing sexual offenders to terms of incarceration seems to have little, if any, impact on sexual and violent recidivism following release." However, punishment tends to have retributionist and deterrent as well as rehabilitative aims. Hence, long sentences are likely to continue even if such sentences have no deterrent or rehabilitative effect.

Having said that, one needs to recognize that long-term studies of cohorts of sex offenders released from prison demonstrate a wide range of outcomes. Broadhurst and Maller (1992) also cast some light on this issue focusing, in particular, on the human and economic costs of preventive incapacitation, concluding that "the solution offered by either categorical or selective incapacitation turns out to be a very costly one once enumerated, and once the limits of predictive methods are understood" (p. 76).

There are a vast range of other types of disposal that are available for sex offenders, just as there are for any type of offender. Some disposals, such as awarding a probation order with a condition of psychiatric treatment (either as in-patient or out-patient)—which in England and Wales was introduced by the Criminal Justice Act 1948—would be available for any offender but was much more freely used for sex offenders, particularly in the 1950s. More recently, there has been the introduction of various forms of sex offender registration and notification laws that are specific for sex offenders. All these are interventions, and the question of their effectiveness is an appropriate one. I return to these after considering the issue of clinical treatment.

Meta-analyses performed by Hall (1995) on 12 studies of treatment with sexual offenders ($n = 1,313$) found a small overall effect size for treatment versus comparison conditions ($r = .12$). The overall recidivism rate for treated sexual offenders was .19 versus .27 for untreated sexual offenders and, thus, gives the scale of the difference. Interestingly, the treatment effect sizes varied quite substantially across studies. Hall reported that effect sizes were larger in studies that had higher base rates of recidivism and had follow-up periods longer than 5 years. He maintains that cognitive-behavioral and hormonal treatments were significantly more effective than behavioral treatments.

As Marshall and Marshall (2007, p. 191) remind, "Harris, Quinsey, and Rice (Harris, Rice, and Quinsey 1998; Rice and Harris 1997, 2003) claim that the only basis upon which to conclude that sexual offender treatment is effective, or not, is evidence from a series of RCT studies." In fact, they point out how government officials and representatives of funding agencies (Breiling 2005) have embraced the notion that the gold standard design for treatment outcome evaluations is the random controlled trial (RCT). In short, an RCT is considered the most reliable form of scientific evidence because it eliminates all forms of spurious causality. Subjects are allocated to treatments at random to ensure that the different treatment groups are "statistically equivalent" (Soothill, Rogers, and Dolan 2008, pp. 597–98). However, the RCT is a good experimental design only in some circumstances. Grossman and Mackenzie (2005) examine some of the limitations of RCTs, particularly in terms of implementation, and, thus, RCTs cannot be considered as always superior to all other types of evidence. Marshall and Marshall (2007) go further and conclude after examining the scientific, practical, and ethical issues surrounding the use of RCTs that "the RCT design is not suitable for determining the effectiveness of sexual offender treatment" (p. 175). No one would dispute their conclusion that "the field is in dire need of more published reports evaluating treatment effectiveness with sexual offenders" (pp. 187–88). While there is no doubt that, in measuring effectiveness, RCTs do provide the most convincing evidence, the problem lies in when this technique is not possible or is not appropriate. Marshall and Marshall provide two alternative strategies for evaluating treatment that should certainly be considered.

In a powerful response, 10 of the leading researchers in this field combine to rebut Marshall and Marshall with the apparently innocuous assertion that "only good science can inform good clinical practices" (Seto et al. 2008, p. 253). The sting in the tail is what is good science. Currently there is a range of view from Marshall and Marshall challenging the efficacy of the RCT design in this field to others who come close to saying that the RCT design is the only design worth considering. Clearly there will be lively methodological debates in the future.

As Tyrer et al. (2009, p. 141) stress, randomized trials are rare in forensic and prison settings, and these authors point out both the advantages and disadvantages "of this ideal form of evaluation of an intervention." However, the insistence on the RCT has been both helpful and harmful. It has been helpful in providing a standard by which measuring the success of intervention can be scientifically assessed. But it has also been harmful in at least two ways. First, it has encouraged a focus on outcome rather than on process. This is neither necessary nor inevitable but is what has happened. In short, there has been a focus on whether there has been a difference between two or more groups rather than on the explanation or description of the process. Second, this focus on intervention being measured only by an RCT has encouraged a rather narrow conception of "intervention." This has perhaps gone unnoticed but is crucial. "Intervention" is generally interpreted as "clinical treatment" in the sense of involving *individuals* in a treatment program. While, of course, such results are important and relevant, particularly for the burgeoning "intervention industry," the study of interventions should have a much wider currency. It is as though the contribution of marriage guidance counselors in preventing divorce is the most important factor in assessing the likelihood of changing the divorce rate. One can develop carefully constructed studies to assess the impact of marriage guidance counselors, but in a society the real action in producing a lower or higher divorce rate is probably taking place elsewhere. Indeed, the institution of marriage means different things in different societies, and there are also changes within a particular society over time that may contribute to different divorce rates. While divorce may often be used as a surrogate measure of an unsuccessful marriage, there are many unsuccessful relationships that do not end in divorce. In short, the analogy is being used to suggest that considering clinical treatment in isolation is rather limit-ing. In fact, there are other approaches. Drake and Aos (2009), for instance, in their meta-analysis on registration/notification identify studies that are aimed at the larger social policy level and are poten-tially much more powerful than the studies about sex offender treat-ment.

Nevertheless, the recent focus has certainly been on RCTs, with commentators often bemoaning the lack of such trials. However, Brooks-Gordon and Bilby (2006), in conducting a meta-analysis on the effects of psychological interventions in relation to sex offending, re-ported that they "found nine trials that were well conducted in terms of randomisation, blinding, loss to follow-up and analysis" (p. 5). These included RCTs with a total of 567 male offenders, 231 of whom were followed up for a decade. The results indicated that "studies on be-havioral treatments were too small to be informative, although statis-tically significant improvements were recorded across some groups of offenders" (Brooks-Gordon, Bilby, and Wells 2006a, p. 60). In short, behavioral treatments for sex offenders have at best only a modest effect on recidivism. There is further doubt of its efficacy increasing when follow-up periods are longer (Brooks-Gordon, Bilby, and Wells 2006a). In a further systematic review on psychological interventions with adult sexual offenders, providing the results of quasi-experimental and qualitative research in this area, the research found 21 studies meeting the criteria for inclusion. Of these, seven studies found sig-nificant effects and 10 revealed no significant effects (Brooks-Gordon, Bilby, and Wells 2006b). There remains the contention about what is the most appropriate treatment. Gordon and Grubin (2004) point to a combination of cognitive behavioral therapy and antilibido medica-tion as "probably the best option in the case of at least some sex of-fenders" (Gordon 2009, p. 169). However, the message about treat-ments has not been a clear and consistent one.

Lösel and Schmucker (2005) report a meta-analysis on controlled outcome evaluations of sexual offender treatment. There is broadly an optimistic message, for despite a wide range of positive and negative effect sizes, the majority of studies confirmed the benefits of treat-ment. In sum, they announce that "treated offenders showed 6 per-centage points or 37 percent less sexual recidivism than controls. Effects for violent and general recidivism were in a similar range" (p. 117). Interestingly, organic treatments (surgical castration and hormonal medication) were reported as showing larger effects than psychosocial interventions. Of the psychological programs, cognitive-behavioral approaches showed the most robust effect. Their methodological discussions are important. An interesting observation, in attempting to explain why small studies seem to reveal a larger effect size than large studies, points to a publication bias, with small studies needing a larger effect size to impress editorial decision makers. Their final demand is that "we need more high-quality outcome studies that address *specific subgroups* of sex offenders as well as more detailed *process* evaluations on various treatment characteristics and components" (p. 138; emphasis added).

In their most recent review Hanson and his colleagues (2009) make a useful contribution in two ways: first, they try to bring treatment for sex offenders into the mainstream of treatment for general offenders and, second, they consider a particular type of treatment. They focus specifically on whether the principles associated with effective treatments for general offenders (risk-need-responsivity: RNR) also apply to sexual offender treatment. Twenty-three recidivism outcome studies met their basic criteria for study quality. The recidivism rates for the treated sexual offenders were lower than the rates observed for the comparison groups for both sexual recidivism (10.9 percent against 19.2 percent) and any recidivism (31.8 percent vs. 48.3 percent). Interestingly, again the importance of treatment quality emerged, with "programs that adhered to the RNR principles [showing] the largest reductions in sexual and general recidivism" (p. i).

In an early study following the Furby, Weinrott, and Blackshaw (1989) review, Rice, Quinsey, and Harris (1991) indicated that "behavioral treatment did not affect recidivism" (p. 381) in relation to a series of child molesters released from a maximum security psychiatric institution. Quinsey et al. (1998) argued that treatment with sexual offenders is largely ineffective. The work of Hanson et al. (2009) is responding to this challenge. There have also been other responses. So, for example, Looman, Abracen, and Nicholaichuk (2000), attempting to improve the methodology of Quinsey et al.'s study, compared the outcome for 89 sexual offenders treated at the Regional Treatment Centre (Ontario) and 89 untreated sexual offenders matched for pretreatment risk. With an average time at risk of 10.3 years for members of the treated group and 9.7 years for members of the untreated group, the treated group had a sexual recidivism rate of 23.6 percent, whereas the untreated group had a sexual recidivism rate of 51.7 percent ($p <$ .0001). This is such an impressive difference that one asks about challenges to this methodology. The authors note that a possible criticism is that the treatment and comparison groups were selected from different regions of Canada, hence raising the question of whether there are different types of offenders found in the different regions. The problem is that the investigators had to use a comparison group from another region since there would have been a selection bias if one assessed offenders from the same region. While future studies must consider in such circumstances perhaps having comparison groups from, say, two regions, the results from this study remain fairly convincing. So what is the secret of this apparent success?

This program is the oldest continuously run sexual offender treatment program offered by the Correctional Service of Canada, and Looman, Abracen, and Nicholaichuk (2000) describe some enhancements to the program over time. Curiously, the study does not seem to discuss whether earlier series members (with treatments prior to the enhancements to the program and with longer periods at risk) fared any better or worse than later members of the series. Certainly quality of treatment is being touted as a crucial variable, and so a further follow-up of the Looman study—if treatment enhancements are proving effective—should show even better results. In fact, elsewhere, multivariate analysis suggests that recidivism is significantly related to quality of treatment involvement (and other variables). Scalora and Garbin (2003), for example, focus on this issue, but it is still not clear whether the impact on recidivism "is due to treatment effectiveness or to higher risk offenders' being more likely to be terminated from intervention" (p. 319). Hence, while promising, the methodological jury is still out.

Some studies have warned of being too complacent following good treatment behavior. In this respect Seto and Barbaree's (1999) oft-cited article is important, for the results are counterintuitive. In fact, the results "did not support the notion that good treatment behavior, defined in terms of positive and appropriate behavior in group sessions, good homework assignments, and positive ratings of motivation and overall change, would be associated with better outcomes" (p. 1244). More specifically, it was found that men who scored higher in psychopathy and who behaved well in treatment were more likely to commit a new offense of some kind and were also much more likely to commit a new serious offense. To explain this finding, Seto and Barbaree suggest that the measure of treatment behavior identified a subset of offenders who were always socially skillful and good at manipulation or that they actually learned skills in treatment that increased the risk for serious recidivism. They note that the latter interpretation is consistent with data from program evaluations that suggest participating in sex offender treatment may increase risk for sexual recidivism, perhaps by exposure to sexually deviant material or by learning about others' modi operandi (Quinsey et al. 1998). These reservations about the involvement of psychopaths in treatment must be seen against the claims of others, with caveats, that psychopaths may respond to treatment with carefully constructed behavioral interventions (e.g., Templeman and Wollersheim 1979; Doren 1987; Newman, Kosson, and Patterson 1992; Hart and Hare 1997; Rice and Harris 1997).

A crucial question is whether changing dynamic factors is actually associated with reductions in sexual recidivism risk. As McGrath, Cumming, and Burchard (2003, p. 1159) indicate, "most programs direct considerable resources toward characteristics that have little or no relationship with recidivism (e.g. offense responsibility, victim awareness, and empathy)." The jury is still out whether programs that target the major predictors of sexual offense recidivism (e.g., lifestyle instability, deviant sexual interests, sexual preoccupations) are actually more effective. In other words, the possible links between identifying risk factors and effective interventions mentioned earlier need to be more carefully explored.

A major change in the last decade or so is the increased interest in what happens to the sex offender in the community. Certainly, for the United States at least, there is a developing body of research on the effects of registration and community notification (Drake and Aos 2009). At one end of the scale this focus has led to severely restrictive conditions for sex offenders in the community that seem to be akin to a punitive reaction, but there has also been interest in producing a more supportive environment for sex offenders in the community that appeals more to a rehabilitative ideal. In a Canadian study (Wilson et al. 2000), the outcome of a community-based sexual offender management protocol combining parole supervision and relapse prevention treatment suggested that valid risk assessment, in combination with a well-defined supervision strategy, is an effective method for the management of sexual recidivism in the community. However, the results are assessed only in relation to those reported at other treatment sites, and this is not a tightly controlled study.

Over the past decade and a half there has been a remarkable rise in community schemes that attempt to monitor the activities of sex offenders after conviction or caution. In most contexts, "it does seem difficult to see it as other than an extension of the offender's punishment" (Soothill and Francis 1998, p. 285). In England and Wales, the enabling act—Sex Offenders Act 1997—focuses on the requirement that certain ex-offenders notify the police of their names and addresses and any subsequent changes to these. While further constraints have come into place, there seems to be little or no systematic research into the effectiveness (or lack of effectiveness) of these new procedures. In contrast, in the United States, where a diversity of practices under the general rubric of sex offender registration/notification laws have until recently been adopted, there has been some attempt to evaluate the effectiveness of these schemes in reducing crime.

In a systematic review Drake and Aos (2009) identified nine rigorous evaluations. Seven of these studies address whether the laws influence "specific" deterrence—that is, the effect on the recidivism rates of convicted sex offenders. The other two studies analyze "general" deterrence—that is, the effect on sex offense rates of the general public, as well as the recidivism rates of convicted sex offenders.

Regarding specific deterrence, the evidence suggests that the laws have had no statistically significant effect on recidivism, whereas for general deterrence, two studies provide some indication that registration laws lower sex offense rates in the public at large. The two studies (Prescott and Rockoff 2008; Shao and Li 2006) on the latter issue are insufficient for a meta-analysis. However, Prescott and Rockoff, analyzing the effect of the laws in 15 states, suggest that "the average registration/notification law produces a statistically significant 10 percent reduction in sex offense rates" (Drake and Aos 2009, p. 5). In the second unpublished study, Shao and Li use UCR panel data for all 50 states from 1970 to 2002 to investigate the impact of registration laws on reported rapes to police. Drake and Aos report that "Shao and Li find a statistically significant negative relationship between registration and reported rapes. The magnitude of their estimate is a 2 percent reduction in reported rapes" (p. 5). The reviewers suggest that "the methodological rigor of Shao and Li's design is . . . very high quality" (p. 5) with sophisticated statistical controls for many factors, but there apparently seems little recognition that reporting rape may vary dramatically over time, and it may be an unreliable surrogate for the actual behavior of rape over time. In short, in terms of probing the effectiveness of these more recent types of intervention, knowledge still remains sparse. In this area, policy implementation outstrips research.

However, there have been other advances. Since the Furby, Weinrott, and Blackshaw (1989) review, the distinctiveness of the needs of young offenders has been recognized. Certainly in the last two decades there has been an increase in research on sexually abusive youth with a commensurate increase in the programs available to treat sexually abusive youth. However, as Fortune and Lambie (2006, p. 1092) state, "it is only in the last 10 years that research has turned to look at the efficacy of these programmes." Fortune and Lambie provide a critical review of the recidivism studies on sexually abusive youth. In broad terms, they maintain that "research indicates that comparison groups of untreated sexually abusive youth have higher rates of sexual and nonsexual re-offending than those who have received treatment" (p. 1078), but their general concerns about research designs mean that caution remains the watchword. They consider the key issues as "the use of comparison groups in order to assist in the interpretation of recidivism rates, definitions of recidivism and the follow-up length" (p. 1093). This challenging list of key issues reflects the fact that outcome research in relation to juveniles and young offenders is in its infancy.

Worling and Curwen (2000) support the efficacy of treatment for adolescents building on the notion that sexual offenders are different from nonsexual offending adolescents. Certainly they argue that the risk of further sexual aggression is related to factors that are unrelated to nonsexual offending. More generally, there seems to be some optimism regarding treatment for juvenile sex offenders.

Reitzel and Carbonell (2006), using data from nine studies on juvenile sexual offender treatment effectiveness, indicated an overall statistically significant effect of treatment on sexual recidivism. Nevertheless, the handling of dropouts and nonequivalent follow-up periods between treatment groups "suggest that results should be interpreted with caution" (p. 401). Their meta-analysis produced an interesting rebuttal to those who might think that apparent success is more likely to be attributable in studies with less strict research designs. Reitzel and Carbonell found the opposite, with higher-quality designs yielding better effect sizes, though the differences between the groups were not significant.

Apart from the need for comparison groups, a methodological footnote is the continuing concern as to what one should do in an analysis with regard to persons who drop out from treatment. It seems remarkable that this remains an issue. One needs to recognize the importance of including noncompleters in the analysis (see Langton et al. 2006). Nunes and Cortoni (2008) compared 52 offenders who dropped out of, or were expelled from, their last sex offender program and a comparison group of 48 program completers. The general criminality items of the Static-99 were significantly associated with dropout/expulsion but the sexual deviance items were not.[3] Crucially, therefore, risk for sexual recidivism and risk for dropout/expulsion from sex offender programs do not appear to be synonymous. However, there remains a substantial overlap between risk of sexual recidivism and risk of program dropout/expulsion.

The research on interventions has produced some guarded optimism, but perhaps even here the mood is changing. Langevin, Curnoe, and Federoff (2006, p. 108) report "a current pessimism among treatment providers of sex offenders" insisting that "results of all treatment efforts with sex offenders over the past 40 years appear to suggest that sexual offending is a persistent problem." They emphasize that this seems to emerge if one examines "*lifetime recidivism* rates among various sex offender groups" (p. 108). In calculating recidivism rates, a crucial choice is the criterion measure used. Langevin, Curnoe, and Federoff examined seven indices of recidivism with very different outcomes.[4] While all their recidivism rates seem remarkably high, thus reflecting the nature of their sample, 61.1 percent for sex offense convictions can be contrasted with 88.3 percent for all sex offenses including detected crimes (Langevin et al. 2004, p. 546, table 4).

In summary, over the past decade or so, the notion of intervention in relation to sexual offending has widened from clinical treatment to a more general interest in what happens to the sex offender in the community.

---

[3] The Static-99 (Hanson and Thornton 2000) is an actuarial instrument designed to assess risk of both sexual and violent recidivism among sexual offenders.

[4] Langevin, Curnoe, and Fedoroff (2006) considered (1) charges for all offenses, (2) convictions for all offenses, (3) charges for sexual offenses, (4) convictions for sexual offenses, (5) number of separate court appearances for all offenses, (6) number of separate court appearances for sexual offenses, and (7) all sex offenses including undetected crimes.

The effectiveness of clinical treatment remains contentious, but progress has been made. There is now a general recognition that "one size does not fit all" in terms of treatment. However, any understanding of the relationship between specific treatments and particular groups of offenders remains modest.

Research evaluations have improved, but a fuller understanding of the role of different methodological approaches (including RCTs) needs to be developed. While optimism about treatment effectiveness has been recently challenged, there should be much more interest in the finding of Reitzel and Carbonell (2006) that higher-quality designs seemed to yield better effect sizes.

There is an increasing interest in the evaluation of the effects of registration and community notification programs, which are discussed further in the next section. However, one crucial point should be noted: almost all of the evaluative work has been dominated by an interest in outcome measures, whereas the dearth of interest in process issues means that, theoretically, there is a shortfall in understanding and ex-plaining what is actually happening.

One final point: In insisting on the need for long-term follow-ups to measure clinical effectiveness or the effectiveness of interventions in general, there is a dilemma. Advocates of a procedure will insist that the practices of their predecessors are now outmoded or outdated. The dilemma of long-term follow-ups is that it takes time to measure cur-rent practices. This leads one to recognize that short- or medium-term follow-ups still have an important role, but at best, they provide only an amber light (indicating "proceed with caution") that may eventually turn to green or red in the longer term. Hence, those involved in policy have a difficult task in interpreting research findings in this area.

IV. Sex Offender Recidivism and Public Policy

There has been a marked change of interest among the public con-cerning sex offenders over the past 20 years. The impact of the media, often using the undifferentiated category of "sexual offender" and en-couraging what I have called the "apartheid of sexual offending" (Soothill and Francis 1997), has impinged unhealthily on the profes-sional sphere. It has impinged even more disconcertingly on the public policy sphere. Increasingly, sexual offenders have had special provisions and procedures that have restricted their movements in the community after conviction. The United States has been at the forefront in developing many of these restrictions. While there are some enabling federal laws, there is not a standardization of practice throughout the states. Elsewhere in the world, some of these practices from the United States have seeped across, but usually in watered-down form. So, for instance, other countries have watched the development of Megan's Law in the United States with interest (e.g., in the United Kingdom, *The Times*'s headline "Should We Import Megan's Law? To Judge by the American Experience, This Legislation Won't Make Children Safer" [Coleman 2006] illustrates the terms of the debate). In the end it seems that other countries have recoiled from a full enactment of this kind of legislation. The source of some of these changes remains an enigma. Sometimes it is debatable whether it is the media orchestrating a moral panic or whether it is the media simply responding to the desire of political leaders to better protect citizens from harm. However, there is little doubt that there is an interactive effect.

While Hood et al. (2002, p. 393), among others, have stressed the importance of "disaggregating" the category "sexual offender," the sustained public outrage, orchestrated by the media in relation to sexual offending, has often clouded sensible public and professional debate. The increased segregation of an undifferentiated category of "sexual offenders," in both policy and practice, has not been helpful and has hindered the more sophisticated development of theorizing. Nevertheless, despite an adverse climate for scholarly work, there have been some advances in understanding, some of which have already been outlined. However, the translation of academic work into public policy has not yet been successfully managed.

In some respects it seems that some public policy initiatives have raced ahead of research. However, this is a sensitive area, for public policy cannot always wait until research is completed, and anyway, most research findings are based on policy initiatives that have been put into place. In fact, the evidence so far suggests that this kind of research is still in its infancy. Indeed, there is little theorizing to recognize that some initiatives, put into place to try to protect the public, might actually produce more sex offending. A challenge on scientific grounds to major initiatives is hazardous, for many of the policies to deal with sex offenders are now fully in the public gaze and, politically, the policies cannot be seen to have failed. However, this essay is written at a time when there is increasingly widespread concern among academics and practitioners about the efficacy of some of the policies that have recently been enacted.

A crucial area is the reintegration process by which an offender rejoins the community after prison. Willis and Grace (2008) have fairly convincingly shown that poor integration planning is a risk factor for recidivism. The introduction of Megan's Law in 1996, which encourages each state to develop procedures to inform communities where sex offenders will be living, had widespread international coverage.

Drake and Aos (2009) have identified nine rigorous evaluations and have seemed to identify a possible effect on "general," rather than "specific," deterrence. In relation to specific deterrence, the studies have widely varying results, with Freeman (2009), for example, finding that those in the registration/notification group had higher recidivism rates and were arrested faster than those in the comparison group. In contrast, however, Duwe and Donnay (2008) maintain that broad community notification, relating to level 3 ("high public risk") sex offenders released from Minnesota prisons between 1997 and 2002, significantly reduced the risk of time to a sex reoffense (rearrest, reconviction, and reincarceration) compared with two control groups.

Why are there such apparent discrepant results? Crucially, there is no indication of the process of what is actually happening. As the original legislation for Megan's Law in the United States left discretion in terms of how it should be put into practice, there was scope for differences in process to emerge. However, this will be less so now with the Adam Walsh Act, which established a national sex offender register and was signed into law in 2006. This act organizes sex offender classification into three tiers. Interestingly, the classification is based solely on the offense of conviction, with a person's likelihood to reoffend no longer being considered. States were ordered to comply with this federal legislation by July 27, 2009, or risk losing 10 percent of a federal law enforcement grant. However, there are still issues with states' compliance. In fact, implementing federal guidelines can still produce differences, and one suspects that current results are not even generalizable in the United States. Nevertheless, there are important points to recognize. So, for instance, Duwe and Donnay (2008) stress that "community notification is . . . a double-edged sword" (p. 443), pointing to earlier research (Zevitz and Farkas 2000) that has clearly demonstrated that Megan's Law imposes many hardships on offenders, who have reported enduring harassment, property damage, and loss of jobs and homes on account of community notification.

Producing such hardships may be counterproductive, and, indeed, they produce more sex offender recidivism rather than less and so explain some of the results in which the imposition of public policy initiatives, supposedly to reduce harm, has produced deleterious effects (e.g., Freeman 2009). Explanations remain contentious. As Freeman notes, "increased awareness, identification and monitoring of sex offenders cannot be ruled out as a possible explanation" (p. 22), but he maintains that the emerging results "are more likely due to the aggregation of stressors related to sexual offending and the stigma experienced as a result of community notification."

In brief, therefore, there may be some unintended consequences resulting from public policy initiatives. This is becoming evident in relation to some other efforts to reduce sex offense recidivism. Local and state governments in the United States are increasingly passing legislation prohibiting sex offenders from living within a certain distance from child congregation locations, such as schools, parks, and day care centers. Some provisions in terms of distance mean that there is simply nowhere for sex offenders to live without transgressing the law. However, so far the main type of challenge to this kind of legislation has been in terms of its ineffectiveness, and following extensive legal challenges, there have been some rulings that restrict the government. Duwe, Donnay, and Tewksbury (2008a) analyzed the offense patterns of every sex offender released from Minnesota correctional facilities between 1990 and 2002 who was reincarcerated for a new sex offense prior to 2006. They maintain that not one of the 224 sex offenses would have likely been prevented by residency restrictions. While Zandbergen (2008) points to some methodological shortcomings in the study, he acknowledges that a more rigorous quantitative characterization of distances would not have altered the paper's principal conclusions. The original authors' rebuttal of Zandbergen's criticisms (Duwe, Donnay, and Tewksbury 2008b) certainly reveals that this is an area where lively academic debate will be more and more forthcoming.

Understanding the development of public policy initiatives is a fine art and is beyond the scope of this essay. However, one needs to recognize that the making of sex offender laws is a complex issue. Zilney and Zilney (2009) provide a powerful historical account of how sex crime laws were created in the United States. Unusually, they ask whether the United States can learn from other countries and actually embrace the consideration of alternatives, coming to the conclusion that the only way to deal with the issue of sexual offending is through sex-positive education and counseling.

Certainly there is a vast range of influences that are brought to bear when an issue becomes one of public concern. Policy makers may respond to a variety of voices from the shrill call of tabloid headline writers to the more measured tones of scientific evidence. For the purposes of this essay, however, just one point needs to be recognized. This widespread concern in the Western world about sex crime recidivism will have different effects in different countries and even in different cities. There may even be the same public policy initiatives in a country, but some cities may impose them more stringently than others, thus causing a different effect. The experiences of the United States and England and Wales (which has followed a paler version of the American pathway) have not yet been fully evaluated. Even so, it perhaps needs to be recognized that particular ways of dealing with sex offenders may not be readily or appropriately exported.

Possible cultural differences are important to recognize, but historical shifts are also crucial to grasp. However, both the public and the professional spheres seem to be becoming increasingly reluctant to consider history. In brief, sex crime and the response to sex crime may be thought to be unchanging. In fact, there are crucial system changes that may affect behavior that need to be confronted. In most of Western society there has been a shift since the Second World War, which has meant that most sexual behavior between consenting adults is no longer proscribed by law. Nowadays the law is focusing much more on nonconsenting sexual behavior, particularly against women and children, whether or not accompanied by violence. However, there has also been some net widening. Viewing pornographic images on the Internet, for instance, has raised concern. It raises the issue as to what should be regarded as relevant to sex offender recidivism.

The pornography issue exemplifies how new areas of concern emerge. Pornography has probably always been a resource for certain sections of society, and there have been the campaigns of the antipornography counterparts (see Walkowitz [1992, pp. 192–95] for examples in nineteenth-century Britain), but its widespread availability on the Internet, together with a more prohibitive culture developing among the religious right, has fueled more general anxiety about its possible effects. Certainly there is recent work on the frequency and type of pornography use on recidivism among sexual offenders. This work is emerging in the context of more general work on pornography and aggression. So, for example, it is argued that the predictive validity of pornography is based on the interaction between various risk characteristics associated with aggression (Malamuth, Addison, and Koss 2000) and that individuals who view sexually explicit material are more likely to offend and/or reoffend when they possess such characteristics (Vega and Malamuth 2007). Kingston et al. (2008), focusing on a sample of 341 child molesters, suggest, for instance, that the frequency of pornography use was primarily a risk factor for higher-risk offenders and that content (i.e., pornography containing deviant content) was a risk factor for all groups. Importantly, after they control for general and specific risk factors for sexual aggression, pornography added significantly to the prediction of recidivism. Interestingly, given the dates of assessment (1982–92) that provided the baseline for this study, there was no opportunity to consider Internet pornography. Hence, there is much scope for more work in this area.

The more widespread use of pornography also reflects changing social attitudes. Indeed, it is important to recognize that different sexual attitudes have evolved historically. In short, there have always been different kinds of social response to sexual behavior, whether licit or illicit, at different times and in different places. There are undoubtedly strong cohort effects in sexual behavior. Hanson (2002, p. 1059) gives the example of sexual intercourse: "almost all, or 95 percent, of those born after 1964 had intercourse prior to age 18 compared to half, or 51 percent, of those born before 1949 (Trocki 1992)." Certainly there has always been an interest in sex crime with moral panics about, say, homosexual activity in one era and child sexual abuse in another, but now the interest in sex crime recidivism is much more widespread. Public and political interest means that further policy initiatives are likely, and hence, researchers need to remain vigilant.

V. To Begin to Conclude

So what impact should this change in public and political interest have on the study of sex offender recidivism? There are at least three themes that have been underplayed in the past but that should come more to the fore in the future. Whether or not they represent a clarion call for a paradigm shift is a moot point, for I want the focus and interests of developmental psychologists to remain, but we need to do much more. The following three themes demand the development of more questions, the interest of more disciplines, and the involvement of different kinds of methodology.

- First, a greater focus on social processes. To date the literature has been dominated by outcome studies, whereas a focus on societal processes has been neglected. Certainly developmental processes of the individual have been scrupulously considered by psychologists. However, questions of *societal* processes are likely to be more adequately answered by sociological rather than psychological approaches. To appreciate processual issues, a greater appeal to qualitative techniques may be appropriate.
- Second, a greater focus on change. While developmental psychologists have been pioneers in the recognition of individual change, there has not been a similar focus on societal change over time. Again, societal change is the fodder of sociological interest, but historians—and their methodologies—should also gain more of a foothold in understanding changes over a long time span.
- Third, a greater focus on the impact of public policy initiatives on sex offender recidivism. In essence, an increased focus on this area should resonate with issues of process and change. There needs to be much more concern among scholars about the most appropriate response to sexual offending at the societal level.

Making an appeal to widen the interest on sex offender recidivism to embrace more fully these three themes may be easy to articulate but much more difficult to accomplish. Simply widening the relevant disciplines to include sociologists, economists, anthropologists, and historians that will need a place at the table in future will not be sufficient.

The last 30 years has been dominated by studies from the United States. Apart from my article from England, all the other papers listed in table 1 emanate from North America. There are two problems caused by a discourse centered almost entirely on material from the United States and Canada. North Americans are not gaining from the experiences and knowledge of other countries, whereas persons from other countries, particularly those working in the public policy community, may be misled into believing that prescriptions for a U.S. audience will also be appropriate in their locations. The notion that risk

factors have a more universal application is under challenge both between and within countries. So, for example, Långström (2004) investigated the predictive validity across ethnicity for the Rapid Risk Assessment for Sexual Offence Recidivism (RRASOR) and the Static-99
actuarial risk assessment procedures in a national cohort of all adult
male sex offenders released from prison in Sweden in 1993–97.[5] He
found that the two tools were equally accurate among Nordic and
European sexual offenders for the prediction of any sexual and any
violent nonsexual recidivism. In contrast, neither measure could differentiate African or Asian sexual or violent recidivists from nonreci-
divists. In short, the study suggests that some risk assessment tools may
not generalize across offender ethnicity or migration status. If there
are *within*-country differences, there will almost certainly be larger
between-country differences. The relative nature of the meaning of sex
offending and the likelihood of recidivism have not yet been fully recognized. More specifically, understanding processual issues—that is,
how various public authorities react to a problem—needs to be more
contextually based. This is where the experiences of other countries
may be relevant.

Both questions and methodology need to be widened. Hence, Worling and Långström (2003) plead for more research on qualitative aspects of sexual offense recidivism, continued inquiry into dynamic,
changeable risk factors for criminal recidivism, and the notion that the
process of decision making concerning assessment and interventions in
clinical contexts should be investigated, all timely concerns.

While there is still much to do, it still needs to be recognized that,
since the benchmark study of Furby, Weinrott, and Blackshaw was published in 1989, there have been some remarkable changes in the focus
on sex offenders over the past 20 years in most Western countries. The
changes have been in both the public and the professional arenas, and
while the changes in the two spheres of the public and the professional
are linked, it has not been a comfortable relationship. In fact, we have
entered a state of confusion about "sex offender recidivism." The discourses of the public and most of the professionals are becoming increasingly discrepant. The public discourse over the past decade or so
has been dangerously molded by the sensational press. The increased

[5] RRASOR (Hanson 1997) is an actuarial tool constructed to yield estimates of risk
for sexual recidivism in sexual offenders based on file-based information. See n. 3 for a
description of Static-99.

focus of the media on the topic of sex crime in general and sex crime recidivism in particular has resulted in what is tantamount to a "moral panic."[6] The consequential demonization of sex offenders has had a devastating effect on the development of ways of dealing with sex offenders. Demonization means that the media encourage the public to focus only on the most extreme and shocking cases, and, misleadingly, these cases start to represent all sex offenders in the public's mind. Sex offenders need to be differentiated but are increasingly being placed in the same box.

Some explicit changes in social policy have been discussed. Public protection has become the clarion call rather than the rehabilitation of offenders. We need to consider more fully whether the balance between public protection and the rehabilitation of offenders is working in harmony. If, for example, public protection measures exclude the possibility of some sexual offenders finding accommodation in a city, this totally militates against any notion of rehabilitation.

In a provocative indictment, Wright (2009, p. 3) maintains that policy responses in the United States "to prevent or address sexual offending, particularly those enacted over the last twenty years, have largely failed" and goes on to suggest that policy responses "have not done any of the following: reduced sex offenders' recidivism rates; provided safety, healing or support for victims; reflected the scientific research on sexual victimization, offending, and risk; or provided successful strategies for prevention" (pp. 3–4).

In recognition that the sexual violation of children, adolescents, and adults is an all-too-common experience with millions of women, men, and children being sexually violated at some time, the demand about *victims'* needs is understandable. However, this essay is focused on "sex *offender* recidivism." Sex offenders have certainly had fewer advocates, and a less popular cause is hard to imagine. And yet there may be a shift. Schultz's (2005) powerful account analyzing the stories of child molesters provides one such example. Establishing from the outset that she is a survivor of child sexual abuse, she declares that "the men who have spoken to me are not monsters, however monstrous the crimes they committed. They all have their own stories, with unique sets of

---

[6] Thompson (1998, p. 7) indicates that "the first published reference to a 'moral panic' was by the British sociologist Jock Young in 1971, when discussing public concern about statistics showing an apparently alarming increase in drug abuse." Since its introduction in 1971, the concept of moral panics has produced a rich literature attracting widespread academic interest and, rather more unusually, acceptance in more popular discourse.

circumstances that led to their crimes, yet there are many similarities as well. Identifying these patterns can give us glimpses of why people molest children and how we should treat offenders to keep them from repeating their crimes" (pp. xvii-xviii). The interaction between offender and victim is highlighted when she stresses that "most importantly, listening to these stories can show what steps we need to take to prevent children from falling victim to these predators" (p. xviii). Listening to and analyzing narratives is a methodology very different from that undertaken to identify risk and to make predictions. On the dustcover of Schultz's book, Robert E. Longo, an independent consultant and trainer, proclaims that "working in the field for almost three decades has taught me that punishment alone will not prevent sexual abuse from occurring." However, punishment has been the framework for the predominant paradigm that has emerged in the public sphere for dealing with sexual offenders, and it has become increasingly difficult for professionals to develop an alternative scenario.

While efforts at treatment have been made in some institutions that house sexual offenders, the social response to the problem of sex offending has been essentially a punitive solution within the operation of the criminal justice system. This approach, heavily endorsed and underpinned by the media, has made opposition difficult to articulate in the public sphere. The approach has created its own myths.

In her inaugural lecture, Lesley McAra (2009) vividly contrasted "myths about what works" and "facts about what works." While discussing contemporary penology in general, her contrast is pertinent to sex offending:

Myths about What Works	Facts about What Works
Punitiveness	Compassion
"Tough" talk is soft on crime!	"Soft" talk is tough on crime!
Criminal justice solutions (alone)	Social justice solutions

In a powerful presentation about juvenile crime, McAra argues that a criminal justice framework of punitiveness with "some posturing tough talk" may not be helpful in the long term. In contrast, a wider framework embracing social justice solutions with more compassion and understanding has had some more effective results. Similar evidence is not currently available that a comparable switch in approach in relation to sex offending would produce comparable results. However, one can readily appreciate that less punitive action and a more compassionate approach would enable many more potential sexual offenders to seek help much earlier in the process. An addiction to watching pornographic images, for example, is too readily assumed to be an inevitable precursor to other types of sex offending, and hence such addicts are less likely to seek help for fear of being so labeled. However, those suffering from such addictions need to be helped for public health rather than criminal justice reasons. Indeed, seeing much more of sex offending within a public health rather than a criminal justice framework needs to be seriously considered.

The crucial stance of the public health approach is to focus on prevention: that is, preventing disease or illness rather than dealing with the health consequences. The first *World Report on Violence and Health* (World Health Organization 2002) has espoused a public health approach to violence with an emphasis on a multidisciplinary approach, making use of "a wide range of professional expertise, from medicine, epidemiology and psychology to sociology, criminology, education and economics" (p. 3). The report has an implicit challenge to medical dominance in matters of health that has hitherto been "largely reactive and therapeutic," with psychiatrists treating individual patients rather than being involved in prevention. The public health approach acts on a wider stage, focusing on the health of communities and populations as a whole rather than on individual patients.

One needs to recognize that developing a public health approach that is essentially a more compassionate paradigm will be difficult to accomplish. Current myths about sex offending have tended to be generated by the media, and facts that do not conform to the myths will tend to be neglected. The danger is that all sex offending is seen as the extreme and dangerous behavior that is reported with such sensational relish by some parts of the media, but most sex offending is not like that.

The advantage of history is that patterns over long trajectories can be explored. It is important to recognize that much behavior that raises concern will reflect the moral values of a particular era: concern, for example, about overt prostitution and obscene language in the late Victorian period and increasing persecution and prosecution of homosexuals in England and Wales up to the liberalization of the late 1960s. Nowadays, for example, we need to assess whether watching some forms of Internet pornography is, indeed, a "serious" offense or simply an aberration that is not potentially harmful to others.[7]

The focus of this essay has been mainly on contemporary empirical work in the United States and the United Kingdom, but we also need to understand the extent to which previous generations and other countries have had to confront similar problems. Knowledge about the scale, nature, and longevity of the threat from sexual offenders is lacking. More pertinently, are we facing a new problem or is sexual recidivism an old problem of which we are now simply more aware? Focusing on history will help to probe such conundrums.

Looking at sex crime over a long time frame is instructive in identifying how some targets of concern alter whereas some remain the same. So, for example, a search of a local newspaper, the *Lancaster Guardian*, over 120 years (1860–1979)—that is, over 6,000 editions—was carried out to identify any mention of sex offending adjudicated by the criminal courts *and* reported in the *Lancaster Guardian*. With these criteria, 1,791 persons—including those convicted as well as those acquitted—were noted as appearing in such cases. One hundred and thirty eight sexual recidivists were identified (Soothill 2003, 2006).[8] However, there were only 19 persons who had been in court on at least two occasions in the Lancaster area for a nonconsensual sexual offense over the 120 years. These can be regarded—by today's standards—as the most serious "sexual recidivists." Hence, there were many sex offender recidivists who would not currently be regarded as a problem, particularly those relating to consensual homosexual activity.

A crucial question remains whether any apparently upward shift in the number of sexual recidivists is the outcome of behavioral or system changes. In short, are there really more sex offenders who recidivate or are we just becoming more vigilant? In other words, the fundamental issue remains whether any changes in sex offender recidivism rates represent a change in *offending* behavior (i.e., whether more persons

---

[7] This point, of course, misleadingly overlooks the possible exploitation of children in the production of some forms of Internet pornography. In short, the issue is more complex than is being portrayed here.

[8] This is likely to be an underestimate of the eventual outcome since others may become recidivists by actions after 1979; but, more seriously, since 1933, English newspapers have not been allowed to reveal the names of juvenile offenders. Hence, there are 57 unnamed juvenile offenders who have been in court for sex offenses; some of these may become sexual recidivists with another court appearance for a sex offense on a later occasion. Also, there may be persons who are charged with sexual offenses in the local area who are not mentioned by the local newspaper.

become engaged in serious sexual offending) or whether they has been any change in *surveillance* (i.e., members of the public being more willing to report incidents and the police taking such reports more seriously).

The almost exclusive focus by psychologists on *behavior* without considering the potential impact of *system* changes on the behavior of offenders has been limiting. In short, processual questions must come more fully into play. Indeed, monitoring the impact of system changes is likely to be—or, at least, should be—the most important aspect in understanding sex offender recidivism over the next decade or so.

The study of history helps to remind us that not all sex offenders are really dangerous; in fact, those who are will be in the minority. However, some sex offenders will be dangerous in other spheres as well: they may be extremely violent men, for instance. Separating out just one form of danger in the analysis of sex crime recidivists may be limiting. In fact, the increasing specialization in the study of sex offending must be curbed. Sex offending research must be more firmly embedded within the framework of mainstream criminal careers research. The tendency of setting apart sexual offending is becoming more marked, particularly in the public arena. The serious/less serious dichotomy is perhaps being eroded, and so, as all sexual offending increasingly becomes regarded as abhorrent, there will be a greater tendency for those committing such offenses to be segregated from offenders committing other type of offenses. Thus, two potential problems should be highlighted: placing all sex crime in one box overestimates the dangerousness issue whereas failing to recognize more widespread danger (beyond sexual activity) from a small minority of offenders may underestimate the dangerousness issue.

This comes to the final plea about the future in considering *sex offender recidivism*. There is the need to place the discussion of sex offender recidivism more firmly in the context of recent advances in understanding recidivism more generally. The technical issues are essentially the same. However, there is something particular about the problems involved in studying sex offender recidivism. It is in the public and political domains to an extent that is unlike any other crime except perhaps terrorism. The main message of the last 30 years is that sex offending is pervasive and that unrecognized it may be repeated. However, the main lesson that still has to be understood is that, as in most crime, a punitive solution alone will not suffice to overcome a pervasive problem. Sexual misbehavior of which sexual offending is a part needs a social response in which compassion may also play a part. To return to the cautionary tale that opened this essay, there is always a bigger picture that we overlook at our peril.

REFERENCES

Allen, Craig M. 1991. *Women and Men Who Sexually Abuse Children: A Comparative Analysis.* Brandon, VT: Safer Society Press.
Andrews, Don A., and James Bonta. 2003. *The Psychology of Criminal Conduct.* 3rd ed. Cincinnati: Anderson.
Barbaree, Howard E., Ray Blanchard, and Calvin M. Langton. 2003. "The Development of Sexual Aggression through the Life Span—the Effect of Age on Sexual Arousal and Recidivism among Sex Offenders." In *Sexually Coercive Behavior: Understanding and Management,* Annals of the New York Academy of Sciences, vol. 989, edited by Robert A. Prentky, Eric S. Janus, and Michael C. Seto. New York: New York Academy of Sciences.
Beech, Anthony, and Hannah Ford. 2006. "The Relationship between Risk, Deviance, Treatment Outcome and Sexual Reconviction in a Sample of Child Sexual Abusers Completing Residential Treatment for Their Offending." *Psychology Crime and Law* 12(6):685–701.
Beech, Anthony, and Tony Ward. 2004. "The Integration of Etiology and Risk in Sexual Offenders: A Theoretical Framework." *Aggression and Violent Behavior* 10:31–63.
Berlin, Fred S., Nathan W. Galbreath, Brendan Geary, and Gerard McClone. 2003. "The Use of Actuarials at Civil Commitment Hearings to Predict the Likelihood of Future Sexual Violence." *Sexual Abuse: A Journal of Research and Treatment* 15:377–82.
Blanton, Hart, and James Jaccard. 2006. "Arbitrary Metrics in Psychology." *American Psychologist* 61(1):27–41.
Breiling, James. 2005. "Lessons from Bio-medical Arena for Determining How Well Treatment Works." Paper presented at the 24th annual Research and Treatment Conference of the Association for the Treatment of Sexual Abusers, Salt Lake City, November.
Broadhurst, Roderick G., and Ross A. Maller. 1992. "The Recidivism of Sex Offenders in the Western Australian Prison Population." *British Journal of Criminology* 32(1):54–80.
Brooks-Gordon, Belinda, and Charlotte Bilby. 2006. "Psychological Interventions for Treatment of Adult Sex Offenders—Treatment Can Reduce Reoffending Rates but Does Not Provide a Cure." *British Medical Journal* 333(7557):5–6.
Brooks-Gordon, Belinda, Charlotte Bilby, and Helene Wells. 2006a. "A Systematic Review of Psychological Interventions for Sexual Offenders I: Ran-

domised Control Trials." *Journal of Forensic Psychiatry and Psychology* 17: 442–66.

———. 2006*b*. "A Systematic Review of Psychological Interventions for Sexual Offenders II: Quasi-Experimental and Qualitative Data." *Journal of Forensic Psychiatry and Psychology* 17:467–84.

Caldwell, Michael F. 2007. "Sexual Offense Adjudication and Sexual Recidivism among Juvenile Offenders." *Sexual Abuse: A Journal of Research Treatment* 19(2):107–13.

Center for Sex Offender Management. 2000. *Community Supervision of the Sex Offender: An Overview of Current and Promising Practices.* Washington, DC: U.S. Department of Justive.

———. 2007. "Female Sex Offenders." http://www.csom.org/pubs/female _sex_offenders_brief.pdf.

Christiansen, Karl O., Mimi Elers-Nielsen, Louis Le Maire, and Gerog K. Sturup. 1965. "Recidivism among Sexual Offenders." In *Scandinavian Studies in Criminology*, vol. 1, edited by Karl O. Christiansen. London: Tavistock.

Coleman, Clive. 2006. "Should We Import Megan's Law? To Judge by the American Experience, This Legislation Won't Make Children Safer." *Times* (London), June 21.

Collins, John A., and Bart C. J. M. Fauser. 2005. "Balancing the Strengths of Systematic and Narrative Reviews." *Human Reproduction Update* 11(2):103–4.

Cortoni, Franca. 2009. "Factors Associated with Sexual Recidivism." In *Assessment and Treatment of Sex Offenders: A Handbook*, edited by Anthony R. Beech, Leam A. Craig, and Kevin D. Browne. Chichester, UK: Wiley-Blackwell.

Craig, Leam A., Anthony R. Beech, and Leigh Harkins. 2009. "The Predictive Accuracy of Risk Factors and Frameworks." In *Assessment and Treatment of Sex Offenders: A Handbook*, edited by Anthony R. Beech, Leam A. Craig, and Kevin D. Browne. Chichester, UK: Wiley-Blackwell.

Davies, Huw T. O., and Iain K. Crombie. 1998. "What Is a Systematic Review?" *Hayward Medical Communications* 1(5):1–5.

Doren, Dennis M. 1987. *Understanding and Treating the Psychopath.* New York: Wiley.

———. 2006. "What Do We Know about the Effect of Aging on Recidivism Risk for Sexual Offenders?" *Sexual Abuse: A Journal of Research Treatment* 18(2):137–57.

Drake, Elizabeth, and Steve Aos. 2009. *Does Sex Offender Registration and Notification Reduce Crime? A Systematic Review of the Research Literature.* Olympia: Washington State Institute for Public Policy, http://www.wsipp.wa.gov/ rptfiles/09-06-1101.pdf.

Duwe, Grant, and William Donnay. 2008. "The Impact of Megan's Law on Sex Offender Recidivism: The Minnesota Experience." *Criminology* 46(2): 411–46.

Duwe, Grant, William Donnay, and Richard Tewksbury. 2008*a*. "Does Residential Proximity Matter? A Geographic Analysis of Sex Offense Recidivism." *Criminal Justice and Behavior* 35(4):484–504.

————. 2008*b*. "Response to Zandbergen." *Criminal Justice and Behavior* 35(11):1452–53.

Falshaw, Louise, Andrew Bates, Vaneeta Patel, Carmen Corbett, and Caroline Friendship. 2003. "Assessing Reconviction, Reoffending and Recidivism in a Sample of UK Sexual Offenders." *Legal and Criminological Psychology* 8(2): 207–15.

Farrington, David P. 2002. "Developmental Criminology and Risk-Focused Prevention." In *The Oxford Handbook of Criminology*, 3rd ed., edited by Mike Maguire, Rod Morgan, and Robert Reiner. Oxford: Oxford University Press.

————. 2003. "Developmental and Life-Course Criminology: Key Theoretical and Empirical Issues—the 2002 Sutherland Award Address." *Criminology* 41(2):221–25.

Farrington, David P., and Jeremy W. Coid. 2003. *Early Prevention of Adult Antisocial Behavior*. Cambridge: Cambridge University Press.

Federal Bureau of Investigation. 2008. *Crime in the United States*. http://www.fbi.gov/ucr/cius2008/index.html.

Ferguson, Niall. 2009. *The Ascent of Money: A Financial History of the World*. London: Penguin.

Finkelhor, David, and Lisa Jones. 2006. "Why Have Child Maltreatment and Child Victimization Declined?" *Journal of Social Issues* 62(4):685–716.

Fortune, Clare-Ann, and Ian Lambie. 2006. "Sexually Abusive Youth: A Review of Recidivism Studies and Methodological Issues for Future Research." *Clinical Psychology Review* 26(8):1078–95.

Francis, Brian, and Keith Soothill. 2000. "Does Sex Offending Lead to Homicide?" *Journal of Forensic Psychiatry and Psychology* 11(1):49–61.

Freedman, Estelle B. 1987. "'Uncontrolled Desires': The Response to the Sexual Psychopath, 1920–1960." *Journal of American History* 74(1):83–106.

Freeman, Naomi J. 2009. "The Public Safety Impact of Community Notification Laws: Rearrest of Convicted Sex Offenders." *Crime and Delinquency OnlineFirst*, http://cad.sagepub.com, doi: m10.1177/0011128708330852.

Freeman, Naomi J., and Jeffrey C. Sandler. 2008. "Female and Male Sex Offenders—a Comparison of Recidivism Patterns and Risk Factors." *Journal of Interpersonal Violence* 23(10):1394–1413.

Friendship, Caroline, and David Thornton. 2001. "Sexual Reconviction for Sexual Offenders Discharged from Prison in England and Wales—Implications for Evaluating Treatment." *British Journal of Criminology* 41(2): 285–92.

Furby, Lita, Mark R. Weinrott, and Lyn Blackshaw. 1989. "Sex Offender Recidivism—a Review." *Psychological Bulletin* 105(1):3–30.

Gendreau, Paul, Tracy Little, and Claire Goggin. 1996. "A Meta-analysis of the Predictors of Adult Offender Recidivism: What Works?" *Criminology* 34: 575–607.

Gerhold, Constanze K., Kevin D. Browne, and Richard Beckett. 2007. "Predicting Recidivism in Adolescent Sexual Offenders." *Aggression and Violent Behavior* 12(4):427–38.

Gordon, Harvey. 2009. Letter to the editor. *Journal of Forensic Psychiatry and Psychology* 20(1):164–65.

Gordon, Harvey, and Don Grubin. 2004. "Psychiatric Aspects of the Assessment and Treatment of Sex Offenders." *Advances in Psychiatric Treatment* 10: 73–80.

Gretton, Heather M., Michelle McBride, Robert D. Hare, Roy O'Shaughnessy, and Gary Kumka. 2001. "Psychopathy and Recidivism in Adolescent Sex Offenders." *Criminal Justice and Behavior* 28(4):427–49.

Grossman, Jason, and Fiona J. Mackenzie. 2005. "The Randomized Controlled Trial: Gold Standard, or Merely Standard?" *Perspectives in Biology and Medicine* 48(Autumn):516–34.

Grove, William M., and Paul E. Meehl. 1996. "Comparative Efficiency of Informal (Subjective, Impressionistic) and Formal (Mechanical, Algorithmic) Prediction Procedures: The Clinical-Statistical Controversy." *Psychology, Public Policy, and Law* 2:293–323.

Grunfeld, Berthold, and Klell Noreik. 1986. "Recidivism among Sex Offenders—a Follow-up-Study of 541 Norwegian Sex Offenders." *International Journal of Law and Psychiatry* 9(1):95–102.

Hall, Gordon C. Nagayama. 1995. "Sexual Offender Recidivism Revisited—a Metaanalysis of Recent Treatment Studies." *Journal of Consulting and Clinical Psychology* 63(5):802–9.

Hanson, R. Karl. 1997. *The Development of a Brief Actuarial Scale for Sexual Offense Recidivism.* User Report no. 1997-04. Ottawa: Department of the Solicitor General of Canada.

———. 2002. "Recidivism and Age—Follow-up Data from 4,673 Sexual Offenders." *Journal of Interpersonal Violence* 17(10):1046–62.

Hanson, R. Karl, Guy Bourgnon, Leslie Helmus, and Shannon Hodgson. 2009. *A Meta-analysis of the Effectiveness of Treatment for Sexual Offenders: Risk, Need, and Responsivity.* Report to Public Safety Canada. Washington, DC: National Institute of Corrections, http://www.nicic.org/Library/023701.

Hanson, R. Karl, and Monique T. Bussière. 1998. "Predicting Relapse: A Meta-analysis of Sexual Offender Recidivism Studies." *Journal of Consulting and Clinical Psychology* 66(2):348–62.

Hanson, R. Karl, Arthur Gordon, Andew J. R. Harris, Janice K. Marques, William Murphy, Vernon L. Quinsey, and Michael C. Seto. 2002. "First Report of the Collaborative Outcome Data Project on the Effectiveness of Psychological Treatment for Sex Offenders." *Sexual Abuse: A Journal of Research and Treatment* 14:169–94.

Hanson, R. Karl, and Andrew J. R. Harris. 2000. "Where Should We Intervene? Dynamic Predictors of Sexual Offense Recidivism." *Criminal Justice and Behavior* 27(1):6–35.

Hanson, R. Karl, and Kelly E. Morton-Bourgon. 2005. "The Characteristics of Persistent Sexual Offenders: A Meta-analysis of Recidivism Studies." *Journal of Consulting and Clinical Psychology* 73(6):1154–63.

Hanson, R. Karl, Kelly E. Morton, and Andrew J. R. Harris. 2003. "Sexual Offender Recidivism Risk—What We Know and What We Need to Know."

In *Sexually Coercive Behavior: Understanding and Management*, Annals of the New York Academy of Sciences, vol. 989, edited by Robert A. Prentky, Eric S. Janus, and Michael C. Seto. New York: New York Academy of Sciences.

Hanson, R. Karl, and David Thornton. 2000. "Improving Risk Assessments for Sex Offenders: A Comparison of Three Actuarial Scales." *Law and Human Behavior* 24:119–36.

Harris, Grant T., Marnie E. Rice, and Vernon L. Quinsey. 1998. "Appraisal and Management of Risk in Sexual Aggression: Implications for Criminal Justice Policy." *Psychology, Public Policy, and Law* 4:73–115.

Hart, Stephen D., and Robert D. Hare. 1997. "Psychopathy, Assessment, and Association with Criminal Conduct." In *Handbook of Antisocial Behavior*, edited by David M. Stoff, James Breiling, and Jack D. Maser. New York: Wiley.

Hood, Roger, Stephen Shute, Martina Feilzer, and Aidan Wilcox. 2002. "Sex Offenders Emerging from Long-Term Imprisonment—a Study of Their Long-Term Reconviction Rates and of Parole Board Members' Judgements of Their Risk." *British Journal of Criminology* 42(2):371–94.

Kingston, Drew A., Paul Fedoroff, Philip Firestone, Susan Curry, and John M. Bradford. 2008. "Pornography Use and Sexual Aggression: The Impact of Frequency and Type of Pornography Use on Recidivism among Sexual Offenders." *Aggressive Behavior* 34(4):341–51.

Knight, Raymond A., and Judith E. Sims-Knight. 2003. "The Developmental Antecedents of Sexual Coercion against Women: Testing Alternative Hypotheses with Structural Equation Modelling." In *Sexually Coercive Behavior: Understanding and Management*, Annals of the New York Academy of Sciences, vol. 989, edited by Robert A. Prentky, Eric S. Janus, and Michael C. Seto. New York: New York Academy of Sciences.

Kubik, Elizabeth K., Jeffrey E. Hecker, and Sue Righthand. 2002. "Adolescent Females Who Have Sexually Offended: Comparisons with Delinquent Adolescent Female Offenders and Adolescent Males Who Sexually Offend." *Journal of Child Sexual Abuse* 11:63–83.

Kuhn, Thomas S. 1962. *The Structure of Scientific Revolutions*. Chicago: University of Chicago Press.

Langevin, Ron, Suzanne Curnoe, and Paul Fedoroff. 2006. "Results by Design: The Artefactual Construction of High Recidivism Rates for Sex Offenders—Reply to Webster, Gartner, and Doob." *Canadian Journal of Criminal Justice* 48(1):107–17.

Langevin, Ron, Suzanne Curnoe, Paul Fedoroff, Renee Bennett, Mara Langevin, Cheryl Peever, Rick Pettica, and Shameen Sandhu. 2004. "Lifetime Sex Offender Recidivism: A 25-Year Follow-up Study." *Canadian Journal of Criminal Justice* 46(5):531–52.

Långström, Niklas. 2004. "Accuracy of Actuarial Procedures for Assessment of Sexual Offender Recidivism Risk May Vary across Ethnicity." *Sexual Abuse: A Journal of Research Treatment* 16(2):107–20.

Långström, Niklas, Gabrielle Sjostedt, and Martin Grann. 2004. "Psychiatric Disorders and Recidivism in Sexual Offenders." *Sexual Abuse: A Journal of Research Treatment* 16(2):139–50.

Langton, Calvin M., Howard E. Barbaree, Leigh Harkins, and Edward J. Pea-
cock. 2006. "Sex Offenders' Response to Treatment and Its Association with
Recidivism as a Function of Psychopathy." *Sexual Abuse: A Journal of Research
Treatment* 18(1):99–120.

Lee, Joseph K. P., Henry J. Jackson, Pip Pattison, and Tony Ward. 2002. "Developmental Risk Factors for Sexual Offending." *Child Abuse and Neglect* 26:
73–92.

Looman, Jan, Jeffrey Abracen, and Terry P. Nicholaichuk. 2000. "Recidivism
among Treated Sexual Offenders and Matched Controls—Data from the
Regional Treatment Centre (Ontario)." *Journal of Interpersonal Violence* 15(3):
279–90.

Lösel, Friedrich, and Martin Schmucker. 2005. "The Effectiveness of Treatment for Sexual Offenders: A Comprehensive Meta-analysis." *Journal of Experimental Criminology* 1:117–46.

MacPherson, Gary J. D. 2003. "Predicting Escalation in Sexually Violent Recidivism: Use of the SVR-20 and PCL: SV to Predict Outcome with Noncontact Recidivists and Contact Recidivists." *Journal of Forensic Psychiatry and
Psychology* 14(3):615–27.

Malamuth, Neil M. 2003. "Criminal and Noncriminal Aggressors: Integrating
Psychopathy in Hierarchical-Mediational Confluence Model." In *Sexually
Coercive Behavior: Understanding and Management*, Annals of the New York
Academy of Sciences, vol. 989, edited by Robert A. Prentky, Eric S. Janus,
and Michael C. Seto. New York: New York Academy of Sciences.

Malamuth, Neil M., Tamara Addison, and Mary Koss. 2000. "Pornography
and Sexual Aggression: Are There Reliable Effects and Can We Understand
Them?" *Annual Review of Sex Research* 11:26–91.

Maltz, Michael D. 1984. *Recidivism*. Orlando, FL: Academic Press.

Marques, Janice K., David M. Day, Craig Nelson, and Mary Ann West. 1994.
"Effects of Cognitive-Behavioral Treatment on Sex Offender Recidivism—
Preliminary Results of a Longitudinal Study." *Criminal Justice and Behavior*
21(1):28–54.

Marshall, William L., and Liam E. Marshall. 2007. "The Utility of the Ran-
dom Controlled Trial for Evaluating Sexual Offender Treatment: The Gold
Standard or an Inappropriate Strategy?" *Sex Abuse: A Journal of Research and
Treatment* 19:175–91.

Martinson, Robert. 1974. "What Works? Questions and Answers about Prison
Reform." *Public Interest* 35:22–54.

Mathews, Ruth, John A. Hunter, and Jacqueline Vuz. 1997. "Juvenile Female
Offenders: Clinical Characteristics and Treatment Issues." *Sexual Abuse: A
Journal of Research and Treatment* 9:187–99.

McAra, Lesley. 2009. "Crime and Punishment in a Small Nation: Why Penology Matters." Inaugural lecture presented at the 8th annual meeting of
the European Society of Criminology, Edinburgh, December 15.

McGloin, Jean Marie, Christopher J. Sullivan, and Alex R. Piquero. 2009.
"Aggregating to Versatility? Transitions among Offender Types in the Short-
Term." *British Journal of Criminology* 49:243–64.

McGrath, Robert J., Georgia Cumming, and Brenda L. Burchard. 2003. *Current Practices and Trends in Sexual Abuser Management*. Brandon, VT: Safer Society Press.

McGuire, James. 1995. *What Works: Reducing Reoffending*. Chichester, UK: Wiley.

Miccio-Fonseca, L. C. 2000. "Adult and Adolescent Female Sex Offenders: Experiences Compared to Other Female and Male Sex Offenders." *Journal of Psychology and Human Sexuality* 11:75–88.

Miller, J., D. Moeller, A. Kaufman, P. Divasto, D. Pathak, and J. Christy. 1978. "Recidivism among Sex Assault Victims." *American Journal of Psychiatry* 135(9):1103–4.

Milner, Joel S., and Jacquelyn C. Campbell. 1995. "Prediction Issues for Practitioners." In *Assessing Dangerousness: Violence by Sexual Offenders, Batterers, and Child Abusers*, edited by Jacquelyn C. Campbell. Thousand Oaks, CA: Sage.

Miner, Michael H. 2002. "Factors Associated with Recidivism in Juveniles: An Analysis of Serious Juvenile Sex Offenders." *Journal of Research in Crime and Delinquency* 39(4):421–36.

Monckton-Smith, Jane. Forthcoming. *Relating Rape and Murder: Narratives of Sex, Death and Gender*. Basingstoke, UK: Palgrave Macmillan.

Motiuk, Laurence L., and Shelley L. Brown. 1996. "Factors Related to Recidivism among Released Federal Sex Offenders." *International Journal of Psychology* 31(3–4):3071.

Newman, Joseph P., David S. Kosson, and C. Mark Patterson. 1992. "Delay of Gratification in Psychopathic and Nonpsychopathic Offenders." *Journal of Abnormal Psychology* 101:630–36.

Nisbet, Ian A., Peter H. Wilson, and Stephen W. Smallbone. 2004. "A Prospective Longitudinal Study of Sexual Recidivism among Adolescent Sex Offenders." *Sexual Abuse: A Journal of Research Treatment* 16(3):223–34.

Nunes, Kevin L., and Franca Cortoni. 2008. "Dropout from Sex-Offender Treatment and Dimensions of Risk of Sexual Recidivism." *Criminal Justice and Behavior* 35(1):24–33.

Nunes, Kevin L., Philip Firestone, Audrey F. Wexler, Tamara L. Jensen, and John M. Bradford. 2007. "Incarceration and Recidivism among Sexual Offenders." *Law and Human Behavior* 31(3):305–18.

Prentky, Robert A., Austin F. S. Lee, Raymond A. Knight, and David Cerce. 1997. "Recidivism Rates among Child Molesters and Rapists: A Methodological Analysis." *Law and Human Behavior* 21(6):635–59.

Prescott, Jane J., and Jonah E. Rockoff. 2008. "Do Sex Offender Registration and Notification Laws Affect Criminal Behavior?" Working Paper no. 13803. Cambridge, MA: National Bureau of Economic Research. Paper presented at the 3rd annual conference on Empirical Legal Studies Papers. Olin Working Paper no. 08-006. Ann Arbor: University of Michigan Law and Economics, http://ssrn.com/abstract=1100663.

Quinsey, Vernon L., Grant T. Harris, Marnie E. Rice, and Catherine A. Cormier. 1998. *Violent Offenders: Appraising and Managing Risk.* Washington, DC: American Psychological Association.

Quinsey, Vernon L., Marnie E. Rice, and Grant T. Harris. 1995. "Actuarial Prediction of Sexual Recidivism." *Journal of Interpersonal Violence* 10(1): 85–105.

Raymond, Nancy C., Eli Coleman, Fred Ohlerking, Gary A. Christensen, and Michael Miner. 1999. "Psychiatric Comorbidity in Pedophilic Sex Offenders." *American Journal of Psychiatry* 156:786–88.

Reitzel, Lorraine R., and Joyce L. Carbonell. 2006. "The Effectiveness of Sexual Offender Treatment for Juveniles as Measured by Recidivism: A Meta-analysis." *Sexual Abuse: A Journal of Research Treatment* 18(4):401–21.

Rice, Marnie E., and Grant T. Harris. 1997. "The Treatment of Adult Offenders." In *Handbook of Antisocial Behavior*, edited by David M. Stoff, James Breiling, and Jack D. Maser. New York: Wiley.

———. 2003. "The Size and Sign of Treatment Effects in Sex Offender Therapy." In *Sexually Coercive Behavior: Understanding and Management*, Annals of the New York Academy of Sciences, vol. 989, edited by Robert A. Prentky, Eric S. Janus, and Michael C. Seto. New York: New York Academy of Sciences.

Rice, Marnie E., Grant T. Harris, Carol Lang, and Catherine Cormier. 2006. "Violent Sex Offenses: How Are They Best Measured from Official Records?" *Law and Human Behavior* 30:525–41.

Rice, Marnie E., Grant T. Harris, and Vernon L. Quinsey. 1990. "A Follow-up of Rapists Assessed in a Maximum Security Psychiatric Facility." *Journal of Interpersonal Violence* 5:435–48.

Rice, Marnie E., Vernon L. Quinsey, and Grant T. Harris. 1991. "Sexual Recidivism among Child Molesters Released from a Maximum Security Psychiatric Institution." *Journal of Consulting and Clinical Psychology* 59(3): 381–86.

Roe, Stephen, Kathryn Coleman, and Peter Kaiza. 2008–9. "Violent and Sexual Crime." In *Crime in England and Wales, 2008/09.* http://www.homeoffice.gov.uk/rds/pdfs09/hosb1109chap3.pdf.

Rogers, Paul, and Keith Soothill. 2008. "Understanding Forensic Mental Health and the Variety of Professional Voices." In *Handbook on Forensic Mental Health*, edited by Keith Soothill, Paul Rogers, and Mairead Dolan. Cullompton, UK: Willan.

Saelens, Brian E., and Karen Glanz. 2009. "Work Group I: Measures of the Food and Physical Activity Environment." *American Journal of Preventive Medicine* 36(4; suppl. 1):S166–S170.

Sample, Lisa L. 2006. "An Examination of the Degree to Which Sex Offenders Kill." *Criminal Justice Review* 31(3):230–50.

Scalora, Mario J., and Calvin Garbin. 2003. "A Multivariate Analysis of Sex Offender Recidivism." *International Journal of Offender Therapy and Comparative Criminology* 47(3):309–23.

Schultz, Pamela D. 2005. *Not Monsters: Analyzing the Stories of Child Molesters.* Lanham, MD: Rowman & Littlefield.

Serin, Ralph C., Donna L. Mailloux, and P. Bruce Malcolm. 2001. "Psychopathy, Deviant Sexual Arousal, and Recidivism among Sexual Offenders." *Journal of Interpersonal Violence* 16(3):234–46.

Seto, Michael C., and Howard E. Barbaree. 1999. "Psychopathy, Treatment Behavior, and Sex Offender Recidivism." *Journal of Interpersonal Violence* 14(12):1235–48.

Seto, Michael C., Janice K. Marques, Grant T. Harris, Mark Chaffin, Martin L. Lalumière, Michael H. Miner, Lucy Berliner, Marnie E. Rice, Roxanne Lieb, and Vernon L. Quinsey. 2008. "Good Science and Progress in Sex Offender Treatment Are Intertwined: A Response to Marshall and Marshall (2007)." *Sex Abuse* 20:247–55.

Shao, L., and J. Li. 2006. "The Effect of Sex Offender Registration Laws on Rape Victimization." Unpublished manuscript. Tuscaloosa: University of Alabama, Department of Economics, Finance, and Legal Studies.

Smallbone, Stephen W., and Mark R. Dadds. 1998. "Childhood Attachment and Adult Attachment in Incarcerated Adult Male Sex Offenders." *Journal of Interpersonal Violence* 13:555–73.

Smith, Wayne R., and Caren Monastersky. 1986. "Assessing Juvenile Sexual Offenders' Risk for Reoffending." *Criminal Justice and Behavior* 13(2): 115–40.

Soothill, Keith. 2003. "Serious Sexual Assault: Using History and Statistics." In *Managing Sex Offenses in the Community: Context, Responses and Challenges*, edited by Amanda Matravers. Cullompton, UK: Willan.

———. 2005. "Capturing Criminology." In *Questioning Crime and Criminology*, edited by Moira Peelo and Keith Soothill. Cullompton, UK: Willan.

———. 2006. "Sex Crime and Recidivism in a Little English City (1860–1979)." In *Le criminel enduci: Récidivbe et récidivistes au moyen âge au 20e siècle*, edited by Françoise Briegel and Michel Porret. Geneva: Droz.

Soothill, Keith, Claire Fitzpatrick, and Brian Francis. 2009. *Understanding Criminal Careers*. Cullompton, UK: Willan.

Soothill, Keith, and Brian Francis. 1997. "Sexual Reconvictions and the Sex Offenders Act 1997." *New Law Journal* 147(September 5):1285–86; 147 (September 12):1324–25.

———. 1998. "Poisoned Chalice or Just Deserts? (the Sex Offenders Act, 1997)." *Journal of Forensic Psychiatry* 9(2):281–93.

———. 2002. "Moral Panics and the Aftermath: A Study of Incest." *Journal of Social Welfare and Family Law* 24(1):1–17.

Soothill, Keith, Brian Francis, and J. Jiayi Liu. 2010. "The Importance of Coconvictions in the Prediction of Dangerous Recidivism: Blackmail and Kidnapping as a Demonstration Study." *Criminology and Criminal Justice* 10: 23–36.

Soothill, Keith, Brian Francis, Barry Sanderson, and Elizabeth Ackerley. 2000. "Sex Offenders: Specialists, Generalists—or Both?" *British Journal of Criminology* 40:56–67.

Soothill, Keith, and Trevor C. N. Gibbens. 1978. "Recidivism of Sexual Offenders: A Re-appraisal." *British Journal of Criminology* 18(3):267–76. Reprinted in *Sex Crimes*, edited by Donald J. West. International Library of Criminology and Criminal Justice. Aldershot, UK: Dartmouth, 1994.

Soothill, Keith, Paul Rogers, and Mairead Dolan, eds. 2008. *Handbook on Forensic Mental Health*. Cullompton, UK: Willan.

Soothill, Keith, and Sylvia Walby. 1991. *Sex Crime in the News*. London: Routledge.

Templeman, Terrel L., and Janet P. Wollersheim. 1979. "A Cognitive-Behavioral Approach to the Treatment of Psychopathy." *Psychotherapy: Theory, Research and Practice* 16:132–39.

Thompson, Kenneth. 1998. *Moral Panics*. London: Routledge.

Thornton, David. 2006. "Age and Sexual Recidivism: A Variable Connection." *Sexual Abuse: A Journal of Research Treatment* 18(2):123–35.

Trocki, Karen F. 1992. "Patterns of Sexuality and Risky Sexuality in the General Population of a California County." *Journal of Sex Research* 29:85–94.

Tyrer, Peter, et al. 2009. "The Assessment of Dangerous and Severe Personality Disorder: Lessons from a Randomised Controlled Trial Linked to Qualitative Analysis." *Journal of Forensic Psychiatry and Psychology* 20:132–46.

Vandiver, Donna M. 2006. "A Prospective Analysis of Juvenile Male Sex Offenders—Characteristics and Recidivism Rates as Adults." *Journal of Interpersonal Violence* 21(5):673–88.

Vega, Vanessa, and Neil M. Malamuth. 2007. "Predicting Sexual Aggression: The Role of Pornography in the Context of General and Specific Risk Factors." *Aggressive Behavior* 33:104–17.

Veysey, Bonita M., and Kristen Zgoba. 2009. "Reducing the Risk of Sex Offenses Reconsidered: Changes in Predictors of Recidivism over Time." Paper presented at the 2009 annual meeting of the American Society of Criminology, Philadelphia, November 4–7.

———. 2010. "Sex Offenses and Offenders Reconsidered: An Investigation of Characteristics and Correlates over Time." *Criminal Justice and Behavior* 37(May):583–95.

Viding, Essi, Henrik Larsson, and Alice P. Jones. 2008. "Review: Quantitative Genetic Studies of Antisocial Behavior." *Philosophical Transactions of the Royal Society* 363(1503):2519–27.

Walkowitz, Judith R. 1992. *City of Dreadful Night: Narratives of Sexual Danger in Late-Victorian London*. London: Virago.

Ward, Tony, and Stephen M. Hudson. 1998. "A Model of the Relapse Process in Sexual Offenders." *Journal of Interpersonal Violence* 13:400–425.

———. 2000. "A Self-Regulation Model of Relapse Prevention." In *Remaking Relapse Prevention with Sex Offenders: A Sourcebook*, edited by D. Richard Laws, Stephen M. Hudson, and Tony Ward. Thousand Oaks, CA: Sage.

Ward, Tony, and Richard J. Siegert. 2002. "Toward a Comprehensive Theory of Child Sexual Abuse: A Theory Knitting Perspective." *Psychology, Crime and Law* 8:319–51.

Webster, Cheryl M., Rosemary Gartner, and Anthony N. Doob. 2006. "Results by Design: The Artefactual Construction of High Recidivism Rates for Sex Offenders." *Canadian Journal of Criminal Justice* 48(1):79–93.

Webster, Stephen D. 2005. "Pathways to Sexual Offense Recidivism Following Treatment—an Examination of the Ward and Hudson Self-Regulation Model of Relapse." *Journal of Interpersonal Violence* 20(10):1175–96.

Wilby, Peter. 2008. "Getting and Spending." Review of *The Ascent of Money: A Financial History of the World*, by Niall Ferguson. *New Statesman* (December 1), http://www.newstatesman.com/books/2008/11/money-financial-ferguson-risk.

Willis, Gwenda M., and Randulph C. Grace. 2008. "The Quality of Community Reintegration Planning for Child Molesters: Effects on Sexual Recidivism." *Sex Abuse* 20(2):218–40.

Wilson, Robin J., Lynn Stewart, Tania Stirpe, Marianne Barrett, and Janice E. Cripps. 2000. "Community-Based Sex Offender Management: Combining Parole Supervision and Treatment to Reduce Recidivism." *Canadian Journal of Criminology—Revue Canadienne de Criminologie* 42(2):177–88.

Woods, Phil, and Gerri C. Lasiuk. 2008. "Risk Prediction—a Review of the Literature." *Journal of Forensic Nursing* 4(1):1–11.

World Health Organization. 2002. *World Report on Violence and Health*. Geneva: World Health Organization, http://www.who.int/violence_injury _prevention/violence/world_report/en/summary_en.pdf.

Worling, James R. 2001. "Personality-Based Typology of Adolescent Male Sexual Offenders: Differences in Recidivism Rates, Victim-Selection Characteristics, and Personal Victimization Histories." *Sex Abuse* 13(3):149–66.

Worling, James R., and Tracey Curwen. 2000. "Adolescent Sexual Offender Recidivism: Success of Specialized Treatment and Implications for Risk Prediction." *Child Abuse and Neglect* 24(7):965–82.

Worling, James R., and Niklas Långström. 2003. "Assessment of Criminal Recidivism Risk with Adolescents Who Have Offended Sexually: A Review." *Trauma Violence Abuse* 4(4):341–62.

Wright, Richard G. 2009. "Introduction: The Failure of Sex Offender Policies." In *Sex Offender Laws: Failed Policies, New Directions*, edited by Richard G. Wright. New York: Springer.

Young, Jock. 1999. "Cannibalism and Bulimia: Patterns of Social Control in Late Modernity." *Theoretical Criminology* 3(4):387–407.

Zamble, Edward, and Vernon L. Quinsey. 1997. *The Criminal Recidivism Process*. Cambridge: Cambridge University Press.

Zandbergen, Paul A. 2008. "Commentary on Duwe, Donnay, and Tewksbury (2008): 'Does Residential Proximity Matter? A Geographic Analysis of Sex Offense Recidivism.'" *Criminal Justice and Behavior* 35(11):1449–51.

Zevitz, Richard G., and Mary Ann Farkas. 2000. *Sex Offender Community Notification: Assessing the Impact in Wisconsin*. Washington, DC: U.S. Department of Justice, National Institute of Justice.

Zilney, Laura J., and Lisa Anne Zilney. 2009. *Perverts and Predators: The Making of Sex Offender Laws*. Lanham, MD: Rowman & Littlefield.

Jonathan P. Caulkins and Peter Reuter

How Drug Enforcement Affects Drug Prices

ABSTRACT

Enforcement against drug selling remains the principal tool of drug control in the United States and many other countries. Though the risk of incarceration for a drug dealer has risen fivefold or more over the last 25 years in the United States, the prices of cocaine and heroin have fallen substantially. Different models of how enforcement affects drug supply may help explain the paradox. There are substantial periods in which drug markets are not in the stable equilibrium that has informed much of the empirical research. Enforcement is likely to be more effective in preventing the formation of a mass market than in suppressing such a market once it has formed. Once a mass market is established, there may be little return to intense enforcement. A modest level of enforcement may generate most of the benefits from prohibition.

The U.S. drug problem has lost some of its political salience since the late 1980s when it was briefly the principal domestic policy concern of the public, but every year there are more than 30,000 deaths from drug-induced causes and roughly 1 million drug-related emergency room visits. More than one-third of AIDS deaths are drug related. Seven and a half million Americans are believed to need drug treatment. The majority of arrestees test positive for at least one illegal drug, and illegal drugs generate an estimated $180 billion per year in social costs (Office of National Drug Control Policy [ONDCP] 2004, 2009).

The nation invests ever-increasing amounts in an effort to control illegal drug markets. In 2007 the federal government probably spent

Jonathan P. Caulkins is professor of operations research and public policy at Heinz College and Qatar Campus, Carnegie Mellon University. Peter Reuter is professor in the School of Public Policy and Department of Criminology, University of Maryland.

$20 billion per year on drug programs,[1] and it devoted almost two-thirds of federal prison space to locking up 100,000 drug offenders. State and local governments made more than 1.5 million arrests for drug offenses and incarcerated 400,000 individuals for drug offenses on any given day. A plausible estimate of the total annual government expenditure for drug control in the United States in the latter part of the first decade of the twenty-first century is about $40 billion, of which approximately three-quarters goes to enforcement, both here and overseas.

Drug enforcement, rather than the demand-side programs of prevention and treatment, is thus the cornerstone of drug policy in the United States. Surprisingly, enforcement also dominates drug control budgets in other countries for which budget estimates are available. This holds even in countries that explicitly embrace less punitive approaches or "harm reduction" regimes that give more attention to the consequences of drug use than to its prevalence in the general population. For example, Moore (2008) finds that enforcement accounts for 55 percent of the $1.3 billion Australia spent on proactive drug control programs, and the majority of the $1.9 billion spent dealing with the consequences of drug use pertained to crime-related consequences. Likewise, Rigter (2006) finds that enforcement accounts for 75 percent of the Netherlands' €2.185 billion spending on drug control in 2003. Both Australia and the Netherlands emphasize harms rather than prevalence as the most important outcomes.

Most enforcement effort and the great bulk of imprisonment for drug-related offenses are focused on people involved in drug distribution rather than on drug users themselves (Sevigny and Caulkins 2004). Though concerns about justice and retribution do play some role, the basic justification for this considerable investment of taxpayer funds and great sacrifice of liberty is the hope that constraining supply will limit drug use and dependence.

Enforcement is directed at all levels of the distribution chain, begin-

[1] In 2003 the Office of National Drug Control Policy (ONDCP) quietly redefined what constituted federal drug control expenditures. Under the new definition, which emphasized those budget items that ONDCP claimed could be controlled ("proactive"), expenditures on prosecution and incarceration were excluded as "reactive." This led to a rebalancing of federal expenditures with a higher share classified as demand reduction, as well as a reduction in estimated total expenditures. The traditional definitions are more informative for present purposes; our $20 billion figure is an educated guess as to what the current budget would be under the traditional reporting rules. For comments on this, see Walsh (2004).

ning with supporting crop eradication and destruction of cocaine processing in Peru, Bolivia, and Colombia, and also arrest of high-level traffickers in Colombia. Even more is spent interdicting drugs at the border and in the "transit zone" between source countries and the United States. There are other types of enforcement, such as programs designed to control the chemical precursors of synthetic drugs such as methamphetamine and diversion of pharmaceuticals that can be abused as recreational drugs. Yet the largest investment is in arrest, prosecution, and incarceration of people involved in drug distribution within the United States. Higher-level domestic wholesale dealers get longer sentences, but there are so many more retail dealers and low-level employees such as couriers that "kingpins" account for a minority of drug-related incarceration.

This essay examines how all of this drug enforcement affects the price of drugs. We focus on that relationship because it is through price and availability that tough enforcement should reduce drug use in the population. We also focus on enforcement aimed at sellers both because that is where most of the resources go and because enforcement against users presents a different set of analytic issues: it constricts demand rather than supply.

The essay draws on a much expanded literature and data that have appeared over the 25 years since *Crime and Justice* published "Risks and Prices" (Reuter and Kleiman 1986, hereafter R&P), the first systematic effort at relating drug enforcement and prices. The essential logic of R&P is that drug dealers are in business to make money, so when enforcement imposes costs on drug dealers, those costs are passed along to users in the form of higher prices. That is easy to understand with respect to seizure of drugs, money, and other assets, but R&P extends the argument to monetary compensation for the nonmonetary risks. Just as miners and deep-sea divers are paid more than construction workers doing otherwise comparable work at relatively safer work sites above ground, R&P likewise attributes a portion of drug dealers' monetary profits to compensation for the risks of arrest and incarceration and also the risk of injury or death at the hands of other criminals.

Twenty-five years later there is no reason to retreat from that fundamental insight, but it now seems incomplete. The traditional R&P argument remains sensible on average in the long run, but a lot of other things can happen on the way to that long run. This essay seeks to describe additional ways that enforcement and also general market dynamics can influence price, mechanisms that can trump the original R&P mechanisms for long enough to be of consequence in at least some markets. Though our focus is on the United States, we make use of experiences and data from other Western nations, particularly Australia and the United Kingdom.

The first section is descriptive. It presents time-trend data for three aspects of cocaine and heroin markets: enforcement (as measured by incarceration), prices (adjusted for purity and inflation), and consumption, particularly as consumption relates to criminally active offenders. Over the period since 1980 incarceration rates (per thousand people) have risen by almost an order of magnitude, while the prices of both cocaine and heroin have fallen substantially. The number of dependent users fell between 1988 and 2000, the only period for which estimates are available, and we conjecture that this decline may have continued.

Sections II through V are the heart of the essay. They present a variety of models for understanding the relationship between enforcement and price. Section II starts with the simple static equilibrium model that was posited in R&P, explaining how, in the long run, tougher enforcement might raise price. Section III then considers a dynamic model that allows for disequilibrium as a market moves toward a new, long-run equilibrium. The subsequent section then discusses models connecting enforcement to emerging drug markets, while Section V considers enforcement during disequilibrium. Section VI reviews empirical evidence supporting the explanatory value of these models, while Section VII briefly presents some policy implications.

The static model of R&P is helpful in explaining some important characteristics of the major drug markets. For example, the fact that most of the earnings, though not the large individual incomes, are from the low level of the distribution system may be explained by the fact that retail dealer risks are distributed over many fewer grams of the drug than are the risks of high-level dealers and smugglers.

However, there is a need for dynamic models to account for how the market behaves in times of rapid change. For example, it is characteristic of psychoactive drugs that an epidemic of initiation starts with explosive growth for a period of months, if not a few years; supply may lag for a number of reasons in adjusting and R&P does not do a good job of accounting for price variation during this time. We also conjecture that there are multiple equilibria in many drug markets and these dynamic models show why it is easier to prevent a market at a lower equilibrium (with few users and high price) from tipping to a high equilibrium than it is to tip a mass market back down to a lower equilibrium.

Most of the advantages of prohibition can be attained with modest levels of overall enforcement coupled with targeting of dealers whose behavior poses a particular risk to the community (e.g., use of juvenile distributors, violence against competitors). Tougher enforcement across the board does not, as a matter of historical observation, seem to raise price much farther or restrict availability; it imposes rather high individual and social costs. However, enforcement may have prevented the emergence of mass markets for various new and attractive drugs. Unfortunately, the very nature of emerging markets makes it difficult to test this proposition empirically.

It is necessary to limit our domain. We say little about efforts to control production in source countries simply because there has been little development since 1986 in understanding that aspect; the pessimistic arguments and judgments of R&P (namely, that interventions in source countries would have minimal effect on retail markets in the United States) hold up well with the historical record.[2] Prices in source countries account for only 1–2 percent of retail prices in developed countries. So even if alternative development, crop eradication, or enforcement in source countries quintupled prices in source countries, the effect on retail prices downstream could be modest. Indeed, prices of coca leaves in Peru and opium in Afghanistan have gyrated dramatically with little or no corresponding observable effect on street prices for crack in Los Angeles or heroin in London. Sometimes source-country interventions reduce production in one country, but unfortunately there seems to be no shortage of peasant farmers and criminals in relatively lawless regions who are willing to take up the slack.

The discussion of markets is restricted to what is necessary for understanding the effects of enforcement on prices. We say much less about drug markets than did R&P; there is now a very large literature on the markets themselves, which we have surveyed elsewhere (Babor

---

[2] Paoli, Greenfield, and Reuter (2009) provide an extensive review for heroin source and transit country control efforts. A briefer analysis that also includes cocaine and amphetamine type stimulants (ATS) is provided in Reuter and Trautmann (2009).

et al. 2010, chap 5; see also Bushway and Reuter 2008). Moreover, some observations about markets—such as their generally competitive rather than monopolistic character—were new and controversial in 1986 and so required extensive discussion, whereas now they are widely accepted. We do not provide systematic discussion of availability because there are few data. Marijuana gets relatively little mention because it is less causally related to crime than are cocaine and heroin.

I. Drug Enforcement, Prices, and Consumption in the United States, 1980–2010

Over the last 30 years the most striking observation about drug markets is that the number of persons serving time in prison for drug offenses in the United States has risen steadily and substantially, while the prices of cocaine and heroin, adjusted for purity, have declined. The price decline was sharp during the 1980s and has been gradual since then. Since there is evidence of a shrinking cocaine and heroin market (discussed below), it is plausible that the risk of incarceration for a cocaine seller in 2005 was more than five times higher than in 1985, even though the price was only 25 percent as high (Fries et al. 2008). Methamphetamine prices have also trended down, with some notable spikes discussed below.

Superficially this is a paradox. Greater pressure on supply has been unexpectedly accompanied by declining, not rising, prices. Technically it is enforcement intensity, not the total number of imprisonments, that R&P predicts should drive up prices, and while variation in demand could play a role, in the rest of this section we argue that the basic paradox remains even after accounting for these issues. This challenge to R&P was a primary motivator of research over the last two decades to improve understanding of drug markets' response to enforcement.

Critics of U.S. drug policy often report trends in total drug arrests to paint a picture of ever-increasing toughness, since total arrests have been increasing steadily since 1980. That is misleading, if not disingenuous. It is rarely sensible to combine marijuana arrests with heroin and cocaine arrests in any analysis. The substances are very different in terms of usage patterns, health risks, enforcement practices, and notably in the consequences of arrest. The vast majority of arrests for marijuana possession, which account for about half of all drug arrests, result in no sentence of incarceration, even to local jail.[3] These arrests present a very different policy issue than do the long terms of incarceration faced by sellers of cocaine, heroin, and methamphetamine.

The rapid increase in cocaine and heroin arrests during the 1980s reflects a deliberate policy choice, and it drove correspondingly large increases in imprisonment. The increase in marijuana arrests starting in the 1990s did not. The George W. Bush administration did make marijuana a priority, but arrests grew faster under the Clinton administration, and in neither period did the arrests lead to big increases in imprisonment. Some of the increase in marijuana arrests stemmed from quality-of-life policing, such as New York City's policy of arresting people for using marijuana in plain view (Golub, Johnson, and Dunlap 2007).

There are different trends for arrests for different drugs and for sales versus possession. Heroin and cocaine arrests rose exponentially during the 1980s to peak in 1989. They fell back down when cocaine markets were disrupted in 1990, and never resumed a consistent upward trend; sales arrests in particular have been ebbing (down one-third from the 1990 peak) as markets have become less flagrant.

Marijuana arrests were stable during the 1980s, and then fell briefly before nearly doubling in the 1990s. There was another lull in growth from 1999 to 2002 before they resumed their upward trend. These substantial shifts in marijuana arrest patterns primarily reflect changes in policing practices, not underlying changes in production, distribution, or consumption patterns.

Figure 1 shows this by plotting the number of persons arrested annually for marijuana offenses and also for either cocaine or heroin (combined) from 1979 to 2007. Figure 1 shows only total marijuana arrests because in all years only 11–21 percent of those arrests were for sale as opposed to possession. For heroin and cocaine the figure shows sales offenses alone as well as the total because the proportion of the total that was for sales changed more over time. The Uniform Crime Reporting program (UCR) does not separate cocaine from heroin offenses, a curious tribute to tradition since there has been intense interest in each separately for at least 25 years (Federal Bureau of In-

---

[3] The only study that we know of that traces the incarceration risks for marijuana possession arrestees is Reuter, Hirschfield, and Davies (2001) for three large counties in the state of Maryland. They report no sentence of jail time, but one-third spent at least one night in jail pretrial.

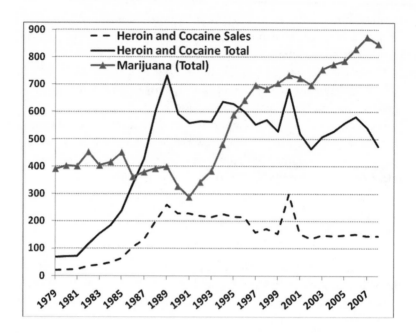

FIG. 1.—Drug arrests (in thousands), 1979–2007. Source: Federal Bureau of Investigation (2009), *Crime in the United States*, various years.

vestigation 2009); UCR data also lump methamphetamine into a heterogeneous "other" category, so figure 1 includes no line for methamphetamine, though by all accounts those arrests grew rapidly in the 1990s.

The arrest figures understate the increase in enforcement intensity over the last quarter century. Arrest is just a part of enforcement and is only a modest penalty by itself, with incarceration being the more substantial penalty to which supply and price trends should respond. However, figure 2 shows that the total number incarcerated for 1980–2002 increased, based on Caulkins and Chandler (2006). The story here is much simpler; the number of those locked up in all three types of correctional facilities (federal prison, state prison, and local jails) rose without cease throughout the period. The growth has been much faster for the state prison population than for local jail inmates. Whereas in 1985 the figures were about even for each, by 2002 the state figure was 225,000 people, whereas that for jails was only 140,000.

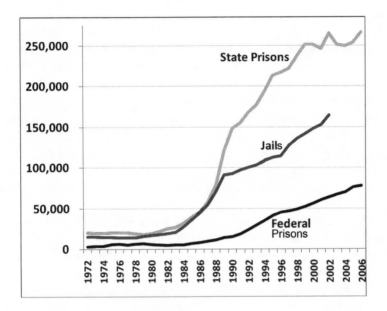

FIG. 2.—Population of inmates awaiting trial or serving time for drug law violations in the United States, by type of penal institution. Source: Caulkins and Chandler (2006).

This may represent increasing severity of penalties meted out for drug offenders.

Sevigny and Caulkins (2004) used the 1997 Survey of Prison Inmates to show that the great majority of those who reported that they were incarcerated for drug possession offenses were involved in drug distribution, albeit often in minor roles. For some, the possession conviction involved a plea bargain. Also, of the 90,000 they estimated to be in state prison for possession (i.e., facing a sentence of more than 12 months), only about one-third said that their actual offense was possession of less than 10 retail units of drugs. One-sixth of them reported that they had a "major role" in drug selling. No analyses have been published for those locked up in jails for drug offenses; a higher share of them are presumably there for simple possession offenses, which rarely result in felony conviction, but the earlier statement that the bulk of incarceration, and the growth in the number, is dominated by selling offenses still holds here.

These arrest and imprisonment figures by themselves give no information about what has happened to the intensity of drug enforcement.

For that one needs to know the ratio of enforcement effort relative to the size of the drug market. For example, it is plausible that cocaine markets expanded even faster than the number of incarcerations for cocaine selling did during the first half of the 1980s (Reuter 1991), in which case the risk faced by a cocaine seller could have been less in 1985 than in 1981. However, that is unlikely for the remainder of the period. Indeed, it appears that total sales (quantity of cocaine and number of transactions) fell through the 1990s (ONDCP 2001).[4] For our purposes, the extent of the decline is a second-order consideration. All we need is for the reader to accept that the stringency of enforcement against cocaine and heroin selling has risen sharply over the period since 1980.

How have prices responded to this increase in enforcement intensity? Cocaine, heroin, and methamphetamine prices are most usefully reported after adjusting for purity since much of the effective variation in price comes through changes in purity (e.g., Caulkins 1994; Rhodes et al. 2007). For example, if 1 gram of a powder that is 50 percent cocaine by weight costs $100, the purity-adjusted price would be $200 per pure gram.

Figure 3 shows that the purity-adjusted price of cocaine declined over the period 1981–2007, expressed in constant dollars. Though there are occasional spikes, none lasted more than a few quarters and none were proportionately large. The big decline occurred in the 1980s, during a period of market expansion. There was not much change during the 1990s, but the decline from 2000 to 2007 was substantial in percentage terms, approximately 25 percent.

The sharp decline in price might be expected to generate a rise in consumption, as even drug users show demand sensitivity to price (Grossman 2005). Yet the available indicators, though not strong, show instead that total consumption has probably declined (ONDCP 2001). Certainly the number of past-year users has declined, at least as reflected in annual surveys of the household population, high school students, and young adults (Johnston et al. 2009; Substance Abuse Mental Health Services Administration [SAMHSA] 2009). It is much harder to measure total consumption. People can more reliably report whether they have used than how much they have used, and, more important, total consumption is dominated by the small subset of past-year users

---

[4] No estimates have been published after 2001, but an update through 2006 is in preparation.

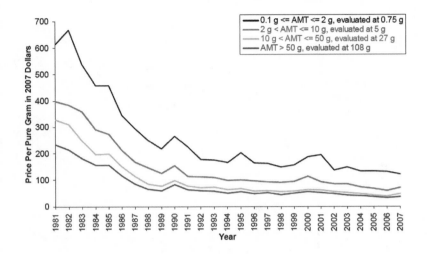

FIG. 3.—The price of cocaine, 1981–2007. Source: ONDCP (2008)

who are heavy or dependent users. Such individuals are more likely to fall outside the surveys' sampling frames (e.g., because they are homeless) or be nonrespondents.

Several teams have stitched together time series for demand by combining various complementary data sets and modeling assumptions (Everingham and Rydell 1994; ONDCP 2001; Caulkins, Behrens, et al. 2004). The general finding is that consumption grew in the 1980s even though prevalence was falling because growth in the number of dependent users more than offset the steep declines in light or occasional users. Since the early 1990s there has been a slow ebbing of demand as the cohort with peak exposure ages, dies, or eventually gives up use. This is a slow process, and there is still some, albeit smaller, inflow of new users, so demand today is probably still within a factor of two of its peak and will not diminish rapidly any time soon.

Figure 4 shows past-month marijuana and cocaine and past-year heroin use as measured by the National Survey on Drug Use and Health since 1974.[5] Prevalence increased during the 1970s and fell during the 1980s. Recorded cocaine and marijuana prevalence is running about 25 percent higher since 2001 than in the 1990s. That may be due to

[5] Data obtained from SAMHDA's online data analysis site, http://www.icpsr.umich .edu/cocoon/SAMHDA/DAS3/00064.xml.

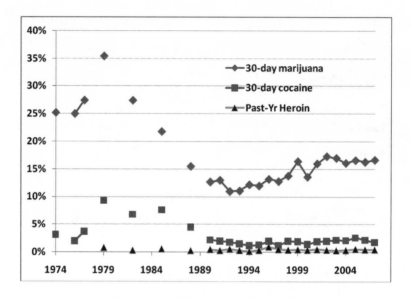

FIG. 4.—Prevalence among 18–25-year-olds as measured by U.S. household surveys, 1974–2007. Source: Authors' analysis of data obtained from SAMHDA's online data analysis site, http://www.icpsr.umich.edu/cocoon/SAMHDA/DAS3/00064.xml. The household survey's name changed from the National Household Survey of Drug Abuse to the National Survey on Drug Use and Health during this time.

changes in survey methodology, including increased response rates after the introduction of $30 payments to incentivize participation in 2002. For example, the number of people reporting having ever used marijuana grew by 10.5 million between 2001 and 2002 even though only 3 million persons reported using for the first time in 2002 (SAMHSA 2003).

Figure 4 also illustrates the enormous differences in prevalence across substances. Marijuana is by far the most commonly used substance, and even past-year heroin use barely registers on the graph when that use is self-reported by the household population. Fewer than one in 200 persons over the age of 12 reported that they had used heroin in the past 12 months in 2007.

Figure 5 shows that the estimated numbers of chronic users[6] of cocaine and heroin have declined in the period 1988–2000, in both cases

[6] Defined as having used on 8 or more days in the previous 30 days.

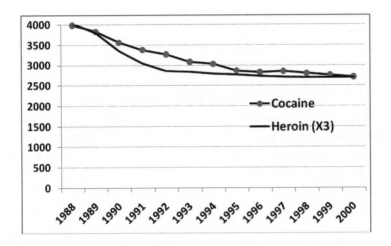

FIG. 5.—Estimated number of chronic cocaine and heroin users (times 3), 1988–2000 (in thousands). Source: ONDCP (2000).

by almost exactly one-third. The heroin numbers are scaled by multiplying by three both to make the heroin trends easier to see and also to highlight how closely the cocaine and heroin trends parallel each other.

These estimates were produced by sophisticated modeling of some weak data sets, and reestimation throughout the 1990s led to substantial changes in the estimates for specific years. For example, the prior set of estimates (ONDCP 2000) found that there had been an increase for heroin in the mid-1990s, almost exactly canceling the decline from 1988 to 1993; that rebound is missing in the most recent published estimate.[7] Thus these estimates should be seen as indicative rather than precise. However, for our purposes what is important is that results agree that there was no expansion in the size of the cocaine and heroin markets from 1988 to 2000. We can safely assume that the massive increase in incarceration outpaced increases in market size, and so indeed generated a very large rise in the legal risks faced by a dealer.

We now turn to the main focus of this essay, assessing four different models of how enforcement affects the purity-adjusted price of drugs. Section II addresses markets in static equilibrium, meaning that prices

[7] Updated estimates were prepared for ONDCP but were never published. See Reuter (2008).

are stable at a level such that the quantity suppliers produce exactly matches the amount customers wish to buy at that price. More precisely, it updates the "risks and prices" framework for comparing two markets, each in equilibrium but differing in the intensity of enforcement. Such analysis attributes difference in price and consumption across the two markets to the difference in enforcement intensity.

The general conclusion from this "comparative statics" analysis is that illegality plus a modest level of enforcement can keep prices much higher and availability much lower than would be the case if there were no prohibition or enforcement. However, for an established market, increases in enforcement beyond that basic level (akin to the enforcement intensity in the United States in 1980) have only modest further effects on price, availability, and use. We take up these policy implications in the concluding section.

The next sections take account of important complications that this model does not consider. Section III discusses what happens when a market for a given substance in a given place and time can have more than one stable equilibrium level of price and use, for example, because the market must attain a certain minimum viable size in order to create general availability. At least in theory, aggressive enforcement may be able to tip a market from a high-level equilibrium to a low-level equilibrium or, more modestly, prevent a market at a low-level equilibrium from tipping up to a high-level equilibrium. We offer some examples of the latter but none of the former; the scarcity of instances of shifting a mass market to a new, small-market equilibrium points to the difficulty of that task.

Section IV extends the analysis to a market that is in the process of moving from one stable equilibrium to another, such as one tipping from a low-use to a high-use equilibrium. Even though price and quantity may be changing over time, they are on an equilibrium path in the sense that at any given moment in time, the market price balances supply and demand. Borrowing a term from thermodynamics, we call them quasi-static equilibria because the changes occur relatively gradually—meaning they take a year or more. The market always clears (meaning users willing to pay the current market price can locate a supplier), and no one is ever surprised by the next week's average market price. The price may be trending higher or lower, but it does so smoothly. This model is important in helping understand price trends in the United States during the 1980s and more generally when a mass market for a drug first emerges.

In Section V, we turn attention to markets that are not in equilibrium, typically due to some shock or surprise. The extreme form of disequilibrium is a market that does not clear, meaning the drug simply is not available no matter how much buyers are willing to pay. The more common form of disequilibrium is when a shock to the system quickly moves the market clearing (purity-adjusted) price and quantity substantially away from the baseline price and quantity, but then price and quantity move again to an equilibrium (whether static or quasi-static). Usually the market returns to its original equilibrium, but in principle if the shock is large enough it could "tip" the market to a different equilibrium. "Quickly" in this context means purity-adjusted price is pushed away from its original equilibrium within a few weeks or months, most often through an adjustment to purity, not (just) a change in the price per raw gram, unadjusted for purity.

A comparison to oil and gasoline markets may be useful. When oil prices spiked to $147 in July 2008, that price did not reflect a long-run equilibrium. However, motorists were always able to buy gasoline, albeit at very high prices. In contrast, during the 1973 oil embargo, sometimes gasoline was simply not available. Both events reflect shocks that pushed prices away from their long-run equilibrium, but only in 1973 were there instances of the market not clearing. It is rare for markets not to clear, but price spikes and troughs are not uncommon in commodity markets, whether legal (e.g., natural resources and farm products) or illegal.

II. Drug Enforcement's Effect on Long-Run Equilibrium Prices: Risks and Prices Theory

Application of the standard competitive model to drug markets is now common in introductory economics texts (e.g., Frank and Bernanke 2004). The most basic concepts in economics are those of demand and supply. A demand curve maps the relationship between price and the quantity consumers are willing to purchase. The supply curve maps the relationship between price and the quantity that producers (distributors) are willing to produce (provide). The market clears at the price at which the quantity demanded by consumers equals the quantity that distributors are willing to supply, that is, at the point where the supply

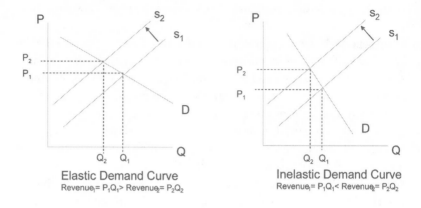

Elastic Demand Curve
$Revenue_1 = P_1Q_1 > Revenue_2 = P_2Q_2$

Inelastic Demand Curve
$Revenue_1 = P_1Q_1 < Revenue_2 = P_2Q_2$

FIG. 6.—Illegal drug markets

and demand curves cross. Interventions can be thought of in terms of how they affect the supply curve or the demand curve and the resulting equilibrium price and quantity.

Consider what the model suggests are the effects of restricting supply, for example, by incarcerating more drug dealers. The standard analysis is that because dealers will only sell in return for more money, the supply curve shifts up and to the left, so that at any given price less is supplied. As figure 6 shows, this increases the market price and reduces the quantity of drugs sold.

Both the magnitude of the reduction in quantity sold and the resulting effect on dealers' revenues depend on the elasticity of demand, which is related to the slope of the demand curve. When the demand curve is relatively flat (high elasticity of demand, as in the left-hand panel of fig. 1), quantity consumed falls a lot, so dealers' revenues decline. If the demand curve is steep (low elasticity, right-hand panel), quantity falls by less, proportionately, than prices rise, so restricting supply actually increases dealers' gross revenues.

Some drug-related consequences are driven by consumption, including overdose, dependence itself, and crime caused by intoxication. Others are driven more directly by spending on drugs; those include corruption, the economic-compulsive crime that users commit to raise funds, and systemic crime between dealers (Goldstein 1985). Hence, the elasticity of demand is perhaps the single most important parameter determining how effective restricting supply is at ameliorating drug-related harms.

Economists have done extensive work on estimating the price elasticity of demand for various drugs, particularly cocaine and marijuana, including the cross-elasticity between illegal drugs and cigarettes or alcohol (e.g., Cameron and Williams 2001; Grossman 2005; Jofre-Bonet and Petry 2008).[8] Almost all serious studies find that consumption responds to changes in price. However, the various studies using different methods and different measures of use produce a range of estimates of just how responsive consumption is to price changes.

Still, the overall logic model should be clear. Supply control drives up prices. Higher prices reduce consumption. The change in consumption, together with the change in price, determines the change in spending. The change in consumption, together with the change in spending, determines the change in drug-related social costs.

"Risks and prices" theory provides the foundation for this logic model by elaborating the simple textbook model of how enforcement imposes costs on drug suppliers. To simplify, enforcement acts almost like a tax. For example, if year in and year out law enforcement seizes one-third of all drugs, the drug distribution system will respond by shipping more drugs, 1.5 kilograms for every kilogram to be consumed. However, the ongoing cost of replacing those seized drugs makes it more expensive to deliver a given quantity to users. Drug dealers are in business to make money, so they pass those costs on to users in the form of higher prices, under plausible assumptions about the structure of drug markets.

Indeed, it is hard to identify any large costs of delivering drugs to final users other than those directly related to illegality and enforcement. One indication of that proposition is that the share of cocaine's retail price accounted for by growing and refining it is less than 1 percent. A gram of a drug that sells for over $100 on the streets of Chicago (in units of less than 1 gram) leaves Colombia at a cost of

[8] The price elasticity of demand is the percentage reduction in demand caused by a 1 percent increase in price; except under exceptional conditions it is negative. There is a similar price elasticity of supply, usually positive. The cross-elasticity of marijuana and alcohol is the percentage change in the demand for marijuana caused by a 1 percent increase in the price of alcohol; the cross-elasticity will be positive if the marijuana and alcohol are substitutes and negative if they are complements. Demand is labeled "inelastic" if the absolute value of the elasticity is smaller than one, since it means that a rise in price will lead to a rise in total revenues.

barely $1 (in units of multiple kilos). Caulkins and Reuter (1998) estimated the breakdown of costs for cocaine in 1990 as follows.

The risk-compensation aspect is somewhat hidden in this decomposition. For example, importation (12 percent of the total) is almost all risk compensation. FedEx will deliver a kilogram of a legal good from Bogotá to Miami for less than $50. In contrast, the price of a landed kilogram of cocaine in Miami is around $15,000, compared to an export price of less than $1,500. That difference between $50 and $13,500 is a consequence of the current prohibition system. (It does not represent monopoly rents; smuggling services are provided in a competitive market.)

Labor costs are high in part because illegality forces the distribution system to operate in inefficient ways. Drugs are diluted and packaged by hand. Simple machines could do that work at a small fraction of the cost (as is done for mass-produced goods such as sugar) except that enforcement makes it risky (i.e., expensive) to maintain dedicated, fixed capital equipment. Sellers need to have protection against robbery, look out for police, and work with small, easily exhausted stock because it is too risky to maintain large quantities at the point of sale.

Two studies provide some data on the rate of sales per dealer. Reuter, MacCoun, and Murphy (1990) estimate that a daily cocaine retailer sold a median of $3,600 worth of drugs each month in 1988 in Washington, DC. The same individuals were estimated to have spent 66 hours per month selling and to earn a median of $7 per hour in the licit labor market. They sacrificed about $462 (66 times $7) in legitimate earnings per $3,600 sold.[9] As Caulkins and Reuter (1998) show, this yields a labor time cost of about 13 percent of the retail value to just compensate the seller's time. Levitt and Venkatesh (2000), working with the financial records of a drug-selling gang in Chicago in the mid-1990s, estimated that the average sales volume per dealer per month was only $1,000 and that the wages per "foot soldier" were about $470. The implied number of sales transactions per day per dealer was only two, suggesting that the costs of time compensation might be higher than estimated in the Reuter et al. study, though the legitimate earnings of this younger and more marginalized population may have been lower in the Levitt and Venkatesh study.

For policy purposes, given the effort that goes into interdicting drugs

---

[9] This assumes that they could have found paid employment for the extra hours.

on their way to the United States, a key analytic issue is how changes in the import price affect retail prices. The R&P model can help understand what parameters are central for that purpose. Assume that a kilogram of heroin sells for $50,000 at import in El Paso and the equivalent of $500,000 per kilogram when sold at retail units of 200 milligrams in Chicago. Now imagine that more effective interdiction boosts the import price by 50 percent to $75,000. How would this affect the retail price of heroin in Chicago?

One theory of vertical price relationships, which Caulkins (1990) has termed the "additive model," argues that the import price is essentially a raw material cost (Reuter and Kleiman 1986). Thus, the wholesaler who previously bought heroin at $50,000 and now pays $75,000 has had roughly $25,000 added to the per-kilo costs. The actual cost increase will be somewhat more than $25,000 per kilo, due to seizures, thefts, and other losses: wholesalers have to buy more than one kilo of drug for each kilo they sell.

In a competitive market, the wholesaler simply passes these increased costs along to the next stage of the distribution chain. The buyer at this stage will thus face an increase of $25,000+ in costs, which will be passed along to the next market level. Eventually, the $25,000+ cost increase reaches consumers, and the end result is that the retail price of heroin increases by $25 per gram (or somewhat more, when all the losses and seizures along the distribution chain are factored in), which is only about 5 percent of the initial retail price. Doing this exercise for cocaine and imported marijuana in the United States, Reuter, Crawford, and Cave (1988) projected, based on some assumptions that were reasonable but not empirically tested, that a doubling of the import price results in only a 10 or 20 percent rise in the retail price. Or, put another way, it would take a quintupling of import prices to effect a doubling of retail prices.

Of the few empirical analyses of interdiction, most have assumed the additive model. And because the replacement cost of seized cocaine and heroin is a small fraction of their final retail price—as little as 1 percent in source countries and usually no more than 20 percent at the point of entry into the final market country—these analyses have concluded that the potential contribution of interdiction to the reduction of drug abuse is small, or at least that it is not cost effective compared to domestic enforcement and treatment (Rydell and Everingham 1994). Although the additive model is conceptually compelling, some scholars have noted that it does not fit very well with some historical price data drawn from the lower end of the distribution chain (Caulkins 1990; Boyum 1992).

Some historical price data appear to be more consistent with what Caulkins has called the "multiplicative model" of vertical price relationships, which holds that a change of a certain percentage in price at one stage of production or distribution brings about a similar percentage change at subsequent stages. The idea behind the multiplicative model is that many of the costs of doing business in the drug trade, such as the risk of employees and other dealers stealing drugs, are more strongly related to the value of drugs bought and sold than to the weight or quantity trafficked. Thus, the multiplicative model predicts that if the import price of heroin rises 50 percent, from \$50,000 to \$75,000, then suppliers' costs all the way down the distribution chain will also increase by 50 percent. So retail prices will also rise 50 percent, from \$500,000 to \$750,000, providing a much more favorable assessment of interdiction.

Cocaine prices in the 1980s and early 1990s followed a remarkably consistent multiplicative relationship between kilogram level and retail prices (Caulkins 1990, 1994). Likewise, Rhodes, Hyatt, and Scheiman (1994), Crane, Rivolo, and Comfort (1997), and DeSimone (1998) argue for a multiplicative model. However, the data that indicated a multiplicative model were far from conclusive (DeSimone 2006). Except during occasional shortages, prices consistently declined during this period, and so it is possible that the factors causing the decline operated at all levels of the market. In other words, it may be that declines in retail prices were not so much caused by the decline in import prices, but rather that both import and retail prices were influenced by other factors. For example, the growth in the cocaine industry internationally, and the development of crack markets domestically, may have created economies of scale that lowered the costs of wholesale and retail operations.

In short, the nature of vertical price relationships in drug markets is an open question. The answer may lie somewhere between the additive and multiplicative models. Indeed, Caulkins (1990) and Boyum (1992) have speculated that the multiplicative model may hold when the drugs' price per unit is very high (e.g., for retail cocaine and heroin transactions in the United States and Europe), but that the additive model may apply when prices are less extreme (e.g., for higher-level

TABLE 1

Components of the Costs of Cocaine, 1990

Component Activity	Percentage of Total Cost
Wholesale price in Colombia	1
Importing of drug	12
Retail labor	13
Higher-level labor	~3
Drug and asset seizure	8–11
Money laundering fees	2–4
Packaging, processing, and inventory costs	~2
Compensation for risk of prison	24
Compensation for physical risk	33
Total	~100

SOURCE.—Caulkins and Reuter (1998).

wholesale transactions). Pietschmann's (2004) analysis of data on heroin prices in the Eastern Hemisphere is consistent with such a mixed model.

It is clear that interdiction imposes considerable costs on drug traffickers; import prices are much higher than they would be if borders were unpoliced. What is uncertain, besides the import-retail price linkage, is whether sizable changes in the interdiction budget would have commensurate effects on import prices. It may be that a 50 percent reduction in interdiction funding would be inconsequential because the remaining effort would be sufficient to induce traffickers to continue to take costly avoidance actions. However, it is also not clear whether even current interdiction spending can preserve the current markups in the long run given increasing globalization of commerce (Stares 1996; Costa Storti and de Grauwe 2009).

We conclude this discussion of the simple risks and prices framework with four observations. First, risk compensation due to violence affects price determination, but that role tends to get short analytic shrift, probably due to the paucity of data available. However, the original R&P noted that it is a risk for which drug dealers need to be compensated. As noted in table 1, Reuter, MacCoun, and Murphy (1990) estimated that compensation risk for violent victimization accounted for one-third of the retail price of cocaine in Washington in the late 1980s. That, however, was a period when the markets were near their peak and had attracted many young men who had high propensities for violence and may not be generalizable across time. Violent crime in the United States generally has declined markedly since the early 1990s, and drug market violence may have fallen substantially as well. The aging of cocaine and heroin users, as indicated in treatment data (e.g., Trunzo and Henderson 2007), suggests that these markets are now populated by older participants, who are probably less violent than they were when younger. For example, in 1992 data on treatment admissions for cocaine, 40 percent of these clients were under the age of 30. By 2006, that figure had dropped to 26 percent, while the fraction of clients over the age of 40 rose from 15 percent to 47 percent between 1992 and 2006. Furthermore, Caulkins, Reuter, and Taylor (2006) offer a theoretical model of drug dealing in which the removal of violent dealers, either through incarceration or homicide, might drive down equilibrium prices. Thus, one force driving down cocaine and heroin prices in the United States may be a decline in compensation for physical risk. However, there is little that can be said empirically on this matter.

Second, David Boyum (1992) offers an important insight, namely, that drug dealing "firms" (almost) never have negative accounting profits. As a consequence of illegal drug markets, the normal Darwinian selection winnowing out inefficient firms, namely, that they lose money, works very weakly. For example, a large rise in the sentence for selling more than one kilogram of cocaine, that should in principle make selling at the current price unattractive and lead some dealers to exit the business and others to raise the wholesale price, may only have those effects with a long lag if it takes time for those in the drug-selling business to learn about this change.

Third, R&P presumes people will move in and out of drug dealing in response to balancing the risk-adjusted return from the dealing against their potential earnings from other activities (whether legal or not). Since R&P was published, advances in behavioral economics and behavioral decision theory have shown repeatedly that people do not always act in ways that maximize their expected gain, even in relatively simple laboratory settings. Decision heuristics routinely fail in certain contexts. People misjudge probabilities (Kahneman, Slovic, and Tversky 1982), discount future events "too heavily" (Laibson 1997), are distracted by irrelevant information, and fail to anticipate how happy or unhappy they will feel in future hypothetical states (Loewenstein,

O'Donoghue, and Rabin 2003). These limitations on human decision making are particularly pronounced for decisions to use or to sell drugs, since both offer immediate rewards with delayed, uncertain consequences. Dependent users' decisions are further clouded by the cravings triggered by withdrawal (Badger et al. 2007). Caulkins and MacCoun (2005) suggest a partially decoupled relationship between drug enforcement and prices. R&P may still apply in the long run as people do gradually move in or out of the market after they finally recognize that it is in their interest to do so, but the adjustment periods may be lengthy.

Fourth, from the perspective of a dealer, enforcement outcomes are random events, akin to fires and traffic accidents in daily life. R&P stresses the idea that greater enforcement intensity increases the expected cost of enforcement for dealers, but enforcement also creates variation in outcomes across dealers because some get arrested but others do not. The point is perhaps best illustrated with some stylized numbers. Suppose enforcement creates for a certain category of dealer a 50 percent risk of receiving a prison term for which those dealers would demand $500,000 in compensation. In other words, in this hypothetical example we imagine that for these dealers $500,000 is the bare minimum they would need to receive—and get to keep—in order to voluntarily serve a prison term for selling. R&P predicts that all dealers in that category will demand $250,000 in additional monetary compensation, since $250,000 equals the 50 percent probability times the $500,000 consequence. However, not all dealers "pay" an enforcement cost of $250,000. Indeed, none do. After the uncertainty about which 50 percent of dealers will be punished, it turns out that half of the dealers are winners and half are losers. The lucky 50 percent made an additional $250,000 without going to prison; the other half are losers who may have made $250,000, but that does not compensate them for the long prison term they received. Both winners and losers at the drug-dealing game are bad for society. Winners make visible, bad role models for impressionable youth who have weak legitimate economic alternatives, and losers suffer in obvious ways. Levitt and Venkatesh (2000) investigate this tournament quality of dealers' wages empirically, and find that there are many losers and just a few big winners, just as with a familiar state lottery and representing the well-known optimism bias that influences so much behavior.

III. Enforcement's Ability to "Tip" Markets from One
Long-Run Equilibrium to Another

Drug markets often experience rapid changes, in particular, periods of explosive growth. Risks and prices is a static framework not well suited to accommodate that phase of market development, which is of particular interest for policy purposes. Are there methods for preventing the growth? For epistemological reasons it is hard to identify law enforcement successes here. Markets that remain small attract neither general public attention nor good measurement.

Many models of markets have multiple stable equilibria separated by an intermediate "tipping point" at which a modest push effects rapid change toward one or another equilibrium. This presents interesting opportunities to time and scale enforcement for the greatest effect. Unfortunately, markets may grow beyond the tipping point quickly, before the associated use has been identified as a "problem situation."

Tipping points have been popularized by Gladwell's (2000) book, but multiple equilibria have long been a mainstay of models of drug markets and drug epidemics (Kleiman 1988, 1993; Baveja et al. 1993; Caulkins 1993; Tragler, Caulkins, and Feichtinger 2001). The scientific notion of a tipping point is more precise than what Gladwell describes (Grass et al. 2008), but the essence is similar.

Stable equilibria are conditions that the system will tend to stay in naturally, without a great deal of control effort being exerted. Many systems have only one such equilibrium: the classic static market described in figure 1. Others systems have more than one condition that tends to persist over time.

Models from development economics offer a familiar example (Skiba 1978). Some macroeconomists speak of very poor countries being stuck in a "poverty trap." What they mean is that, even should the income gap between affluent countries and middle-income countries tend to diminish over time through "convergence" or technological catch-up, prospects for the world's "bottom billion" may be less favorable (Collier 2007). Those countries, according to some schools of thought, are trapped in a different, much poorer stable state than the stable high-income state enjoyed by developed countries.

If there are two or more states the system can remain in stably over time, and if at the moment the system is near a balance point in between two of them, the "tipping point," then even a little shove can have very large effects if it tips the system into a trajectory to approach one equilibrium instead of another (what in lay jargon is referred to as a "butterfly effect").

For drug markets, the basic intuition is that when few people are using or selling the drug, it is relatively easy to keep the drug from spreading, so that is one (low-use) equilibrium. Reasons include the following: in a "thin" market, sellers and buyers have a hard time locating each other, behaviors that are uncommon are more likely to be socially stigmatized, and a modest level of enforcement effort can create high risks for each of the relatively small number of people over whom that effort is distributed (Kleiman 1993). The other extreme is a high-volume equilibrium, when the drug is very widely used. That situation may also be stable because having one more or one fewer person use might have very little effect on the behavior of others. Potential users will be offered the drug multiple times anyway and, if they choose to use, will be able to locate multiple suppliers (Riley 1997). So there are not feedback effects that amplify movements away from the high-volume equilibrium. In between, however, there may be a tipping point where the market is still of modest size, but close to reaching a critical mass that will enable it to spread widely.

Kleiman (2009) lays out the general theory behind multiple equilibria, but some of the key ideas are captured in his (1993) paper on "enforcement swamping." Drug enforcement's effect on the risk of trafficking a kilogram and, hence, the resulting price per kilogram depends not on the total level of enforcement effort but rather on the enforcement intensity per kilogram sold. When the market is small, a given level of enforcement effort can make selling quite risky, but if the market grows tenfold while enforcement resources grow only fivefold, then the enforcement risk experienced per dealer or per kilogram sold falls by 50 percent.

Dynamic analysis of drug markets is a relatively recent phenomenon, and empirically validating and parameterizing models is very difficult. However, in almost all models constructed to date, the tipping point is not halfway between the low- and high-use equilibria; it is much closer to the low-level equilibrium. That is, only with very low levels of use are those low levels stable. If use rises to even a modest fraction (perhaps one-tenth or one-fifth) of the long-run steady state, then that is enough to place the system on a trajectory approaching a higher-use steady state.

If one believes drug markets operate in this way, the implications are as follows: If a market is at a low-level equilibrium, it should take little enforcement effort to hold it there, and that effort may be a tremendously cost-effective investment, even if the drug does not seem to be very threatening, precisely because it is not widely used. Conversely, if a market is at a high-level equilibrium, suppressing use is difficult because one is pushing against the tide. Moderately strenuous efforts might reduce consumption somewhat for a time, but as soon as the extra efforts are relaxed, use will rapidly rise back to that stable, high-level equilibrium. A very aggressive effort sustained long enough might eventually tip the market back to its low-level equilibrium, but it would take great determination. Finally, if one happens to catch the market after it has begun moving toward the high-level equilibrium but before it has approached that equilibrium, then it might be wise to act very quickly and decisively, because it is much easier to stuff a genie that is halfway out of the bottle back in than it is to corral a genie after it has escaped completely.

There are very few examples of entire countries being able to put a genie back in the bottle. Communist China's suppression of its opium market in the 1950s is perhaps the last example. Paoli, Greenfield, and Reuter (2009) note that the irredentist movement controlling the dominant opium producer in Myanmar managed to reduce production there drastically in the period 1998–2007.[10] It is not clear whether suppression of the U.S. cocaine and heroin markets between 1900 and 1930 counts. That might instead be seen as an original imposition of prohibition that drove users out of the market who would not participate in a black market, rather than an increase in enforcement tipping a large, already illegal market down to a small market equilibrium.

There are more instances at the local level, where the two equilibria are not between levels of use but rather between levels of flagrancy in dealing (each supporting roughly the same amount of use). Surreptitious dealing is one possible equilibrium. Even if there are 1,000 dealers in a city, if all are hidden from the police and the public eye, and you become the only dealer brazenly selling on a street corner, then your drug dealing career will be very short.

---

[10] Both episodes involved use of coercion not compatible with even a modest level of civil rights and democratic process. We know of no similar success on the part of a democratic government.

Unfortunately, another equilibrium is one in which all or most dealers sell brazenly in public markets. Such selling does not make them immune to arrest. Indeed, when there are flagrant street markets, the police sometimes can make more arrests than the rest of the criminal justice system could handle. However, the arrest risk per dealer may be tolerably low if physical presence in the street market increases opportunities to obtain customers. The risk is a bit akin to small fish swimming in schools. It is easy for big fish to see the school, so schooling does not deter predation. But, from the perspective of an individual fish, it decreases the individual likelihood that it gets eaten.

Enforcement does have instances of success tipping large black markets from high flagrancy equilibrium into the lower equilibrium. There are a variety of case studies of aggressive "crackdowns" suppressing at least the flagrancy of dealing activity (Zimmer 1987; Kleiman 1988; Caulkins, Larson, and Rich 1993; Braga et al. 2001), and a complementary set of theoretical papers on the topic (Baveja et al. 1993; Caulkins 1993; Tragler, Caulkins, and Feichtinger 2001). More generally, the idea that markets can be tipped from brazen to covert modes of operation is a plausible interpretation of the changes in local U.S. markets between the 1980s and 2000s when flagrant, place-based markets supporting anonymous transactions were largely replaced by transactions arranged through some electronic contact (cell phone, beeper, etc.).

Perhaps enforcement has many more instances of success tipping small black markets into low equilibrium, or expunging them entirely. After all, very many substances are prone to abuse. Yet a rather modest number of substances account for most use of purely illegal drugs (as opposed to diverted pharmaceuticals). These standbys (marijuana, opiates, cocaine/crack, and certain of the amphetamine type stimulants) may be widespread because they are more appealing than other drugs, but it is also possible that law enforcement has instead succeeded in preventing an otherwise robust market from forming for these other substances as well: PCP, GHB, Rohypnol, LSD, ketamine, methcathinone, peyote, and mescaline. If so, then law enforcement might be very effective at controlling those smaller markets, and we have no way to know because the prevention of a potential outcome, or counterfactual and nonevents, are intrinsically hard to document or disprove.

IV. Enforcement's Effects on Emerging Markets

The general conclusion of the R&P model is that after simple illegality, backed by enough enforcement to realize the "structural consequences of product illegality" (Reuter 1983), drives prices quite high, expanding drug law enforcement against an already established market has little further effect on the price of illegal drugs. The purpose of this section is to note that this conclusion may not apply to new or emerging markets.

That is not to say that there is strong evidence that enforcement is able to drive up prices in emerging markets. Rather, there is little empirical evidence one way or another. However, there are deductive arguments suggesting that enforcement might be relatively more successful at keeping prices high in small or emerging markets, at least for a time. We discuss those hypotheses after first clarifying what we mean by an emerging market.

A. Concept of an Emerging Market

Drug use emerges over time in ways that reflect what is sometimes called an "epidemic cycle." Initially, drug use is rare, but then something on the supply (increased availability) or demand side (e.g., a counterculture or youth movement) kicks off a period of rapid expansion in drug use. Drug use diffuses by word of mouth, with existing users introducing friends and associates to the substance (Ferrence 2001). Such "contagious" spread tears through networks quite literally to create exponential growth. That rapid growth cannot go on indefinitely. There are competing explanations for what typically brings an end to the rapid growth, including exhaustion of the pool of individuals susceptible to initiation and lagging negative feedback that begins once enough users escalate to dependent or problematic use to give the drug a reputation for being dangerous (Musto 1987; Behrens et al. 1999, 2000; Rossi 2001).

Whatever the mechanism, initiation rates for many substances drop substantially from their initial peaks. For some drugs, prevalence (the percentage of the population using) also spikes up above ("overshoots") its long-run equilibrium. As time goes on, the mix of users shifts as well, with a growing number of dependent users. Nondependent users generally remain in the majority by number, but dependent users consume so much more per capita that they come to dominate consumption by quantity of drug. In the United States today, dependent users account for much more than half of the consumption of all the major illegal drugs (heroin, cocaine/crack, methamphetamine, and cannabis). For example, by ONDCP (2001) estimates, the relatively small number of cocaine users who are "hard core" account for 84 percent of total spending on the drug; the corresponding figure for heroin is 93 percent. Once initiation has passed its peak and demand becomes dominated by dependent users, drug use is less likely to vary sharply over time; dependent users make stable customers.

The markets can likewise evolve in terms of both size and sophistication. Obviously, a growing number of drug users implies a growing total quantity supplied. Larger drug markets may be more efficient and more robust to enforcement actions. While the exact threshold of size needed for an emerging market to resist enforcement efforts is not clear, the qualitative result is that although it may be cheaper to find and arrest people when markets are large, the cost effectiveness of arresting an additional dealer may be higher when markets are small.

Also, drug production and distribution can become more sophisticated over time, with smugglers constantly developing new and more sophisticated methods (submarines, tunnels under the border, embedding drugs within other materials, etc.). Drug enforcement also innovates. Indeed, drug smuggling is often depicted as something of an "arms race" between smugglers and law enforcement. However, there is some reason to believe that smugglers' risk of arrest is particularly high the first few times that an organization tries a particular route or tactic (Caulkins, Burnett, and Leslie 2009), and enforcement's early edge might tend to erode over time.

A counterpart of sophistication at the production and smuggling levels can be "professionalization" of retail distribution, meaning an increasing share of demand is supplied by people who derive much of their income from drug distribution. Professional selling can be distinguished from distribution within social networks, where the retail transaction occurs between people who interact for reasons other than the distribution of drugs and the supplier has some other principal source of income.[11]

---

[11] By this definition, stereotypical street markets for crack or heroin involve professional sellers, whereas most marijuana users obtain their drugs within social networks. Indeed, Caulkins and Pacula (2006) report that 89 percent of household survey respondents report obtaining their marijuana most recently from a friend or relative. However, the small numbers of users who obtain their marijuana from professional sellers tend to be disproportionately heavier users.

There is little written about the supply side of nascent or emerging drug markets. Thus our description is largely inferential. It does suggest, however, that emerging markets may be more fragile to various kinds of enforcement efforts.

B. Why Enforcement Might Be More Effective against Small or Emerging Markets

There are three distinct reasons why enforcement might be relatively more effective at constraining small and/or emerging markets than it is at addressing larger, more established markets: differential effects on dealers' costs, dynamic growth, and epidemic effects.

1. *Differential Effects on Dealers' Costs.* In the comparative statics ("risks and prices") framework outlined above, enforcement affected retail prices by increasing dealers' costs. Enforcement can also increase dealers' costs in an emerging (dynamic or "quasi-static") market, and may do so more efficiently.

Late in the epidemic, there may be a steady stream of convicted drug traffickers being released from prison. If, as is likely, their prison record makes it difficult to secure legitimate employment, they may see few options other than a return to dealing. Such "barriers to exit" from dealing might make replacing newly incarcerated dealers easier for an established market than in an earlier one. The released traffickers can act as replacements to new arrestees, creating a revolving door where investment in arrests simply maintains the status quo.

A more subtle factor is that the distribution network is more robust in larger markets. Drug distribution networks are embedded within a larger social network.[12] The larger the drug market, the denser is the embedded distribution network. Denser networks have more redundant linkages, making it harder for enforcement to isolate a subnetwork through judicious elimination of certain nodes or arcs. In the language of engineers who study network reliability in telecommunications and other fields, dense networks are more "robust" to disruption. Also, the denser the network, the better the information flows are likely to be and the more like a competitive market it becomes. If a denser network means that buyers at various levels know more sellers, then they are

---

[12] Social networks can be visualized as a sea of dots—called "nodes"—connected by lines ("arcs") indicating that the two nodes at either end of that arc interact with each other. In the embedded distribution network, an arc would represent a supplier-customer relationship.

better able to force those sellers to compete on price, driving the price bar down farther on.

2. *Greater Effects When Supply Is Constrained.*   Distinct from these cost effects is the possibility that, early on in a drug epidemic, supply capacity at some market levels might simply not be able to keep up with exponential growth in demand. So eliminating some of the supply network's scarce throughput capacity (e.g., by arresting a particular seller) might cause a greater disruption than would the same arrest 5 years later, when the market has stabilized and has excess supply capacity.

Constrained capacity is unlikely at lower distribution levels where it is relatively easy for outsiders to break into the business. However, not just anyone can decide to be a successful international smuggler or high-level drug dealer. The main barrier to entry does not appear to be skill per se. Studies of incarcerated sellers (e.g., Reuter and Haaga 1989; Matrix Knowledge Group 2007; Decker and Chapman 2008) often report that drug dealing requires few specialized skills. Even high-level domestic distribution is essentially just brokerage activity. One needs a source and customers, but there is next to no physical processing of the drugs.

However, a certain amount of tacit knowledge seems to be required, and the primary source of this tacit knowledge is by working with an existing dealer. Existing dealers can spread this knowledge to others intentionally (e.g., by introducing a friend to the business when demand exceeds what one person can supply) or unintentionally (e.g., when a former employee begins to sell on his or her own).

This suggests that expanding higher-level supply capacity in an emerging market should not be thought of as drawing on a limitless pool of labor that rapidly flows in to bid away wage differences whenever profits from dealing exceed profits available from legitimate work. Rather, when selling is profitable (e.g., because there is excess demand) then existing dealers spawn new dealers, akin to the way existing users are the principal vector for inducing initiation of new users. Hence, when the current number of sellers at these higher market levels is very small, the inflow of new dealers is also small. In short, there may be "word of mouth" diffusion of drug dealing throughput capacity, at least at the rate limiting market level.

The key insight is that if drug use spreads faster (is "more contagious") than is drug selling, then during the explosive stage of a drug epidemic, the ratio of demand to supply may grow very large.[13] In particular, if the rate of growth for both is proportional to the current numbers, as in standard diffusion models, then the ratio of customers to supply would tend to grow exponentially over time.

The ratio of customers to sellers cannot grow exponentially forever. At some point the relative shortage of distribution capacity limits the rate at which drug use can spread. When supply capacity limits the spread of use, eliminating sellers at that constrained market level could directly constrain growth in use. Later on, once use has hit a plateau and distribution capacity has had time to catch up, eliminating the same number of sellers might have much less effect. More precisely, the "risks and prices" deterrence effect exists both early and late, but the incapacitation effect of leaving insufficient distribution network throughput capacity only pertains early in an epidemic.

There is no appreciable incapacitation effect late in an epidemic because most dealers in mature markets could quickly increase the quantity distributed. If the demand were there, they could simply ask their supplier for more, and the supplier would in turn ask his or her supplier for more, on up the distribution chain. That is, in equilibrium, lost network capacity can be made up not only by bringing in new dealers but also by having the remaining dealers sell more per unit time.

3. *Multiplier Effects.* The previous subsections gave reasons why it is easier for enforcement to constrain supply earlier in a drug epidemic. It is also plausible that a given constraining of supply has a bigger effect on drug use when the constraining happens early in an epidemic. That is, if one could conceptualize one "unit" of supply reduction (e.g., an increase in the market clearing price by a given amount for a given duration of time), then early in an epidemic it may not only be easier (cheaper) for enforcement to produce that effect, but also that unit reduction in supply might yield a larger reduction in drug consumption.

This could happen if initiation and light use are more price responsive than is dependent use because early in an epidemic, initiation is

---

[13] In symbols, let $U(t)$ and $S(t)$ denote the number of users (demand) and selling or throughput capacity, respectively, where we specifically mean the capacity at the most constrained market level (e.g., the import level). If growth is proportional to current numbers, then both demand and throughput capacity grow exponentially ($U(t) = e^{\alpha t}$ and also $S(t) = e^{\beta t}$), and so the ratio of customers to supply would also grow exponentially over time since $U(t)/S(t) = e^{(\alpha-\beta)t}$ and $\alpha > \beta$.

high and dependent use is low (Caulkins, Behrens, et al. 2004).[14] Also, an intervention that directly prevents one person from using may indirectly affect the use of others. The magnitude of this so-called social multiplier effect can vary over the course of a drug epidemic (Caulkins et al. 2002). For example, Caulkins, Behrens, et al. (2004) observe that one proxy for infectiousness, the ratio of new initiations per current user, changed quite dramatically over the course of the U.S. cocaine epidemic, and simulations of drug epidemics reach the same conclusion (Winkler et al. 2004; Caulkins et al. 2009). Hence, early on, when drug use is spreading rapidly, eliminating one initiation may prevent a cascade of subsequent initiations in the same way that preventing one case of an infectious disease can avert additional secondary infections.

C. Summary

Drug markets evolve over time. Drug use often follows an epidemic cycle, and drug distribution networks mature. A modeling literature (e.g., Tragler, Caulkins, and Feichtinger 2001) and a variety of armchair arguments suggest that supply control may be more effective earlier in this process than later, after drug use has become endemic and the markets have matured.

Hence, although we are fairly confident in the central conclusion of the preceding sections, namely, that it is difficult for enforcement to suppress endemic use that is supported by a large, well-established market, we recognize that this conclusion may not apply to small or emerging markets. Unfortunately, there is limited potential to replace the many conjectures in this section with empirical evidence. The great bulk of data and analysis pertain to drugs whose use is endemic and whose markets are mature.

Also, as in the previous section, there is a problem of measuring dogs not barking. How can we measure instances in which enforcement tempers or delays an emerging market? Consider, for example, methamphetamine use in Missouri. Methamphetamine is widely used in Missouri today, but it was not 15 years ago, even though methamphetamine was already popular on the West Coast. It is hard to imagine that Missourians in 1995 intrinsically liked meth less than did Califor-

---

[14] Elasticities estimated from use self-reported in surveys tend to be higher than those based on measures associated with heavy or dependent use (e.g., Dave 2008). Evidence on the elasticity of initiation relative to the elasticity of nondependent use is weak, but a recent meta-analysis (Cicala 2006) reports cocaine participation elasticities that are slightly higher than elasticities for current users.

nians in 1995 or Missourians in 2010. More plausibly, the big differences in use are attributable to differences in availability and price.

Legal consumer goods tend to diffuse very quickly, so it is possible that enforcement deserves credit for sparing Missouri from some number of meth-related deaths and other problems for a decade or more. More generally, it seems entirely plausible that prohibition plus enforcement can at least temporarily constrain some emerging drug markets, even though there is next to no direct empirical evidence of quality one way or another.

V. Reducing Supply through Disequilibrium Effects

Introductory economic texts focus on equilibrium in markets,[15] yet markets—including drug markets—can also be out of equilibrium. Disequilibrium presents challenges and opportunities both analytically and for enforcement choices. The question of interest here is, how can and how has enforcement affected disequilibrium prices in drug markets? Ideally we would also like to know whether such enforcement is a cost-effective form of drug control, but by and large the literature lacks empirical estimates of cost effectiveness.

A. Historical Examples of Market Disruptions

Markets for illicit drugs are frustratingly resilient, but there have been significant disruptions. In one extreme case, purity-adjusted prices at least tripled and overdoses fell by as much as 80 percent within 3 months during the Australian heroin drought (Moore et al. 2005). There is a modest literature debating whether it was supply control or other circumstances that created that shock (e.g., Weatherburn et al. 2003; Degenhardt, Reuter, et al. 2005; Wood et al. 2006a, 2006b; Wodak 2008), and a larger literature documenting the resultant effects on outcomes such as overdose, crime, and the use of other substances in Australia (Baker et al. 2004; Longo et al. 2004; Degenhardt, Conroy, et al. 2005).

Supply shocks include not only literal shortages, when customers are physically unable to locate a supplier, but also large spikes in (purity-adjusted) prices, most often taking the form of troughs in purity. (If

---

[15] One exception to this is discussion of the cobweb cycle for agricultural markets, where a high price in season 1 leads growers to plant large quantities in season 2, which leads to low prices and thus decisions to plant smaller quantities in season 3, and so on.

the price spike is large enough to induce additional suppliers to enter the market, then by definition the market is not in equilibrium.)

Supply shocks and disequilibrium are the exceptional cases. At any given time, prices in most drug markets are stable or exhibit some long-run trend (Caulkins, Behrens, et al. 2004), and the great majority of users usually report success at being able to locate a drug supplier (National Institute of Justice 2003). However, there are enough exceptions to merit study.

In the United States, every major drug has witnessed significant market disruptions. There was the 1969 marijuana shortage (McGlothlin, Jamison, and Rosenblatt 1970; Gooberman 1974; Craig 1980); the heroin drought of the early 1970s associated with the Turkish opium ban, a literal drought, and the "French connection" case (DuPont and Greene 1973); multiple rounds of methamphetamine shortages associated with precursor controls (Cunningham and Liu 2003, 2005, 2008; Dobkin and Nicosia 2009); and the cocaine shortage of 1989–90 as well as a possible, briefer one in 1995 associated with the Peruvian air bridge interdiction (Crane et al. 1997; Caulkins et al. 2009).

The earlier cocaine shortage apparently stemmed from a combination of U.S. efforts and the "war" between the Colombian government and the Medellin-based traffickers. It led to a sharp (50–100 percent at its peak) increase in cocaine prices that lasted about 18 months (Crane, Rivolo, and Comfort 1997; Caulkins, Pacula, et al. 2004). The "Peruvian air bridge" refers to a period in which the Peruvian Air Force, assisted by U.S. agencies, began to intercept planes flying coca paste from Peru to Colombia; that had previously been the dominant source of cocaine, but the markets have since innovated around that tactic. It is harder to identify instances of true market gluts with excess supply, but some authors have mentioned the possibility in Australia with respect to heroin (Dietze and Fitzgerald 2002) and MDMA (Hall, Spillane, and Camejo 2000).

Two facts limit historical data on market disruptions. First, price reports are usually annual; market disruptions, by contrast, are relatively brief, usually lasting less than one year. Second, most sources report prices not adjusted for purity, and often most of the effective price change comes about through changes in purity (Caulkins, Pacula, et al. 2004; Caulkins 2007; Caulkins et al. 2009). Still, table 2 summarizes price changes associated with some of the more prominent

TABLE 2

Price per Pure Gram Before and During Various Market Disruptions

Country	Drug	Baseline		Disruption		Change in Price (%)
		Year	Price ($)	Year	Price ($)	
United States	Cocaine	1989	190	1990	235	+24
United States	Crack	1989	198	1990	255	+28
United States	Meth	1994	160	1995	254	+59
United States	Meth	1997	178	1998	256	+44
Australia	Heroin	2000	750	2001	2,250	+200
				2002	1,500	+100
				2003	1,500	+100

SOURCE.—Caulkins, Pacula, et al. (2004b) for U.S. data and Moore et al. (2005) for Australia.

market disruptions that have occurred in times and places with relatively good price monitoring.

We focus on purity-adjusted prices as an outcome that combines enforcement's effects on purity and price into a single metric. Thus, halving purity at a given price per gram and doubling the price per gram when purity is held constant are seen as equivalent changes in the effective price for users. This is sensible from a theoretical perspective. Diluents and adulterants typically account for a trivial share of the dealers' cost of producing and distributing drugs (as shown in table 1), and users primarily care about pure milligrams of the principal intoxicant.[16] It also has empirical support. Purity-adjusted prices often correlate much more strongly with other indicator series such as treatment admissions and emergency department mentions than do prices not adjusted for purity (e.g., Hyatt and Rhodes 1995).

B. Mechanisms of Supply Disruption

Given this description of the types of market shocks, the next question is, how can policy go about creating them? There are at least two ways: eliminating in one fell swoop a large proportion of suppliers at some critical market level, and eliminating for all suppliers a common operating practice or tactic that forces everyone to adapt. The former

---

[16] Diluents such as mannitol are psychopharmacologically inert, so they merely dilute the mixture; adulterants such as caffeine have some psychopharmacological effect. The distinction is more important for some amphetamine type stimulants (e.g., when ecstasy is "cut" with amphetamine) than for cocaine or heroin.

is the goal of crackdowns in which multiple arrests are executed simultaneously (Kleiman 1988). A good example of the latter would be imposing controls on precursor chemicals used in the drug manufacturing process (Cunningham and Liu 2003, 2005, 2008). Other examples include eliminating the Peruvian air bridge (Crane, Rivolo, and Comfort 1997) and Operation Intercept's closing of the U.S.-Mexican border to marijuana smugglers (and many others) in 1969.

There are no clear examples of the simultaneous arrest of large numbers of dealers disrupting a market. The challenges faced by this tactic when employed at the retail level become clear when one considers the numbers. Roughly 1 million Americans sell cocaine at retail every year (Caulkins and Reuter 1998), so an average metropolitan area with a population of 1 million (i.e., the size of Raleigh, North Carolina, or Birmingham, Alabama) might be expected to have about 3,300 cocaine sellers. Police departments consider crackdowns to be large if they simultaneously arrest a few hundred people at a time, which would still be only about 10 percent of retail sellers in such a metropolitan area.

Strategies that credibly threaten arrest without actually arresting very large numbers may be more effective (e.g., Braga et al. 2001) and avoid overwhelming the criminal justice system (see Zimmer 1987). David Kennedy has effectively promoted such efforts; for example, in High Point, North Carolina (a city of 100,000), police accumulated credible evidence for cases against well-established drug sellers and used that evidence to persuade them to quit the business (Kennedy 2009). Similarly, arrests or threat of arrests are likely more effective in small or isolated markets. Grimm (2009) offers a credible account of the drying up of LSD supply around 2001 as the result of the incarceration of a few key producers.[17]

Parallel arguments apply with respect to disrupting crop production for the crop-based drugs (cocaine/crack, marijuana, and opiates including heroin). The number of market participants at a given market level decreases as one moves up from retail to upstream activities, but only to a point. The level of the greatest market concentration (i.e., smallest number of participants and organizations) may be at export (e.g., from Colombia) and smuggling and transshipment countries (e.g., through

---

[17] Grimm's (2009) account stresses the role of social networks in the distribution of LSD. Grateful Dead concerts were important events for distributors, and the death of Jerry Garcia in 1995 created a major problem for them, exacerbated when the band Phish stopped touring in 2000 (p. 7). The final blow seems to have been the imprisonment of the largest producer in 2001.

Mexico). It is not even clear whether these narrower parts of the distribution system constitute true "bottlenecks"; even for smuggling of cocaine and heroin there are many competent potential entrants.

However, what is clear is that still further up the distribution chain the funnel begins to broaden out again (Babor et al. 2010, chap. 5). There are many small-time processing labs that convert coca leaves into paste and paste into base. The number of farmers cultivating crops is another order of magnitude larger still. For Afghanistan it is estimated that over 2 million individuals were involved in poppy growing and opium harvesting in the middle of this decade (Paoli, Greenfield, and Reuter 2009).

It is perhaps not surprising that source-country control efforts have rarely had any discernible effect on the quantity of drugs available for consumption downstream in high-income countries. The most notable exceptions are the Turkish opium ban, which in conjunction with the breaking of the French connection contributed to a heroin drought in the United States in the early 1970s, and the Taliban's opium eradication campaign in Afghanistan, which appears to have affected prices in European markets (Paoli, Greenfield, and Reuter 2009). Even for cocaine, whose production is concentrated in one continent and has long been the focus of U.S. efforts, coca farming did not begin to decline until 2002 (United Nations Office on Drugs and Crime [UNODC] 2004), and prices continued to decline at least until 2007, as shown in figure 3.[18]

For countries with defensible borders, such as Australia and Canada, interdiction is different than source-country control in this regard, even though both are "international" programs. Interdiction has been credited with occasional, significant, short-term disruption of U.S. cocaine markets, notably through 1989–90 and mid-1995 (Crane, Rivolo, and Comfort 1997), and it is the most plausible explanation for the Australian heroin drought (Degenhardt, Reuter, et al. 2005).

Note that seizures in and of themselves should not generally be expected to disrupt the market unless they are extremely large since usually suppliers can easily replace the lost drugs at wholesale costs (Reuter 1988). If the seizure is associated with dismantling an organization that had a substantial share of market throughput capacity, then one might

---

[18] Peruvian production began to fall in the mid-1990s, and Bolivian production in the late 1990s, but until recently expansion in Colombia made up the difference. U.S. government figures are slightly different but tell the same basic story.

observe a correlation between seizures and price changes, as Smithson et al. (2004, 2005) found for the Canberra (Australia) metropolitan area. However, inasmuch as seizures are just a proxy for an unmeasured, true causal variable (destruction of throughput capacity), such a relationship will not always be apparent (see DiNardo 1993; Yuan and Caulkins 1998).

Three large heroin seizures in 2000 involving a multinational smuggling organization serving Australia and Canada instruct us in this regard. The first seizure (126 kilograms seized in January 2000 in the Bangkok airport) is not claimed to have affected markets in either Australia or Canada. Indeed, it evidently did not put even that particular smuggling organization out of business. The second (~100 kilograms on September 2 in Vancouver) did not lead to detectable changes in Vancouver's heroin markets over the next 30 days as compared to the previous 30 days (Wood et al. 2003). However, Royal Canadian Mounted Police investigation of the seizure provided evidence that led back to a Fijian front company (Prime Success Enterprises) that was then dismantled in October. That operation led to the third seizure (357 kilograms in October), which, in the AFP account, "rendered ineffective a sophisticated concealment methodology, identified a legitimate cargo stream, and removed some very important facilitators [smugglers]" (Hawley 2002, p. 48). This has been credited by some (e.g., United Nations Office for Drug Control and Crime Prevention 2002), though by no means all (see Wodak [2008] for a contrary view), with precipitating the Australian heroin drought by convincing Asia-based trafficking syndicates to look for easier distribution markets.

C. Effects of Short-Term Disruptions

It is easy to dismiss market disruptions as inconsequential, since in most cases prices return to equilibrium levels within a year or two (Dobkin and Nicosia 2009). The price increases do not last because suppliers adapt by modifying tactics and operations or by replacing lost resources (Reuter 1988; Reuter, Crawford, and Cave 1988). For example, at one time or another over the last 25 years, four different regions have been the principal supplier of heroin to the United States (Mexico, South America, Southwest Asia, and Southeast Asia). Similarly, in the late 1970s Colombia quickly replaced Mexico as the principal supplier of marijuana to the United States in response to paraquat spraying and fears of adverse health effects of using sprayed marijuana (Kleiman 1992).

However, even transient price increases can have meaningful effects. Lives are saved even if overdoses decline only temporarily, as hospital data suggest they did after the 1989/1990 cocaine supply disruption, the 1995 interdiction of the Peruvian air bridge, and the imposition of controls on chemical precursors for methamphetamine (Crane, Rivolo, and Comfort 1997; Cunningham and Liu 2003; Dobkin and Nicosia 2009).

Furthermore, some effects of transient disruptions may be long-lasting. Tighter supplies can induce users to enter into drug treatment (Weatherburn and Lind 2001), and some of those individuals may not return to the former patterns of use, even once supply is restored. Likewise, Day, Degenhardt, and Hall (2006) document the Australian heroin drought's effects on initiation. As Moore (1990) notes, most people initiate within a narrow band of ages. If they pass through that "window of vulnerability" during a supply shortage, their initiations may be prevented, not merely delayed.

However, not all of the effects of market disruptions are positive. For example, transient shortages have been blamed for increasing needle sharing and, hence, the spread of HIV (Maher and Dixon 2001), and they can lead both users and sellers to substitute one drug for another (Cunningham, Liu, and Muramoto 2008). Kleiman (1992) wonders whether successful interdiction of marijuana (which is relatively bulky and hard to conceal) induced smugglers to substitute into cocaine. Some have raised similar concerns about the Australian heroin drought inducing substitution into amphetamine use (Longo et al. 2004; but see Snowball et al. [2008] for an opposing view).

Perhaps the most common concern pertains to the effect on users' spending on drugs. Recall that some drug-related consequences are driven by consumption (e.g., overdose); others are driven by spending on drugs (e.g., economic-compulsive and systemic crime). Constraining supply shifts back the supply curve, leading to higher prices and lower consumption. Whether drug spending goes up or down depends on how great a percentage decline in consumption is caused per 1 percent increase in price, a parameter that is called the elasticity of demand. The elasticity of demand is always negative. (Use goes down when price goes up.) If the elasticity is smaller than 1.0, in absolute value, then constraining supply will actually increase, not decrease, spending on drugs (and thus drug dealers' revenues).

Everything in the paragraph above applies equally to supply restrictions that are sustained (shifting the long-run equilibrium) as well as shocks. However, even if the elasticity of demand is large (in absolute value) in the long run, drug use may be less price responsive over the course of a transient price spike. The few empirical studies that investigate this possibility for illegal drugs seem to support this concern.[19]

We close by mentioning two more speculative potential effects of market shocks, both of which would enter on the positive side of the ledger. First, there are mathematical models of drug epidemics incorporating endogenous nonlinear feedback for which a temporary change in drug use can have lasting effects (e.g., Behrens et al. 1999, 2000; Winkler et al. 2004; Bultmann et al. 2008). There are also four noteworthy instances of drugs spreading rapidly up until a major market disruption and then stabilizing thereafter: the mid-1970s Turkish opium ban and French connection cases coinciding with the end of the U.S. heroin epidemic (DuPont and Greene 1973), the 1989/90 U.S. cocaine market disruption marking the end of the 1980s expansion in cocaine-related problems (Crane, Rivolo, and Comfort 1997), the Australian heroin drought of 2001, and—though less documented— the Taliban opium ban and marked 2003 disruption in U.K. heroin purity roughly coinciding with the end of a long period of increasing heroin dependence in the United Kingdom (Reuter and Stevens 2007). Absence of a counterfactual makes it very difficult to know whether these market disruptions were actually what broke the momentum of some epidemic-type positive feedback loop, but the coincidence is intriguing.

Second, an early observation in drug policy was that increasing nondollar costs of drug use was generally more appealing than increasing the dollar price (Moore 1977; Kleiman 1988). Both discourage use, but only higher dollar prices increase market revenue per gram consumed. Hence, a consumption reduction created by increasing so-called search

---

[19] Dave (2008) estimated a long-run elasticity of arrestees testing positive for heroin that was almost twice the corresponding short-run elasticity. Becker, Grossman, and Murphy (1994) and Saffer and Chaloupka (1999) obtained similar results for cigarettes and for cocaine, respectively. Although perhaps less relevant to the modern era, van Ours (1995) used 1922–38 records from the Dutch East Indies Opium Regie to estimate the short-term and long-run elasticity for opium to be −0.70 and close to −1.0, respectively. Liu et al. (1999) similarly found that opium use in Taiwan between 1895 and 1945 had short- and long-run elasticities of −0.48 and 1.38, respectively.

time costs is more valuable than an equally large reduction in consumption created by driving up price.

We neglected this possibility in the comparative statics discussion above because even though regular users do spend considerable time locating a seller (Rocheleau and Boyum 1994), that may be due primarily to the structural consequences of product illegality, not something that scales linearly in the toughness of enforcement. Two observations supporting that speculation are that heavy users (who account for the majority of demand for most drugs) report knowing multiple alternative suppliers (e.g., Riley 1997), and that a mature market's distribution network tends to have multiple redundant linkages. (See Caulkins [1998] for some illustrative calculations.)

However, reports of market disruptions ranging from Operation Intercept to the Australian heroin drought describe users having trouble locating supplies (Gooberman 1974; Degenhardt, Conroy, et al. 2005; Degenhardt, Reuter, et al. 2005). Hence, there may be greater potential for disequilibrium shocks to increase search times than for routine enforcement pressure to drive up search times on an ongoing basis.

D. Cost Effectiveness of Disrupting Drug Markets

The discussion above underscores how little is understood about how to quantify the benefits of disrupting drug markets. Unfortunately, the situation is equally bleak with respect to the other half of a cost-effectiveness ratio. There are no serious estimates of the cost of producing market disruptions.

Some law enforcement operations have fairly predictable production functions. For example, suppose police investigating retail selling operations in a certain city produce an average of 20 arrests per officer per year. In that case, one can reasonably expect that assigning another officer to that activity will increase arrests by about 20 per year. The actual number may be higher or lower since the marginal officer's productivity may differ from the average, and it could increase or decrease somewhat from year to year as police develop new tactics and the market adapts. However, in some sense taxpayers can just "order" a certain number of additional low-level drug arrests by increasing police budgets by a certain amount.

Market disruptions, however, cannot just be ordered. It seems plausible that the greater the level of enforcement effort, the greater the likelihood that such a disruption will occur. However, historically most

TABLE 3

The Price of Cocaine at Some Market Levels between Farm Gate
and Retail

| Stage | Cocaine—1 Kilogram | | | |
	Raw Price ($)	Purity (%)	100% Pure ($)	Location
Farm gate	800	100	800	Colombia
Export	2,200	91	2,400	Colombia
Import/wholesale (kg.)	14,500	76	19,000	Los Angeles
Mid-level/wholesale (oz.)	19,500	73	27,000	Los Angeles
Typical retail price	78,000	64	122,000	U.S.

SOURCE.—Kilmer and Reuter (2009).

market disruptions have been the result of a convergence of fortuitous circumstances, not all of which are under policy makers' control. So it is not useful to think of market disruptions created per million dollars. That inherently limits the ability to bring the drug control tactic of creating temporary market disruptions within a cost-effectiveness framework or to compare it in such terms to other drug control strategies.

VI. Empirical Evidence

Above we mentioned specific data to illustrate the various models of how enforcement affects prices, but in this section we present some broader evidence supporting the view that drug markets can be understood with these economic models.

A. Markups across Levels of the Distribution System

We start by noting how cocaine prices increase along the distribution chain from coca growing to retail price, as presented in table 3. An essentially identical chain applies to heroin and to other Western countries. What is relevant for our purposes is that most of the markup occurs at the bottom of the distribution chain. Though the large fortunes are made by controlling the higher levels of the trade (smuggling, wholesaling), these levels account for a small share of the retail price. Risks and prices theory accounts for that nicely, as suggested by the following hypothetical calculation.

At the bottom of the system, very large numbers of retailers and low-level wholesalers make modest incomes (Reuter, MacCoun, and

Murphy 1990; Levitt and Venkatesh 2000). Smugglers and high-level wholesalers (selling ounces of heroin or kilos of cocaine) have much higher incomes. For purposes of calculation, suppose that smugglers demand as compensation for the risks of enforcement 100 times as much income per year ($5 million per year) as does a typical retail seller (only $50,000 per year). That demand might be rooted in some combination of greater objective risk of receiving a long sentence if caught and a higher value of freedom, for example, because smugglers might be forgoing better alternatives in the legitimate labor market.

Even so, if the smuggler typically handles 500 kilograms of cocaine each year (five shipments of 100 kilograms each) and the retailer sells a total of 0.5 kilogram (2 grams each day for 250 days of the year), then the smuggler spreads his or her risk over 1,000 times as many kilograms of cocaine. Even with a greater valuation of freedom and longer expected sentence, the smuggler's risk compensation cost per gram is one-tenth that of the retailer.[20] As the observed markups show, and as R&P predicts, the risk compensation costs per gram are much higher at the lowest level of the trade than at the higher levels. While these specific figures are obviously entirely speculative, their general relationship is not. Absolute markups are highest at the bottom of the distribution system because risks are distributed over such small quantities.

B. Differences across Countries

There are persistent differences in the purity-adjusted price across countries. We focus here on the United States versus the United Kingdom, another country with price and purity data over a substantial period of time. Within those markets, we compare U.S. cocaine with U.K. heroin since those are the dominant drugs in the respective countries.

Over very broad ranges of market levels, price per pure gram can be well modeled as being proportional to pure quantity raised to an exponent (Caulkins and Padman 1993; Caulkins 1994; Crane, Rivolo, and Comfort 1997). An exponent of 1.0 would indicate that the transaction value is simply proportional to quantity, so the price per pure

---

[20] It would be slightly more realistic to speak of a smuggling organization, not a single individual smuggler, but the point carries through. If the organization collectively demands income of $5 million per year and spreads it over 500 kilograms, the risk compensation per gram is the same as if an individual smuggler did so.

TABLE 4
Price Markup Coefficients in the United States and United Kingdom

| | United Kingdom, Matrix Data (Avg.) | Caulkins and Padman (1993) | United States | | | |
| | | | Arkes et al. (2004) | | | |
			Retail	Mid-Low Level	Mid-Level	Top-Level
Cannabis	.817	.72 imported .76 domestic	.573		.802	.783
Sinsemilla		.850				
Cannabis resin	.851					
Hashish		.770				
Cocaine	.869	.830	.716	.751	.787	.813
Crack	.827	.790	.731	.661		.833
Heroin	.834	.83 brown .84 white	.531		.718	.764

SOURCE.—Caulkins et al. (2009).
NOTE.—Smaller values indicate greater markups as the drugs move down the distribution chain.

gram is the same across market levels. In reality, the exponents are less than 1.0. The smaller the exponent, the greater the markup as drugs move down the distribution chain. Inasmuch as the United States has particularly tough domestic enforcement, one would expect price regressions to produce smaller exponents in the United States than abroad. Table 4, reproduced from Caulkins, Burnett, and Leslie (2009), shows that this tends to be the case. Predictably, Moore et al.'s (2005) heroin prices across market levels in Australia imply an exponent (0.82) closer to that of the United Kingdom than to the United States.

C. Changes over Time

Drug price trends over time also support the idea that the main driver of retail price is events in the final market country. When examining heroin and cocaine price trends in the United States (e.g., Fries et al. 2008) and in Europe (e.g., Farrell, Mansur, and Tullis 1996), the striking observation is that cocaine prices in one location are more strongly correlated over time with heroin prices in that same location than they are with cocaine prices in the other location. Similarly, heroin prices in Europe are more highly correlated with cocaine prices in Europe than with heroin prices in the United States.

That is hard to reconcile with models of price determination that focus on global production or other events in source countries. It is much easier to reconcile with the idea that retail prices are determined primarily by risks and other factors in the final market country. Indeed, it is even suggestive that there is some balancing of supply and demand across drugs within a domestic country. That is a plausible topic for further research given that most demand stems from polydrug users and most domestic drug enforcement policy shifts lump hard drugs together (symbolized by the fact that in the United States the arrest data report cocaine and heroin arrests in aggregate, not separately).

There remains the question of general trends. Although there are no quotable standard data sources, the discussion in Section I makes clear that at least in the mid-1980s the intensity of enforcement, as measured by the expected prison time per unit of cocaine sold, has apparently increased substantially in the United States. During that period the purity-adjusted price of cocaine has fallen, substantially in the 1980s and more gradually since. The slow ebbing since 1990 might be attributed to a decline in demand and declining risks of violence, but not the sharp decline in the 1980s.[21] The conflicting price and enforcement trends of the 1980s would be a puzzle if the markets had been in long-run equilibrium.

However, the 1980s were clearly a time of quasi-static, not static equilibrium. The cocaine epidemic was still unfolding, with drug consumption expanding markedly as the mix of users shifted to include more dependent users. Distribution routes and tactics were evolving; Miami was a principal port of entry in 1980, but by 1990 had been supplanted by the Southwest border. Likewise, retail distribution evolved from relatively affluent people supplying friends in nightclubs and other discreet settings to flagrant street corner markets "staffed" by dealers for whom dealing was their principal form of employment. In short, we were still in the process of tipping from the low cocaine equilibrium to the high cocaine equilibrium. Furthermore, since enforcement swamping pertains to total drug volume (which is dominated by cocaine in the United States), not just or primarily drug-specific market volume, there is a simple explanation for why the explosion in cocaine use could have eroded price markups for heroin. Two pieces of empirical support for this are that by the 1990s the risks and prices

---

[21] Demand refers to the quantity that users desire to purchase at a given price; it is a relationship between price and quantity. Consumption refers to actual quantity purchased at the observed price.

story roughly added up (Caulkins and Reuter 1998), and Kuziemko and Levitt (2004) estimate empirically that in the absence of expanding toughness, U.S. cocaine prices would have fallen even farther.

VII. Conclusion

The simple sound bite summary of the foregoing is this: prohibition plus a base level of enforcement can drive prices up far above the legalized price, but for most established markets, expanding enforcement beyond that base level is a very expensive way to purchase further increments in price. Overall the United States is far into the region of diminishing returns; toughness could be cut with modest effects on prices and use. Alternately, toughness could be focused on the forms of dealing that are most violent or otherwise noxious, rather than feeling compelled to treat all dealers operating at a particular volume or market level as equivalent. We did note that the dynamics of drug markets might offer specific opportunities, a matter we return to at the end of this section.

We start our elaboration of the sound bite by drawing in two topics that have only been at the margin of this analysis—enforcement against marijuana and against users. Marijuana presents a distinctive policy problem (Room et al. 2010). Contrary to popular belief, marijuana toughness is already low. In 1997 there were only about 27,000 offenders in state prison for marijuana offenses (Sevigny and Caulkins 2004),[22] while the number of marijuana sellers is in the millions. Indeed, on the basis of self-reports to the National Survey on Drug Use and Health, it is estimated that 1.1 million individuals sell some of their most recent marijuana acquisition (Caulkins and Pacula 2006), and estimates based on self-report to a government-run survey are almost certainly underestimates. Hence, marijuana distributors can certainly expect to spend at least 40 years (1.1 million/27,000) selling per year of incarceration, and the actual figure is probably close to 100. By comparison, Reuter, MacCoun, and Murphy (1990) estimated that the street sellers of cocaine and heroin spent about one-fifth of their time incarcerated. The upshot is that even if easing up on toughness against

---

[22] The number in prison with marijuana offenses is larger, but 27,000 is the figure for those for whom the marijuana offense had the greatest sentencing potential. For example, it excludes instances in which someone was convicted of possessing both wholesale quantities of cocaine and personal-use quantities of marijuana.

cocaine, heroin, and methamphetamine is a plausible strategy for substantially reducing incarceration rates in the United States (Caulkins and Reuter 2006), there are no such easy savings from reducing marijuana toughness.

Likewise, the imprisonment risk just for *users* of the "expensive drugs" (cocaine, heroin, and methamphetamine) who are not also even peripherally involved in distribution accounts for 10 percent or less of drug-related imprisonment, resulting in a risk of only about 1 and a half days in prison per year of use. For marijuana it is about one hour in prison per year of use, even if all incarceration for polydrug use involving marijuana is attributed entirely to marijuana, and only 30 minutes of it is attributed to the other drug (Caulkins and Sevigny 2005). Though many of the seven hundred thousand individuals who are arrested each year for simple marijuana possession were only users, the average time served per arrest is already less than 2 days. So for users, it might be possible to reduce arrests greatly, but there is little scope for reducing imprisonment dramatically by cutting prison terms for users who were not also involved in distribution.

The policy implications for enforcement against the domestic suppliers of cocaine, heroin, and methamphetamine are as follows: markets can stably remain at either a low- or high-volume equilibrium. If the market is negligible (e.g., with GHB or methamphetamine in New England), use enforcement to keep it there. That is feasible and in some instances can prevent very serious harms. The consequences of a crackdown are unlikely to be harsh at the population level since few individuals are yet involved in distribution or production.

If the market is past its tipping point and is currently in epidemic expansion toward a higher-level steady state, use enforcement to delay that expansion; eradicating the market may not be realistic, but it is worth fighting a holding action rather than giving up on enforcement entirely. This policy of "grudging toleration" may be relevant to cocaine in parts of Europe today.

An important implication of the discussion surrounding these markets that are in quasi-static equilibrium is that the endogenous market forces may overwhelm enforcement efforts, even if those enforcement efforts are serving a valuable role. Hence, even if prices fall and use expands, that is not prima facie evidence that enforcement was mismanaged or counterproductive.

Established markets force a discrete choice. One might try to effectively "eradicate" the market by tipping it back to low levels of use, but that takes enormous effort and patience; probably it is not feasible for most established drugs, at least in countries with strong traditions of freedom.

Practically speaking, one must accommodate most established markets. The marginal value of enforcement intensity beyond those basic levels is probably very low. That means doing enough enforcement to keep everyone's heads down, both to realize the structural consequences of product illegality and because brazen selling is more harmful to society per kilogram sold than is surreptitious selling. Ongoing toughness may also increase the likelihood that one stumbles into a significant market disruption, although that takes considerable luck. Inasmuch as the United States has expanded enforcement intensity far beyond the levels needed to achieve the structural consequences of product illegality, it has the ability to reduce enforcement intensity with only modest adverse consequences on use and dependence.

Concretely, one way to cut back cocaine and probably heroin toughness without large adverse effects would be to reduce the number of drug prisoners to 250,000 rather than 500,000 (Caulkins and Reuter 2006). This would hardly be going soft on drugs. It would still be a lot tougher than the Reagan administration ever was. It would ensure that the United States still maintained a comfortable lead over any other Western nation in its toughness toward drug dealers, to put it in the most cynical terms. Furthermore, not all incarcerated drug-law violators are equal. The minority who are very violent or unusually dangerous in other ways may be getting appropriate sentences, and with less pressure on prison space, they might serve more of their sentences. Deemphasizing sheer quantity of drug incarceration could usefully be complemented by greater efforts to target that incarceration more effectively.

There is no magic formula suggesting a halving of drug incarceration as opposed to cutting it by one-third or two-thirds. The point is simply that dramatic reductions in incarceration are possible without entering uncharted waters of permissiveness, and the expansion to today's unprecedented levels of incarceration seems to have made little contribution to the reduction in U.S. drug problems.

Drug treatment as an alternative to incarceration has become a standard response, but it is not really an alternative. It is a separate policy that stands or falls on its own merits. We can compare the cost effectiveness of locking up drug sellers to the cost effectiveness of treating drug users, but no agency or decision maker divides a constrained budget between these two policy choices. Furthermore, many of the most promising approaches to dealing with drug abusing offenders rely on frequent drug testing backed with the threat of enforcement,[23] and Hawken (2010) notes how such coerced or mandated abstinence programs (Kleiman 2009) may usefully prioritize scarce treatment slots via what she calls "behavioral triage." Likewise, enforcement has a key role to play in managing drug market harms (Caulkins and Reuter 2009). So backing away from long sentences for dealers in no way implies relegating enforcement to a minor role in drug policy.

A democracy should be reluctant to deprive its citizens of liberty, a reluctance reinforced by the facts that imprisonment falls disproportionately on poor minority communities and that many U.S. prisons are nasty and brutalizing institutions. Further, there is growing evidence that the high incarceration rates have serious consequences for communities. A recent study suggests that differences in black and white incarceration rates may explain most of the sevenfold higher rate of HIV among black males as compared to white males. If locking up typical dealers for 2 years rather than one has minimal effect on the availability and use of dangerous drugs, then a freedom-loving society should be reluctant to do it.

Yet we are left with an enforcement system that runs on automatic, locking up increasing numbers on a faded rationale despite the high economic and social costs of incarceration and its apparently quite modest effects on drug use. Truly "solving" the nation's drug problem, with its multiple causes, is beyond the reach of any existing intervention or strategy. But that should not prevent decision makers from realizing that money can be saved and justice improved by simply cutting in half the number of people locked up for drug offenses.

[23] Drug courts are well known (Belenko 2001). Hawaii's Opportunity Probation with Enforcement (HOPE) and South Dakota's 24/7 Sobriety programs are in some sense similar but empower other criminal justice personnel to do the supervision that judges do in drug courts, which greatly enhances the potential to scale these program up (Kleiman and Hawken 2004; Caulkins and DuPont 2010).

REFERENCES

Arkes, Jeremy, Rosalie Liccardo Pacula, Susan Paddock, Jonathan P. Caulkins, and Peter Reuter. 2004. "Technical Report for the Price and Purity of Illicit Drugs through 2003." Report prepared by RAND and published by the Office of National Drug Control Policy, no. NCJ 2007769.

Babor, Thomas, Jonathan Caulkins, Griffith Edwards, David Foxcroft, Keith Humphreys, Maria Medina Mora, Isidore Obot, Jurgen Rehm, Peter Reuter, Robin Room, Ingeborg Rossow, and John Strang. 2010. *Drug Policy and the Public Good*. Oxford: Oxford University Press.

Badger, G. J., W. K. Bickel, L. A. Giordano, E. A. Jacobs, and G. Loewenstein. 2007. "Altered States: The Impact of Immediate Craving on the Valuation of Current and Future Opioids." *Journal of Health Economics* 26(5):865–76.

Baker, A., N. K. Lee, M. Claire, T. J. Lewin, T. Grant, S. Pohlman, J. B. Saunders, and F. Kay-Lambkin. 2004. "Drug Use Patterns and Mental Health of Regular Amphetamine Users during a Reported 'Heroin Drought.'" *Addiction* 99(7):875–84.

Baveja, Alok, Rajan Batta, Jonathan P. Caulkins, and Mark H. Karwan. 1993. "Modeling the Response of Illicit Drug Markets to Local Enforcement." *Socio-economic Planning Sciences* 27(2):73–89.

Becker, Gary S., Michael Grossman, and Kevin M. Murphy. 1994. "An Empirical Analysis of Cigarette Addiction." *American Economic Review* 84: 397–418.

Behrens, Doris A., Jonathan P. Caulkins, Gernot Tragler, Josef L. Haunschmied, and Gustav Feichtinger. 1999. "A Dynamical Model of Drug Initiation: Implications for Treatment and Drug Control." *Mathematical Biosciences* 159:1–20.

———. 2000. "Optimal Control of Drug Epidemics: Prevent and Treat—but Not at the Same Time." *Management Science* 46(3):333–47.

Belenko, Steven R. 2001. *Research on Drug Courts: A Critical Review; 2001 Update*. New York: National Center on Addiction and Substance Abuse at Columbia University.

Boyum, David. 1992. "Reflections on Economic Theory and Drug Enforcement." PhD dissertation, John F. Kennedy School of Government, Harvard University.

Braga, Anthony A., David M. Kennedy, Elin J. Waring, and Anne M. Piehl. 2001. "Problem-Oriented Policing, Deterrence, and Youth Violence: An Evaluation of Boston's Operation Ceasefire." *Journal of Research in Crime and Delinquency* 38(3):195–225.

Bultmann, Roswitha, Jonathan P. Caulkins, Gustav Feichtinger, and Gernot Tragler. 2008. "How Should Drug Policy Respond to Disruptions in Markets for Illegal Drugs?" *Contemporary Drug Problems* 35(2–3):371–96.

Bushway, Shawn, and P. Reuter. 2008. "Economists' Contribution to the Study of Crime and the Criminal Justice System." In *Crime and Justice: A Review of Research*, vol. 37, edited by Michael Tonry. Chicago: University of Chicago Press.

Cameron, Lisa, and Jennifer Williams. 2001. "Cannabis, Alcohol and Cigarettes: Substitutes or Complements?" *Economic Record* 77:19–34.

Caulkins, Jonathan P. 1990. "The Distribution and Consumption of Illicit Drugs: Some Mathematical Models and Their Policy Implications." PhD dissertation, Operations Research Center, Massachusetts Institute of Technology.

———. 1993. "Local Drug Markets' Response to Focused Police Enforcement." *Operations Research* 41(5):848–63.

———. 1994. *Developing Price Series for Cocaine.* Santa Monica, CA: RAND.

———. 1998. "The Cost-Effectiveness of Civil Remedies: The Case of Drug Control Interventions." In *Crime Prevention Studies*, vol. 9, edited by Lorraine Green Mazerolle and Janice Roehl. Monsey, NY: Criminal Justice Press.

———. 2007. "Price and Purity Analysis for Illicit Drugs: Data and Conceptual Issues." *Drug and Alcohol Dependence* 90:S61–S68.

Caulkins, Jonathan P., Doris A. Behrens, Claudia Knoll, Gernot Tragler, and Doris Zuba. 2004. "Markov Chain Modeling of Initiation and Demand: The Case of the U.S. Cocaine Epidemic." *Health Care Management Science* 7(4): 319–29.

Caulkins, Jonathan P., Honora Burnett, and Edward Leslie. 2009. "How Illegal Drugs Enter an Island Country: Insights from Interviews with Incarcerated Smugglers." *Global Crime* 10(1):66–93.

Caulkins, Jonathan P., and Sara Chandler. 2006. "Long-Run Trends in Incarceration of Drug Offenders in the U.S." *Crime and Delinquency* 52(4):619–41.

Caulkins, Jonathan P., and Robert L. DuPont. 2010. "Is 24/7 Sobriety a Good Goal for Repeat DUI Offenders?" *Addiction* 105(4):575–77.

Caulkins, Jonathan P., Richard C. Larson, and Thomas F. Rich. 1993. "Geography's Impact on the Success of Focused Local Drug Enforcement Operations." *Socio-economic Planning Sciences* 27(1):119–30.

Caulkins, Jonathan P., and Robert MacCoun. 2005. "Analyzing Illicit Drug Markets When Dealers Act with Limited Rationality." In *The Law and Economics of Irrational Behavior*, edited by Francesco Parisi and Vernon L. Smith. Stanford, CA: Stanford University Press.

Caulkins, Jonathan P., and Rosalie Pacula. 2006. "Marijuana Markets: Inferences from Reports by the Household Population." *Journal of Drug Issues* 36(1):173–200.

Caulkins, Jonathan P., Rosalie L. Pacula, Jeremy Arkes, Peter Reuter, Susan Paddock, Martin Iguchi, and Jack Riley. 2004. *The Price and Purity of Illicit Drugs: 1981 through the Second Quarter of 2003.* Report prepared by RAND and published by the Office of National Drug Control Policy as publication no. NCJ 207768, November.

Caulkins, Jonathan P., Rosalie Pacula, Susan Paddock, and James Chiesa. 2002. *School-Based Drug Prevention: What Kind of Drug Use Does It Prevent?* Santa Monica, CA: RAND.

Caulkins, Jonathan P., and Rema Padman. 1993. "Quantity Discounts and

Quality Premia for Illicit Drugs." *Journal of the American Statistical Association* 88(423):748–57.

Caulkins, Jonathan P., and Peter Reuter. 1998. "What Price Data Tell Us about Drug Markets." *Journal of Drug Issues* 28(3):593–612.

———. 2006. "Re-orienting Drug Policy." *Issues in Science and Technology* 23 (1).

———. 2009. "Toward a Harm Reduction Approach to Enforcement." *Safer Communities* 8(1):9–23.

Caulkins, Jonathan P., Peter Reuter, and Lowell Taylor. 2006. "Can Supply Restrictions Lower Price? Violence, Drug Dealing, and Positional Advantage." *Contributions to Economic Analysis and Policy* 5(1), art. 3. http://www.bepress.com/bejeap/contributions/vol5/iss1/art3.

Caulkins, Jonathan P., and Eric Sevigny. 2005. "How Many People Does the U.S. Incarcerate for Drug Use, and Who Are They?" *Contemporary Drug Problems* 32(3):405–28.

Cicala, Steven J. 2006. "The Demand for Illicit Drugs: A Meta-Analysis of Price Elasticities." Working paper. Chicago: Becker Center on Chicago Price Theory, University of Chicago.

Collier, Paul. 2007. *The Bottom Billion: Why the Poorest Countries Are Failing and What Can Be Done about It.* Oxford: Oxford University Press.

Costa Storti, Cláudia, and Paul De Grauwe. 2009. "Globalization and the Price Decline of Illicit Drugs." *International Journal of Drug Policy* 20(1):48–61.

Craig, Richard B. 1980. "Operation Intercept: The International Politics of Pressure." *Review of Politics* 42(4):556–80.

Crane, Barry D., A. R. Rivolo, and Gary C. Comfort. 1997. *An Empirical Examination of Counterdrug Interdiction Program Effectiveness.* Alexandria, VA: Institute for Defense Analysis.

Cunningham, James K., and Lon-Mu Liu. 2003. "Impacts of Federal Ephedrine and Pseudoephedrine Regulations on Methamphetamine-Related Hospital Admissions." *Addiction* 98:1229–37.

———. 2005. "Impacts of Federal Precursor Chemical Regulations on Methamphetamine Arrests." *Addiction* 100(4):479–88.

———. 2008. "Impact of Methamphetamine Precursor Chemical Regulation, a Suppression Policy, on the Demand for Drug Treatment." *Social Science and Medicine* 66:1463–73.

Cunningham, James K., Lon-Mu Liu, and Myra Muramoto. 2008. "Methamphetamine Suppression and Route of Administration: Precursor Regulation Impacts on Snorting, Smoking, Swallowing and Injecting." *Addiction* 103(7):1174–86.

Dave, Dhaval. 2008. "Illicit Drug Use among Arrestees: Prices and Policy." *Journal of Urban Economics* 63:694–714.

Day, Carolyn, Louisa Degenhardt, and Wayne Hall. 2006. "Changes in the Initiation of Heroin Use after a Reduction in Heroin Supply." *Drug and Alcohol Review* 25:307–13.

Decker, Scott H., and Margaret Townsend Chapman. 2008. *Drug Smugglers* on *Drug Smuggling: Lessons from the Inside*. Philadelphia: Temple University Press.

Degenhardt, Louisa, Elizabeth Conroy, Stuart Gilmour, and Linette Collins. 2005. "The Effect of a Reduction in Heroin Supply in Australia upon Drug Distribution and Acquisitive Crime." *British Journal of Criminology* 45(1): 2–24.

Degenhardt, Louisa, Peter Reuter, Linette Collins, and Wayne Hall. 2005. "Evaluating Explanations of the Australian Heroin Drought." *Addiction* 100: 459–69.

DeSimone, Jeffrey S. 1998. "The Relationship between Marijuana Prices at Different Market Levels." http://www.ecu.edu/econ/wp/99/ecu9915.pdf.

———. 2006. "The Relationship between Illegal Drug Prices at Different Market Levels." *Contemporary Economic Policy* 24(1):64–73.

Dietze, Paul, and John Fitzgerald. 2002. "Interpreting Changes in Heroin Supply in Melbourne: Drought, Gluts or Cycles?" *Drug and Alcohol Review* 21: 295–303.

DiNardo, John. 1993. "Law Enforcement, the Price of Cocaine, and Cocaine Use." *Mathematical and Computer Modelling* 17(2):53–64.

Dobkin, Carlos, and Nancy Nicosia. 2009. "The War on Drugs: Methamphetamine, Public Health, and Crime." *American Economic Review* 99(1): 324–49.

DuPont, Robert L., and Mark H. Greene. 1973. "The Dynamics of a Heroin Addiction Epidemic." *Science* 181:716–22.

Everingham, Susan S., and C. Peter Rydell. 1994. "Modeling the Demand for Cocaine." Research project no. MR-332-ONDCP/A/DPRC. Santa Monica, CA: RAND.

Farrell, Graham, Kashfia Mansur, and Melissa Tullis. 1996. "Cocaine and Heroin in Europe, 1983–1993: A Cross-National Comparison of Trafficking and Prices." *British Journal of Criminology* 36:255–81.

Federal Bureau of Investigation. 2009. *Crime in the United States, 2008*. Washington, DC: U.S. Department of Justice. http://www.fbi.gov/ucr/cius2008/index.html.

Ferrence, Roberta. 2001. "Diffusion Theory and Drug Use." *Addiction* 96: 165–73.

Frank, Robert H., and Ben S. Bernanke. 2004. *Principles of Microeconomics*, 2nd ed. New York: McGraw-Hill.

Fries, Arthur, Robert W. Anthony, Andrew Cseko Jr., Carl C. Gaither, and Eric Schulman. 2008. *The Price and Purity of Illicit Drugs: 1981–2007*. Alexandria, VA: Institute for Defense Analysis.

Gladwell, Malcolm. 2000. *The Tipping Point: How Little Things Can Make a Big Difference*. Boston: Little Brown.

Goldstein, Paul J. 1985. "The Drugs/Violence Nexus: A Tripartite Conceptual Framework." *Journal of Drug Issues* 15(4):493–506.

Golub, Andrew, Bruce Johnson, and Eloise Dunlap. 2007. "The Race/Ethnicity Disparity in Misdemeanor Marijuana Arrests in New York City." *Criminology and Public Policy* 6(1):301–35.

Gooberman, Lawrence A. 1974. *Operation Intercept: The Multiple Consequences of Public Policy*. Elmsford, NY: Pergamon.

Grass, Dieter, Jonathan P. Caulkins, Gustav Feichtinger, Gernot Tragler, and Doris Behrens. 2008. *Optimal Control of Nonlinear Processes: With Applications in Drugs, Corruption, and Terror*. Berlin: Springer-Verlag.

Grimm, Ryan. 2009. *This Is Your Country on Drugs*. Hoboken, NJ: Wiley.

Grossman, Michael. 2005. "Individual Behaviors and Substance Use: The Role of Price." In *Substance Use: Individual Behavior, Social Interactions, Markets, and Politics, Advances in Health Economics and Health Services Research*, vol. 16, edited by Björn Lindgren and Michael Grossman. Amsterdam: Elsevier.

Hall, James N., Joe Spillane, and Madeline Camejo. 2000. "Drug Abuse in Miami and South Florida." In *Proceedings of the Community Epidemiology Work Group*, vol. 2, *Epidemiologic Trends in Drug Abuse*, edited by the Community Epidemiology Work Group. Bethesda, MD: National Institute on Drug Abuse.

Hawken, Angela. 2010. "Behavioral Triage: A New Model for Identifying and Treating Substance-Abusing Offenders." *Journal of Drug Policy Analysis* 3 (1).

Hawley, Michael. 2002. "Heroin Shortage: The Cause." *Platypus Magazine* 76: 43–48.

Hyatt, Raymond R., and William Rhodes. 1995. "The Price and Purity of Cocaine: The Relationship to Emergency Room Visits and Deaths, and to Drug Use among Arrestees." *Statistics in Medicine* 14:655–68.

Jofre-Bonet, Mireia, and Nancy M. Petry. 2008. "Trading Apples for Oranges? Results of an Experiment on the Effects of Heroin and Cocaine Price Changes on Addicts' Polydrug Use." *Journal of Economic Behavior and Organization* 66:281–311.

Johnston, Lloyd D., Patrick M. O'Malley, Jerald G. Bachman, and John E. Schulenberg. 2009. *Monitoring the Future National Survey Results on Drug Use, 1975–2008*, vol. 1, *Secondary School Students* (NIH Publication no. 09-7402). Bethesda, MD: National Institute on Drug Abuse.

Kahneman, Daniel, Paul Slovic, and Amos Tversky, eds. 1982. *Judgment under Uncertainty: Heuristics and Biases*. New York: Cambridge University Press.

Kennedy, David. 2009. "Drugs, Race and Common Ground." *NIJ Journal*, no. 262. http://www1.cj.msu.edu/~outreach/psn/DMI/NIJJournal262.pdf.

Kilmer, Beau, and Peter Reuter. 2009. "Prime Numbers." *Foreign Policy*, November/December, pp. 34–35. http://www.foreignpolicy.com/category/section/prime_numbers.

Kleiman, Mark A. R. 1988. "Crackdowns: The Effects of Intensive Enforcement on Retail Heroin Dealing." In *Street-Level Drug Enforcement: Examining the Issues*, edited by Marcia R. Chaiken. Washington, DC: National Institute of Justice.

———. 1992. *Against Excess: Drug Policy for Results*. New York: Basic.

———. 1993. "Enforcement Swamping: A Positive-Feedback Mechanism in Rates of Illicit Activity." *Mathematical and Computer Modeling* 17:65–75.

———. 2009. *When Brute Force Fails: Strategy for Crime Control*. Princeton, NJ: Princeton University Press.

Kleiman, Mark A. R., and Angela Hawken. 2004. "Fixing the Parole System." *Issues in Science and Technology* 24 (4). http://www.issues.org/24.4/index.html.

Kuziemko, Ilyana, and Steven D. Levitt. 2004. "An Empirical Analysis of Imprisoning Drug Offenders." *Journal of Public Economics* 88(9–10):2043–66.

Laibson, David. 1997. "Golden Eggs and Hyperbolic Discounting." *Quarterly Journal of Economics* 112:443–77.

Levitt, Steven, and Sudhir A. Venkatesh. 2000. "An Economic Analysis of a Drug-Selling Gang's Finances." *Quarterly Journal of Economics* 115(3):755–89.

Liu, Jin-Long, Jin-Tan Liu, James K. Hammitt, and Shin-Yi Chou. 1999. "The Price Elasticity of Opium in Taiwan, 1914–1942." *Journal of Health Economics* 18:795–810.

Loewenstein, George, Ted O'Donoghue, and Matthew Rabin. 2003. "Projection Bias in Predicting Future Utility." *Quarterly Journal of Economics* 118: 1209–11.

Longo, Marie C., Susan M. Henry-Edwards, Rachel E. Humeniuk, Paul Christie, and Robert L. Ali. 2004. "Impact of the Heroin Drought on Patterns of Drug Use and Drug-Related Harms." *Drug and Alcohol Review* 23(2):143–50.

Maher, Lisa, and David Dixon. 2001. "The Cost of Crackdowns: Policing Cabramatta's Heroin Market." *Current Issues in Criminal Justice* 13(1):5–22.

Matrix Knowledge Group. 2007. *The Illicit Drug Trade in the United Kingdom.* Home Office Online Report 20/07. London: Home Office.

McGlothlin, William, Kay Jamison, and Steven Rosenblatt. 1970. "Marijuana and the Use of Other Drugs." *Nature* 228:1227–29.

Moore, Mark H. 1977. *Buy and Bust: The Effective Regulation of an Illicit Market in Heroin.* Lexington, MA: Lexington Books.

———. 1990. "Supply Reduction and Drug Law Enforcement." In *Drugs and Crime,* edited by Michael Tonry and James Q. Wilson. Vol. 13 of *Crime and Justice: A Review of Research,* edited by Michael Tonry and Norval Morris. Chicago: University of Chicago Press.

Moore, Timothy J. 2008. "The Size and Mix of Government Spending on Illicit Drug Policy in Australia." *Drug and Alcohol Review* 27:404–13.

Moore, Timothy J., Jonathan P. Caulkins, Alison Ritter, Paul Dietze, Shannon Monagle, and Jonathon Pruden. 2005. *Heroin Markets in Australia: Current Understanding and Future Possibilities.* DPMP Monograph Series. Fitzroy, Australia: Turning Point Alcohol and Drug Centre.

Musto, David F. 1987. *The American Disease.* New Haven, CT: Yale University Press.

National Institute of Justice. 2003. *2000 Arrestee Drug Abuse Monitoring: Annual Report.* Washington, DC: U.S. Department of Justice.

Office of National Drug Control Policy (ONDCP). 2000. *What America's Users Spend on Illicit Drugs, 1988–1998.* Washington, DC: Executive Office of the President.

———. 2001. *What America's Users Spend on Illicit Drugs, 1988–2000.* Washington, DC: Executive Office of the President.

———. 2004. *The Economic Costs of Drug Abuse in the United States, 1992–2002.* Washington, DC: Executive Office of the President.

———. 2008. *The Price and Purity of Illicit Drugs, 1091–2007.* Washington, DC: Executive Office of the President.

———. 2009. *ADAM II. 2008 Annual Report.* http://www.whitehousedrug policy.gov/publications/pdf/adam2008.pdf.

Paoli, Letizia, Victoria Greenfield, and Peter Reuter. 2009. *The World Heroin Market: Can Supply Be Cut?* New York: Oxford University Press.

Pietschmann, Thomas. 2004. "Price-Setting Behavior in the Heroin Market." *Bulletin on Narcotics* 56(1–2):105–39.

Reuter, Peter. 1983. *Disorganized Crime: The Economics of the Visible Hand.* Cambridge, MA: MIT Press.

———. 1988. "Quantity Illusions and Paradoxes of Drug Interdiction: Federal Intervention into Vice Policy." *Law and Contemporary Problems* 51:233–52.

———. 1991. "On the Consequences of Toughness." In *Searching for Alternatives: Drug Control Policy in the United States*, edited by Edward Lazear and Melvyn Krauss. Stanford, CA: Hoover Institution.

———. 2008. "Assessing U.S. Drug Policy and Providing a Base for Future Decisions." Testimony before the Joint Economic Committee, June 19.

Reuter, Peter, Gordon Crawford, and Jonathan Cave. 1988. *Sealing the Borders: The Effects of Increased Military Participation on Drug Interdiction.* Santa Monica, CA: RAND.

Reuter, Peter, and John Haaga. 1989. *The Organization of High-Level Drug Markets: An Exploratory Study.* Santa Monica, CA: RAND.

Reuter, P., P. Hirschfield, and K. Davies. 2001. "Assessing the Crackdown on Marijuana in Maryland." Unpublished manuscript. College Park: University of Maryland. http://www.drugpolicy.org/docUploads/md_mj_crackdown.pdf.

Reuter, Peter, and Mark Kleiman. 1986. "Risks and Prices: An Economic Analysis of Drug Enforcement." In *Crime and Justice: A Review of Research*, vol. 7, edited by Michael Tonry and Norval Morris. Chicago: University of Chicago Press.

Reuter, Peter, Robert MacCoun, and Patrick Murphy. 1990. *Money from Crime: A Study of the Economics of Drug Dealing in Washington, D.C.* Santa Monica, CA: RAND.

Reuter, Peter, and Alex Stevens. 2007. *An Analysis of U.K. Drug Policy.* London: U.K. Drug Policy Commission.

Reuter Peter, and Franz Trautmann, eds. 2009. *Assessing the Operations of the Global Illicit Drug Markets, 1998–2007.* Report for the European Commission. http://ec.europa.eu/justice_home/doc_centre/drugs/studies/doc_drugs _studies_en.htm.

Rhodes, William, Dana Hunt, Meg Chapman, Ryan Kling, Doug Fuller, and Christina Dvous. 2007. *Using ADAM Data to Investigate the Effectiveness of Drug Enforcement.* Cambridge, MA: Abt.

Rhodes, William R., Raymond Hyatt, and Paul Scheiman. 1994. "The Price of Cocaine, Heroin, and Marijuana, 1981–1993." *Journal of Drug Issues* 24: 383–402.

Rigter, Henk. 2006. "What Drug Policies Cost: Drug Policy Spending in the Netherlands in 2003." *Addiction* 101:323–29.

Riley, Kevin Jack. 1997. *Crack, Powder Cocaine, and Heroin: Drug Purchase and Use Patterns in Six U.S. Cities.* Washington, DC: National Institute of Justice.

Rocheleau, Ann Marie, and David Boyum. 1994. *Measuring Heroin Availability in Three Cities.* Washington, DC: Office of National Drug Control Policy.

Room, Robin, Benedikt Fischer, Wayne Hall, Simon Lenton, and Peter Reuter. 2010. *Cannabis: Moving Beyond the Stalemate.* Oxford: Oxford University Press.

Rossi, Carla. 2001. "A Mover-Stayer Type Model for Epidemics of Problematic Drug Use." *Bulletin on Narcotics* 53(1):39–64.

Rydell, C. Peter, and Susan S. Everingham. 1994. *Controlling Cocaine: Supply versus Demand Programs.* Santa Monica, CA: RAND.

Saffer, Henry, and Frank J. Chaloupka. 1999. "The Demand for Illicit Drugs." *Economic Inquiry* 37(3):401–11.

Sevigny, Eric, and Jonathan P. Caulkins. 2004. "Kingpins or Mules? An Analysis of Drug Offenders Incarcerated in Federal and State Prisons." *Criminology and Public Policy* 3(3):401–34.

Skiba, A. K. 1978. "Optional Growth with a Convex-Concave Production Function." *Econometrica* 46:527–39.

Smithson, Michael, Michael McFadden, and Sue-Ellen Mwesigye. 2005. "The Impact of Federal Drug Law Enforcement on the Supply of Heroin in Australia." *Addiction* 100(8):1110–20.

Smithson, Michael, Michael McFadden, Sue-Ellen Mwesigye, and Tony Casey. 2004. "The Impact of Illicit Drug Supply Reduction on Health and Social Outcomes: The Heroin Shortage in the Australian Capital Territory." *Addiction* 98:340–48.

Snowball, Lucy, Steve Moffatt, Don Weatherburn, and Melissa Burgess. 2008. *Did the Heroin Shortage Increase Amphetamine Use?* Crime and Justice Bulletin no. 114. Sydney: NSW Bureau of Crime Statistics and Research.

Stares, Paul B. 1996. *Global Habit: The Drug Problem in a Borderless World.* Washington, DC: Brookings Institution.

Substance Abuse and Mental Health Services Administration (SAMHSA). 2003. *Results from the 2002 National Survey on Drug Use and Health: National Findings.* Office of Applied Studies, NHSDA Series H-22, DHHS Publication no. SMA 03-3836, Rockville, MD.

———. 2009. Data tables published on line, table 8.40B. http://www.oas.samhsa.gov/NSDUH/2K8NSDUH/tabs/Sect8peTabs1to43.htm#Tab.

Tragler, Gernot, Jonathan P. Caulkins, and Gustav Feichtinger. 2001. "Optimal Dynamic Allocation of Treatment and Enforcement in Illicit Drug Control." *Operations Research* 49(3):352–62.

Trunzo, D., and L. Henderson. 2007. "Older Adult Admissions to Substance Abuse Treatment: Findings from Treatment Episode Data System, 1992–2005." Presentation to American Public Health Association annual meetings, November 6.

United Nations Office for Drug Control and Crime Prevention. 2002. *Global Illicit Drug Trends, 2002.* New York: United Nations Office for Drug Control and Crime Prevention.

United Nations Office on Drugs and Crime. 2004. *2004 World Drug Report.* Oxford: Oxford University Press.

Van Ours, J. C. 1995. "The Price Elasticity of Hard Drugs: The Case of Opium in the Dutch East Indies, 1923–1938." *Journal of Political Economy* 103:261–79.

Walsh, John. 2004. "Fuzzy Math: Why the White House Drug Control Budget Doesn't Add Up." *Drug Policy Analysis Bulletin*, no. 10. http://www.fas.org/drugs.

Weatherburn, Don, Craig Jones, Karen Freeman, and Toni Makkai. 2003. "Supply Control and Harm Reduction: Lessons from the Australian Heroin 'Drought.'" *Addiction* 98:83–91.

Weatherburn, Don, and Bronwyn Lind. 2001. "Street Level Drug Law Enforcement and Entry into Methadone Maintenance Treatment." *Addiction* 96(4):577–87.

Winkler, Doris, Jonathan P. Caulkins, Doris Behrens, and Gernot Tragler. 2004. "Estimating the Relative Efficiency of Various Forms of Prevention at Different Stages of a Drug Epidemic." *Socio-economic Planning Sciences* 38(1): 43–56.

Wodak, Alex. 2008. "What Caused the Recent Reduction in Heroin Supply in Australia?" *International Journal of Drug Policy* 19(4):279–86.

Wood, Evan, Jo-Anne Stoltz, Kathy Li, Julio S. G. Montaner, and Thomas Kerr. 2006*a*. "The Cause of the Australian Heroin Shortage: Time to Reconsider?" *Addiction* 101(5):623–25.

———. 2006*b*. "Changes in Canadian Heroin Supply Coinciding with the Australian Heroin Shortage." *Addiction* 101(5):689–95.

Wood, Evan, Mark W. Tyndall, Patricia M. Spittal, Kathy Li, Aslam H. Anis, Robert S. Hogg, Julio S. G. Montaner, Michael V. O'Shaughnessy, and Martin T. Schechter. 2003. "Impact of Supply-Side Policies for Control of Illicit Drugs in the Face of the AIDS and Overdose Epidemics: Investigation of a Massive Heroin Seizure." *Canadian Medical Association Journal* 168(2): 165–68.

Yuan, Yuehong, and Jonathan P. Caulkins. 1998. "The Effect of Variation in High-Level Domestic Drug Enforcement on Variation in Drug Prices." *Socio-economic Planning Sciences* 32(4):265–76.

Zimmer, Lynn. 1987. "Operation Pressure Point: The Disruption of Street-Level Drug Trade on New York's Lower East Side." Occasional Papers from the Center for Research in Crime and Justice. New York: New York University School of Law.

Michael Tonry

The Social, Psychological, and Political Causes of Racial Disparities in the American Criminal Justice System

ABSTRACT

Imprisonment rates for black Americans have long been five to seven times higher than those for whites. The immediate causes are well known: high levels of black imprisonment resulting in part from higher black than white arrest rates for violent crime and vastly higher black drug arrest rates. Drug arrest disparities result from police decisions to concentrate attention on drugs blacks sell and places where they sell them. Prison disparities are aggravated by laws prescribing sentences of unprecedented severity for offenses for which blacks are disproportionately arrested. Those practices and policies were shaped by distinctive sociological, psychological, and political features of American race relations. Work on the psychology of American race relations shows that many white Americans resent efforts made to help black Americans overcome the legacy of racism; that stereotypes of black criminality support whites' attitudes toward drug and crime control policy; and that statistical discrimination, colorism, Afro-American feature bias, and implicit bias cause black offenders to be treated especially severely. Sociological work on racial stratification shows that whites support policies that maintain traditional racial hierarchies. Contemporary drug and crime control policies are components of the Republican Southern Strategy, shaped by and exacerbating those phenomena,

Michael Tonry is professor of law and public policy, University of Minnesota Law School, and senior fellow, Netherlands Institute for the Study of Crime and Law Enforcement. This essay appears in a different version as chap. 4 of Michael Tonry's *Punishing Race: A Continuing American Dilemma* (Oxford: Oxford University Press, 2010).

273

to use crime as a "wedge issue" to appeal to whites' racial anxieties and resentments.

Imprisonment rates for black Americans have been five to seven times higher than those for whites since the mid-1980s. A third of black men in their 20s are in prison or jail or on probation or parole. A third of black baby boys born in 2001 will spend part of their lives as inmates in a federal or state prison. These are extraordinary numbers that raise fundamental questions about racial, social, and criminal justice in twenty-first-century America.

Two important causal questions are raised. The first is how those numbers happened. Those answers are clear. Although violent crime arrest rates for blacks are higher than for whites, the differential has long been declining. Group differences in violent crime do not explain racial disparities in prison. What does explain them is a combination of police practices and legislative and executive policy decisions that systematically treat black offenders differently, and more severely, than whites. Policy makers emphasized law enforcement approaches to drug abuse over preventive ones. Police drug law enforcement focused effort on inner-city, primarily minority, neighborhoods, where many black Americans live, and on crack cocaine, of which blacks are a large majority of arrested sellers. Police officers engaged in widespread racial profiling and stopped blacks on streets and sidewalks much more often than is justifiable in terms of objective, race-neutral criteria. More broadly, legislatures and administrative agencies established policies in the 1980s and 1990s that mandated sentences of historically unmatched severity for violent and drug crimes, for both of which blacks are disproportionately often arrested and prosecuted.

The second question is, inevitably, Why? Possible answers range from deliberate antiblack racism to innocent inadvertence. Racism in its most blatant forms is not the answer. Conscious racial discrimination is not so pervasive in the early twenty-first century, nor was it in the last two decades of the twentieth, that it is likely that policy makers and police officials were primarily motivated by invidious aims or beliefs.

Nor is inadvertence believable—that policies were chosen and practices were followed in good faith—and it simply never occurred to anyone that black Americans would disproportionately suffer. No credible case can be made that gross racial disparities were unforeseeable. Everyone, we know, sees the world through filters shaped by personal values and ideologies, and reasonable people accordingly differ in their assessments of the scientific evidence about the effectiveness of drug and crime control policies. Reasonable people, however, cannot have failed to recognize that policies adopted since the mid-1980s would produce foreseeable undesirable side effects. No informed person could have failed, for example, to foresee that unprecedentedly harsh penalties for crack offenses would hit black drug dealers especially hard. Nor, since black arrest rates for serious violent crimes have long been higher than white rates, could any informed person have failed to understand that three-strikes, lengthy mandatory minimum sentence, truth-in-sentencing, and life without possibility of parole laws would disproportionately send black offenders to prison and keep them there.

One possible explanation is uncomfortably close to racism: officials knew that blacks would disproportionately suffer but did not care. For reasons of political self-interest, ideology, or partisanship, they enacted disparity-causing policies anyway. At least for some policy makers, this is what happened. They acted as if it were more important to score political and ideological points than to worry about the effects on individual human beings of the policies they promoted. Similar things have happened in many policy realms in recent decades, and there is little reason to doubt that it happened in relation to drugs and crime.

Americans have lived through three decades in which many conservative politicians at the federal level—and in some states, most notably California and Texas—adopted scorched earth political strategies in which ideological purity, frustrating Democratic policy initiatives, or obeisance to key constituencies have been more important to them than formulating sensible public policies. Examples outside the criminal justice system include the decision to shut down the federal government in the early 1990s rather than negotiate budget reforms, health care reform during the early years of the Obama administration, and refusal to support meaningful gun control legislation despite heavy public support for it. Examples inside the justice system are countless.

One stark example was the persistent refusal of federal policy makers to amend or repeal the 100-to-one law for sentencing of cocaine offenders.[1] No one questions that the law produces unwarranted racial

---

[1] This refusal is the more striking because the 100-to-one law is the one contemporary crime control policy that whites oppose when they become aware of the racial disparities it causes. Levels of whites' support for capital punishment do not significantly change when they learn that blacks are much more likely to be sentenced to death than whites or that black killers of white victims are much more likely than any other killers to be

disparities, and almost everyone agrees that it is unjust. Three Republican administrations and Bill Clinton's, however, refused to change it. In 2008 former President Clinton called the law a "cancer" and said, "I regret more than I can say that we didn't do more on it" (Wickham 2008). However, his administration was unwilling to act, from fear of opening itself to Republican accusations of softness. The Clinton White House rejected proposals by the U.S. Sentencing Commission, initially endorsed by Attorney General Janet Reno and "drug czar" Barry McCaffrey, to eliminate the 100-to-one difference. Congress passed legislation to reject the commission proposal; Clinton signed it. That was more then 15 years ago. Finally, in August 2010, President Obama signed legislation to reduce the crack/powder differential to 18-to-one. This is a half-a-loaf compromise.[2]

The challenge is to understand why for a quarter century most urban police leaders and many state and federal policy makers adopted and supported disparity-causing policies and practices. The answer is not uncomplicated, but it is gradually becoming clear. Three powerful forces in the history and culture of American race relations interacted. The first is a psychology of race relations characterized by stereotypes of black criminals, by unconscious preferences for whiteness over blackness, and by a resulting lack of empathy among whites for black offenders and their families. The second, which shaped the first, is a three-century-old pattern of economic, political, and social dominance of blacks by whites. The third, enabled by the first two, is the Republican Southern Strategy of appealing to racial enmities and anxieties by use of seemingly neutral code words.

Research on social stratification shows how contemporary drug and crime control policies have helped sustain a historic pattern of white political and economic dominance over blacks. Few police officials and other policy makers have been consciously motivated by that goal. In-

---

sentenced to death. Whites' support for the 100-to-one law plummets when they learn of its racially skewed effects (Bobo and Johnson 2004).

[2] The U.S. Sentencing Commission (2007) revised its crack and cocaine guidelines in 2007. Twenty years earlier the commission, then differently constituted, made guideline sentences for crack offenses even more severe than the legislation required; those earlier guidelines provisions were repealed. Those changes, a *New York Times* article reported, merely nibble at the edges because the federal statute continued in force unaltered: "The sentencing commission's striking move on Tuesday, meant to address the wildly disproportionate punishments for crack and powder cocaine, will have only a minor impact. Unless Congress acts, many thousands of defendants will continue to face vastly different sentences for possessing and selling different types of the same thing" (Liptak 2007, p. A21).

stead they have viewed the world through what might be called white eyes. The minds behind the eyes, we know better than we once did, were influenced by stereotypes of black street criminals and drug dealers and saw disparities as "chips falling where they may." Some, in a more melancholy mood, may have thought, "Life is unjust but there is nothing we can do about it." The minds behind the eyes, we also now know better than before, often lacked empathy for black offenders, largely because of social distance and lack of personal contact, and partly because of widely held resentments toward black people in the aftermath of the civil rights movement.

A half dozen different intertwined literatures on the psychology of race relations show how insensitivity to the interests of black people became a theme of crime and drug control policy. One demonstrates that the mass media—news and entertainment both—regularly portray criminals as black and victims as white and that those stereotypes seep into people's thinking. When asked to envision a drug addict or a violent criminal, most white people assume the typical offender to be black. Because these findings have long been known, I do not discuss them at length. A second literature on "implicit bias" shows that when asked to associate black and white with such qualities as pleasant and unpleasant or dangerous and safe, most people (including often black people) associate black with unpleasant and dangerous and white with pleasant and safe. These reactions are near instantaneous and unconscious but influence what people think and do. A third, on "colorism," shows that the darker the skin tone of a black suspect, the likelier people are to believe him to be a criminal, and the more severely he is likely to be punished. A fourth, on "Afro-American feature bias," provides parallel findings concerning people (whites as well as blacks) whose facial features match prevailing Afro-American stereotypes. Observers associate stereotypically black faces with crime and criminals. People with such faces get punished more severely, even unto death. Finally, a fifth literature on public attitudes and opinions shows that whites have much more punitive attitudes toward offenders and that racial animus and resentment toward blacks are the strongest predictors of those attitudes.

More important, however, than unconscious processes, though made easier by them, was the deliberate decision of Republican political strategists beginning in the 1960s to use stereotypes of black criminals and proposals for tough crime policies as devices to appeal to white voters. Kevin Phillips, an architect of the Republican Southern Strategy, observed that liberalism and Democrats in the South "lost the support of poor whites" as the civil rights movement progressed: "The Negro socioeconomic revolution gave conservatism a degree of access to poor white support which it had not enjoyed since the somewhat comparable Reconstruction era" (1969, p. 206). Phillips proposed that Republican candidates depart from the party's historical support for civil rights, from Abraham Lincoln through the 1960s, and instead work to manipulate whites' racial animus and anxiety in order to win votes.

The Republican Southern Strategy was premised on an extraordinary non sequitur—that black/white differences in the South in the 1960s were indistinguishable from ethnic differences at other times and places in American history. In the preface to *The Emerging Republican Majority*, the book announcing and justifying the Republican Southern Strategy, Kevin Phillips wrote that "few people realize the extent of ethnic influences in American politics. Historically, our party system has reflected layer upon layer of group oppositions: Irish against Yankee, Jewish against Catholic, French against English and so forth. Racial and ethnic polarization has neither stopped progress nor worked repression on the groups out of power" (1969, p. 22).

Those words were written late in 1968, the year when George Wallace ran as an openly racist candidate for president and Martin Luther King was assassinated. It was the end of the decade made famous by the march on Selma, notorious killings of activists, and the civil rights movement. It was the end of three centuries of white supremacy in the South. The proposition that racial polarization has "neither stopped progress nor worked repression on the groups out of power" is a mite saccharine.

Phillips's premise was that ethnic group conflict has always characterized American politics. "Southern politics," he observed, "like those of the rest of the nation, cleave along distinct ethnic (racial in this case) lines. Whereas in New York City, the Irish are lined up against the Jews, in the South it is principally a division between Negroes and whites" (1969, pp. 287–88). That is why the party "decided to break with its formative antecedents and make an ideological bid for the anti–civil rights South" (p. 33). The "formative antecedents" were the Republican Party's historic commitment from Abraham Lincoln onward to civil rights.

Phillips's conclusion was that manipulation of racial passions would enable Republicans to achieve political dominance in the South and strengthen their appeal to working-class whites elsewhere. As a result, Phillips favored aggressive federal enforcement of civil rights laws and decisions, not because it was the right thing to do but because it would alienate white Democrats. Enforcement of "Negro voting rights in Dixie," he wrote, "is essential if southern conservatives are to be pressured into switching to the Republican Party—for Negroes are beginning to seize control of the national Democratic Party in southern regions" (1969, p. 464).

Elaborating on the logic of the Southern Strategy in an interview published in the *New York Times* in 1970, Phillips observed, "From now on, the Republicans are never going to get more than 10 to 20 percent of the Negro vote and they don't need more than that . . . but Republicans would be shortsighted if they weakened enforcement of the Voting Rights Act. The more Negroes who register as Democrats in the South, the sooner the Negrophobe whites will quit the Democrats and become Republicans. That's where the votes are" (Boyd 1970, p. 106).

Lee Atwater, the first President Bush's Karl Rove and developer of the Willie Horton ads used in the 1988 presidential campaign against Michael Dukakis, in a 1981 interview told a blunter story:

You start out in 1954 by saying, "Nigger, nigger, nigger." By 1968 you can't say "nigger"—that hurts you. Backfires. So you say stuff like forced busing, states' rights and all that stuff. You're getting so abstract now [that] you're talking about cutting taxes, and all these things you're talking about are totally economic things and a by-product of them is [that] blacks get hurt worse than whites.

And subconsciously maybe that is part of it. I'm not saying that. But I'm saying that if it is getting that abstract, and that coded, that we are doing away with the racial problem one way or the other. You follow me—because obviously sitting around saying, "We want to cut this," is much more abstract than even the busing thing, and a hell of a lot more abstract than "Nigger, nigger." (Herbert 2005)

In the social turbulence associated with the 1960s in general, and the civil rights movement in particular, conservative Republican politicians saw an opportunity to appeal to southern and working-class white voters who traditionally voted Democratic, a group referred to later on, in the 1980s, as "Reagan Democrats." They did so by focusing on issues—crime, welfare fraud, "forced" busing, states' rights, affirmative action—that served as proxies for race, "wedge issues" as they have since become known (Edsall and Edsall 1991).

The Southern Strategy is no longer official Republican Party policy, but it need not be. It achieved its short-term aim—winning elections. In the long term, however, it helped shape and reinforced prevailing negative white attitudes toward black people. As time passed, most white people abandoned ideas about black racial inferiority but replaced them with racial resentments: that disadvantaged black people have received too much support from the state and are responsible for the adverse social and economic conditions of their lives.

The rest of this essay tells that story in three parts. Section I examines recent writings on the social psychology of American race relations in connection with crime and punishment. They document and investigate mental processes that lead officials and others to engage in statistical discrimination, in which they attribute characteristics of groups to individuals, and to treat black people more severely on the basis of skin tone and distinctive Afro-American facial characteristics. A literature on public opinion and attitudes examines the causes and correlates of racial differences in attitudes toward punishment. The key findings are that much larger percentages of whites than blacks support harsh punishments, including the death penalty, for reasons that include widely held resentments toward and stereotypes about black criminals. Many fewer blacks support harsh punishments. The overwhelmingly influential reasons are widespread beliefs that the justice system is racist and treats black people unfairly (large majorities of whites disagree).

Section II examines the history of American race relations. Scholars who study "social stratification" and "racial hierarchy" have shown that American social, economic, and legal institutions have evolved over time in ways that have maintained white dominance and protected the interests of whites as a class. When one mechanism for maintaining white domination broke up, another replaced it. Slavery did the job for centuries, until the Civil War. Within decades after the war, "Jim Crow" laws restored overwhelming white predominance. After millions of blacks moved from the South to the North in the 1910s and 1920s to escape Jim Crow, the big-city ghettos, housing discrimination, and racial bias kept blacks in their subordinate place. Contemporary wars on drugs and crime took over more recently.

Section III says a bit more about the Republican Southern Strategy. Some of its most influential designers and practitioners in retrospect repudiated it and expressed regret for the roles they played. It has, alas, done lasting damage. The appeals to overt racism made by the George Wallaces and Lester Maddoxes in the 1960s were followed by the appeals to racial animus made by Richard Nixon, Ronald Reagan, and George Herbert Bush. Beliefs in the inferiority of black people were succeeded by beliefs that unfair efforts were made to help blacks overcome the legacies of slavery and racial discrimination and that blacks failed to take advantage of them. Ideological battles over affirmative action, busing, "quotas," and "reverse racism" shaped many white people's beliefs that the time for remediation is past and that further efforts to help disadvantaged black people unfairly deny jobs, school admissions, opportunities, and resources to whites. Those racial resentments are a principal reason why so many whites support drug and crime control policies that do so much damage to black people.

I. The Social Psychology of American Race Relations

Some Americans, including no doubt some public officials and practitioners, are racists and are biased against blacks. Larger numbers are affected by conscious stereotypes ("Many young black men are dangerous and this young black man probably is also"). Almost everyone—black Americans included—is influenced by subconscious negative associations of black people with crime and criminality. Different words are used to describe those influences—"colorism," "Afro-American feature bias," "implicit bias"—and different groups of researchers study them. In the end, they come to the same conclusion: Americans, especially white Americans, are predisposed to associate blackness with crime and dangerousness and are prepared to treat black offenders especially harshly as a result.

Sociologists use the term "statistical discrimination" to describe one outcome of those predispositions. Statistical discrimination is the attribution to individuals of traits that characterize groups of which they are members. Sociologist William Julius Wilson in *The Truly Disadvantaged: The Inner City, the Underclass, and Public Policy* (1987) showed how this operates in employment. Many young black inner-city men have not been socialized into habits that employers want: coming to work on time, sticking with monotonous jobs, dressing in mainstream ways, speaking in mainstream English, and observing conventional forms of politeness. Many employers as a consequence are skeptical about hiring young black men. Employers may be correct that young minority men who dress in trousers with drooping crotches and affect stereotypical behaviors are on average more likely than other people to be unreliable workers. However, those preconceptions in many cases lead them to reject job applicants who would be reliable workers. Extensive subsequent research, most prominently by Princeton sociologist Devah Pager (2007), has confirmed Wilson's assertions. Pager conducted a series of projects in which black and white researchers applied for the same jobs and presented identical resumes and made identical applications. The white "applicants" were much more likely to be hired.

Novelist Tom Wolfe in *Bonfire of the Vanities* (1987) describes the power of statistical discrimination in the criminal courts. Stereotypes of black criminals matter. The lawyer for a young black defendant has tried, with some success, to persuade the judge that his client is a nice kid, young, impressionable, and salvageable; played a minor role in a street robbery; and deserves a break. Then the defendant appears:

> He had the same pumping swagger that practically every young defendant in the Bronx affected, the Pimp Roll. Such stupid self-destructive macho egos, thought Kramer [a prosecutor]. They never failed to show up with the black jackets and the sneakers and the Pimp Roll. They never failed to look every inch the young felon before judges, juries, probation officers, psychiatrists, before every single soul who had any say in whether they went to prison. . . . The defendant's comrades always arrived in court in their shiny black thermal jackets and go-to-hell sneakers. That was very bright too. That immediately established the fact that the defendant was not a poor defenseless victim of life in the ghetto but part of a pack of remorseless young felons. (Pp. 13–14)

The defendant does not get the break.

Statistical discrimination is a central problem in racial profiling by the police. If many young black men in particular neighborhoods, who adopt particular styles of dress, are involved in gang activities or drug dealing, police seeing a young man in that neighborhood who fits that pattern may believe it likely that he is a gang member or drug dealer and stop him, even if the individualized basis for a stop that the law requires does not exist.

The situation with court officials may be somewhat different. On the basis of personal interactions over decades with judges in many American jurisdictions, I do not believe that invidious racial bias and gross stereotypes substantially affect sentencing decisions. This is a subject judges worry about, are taught about at judicial conferences, and discuss often among themselves and with others. Sentencing research showing that there are few racial differences in sentence lengths is consistent with this belief (e.g., Spohn 2000, 2002). Judges, however, are no doubt affected by the unconscious stereotyping described in the following pages.

A. Negative Cultural Stereotypes of Black People

It is not surprising that the racial profiling literature documents excessive and poorly justified stops of black people. Two decades of research document that the media commonly portray a world of black offenders and white victims and that, when asked to describe typical violent criminals and drug dealers, white Americans describe black offenders (e.g., Entman 1992; Reeves and Campbell 1994; Beckett and Sasson 2004). Psychological processes much subtler than the crude stereotypes Tom Wolfe describes, however, are also at work. Research on the influence of skin tone and "Afrocentric" features shows that negative stereotypes are deeply embedded in American culture and operate to the detriment of blacks in the criminal justice system. They cause black offenders to be punished more severely than whites, and among blacks they cause dark-skinned people, and people with distinctively "African" facial features, to be punished more severely than light-skinned people and people with more "European" features.

"Colorism" is the "tendency to perceive or behave toward members of a racial category based on the lightness or darkness of their skin tone" (Maddox and Gray 2002, p. 250). The research field is comparatively new, but the phenomenon is old. Two-thirds of a century ago, Gunnar Myrdal observed in *An American Dilemma: The Negro Problem and Modern Democracy* that "without a doubt a Negro with light skin and other European features has in the North an advantage with white people" (1944, p. 697). A few years later, an American Council on Education report observed, "What is really crucial behind the color point is class; the implications that light color goes with higher status and the Negroid appearance with lower status, is what makes these characteristics so important" (Davis, Dollard, and American Youth Commission 1946, p. 137).

Among American black people, dark-skinned people are at a comparative disadvantage. Harvard political scientist Jennifer Hochschild, one of the leading scholars of the subject, and her colleague Vesla Mae Weaver recently offered this summary: "Relative to their lighter-skinned contemporaries, dark-skinned blacks have lower levels of education, income, and job status. They are less likely to own homes, or to marry; and dark-skinned blacks' prison sentences are longer. Dark-skin discrimination occurs within as well as between races" (Hochschild and Weaver 2007, p. 644).

There has not been much research on the effects of colorism on people suspected or accused of crimes, but what there is suggests that dark-skinned people are more likely to be suspected and are punished more severely. Dark skin evokes fears of criminality (Dasgupta, Banaji, and Abelson 1999). Darker skin is a more easily remembered characteristic of a purportedly criminal face (Dixon and Maddox 2005).

An analysis of more than 67,000 male felons incarcerated in Georgia for their first offense from 1995 through 2002 showed that black offenders with dark skins received longer sentences than light-skinned blacks. Overall, white sentences averaged 2,689 days. The black average was 378 days longer. When the figures for blacks were broken down, however, light-skinned black people received sentences three and a half months longer than the white average, medium-skinned blacks a year longer, and dark-skinned blacks a year and a half longer.

When the type of offense, socioeconomic characteristics, and demographic factors were controlled for statistically, light-skinned defendants received sentences indistinguishable from those of whites. Medium- and dark-skinned defendants received longer ones (Hochschild and Weaver 2007, p. 649).

Scholars of Afrocentric feature bias take the analysis one step further (Blair, Judd, and Chapleau 2004). If skin tone affects stereotypes about crime and criminals, analysts hypothesized that certain stereotypically African American facial features (e.g., dark skin, wide noses, full lips) also influence decision makers' (and research subjects') judgments. The evidence confirms the hypothesis. One study found that the larger the number of Afrocentric features an individual possessed, the more "criminal" that individual appeared to be in the eyes of observers (Eberhardt et al. 2004). Other studies have shown that Afrocentric features are associated with longer prison sentences and increased the likelihood that murderers were sentenced to death.

Several important studies have tried to assess the significance of Afrocentric feature bias. Blair et al. (2002) found that individuals with more Afrocentric features were judged by college undergraduates to have stereotypical African American traits. Blair, Chapleau, and Judd (2005) showed that observers believed that individuals with more Afrocentric features were more likely than others to behave aggressively.

Jennifer Eberhardt and three colleagues asked 182 police officers to examine photographs of male students and employees at Stanford University. Half were shown white faces and half were shown black faces. One-third of the officers were asked to rate the stereotypicality of each face on a scale, that is, how stereotypical each face was of members of that person's race. Another third, told that some of the faces might be of criminals, were asked to indicate whether the person "looked criminal." The last third were asked to rate attractiveness on a scale. Each officer completed only one of the three measures.

More black than white faces were thought to look criminal. Black faces rated above the median for stereotypical black features were judged as criminal significantly more often than were black faces rated below the median. The authors concluded that the police officers thought that black faces looked more criminal and that "the more black, the more criminal" (Eberhardt et al. 2004, p. 889).

Blair, Judd, and Chapleau (2004) analyzed the faces of inmates in the Florida Department of Corrections to learn whether facial features were associated with longer sentences. They asked undergraduates to rate the faces of a randomly selected sample of 100 black and 116 white inmates, in terms of the "degree to which each face had features that are typical of African Americans" (p. 676). The results showed that facial characteristics were a significant predictor of the lengths of sentences the prisoners were serving. After the authors controlled for race and criminal history, stereotypical black features were a significant predictor of sentence length. Within each race, more stereotypical black features were associated with longer sentences. Even those whites who had facial features that "looked black" had received longer sentences than other white prisoners.

Pizzi, Blair, and Judd (2005) investigated the effect of facial features on sentencing, starting from a presupposition that conscious bias is not likely to be a significant cause of disparities. They reasoned that judges and prosecutors have learned to be sensitive to the possibility that they treat blacks differently and have become sensitive to some stereotypical differences. They concluded, however, that practitioners continue to treat offenders differently on the basis of the presence or absence of Afrocentric features: "Racial stereotyping in sentencing decisions still persists. But it is not a function of the racial category of the individual; instead, there seems to be an equally pernicious and less controllable process at work. Racial stereotyping in sentencing still occurs based on the facial appearance of the offender. Be they white or African American, those offenders who possess stronger Afrocentric features receive harsher sentences for the same crimes" (p. 351).

Even the chance that offenders will be sentenced to death is influenced by facial features. Eberhardt et al. (2006, p. 383), looking at cases in Philadelphia in which death had been a possible sentence, "examined the extent to which perceived stereotypicality of black defendants influenced jurors' death-sentencing decisions in cases with both white and black victims." Stanford undergraduates were shown pictures of 44 death penalty–eligible defendants, presented randomly and edited for uniformity, and asked to rate the stereotypicality of each black defendant's appearance. With stereotypicality as the only independent variable, 24.4 percent of black defendants rated below the median had been sentenced to death, compared with 57.5 percent of black defendants rated above the median.

Unconscious attribution of criminality to black people is a serious problem, and it is one that influences even other black people. Yet another source of evidence comes from the Implicit Association Test (IAT), a test developed by psychologists to assess peoples' implicit attitudes toward different groups. The IAT, which by 2008 had been taken by 4.5 million on the Internet and elsewhere, asks individuals to categorize a series of words or pictures into groups.[3] Two of the groups are racial—"black" and "white"—and two of the groups are characterizations of words as "good" or "pleasant" (e.g., joy, laugh, happy) or "bad" or "unpleasant" (e.g., terrible, agony, nasty). To test for implicit bias, one version of the IAT asks respondents to press one key on the computer for either "black" or "unpleasant" words or pictures and a

---

[3] The test, available since 1998, is offered by Project Implicit (http://www.project implicit.net/), which describes itself as combining "basic research and educational outreach in a virtual laboratory at which visitors can examine their own hidden biases." The test can be taken at https://implicit.harvard.edu/implicit/.

different key for "white" or "pleasant" words or pictures. In another version, respondents are asked to press one key for "black" or "pleasant" and another key for "white" or "unpleasant." Implicit bias is defined as faster responses when "black" and "unpleasant" are paired than when "black" and "pleasant" are.

The results have consistently shown that implicit bias against blacks is "extremely widespread" (Jolls and Sunstein 2006, p. 971). The consensus view demonstrates the existence of a real unconscious bias by whites against blacks (Rachlinski et al. 2009). Almost all demographic groups show a significant implicit preference for whites over blacks. The major exception is blacks: equal proportions show implicit preferences for blacks and for whites, though blacks—unlike whites—do not show a preference for their own group.

Since the consensus view of the existence of implicit racial bias is based on the results of millions of tests of every imaginable group in the population, it would be remarkable if criminal justice practitioners were not affected by it. Much recent research as a consequence investigates the effectiveness of possible ways to alert officials to their implicit biases, so that they can attempt to reduce the biases' influence in the same ways that practitioners have become sensitized to cruder stereotypes based on dress or hairstyles (e.g., Levinson 2007).

Some research has explicitly examined practitioners' possible biases. Jeffrey Rachlinski and his colleagues (2009) recruited 133 judges from three jurisdictions to take implicit bias tests and to sentence hypothetical cases in which the defendant's race was varied. The bias test, as expected, revealed implicit biases against blacks among white judges and no clear pattern among black judges. The sentencing exercise also showed a statistically significant (though not large) relationship between individual judges' biases and the sentences they said they would impose.

Other research has focused on police. In one study, participants were shown pictures of black and white criminal suspects who were and were not carrying guns. Participants were told to imagine they were police officers and that they should shoot suspects holding guns. The findings strongly confirmed hypotheses about implicit bias. Among suspects carrying guns, whites were less likely than blacks to be "shot"; among suspects not carrying firearms, blacks were more likely to be shot (Plant, Peruche, and Butz 2005).

When George Bush used images of Willie Horton to symbolize Michael Dukakis's softness on crime in the 1988 presidential election, he was pushing a button that was waiting to be pushed, and one that manipulated and exacerbated deeply ingrained predispositions among whites to associate blackness with criminality.

B. Racial Resentments and Public Opinion about Crime and Punishment

White Americans, especially politically conservative and fundamentalist Protestant white Americans, tend to support harsh punishments, including the death penalty. Black people tend to support harsh punishments at much lower rates. Whites have substantially greater confidence in the justice system and its practitioners than do blacks. Researchers repeatedly find that measures of racial animus and resentment are strong influences on whites' punitive attitudes. Reciprocally, low levels of confidence in the fairness of the justice system are a major influence on blacks' attitudes. Most black Americans believe that the criminal justice system is racially biased and that black suspects and defendants are treated unfairly. Most whites do not.

A substantial literature on racial differences in attitudes toward and opinions about crime control policy shows that whites have rationalized a criminal justice system that is disparately severe toward blacks. Early research on the influence of race on attitudes toward the criminal justice system found that racial prejudice (measured by support for racial segregation and belief in black inferiority) was associated with whites' support for harsh sentencing (Cohn, Barkan, and Halteman 1991), as were negative racial stereotypes (Hurwitz and Peffley 1997) and racial antipathy (a preference for maintaining social distance from blacks; Gilliam and Iyengar 2000).

More recent work has struggled to find nuanced ways to disentangle the influence of racial beliefs and attitudes, distinguishing among racial bigotry, racial resentments, and negative racial stereotyping. Findings consistently show that whites' belief in inherent black inferiority has almost disappeared. Encouraging as that is, however, findings also demonstrate widely shared white resentments of post–civil rights era efforts to integrate blacks into mainstream American society and a powerful association between those resentments and support for the crime control and drug policies that have ensnared so many black Americans.

The relevant literature has exploded in recent years. The initial focus was on racial differences in support for harsh sentencing policies and for the death penalty. The death penalty literature began to develop after the U.S. Supreme Court decided *Furman v. Georgia*, 408 U.S. 228 (1972), which suspended use of capital punishment in the United States, and *Gregg v. Georgia*, 428 U.S. 153 (1976), which reinstituted it. Researchers examined a wide range of issues, including characteristics of death penalty supporters and opponents, whether peoples' views changed if they learned more about the subject (sometimes), whether the availability of sentences of life without possibility of parole changed opinions (sometimes), and whether blacks and whites had different views (yes).

The most comprehensive survey of that literature shows that there was a 30-point racial gap in support for capital punishment in 2004 (whites: 72.5 percent; blacks: 41.7 percent). That gap had not changed since 1974 (whites: 69.8 percent; blacks: 39.9 percent) and held steady in between. The obvious question is what explains the gap. The strongest predictor of whites' support for capital punishment in our time is racial resentment: "Taken together, the extant studies reach remarkably consistent results: negative views toward African Americans—what scholars in this area have called 'racism' or 'racial animus'—predict a range of political attitudes, including greater support for capital punishment" (Unnever, Cullen, and Lero Jonson 2008, p. 53).

Efforts were made to see whether peoples' attitudes changed if they realized that blacks disproportionately occupy death row cells and that the race of the victim is a primary determinant of whether a convicted murderer is sentenced to death. Lawrence Bobo and Devon Johnson (2004) examined blacks' and whites' support for capital punishment and the crack cocaine 100-to-one law and the extent to which opinions changed in the light of information about the racial dimensions of those problems (e.g., the disproportionate presence of blacks on death rows; that killers of whites are much more likely to be sentenced to death than are killers of blacks; that most crack dealers are black). In general, except concerning the 100-to-one law, information did not significantly affect whites' opinions. Racial resentment was powerfully related to support for the death penalty:

> The most consistent predictor of criminal justice policy attitudes is, in fact, a form of racial prejudice. While white racial resentment does not ever explain a large share of the variation in any of the attitudes we have measured, it is the most consistently influential of the variables outside of race classification itself. This pattern

has at least two implications. It further buttresses the concern that some of the major elements of public support for punitive criminal justice policies are heavily tinged with racial animus and thus quite likely to be resistant to change based on suasion and information-based appeals." (Bobo and Johnson 2004, pp. 171–72)

James Unnever and colleagues have tried to isolate the influence of racial resentments on other issues. One analysis examined data from the 2006 African American Survey undertaken for the *Washington Post*, the Henry J. Kaiser Foundation, and Harvard University to explore peoples' explanations for racial disparities in imprisonment. This is a huge survey of 1,328 African American men, 507 African American women, and 1,029 members of other racial and ethnic groups. Blacks were substantially likelier than whites to give denial of jobs and bad schools as "big reasons" for the disparity, but the largest differences concerned bias in the legal system. Seventy-one percent of blacks, but only 37 percent of whites, believed that police bias was a primary cause of disparities. Similarly, 67 percent of blacks blamed "unfair courts" but only 28 percent of whites (Unnever 2008, table 1). The degree to which black respondents had personally experienced what they perceived as racial discrimination "predicts whether African Americans believe that criminal injustices, such as whether the police target black men and whether the courts are more willing to convict African-American men, are reasons for the high incarceration among black men" (p. 527).

The racial difference in perceptions of bias in the justice system that Unnever found is echoed in findings from many other projects. The leading scholar of the subject, Harvard sociologist Lawrence Bobo, organized two representative national surveys on race, crime, and public opinion. The 2001 Race, Crime, and Public Opinion Study included 1,010 black respondents and 978 whites. Only 38 percent of whites said they believed that the criminal justice system is biased against blacks; 89 percent of blacks said that it was. Only 8 percent of blacks said that the justice system "gives blacks fair treatment"; 56 percent of whites said that it did. Seventy-eight percent of whites expressed confidence that judges treat blacks and whites equally, compared with only 28 percent of blacks. Concerning police, the gap was even bigger: 68 percent of whites expressed confidence in the police and only 18 percent of blacks did (Bobo and Thompson 2006, p. 456).

Approaching the same kinds of issues from another angle, Unnever,

Cullen, and Jones (2008) analyzed data from the 2000 National Election Study to investigate racial differences in support for social policies to address economic and social causes of crime. Respondents were asked whether they thought "the best way to reduce crime is to address social problems or to make sure criminals are caught, convicted, and punished, or something in between." A series of follow-up questions asked whether the preferred approach was a "much" or "somewhat" better way to reduce crime. Their main aim was to investigate whether and how peoples' attachment to egalitarian beliefs influenced their attitudes toward adoption of nonpunitive anticrime policies (a lot, was the answer). Their premise was that people with strong commitments to equality are more likely than others to support social policies aimed at preventing crime by reducing the social and economic inequalities associated with it. A variety of demographic (age, sex, race, education, place of residence) and attitudinal (egalitarian beliefs, racial stereotypes, racial resentment) variables were analyzed. Blacks were much more likely than whites to support social policy approaches to crime reduction. Whites with racial resentments toward blacks were much more likely to oppose social policy approaches and to support criminal justice approaches.

Devon Johnson has completed the most comprehensive analysis of the sources of racial differences in attitudes toward punishment. I describe her analysis in considerable detail to show the basis of the conclusions she drew. The data came from the 2001 Race, Crime, and Public Opinion Study. A "punitiveness index" was calculated on answers on a 1–4 scale (1 = "strongly disagree," 4 = "strongly agree") to four questions: Do you favor life sentences for third-time felons? Should parole boards be more strict, less strict, or continue current practices? Should 14–17-year-olds accused of violent crimes be tried and sentenced in adult courts? Are current punishments for violent crimes too harsh, too light, or just about right? Whites were much more likely than blacks to favor three-strikes laws and trying young people as adults, to believe that parole boards should be more strict, and to believe that punishments for violent crimes are too light.

To find out whether and how racial attitudes and beliefs influence punitive attitudes, Johnson developed a measure of perceived racial bias in the justice system and various measures of racial prejudice. Perceived racial bias was calculated from responses to three questions about confidence that the police, prosecutors, and judges treat blacks and whites equally.

Racial prejudice was measured in three ways. To calculate "racial resentment," respondents were asked to indicate agreement or disagreement with six propositions (shortened and paraphrased here).

First, members of other ethnic groups have overcome prejudice and succeeded; blacks should do the same without special favors.

Second, blacks in recent years have gotten less than they deserve.

Third, government officials pay less attention to requests and complaints from black than from white people.

Fourth, blacks who receive welfare could get along without it if they tried.

Fifth, if blacks would only try harder, they would do as well as whites.

Sixth, generations of slavery and discrimination created conditions that make it hard for blacks to work their way out of the lower class.

To calculate "negative affect," general attitudes to black people, respondents were asked two questions. How often have you felt sympathy for blacks? How often have you admired blacks?

Finally, to calculate "racial stereotypes," respondents were asked on a 1–10 scale to characterize as accurate or inaccurate four negative descriptions of black people: as lazy, aggressive or violent, preferring to live on welfare, and complaining.

The analysis took account of many other characteristics of the survey respondents including demographic characteristics such as age, sex, income, education, and place of residence and other characteristics such as political beliefs, fear of crime, and having a relative or friend imprisoned. When all these characteristics were taken into account, two factors stood out. For blacks, perceptions of racial bias in the system were the major distinguishing characteristic. For whites, it was racial resentment. The other two measures of prejudice—negative affect and racial stereotypes—had discernible effects that were dwarfed by the power of racial resentment.

It might in some sense seem encouraging that whites are less likely than in earlier times to hold beliefs about racial inferiority or about race-based negative characterizations of laziness, violence, and querulousness. Their displacement, however, by racial resentments is no

cause for celebration. The consequence in some ways is more pernicious, especially in light of what we now know about statistical discrimination, colorism, Afro-American feature bias, and implicit bias.
Widespread beliefs that blacks are racially inferior have been replaced
by beliefs that the conditions of life that lead some black people to
crime are their own fault and they deserve whatever punishment they
get. Put differently, racial resentments provide a powerful basis for lack
of sympathy for people caught up in the legal system. And if disproportionate numbers of blacks are arrested for drug dealing and for
violent crimes, they have no cause to complain.

Devon Johnson summed up where things stand:

> Given the association between race and crime in political dis-
> course, in media accounts, and in the minds of many whites, it is
> likely that racial prejudice will continue to play a significant role in
> whites' political support for punitive policies for some time. More-
> over, in light of the . . . inability of those in privileged positions
> to perceive racial discrimination in the administration of justice (or
> their unwillingness to acknowledge it), it is unlikely that blacks'
> cynicism toward the criminal justice system will markedly improve
> in the short term. (2008, p. 205)

That seems right. However, it also seems remarkable. How could
the initial dynamic, with its assumptions about black inferiority, have
worked? And when it became untenable, how could its reincarnation
on the basis of racial resentments have continued to work? Part of the
answer can be found in the history of American race relations.

II. The History of Race Relations

Ideas about statistical discrimination and social stereotyping, and about
the unconscious effects of colorism and Afrocentric facial features, may
be unfamiliar to some readers, but they are not difficult to grasp. Similarly pernicious effects of social stereotypes and unrecognized biases
about women and gay and lesbian people were in due course recognized, and social attitudes, actions, and policies changed as a result.
Few people any longer believe that menstruation makes women emo-
tionally unstable and unsuited for leadership positions or that women
lack the physical stamina and self-discipline to participate in physically
demanding work or sports. Likewise, few people any longer believe
that gays and lesbians' lives are governed by their sexual appetites (or

no more anyway than is true of heterosexuals) or are incapable of being successful parents. No similar changes have occurred concerning the experiences of black people in the criminal justice system. Stereotypes about racial inferiority may have been replaced by racial resentments, but to disproportionate numbers of blacks on death row or in prisons, or to black defendants in crack cocaine cases, that is a distinction without a difference.

So the question is why the effects of racial resentments persist and make many whites unsympathetic to the experiences of blacks in the criminal justice system. The most likely explanation for adoption of disparity-causing policies, and their continuation long after their effects became known, and why racial resentments have such blinding power, is the subtlest and hardest to grasp. It is that we white Americans as a class are so accustomed to seeing the world from the perspective of our own self-interest that we unconsciously support policies that ensure our social, political, and economic dominance. Anti-immigrant policies are a vulgar recent example: people hostile to immigrants may talk about the rule of law and illegal immigration, but their real, underlying concerns relate to competition for jobs, fear of social change, and worry that their own well-being will suffer. Rational analyses of economic and social effects of immigration are beside the point. Drug and criminal justice policies that destabilize poor black communities and sustain white dominance are a subtler instance of a similar phenomenon.

The stereotyping, resentments, and attributions discussed in the preceding section are unlikely by themselves to have produced and perpetuated racial profiling and 100-to-one, three-strikes, and similar laws. Police officials and other policy makers are sometimes influenced by base political considerations, but comparatively few are likely to be motivated by invidious racial bias. Conscious stereotypes and statistical discrimination no doubt play roles, especially in explaining police decisions to stop citizens on the street and judges' sentencing decisions to send to prison people they believe (often wrongly) to be dangerous. Unconscious stereotyping no doubt operates at the level of the individual case, and people with typical black features suffer as a result. All of these factors, however, are likely to be most important in individual cases and unlikely to be major causes of passage of laws and policies that treat black people especially severely.

A literature that has developed over the past 20 years explains what happened. Contemporary drug and crime control policies are in large part products of unconscious efforts by the white majority to maintain political, social, and economic dominance over blacks.

Sociologist Loïc Wacquant's work provides insight into enduring features of American history and culture that help explain racial disparities in the justice system. His basic claim is that American cultural practices and legal institutions have operated to maintain patterns of racial dominance and hierarchy for three centuries. When one mechanism for maintaining white domination broke down, another replaced it. Until the Civil War, slavery did the job. Within 30 years after the war, the practices and legal forms of discrimination known as "Jim Crow" laws restored overwhelming white dominance. In the Great Migration in the 1910s and 1920s, millions of blacks moved from the South to the North to escape Jim Crow; the big city ghettos, housing discrimination, and other forms of discrimination kept blacks in their subordinate place (Lieberson 1980). And when deindustrialization and the flight of jobs and the middle class to the suburbs left disadvantaged blacks marooned in the urban ghettos, the modern wars on drugs and crime took over (Wacquant 2002*a*, 2002*b*).

More recently, Wacquant has explained how that happened: "Unlike Jim Crow, the ghetto was not dismantled by government action. It was left to crumble onto itself, trapping lower-class African-Americans in a vortex of unemployment, poverty, and crime, abetted by the joint withdrawal of the wage-labor market and the welfare state. . . . As the ghetto lost its economic function and proved unable to ensure ethnoracial closure, the prison was called upon to help contain a population widely viewed as deviant, destitute, and dangerous" (2008, p. 65). That is a major reason why a third of black baby boys are eventually bound for prison, why a third of young black men are under the control of the criminal justice system, and why imprisonment rates for blacks have been five to seven times those for whites since 1980.

Wacquant's argument concerns what criminal justice policies and practices do rather than what they are consciously intended to do. Thought of that way, it is hard not to see that the machinery of the criminal justice system produces devastatingly reduced life chances for black Americans.

There has to be a powerful underlying reason why the Republican Southern Strategy was adopted and why it worked, why the criminal justice system treats black Americans so badly, and why foreseeable racially disparate effects of crime control and drug policies are disregarded. For people who do not believe that conscious racism is the reason, Wacquant's analysis provides a better explanation.

Wacquant is not alone in suggesting that contemporary American criminal justice practices are the latest in a series of social policies that operate to keep poor blacks in their places. Douglas Massey, author (with Nancy Denton) of *American Apartheid* (1993), a widely praised and decidedly nonpolemical account of housing discrimination, argued in *Categorically Unequal*, his 2007 book on social stratification, that crime policy supports white interests:

> Whether whites care to admit it or not, they have a selfish interest in maintaining the categorical mechanisms that perpetuate racial stratification. As a result, when pushed by the federal government to end overt discriminatory practices, they are likely to innovate new and more subtle ways to maintain their privileged position in society. If one discriminatory mechanism proves impossible to sustain, whites have an incentive to develop alternatives that may be associated only indirectly with race and are therefore not in obvious violation of civil rights law. The specific mechanisms by which racial stratification occurs can thus be expected to evolve over time. (P. 54)

> The new emphasis on retribution and punishment was achieved . . . through the deliberate racialization of crime and violence in public consciousness by political entrepreneurs. (P. 94)

> As discrimination moved underground, new mechanisms for exclusion were built into the criminal justice system for Afro Americans. (P. 251)

Economist Glenn C. Loury observed in *The Anatomy of Racial Inequality* that "the deeper truth is that, for three centuries now, political, social, and economic institutions that by any measure must be seen as racially oppressive, have distorted the communal experience of the slaves and their descendants" (2002, p. 104). Later on, in introducing his 2007 Tanner Lectures at Stanford, he elaborated: "We have embraced what criminologist Michael Tonry . . . calls a policy of 'malign neglect,' and in doing so we, as a society, have stumbled more or less wittingly into a God-awful cul de sac. . . . The connection of this apparatus to the history of racial degradation and subordination in our country (lynching, minstrelsy, segregation, ghettoization) is virtually self-evident. . . . The racial subtext of our law and order political discourse over the last three decades has been palpable" (Loury 2007; references omitted).

More recently, Loury has written, "Mass incarceration has now become a principal vehicle for the reproduction of racial hierarchy in our society" (2008, pp. 36–37). To like effect, the finding discussed earlier that racial resentment is the strongest predictor of whites' support for severe punishment policies led Lawrence Bobo and Devon Johnson to conclude, "This pattern reinforces the claim . . . that one major function of the criminal justice system is the regulation and control of marginalized social groups such as African Americans" (2004, pp. 171–72).

These are functionalist arguments, about what criminal justice policies and practices do, rather than political ones about what those practices and policies are intended to do. The argument is not that a cabal of racist whites consciously acts to favor white interests but that deeper social forces collude, almost as if directed by an invisible hand, to formulate laws, policies, and social practices that serve the interests of white Americans. Thought of that way, if one thinks of what the machinery of the criminal justice system produces, it is hard not to see that it produces devastatingly reduced life chances for black Americans. If its aims were to reduce poor black men's chances of earning a decent living, being successfully married and a good father, or being socialized into prosocial values, it is hard to see how the criminal justice system could do those things better (Western 2006). There has to be a reason why the criminal justice system treats American blacks so badly, why its foreseeable disparate impacts on blacks and whites are disregarded. Wacquant's and the others' analyses provide a better explanation than any other that has been offered.

Once the racial hierarchy/status anxiety analysis that Wacquant, Massey, Loury, and Bobo and Johnson offer is recognized, much else falls into place. David Garland, in his writing on lynchings in America during their 1890–1930 heyday, observes, "The penal excess of the lynching spectacle said things that a modernized legal process could not. . . . [I]t reestablished the correlative status of the troublesome black man, which was as nothing, with no rights, no protectors, no personal dignity, and no human worth" (2005, p. 817).

Lest the preceding discussion of racial hierarchy seem fanciful, there are plenty of other subjects concerning which similar things have happened. Housing policy offers an example. Federal housing policies of the 1950s and 1960s, though proposed and explained in neutral terms of credit risk and sound stewardship of federal dollars, operated to block blacks from moving into newly developing white suburbs and, through redlining "risky neighborhoods," to deny federally insured mortgages to residents of urban minority neighborhoods. The effect was to lock black people into deteriorated inner-city areas. In retrospect, those federal policies have been discredited and are widely recognized to have been a significant contributor to perpetuation of racially segregated housing (Massey and Denton 1993).

Nineteenth-century temperance and prohibition movements provide another example of a conflict over crime and drug policy that appeared to be about one thing (the dangers of alcohol) but was really about status conflicts between ethnic groups. Nineteenth-century movements to prohibit alcohol, in their proponents' arguments, were precipitated by the problems associated with alcohol use and were motivated to address them. In retrospect, nineteenth-century prohibition was in large part a proxy for social and status conflicts between Protestant descendants of earlier waves of British and German settlers, anxious to protect their newly acquired social status and political power, and newly arrived Irish Catholics. Many of the earlier settlers were teetotalers; many of the bibulous Irish were enthusiastic drinkers. Moralistic crusades against alcohol served as devices for expressing disapproval and social distance from newcomers that was sometimes unacknowledged or unrecognized by the prohibitionists themselves. Attacking drinking as immoral was a way to assert the moral superiority of the attackers and the moral inferiority of the attacked (Gusfield 1963).

Criminalization of particular substances reflected similar ethnic group dynamics each time it happened in the twentieth century. When heroin and cocaine were criminalized by the federal Harrison Act in 1914, the prevailing images of the "immorality" of drug use were provided by groups other than the white majority: Chinese users of opiates and black users of cocaine (Musto 1973; Courtwright 1982). The Marijuana Tax Act, the first federal criminalization of marijuana, was aimed at pot-smoking Mexican laborers whose migration into western states in search of work precipitated hostile reactions from whites not unlike those occurring early in the twenty-first century (Whitebread and Bonnie 1974). In the 1980s, the targets of unprecedentedly tough laws aimed at crack cocaine were inner-city blacks (Massing 1998, chap. 14)

A similar dynamic, though between generations rather than between ethnic groups, characterized recent drug wars generally. The first was announced by President Richard M. Nixon on July 14, 1969, in his "Special Message to the Congress on Control of Narcotics and Dangerous Drugs." The primary status conflict of the time concerning drugs was not between whites and blacks or members of other ethnic minorities, but between generations. The alcohol-using and alcohol-abusing generations that moved in the corridors of power in the 1960s and 1970s were befuddled by a troubling and disrupted world and threatened by challenges to their political and moral authority. Marijuana and hard drug use by young people encapsulated those challenges. Marijuana was widely available and widely used. LSD and cocaine had visible and outspoken proponents. Officials said, and probably believed, that they wanted to protect young people from the ravages of drug use, and in any case that drug use is irresponsible and immoral. Young people believed that the dangers were slight and that the choices should be theirs, not the state's, to make. As was true of nineteenth-century prohibition, more recent disagreements about protection of important moral standards can as readily be understood as conflicts over whose moral standards are to be preferred and expressed in the criminal law. The words of the planners of successive modern drug wars may have been about safety and responsibility, but the music was about protection of their views of the world and of the places in it of people like them (Musto and Korsmeyer 2002, p. 60).

Harvard philosopher Tommie Shelby has observed, "It is a truism about human nature—one emphasized by Max Weber—that the privileged want to maintain that they merit their advantages and that the disadvantaged deserve all their hardships" (2008, p. 80). Concerning the criminal justice system, about which concern about racial disparities in imprisonment might be expected, whites can take comfort in racial stereotypes, such as that black Americans are especially criminal, so of course so many are in prison.

The incentive to rationalize is clear. System justification theory posits "a general human tendency to support and defend the social status quo, broadly defined" (Blasi and Jost 2006, p. 1123). People, regardless of their situation, try to rationalize the injustices and inequities they see. Stereotypes (such as that the rich are smart, the poor are lazy, and blacks are criminal) are often employed to demonstrate that all members of society deserve their status. People who believe in a just world experience, by and large, have more positive emotions than people who believe in an unjust world. For example, poor people who blame themselves for their own poverty are happier and more satisfied with life in general. By rationalizing the racial inequities in the American criminal justice system, white Americans persuade themselves that the problem is not in the policies they and people like them set and enforce, but in social forces over which they have no control.

Current crime and drug control policies, however, were not written by an invisible hand. They were enacted and implemented by human beings influenced by mixed motives, some idealistic, some cynical, some self-serving. Insofar as they were enacted as fruits of the Republican Southern Strategy, they represented deliberate manipulations of racist biases and fears and racial stereotypes and attributions to achieve partisan political aims.

III. The Southern Strategy

It is common as I did in the introduction to this essay to date the beginning of the Republican Southern Strategy in the 1960s and to describe Kevin Phillips's *The Emerging Republican Majority* (1969) as its basic text. Both things are true: the Republican Southern Strategy was first commonly used to characterize Republican Barry Goldwater's 1964 presidential campaign, and Phillips was a strategist in Richard Nixon's 1968 campaign who later published a book making a case for it, but that account oversimplifies.

Proposals that southern segregationist Democrats combine with Republican conservatives were first seriously promoted in the 1940s. Civil rights advocates began to win legal and political victories, and white supremacists began to worry. Democratic President Franklin Delano Roosevelt on June 25, 1941, signed Executive Order 8802, which established the Federal Employment Practices Commission. The order forbade racial discrimination by federal contractors and empowered the FEPC to investigate complaints. After Roosevelt's death, segregationists hoped that Harry S. Truman would be more sympathetic. Their hopes were misplaced. Within 2 months of taking office, Truman proposed legislation to make the FEPC permanent. Truman later appointed a biracial Committee on Civil Rights, which, in *To Secure These Rights* (1947), recommended enactment of antilynching, anti–poll tax, and fair employment legislation. The committee also proposed prohibition of discrimination in interstate transportation and desegrega-tion of the armed forces. In his January 7, 1948, State of the Union address, Truman announced his intention to carry out the committee's proposals (Lowndes 2008, chap. 2).

Segregationist southern Democrats were stunned. Mississippi Sen-ator James Eastland declared, "The South we know is being swept to its destruction." Southern governors convened to denounce Truman's desegregation effort and approved a resolution mostly written by South Carolina Governor Strom Thurmond warning that the South would not "stand idle and let all of this happen" (Lowndes 2008, p. 27). Among the results was opposition to Truman's bid for reelection and the nomination of Strom Thurmond as the "Dixiecrat" candidate for president in 1948. He received 20 percent of the southern vote and carried Alabama, Mississippi, Louisiana, and South Carolina.

I stop retelling the story at that point and skip to the 1960s. A number of fine books tell it in detail and carry it forward from the 1940s (Carter 1996; Black and Black 2002; Murakawa 2005; Lowndes 2008). My aim in going back to the 1940s is to show that what became widely known as the Southern Strategy had its roots in earlier efforts by segregationists to maintain white supremacy in the South.

Barry Goldwater's 1964 campaigns first for the Republican nomi-nation and then for the presidency were the first national campaigns in which Republicans openly played the race card. The Republican National Committee since 1961 had been pouring money into "Op-eration Dixie," an effort to reach out to conservative and segregationist southern Democrats, and recruiting segregationist candidates. Gold-water trod a fine line. He condemned President John F. Kennedy for sending troops to the University of Mississippi in 1962 to assure ad-mission of the first black students. While supporting voting rights for black people, he also insisted on southerners' right to control their own destiny. Historian Joseph Lowndes observes, "As long as Gold-water held high the banner of states' rights, he could appear to split real questions of racial domination from an abstract commitment to the Tenth Amendment, and allow conservatives to show clean hands while building a segregationist party in the South" (2008, p. 67).

Other Republicans knew what was going on. New York's liberal Re-publican Senator Jacob Javits in 1964 accused Operation Dixie "and what was now being called the 'southern strategy' of wrecking the party by appealing to the worst in southern racial sentiment" (Lowndes 2008,

p. 63). At the Republican convention, the liberal Ripon Society declared that the party had to choose "whether or not to adopt a strategy that must inevitably exploit the 'white backlash' to the Civil Rights Movement in the South and the suburbs of the North" (*New York Times* 1964, p. 31).

The historical accounts make it clear that Goldwater meant to appeal to white supremacist voters. Conservative scholars Stephen and Abigail Thernstrom, for example, refer to use of race-coded issues as "rhetorical winks" that have allowed "a variety of candidates—for instance, Barry Goldwater, with his talk of states rights—to play on white racial resentment" (Thernstrom and Thernstrom 1997, p. 309).

Goldwater lost dismally, winning only 38.5 percent of the vote and six states (Arizona, Louisiana, Mississippi, Alabama, Georgia, and South Carolina), but the pattern was set. In 1968, George Wallace ran as a third-party candidate appealing openly to antiblack sentiments. Nixon ceded the segregationist Deep South to Wallace.

Goldwater showed that conservative Republicans could win elections in the Deep South by use of veiled appeals to race. However, he also showed that the ugliness of open racism could alienate voters elsewhere. Former President Richard Nixon, in a 1988 interview, observed of Goldwater that he "ran as a racist candidate . . . and he won the wrong [southern] states" (Lowndes 2008). By this Nixon meant that overt or barely disguised racist appeals that were successful in the Deep South would not win elsewhere unless made more subtly.

Goldwater, however, had cast the die, and conservative Republicans continued to cast the dice for another 25 years. Nixon's code words were law and order and busing. The historical accounts make it clear that Nixon in 1968 tried to walk a fine line between repudiating the vulgar, overtly racist appeals of George Wallace and appealing to whites' racial resentments and animus. One of the gentler critiques observes that supporters of the Southern Strategy, "including southern politicians and Richard Nixon and his aides, seem to have been quite conscious of the fact that the voters they targeted for mobilization were white and had racial concerns" (Mendelberg 2001, p. 11).

Racial appeals did not play a big role in the 1972 (Nixon and Mc-Govern) or 1976 presidential campaigns but reappeared prominently in the 1980 campaign between Ronald Reagan and Jimmy Carter. Reagan's 1980 presidential campaign was launched in Philadelphia, Mississippi, a town notorious in the history of the civil rights movement for the 1964 murders of civil rights workers James Cheney, Michael Schwerber, and Andrew Goodman. Reagan assured those present of his adamant support for "states' rights." Lowndes observes, "Reagan could now seamlessly combine conservatism, racism, and antigovernment populism in a majoritarian discourse—and with it founded the modern Republican regime" (2008, p. 160).

The low point in race-coded political symbolism occurred in the Bush-Dukakis presidential campaign in 1988 and centered on Willie Horton.[4] Horton had been convicted of a particularly gruesome murder in Massachusetts. Released under a Massachusetts prison furlough program, he absconded. Months later he broke into a suburban Maryland house, where he assaulted and tied up the man and raped his fiancée. A photograph of the bleary-eyed and disheveled Horton, taken shortly after his arrest, became a prominent image in the campaign to represent Dukakis's softness on crime.

Although Lee Atwater, the creator of the Willie Horton strategy, and others later denied that they were playing a race card, subsequent reconstructions make it clear that they were. A focus group of 30 people who had voted for Reagan in 1984 but planned to vote for Dukakis was convened in Paramus, New Jersey, in late May 1988, a time when Bush was running far behind Dukakis in the polls. Small numbers of participants reacted negatively to Dukakis when they learned that he opposed capital punishment and as governor of Massachusetts had vetoed legislation permitting prayers in schools. And then, "paydirt," as historian Dan Carter describes it. On learning the Willie Horton story, "fifteen of the thirty voters said they had changed their minds. They would never vote for Dukakis. Lee Atwater had found his silver bullet" (1996, pp. 72–73).

A few days later, on Memorial Day 1988, Atwater showed films of the focus group's discussions at a campaign strategy meeting at Bush's summer home in Kennebunkport, Maine, and proposed a campaign strategy. Within 10 days, first in Texas, then elsewhere, Bush began mentioning Horton in his campaign speeches.[5] The campaign arranged

---

[4] Horton did not call himself Willie, but William. Bush's campaign advisor Lee Atwater chose to use "Willie," which was more in keeping with the southern white practice of Atwater's childhood of "referring to black men with overstated familiarity" (Mendelberg 2001, p. 142; see also Jamieson 1992).

[5] Two of those in Kennebunkport later told a reporter, off the record, that Bush never hesitated about adopting Atwater's proposal. He expressed concern that it might backfire, but that was all. "As far as I could tell, he had no qualms about it," one staff member

for *Reader's Digest* to run a July story on Horton, and Atwater under the aegis of the Bush election committee developed and released a hard-hitting television commercial. Another Republican group, Americans for Bush, blanketed CNN with Bush campaign advertisements showing a picture of black, bleary-eyed Horton staring dully into the camera. Dukakis never recovered.

The Republican Southern Strategy, and its more subtly coded successors, cynically manipulated the anxieties of southern and working-class whites by focusing on issues such as crime and welfare fraud that served as code words for race. The times were ripe in the decades after enactment of the Civil Rights Act of 1964. Life in the United States was turbulent. The civil rights movement continued: busing to integrate schools, aggressive legal efforts to assure employment and housing opportunities to black people, and political developments such as the emergence of the Black Panthers and Elijah Muhammad's Nation of Islam followed in its wake. Riots broke out in black areas of cities across the country in the late 1960s. The Vietnam War ripened, provoked years of demonstrations and resistance, and ended ignominiously. Robert Kennedy and Martin Luther King were assassinated in 1968, and George Wallace was permanently crippled by an attempt on his life in 1972. The women's and gay liberation movements became newly assertive and challenged long-standing social practices and norms. OPEC declared its first embargo in the 1970s, and the first major modern economic restructuring, disproportionately affecting unionized and low-level white-collar workers, took place.

People were on edge and ready to look for scapegoats. It was a time when virtuous political leaders should have tried to reassure people, to develop practical solutions to troubling problems, and to foster improved race relations. Conservative politicians instead fostered racial conflict. It worked. David R. Roediger, a leading historian of American race relations, recently observed that Republican President Ronald "Reagan's sure command of divisive code words such as 'state's rights,' 'welfare moms,' 'quotas,' and 'reverse racism' came to be seen as key to his success at winning over 'Reagan Democrats' via racial appeals" (2008, p. 207).

In our time, politicians must tread a fine line in making appeals to

---

recalled. "It was just the facts of life. He realized that as far behind as he was it was the only way to win" (Schieffer and Gates 1989, p. 360).

race. Racial appeals can mobilize white voters, but as Nixon sensed, they will fail if they are seen as overtly racist. Most Americans no longer believe in the racial inferiority of black people, and most believe that racial discrimination is wrong. Reflecting the conclusions of most scholars who study race relations, Thernstrom and Thernstrom (1997, pp. 498–501) show that from the 1970s onward large majorities of whites have believed that blacks are of equal intelligence, favor integrated schools, and do not object to having blacks of their own social class as neighbors.

The most thoughtful and detailed analysis of the role of issues related to race in American politics surveys research on racial attitudes and concludes that Americans' endorsement of norms of racial equality are nearly universal:

> In the age of equality, neither citizens nor politicians want to be perceived or perceive themselves as racist. The norm of racial equality has become descriptive and injunctive, endorsed by nearly every American. For most white Americans, it is a personal norm as well. Whites do not simply pay lip service to equality and continue to derogate blacks in private. Almost all whites genuinely disavow the sentiments that have come to be most closely associated with the ideology of white supremacy—the immutable inferiority of blacks, the desirability of segregation, and the just nature of discrimination in favor of whites. In this sense, nearly every white person today has a genuine commitment to basic racial equality in the public sphere. (Mendelberg 2001, pp. 18–19)

If it is true, as I believe it is, as Mendelberg and the Thernstroms conclude, that most Americans believe in racial equality and that base forms of invidious racism are no longer commonplace in American life, how is it possible that coded allusions to race and to racial resentment so long remained so common and so effective? Part of the answer can be found in the psychology of race relations that I discussed earlier. White Americans are influenced by stereotypes of black criminals, as the research on colorism, Afro-American feature bias, and implicit bias shows. And, as the research on public opinions and attitudes shows, overtly racist attitudes have been replaced by racial resentments, which are the single most powerful explanation for why many more whites than blacks support harsh criminal justice policies.

Coded racial appeals have long been effective in American politics precisely because they are coded, as Mendelberg shows in an exhaustive analysis of media handling of the Willie Horton advertisement in the 1988 presidential campaign and afterward. The key distinction is between explicit and implicit appeals to racial stereotypes and resentments. Because of Americans' commitment to norms of racial equality, explicit appeals no longer work. They backfire, and their practitioners are widely disparaged. The successive campaigns for Louisiana governor and U.S. senator by former Ku Klux Klansman David Duke provide a vivid illustration.

Implicit appeals, however, can work: "White voters respond to implicit messages [such as Willie Horton and Reagan's 'Welfare Queen'] because they do not recognize these messages as racial and do not believe their favorable response is motivated by racism. In fact, the racial reference in an implicit message, while subtle, is recognizable and works most powerfully through white voters' racial stereotypes, fears, and resentments" (Mendelberg 2001, p. 7).

Appeals to racial issues in modern American politics, once explicit, became implicit. White segregationists in the 1960s and 1970s, who were not reconciled to the success of the civil rights movement, were motivated by invidious considerations and made explicit racial appeals when they could. Opponents of the civil rights movement, rather than continue openly to fight battles they had lost, and whose loss made open appeals to bigotry no longer politically acceptable, "shifted attention to a seemingly race-neutral concern over crime," as Glenn Loury (2008, p. 13) put it. A history of law and order politics in the 1960s similarly observed, "For conservatives, black crime would become the means by which to mount a flank attack on the civil rights movement when it was too popular to assault directly" (Flamm 2005, p. 22). Vesla Weaver explained, "Much of the legislative activity on crime came from the same hand that fed the early opposition to civil rights. . . . Through a frontlash, rivals of civil rights progress defined racial discord as criminal and argued that crime legislation would be a panacea to racial unrest" (Weaver 2007, p. 265).

Other activists, influenced by the history and social psychology of American race relations and blinded by political opportunism, were unable fully to appreciate the implications of what they were doing. Some of the latter, especially in hindsight, recognized those implications and expressed regret for their earlier actions and blindness. The most striking refutation came from Lee Atwater, creator of the Willie Horton campaign. On his deathbed, Atwater apologized for the "naked cruelty" of the attacks on Democratic candidate Michael Dukakis: "In 1988, fighting Dukakis, I said I would 'strip the bark off the little bastard' and 'make Willie Horton his running mate.' I am sorry for both statements" (Associated Press 1991, p. 16). Harry Dent, Strom Thurmond's senior aide in the 1960s and chairman of the Republican National Committee in the 1970s, was a prime implementer of the Southern Strategy. In a 1980 interview, he expressed regret for anything he did "that stood in the way of black people" (Stout 2007, p. B7).

James Unnever and his colleagues, at the end of an article on racial attitudes toward the justice system, offered an assessment of the consequences of the Southern Strategy: "the disturbing part of our research is not only that Americans with racial resentments were more likely to endorse the punitive approach to resolving the crime problem, but also that racial animus was the most robust predictor. . . . We did not find any evidence that having negative stereotypes of African Americans was predictive of how individuals perceive solutions to reducing crime. . . . Together, these findings are suggestive that the Republican political elites' southern strategy 'worked'" (Unnever, Cullen, and Jones 2008, pp. 25–26).

There are no easy paths out of the racial dead end in which the American criminal justice system finds itself. The damage has been done to living black Americans—lives blighted, families fractured, life chances reduced, communities undermined. Even radical changes in American crime policies cannot undo the damage.

For the future, there are things that can be done. The greatest damage to black Americans as a class has been done by the unprecedented severity of American crime and drug control policies. The things that need to be done include radical decarceration; fundamental changes in drug policy; repeal of mandatory minimum, three-strikes, and life without possibility of parole laws; and creation of new mechanisms for reducing the sentences of historically unprecedented length that many American prisoners now serve.

Less radical changes, which will make America a better place but not greatly reduce racial disparities, also need doing. These include training of criminal justice practitioners to make them more aware of the power of racial stereotypes, colorism, and Afro-American feature bias and development of requirements that existing policies be subjected to racial disparity audits and legislative proposals to disparity impact projections.

Much of what is proposed in the preceding paragraphs may appear fanciful, and it may be. However, those proposals would do no more than return American criminal justice policies and practices to where they were 30 years ago and to where the policies and practices of other Western countries now are. It seems unlikely that Americans 30 years ago would have chosen the criminal justice system we now have. The social psychology, sociology, and politics of American race relations have brought us to a place where no one should want to be, but there is no good reason to stay here.

REFERENCES:

Associated Press. 1991. "Gravely Ill, Atwater Offers Apology 25 Years for a Slice of Pizza." *New York Times*, January 13, sec. 1, pt. 1, p. 16.

Beckett, Katherine, and Theodore Sasson. 2004. *The Politics of Injustice*. 2nd ed. Beverly Hills, CA: Sage.

Black, Earl, and Merle Black. 2002. *Southern Republicans*. Cambridge, MA: Harvard University Press.

Blair, Irene V., Kristine M. Chapleau, and Charles M. Judd. 2005. "The Use of Afrocentric Features as Cues for Judgment in the Presence of Diagnostic Information." *European Journal of Social Psychology* 35:59–68.

Blair, Irene V., Charles M. Judd, and Kristine M. Chapleau. 2004. "The Influence of Afrocentric Facial Features in Criminal Sentencing." *Psychological Science* 15(10):674–79.

Blair, Irene V., Charles M. Judd, Melody S. Sadler, and Christopher Jenkins. 2002. "The Role of Afrocentric Features in Person Perception: Judging by Features and Categories." *Journal of Personality and Social Psychology* 83(1): 5–25.

Blasi, Gary, and John T. Jost. 2006. "System Justification Theory and Research: Implications for Law, Legal Advocacy, and Social Justice." *California Law Review* 94:1119–68.

Bobo, Lawrence D., and Devon Johnson. 2004. "A Taste for Punishment: Black and White Americans' Views on the Death Penalty and the War on Drugs." *Du Bois Review* 1:151–80.

Bobo, Lawrence D., and Victor Thompson. 2006. "Unfair by Design: The War on Drugs, Race, and the Legitimacy of the Criminal Justice System." *Social Research* 73(2):445–70.

Boyd, James. 1970. "Nixon's Southern Strategy: 'It's All in the Charts.'" *New York Times*, May 17.

Carter, Dan T. 1996. *From George Wallace to Newt Gingrich—Race in the Republican Counterrevolution, 1993–1994*. Baton Rouge: Louisiana State University Press.

Cohn, S., S. Barkan, and W. Halteman. 1991. "Public Attitudes toward Criminals: Racial Consensus or Racial Conflict." *Social Problems* 38:287–96.

Committee on Civil Rights. 1947. *To Secure These Rights*. Washington, DC: U.S. Government Printing Office.

Courtwright, David T. 1982. *Dark Paradise: Opiate Addiction in America before 1940*. Cambridge, MA: Harvard University Press.

Dasgupta, Nilanjana, Mahzarin Banaji, and Robert Abelson. 1999. "Group Entitavity and Group Perception: Associations between Physical Features and Psychological Judgment." *Journal of Personality and Social Psychology* 77(5): 991–1003.

Davis, Allison, John Dollard, and American Youth Commission. 1946. *Children of Bondage: The Personality Development of Negro Youth in the Urban South*. Washington, DC: American Council on Education.

Dixon, Travis, and Keith Maddox. 2005. "Skin Tone, Crime News, and Social Reality Judgments: Priming the Stereotype of the Dark and Dangerous Black Criminal." *Journal of Applied Social Psychology* 35(8):1555–70.

Eberhardt, Jennifer L., Paul G. Davies, Valerie J. Purdie-Vaughns, and Sheri Lynn Johnson. 2006. "Looking Deathworthy: Perceived Stereotypicality of Black Defendants Predicts Capital-Sentencing Outcomes." *Psychological Science* 17(5):383–86.

Eberhardt, Jennifer L., Phillip Atiba Goff, Valerie J. Purdie, and Paul G. Davies. 2004. "Seeing Black: Race, Crime and Visual Processing." *Journal of Personality and Social Psychology* 87(6):876–93.

Edsall, Thomas, and Mary Edsall. 1991. *Chain Reaction: The Impact of Race, Rights, and Taxes on American Politics*. New York: Norton.

Entman, Robert. 1992. "Blacks in the News: Television, Modern Racism, and Cultural Change." *Journalism Quarterly* 69(2):341–61.

Flamm, Michael W. 2005. *Law and Order: Street Crime, Civil Unrest, and the Crisis of Liberalism in the Sixties*. New York: Columbia University Press.

Garland, David. 2005. "Penal Excess and Surplus Meaning: Public Torture Lynchings in 20th Century America." *Law and Society Review* 39:793–833.

Gilliam, F. D., and S. Iyengar. 2000. "Prime Suspects: The Influence of Local Television News on the Viewing Public." *American Journal of Political Science* 44:560–73.

Gusfield, Joseph. 1963. *Symbolic Crusade: Status Policies and the American Temperance Movement*. Urbana: University of Illinois Press.

Herbert, Bob. 2005. "Impossible, Ridiculous, Repugnant." *New York Times* (October 6).

Hochschild, Jennifer L., and Vesla Mae Weaver. 2007. "The Skin Color Paradox and the American Racial Order." *Social Forces* 86(2):643–70.

Hurwitz, J., and M. Peffley. 1997. "Public Perceptions of Race and Crime: The Influence of Racial Stereotypes." *Journal of Politics* 67:375–401.

Jamieson, Kathleen Hall. 1992. *Dirty Politics*. Oxford: Oxford University Press.

Johnson, Devon. 2008. "Racial Prejudice, Perceived Injustice, and the Black-White Gap in Punitive Attitudes." *Journal of Criminal Justice* 36:198–206.

Jolls, Christine, and Cass R. Sunstein. 2006. "The Law of Implicit Bias." *California Law Review* 94:945–96.

Levinson, Justin D. 2007. "Forgotten Racial Equality: Implicit Bias, Decision-making, and Misremembering." *Duke Law Journal* 57(1):345–424.

Lieberson, Stanley. 1980. *A Piece of the Pie: Blacks and White Immigrants since 1980*. Berkeley: University of California Press.

Liptak, Adam. 2007. "Whittling Away, but Leaving a Gap." *New York Times*, November 17, p. A21.

Loury, Glenn C. 2002. *The Anatomy of Racial Inequality*. Cambridge, MA: Harvard University Press.

———. 2007. "Racial Stigma, Mass Incarceration and American Values." Tanner Lectures in Human Values delivered at Stanford University, April 4 and 5, http://www.econ.brown.edu/fac/Glenn_Loury/louryhomepage/.

———. 2008. "Race, Incarceration, and American Values." In *Race, Incarceration, and American Values*, edited by Glenn Loury, with Pamela S. Karlan, Tommie Shelby, and Loïc Wacquant. Boston Review Book. Cambridge, MA: MIT Press.

Lowndes, Joseph. E. 2008. *From the New Deal to the New Right: Race and the Southern Origins of Modern Conservatism*. New Haven, CT: Yale University Press.

Maddox, Keith B., and Stephanie A. Gray. 2002. "Cognitive Representations of Black Americans: Re-exploring the Role of Skin Tone." *Personality and Social Psychology Bulletin* 28:250–59.

Massey, Douglas S. 2007. *Categorically Unequal*. New York: Russell Sage Foundation.

Massey, Douglas S., and Nancy Denton. 1993. *American Apartheid: Segregation and the Making of the Underclass*. Cambridge, MA: Harvard University Press.

Massing, Michael. 1998. *The Fix*. New York: Simon & Schuster.

Mendelberg, Tali. 2001. *The Race Card: Campaign Strategy, Implicit Messages, and the Norm of Equality*. Princeton, NJ: Princeton University Press.

Murakawa, Naomi. 2005. "Electing to Punish: Congress, Race, and the American Criminal Justice State." Ph.D. dissertation, Princeton University, Department of Political Science.

Musto, David F. 1973. *The American Disease: Origins of Narcotic Control*. New Haven, CT: Yale University Press.

Musto, David F., and Pamela Korsmeyer. 2002. *The Quest for Drug Control: Politics and Federal Policy in a Period of Increasing Substance Abuse, 1963–1981*. New Haven, CT: Yale University Press.

Myrdal, Gunnar. 1944. *An American Dilemma: The Negro Problem and Modern Democracy*. New York: Harper & Brothers.

New York Times. 1964. "GOP Moderates Score Goldwater." July 5, p. 31.

Pager, Devah. 2007. *Marked: Race, Crime, and Finding Work in an Era of Mass Incarceration*. Chicago: University of Chicago Press.

Phillips, Kevin P. 1969. *The Emerging Republican Majority*. New Rochelle, NY: Arlington.

Pizzi, William T., Irene V. Blair, and Charles M. Judd. 2005. "Discrimination in Sentencing on the Basis of Afrocentric Features." *Michigan Journal of Race and Law* 10:327–53.

Plant, E. Ashby, B. Michelle Peruche, and David A. Butz. 2005. "Eliminating Automatic Racial Bias: Making Race Non-diagnostic for Responses to Criminal Suspects." *Journal of Experimental Social Psychology* 42:141–56.

Rachlinski, Jeffrey J., Sheri Lynn Johnson, Andrew J. Wistich, and Chris Guthrie. 2009. "Does Unconscious Racial Bias Affect Trial Judges?" *Notre Dame Law Review* 84(3):1195–1246.

Reeves, Jimmie L., and Richard Campbell. 1994. *Cracked Coverage: Television News, the Anti-cocaine Crusade, and the Reagan Legacy*. Durham, NC: Duke University Press.

Roediger, David R. 2008. *How Race Survived U.S. History*. London: Verso.

Schieffer, Bob, and Gary Paul Gates. 1989. *Acting President*. New York: Dutton.

Shelby, Tommie. 2008. "Commentary." In *Race, Incarceration, and American Values*, edited by Glenn Loury, with Pamela S. Karlan, Tommie Shelby, and Loïc Wacquant. Boston Review Book. Cambridge, MA: MIT Press.

Spohn, Cassia. 2000. "Thirty Years of Sentencing Reform: The Quest for a Racially Neutral Sentencing Process." In *Criminal Justice 2000*, vol. 3, edited by the U.S. National Institute of Justice. Washington, DC: National Institute of Justice, U.S. Department of Justice.

———. 2002. *How Do Judges Decide? The Search for Fairness and Justice in Punishment*. Thousand Oaks, CA: Sage.

Stout, David. 2007. "Harry Dent, an Architect of Nixon 'Southern Strategy,' Dies at 77." *New York Times*, October 2, p. B7.

Thernstrom, Stephen, and Abigail Thernstrom. 1997. *America in Black and White: One Nation, Indivisible*. New York: Simon & Schuster.

Unnever, James D. 2008. "Two Worlds Far Apart: Black-White Differences in Beliefs about Why African-American Men Are Disproportionately Imprisoned." *Criminology* 46(2):511–38.

Unnever, James D., Francis T. Cullen, and James D. Jones. 2008. "Public Support for Attacking the 'Root Causes' of Crime: The Impact of Egalitarian and Racial Beliefs." *Sociological Focus* 41(1):1–33.

Unnever, James D., Francis T. Cullen, and Cheryl N. Lero Jonson. 2008. "Race, Racism, and Support for Capital Punishment." In *Crime and Justice: A Review of Research*, vol. 37, edited by Michael Tonry. Chicago: University of Chicago Press.

U.S. Sentencing Commission. 2007. *Cocaine and Federal Sentencing Policy*. Washington, DC: U.S. Sentencing Commission.

Wacquant, Loïc. 2002*a*. "Deadly Symbiosis: Rethinking Race and Imprisonment in Twenty-first-Century America." *Boston Review* 27(April/May):22–31.

———. 2002*b*. "From Slavery to Mass Incarceration." *New Left Review* 13 (January–February):41–60.

———. 2008. "Commentary." In *Race, Incarceration, and American Values*, edited by Glenn Loury, with Pamela S. Karlan, Tommie Shelby, and Loïc Wacquant. Boston Review Book. Cambridge, MA: MIT Press.

Weaver, Vesla Mae. 2007. "Frontlash: Race and the Development of Punitive Crime Policy." *Studies in American Political Development* 21(Fall): 230–65.

Western, Bruce. 2006. *Punishment and Inequality in America.* New York: Russell Sage Foundation.

Whitebread, Charles H., II, and Richard J. Bonnie. 1974. *The Marihuana Conviction: The History of Marihuana Prohibition in the United States.* Charlottesville: University Press of Virginia.

Wickham, Dewayne. 2008. "Bill Clinton Expresses 'Regret' on Crack Cocaine Sentencing." *USA Today*, March 4, http://www.nacdl.org/public.nsf/media sources/20080304a?opendocument.

Wilson, William Julius. 1987. *The Truly Disadvantaged: The Inner City, the Underclass, and Public Policy.* Chicago: University of Chicago Press.

Wolfe, Tom. 1987. *The Bonfire of the Vanities.* New York: Bantam.

Philip J. Cook, Denise C. Gottfredson, and Chongmin Na

School Crime Control and Prevention

ABSTRACT

School violence, drug use, vandalism, gang activity, bullying, and theft are
costly and interfere with academic achievement. Fortunately, crime victimization in schools for students and teachers followed the downward trend
in national crime rates during the 1990s and has remained at a relatively
low level since 2000. Youths are as likely to be victimized in school as out
when it comes to theft and minor assaults, but the most serious assaults
tend to occur outside of school. Despite the high rates of crime in school,
school crime plays a relatively minor role in juvenile criminal careers.
Nonetheless, school crime deserves public concern. The composition and
operation of schools influence crime. A variety of instructional programs
can reduce crime, such as those that teach self-control or social competency skills using cognitive-behavioral or behavioral instructional methods.
School discipline management policies and practices are also important.
Schools in which rules are clearly stated, are fair, and are consistently enforced, and in which students participate in establishing mechanisms for
reducing misbehavior, experience less disorder.

School violence, drug use, vandalism, gang activity, bullying, and theft
are costly and interfere with academic achievement. Student misbehavior interferes with teaching and learning and is one of the primary
sources of teacher turnover. Gallup polls from the past 20 years show
that the percentage of parents who report being concerned about the
physical safety of their children while at school has ranged from 15
percent to 55 percent, with the highest percentages just after the in-
famous school shootings at Columbine High School in 1999. Reducing

Philip Cook is ITT/Sanford Professor of Public Policy in the Sanford School of Public
Policy, Duke University. Denise Gottfredson is a professor and Chongmin Na a doctoral
student in the Department of Criminology and Criminal Justice, University of Maryland.

crime rates has become an increasingly high priority for America's schools.

Middle and high schools aggregate youths who are in their peak crime years. Hence it is not surprising that crime rates in schools are high. Victimization rates are about the same in school as out, despite the fact that youths spend only about one-fifth of their waking hours in school. And other things equal, youth violence rates tend to be higher when school is in session than not.

However, since 1993 schools have enjoyed a strong downward trend in crime of all types that mimics the downward trend in overall youth victimization. That coincidence reflects one of the important findings in the school crime literature: school crime is linked closely to community crime rates. The schools have benefited from the remarkable crime drop in America.

There has also been an important trend in the official response to school crime. It has become increasingly formal over the last 20 years, with greater recourse to arrest and the juvenile courts rather than school-based discipline—a trend that has been dubbed the "criminalization" of student misbehavior (Hirschfield 2008). To some extent this trend has been furthered by federal law that has imposed zero-tolerance rules for some offenses and has subsidized the hiring of uniformed officers to police the schools. The shift has been from administrative discretion to mandatory penalties and from in-school discipline to increasing use of suspension or arrest. At the same time, there has been a considerable investment in the use of surveillance cameras and metal detectors.

While the increasing formality has coincided with the declining crime rates, there is no clear indication whether the new approach deserves any of the credit. Indeed, the evaluation literature we examine here has very little to say about the likely effects of these changes. As so often happens, there appears to be a disconnect between policy and research.

A variety of other school reforms have had important effects on the quality of schooling and school life. Some are dictated by the recent push toward improved academic performance through school accountability. A question of considerable interest is whether reforms designed to improve academic performance are likely to increase or reduce crime rates in school. We find that for the most part the two goals of better academic performance and safer schools are compatible, as would be expected given that most delinquents have academic problems. One exception is the practice of retaining students who perform poorly on end-of-grade tests, a practice that has been broadly implemented as part of the effort to establish higher academic standards but has the effect of holding back and concentrating delinquency-prone youths. The goal of safer schools may also run afoul of the literal meaning of no child left behind. The growing use of suspension or expulsion may make schools safer, but at the cost of further limiting delinquents' chance to succeed in school. School officials face similar dilemmas in policies regarding truancy, dropout, and alternative schools.

There are alternatives to the get-tough approach. We know that some schools do a much better job than others in controlling the behavior of their students. Characteristic of successful schools is that they are close-knit communities in which rules of acceptable behavior are clearly communicated and consistently (even if not harshly) enforced. In addition to good management practices, there is much that can be done in the classroom that has demonstrated effectiveness in improving behavior. Admittedly, the challenge to establishing a well-ordered community is much greater if a high proportion of the students are at risk.

For those who want to identify what works and go with that, it is distressing that major reforms are adopted without evaluation. The get-tough exclusionary policies are the most glaring example. From a different part of the political spectrum is the high-profile push to break up large high schools into smaller ones, led by a billion dollar commitment from the Gates Foundation. That effort was deemed a disappointment by the foundation and discontinued in 2008 on the basis of an evaluation of its effects on academic progress. Our own analysis suggests that while smaller schools may or may not be more conducive to academic achievement, they are not safer.

In this essay, we focus on the characteristics of schools related to the problem behaviors of the current student population. That is, we consider those school characteristics that influence concurrent levels of crime, victimization, violence, and substance use in and out of schools. Some of the mechanisms linking school characteristics with offending behavior (such as surveillance practices) can be expected to influence only crime that is perpetrated within the school, whereas others (such as truancy prevention and use of disciplinary suspension) can be expected to influence the level of offending in and out of school.

Among our findings are the following:

- There are a variety of sources of statistics on crime in schools, but these sources provide differing results on levels, patterns, and trends.
- Crime victimization in schools (for both students and teachers) followed the downward trend in national crime rates during the 1990s and remains at a relatively low level since 2000.
- A great deal of crime in schools is perpetrated by and against students, with victimization rates that are similar to rates experienced outside of school, even though students spend less than one-fifth of their waking hours in school.
- A much higher percentage of minor assaults than serious assaults occur in schools.
- The rate of crime reported by principals is much higher for middle schools than for elementary or high schools, somewhat higher for city schools than for those in suburban or rural communities, and higher in predominantly minority schools than in those that are less than half minority. There is little relationship between the size of the school and school crime rates.
- Despite the high rates of crime in school, school crime plays a relatively minor role in juvenile criminal careers. Eighty-five percent of juvenile arrests are for crimes committed away from school.
- Keeping school-aged children in school reduces the probability of later crime, arrest, and incarceration. This suggests that policies that exclude students from school may increase crime in the long run.
- Which school a student attends matters. Characteristics of the way schools are composed and operated are reliably related to crime and disorder in the schools. Some findings related to school effectiveness include the following:

  a.   The concentration of different types of students has important implications for the amount of crime in the school. The grade levels included in the school or average age of the students in the school, the percentage male students, the social class composition, and the racial and ethnic composition of the schools are related to measures of problem behavior.

  b.   Some policies that alter the composition of classes, grades, or schools have been shown to reduce problem behavior: Keeping sixth graders in elementary schools as opposed to moving them to middle schools reduces disciplinary infractions, and retaining students in a grade increases conduct problems both for the "old-for-grade" students and for nonretained students.

c.   Although reducing school size is unlikely to reduce crime, some evidence suggests that it may be fruitful to reorganize schools (regardless of their size) by creating smaller groups of students who stay together for an extended period during the school day and who are taught by a small group of teachers. Such efforts might be effective for increasing youths' sense of connection, which serves to hold criminal behavior in check. School-based mentoring programs also hold considerable promise for crime prevention. More research is needed to more fully explore these approaches.

d.   Many instructional programs have been demonstrated to be effective for reducing crime. In particular, those that teach self-control or social competency skills using cognitive-behavioral or behavioral instructional methods are effective. These programs are most effective when targeted at youths who are at elevated risk for subsequent problem behavior.
e.School discipline management policies and practices are important determinants of school crime. Schools in which rules are clearly stated, are fair, and are consistently enforced, and in which students have participated in establishing mechanisms for reducing misbehavior, experience less disorder. Programs that employ behavioral strategies to monitor and reinforce student behavior are effective both for controlling behavior in school and for reducing subsequent crime.

We begin in Section I with a review of the statistics on crime in school and youth crime more generally, documenting trends and patterns using a variety of data sources (which unfortunately tend to give different answers). Section II makes the case that crime in school is not simply the sum of criminal propensities of the enrolled students and that the organizational characteristics of the school have considerable influence. Sections III–V consider just what aspects of school organization or "climate" matter, including such factors as school size and composition of the student body (Sec. III), school discipline and delinquency prevention curricula (Sec. IV), and culture (Sec. V). Section VI discusses next steps in research and policy.

I. School Crime: Patterns and Trends

By rights, schools should be sanctuaries against criminal victimization, but the truth shows otherwise. Youths are required by law to attend school until their late teens, but that requirement does not come with any assurance that they will be safe. Students report victimization rates at school similar to those away from school, even though they spend many fewer waking hours in school. The important exception is for the most serious violent crime, murder, where the relative risks are decidedly reversed; only about 1 percent of murders of school-aged youths occur on school grounds. But lesser crimes, the fights and strong-arm robberies and larcenies, are common enough to have an important effect on the school experience for many students. Nor are schools a safe haven against drug abuse: in 2007, 22 percent of high school students reported being offered an illegal drug on school grounds in the previous 12 months (Centers for Disease Control and Prevention 2008, table 59).

Not just students, but also teachers are threatened by crime in schools. In 2003–4, 7 percent of teachers reported that they were threatened with injury in the previous year, and over 3 percent said they had been physically attacked (Dinkes, Kemp, and Baum 2009). The more crime-ridden schools have greater difficulty in recruiting and keeping qualified teachers (Ingersoll 2001). Crime prevention in schools also burdens school budgets. For example, 72 percent of high schools have security officers present (Jekielek et al. 2007), 61 percent use drug-sniffing dogs for random drug checks, and 11 percent use metal detectors for random checks (Dinkes, Kemp, and Baum 2009). The corresponding percentages for middle schools are lower, but not by much.

A threatening environment is not conducive to academic success. The federal law implementing No Child Left Behind (the national education reform initiative) stipulates that school systems must have programs in place to reduce levels of violence. There does appear to be some progress on this score, although the problem remains: the National Crime Victimization Survey (NCVS) School Crime Supplement data indicate that in 2007, approximately 5 percent of students aged 12–18 reported that they were afraid of attack or harm at school, compared with 12 percent in 1995 (Dinkes, Kemp, and Baum 2009).[1] The legislation authorizing No Child Left Behind has a specific provision that "persistently dangerous" schools be identified by the states and that students attending such schools be given the option of transferring to another school. The definition of "persistently dangerous" was left to each state, and only 46 schools out of the 94,000 in the United States were so identified in 2007 (Hernandez 2007). One problem is the tendency of school officials to underreport serious crimes to the police and to the public.

As it turns out, obtaining reliable information about crime in schools is a challenge for researchers as well as for state and federal officials. There are several sources of data in addition to the schools' own reports, but each source is error-prone and there are some rather remarkable differences among them with respect to estimated crime rates and patterns. We begin with a brief summary of data sources and then summarize some of the statistical results and conundrums.

A. Data Sources

The primary source of crime data for many purposes is the FBI's Uniform Crime Reports (UCR; http://www.fbi.gov/ucr/ucr.htm) compiled from crimes known to the police and reported by police departments. The UCR crime data do not provide information on the characteristics of victims and are of little help in estimating crime in schools. Some jurisdictions have begun reporting crimes in much more detail through the National Incident Based Reporting System (NIBRS; http://www.fbi.gov/ucr/ucr.htm#nibrs). In this system police agencies submit a record of each known crime that includes the age, sex, and race of the victim, the location of the crime, and the characteristics of the perpetrator (when known). These data can be used to provide a detailed description of crimes involving school-aged youths, distinguishing, for example, between crimes on school grounds and elsewhere (Jacob and Lefgren 2003). There are two problems, however, with this source. First, participation rates are very low: only 20 percent

[1] In 2007, only 3 percent reported that they were afraid of being attacked away from school.

of police agencies, representing 16 percent of the U.S. population, were participating in the NIBRS as of 2003 (http://www.ojp.usdoj.gov/bjs/nibrsstatus.htm). And second, crimes committed on school property may be less likely to become known to the police than crimes occurring elsewhere.[2]

As a result of the limitations of police data, school crime statistics are usually generated from school reports or surveys. In the School Survey on Crime and Safety (SSCS; http://nces.ed.gov/surveys/ssocs), public school principals are asked to report to the U.S. Department of Education the number of violent incidents and thefts and to indicate how many of these incidents were reported to the police. In addition, there are several recurrent sample surveys: the NCVS and the biannual School Crime Supplement to this survey (sponsored by the National Center for Education Statistics, or NCES) and the Youth Risk Behavior Surveillance System (YRBSS; http://www.cdc.gov/HealthyYouth/yrbs) sponsored by the Centers for Disease Control and Prevention (CDC). The NCES compiles data from all these sources into a report called the *Indicators of School Crime and Safety* (e.g., Dinkes, Kemp, and Baum 2009). When the estimates from these alternative sources are compared, there emerge some rather dramatic differences, leaving the investigator with the challenge of deciding where the truth lies.

B. *Youthful Victimization in School and Out*

Here we report crime victimization rates for school-aged youths, comparing, when possible, the rates at school and at other locations. We begin with murder, which is the only crime for which the statistics are reasonably accurate. Figure 1 depicts the trend in murders on school property for youths aged 5–18, compared with the overall murder count for that age group. There were about 30 school murders of youths each year from 1992–93 to 1998–99, a period notorious for the series of school rampage shootings that culminated with Columbine High School on April 20, 1999. During that event 12 students and a teacher were murdered, and 23 students injured, before the shooters

---

[2] One analysis of NCVS data found that only 9 percent of violent crimes against teenagers occurring in school were reported to the police compared to 37 percent occurring on the streets (Whitaker and Bastian 1991). But our analysis of the 2005 NCVS finds that the gap has narrowed or disappeared for violent crimes: 30 percent in school were reported to the police compared with 35 percent out of school. There remains a large difference in property crimes: the 2005 NCVS indicates that thefts outside of school are about twice as likely to be reported as those in school.

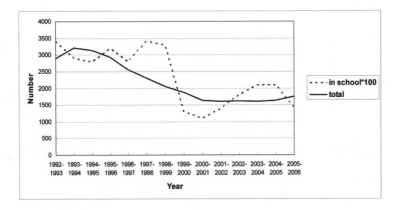

FIG. 1.—Number of homicides involving young victims, in school and out, 1992–93 to 2005–6. Note: "In school" includes on school property, on the way to or from regular sessions at school, and while attending or traveling to or from a school-sponsored event. Source: Data on number of homicides in school are from School-Associated Violent Deaths Surveillance Study (SAVD), tabulated in *Indicators of School Crime and Safety* (Dinkes, Cataldi, and Lin-Kelly 2007, p. 68); data on total number of homicides are from National Center for Injury Prevention and Control, Web-based Injury Statistics Query and Reporting System Fatal (WISQARSTM Fatal), from http://cdc.gov/ncipc/wisqars.

committed suicide. In the year following Columbine the national in-school murder count dropped sharply and has remained relatively low since then. The murder rate for the same age group follows a similar pattern, though the decline began earlier and is less abrupt. The most important lesson from these data is that only about one in 100 murders of this age group occurs in school. That was true during the peak years of the early 1990s and also true a decade later. By this measure, then, school appears much safer than other locations for school-aged youths.

However, schools have a much larger share of the nonfatal crimes with school-aged victims. Figure 2 depicts the trend for victimization rates of youths aged 12–18, including both theft and violence.[3] The rates per 1,000 follow the trend for youth homicide (as well as the national trend for criminal victimization for all age groups)—a sustained and rather dramatic reduction, so that the 2006 figures are about one-third of the peak in 1993. For our immediate purpose here, the important thing to notice is that the victimization rate in school is

---

[3] Youths who have completed 12 years of school are excluded from this tabulation.

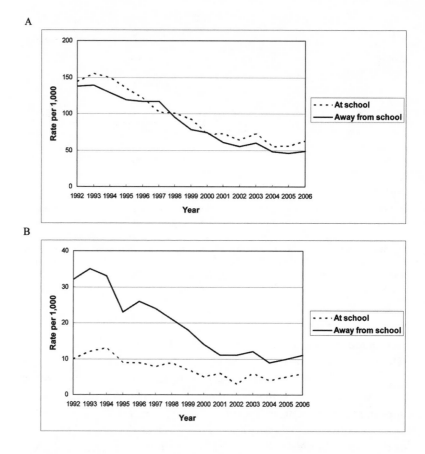

Fig. 2.—*A*, Victimization rates at school and out for youths aged 12–18, 1992–2006: theft and violence. *B*, Victimization rates at school and out for youths aged 12–18, 1992–2006, serious crimes of violence. Note: Theft includes purse snatching, pickpocketing, and all attempted and completed thefts except motor vehicle thefts. Theft does not include robbery in which threat or use of force is involved. Violence includes serious crimes of violence and simple assault. Serious crimes of violence include rape, sexual assault, robbery, and aggravated assault. "At school" includes inside the school building, on school property, or on the way to or from school. Source: NCVS, tabulated in Dinkes, Kemp, and Baum (2009, p. 76).

about the same as out of school. That parity is the net result of theft, which has higher rates at school, and violence, which for most of the period has lower rates at school (although in-school and out-of-school rates of violence converged in 2004). Note that since youths spend over 80 percent of their waking hours during a calendar year out of school (D. Gottfredson 2001, p. 21), the parity in victimization rates implies that youths are far more likely to be victimized during an hour in school than during an hour elsewhere.

For the serious violent crimes of rape, robbery, and aggravated assault, NCVS victimization rates are twice as high away from school as at school during recent years, as shown in figure 2B. Since the corresponding ratio for murder is 100 to one, we conclude that serious violent crimes committed out of school are far more likely to become murders than is true for similar crimes in school.[4]

Survey data on crime are notoriously unreliable. In particular, crime survey results are exquisitely sensitive to the details of how the data are collected. One survey that provides an alternative to the NCVS for estimating victimization rates is the YRBSS, sponsored by the CDC. This survey yields estimates of victimization rates for serious violent crimes that are an order of magnitude higher than the NCVS rates. For example, in the 2005 YRBSS, 8 percent of students in grades 9–12 reported being threatened or injured with a weapon on school property during the previous 12 months. That compares with the serious-violence victimization rate at school for 15–18-year-olds in the NCVS of 0.4 percent. Thus the YRBSS rate is 20 times as high, even though logic suggests that it should be less, given that the YRBSS refers to prevalence of victimization and the NCVS figure is overall incidence (so that multiple victimizations reported by the same respondent are included in computing the rate). Further, the NCVS category of "serious violence" encompasses more types of crime than the YRBSS category of "threatened or injured with a weapon."

What could account for this vast difference in results? First, the NCVS sample is interviewed every 6 months, and the previous interview serves as a bracket to help the respondent place events in time. Thus the NCVS sample members are asked to report on events that occurred since the previous interview. The YRBSS, however, is a one-shot survey with no natural bracket on the time interval; respondents

[4] Soulé, Gottfredson, and Bauer (2008) report that the crime that occurs in schools tends to be of a less serious nature than the crime that occurs outside of school.

are asked to report on the previous 12 months, which creates the likelihood that some will report on serious events that occurred outside the designated period (a phenomenon known as "telescoping"). A second important difference is that all YRBSS respondents are asked the specific question about whether they were threatened or injured with a weapon on school property, whereas the only NCVS respondents who are asked about such an incident are those who first respond affirmatively to a more general screener question. Third, the NCVS questionnaire is administered to the respondent (in person or over the telephone) at home, whereas the YRBSS questionnaire is self-administered by the respondent while in school. These and other differences, none of which are relevant in a literal sense, appear to be hugely important to the respondents' answers in practice.[5]

Given the disparate results from surveys, it is of interest to consider administrative data. The SSCS gathers reports from public school principals about crimes occurring during school hours. For the 2005–6 school year, principals for middle and high schools reported a total of 928,000 violent crimes and 206,000 thefts (see table 1). While these counts are not precisely comparable to the NCVS results for 12–18-year-olds,[6] they should be close. In fact, the violence reports are half again as high in the SSCS as in the NCVS for 12–18-year-olds, whereas the SSCS theft reports are much lower. These discrepancies might be due in part to different definitions of crimes used in the two series. Although they are close (see the table 1 note), the SSCS limits theft offenses to those involving losses over $10. The discrepancies arise also undoubtedly partly because the SSCS includes only incidents that came to the attention of the principal. It is not surprising that school officials do not know about many of the thefts that occur on school property, but that they are aware of more violence than shows up in the NCVS defies ready explanation.

Thus the truth about crime in school—or even a rough approximation of the truth—is elusive. Our inclination is to believe that the SSCS reports provide a reliable lower bound for the "true" volume of crime, understating the true total to the extent that officials are never made aware of some crimes and may generally be inclined to under-

[5] Cook (1987) notes that the Safe Schools study estimated 1 million robberies in schools, compared with the estimate of 30,000 in the NCVS for the same period.

[6] Unlike the NCVS, the SSCS is limited to public schools. The NCVS age range of 12–18 is roughly but not exactly comparable to the SSCS category of "middle and high school."

TABLE 1

Comparison of SSCS and NCVS Crime Counts

	SSCS Crime Count: Public Middle and High Schools, 2005–6 School Year	NCVS Crime Count in School, Ages 12–18, 2005
Violent crimes	928,000	628,000
Theft	206,000	868,000

SOURCE.—Nolle, Guerino, and Dinkes (2007); Dinkes, Cataldi, and Lin-Kelly (2007, table 2.1).

NOTE.—In the NCVS, theft includes purse snatching, pickpocketing, and all attempted and completed thefts except motor vehicle thefts. Theft does not include robbery in which threat or use of force is involved. Violence includes serious crimes of violence and simple assault. In the SSCS, violent crimes recorded include rapes, sexual batteries other than rape, robberies with or without a weapon, physical attacks or fights with or without a weapon, and threats of physical attack with or without a weapon. Theft includes taking things worth over $10 (without personal confrontation) and includes pickpocketing, stealing a purse or backpack (if left unattended or no force was used to take it from its owner), theft from a building, theft from a motor vehicle or of motor vehicle parts or accessories, theft of a bicycle, theft from a vending machine, and all other types of thefts.

report in order to make their schools look as safe as possible. If true, then the NCVS appears to provide a notable underestimate of the volume of violence in schools, but the difference is nothing like that suggested by the very high YRBSS results. We are inclined to believe that the NCVS data are superior to the YRBSS because the method of administration discourages exaggeration by respondents, and the bracketing provides some discipline on memory. We also note that the downward trend in NCVS rates (shown in fig. 2) reproduces well-documented trends during that period for the entire U.S. population and hence is credible. The YRBSS victimization rates, however, exhibit no such trend during this period, showing if anything an upward tilt since 1993. For those reasons we report additional NCVS results in what follows, even though we are willing to believe that they are also far off the mark.

Table 2 summarizes demographic patterns in victimization rates at school for youths aged 12–18.[7] The rates shown here are averaged over the three most recent years of the School Supplement of the NCVS.

[7] It should be noted that these data exclude the responses of students who have already completed 12 years of schooling. They do not exclude school dropouts.

TABLE 2

At-School Victimization Rates/1,000 for Youths Aged 12–18

	Total	Theft	Violence	Serious Violence
Male	73	41	32	7
Female	61	41	21	4
Ages 12–14	75	42	33	6
Ages 15–18	61	40	21	5
Urban	75	41	34	9
Suburban	67	43	24	5
Rural	58	37	22	2
White	72	45	27	4
Black	64	38	27	5
Hispanic	55	29	26	5
Other	53	33	20	2
Overall	67	41	27	6

SOURCE.—National Crime Victimization Survey (NCVS), tabulated in *Indicators of School Crime and Safety* (Devoe et al. 2003, pp. 55–66; Devoe et al. 2005, pp. 72–73; Dinkes, Cataldi, and Lin-Kelly 2007, pp. 70–71).

NOTE.—Theft includes purse snatching, pickpocketing, and all attempted and completed thefts except motor vehicle thefts. Theft does not include robbery in which threat or use of force is involved. Violence includes serious crimes of violence and simple assault. Serious crimes of violence include rape, sexual assault, robbery, and aggravated assault.

Note that "theft" and "violence" sum to the total; "serious violence" is included in "violence."

Theft rates are remarkably uniform across all demographic categories, averaging 41/1,000. Violence rates are a bit lower overall and more textured, although the differences among groups are still not as large as one might expect. Males are half again as likely to be victims of violence as females, and youths 12–14 are half again as likely as older youths. Urban schools experience a higher per capita rate of violent incidents than suburban or rural schools. Most surprising is that whites, blacks, and Hispanics report virtually the same rates of violence and serious violence.

The same NCVS data provide estimates for victimization rates away from school. The patterns are not much different, with two exceptions. First, blacks report a higher rate of serious violent crimes (17/1,000) than whites and Hispanics (both at 10/1,000). Second, and perhaps most intriguing, is that the age pattern away from school is the reverse of the age pattern at school. The younger group, aged 12–14, has somewhat higher victimization rates at school than the older group, but the older group has much higher victimization rates than the younger group away from school. The results are depicted in figure 3. The explanation may in part be that the older group includes a number of school dropouts who, since they are not attending school, are unlikely to be victimized on school property. Perhaps more important is that older youths have greater mobility and freedom outside of school and thus more opportunity to get into trouble.

Finally, we note the high prevalence of bullying in school. While not necessarily a crime, bullying can greatly color the school experience for some children. The NCVS School Crime Supplement found that 28 percent of youths aged 12–18 in 2005 reported being bullied in school; of those, 79 percent said they were bullied inside school, 28 percent outside on school grounds, and 8 percent on the school bus (Dinkes, Cataldi, and Lin-Kelly 2007, p. 95).

C. Teachers as Crime Victims

While crime in schools for the most part involves students as both perpetrators and victims, the teaching staff is not spared. The best source of information on teacher victimization rates is the recurrent School and Staffing Survey (SASS). This survey selects a stratified sample of schools and collects data from up to 20 teachers in each of the sample schools. Teachers are asked whether they had been threatened with injury or physically attacked by a student from their school in the previous 12 months. In 2003–4, an estimated 7 percent of teachers were threatened with injury, and 3 percent reported being physically attacked. These percentages are lower than in the previous wave (1999–2000) and substantially lower than in 1993–94: in that year, 12 percent of teachers were threatened, and 4 percent were attacked (Dinkes, Cataldi, and Lin-Kelly 2007).

The rates of teacher victimization differ somewhat along two dimensions that are reported in the SASS: first, whether the school is in a city, suburb, town, or rural area and, second, whether the school is elementary (through sixth grade) or secondary. Figure 4 depicts the results for threats and physical attacks. In both cases the city schools have the highest victimization rates. Interestingly, in every location the teachers are more likely to be threatened in secondary schools but more likely actually to be attacked in elementary schools. This finding is consistent with epidemiological studies showing that violent behavior is learned at a very early age (by 24 months) and that the frequency of

A

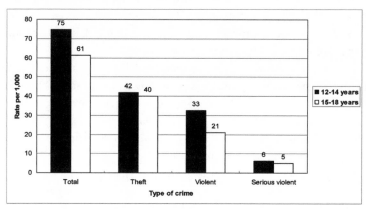

B

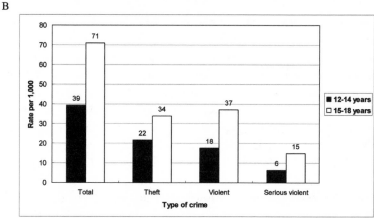

FIG. 3.—*A*, Victimization rates at school for youths aged 12–14 and 15–18. *B*, Victimization rates away from school for youths 12–14 and 15–18. Note: Total crimes include theft and violent crimes. Theft includes purse snatching, pickpocketing, and all attempted and completed thefts except motor vehicle thefts. Theft does not include robbery in which threat or use of force is involved. Violent crimes include serious violent crimes and simple assault. Serious violent crimes include rape, sexual assault, robbery, and aggravated assault. "At school" includes inside the school building, on school property, or on the way to or from school. NCVS results are averaged for 2001, 2003, and 2005.

A

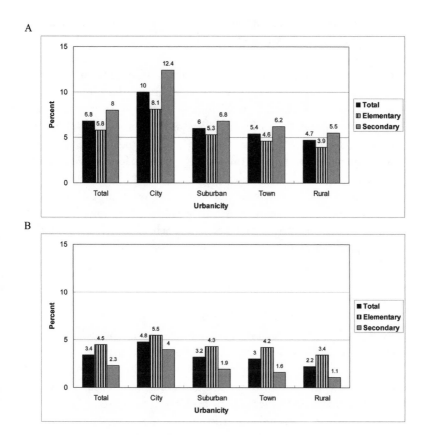

B

FIG. 4.—*A*, Prevalence of injury threats to school teachers, 2003–4. *B*, Prevalence of physical attacks on school teachers, 2003–4. Source: Schools and Staffing Survey (SASS), tabulated in Dinkes, Cataldi, and Lin-Kelly 2007, pp. 77–78).

violent behavior declines steadily from preschool through old age (Tremblay 2006). During the elementary school years, many children are still learning to control their violent behavior. Of course, this difference also illustrates the importance of taking account of differing meanings attached to a particular crime when comparing results across surveys or even within surveys for different grade levels. A "physical attack" of a teacher by an elementary school student is likely to carry much less consequence than one by a high school student.

It is interesting to reflect on these results. In what other professions that require a college degree are workers so likely to be threatened and physically attacked? After military officers, psychiatric nurses, and perhaps divorce lawyers, we suspect that teachers are among the most victimization-prone.

Of course, teacher victimization and school disorder more generally interfere with the school's ability to conduct its educational mission. Teachers find it difficult to teach when students disrupt their classrooms. Many leave the profession all together. Ingersoll (2001), using data from the NCES's SASS from the 1990–91 school year, showed that the likelihood of teacher turnover by the year following the survey was higher in schools in which teachers reported higher levels of student discipline problems, as measured by an index of problems ranging in seriousness from nonattendance to weapon possession. Analyses of reasons for leaving provided by teachers who had left showed that, among those who left because they were dissatisfied, 30 percent cited discipline problems as a reason for their dissatisfaction.

D. Differences among Schools

Up until this point we have described crime patterns primarily with respect to the characteristics of the victims. From another perspective, school crime is a characteristic of the school, and there is strong evidence that school characteristics and policies influence crime victimization rates. While we postpone the discussion of the causal influence of school climate and other school features until subsequent sections, here we summarize several patterns.

The 2005–6 SSCS classifies schools by grade level, enrollment size, urbanicity, and percentage of minority enrollment. The rate of violent incidents reported by principals is much higher for middle schools than for either elementary or high schools,[8] somewhat higher for city schools than for those in suburban or rural communities, and higher in predominantly minority schools than in those with less than half minority. Notably, there is little relationship between the size of the school and the violence victimization rate. The results for theft tend

---

[8] This finding appears to contradict data presented earlier showing that elementary school teachers are more likely than secondary school teachers to be physically attacked. The apparent discrepancy is most likely due to differences between the two surveys in respondents (i.e., teachers reporting on attacks against themselves vs. principals reporting on violent incidents recorded in the office). Elementary school teachers are more likely to handle an "attack" by a young child themselves rather than reporting it to the office. Violence rates decline from middle to high school in part because of the maturation process, but also because youths prone to violent behavior drop out of high school at relatively higher rates.

TABLE 3

Crime Rates by School Characteristic

	Violence Rate/ 1,000 Students	Theft Rate/ 1,000 Students
Level:		
Primary	25.2	1.6
Middle	51.6	7.8
High school	25.7	8.7
Enrollment:		
< 300	34.5	4.3
300–499	34.0	3.3
500–999	30.9	4.5
1,000 or more	28.6	7.2
% minority enrollment:		
< 5%	26.9	4.8
5%–20%	22.9	5.2
20%–50%	28.4	5.5
50% or more	39.9	4.8

SOURCE.—Nolle, Guerino, and Dinkes (2007, table 1).

to be less patterned, but recall that the theft statistics appear less reliable in this survey. Table 3 summarizes the results.

To some extent these patterns are at odds with NCVS victimization patterns. In the administrative data in table 3, violence is much more common than theft, whereas NCVS victimization rates are about equal. Further, it appears that the relatively high rate of violence in minority schools contradicts the NCVS finding that there is little difference in victimization rates by race. These differences could be due to the differences in coverage (since the SSCS includes all ages and the NCVS only ages 12–18). More likely it reflects problems with underreporting of violence in the NCVS that we encountered above.

The same source, the SSCS, reports information on gang-related crime. In 2005–6, 11 percent of middle schools and 16 percent of high schools reported at least one crime that was gang-related. Gang-related crimes were concentrated in large, urban, and predominantly minority schools (Nolle, Guerino, and Dinkes 2007, table 4).[9]

[9] Some confirmation for these patterns comes from the NCVS School Supplement data. Students were asked about gangs in their schools. Affirmative responses were much more likely given by black and Hispanic students and by students in urban areas.

TABLE 4

Arrestees Aged 5–18 in NIBRS Jurisdictions, by
Offense Type and Location: 2006

Offense Type	Total Arrests	Percent in School
Murder	339	.9
Forcible rape	1282	3.6
Robbery	6331	4.4
Aggravated assault	13,242	12.1
Simple assault	58,778	27.8
Burglary	18,663	7.8
Larceny	74,1582	7.6
Motor vehicle theft	7,071	1.5
Arson	1,765	20.5
Vandalism	27,017	13.2
Drug/narcotic violations	55,418	17.9
Total	264,058	14.9

SOURCE.—Original tabulations from data files, National Incident-Based Reporting System (2006).
NOTE.—"In school" refers to the location of the offense that led to an arrest. "Total" includes some offenses that are not listed above.

E. Arrests and Juvenile Criminal Careers

Our final perspective on crime in schools is in terms of arrests of school-aged youths. While school-aged youths are about equally likely to be victimized in school as out, they are much more likely to be arrested for offenses occurring outside of school. We draw that conclusion from the admittedly imperfect data provided by the NIBRS— imperfect because, as mentioned above, only about one in five jurisdictions participate in this system, with no guarantees about just how representative participating police agencies are with respect to national arrest patterns. What we see from table 4 is that just 15 percent of all arrests of youths aged 5–18 occur in conjunction with offenses committed in school. To some extent the arrest patterns follow the victimization patterns. For example, a much higher percentage of simple assault arrests (28 percent) occur in school as compared to aggravated assault arrests (12 percent) or murder arrests (0.9 percent). The percentages of arrests for larceny and robbery that occur in school are remarkably low given what we know about victimization patterns for this group.

What accounts for the low percentage of arrests that occur in school, as compared with the percentage of victimizations that occur in school?

We believe that may reflect the reality of juvenile crime careers: the bulk of crimes committed by juveniles outside of school are committed against adults or commercial or residential targets. Thus it is plausible that there be a large difference between the distribution of locations of youth victimization and the location of delinquent acts. In school there is a close match between the ages of perpetrators and victims, but out of school that is not the case.

F. Concluding Thoughts

There are a variety of sources of statistics on crime in schools, which unfortunately provide differing results on levels, patterns, and trends. Anyone wishing to make sense of the available statistics should first become informed on the details of how the data are generated and consider the likely biases.

We believe that the homicide statistics are close to accurate but that other police data on school crime are not to be trusted. For nonfatal crimes, we place some credence in the NCVS for students and the SASS for teachers, both of which are recurrent surveys and are implemented by the U.S. Census Bureau. What one learns from these sources is that crime victimization in schools (for both students and teachers) followed the downward trend in national crime rates during the 1990s and remained at a relatively low level after 2000. That there would be a common trend makes sense and is one illustration of a more general result that crime in schools is closely linked to crime in the community.

Another credible result is that there is a great deal of crime in schools perpetrated by and against students, with victimization rates that are similar to rates experienced outside of school, even though students spend less than one-fifth of their waking hours in school. Fortunately, homicide is very rare in school (relatively and absolutely). In general, a much higher percentage of minor assaults occur in schools than serious assaults. Teachers are somewhat less likely to be victims of threats and attacks by students, but teaching is without a doubt a risky profession. It is particularly frustrating that we lack good data on injuries to teachers resulting from physical attacks.

Despite the high rates of crime in school, school crime plays a relatively minor role in juvenile criminal careers. Eighty-five percent of juvenile arrests are for crimes committed away from school. When in school, delinquents primarily victimize their peers, but outside of school a large percentage of their victims are older and the crimes are more serious.

II. Schools' Potential to Influence Crime

Schools share the responsibility with families and communities for socializing youths to become law-abiding and productive citizens. For current students, schools have primary responsibility for providing a safe environment on school property and a shared responsibility for limiting delinquent behavior elsewhere. Our focus in this essay is on how schools can and do influence the behavior of students while they are enrolled. However, we begin with a brief account of the role of schools and schooling in influencing subsequent behavior.

A. Does Schooling Influence Criminal Careers?

It seems reasonable to expect that formal schooling would tend to provide licit skills and social capital that would compete effectively with the allure of criminal activity. Research on the relationship between school attainment and criminal careers is challenged by the difficulty in identifying the effect on crime of schooling per se, as distinguished from the underlying factors that influence both educational attainment and crime. This difficulty is evident in the mixed results from research on school dropout and crime. All studies find that dropouts engage in more criminal behavior than their peers who graduate from high school, but the conclusions differ depending on how the selection artifacts are handled. Some studies have concluded that, net of controls for factors that influence both educational attainment and crime such as school performance and socioeconomic status, dropping out of school is related to an increase in subsequent crime (Thornberry, Moore, and Christenson 1985) and that the number of offenses committed per year is lower when youths are enrolled in school as opposed to out of school (Farrington et al. 1986). Other studies have concluded that graduation status is unrelated to subsequent crime when statistical controls are applied (Bachman, O'Malley, and Johnston 1978; LeBlanc, Vallières, and McDuff 1993; Sweeten, Bushway, and Paternoster 2009) or that problem behaviors such as substance use increase the likelihood of dropping out of school (Mensch and Kandel 1988; Garnier, Stein, and Jacobs 1997; but see Cook and Hutchinson 2007).[10] Another study

---

[10] Hjalmarsson (2009) investigates the reverse causal process. Her question is whether

(Jarjoura 1993) found that the relationship between dropout and later delinquent behavior is conditioned by the reason for dropping out.

One recent study used a quasi-experimental method to identify the influence of educational attainment on subsequent crime. Lochner and Moretti (2004) used changes in state compulsory education laws over time to provide an exogenous instrument influencing schooling decisions. They found that schooling significantly reduces the probability of incarceration, arrest, and crime. They note several mechanisms that may account for these findings: First, additional years of schooling might increase the opportunity cost of prison by providing more attractive licit employment opportunities. Additionally, the stigma of criminal conviction is likely to be higher for more highly educated individuals, and schooling may alter individual levels of risk aversion or "tastes for crime." It is also true that many school-based prevention programs seek to reduce participation in violence, substance use, and crime by increasing individuals' social bonding, social and cognitive skills related to future success, and social capital.

We conclude that compulsory education laws have a preventive effect on criminal activity. The effects on crime of other policies to extend school careers have not been tested adequately.

We now turn to our main focus, the effect of schools on the problem behaviors of the current student population. That is, we consider those school characteristics that influence concurrent levels of crime, victimization, violence, and substance use.

B. School Organization Matters

Contrary to the research demonstrating that staying in school for more years decreases subsequent crime, the data on how school attendance affects concurrent criminal activity are mixed. Two recent studies find that the causal effect of being in school differs by type of crime. Jacob and Lefgren (2003) exploit the quasi experiment provided by teacher in-service days (i.e., days on which students do not attend school because teachers are engaged in professional development), finding that these days were associated with a 28 percent reduction in violent crimes known to the police but a 14 percent increase in property crimes. Another analysis using variation in attendance caused by

---

incarceration for delinquents reduces the chance that they will graduate from high school. She finds mixed results.

teacher strikes finds similarly mixed results: teacher strikes in Washington State are associated with a 34 percent reduction in juvenile arrests for violence and a 29 percent increase in arrests for property crimes (Luallen 2006). It is not clear from these studies whether overall property crime rates increase when students are out of school; it is quite possible that property crime by students simply is relocated from school to the community, with crime in the community much more likely to become known to the police.

Regardless of the effect of school on juvenile crime commission, we know that higher youth victimization rates in school than out are most likely due to increased exposure to other deviant youths. An increase in delinquency perpetration is also likely to be encouraged during the school day by the presence of social norms that support (or at least appear to youths to support) delinquent behavior and by peer reinforcement for the expression of deviant attitudes, beliefs, and behaviors. Dishion and Dodge (2006) discuss this "deviant peer contagion" process (which has mainly been of concern in the context of intervention programs that group high-risk youths together for services) and how this process is facilitated by ecological factors such as the school and community contexts. They suggest, for example, that peer reinforcement of deviant behavior may be particularly potent in school contexts that fail to reinforce nondeviant behavior. An extensive body of "school effects" research has investigated what features of the school environment might be important for influencing students' deviant behavior.

Research on school organizations and crime in the United States was born out of the major shifts in public education of the 1960s that resulted from forced school desegregation and "white flight" from city schools. These events led to increasing concerns about the condition of schools and considerable media coverage emphasizing the general deterioration and safety problems in the inner-city schools. The American Federation of Teachers was instrumental in raising public awareness related to teacher safety. In response to these pressures, the U.S. Congress held a series of hearings in 1975 and 1976 on the topic of school disorder. Subsequently, Congress mandated the National Institute of Education to conduct a study to learn more about school safety. This Safe School Study (National Institute of Education 1978), conducted in 1976 by Research Triangle Institute, became the first large-scale study of school climate and delinquency.

At approximately the same time, another early influential study was conducted by Michael Rutter and colleagues (1979) in which 12 city schools in Great Britain were compared. Rutter and Maughan (2002) describe their research team's early discovery of school effects on problem behavior as somewhat opportunistic. While studying reading difficulties and emotional/behavioral problems in communities, they noticed that the rates of problem behavior differed considerably from school to school. This observation coincided with those of several smaller-scale studies conducted in the 1970s that demonstrated large variability in behavioral outcomes across schools.

Of course, school crime rates might differ not because schools influence these outcomes, but rather because the input characteristics of the students differ from school to school. Early work on school organization and problem behavior included only fairly crude controls for the characteristics of surrounding communities and student input. In the mid-1980s, Gottfredson and Gottfredson (1985) reanalyzed the Safe School Study data to provide a more precise estimate of the extent to which characteristics of schools influence the incidence of problem behaviors. They aggregated data from principal, teacher, and student surveys collected from 642 secondary schools to the school level to model the effects of school characteristics on school disorder, as measured by rates of victimization. They merged these reports of school disorder and school characteristics with census data pertaining to the school communities. They found that input characteristics of the students and communities in which the schools were located accounted for 54 percent and 43 percent of the between-school variance in teacher victimization rates in junior and senior high schools, respectively. However, controlling for these exogenous characteristics, they found that characteristics of the schools (e.g., school and discipline management practices and school culture and climate factors) accounted for an additional 12 percent (junior high) and 18 percent (senior high) of variance.

More recent studies of schools and problem behavior have replicated these findings. In data from another nationally representative sample of schools collected in the late 1990s, G. Gottfredson et al. (2005) again merged census characteristics describing the communities surrounding the schools onto school-level files containing reports from the principals, teachers, and students regarding their experiences with victimization and delinquency and the characterizations of their schools. As in earlier studies, school and community characteristics explained a considerable proportion of the between-school variability in problem behavior. (The list of community characteristics included racial composition of the schools, size of school, urban location, community poverty and disorganization, residential crowding, grade levels included in the school, and males as a percentage of the student body.)[11] But compared with the results of the earlier Safe School Study data (Gottfredson and Gottfredson 1985), this more recent research found that a lower percentage of variance in school disorder is accounted for by these exogenous characteristics: 12 percent for measures of student delinquency, 23 percent for student victimization, and 25 percent for teacher victimization. Similarly, the more recent study documented that a larger percentage of the variance in these outcomes is explained by school characteristics. While the earlier study found that characteristics of the schools accounted for an additional 12 percent (junior high) and 18 percent (senior high) of the variance of teacher victimization rates, the more recent study found that 30 percent of the between-school variance in teacher victimization is accounted for by six different measures of school organization.

A recent study by Cullen, Jacob, and Levitt (2006) capitalized on a natural experiment in the Chicago Public Schools to demonstrate that schools matter for problem behavior outcomes. By analyzing data from Chicago's school choice program, they showed that ninth graders who had won the lottery to attend a high-achieving high school reported arrests at a rate 60 percent lower than those who lost the lottery. This pattern of self-reports was corroborated by administrative data on incarceration rates for these students (p. 1223). Similarly, Deming (2009) analyzed data from a public school choice lottery in the Charlotte-Mecklenburg, North Carolina, school district. This school district implemented a districtwide open enrollment school choice plan in 2002. Students were guaranteed placements in their neighborhood schools but could also request "nonguaranteed" schools. Nearly all students in the school district submitted at least one choice, and 40 percent re-

---

[11] Note that different studies have drawn different dividing lines between "community" and "school" characteristics. For example, Gottfredson and Gottfredson (1985) defined average demographic characteristics and grade level of the school's students as a community characteristic, but school size and staffing characteristics such as the racial composition of the school's teachers as school characteristics. G. Gottfredson et al. (2005) included teacher and student demographics as well as school size as "externally determined" characteristics. In this essay, we define "school climate" more broadly to include both demographic and ecological "inputs" that, although determined external to the school building, nevertheless may influence school crime. See below.

quested a nonguaranteed school. Enrollment in oversubscribed schools (which were demonstrated to be of higher quality) was allocated using a lottery system. Analyzing official criminal records data for students whose probability of attending a nonguaranteed school was not zero or one, Deming found that lottery winners were arrested for fewer and less serious crimes 7 years later and spent fewer days incarcerated. The effects were concentrated among African American students and students who were at elevated risk for crime. Because of the chance allocation of school choice in these studies, the estimates of school effects on crime are not confounded with the characteristics of the students or of their community of residence. Thus there is something about schools themselves that is important for shaping the behavior of youths in the schools.

But what mechanisms link the school context to misbehavior? Criminological theory tells us that youths engage in proscribed behaviors when they believe that doing so will result in pleasure or profit and when they perceive opportunities to do so. They are especially likely to anticipate pleasure or profit if they have been reinforced in the past or seen others being reinforced for these behaviors. Fortunately, the application of controls reduces the likelihood that youths will act on their impulses. Some of these controls influence behavior by threatening undesirable consequences if caught. These include sanctions applied by parents, schools, and the police. But these sanctions tend to be less effective if the sanctioning process is not perceived as legitimate and fair. Some controls are more implicit in the process of socialization. These "informal" controls bond youths to the social order through emotional attachments, investments in certain futures, and beliefs about what is right and wrong. They control behavior to the extent that youths believe that by engaging in proscribed behaviors they risk losing the respect of loved ones, gambling with a good future, or suffering a bad conscience. Finally, some youths hold their own behaviors in check through the application of self-control. This basic understanding of the mechanism underlying crime and other forms of misbehavior implies that schools can reduce these behaviors in the following ways:

- reducing availability of opportunities to engage in problem behaviors;
- reducing positive reinforcement of problem behaviors;
- increasing formal controls (e.g., increasing the probability of formal sanction as a consequence of problem behavior as well as the

perceived legitimacy of the sanctioning process);
- increasing informal controls (e.g., increasing emotional attachments, investments in goals inconsistent with engaging in crime, and beliefs about right and wrong behavior); and
- increasing self-control.

Of course, these mechanisms are influenced in large part by the community, the family, and individual predispositions. But several aspects of the way schools are organized and managed influence these crime-producing mechanisms. First, as will be developed in greater detail, school system decisions influence the demographic composition of schools and the number and types of other students to whom a child is exposed. School or school district decisions regarding how students are organized for instruction (e.g., academic or behavioral tracking, or departmentalization) further narrow the characteristics of other students to whom youths will be exposed. Importantly, these decisions determine the pool of youths from which highly influential peers will be selected as well as the dominant peer culture in the school. Second, curricular content and teaching methods determine student success in school and decisions to persist in school. Specialized curricula are often used directly to influence problem behaviors (e.g., social competency skills instruction, drug prevention curricula). Third, policies and procedures governing discipline management directly affect the extent to which formal sanctions are applied and the effectiveness of these sanctions. And fourth, the school social organization sets the stage for the application of social controls by influencing the nature of interactions among teachers and students and the school culture.

C. School Climate

The relevant aspects of the school environment are brought together under the umbrella term "school climate." The research literature relating characteristics of school climate to crime-related youth outcomes has grown at a rapid pace in the past 10 years (see fig. 5).

The largest challenge to accumulating knowledge from this growing research base is that school climate is defined and measured very differently from study to study. School climate is rarely explicitly defined but simply treated as a feature of the school environment that is larger than the individual student. While some studies measure school climate according to the average demographic characteristics of the students in the school, others measure it according to externally determined

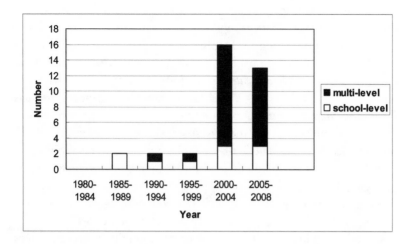

FIG. 5.—Number of school climate and problem behavior studies, 1980–2008

characteristics of the school's organization such as size or student/ teacher ratio. Still others use students' subjective assessments of their schools. It is necessary to organize these different conceptions of school climate before trying to summarize its influence on school crime. Although many organizing frameworks exist, we adopt one introduced by Tagiuri (1968) and used in an earlier review of school climate research (Anderson 1982).

Tagiuri (1968) defined organizational climate as follows: "Organizational climate is a relatively enduring quality of the internal environment of an organization that (a) is experienced by its members, (b) influences their behavior, and (c) can be described in terms of the values of a particular set of characteristics (or attributes) of the organization" (p. 27). His definition emphasizes the importance of the perceptions of members of the organization in defining the climate. Tagiuri distinguishes four important features of organizational environments. *Ecology* refers to physical and material features of the environment. In the school context, these are largely externally determined, and they determine resources available and define patterns of interaction broadly speaking. They include school finances, physical features of buildings, school size and its derivative, and student/teacher ratio. *Milieu* characteristics are average input characteristics of people in the organization—the composition of the organization in terms of participating people and groups. The *social system* concerns patterned relationships of persons and groups in the organization or the rules of operating and interacting in the organization. It is useful to divide the school social system into two major subcategories, *school organizational structure* and *school administration/management*: the organizational structure refers to how the work in the organization is conducted. It includes the level of departmentalization and specialization, the curricular offerings and organization, and the way students are scheduled into classes and grouped for instruction, for example. School administration/management includes the methods used for discipline management and for managing the organization more generally. Practices and procedures aimed at increasing goal clarity, effective communication and decision-making/problem solving, and coordination of resources are included in this category. Finally, *culture* refers to the prevailing beliefs, values, norms, and attitudes of the people in the organization and pertains more to the quality of human relationships than to the formal social organization. Two important aspects of organization culture in the school context are the peer culture and the extent to which the organization is communally organized.

In order to summarize recent research on school climate and problem behavior, we conducted a search for such studies conducted since 1980. We searched for empirical research categorized under the following keywords: school climate, school culture, school environment, school organization, or school milieu *and* substance use, delinquency, crime, victimization, misbehavior, or problem behavior. We also searched for articles that had cited one of three earlier reviews of school climate research (Anderson 1982; Purkey and Smith 1983; Lee, Bryk, and Smith 1993), and we included additional studies already known to us. We identified 72 studies for potential inclusion. About half (37) were eliminated in our first reading, mainly because they did not report on an empirical study. The remaining 35 studies were coded to capture aspects of their methodologies, the nature of the student outcomes and school variables examined, and the associations found. The measures of school climate were coded according to the elements of Tagiuri's classification just described.

The studies are based on predominantly U.S. samples (86 percent), approximately half of the studies (57 percent) use nationally representative samples of schools, and approximately half (51 percent) include both middle and high schools. Some include only middle schools (34 percent) or only high schools (14 percent). The number of schools per study averages 339 (range: 11–2,270).

These studies are divided into two major classes according to their designs. School-level studies model only between-school variation relating school characteristics to school mean levels of student problem behaviors. Multilevel studies model individual-level student variability in problem behaviors from both individual-level predictors and school-level predictors. (Intervention studies that report the results of experimental or quasi-experimental changes in some feature of school organization are treated in subsequent sections separately from the observational studies.) The large number of studies of school-based interventions required that we conduct more focused literature searches only on specific types of interventions.

Although school-level studies are useful for identifying school-level associations, multilevel models allow for more precise decomposition of these aggregate correlations into a segment that is due to individual-level processes and another due to contextual effects. For example, we know that most problem behaviors are elevated for males relative to females. A school-level association between percentage students male and average delinquency level may reflect only this underlying individual-level correlation, but it might also reflect a contextual effect in which youths who attend schools with a higher concentration of males engage in more delinquency than they would if they attended a school with a lower concentration of males.

In both types of studies, school characteristics are measured in a variety of ways, including the following: average student or teacher reports of their own characteristics and experiences (e.g., average teacher job satisfaction or youth reports of delinquent peers), average student or teacher reports of school characteristics (e.g., teacher reports of principal's administrative style or student reports of fairness of school rules), principal reports of school characteristics (e.g., presence of gangs in the school), school archival records (e.g., school size), and average census characteristics (e.g., poverty level in the area surrounding the school). Individual-level characteristics are almost always measured using youth self-reports.

In the following sections, we consider each major type of school climate characteristic included in Tagiuri's classification. Ecology and milieu are considered in the next section (titled "inputs"). The remaining categories (school system and culture) are reviewed in Sections

IV and V, respectively. In each section, we first summarize evidence from the observational studies that relate aspects of school climate to measures of youth substance use, delinquency, victimization, and other problem behaviors such as misbehavior or classroom disorder. The details underlying these summaries are contained in the appendix. Appendix tables A1 and A7 provide overviews of the school-level and multilevel studies included in the summary. Appendix tables A2–A6 and A8–A12 provide more detail showing the actual measures used as indicators of school climate and the nature of the associations observed. The results from observational studies are followed by discussions of intervention research that has attempted to alter each school's characteristics of interest.

III. School Inputs

The four dimensions that constitute "school climate" include two that refer to what might be called the "inputs" in the process that produce school-related misbehavior. Those inputs include, first, the "ecology" of the school—physical features of the building, the ratio of students to adults in the school, and school size (size is of particular interest because of the widespread belief that smaller schools are better places to learn). Second is the "milieu" of the school, meaning the characteristics of the students and adults who are present in the school on any given day.

A. Ecology

Most studies listed in appendix tables A2 and A8 include a measure of school size—number of students in the school or in the grade. A few studies include measures of other aspects of ecology such as resources available for teaching (Gottfredson and Gottfredson 1985), per-pupil expenditure (Eitle and Eitle 2004), student/teacher ratio, or average class size. Only one study measured physical features of the environment (Kumar, O'Malley, and Johnston 2008). The reports of associations of problem behaviors with these aspects of school ecology other than school size are generally consistent with expectations, but the small number of studies reporting on such associations limits what can be learned from them. The discussion here focuses on school size, providing a summary of the literature and some new results.

School size is thought to have a major influence on the internal organization of schools and on subsequent student outcomes. Lee, Bryk, and Smith (1993) suggest that larger schools are likely to have increased capacity to tailor programs and services to meet the diverse needs of students in the school. The extreme example of low specialization is a one-room schoolhouse in which one teacher teaches all students all day. In small schools, the typical teacher teaches a smaller number of different students and gets to know these students well. Students in such schools may develop a greater sense of trust in the adults and be more likely to communicate potentially dangerous situations to them. Large schools are likely to be organized more bureaucratically and to involve more formalized social interactions among members of the school population. As a result, communication may be less frequent or less direct, cohesiveness may be reduced, management functions (including the management of discipline) may become less nuanced, and individuals may share less of a common experience in the school. Alienation, isolation, and disengagement may result. All of these mechanisms are plausible but speculative.

As it turns out, school size has not received much focused attention in research on schools and crime. However, many studies have included a measure of school size as a control variable when focusing on the effects of other aspects of school climate. Appendix table A2 summarizes the associations between measures of school size and problem behavior in school-level studies. The nine school-level studies are based on data from seven different data sources, although unambiguous associations with school size cannot be obtained from two of the data sources (used in three of the studies) because the school size measures were combined with other background measures. In two of the remaining studies (both using SSCS data), the dependent variable is the raw count of criminal incidents (rather than a rate per student), and therefore the association with school size is not very interesting. The remaining studies reach differing conclusions, depending among other things on the measure of problem behavior. Positive associations between school size and measures of minor misbehavior are reported for the High School and Beyond high school data and the NELS eighth graders, but the associations with more serious forms of misbehavior are not statistically significant. In another data source (Safe School Study), school size is not significantly related to student victimization but is positively related to teacher victimization. That study also shows that the effect of school size on teacher victimization is mediated by aspects of the school social organization and culture to be discussed below. No significant relationship with school size is found in the remaining study of middle schools in Philadelphia.

The multilevel studies shown in appendix table A8 provide no support for the "smaller is better" viewpoint. We summarize 15 different research reports based on nine different data sources. In these studies, which generally control for community characteristics as well as characteristics of the students who attend the school, only one data source (NELS tenth graders, as reported in Stewart [2003]) produces a significant positive association between school size and a measure of problem behavior, and the measure of problem behavior used in this study is unusual because it contains mainly school responses to misbehavior (e.g., being suspended or put on probation) rather that actual youth behavior. Hoffmann and Dufur (2008) also report on the association of school size and a broader measure of problem behaviors including substance use, arrest, and running away using the NELS tenth grade sample and find no significant association. Reports from a sample of Israeli schools containing seventh and eleventh grades document a positive association between average class size and student victimization but no significant association with school size. One of the multilevel studies reports a significant negative association between school size and student victimization, but this sample is unusual in that it includes only rural schools located in New Brunswick, Canada, whose average size was 39 and 53 students, respectively, for sixth and eighth grades. Most of the multilevel studies suggest that school size is not reliably related to student problem behavior once characteristics of the students who attend the schools are controlled.

However, these studies often report on the association between school size and problem behavior from models that may provide too conservative a test. The student characteristics that are controlled in the multilevel studies are often exactly those student characteristics that Lee, Bryk, and Smith (1993) hypothesized to be influenced by school size (e.g., school attachment, involvement, perceived positive social climate). Also, most of the associations with school size reported in the studies are from models that partial out influences not only of the communities in which the schools are located and the average demographic characteristics of the students attending the schools, but also of other school climate characteristics such as school culture and the administration/management of discipline, hypothesized to mediate the influence of school size on student outcomes. For example, Hoffmann and Dufur's (2008) study reports a negative association between school size and delinquency in the NELS data, but the equation also contains measures of "school quality," a composite measure assessing youths' perceptions of their school as fair and their teachers and fellow students as caring and trustworthy. Unfortunately, most of these reports do not report the association of school size with problem behavior in models that do not control for potential effects of school size.

New Results. We analyzed data from the 2007–8 SSCS (Neiman and DeVoe 2009) in an attempt to establish baseline descriptive results on how school size relates to school crime. Principals were asked how many incidents of various types of crime had occurred at school during the last school year. They were asked about violent crimes (rape, sexual battery other than rape, physical attack or fight with or without a weapon, threat of physical attack with or without a weapon, and robbery with or without a weapon) and about theft and larceny. We calculated rates per 1,000 students for each school. Because school size is highly related to location and level, it is necessary to look at the association of crime rates and enrollment while controlling for these factors.

Figure 6 shows median rates per 1,000 students for theft/larceny and violent crimes, according to school principals. The figures make clear that crime rates are not systematically related to school size within level and location. However, there is some suggestion that the association between size and principal reports of crime varies according to type of crime, level, and location: in urban locations, principals in smaller elementary and middle schools report more violent crimes. This is not the case in rural/suburban schools or in urban high schools.

We conclude that school size is not generally related to principal reports of school crime and that whatever differences observed favor larger schools over smaller schools.

It is likely that the ratio of adults to students rather than the actual number of students in the school is related to problem behavior. Five of the studies summarized in appendix tables A2 and A8 looked at the association of problem behavior to student/teacher ratio. Only one of the five studies reported a significant relationship, D. Gottfredson and DiPietro (forthcoming), a multilevel study using the National Study of Delinquency in Schools (NSDPS) data in which a positive association of student/teacher ratio was observed for a measure of personal but

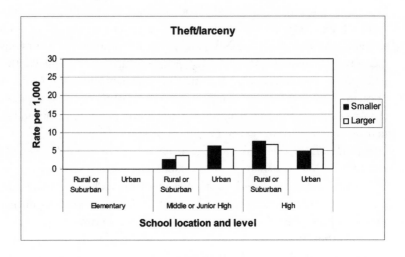

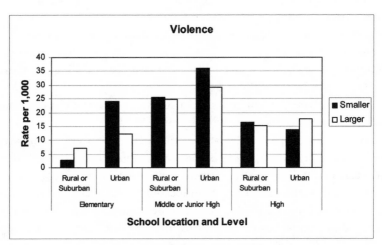

FIG. 6.—Principal reports of crimes recorded by school, by school enrollment, location, and level—median rates per 1,000 students. Note: Size is split at the median total enrollment for each school level: 452, 585, and 885 for elementary, middle, and high school, respectively. One outlier (a small alternative school for delinquent youths with a very high crime rate) is excluded. Violent crimes include rapes, sexual batteries other than rape, robberies with or without a weapon, physical attacks or fights with or without a weapon, and threats of physical attack with or without a weapon. Theft includes taking things worth over $10 (without personal confrontation) and includes pickpocketing, stealing a purse or backpack (if left unattended or no force was used to take it from the owner), theft from a building, theft from a motor vehicle or (of) motor vehicle parts or accessories, theft of a bicycle, theft from a vending machine, and all other types of thefts. Source: Original tabulation from data files, SSCS 2007–8, http://nces.ed.gov/surveys/ssocs.

not property crime victimization. We believe that a more sensitive measure of adult presence would be the ratio of all adults (rather than just teachers) to students. Many schools use parent volunteers and teacher aides in addition to teachers to help maintain order. The ratio of the total number of adults to students would reflect variability in the use of such auxiliaries. Unfortunately, no studies have reported on this association. Still more troublesome is the dearth of studies on how school finances affect school crime rates. Whether a better-financed school is a safer school is surely an interesting question for future research.

As far as we know, there are no intervention-based studies of how school size or resources affect school crime. Case studies of instances in which an established school is divided in smaller units are available, but they almost never assess effects on crime, and they do not provide a clean test of the effects of changing school size because other factors (such as the curriculum, aspects of the physical space, and school finances) are always altered simultaneously.

B. Milieu

As discussed in Section I, rates of problem behavior differ with demographic characteristics, a finding that is reflected in school-level rates in the obvious way. Middle schools have higher rates of delinquency than elementary or high schools (the partial exception is substance use, which increases through high school). Schools with 50 percent or more minority enrollment experience higher rates of violence than majority white schools (see table 3). Socioeconomic status of the student body is also associated with delinquency rates (Brooks-Gunn et al. 1993; Bryant et al. 2003; Gottfredson and Gottfredson 2005). Appendix table A3 summarizes these associations from the school-level studies.

More interesting from a policy perspective is the extent to which the mix of students in the school or the classroom influences the likelihood that any given student will misbehave. The mechanisms of deviant peer influence are both direct and indirect. The direct effects may arise as a result of deviant peer influence: learning and imitation, social reinforcement for deviant acts, and the creation of opportunities for deviant activities (Dishion and Dodge 2006). All these mechanisms are relevant for involvement with delinquency both in and out of school, including drugs and alcohol, and participation in gangs (Reid,

Patterson, and Snyder 2002).[12] The indirect effects may come about as a result of the dilution of authority: a teacher who can manage one or two disruptive students may lose control of the classroom when there are more than two. The same phenomenon can occur at the school level, where a high "load" of troublesome students may swamp the mechanisms of control in the corridors, cafeteria, lavatories, and grounds.

Given the real possibility of peer influence (Carrell and Hoekstra 2008), the actual behavior of youths with a given propensity to deviant or criminal activity may well depend on whom they encounter in their classes and in the other locations in the school. A variety of policies are relevant to influencing the mix of students. At the level of the school district, the distribution of students among schools will be influenced by which grade spans are included in the middle schools, the extent to which low-performing students are held back, and whether school assignments are tied largely to place of residence or tailored to promote integration or parental choice. For a given pattern of assignments to schools, the number and characteristics of students who are actually in the building on a school day will depend on absenteeism and use of out-of-school suspension. And for a given population of students who are actually attending the school on any given day, social influence will likely be mediated by policies that influence the extent to which deviant students are concentrated, such as in-school suspension or academic tracking.

Appendix table A9 summarizes the results from 18 multilevel studies based on 14 data sets showing associations between the milieu of the school and measures of problem behavior, controlling for individual-level demographics as well as for related characteristics of the communities from which the student body is drawn. These studies are largely consistent in showing that the grade levels included in the school or average age of the students in the school, the percentage of male students, the social class composition, and the racial and ethnic composition of the schools are related to measures of problem behavior. These associations sometimes do not reach statistical significance, but they are nearly always in the expected direction. Here we discuss

---

[12] The potential for deviant learning is illustrated by a study of Florida reformatories, which finds suggestive evidence that youths with similar criminal specialties learn from each other and are more likely to recidivate if exposed to a high concentration of similar youths (Bayer, Hjalmarsson, and Pozen 2009).

several of the strongest studies relevant to evaluating the impact of policy choices concerning grade span, grade retention, truancy prevention, racial segregation, and use of alternative schools.

1. *Grade Span.*   One recent study demonstrates that the grade composition in a middle school influences the rates of misbehavior of the students. A generation ago most elementary schools included sixth grade, but now most sixth graders attend middle school. Using a quasi-experimental approach, Cook et al. (2008) compare the school records of North Carolina students whose sixth grade was located in a middle school with those whose sixth grade was in an elementary school (the sample of sixth grades in middle school was trimmed to match the sixth grades in elementary school in several dimensions). While the two groups of students had similar infraction rates in fourth and fifth grades, those who moved to a middle school for sixth grade experienced a sharp increase in disciplinary infractions relative to those who stayed in elementary school. More interesting, perhaps, is that the elevated infraction rate persisted through ninth grade. A plausible interpretation of these findings is that sixth graders are at a highly impressionable age, and if placed with older adolescents, they tend to be heavily influenced by their inclination to break the rules (Warr 1993; Jang 1999). This example of negative peer influence is quite large and extends to all types of infractions, including violence and drug violations.

2. *Retention Policies.*   The age mix in a school is closely related to the grade span, but that is not the only determinant; the school district's retention policies also play a role. In response to high-stakes accountability programs (including No Child Left Behind), many school systems have ended social promotion for students who fail end-of-grade tests, thus increasing the number of old-for-grade students (Jimerson and Ferguson 2007). Entry-level at-risk students are often held back for a year before making the transition to second grade. The effect of retention on behavior of the retained students has been extensively studied. Most studies have focused on academic outcomes: meta-analyses of this literature conclude that the long-term effect on academic achievement is null or negative, with a greatly elevated risk of dropping out (Jimerson et al. 2006). Hence, given the robust general finding that students with academic difficulties are more prone to antisocial behavior (Nagin et al. 2003), it is not surprising that grade retention appears to increase conduct problems (Jimerson 2001; Pagani

et al. 2001; but see D. Gottfredson, Fink, and Graham 1994). One of the most sophisticated studies, using Richard Tremblay's longitudinal data on Montreal school children, found that the effect of grade retention on classroom physical aggression (as measured by teacher reports) is conditioned by the developmental history of the child: those showing no aggression or chronic aggression levels were not affected, whereas those whose trajectory of aggression was declining over time increased their aggression more so if retained than if not retained (Nagin et al. 2003).

There has been less attention to the contextual effect of having old-for-grade students in the classroom and school. One exception is a recent study that uses a comprehensive data set of North Carolina students.[13] Muschkin, Glennie, and Beck (2008) conduct a cross-section analysis of infraction rates by seventh graders, finding that the prevalence and incidence of infractions increase with the prevalence of retained students (students who were retained at least once in the previous 3 years) and the prevalence of old-for-grade students who were not retained during that 3-year period. These results hold after they control for various characteristics of the student body and the schools and the inclusion of district fixed effects. The authors also find evidence that susceptibility differs among types of students; in particular, the old-for-grade seventh graders were themselves especially susceptible to the influence of the concentration of other old-for-grade students in their school. Similar results were found when the outcome variable was the likelihood of being suspended.

3. *Truancy Prevention.* The mix of students who are in the school building on any given day will be affected by absenteeism and tardiness. School attendance laws require that youths between specified ages (e.g., 7–16 in North Carolina and 5–18 in New Mexico) attend school, with possible exceptions for home schooling. This is a legal obligation for which both the child and parents are liable. In many school districts, however, these laws are widely flouted. For example, the absentee rate in Washington, DC, public high schools in the 2006–7 school year averaged 17 percent (*Washington Times* 2008).

The rate of unexcused absences determines not only the number of students in the school building but also the behavioral propensities of those students. Chronic truants are not a representative sample of the

---

[13] A similar study that also found deleterious effects on behavior is Lavy, Paserman, and Schlosser (2008).

student body but rather tend to come from dysfunctional families and be at risk for delinquency, violence, and substance abuse (McCluskey, Bynum, and Patchin 2004). It is also true that chronic truancy engenders academic problems and is associated with failure to graduate from high school and a variety of poor life outcomes, including involvement with serious crime. As a logical matter, then, programs that are effective in improving attendance rates may have several effects. First, if they get delinquent youths off the street and into school, the result may be reduced crime rates in the community. Indeed, communities concerned about the daytime crimes committed by truants have increasingly enlisted the police and the juvenile court to combat truancy (Bazemore, Stinchcomb, and Leip 2004). Second, effective truancy-prevention programs may come at the cost of higher crime rates within the school. And third, if at-risk youths are persuaded to attend school more faithfully, the long-term result may be to improve their chances of graduation and subsequent success.

A number of school-based programs have been evaluated in part by their effect on school attendance. Some of these programs are reviewed in Sections IV and V. Several of these studies demonstrate that it is possible to increase school attendance among delinquency-prone youths and that doing so also reduces delinquency (e.g., Tierney, Grossman, and Resch 1995), school dropout rates (Sinclair et al. 1998), and subsequent crime rates (Bry 1982). Unfortunately, there are no studies, insofar as we know, that evaluate the effect of attendance-promoting programs on school crime rates or overall (community plus school) crime rates.

4. *School Desegregation.*   In compliance with the 1954 Supreme Court ruling *Brown v. Board of Education*, federal courts issued a series of desegregation orders to public school districts. These orders forced a considerable increase in the extent to which African American students attended school with whites during the 1960s and 1970s. A vast literature on the effects of school segregation and desegregation has focused on academic outcomes. The results of this research offer support to the conclusion that integrated schools promote black achievement and increase black high school graduation rates, college attendance and graduation rates, and occupational success (LaFree and Arum 2006). A persuasive quasi-experimental study of the effect of desegregation plans found that they reduced black dropout rates by 2–3 percentage points, with no detectable effect on whites (Guryan

2004). The termination of many of these desegregation plans during the 1990s appears to have had similar effects in the other direction (Lutz 2005).

Given the tight link between academic success and school behavior, it is entirely plausible that the degree of segregation has a direct influence on delinquency in schools. But we are not aware of any direct evidence on the subject; segregation studies have not used school crime as an outcome variable.

There have been two persuasive studies concerning the effects of segregation on crime outside of school. LaFree and Arum (2006) analyzed the incarceration rates for black males who moved to a different state following school. For any given destination state, they found that those who moved from a state with well-integrated schools had a substantially lower incarceration rate than those who moved from a state where the schools were more segregated. A more recent study (Weiner, Lutz, and Ludwig 2009) uses a quasi-experimental approach in which the court desegregation orders serve as the experimental intervention: they report that these orders reduced black and white homicide victimization rates for 15–19-year-olds. The authors explore several mechanisms that may account for this result, including both the direct effects of changing the mix of students in the schools and indirect effects associated with police spending and relocation of some white students. In any event, since all but a handful of these homicides occurred outside of school (see Sec. I), we are still waiting for direct evidence on crime in schools.

5. *Alternative Schools.*   A recent survey found that 39 percent of public school districts administered at least one alternative school for students at risk of educational failure. As of October 2000, 613,000 students were enrolled in these schools, 1.3 percent of nationwide total enrollment. Urban districts, large districts (those with 10,000 or more students), districts in the Southeast, districts with high minority student enrollments, and districts with high poverty concentrations were more likely than other districts to have alternative schools and programs for at-risk students (Kleiner, Porch, and Farris 2002). Despite the widespread use of these schools as a means of removing antisocial and violent students from the regular classrooms, there have been no systematic studies of the effects on school crime rates. The effects on the behavior of youths who are given alternative-school placements have been studied, with mixed results. Indeed, there is unlikely to be

any generic answer, since effects will depend on the quality of the programming and on which students are selected (D. Gottfredson 2001). Best-practice judgments tend to rely on expert opinion rather than on evaluation studies with strong designs (Van Acker 2007).

6. *Grouping within Schools.*   Academic tracking is nearly universal in U.S. secondary education. The attraction of separating students into tracks that are more or less demanding academically is the belief that this is the best way to tailor coursework to the differing background, ability, and motivation of the students. Tracking tends to have the result of concentrating minorities and students from lower socioeconomic status households in certain classrooms. Given the strong association between academic success and delinquency involvement, it also has the effect of concentrating crime-prone students, setting the stage for negative peer influence (Reinke and Walker 2006).

As a device to improve academic progress, tracking has had more detractors than advocates among education specialists. The evidence base is thin: most notably, Mosteller, Light, and Sachs (1996) identified only 10 randomized experimental evaluations comparing the performance of students in tracked (homogeneous) and untracked (heterogeneous) classrooms. When these studies were combined, the best estimate was a zero difference in average academic performance. Still thinner is any evidence on how tracking affects misbehavior.[14] Thus we conclude that the possibility of deviant peer influence due to tracking is plausible but unproven.

7. *Concluding Thoughts.*   School reform is typically shaped by theories of how to improve students' academic performance. But to the extent that school safety is an important goal, somewhat distinct from academic progress, the potential impacts on safety should be considered in any evaluation.

One of the most prominent reform efforts since 2001 has been the campaign funded largely by the Gates Foundation to create small high schools. While that effort was abandoned in 2008 as a result of disappointing results on academic progress, it would also be of interest to know the effect on school crime and juvenile delinquency. Given

---

[14] An early study by Wiatrowski et al. (1982) used a national longitudinal sample and found that change in delinquency involvement after tenth grade was not affected by track status in eleventh grade, controlling for grades and such variables as school attachment and "college encouragement" (which may themselves be influenced by tracking). In this study delinquency is self-reported and is only slightly correlated with academic track in the cross section.

the fact, reported here, that small schools are not systematically safer than large schools (controlling for urbanicity and grade level), it appears doubtful that smaller is better in this domain.

There is very good reason to believe that the mix of students who are assembled in a school or any one classroom may influence the behavior of all. Two relevant mechanisms are deviant peer influence and "resource swamping," both implying that overall crime rates within school may increase in nonlinear fashion with the addition of deviant students to the mix (Cook and Ludwig 2006). This concern is relevant in evaluating policies regarding grade retention, truancy prevention, use of suspension and expulsion, use of alternative high schools, and even academic tracking. In each case, however, we found that relevant evaluations were lacking.

IV. School Social System

In this section, we discuss Tagiuri's (1968) social system dimensions. We remind the reader that our conception of the *social system* includes both *school organizational structure* (e.g., how the school is organized to conduct its work) and *school administration/management*: not surprisingly, a sizable research literature describes attempts to alter many aspects of the school social system. More than a dozen narrative reviews and meta-analyses of school-based interventions aimed at reducing conduct problems and delinquent behavior have been published in the last 15 years (Dryfoos 1990; Lipsey 1992; Lipsey and Wilson 1993; Institute of Medicine 1994; Durlak 1995; Tremblay and Craig 1995; D. Gottfredson 1997, 2001; Stage and Quiroz 1997; Catalano et al. 1998; Hawkins, Farrington, and Catalano 1998; Samples and Aber 1998; Wilson, Gottfredson, and Najaka 2001; D. Gottfredson, Wilson, and Najaka 2002; Hahn et al. 2007; Wilson and Lipsey 2007). This growing research base has led to a rapid increase in use of research by government and professional organizations seeking to promote the use of "evidence-based" practices. In the past 10 years, we have seen several large-scale efforts to publicize and disseminate effective prevention practices for use in schools. Early examples include the CDC's *Sourcebook for Community Action* (Thornton et al. 2000), the U.S. Department of Education's Expert Panel on Safe, Disciplined, and Drug-Free Schools (http://www.ed.gov), the U.S. Surgeon General's *Report on Youth Violence* (http://www.surgeongeneral.gov/library/youthviolence/

summary.htm), and the American Psychological Association's Commission on Violence and Youth (American Psychological Association 1993). These efforts to catalogue and disseminate research information have become increasingly rigorous over time.

Two contemporary efforts to disseminate information about effective school-based prevention practices are the University of Colorado Center for the Study and Prevention of Violence's Blueprints for Violence Prevention program (BVP; http://www.colorado.edu/cspv/blueprints) and the U.S. Department of Education's What Works Clearinghouse (WWC; http://ies.ed.gov/ncee/wwc). Both of these efforts apply rigorous standards of evidence in identifying effective programs. BVP requires evidence of a deterrent effect on a measure of violence, delinquency, and/or drug use in a study using a strong research design (e.g., randomized controlled trial or strong quasi-experimental design), evidence that effects are sustained for at least a year after the intervention has ended, and multiple site replication. To date, 11 model programs have been identified. Several others have been designated as "promising" on the basis of initial positive effects in a rigorous study, but their effects must be replicated or shown to last beyond the project period before they can be identified as model programs.

The WWC was established in 2002 by the Institute of Educational Sciences at the U.S. Department of Education. It is intended to provide an unbiased summary of scientific evidence about effective practices in education. Much broader in scope than the BVP, it provides summaries of evidence in topics such as beginning reading, character education, dropout prevention, early childhood education, elementary school math, English language learners, and middle school math. Although the WWC does not endorse specific programs as effective, it provides ratings for each reviewed program based on the type of design used in the study, the quality of the data, and the adequacy of the study's statistical procedures. The criteria used are very similar to those used in the BVP effort. A "positive effect" WWC rating for an intervention means that two or more studies showed statistically significant positive effects on an outcome of interest and that at least one of the studies used a randomized design. Such a rating also requires that no studies of the intervention showed statistically significant or substantively important negative effects. Most central to our essay are the WWC reviews of character education and dropout prevention, although as we will see, efforts aimed at improving academic performance may also reduce crime.

In this section, in addition to the observational studies summarized in appendix tables A4, A5, A10, and A11, we also rely on several existing reviews to summarize effective school-based crime prevention practices. A thorough review of the evaluation research on school-based prevention would be redundant with these other efforts. Instead, we rely primarily on earlier narrative and meta-analytic summaries of school-based prevention (D. Gottfredson 2001; Wilson, Gottfredson, and Najaka 2001; D. Gottfredson, Wilson, and Najaka 2002). These reviews are based on 178 studies located through a bibliographic search. The criteria included studies that reported on an evaluation of a school-based intervention intended to reduce problem behaviors among children and youths, used a comparison group against which to compare outcomes for treated youths, and measured at least one of the following outcomes:[15] crime or delinquency; alcohol or other drug use; withdrawal from school (e.g., dropout, truancy); rebellious, antisocial, aggressive, or defiant behavior; or suspension or expulsion. As these reviews are somewhat dated, we rely also on two very recent reviews of school-based delinquency prevention efforts (Hahn et al. 2007; Wilson and Lipsey 2007). We briefly summarize the conclusions from these reviews about the effectiveness of different types of school-based interventions. Findings from these reviews are reported as standardized mean difference effects sizes (ESs), which are measures of the difference between program and comparison groups on an outcome relative to the standard deviation of the outcome measure.[16] We also provide a few examples of specific programs that have been demonstrated to be effective for reducing problem behaviors. We rely on the BVP and WWC efforts to identify particularly effective programs.

A. School Organizational Structure

Schools differ in the rules that govern the operations of the school and the way people interact to conduct the school's business. Much has been written in the educational literature about the importance of

---

[15] See D. Gottfredson, Wilson, and Najaka (2002) for a more detailed account of outcomes included in the review.

[16] To provide a benchmark against which to compare the ESs reported in this section, we note that the typical ES for delinquency prevention programs is small. Lipsey (1992) showed that the average ES across 397 delinquency treatment and prevention evaluations was 0.17.

features of the school organizational structure for determining levels of student academic achievement. Lee, Bryk, and Smith (1993) summarize research relating the internal organization of schools to educational outcomes. Among these important organizational features are the extent to which teachers act in the role of subject matter specialists versus having broader roles in socializing students, the content of the curriculum (e.g., emphasizing college vs. vocational preparation), how students are "mapped into" the curriculum, and how decisions are made about which teachers and students are assigned to curricular tracks and courses within those tracks.

Although the effects of variations of these school organizational features on crime have for the most part not been studied, it is tempting to conclude that attempts to improve academic performance, if successful, would also result in a reduction in crime because academic performance is highly correlated with youthful offending. Of course, much of the association between academic performance and crime is due to common causes including lower intelligence, attention problems (Maguin and Loeber 1995), and low self-control (Felson and Staff 2006), suggesting that school-based interventions that target these common causes early in the school career will both decrease crime and increase academic performance. Below we review evaluation research demonstrating the crime prevention potential of such interventions. Notwithstanding these common influences on both outcomes, other research suggests that interventions targeting school performance are also likely to reduce crime.

Najaka, Gottfredson, and Wilson (2001) provide evidence from experimental and quasi-experimental studies of school-based interventions that improving academic performance reduces problem behaviors. Using the meta-analytic database described above, they regressed changes in problem behavior resulting from school-based interventions on changes in risk factors for problem behavior also resulting from the interventions. They found that increases in social bonds—attachment and commitment to school—resulting from the interventions were by far the largest correlates of reductions in problem behaviors. Increases in academic performance resulting from the interventions were also modestly related to changes in problem behaviors. Of course, direct experimental evidence of the crime rate effects of interventions aimed at improving academic performance would be more convincing. But the meta-analysis results suggest that interventions aimed at increasing academic performance do reduce crime, especially if these interventions are also successful in increasing attachment and commitment to school. Also, to the extent that interventions aimed at improving academic success reduce subsequent school dropout, they can be expected to reduce later crime as well. The crime reduction potential of manipulating the aspects of school organization known to be related to academic performance should be more thoroughly studied. A good starting point would be studies of the organizational features identified by Lee, Bryk, and Smith (1993), including teacher roles, the academic content of the curriculum, and how students are assigned to curricular tracks and courses within those tracks.

1. *Class Size and Schools-within-Schools.* That said, a small body of research does link certain aspects of the way schools are organized for instruction to crime. A handful of studies have examined the influence of the number of different students taught by the average teacher on problem behaviors. Gottfredson and Gottfredson (1985) in their appendix table 4 show that the number of different students taught by the average teacher is positively related to teacher victimization rates in senior high schools, net of community factors and the demographic composition of the school. The zero-order correlation with student victimization is also statistically significant but is reduced to nonsignificance once control variables are added to the equation. Two multilevel studies of a more contemporary nationally representative sample of schools, the National Study of Delinquency Prevention in Schools (G. Gottfredson et al. 2000), have also examined the influence of number of different students taught (app. table A10). Payne (2008) finds no effect on student reports of delinquent behavior in general, but D. Gottfredson and DiPietro (forthcoming) find that in schools in which the typical teacher teaches more students, student reports of property victimization at school are elevated. O'Neill and McGloin (2007), analyzing a third nationally representative sample of schools from the SSCS, find that a related measure of school organizational structure, the number of classroom changes throughout the day, is related to higher levels of violent and property crime perpetration.

These findings dovetail with findings from educational research suggesting that school organizational features that promote more cohesive teacher-student relationships promote learning (Lee et al. 2000). Schools in which the typical teacher interacts on a regular basis with fewer different students might facilitate more cohesive student-teacher relationships. Organizational arrangements that can be expected to reduce the number of different students taught include reducing class size and organizing instruction so that smaller groups of students remain together for an extended period during the school day and are taught by a small group of teachers. Some schools accomplish such reorganizations by breaking into smaller "schools-within-schools" (SWS) and others through creative use of block scheduling.

A recent review of research on class size (Finn, Pannozzo, and Achilles 2003) summarizes results from 19 studies, including five large-scale class size reduction initiatives conducted in Indiana, Tennessee, North Carolina, Wisconsin, and California. The research clearly demonstrates positive effects of reduced classroom size in the early elementary grades on both academic achievement and negative or antisocial behaviors. Lasting effects on academic outcomes of having attended smaller classes were also observed. Finn, Gerber, and Boyd-Zaharias (2005), reporting on long-term effects from the Tennessee class size experiment, found that high school graduation was more likely for students who had attended smaller classes for 3 or more years. Analyses of possible mechanisms linking class size to these outcomes conclude that the positive effects are at least in part due to teachers getting to know students better in smaller classes, which increases students' sense of belonging in the classroom. Also, teachers in smaller classes are better able to "nip discipline problems in the bud," therefore reducing time that must be spent on discipline management. Although not mentioned in the reviews, reducing discipline problems in the early grades is also likely to reduce subsequent problem behaviors by limiting student exposure to the modeling of misbehavior and its reinforcement.

Although these reports suggest that reducing class size is likely to reduce student misbehavior by increasing teachers' attention to students, increasing student engagement and sense of belonging in the school, and facilitating more effective management of classroom behavior, only one study that we know of relates class size to actual crime, most likely because most of the research on class size is conducted at the elementary school level. One of the studies summarized earlier (Khoury-Kassabri et al. 2004; Khoury-Kassabri, Benbenishty, and Astor 2005) demonstrated that in a sample of Israeli schools containing seventh and eleventh grades, smaller class size was related to lower levels of student victimization. But others have speculated that the benefits of smaller classes that are evident in elementary schools may not be observed in middle and high schools because higher-level schools tend to rotate students through different classes during the school day rather than keeping them with one teacher. Finn, Gerber, and Boyd-Zaharias (2005) suggest that the positive effect of reduced class size may be offset by a simultaneous negative effect of changing classes. Future studies should attempt to isolate the effects of class size and class changing in the upper grades.

It may be possible, however, to achieve an increase in sense of community without altering class size directly. Nearly 20 years ago, two different studies reported on efforts to reorganize secondary schools to create small groups of students who stay together for an extended period during the school day and who are taught by a small group of teachers. Although neither of these studies meets contemporary standards for scientific rigor in establishing intervention effectiveness (Flay et al. 2005), both offer suggestive evidence of reductions in problem behaviors resulting from the reorganizations. Felner and Adan (1988) reported that students who had been assigned to an SWS program rather than to the typical ninth grade experience had higher grades, better attendance, and lower dropout rates later in their high school years. D. Gottfredson (1990) reported that delinquency-prone students who were randomly assigned to a 2-hour per day integrated curriculum in which students were team-taught by a small number of teachers reported lower levels of delinquent behavior and drug use than their counterparts in the regular school setting. These experimental students also experienced higher academic achievement, persisted longer in school, and reported higher levels of attachment to school and lower levels of negative peer influence.

A more recent effort to study the effect of a similar intervention—"accelerated middle schools" (AMS)—on school dropout is included in the WWC. AMSs are self-contained academic programs designed to help middle school students who are behind grade level catch up with their age peers before entering high school. The programs target students who have been retained in a grade at least once and give them the opportunity to cover an additional year of curriculum during their 1–2 years in the program. AMSs can be structured as separate schools or as schools within traditional middle schools. The SWS model is similar in many respects to the intervention reported by D. Gottfredson (1990). Dynarski et al. (1998) reported on three different implementations of AMSs, only one of which (the New Jersey experiment) used the SWS model. The New Jersey experiment, which met the WWC's high standards for evidence, used a randomized controlled research design and a sample of 620 sixth and seventh graders. Treatment students were assigned to a special program serving about 50 students, taught by a team of four teachers who each covered one of four subjects: English, math, basic skills, and science/social studies. Sixth graders stayed in the program for 2 years and seventh graders for 1. All students were followed for 3 years to determine their dropout rates and highest grade completed. The study found that students who were assigned to the AMS program completed significantly more years of schooling (highest grade completed after 2 years was 7.8 vs. 7.5 for the treatment vs. the control cases, with an effect size of 0.38). Dropout rates after 2 years were low for both groups and not significantly different. Although effects on crime were not reported, a smaller percentage of treatment than control subjects were sent to the office for doing something wrong (46 percent vs. 59 percent) and reported that they drank alcohol in the previous month (11 percent vs. 19 percent) during the school year of the 3-year follow-up.

A much larger-scale effort to mimic the small school environment is seen in the recent SWS movement that is sweeping the nation. In light of evidence documenting greater achievement gains in smaller schools (e.g., Lee and Smith 1995), researchers and professional educator organizations such as the National Association of Secondary School Principals began calling for smaller schools. Although the high cost of rebuilding schools precludes such a radical shift, many school districts caught on to the less costly alternative of dividing large high schools into several smaller SWSs. The reform was expected to result in closer, more personalized relations among teachers and students, which was expected to increase student engagement in the learning process and improve their academic performance. Although our analysis (in Sec. III) found no consistent relationship between school size per se and crime rates, it is not unreasonable to expect that reorganizing large schools into smaller units could reduce crime if such reorganizations result in increased informal social control.

The SWS idea came into full swing in the last decade, with the U.S. Department of Education awarding $100 million through its Smaller Learning Communities Grants program, the Bill and Melinda Gates Foundation investing over a billion dollars in similar initiatives, and other charitable organizations following suit. Large urban centers including Philadelphia, Chicago, and Baltimore have systematically converted their large comprehensive high schools to smaller SWSs (Lee and Ready 2007) and, in some cases, have also opened new smaller schools.[17]

Lee and Ready (2007) summarize what was learned from evaluations of these major reform efforts. First, all of the studies found that social relations in the SWSs were more positive than in the traditional comprehensive schools. However, findings were inconsistent across studies regarding effects on other outcomes such as attendance and academic achievement, and little can be said about the mechanisms underlying the changes that were observed. In many cases, the changes to the school organization were completely confounded with changes in the curriculum and other aspects of the schooling experience so that the effects of these multiple changes could not be disaggregated. Sadly, the studies produced no evidence whatsoever about the effects of the reforms on crime. The findings related to the more beneficial social relations in the SWSs are promising, but it is left to future research to determine how this major shift in school organization influences crime.[18] In the meantime, Bill and Melinda Gates have given up on this initiative (Gates 2008).

2. *Prevention Curricula.* Another aspect of school organizational structure whose effects on crime have been studied is curricular content. While Lee, Bryk, and Smith (1993) focus primarily on the academic content of the curriculum, prevention researchers are more concerned with investigating attempts to incorporate content related to the prevention of problem behaviors into the school curriculum. Evaluations of these efforts have shown positive effects on crime and crime-related outcomes. D. Gottfredson, Wilson, and Najaka's (2002) review

---

[17] Evaluations of these efforts to create new small schools fail to separate selection effects from outcomes of having attended these smaller schools. Most often, the criteria for entry into the smaller schools render the remaining large schools grossly nonequivalent for evaluation purposes. For this reason, we limit our discussion to the efforts to create smaller SWSs. The populations in these reorganized schools are more similar to the populations in the original large high schools.

[18] One recent study of "career academies," small learning communities within large high schools, demonstrated that among a highly motivated group of students who volunteered for the program, those who participated in the career academies were earning higher salaries 8 years after their scheduled graduation than randomly assigned control cases (males only). No effects were found on graduation rates, criminal activity, or substance use, however. The absence of findings may be due to the highly selective study population. Graduation rates were very high and crime rates very low for both the treatment and control groups at follow-up (Kemple and Willner 2008). More research of this nature, using rigorous research designs with more at-risk populations, is needed.

of studies of school-based prevention found that certain types of curricular change are effective for reducing problem behaviors. They reported average effect sizes ranging from 0.05 ($p < .05$) for alcohol and drug use to 0.30 ($p < .05$) for antisocial behavior and aggression due to instructional programs that teach self-control or social competency using cognitive-behavioral or behavioral instructional methods. This category of intervention seeks to develop students' skills in recognizing situations in which they are likely to get into trouble, controlling or managing their impulses, anticipating the consequences of their actions, perceiving accurately the feelings or intentions of others, or coping with peer influence that may lead to trouble. These interventions use instructional methods that explicitly teach principles for self-regulation and recognize antecedents of problem behavior. They provide cues to help young people remember and apply the principles, use modeling to demonstrate the principles and associated behavior, encourage goal setting, provide opportunities for rehearsal and practice of the behavior in social situations (role playing), provide feedback on student performance, and promote self-monitoring and self-regulation.

A closely related type of school-based intervention that teaches similar cognitive content, often coupled with behavior change strategies (to be discussed in greater detail later), and most often targets higher-risk youths rather than entire classrooms, also has positive effects on measures of antisocial behavior and aggression (average effect size = 0.34, $p < .05$). More recent reviews of school-based prevention curricula (Hahn et al. 2007; Wilson and Lipsey 2007) concur that this type of prevention curriculum is moderately effective for reducing a variety of forms of problem behavior. Also of interest is the conclusion from these reviews (Wilson, Gottfredson, and Najaka 2001; Wilson and Lipsey 2007) that school-based interventions targeting more at-risk populations produced larger effect sizes on measures of delinquent, disruptive, and aggressive behaviors than those targeting the general population.

The reviews identify a large number of programs of the general type found to be effective. These effective programs are heterogeneous in terms of age group (ranging from prekindergarten through high school), duration, and targeting strategies. The most ambitious demonstration of the effectiveness of an intervention primarily targeting cognitive and social cognitive skill development to date is Fast Track (Conduct Problems Prevention Research Group 1999, 2002, 2007,

2009, forthcoming). The multicomponent intervention, which began in first grade and continued for 10 years, provided training for parents in family management practices, frequent home visits by program staff, social skills coaching for children delivered by program staff using a model that focused on social competency skill development as described earlier, and academic tutoring. The intervention also included a universal classroom instructional program (the PATHS curriculum: Greenberg and Kushé 1993, 1996; Greenberg et al. 1995), which reinforced social-competency skill development in students and provided classroom management strategies for the teacher. Thus, the program provided both universal and selective programming, mostly focused on social-cognitive skill development, to participating youths during elementary school. It is exactly the type of early intervention we suggested above that had the potential both to decrease crime and to increase academic performance by addressing the common causes of both behaviors. Less intensive services were also provided in Fast Track during the middle and early high school years: families were invited to participate in meetings addressing adolescent development issues, and youths were invited to participate in "youth forums" addressing issues related to vocational preparation.

The evaluation of this intervention involved 891 subjects who were screened and found to be at risk for conduct disorder while in kindergarten. These subjects have been followed for 12 years so far. Early reports from the project (Conduct Problems Prevention Research Group 1999, 2002) found positive effects on several of the intermediate behaviors targeted by the program (e.g., parent involvement in the child's education and child social-cognitive skills) and less aggressive behavior in the classroom. By the end of elementary school, the intervention children reported lower rates of antisocial behavior (Conduct Problems Prevention Research Group 2007). Effects of the intervention on problem behaviors during the middle school years seemed to fade but began to reemerge in high school. Interestingly, by the end of high school, the rates of diagnosed conduct disorder for the program children were half as high as those for the control group. But, when broken down by initial risk level, only those with the highest initial risk exhibited gains (Conduct Problems Prevention Research Group 2009). Rates of court-recorded juvenile arrests[19] and onset of arrests

---

[19] The measure of juvenile arrests was a severity-weighted frequency of juvenile arrests. Each offense for each arrest was assigned a severity score ranging from 1 to 5. The

were also significantly lower for the intervention than for the control children at the end of twelfth grade. For example, among intervention youths, the odds of being in a higher juvenile arrest activity group were only 71 percent of the odds for control youths, a finding that was not conditioned by initial risk level. Surprisingly (given these results), neither self-reports of a wide range of delinquent behaviors nor adult arrest rates from official sources differed significantly for the treatment and control groups (Conduct Problems Prevention Research Group, forthcoming). Fast Track appears effective for reducing crime, but the effects are evident only for the presumably more serious offenses that come to the attention of the police, and subsequent follow-ups will be required to establish lasting effects on adult crime rates.

The Fast Track intervention is considered a promising program on the BVP Web site, pending replication. The universal prevention curriculum component of Fast Track (PATHS), though, has been studied more extensively and is identified by BVP as one of its 11 model programs. The Fast Track research clearly demonstrates that an intensive, long-term effort that begins early and involves both the family and the school in teaching self-control and social-competency skills can reduce arrests of students. It also provides a solid example of the benefits of targeting higher-risk youths for intervention. But can shorter-duration school-based programs also work? Both Hahn et al. (2007) and Wilson and Lipsey (2007), examining the effect of a wide assortment of school-based programs intended to reduce violence and aggressive behaviors, conclude that moderately large effect sizes are observed on aggressive and disruptive behavior for programs targeting all age groups (elementary, middle, and high school). For example, Hahn et al. report a 29.2 percent reduction in violent behavior for programs targeting high school students, a 7.3 percent reduction for middle school students, and an 18.0 percent reduction for elementary school students. Further, both studies reported that the duration of the program does not influence the observed effect sizes. It is possible that a 10-year intervention beginning in elementary school will produce more durable effects in the long run, but programs of more limited duration delivered much later in the educational career also produce reductions in problem behavior.

---

severity levels of the most severe offense from each arrest were summed. This sum was then broken into four categories for analysis.

Finally, we note that there may be unintended benefits of providing effective prevention services for high-risk youths. The Fast Track results as well as the research summaries clearly suggest that the strongest effects are observed for the highest-risk youths receiving the services. While most studies have examined intervention effects only on the targeted group, a recent CDC-sponsored study measured effects of both universal and selective violence prevention programs on the general populations in the participating middle schools. In this study (Multisite Violence Prevention Project 2008, 2009), 37 schools were randomly assigned to receive a universal prevention curriculum for all sixth grade students, a selective family intervention for high-risk sixth graders, both the universal and the selective intervention, or a no-intervention control condition. The study found negative effects of the universal intervention both at the immediate posttest and in growth parameters over the following 2 years. It found positive effects of the selective intervention that emerged only over time (i.e., no immediate effects were observed on aggression measures). Interestingly, the effects of both the selective and universal interventions at the end of the intervention year differed according to preintervention risk status: students at low initial risk increased in aggression relative to controls, whereas students at high initial risk decreased (Multisite Violence Prevention Project 2009). This pattern of findings not only supports the conclusion that targeting high-risk youths for prevention programming is more beneficial than providing universal programming in the long run but also suggests that universal programming may actually increase aggression among the lower-risk segment of the population. Even more interesting, the study found that the selective intervention produced significant long-term reductions in aggression for the entire sixth grade cohort. It is not clear how much of this overall effect is due to the specific effect of the program on the targeted high-risk youths' aggression or to an ecological effect of these students on the larger group, but the results again remind us that it is important to examine effects of programming not only on the youths who receive it directly but also on those who are in the part of the same social network as those who receive the intervention. Unexpected positive "spillover" effects as well as negative effects may be observed.

B. Administration/Management Structure

The second aspect of the school social system, administration/management structure, has been studied extensively. Appendix tables A5 and A11 summarize findings from four school-level and eight multilevel studies, representing 10 different data sources. The results for discipline management show remarkable consistency:[20] when schools monitor students and control access to the campus, and when students perceive that school rules are fair and consistently enforced, schools experience lower levels of problem behavior. Inclusion of students in establishing school rules and policies for dealing with problem behaviors has also been found to be related to lower levels of problem behavior, most likely because students are likely to internalize school rules if they have helped to shape them. However, severity of sanctions is not related to a reduction in problem behaviors. These findings conform to the main findings from deterrence research that the certainty of punishment has a greater deterrent effect than the severity of punishment (Cook 1980; Nagin 1998).

Of course, there has been considerable policy attention to school disciplinary practices, especially in response to the spate of school shootings experienced in the 1980s and 1990s. Most schools employ security and surveillance strategies aimed at keeping intruders out and preventing weapons from coming into the schools. Common practices include controlled entry and identification systems, metal detectors, security personnel or volunteers who challenge intruders, or doors fitted with electromagnetic locks. The NSDPS described earlier showed that over half of schools in the United States employ one or more such procedures (Gottfredson and Gottfredson 2001). Unfortunately, our search for evidence on the effectiveness of these practices yielded only one outcome study of reasonable scientific rigor—a study of metal detectors in high schools in New York City. Ginsberg and Loffredo

---

[20] Although discipline management is by far the most studied aspect of school administration and management, app. tables A5 and A11 also report findings related to broader aspects of school administration. These studies show that practices and procedures aimed at increasing goal clarity, effective communication, decision making/problem solving, and coordination of resources have inconsistent effects on problem behaviors. Both Gottfredson and Gottfredson (1985) and G. Gottfredson et al. (2005) show that teacher reports of victimization are more highly related to these aspects of school management than student reports of victimization, and Welsh (2000, 2001) reports that student victimization but not delinquency is related to student reports of the extent to which their schools take action to improve the school. Similarly, the studies show that involving students in the management of the school more broadly is not consistently related to the level of problem behavior experienced in the school.

(1993) compared the frequency of weapon carrying in schools with and without metal detectors and found that students in schools with metal detectors were half as likely to carry a weapon to school as students in schools without metal detectors.

Since the late 1990s, school resource officers (SROs) have been especially popular in secondary schools as a way to prevent violence, encouraged by federal subsidies. Kochel, Laszlo, and Nickles (2004) reported that as of October 2004, the U.S. Department of Justice had invested $746 million to place more than 6,500 SROs in schools and an additional $20 million to train them to implement community policing in schools. According to the School Crime Supplement to the NCVS described in Section I, the percentage of students aged 12–18 who reported the presence of security guards and/or assigned police officers at their schools increased from 54 percent in 1999 to 68 percent in 2005. A recent *New York Times* article (January 4, 2009) reported that more than 17,000 police officers are now placed in the nation's schools. As with other security strategies, little high-quality evaluation research has been conducted to assess SRO effectiveness, but it seems reasonable that the increased presence of SROs in schools at the very least increases the referral of problem behaviors to law enforcement agencies. Using SSCS data for the 2003–4 school year (Guerino et al. 2006), we find that schools in which the principal reports the presence of at least one SRO or other sworn law enforcement officer are much more likely to report criminal incidents to the police. Figure 7 shows that of the 14 offenses reported in the survey, only referrals for the robbery with weapon are not related to the presence of an SRO or other law enforcement officer (these crimes are rare, and the rates of referral to the police are uniformly high). The presence of an officer in the school results in a doubling of the rate of referrals to law enforcement for the most common crime perpetrated by students in schools—simple assault without a weapon.

We do not know if the increase in referrals to law enforcement deters future crime. Regardless of the impact, the cost of adding SROs to schools is high, not only in personnel costs but also in extra costs related to formal processing of misbehaviors that would otherwise be handled in the school. There are also civil liberties issues to be considered. As reported in the *New York Times* (January 4, 2009), an American Civil Liberties Union inquiry into school-based arrests in Hartford, Connecticut, found that they disproportionately affected minority

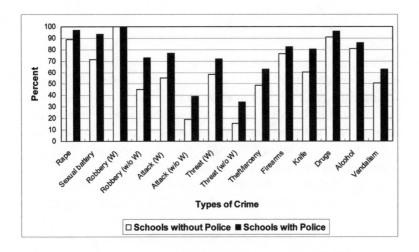

FIG. 7.—Crimes reported by police, by presence of police in schools Source: SSCS (2003–4), U.S. Department of Education, http://nces.ed.gov/surveys/ssocs.

youths. Clearly, research is needed to assess the effectiveness of popular but costly security and surveillance practices, especially in light of the high potential for net-widening and disproportionality in the consequences of their use.

A closely related discipline strategy is the use of zero-tolerance policies in schools—another "tough on crime" practice engendered by the epidemic of youth violence in the late 1980s and the school rampage shootings of that decade and the next. Congress adopted the Gun-Free Schools Act in 1994, mandating that students be suspended for 1 year if they brought a gun to school. A large majority of school districts adopted zero-tolerance policies for alcohol, tobacco, drugs, and violence (Simon 2006). The use of suspension, especially long-term suspension, is thought to have a disproportionate impact on minority and special education populations (McFadden and Marsh 1992; Gregory 1995), whose behavior places them more at risk for suspension. Civil liberties advocates have argued that zero-tolerance policies rob youths of their right to a public education (Skiba 2000). As with the other security-related school policies, little high-quality evidence is available to guide decisions about which discipline management policies produce the most desirable outcomes. The issue is complex, requiring consideration of the trade-offs between in-school versus out-of-school crime, the welfare of the youths who perpetrate the school-based offenses versus that of the other youths in the school, and long-term versus short-term outcomes.

Clearly, removing troublemakers from school helps to maintain an environment more suitable for learning for the remaining students. But what are the costs for the offenders and society? A recent econometric analysis of discipline data from middle schools in three North Carolina counties (Kinsler 2009) found that suspension reduces subsequent in-school problem behavior among the suspended youths without reducing subsequent academic performance among them (possibly because suspended youths are already disengaged from the learning process). Further, Kinsler found that disruptive behavior reduces academic achievement for the general student population, suggesting that strict discipline policies that make liberal use of suspension for misbehavior are a rational course of action for school administration seeking to increase overall achievement.

Of course, this analysis is limited in scope and based on nonexperimental evidence. A more complete analysis of the effect of zero-tolerance policies on youth crime would consider the displacement of crime from school to the community as well as consequences for the suspended youths' long-term criminal and academic careers. As youths lose more days of school to suspension, promotion to the next grade becomes less likely. And as youths fall farther behind a grade, they become much less likely to graduate (Alexander, Entwisle, and Horsey 1997; Entwisle, Alexander, and Olson 1997; Lee and Burkam 2003; Jimerson et al. 2006), and dropout, as we have seen, is likely to increase subsequent crime. Clearly, although zero-tolerance policies benefit the classmates of troublesome youths, a rational discipline policy would also have to consider the broader consequences of such policies for the community.

More consistent with the research on effective crime deterrents are school discipline policies that emphasize the certainty of response to misbehavior over the severity of the response. Among the most effective school-based strategies for reducing youth violence, aggression, and problem behavior are behavioral interventions that target specific behaviors, systematically remove rewards for undesirable behavior, and apply contingent rewards for desired behavior or punishment for undesired behavior.[21] These interventions are often applied to the high-

---

[21] These behavioral interventions are often extended to work on cognitive skills as well.

risk youths who are most at risk for being suspended from school under zero-tolerance policies and as such could be incorporated into school routines for discipline management. D. Gottfredson, Wilson, and Najaka's (2002) meta-analysis reported average effect size on measures of antisocial behavior and aggression of 0.34 ($p < .05$) across 12 studies of this type of behavioral intervention.

Examples of particularly effective behavioral interventions currently in use in schools are the Good Behavior Game (GBG; Dolan et al. 1993; Kellam, Rebok, et al. 1994; Kellam, Brown, et al. 2008), "home-based reinforcement" (Schumaker, Hovell, and Sherman 1977), and the Behavioral Monitoring and Reinforcement Program (Bry and George 1980; Bry 2003). GBG is a classroom-based application of behavioral principles in which elementary school children are divided into small teams, and the teams are rewarded when the classroom behavior of the entire team meets or exceeds a preestablished standard. The GBG is played several times per week throughout the school year. The intervention was evaluated through a randomized trial involving 19 schools in Baltimore, with posttests conducted immediately following the intervention as well as 6 and 14 years later. The results of this study indicate that participation in GBG is related to immediate reductions in aggressive behavior, rates of diagnosed antisocial personality disorder, and long-term effects (14 years later) on drug and alcohol use and smoking. GBG is considered a promising program in the BVP classification.

Home-based reinforcement (HBR), applied to individual students displaying behavior problems, requires cooperation between teachers and parents in the management of the child's behavior. After agreeing on specific child behaviors to be extinguished or encouraged and establishing a baseline for these behaviors, teachers systematically record data on the target behavior on a "daily report card" that goes home to the parents. The parents, who generally have access to a wider array of reinforcers and punishments than the teachers do, use the teacher's information to guide the application of rewards and punishments. As the desired behavior emerges, the frequency of reports home is re-

---

These cognitive-behavioral interventions are often based on research indicating that aggressive or delinquent children and youths tend to be impulsive, tend not to make self-attributions for negative personal outcomes, tend to have hostile attributional bias in interpreting ambiguous social cues, fail to consider alternative solutions to problems, and lack effective communication skills (Dodge, Bates, and Pettit 1990).

duced, and the schedule of contingencies is relaxed. In the earliest research on HBR, application of this technique to junior high school students showed that school rule compliance, teacher satisfaction with the student, and academic performance improved as a result of participation in an HBR program (Schumaker, Hovell, and Sherman 1977). A recent review of 18 empirical studies of school-home collaboration interventions (Cox 2005) concluded that behavioral interventions using the daily report card strategy had the strongest effects on problem behavior. Lasting effects on crime are unknown.

The Behavioral Monitoring and Reinforcement Program (Bry and George 1979, 1980; Bry 1982), also a promising program on the BVP Web site pending replication, was among the first published studies demonstrating the effectiveness of a school-based behavioral intervention with high-risk middle school youths. Students were randomly assigned to the treatment and control conditions in this study. Tardiness, class preparedness, class performance, classroom behavior, school attendance, and disciplinary referrals were monitored weekly for 2 years. Students met with program staff weekly and earned points contingent on their own behavior that could be used for a class trip of the student's choosing. Frequent parent notification was used. Experimental students had significantly better grades and attendance at the end of the program than controls did, but the positive effects did not appear until the students had been in the program for 2 years (Bry and George 1979, 1980). Bry (1982) reported that in the year after the intervention ended, experimental students displayed significantly fewer problem behaviors at school than controls did, and in the 18 months following the intervention, experimental students reported significantly less substance abuse (ES = −.44) and criminal behavior (ES = −.30). Five years after the program ended, experimental youths were 66 percent less likely to have a juvenile record than controls were (ES = −.50). The program has been updated and is currently in use in numerous school systems in the United States (Bry 2003).

These relatively simple and inexpensive behavioral interventions represent a potentially potent school-based prevention strategy that might be incorporated into routine school practice. The 1997 reauthorization of the Individuals with Disabilities Education Act (IDEA) (Public Law 105-17) required functional assessment and behavioral intervention procedures to be implemented in the disciplining of students with disabilities. The evidence-based programs described here would meet these federal requirements.

Behavioral principles have also been incorporated into schoolwide discipline management systems. These systems are typically designed to clarify expectations for behavior. They establish school and classroom rules, communicate these rules as well as consequences for breaking them clearly to parents and students, establish systems for tracking both youth behavior and consequences applied by the schools, and monitor the consistency of the application of consequences for misbehavior. Schoolwide discipline management efforts, most often implemented by a school-based team of educators, are highly consistent with the research summarized earlier suggesting that students' perceptions of school rules as fair and consistently enforced are related to reductions in problem behavior. The meta-analysis described earlier (D. Gottfredson, Wilson, and Najaka 2002) also examined the effectiveness of this type of schoolwide effort to improve discipline management and reported average effect size on measures of crime (0.27, $p < .05$) and alcohol and other drug use (0.24, $p < .05$). Among the studies included in the meta-analysis are two early studies of the effects of schoolwide discipline management systems on problem behavior outcomes. Students in the intervention schools in the first of these efforts (Project PATHE implemented in nine Charleston, South Carolina, schools) reported less delinquent behavior and drug use and fewer punishments in school relative to the students in the comparison schools (D. Gottfredson 1986). A similar intervention was tested in a troubled Baltimore junior high school, with a special emphasis on replacing the school's reliance on out-of-school suspension with a wider array of consequences for misbehavior. This intervention, which also added positive reinforcement for desired behavior to the mix of consequences routinely used, also showed positive effects on student delinquency and rebellious behavior (D. Gottfredson 1987). This early research, although based on relatively small numbers of schools and lacking randomization to condition, suggested that behavioral principles could be incorporated into "normal" school disciplinary practices and that an emphasis on consistency of rule enforcement as opposed to severity of punishment provided an effective deterrent.

Contemporary approaches to discipline management incorporate behavioral principles into comprehensive systems that include schoolwide discipline policies and practices as well as targeted behavioral interventions. One popular approach is "school-wide positive behavior support" (SWPBS), a "whole-school approach emphasizing effective systemic and individualized behavioral interventions for achieving social and learning outcomes while preventing problem behaviors" (Sugai and Horner 2008, p. 69). This system, adopted by over 5,600 schools throughout the United States, uses a school team approach to apply behavioral interventions at different levels of intensity for students at different levels of need. Universal interventions focus on clarity of school and classroom rules and consistency of enforcement and on screening for more serious behavior disorders. Group-based behavioral interventions are employed with the 5–10 percent of youths who do not respond to the universal interventions. In addition, intensive, individualized behavioral interventions are employed to manage the behavior of the small segment of the population that is especially at risk. Unfortunately, the research on the effectiveness of SWPBS is not as sophisticated as it should be for such a widely disseminated program. Although dozens of studies have demonstrated that problem behavior decreases after the intervention is put in place, only one (Sprague et al. 2001) compared change in the intervention school(s) with the change that might be expected in the absence of an intervention. Even this study is not useful for isolating the effects of the behavior management strategies because it also included the introduction of a prevention curriculum along with the schoolwide behavioral supports. Higher-quality research is needed to assess the effects of this promising approach on crime both in and out of school.

Recent high-profile efforts to manage student behavior in urban centers also reflect an emphasis on behavioral principles. Under the direction of Roland G. Fryer of the American Inequity Lab at Harvard University, students in 14 Washington, DC, middle schools are being given the opportunity to earn up to $100 every 2 weeks contingent on their school attendance and behavior. The program, Capital Gains, is described by Washington, DC's, mayor as the kind of "outside the box" thinking required to turn around a failing urban school district (Haynes and Birnbaum 2008). The program mimics Fryer's similar efforts currently being tested in the New York City and Chicago public schools. This type of intervention, focusing on reinforcing the positive, is similar to the effective Behavioral Monitoring and Reinforcement Program (Bry and George 1979, 1980; Bry 1982) described above. It holds more promise for reducing crime in the long run than zero-tolerance and other policies and practices that exclude misbehaving youths from school.

C. Conclusion

We began this section by considering research on the efforts to change the way secondary students are organized for instruction. We noted that relatively little is known about the crime reduction potential of manipulating school organization, and we suggested that this is an area ripe for additional research. The little available research suggests, however, that it may be fruitful to reorganize schools by creating smaller groups of students who stay together for an extended period during the school day and who are taught by a small group of teachers. The research on these efforts suggests that such efforts might be effective for increasing youths' sense of connection, which serves to hold criminal behavior in check.

Much more is known about the effectiveness of prevention curricula for reducing problem behaviors. We summarized evidence showing that instructional programs that teach self-control or social competency using cognitive-behavioral or behavioral instructional methods are effective and that the largest crime prevention potential results when youths who are at elevated risk for subsequent problem behavior are targeted for such school-based programs. We also summarized research suggesting that programs that are effective for reducing problem behavior among high-risk youths may have beneficial effects for the general population as well, and we suggested that more research is needed to document such unanticipated "spillover" effects.

This section also summarized research on school discipline management policies and practices and showed that they are important determinants of school crime. The studies reviewed consistently showed that in schools in which students report that the school rules are clearly stated, are fair, and are consistently enforced and in schools in which students have participated in establishing mechanisms for reducing misbehavior, students are less likely to engage in problem behaviors. We showed that evaluations of specific school-based programs that employ behavioral strategies to monitor and reinforce student behavior are effective both for controlling behavior in school and for reducing subsequent crime. Also, altering schoolwide discipline management policies and practices to incorporate behavioral principles, clarify expectations for behavior, and consistently enforce rules reduces problem behavior. We discussed popular "get-tough" approaches to school discipline, including zero-tolerance policies and the use of law enforcement officers in schools. Although the effects of these policies on crime are not known, we argued that they might actually increase crime outside of school. There is a clear need for rigorous research on the effects of these policies.

V. School Culture

The final category of school climate to be considered is school culture—potentially the most potent aspect of school climate because it involves proximal interpersonal influences on student behavior. *School culture* refers to the quality of human relationships in the school and includes both peer culture and the extent to which the organization is communally organized. All these dimensions influence youth crime and can be successfully manipulated to reduce it.

We rely in this section on the same resources we did in the previous section. We first summarize results from observational studies relating features of school culture to measures of problem behavior (results summarized in app. tables A6 and A12). The same meta-analyses discussed in the previous section are used to identify effective categories of school-based prevention practice, and the WWC and BVP initiatives are referenced to identify particularly effective programs.

A. Behavioral Norms

Cultural norms, expectations, and beliefs influence all behaviors. Considerable research has focused, for example, on the notion that academic achievement is devalued in contemporary youth culture, especially among African American youths who associate academic achievement with an oppressive white culture (Fordham and Ogbu 1986). Although the best empirical evidence does not support the claim that a racialized "oppositional culture" is commonplace, it is plausible that peer pressure against being "nerdy" and working hard in school influences the academic achievement of youths in general (Cook and Ludwig 1997, 1998; Tyson, Darity, and Castellino 2005). Early research on characteristics of effective schools documented that schools have a distinctive "ethos" that influences students' academic as well as social behaviors (Rutter et al. 1979). Norms and expectations for behavior, both peers and adult, have been shown to be powerful determinants of behavior. Appendix tables A6 and A12 summarize findings from studies that have related some aspect of school culture to student problem behaviors.

Culture is variously operationalized in these studies. Many studies use a measure of the average level of some form of misbehavior (e.g., truancy, bullying, or classroom misconduct) among students in the school to measure norms for misbehavior. These studies most often control for individual-level measures of the same behavior to demonstrate that net of the individual's own level of misbehavior, school norms influence more serious forms of misbehavior such as substance use or delinquency. Another common method for assessing school culture is to ask students to report on the availability of illegal substances in the school or the extent to which other students in the school engage in problem behaviors. These approaches to measuring "culture" are suspect because they confound cultural values with other determinants of school crime rates.

A purer operationalization of culture asks youths to report on their own beliefs about morality. An observed effect on problem behaviors of school average beliefs, net of individual-level beliefs, is taken as an indication of a school culture effect. Appendix tables A6 and A12 show that most studies that have measured school culture using one of these methods have produced evidence in support of a school culture effect on problem behavior.

Of course, the school "inputs" discussed in Section III are key determinants of the predominant cultural beliefs in the school. As we discussed, school desegregation and retention policies as well as the grade span of the school can influence school culture by altering the mix of students in the school. But several more programmatic attempts to alter school culture have also been studied. These programs have in common a focus on clarifying behavioral norms. That is, in contrast to the instructional programs described in the previous section that focus on teaching youths specific social competency skills, these normative change programs focus on clarifying expectations for behavior. Some signal appropriate behavior through media campaigns or ceremonies, others involve youths in activities aimed at clarifying misperceptions about normative behavior, and still others increase exposure to prosocial models and messages.

Several studies of attempts to clarify norms for behavior have been reported. D. Gottfredson, Wilson, and Najaka (2002) summarized effects reported in 13 studies and concluded that such programs are effective for reducing crime, substance use, and antisocial behavior. Two of the better-known examples of programs in this category are the Bullying Prevention Program (Olweus, Limber, and Mihalic 1999) and the Safe Dates Program (Foshee, Linder, et al. 1996; Foshee, Bauman, et al. 1998). Olweus's program is designated as one of the 11 BVP model programs.

Olweus's antibullying program includes schoolwide, classroom, and individual components. Schoolwide components include increased adult supervision at bullying "hot spots" and schoolwide discussions of bullying. Classroom components focus on developing and enforcing rules against bullying. Individual counseling is also provided to children identified as bullies and victims. A large-scale evaluation of this program in Norwegian schools demonstrated that it led to reductions in student bullying and victimization and decreases in the incidence of vandalism, fighting, and theft (Olweus, Limber, and Mihalic 1999). A very recent review of antibullying programs summarizing results from 59 studies conducted between 1983 and 2008 (Farrington and Ttofi 2009) confirmed that antibullying programs are effective for reducing bullying and student victimization and that Olweus's program is particularly effective.

The Safe Dates Program targets norms for dating violence among adolescents. The school portion of the intervention includes a theater production performed by peers; a 10-session curriculum addressing dating violence norms, gender stereotyping, and conflict management skills; and a poster contest. The community portion of the intervention includes services for adolescents experiencing abuse and training for community service providers. Foshee, Bauman, et al. (1998) found that intervention students reported less psychological abuse and violence against dating partners than control students did.

On the basis of these and other relatively rigorous evaluations, D. Gottfredson, Wilson, and Najaka (2002) concluded that interventions aimed at establishing norms or expectations for behavior can be effective in preventing substance use, delinquency, aggression, and other problem behaviors. It should be noted, however, that evaluations of these programs seldom provide clean tests of the proposition that culture matters, since the programs more often than not combine attempts to alter norms with other components aimed at increasing levels of supervision and enforcement (e.g., Olweus) or improving social competency skills (Foshee).

Another type of school-based program that fits into the more general class of programs aimed at changing perceived norms for behavior has recently been highlighted in the U.S. Department of Education's WWC. These "character education" programs are defined in the WWC as educational efforts to support the positive character development of children and adults, where "character" refers specifically to moral qualities such as respect, responsibility, trustworthiness, fairness, caring, and citizenship. Such initiatives were specifically encouraged and supported in the No Child Left Behind Act of 2001. In criminological language, character education programs seek to develop internal controls for behavior by clarifying beliefs about right and wrong behavior. Unfortunately, the majority of character education studies reviewed by the WWC were found to have insufficient evidence to ascertain their effectiveness. We believe that the evidence supporting character education programs does not warrant the level of attention these programs have been given of late. However, the evidence supporting the effectiveness of norm-clarification programs, whether or not it focuses on fostering moral development, is more persuasive.

We would be remiss if we failed to mention that sometimes school-based practices that seek to clarify norms for behavior backfire. One example is a peer counseling program that deliberately mixed delinquent and nondelinquent youths in counseling sessions in which youths were encouraged to share their problems. The intent was that the negative beliefs and attitudes voiced by the delinquent youths would be corrected through interaction with the nondelinquent youths. A randomized experiment testing this program as implemented in the Chicago Public Schools (G. Gottfredson 1987) reported predominantly harmful effects for high school students: high school treatment youths reported significantly more delinquent behavior than controls. A more recent large-scale evaluation of the Reconnecting Youth program (Cho, Hallfors, and Sánchez 2005) also found negative effects for a group counseling program for at-risk high school students. This program sought to "reconnect" truant, underachieving high school students (and to reduce their deviance and substance use) by developing a positive peer group culture. Students were grouped together in classes of 10–12 students for a full semester during which a trained group leader (following a standardized curriculum) attempted to develop a climate conducive to building trust. The evaluation reported only negative effects 6 months following the end of the intervention. Treatment students showed greater bonding to high-risk peers, lower bonding to school and conventional peers, lower grade point average (GPA), and higher anger than control students at the 6-month follow-up.

B. Communal Social Organization

A second aspect of school culture that has been studied extensively pertains to the affective bonds between students and teachers and among adults in the school. The concept of "communal social organization" (CSO) was first introduced as part of the effective schools debate in the 1980s (e.g., Purkey and Smith 1983; Firestone and Rosenblum 1988) and studied by Bryk and colleagues (Bryk and Driscoll 1988) mostly in the context of predictors of school achievement. Communally organized schools are schools in which "members know, care about, and support one another, have common goals and sense of shared purpose, and . . . actively contribute and feel personally committed" (Solomon et al. 1997, p. 236). This aspect of school culture is especially important for school crime research because we know that individual-level student affective bonds are an important predictor of delinquency (Hirschi 1969), and it seems reasonable to hypothesize that schools high on CSO would produce higher levels of student bonding to school.

Four studies have measured CSO and nine studies have related some measure of student affective bonds (at the school level) to problem behaviors. These studies, summarized in appendix tables A6 and A12, are compatible with the conclusion that average student attachment to school and CSO more generally do inhibit student problem behaviors. The most comprehensive test of this linkage was provided by Payne, Gottfredson, and Gottfredson (2003) using data from the NSDPS. This study demonstrated that more communally organized schools experience less student delinquency and teacher victimization and that the effect of CSO on student delinquency is mediated by average student bonding.

This survey research dovetails nicely with an ambitious ethnographic study of school violence conducted for the National Research Council. In 2003, the Committee to Study Youth Violence in Schools published its report on the circumstances surrounding several incidents involving extreme lethal violence that had occurred in the nation's schools (National Research Council 2003). The report was based on detailed case studies of six schools and communities that had experienced school shootings resulting in death. Among the committee's several insights into the factors leading to the incidents is the following: "the sense of community between youth and adults in these schools . . . was lacking. In the worst example, the school allowed a school newspaper to print an article that humiliated one of the students who became a shooter. The adults involved may have been too distant from the students to prevent some social processes leading to the potential for violence or resulting in an intolerable humiliation from some potentially vulnerable youth" (p. 256).

This observation is consistent with the research on more mundane forms of school violence just summarized. It suggests that strategies that increase social bonds between students and others in their schools will reduce misbehavior by increasing informal controls. Students who care what adults in the school think about them will be less likely to act in ways that jeopardize their positive regard. More concretely, students who have close ties to the adults in the school will be more likely to report on rumors of impending attacks. But how can such bonds be built or maintained? Possibilities noted in previous sections of this essay include organizing the school so that the typical teacher interacts with fewer students, reducing class size, and creating more "communal" social environments in which members are more tightly joined together by common goals and in which members are held in place by the support and positive regard of others in the organization.

In the previous section, we summarized evidence suggesting that reorganizing schools to create a smaller feel to the schooling experience is an effective strategy for increasing youths' sense of connection and that enhanced connectedness should hold criminal behavior in check. A less drastic intervention with the same objectives is mentoring. Youth mentoring programs often target youths at risk of behavioral problems, assigning them to an adult mentor who spends time with the young person, provides support and guidance, and provides general guidance. Evaluations of such programs have been mixed, but often null or weak results can be attributed to implementation failure. As with any voluntary program, mentoring programs in practice are often not as intensive as intended (e.g., Karcher 2008). However, a recent meta-analysis of mentoring programs (Eby et al. 2007) demonstrated small but positive effects of mentoring programs on several behaviors of interest in this essay: withdrawal behaviors (e.g., school dropout, truancy—18 studies), deviance (e.g., suspension from school, aggressive behavior, property crime—15 studies), and substance use (seven studies). This review included a wide range of types of mentoring programs, but outcomes for youth mentoring programs were as strong on these outcomes as the other types of mentoring programs (academic and workplace mentoring) included in the review.

One of the better-known models for adult mentoring, the Big Brothers–Big Sisters program (BBBS), is a community-based program identified by BVP as a model primarily on the basis of evidence from a large-scale randomized trial that found that mentored youths were 46 percent less likely than control youths to initiate drug use, 27 percent less likely to initiate alcohol use, and almost one-third less likely to hit someone during the study period (Tierney, Grossman, and Resch 1995). Community-based mentoring involves meetings between the mentor and mentee at times and places selected by the pair. Many schools now provide "school-based mentoring" (SBM), which involves meetings primarily in school during the school day. A recent evaluation of the BBBS SBM model, also involving random assignment of a large number of youths, shows that although it is not as effective as the community-based alternative, SBM does improve academic performance, reduce truancy, and reduce serious school infractions (Herrera et al. 2007) at least during the first year of mentoring. Consistent with results from smaller-scale randomized trials of SBM showing positive effects on increasing connectedness to school (Karcher 2005) and perceived social support (Karcher 2008), Herrera et al. found that mentored youths reported more often than controls the presence of a nonparental adult in their life who provides social support. At the end of the second year of the study during which minimal SBM was provided, the positive program effect on truancy was sustained but the other positive effects were not. Herrera et al. conclude that although the SBM model is promising, it needs to be strengthened to ensure longer and higher-quality mentor/mentee matches than are typically found in schools.

A similar program is described in the WWC review of dropout prevention research. The Check & Connect program involves monitoring of school performance, mentoring, and case management for at-risk high school students. Program staffers closely monitor student attendance, performance, and behavior in school. They also provide individualized attention to participating students, encouraging them to stay in school. One study—a randomized controlled trial that included 94 high school students from the Minneapolis public schools with learning, emotional, or behavioral disabilities—met the WWC standards for evidence (Sinclair et al. 1998). That study reported that 9 percent of ninth grade students enrolled in Check & Connect compared with 30 percent of controls dropped out of school at the end of the first follow-up year. This intervention is interesting because it combines aspects of adult mentoring with aspects of behavior management described earlier as having crime prevention potential.

C. Summary

In this section, we summarized findings from observational studies relating measures of school culture and student delinquency, victimization, substance use, and other forms of problem behavior. These studies suggest that perceptions of social norms for behavior are related as expected to problem behavior, net of individuals' personal beliefs. In schools in which the prevailing norm is to condone delinquent activities, students are more likely to do so regardless of their own personal dispositions to engage in these behaviors. But we showed that schools can intervene to change perceptions of norms and expectations for behavior and that doing so reduces delinquency, although attempts to do so sometimes backfire.

We also found evidence in observational studies that in schools in which students feel an emotional attachment to the adults in the school, their misbehavior is restrained. We referred to our earlier discussion of efforts to create smaller learning environments (SWSs) aimed at increasing youths' sense of connection to the school, reminding the reader that such attempts to reorganize schools are promising to the extent that they are successful at creating more communal social organizations. We reviewed research on school-based mentoring programs and showed that they also hold considerable promise for crime prevention. Although research documents positive effects of these programs on social relations outcomes, more work is needed to test the full potential of more potent models of school-based mentoring than have been tested to date.

VI. Where Now for Policy and Research?

While only 1 percent of homicides of school-aged youths take place in schools, nonlethal victimization rates for theft and violence in school are as high as in all other locations combined. The concentration of crime in schools reflects the reality that schools, especially middle and high schools, concentrate youths near the peak of their delinquent careers. The regimentation of school life and extensive adult supervision are surely helpful in controlling behavior but are not sufficient to negate the basic fact of exposure. Other things equal, a school-aged youth is more likely to be mugged or beaten up on a day when school is in session than when it is not.

Still, there is good news of a sort. In 2005 school crime victimization rates were only about one-third what they were in the early 1990s. The school rampage shootings that culminated in the Columbine disaster in April 1999 are largely a thing of the past. Students and teachers alike are far less likely to be victims of larceny, robbery, or assault while in school.

What can we learn from this remarkable crime drop? A possible explanation is given in terms of the redirection of school discipline and crime-prevention policy that occurred during the 1990s and beyond. During that period schools have greatly expanded the use of school resource officers (police), adopted zero-tolerance policies that have increased suspensions and expulsions, referred more crimes to the juvenile justice system, and generally "criminalized" behavior that used to be dealt with internally and less formally. The problem with crediting this shift in policy, however, is that youth victimization rates were declining outside the schools as fast as or faster than in the schools. Occam's Razor would suggest that any explanation for the trend in school crime takes note of the close link between school crime and community crime and that the crime drop in the community fully accounts for the crime drop in schools since 1993. In sum, and perhaps unsatisfactorily, the primary reason school crime rates have dropped is that community crime rates have dropped.

This conclusion does not imply that there is nothing that schools themselves can do to control the criminal activity by their students. Crime rates differ widely among schools, even those that are similar with respect to grade span, urbanicity, and demographic characteristics of the students. Experimental evidence suggests that the crime involvement of any given student at risk is influenced by the school that he or she attends. That fact motivates our scientific quest to find the school-level determinants of criminal activity by school-aged youths.

In Sections III–V, we summarized findings from 35 studies of school climate and crime conducted since 1980 and discussed numerous additional studies that reported on attempts to manipulate aspects of school climate. The review was organized around the four categories of school climate described by Tagiuri (1968). The school climate studies revealed sturdy associations between measures of school climate and measures of student delinquency, victimization, substance use, or other forms of problem behavior, summarized in table 5.

A starting point in accounting for interschool differences in crime is the criminal propensities of the students. Schools in which many of the students are active delinquents outside school start with a far greater challenge than those in which the students are largely law-abiding. The school crime rate of a student body with high crime propensity may be greater than the sum of the parts, for two reasons. First, if the school lacks the adult resources to manage the "load" of misbehavior, then the school may become progressively more chaotic, spinning out of control. Further, delinquent and deviant youths may have a negative influence on each other and other students as well, further amplifying the problem. In short, the crime rate in school is not just the sum of the parts but does reflect the ecological effects of the mix of students in the building.

Schools and school districts have a good deal of control over the makeup of the student body. Schools can be based on neighborhood residential patterns or integrated across race and class. The grade span for elementary and middle schools can be adjusted. Truancy and dropout prevention programs can be pursued with more or less vigor and troublesome students reassigned. Whether failing students are retained in a grade or given a social promotion influences the extent of age homogeneity within classrooms. Students who are enrolled in the school can be tracked on the basis of academic potential or mixed together. And so forth. This array of policy choices all have the potential to influence the "load" on teachers and other adults and the opportunity for deviant peer influence. Some of these policies have been evaluated for these ecological effects, but the evidence base is quite thin.

Aspects of school culture have the most robust associations with problem behavior. In schools in which the prevailing norm is to engage

TABLE 5

School Climate and Problem Behaviors: Summary of Evidence

Tagiuri (1968) Classification	Feature of School Environment	Evidence from Observational Studies
Ecology	School size	School size generally unrelated to levels of problem behavior (weak evidence)
Milieu	Demographic characteristics of students in the school	Demographic composition of the school matters for level of problem behavior, net of individual demographics; important compositional characteristics include grade levels included in the school or average age of the students in the school, the percentage male students, and the social class composition of the school (strong evidence)
Social system	Organizational structure: Number of different students taught by teacher/number of classroom changes	Teaching more students and allowing more classroom changes promotes higher levels of problem behavior (moderate evidence)
	Administration/management: Discipline management	Schools that establish and maintain rules, effectively communicate clear expectations for behavior, monitor student behavior, consistently enforce rules, experience lower levels of problem behaviors (strong evidence)

Student involvement	Giving students a meaningful role in establishing mechanisms for reducing misbehavior reduces problem behaviors (moderate evidence)
General school management	Effective management of the school reduces problem behaviors (moderate evidence)
Culture	
School norms related to problem behaviors	The attitudes, beliefs, and behaviors of students in the school predict the level of problem behavior (strong evidence)
Students' affective bonds/communal social organization (CSO)	Average student attachment to school and CSO more generally do inhibit student problem behaviors (strong evidence)

in delinquent activities, students are more likely to do so regardless of their own personal dispositions to engage in these behaviors. We also found strong evidence that in schools in which students feel an emotional attachment to the adults in the school, their misbehavior is restrained. The challenge is to find interventions that are effective in changing school culture. We provided evidence to suggest that reorganizing secondary schools so that the typical teacher interacts with fewer students may help to create school environments that limit problem behaviors. We reviewed research on efforts to change the way secondary students are organized for instruction, creating smaller groups of students who stay together for an extended period during the school day and who are taught by a small group of teachers. The research on these efforts suggested that such reorganization efforts might be effective for increasing youths' sense of connection with school, which serves to hold criminal behavior in check. These interventions should be put to more rigorous tests to document their effects on crime. Mentoring programs can also be expected to reduce crime by creating connections with adults, but more work is needed to test the full potential of more potent models of school-based mentoring than have been tested to date.

School discipline management policies and practices are important determinants of school crime. The studies we reviewed consistently showed that in schools in which students report that the school rules are clearly stated, are fair, and are consistently enforced and in schools in which students have participated in establishing mechanisms for reducing misbehavior, students are less likely to engage in problem behaviors. Altering school discipline management to incorporate behavioral principles, clarify expectations for behavior, and consistently enforce rules reduces problem behavior. We discussed popular "get-tough" approaches to school discipline, including zero-tolerance policies and the use of law enforcement officers in schools. Although the effects of these policies on crime are not known, we argued that they might actually increase crime outside of school. There is a clear need for rigorous research on the effects of these policies.

Finally, we noted that evidence does not support the conclusion that smaller schools are more effective for limiting problem behaviors than larger schools, but it does suggest that conditions that make a school environment "feel" smaller and more communally organized are related to levels of problem behavior.

The findings from the review of existing research dovetail nicely with our earlier discussion of the mechanisms involved in the production of crime and the features of schools that might influence these mechanisms. We noted that decisions that influence the demographic composition of schools are important because they determine the prevailing cultural beliefs in the school as well as the pool of youths from whom friends can be selected. We noted that policies and procedures governing discipline management are important because they influence the extent to which formal sanctions are applied and the effectiveness of these sanctions. And we noted that the school social organization is important because it influences the level of social control to which students in the school are exposed.

Recommendations.   Given the limitations of the evidence base, we are more confident in making recommendations about research priorities than about effective policy. Indeed, this field is burdened by a lack of timely policy research and a tendency to launch major initiatives without first (or ever!) doing a high-quality evaluation. Note in this regard the various get-tough policies that have been encouraged by the federal government and adopted nationwide since the 1990s, the School-Wide Positive Behavior Support package that has been adopted by 5,500 schools, or the nationwide shift beginning in the 1970s toward a middle school grade configuration that included sixth graders. To the contrary, a model approach is the series of experiments being conducted by Roland Fryer on providing cash incentives to students to come to class, do the school work, and stay out of trouble. Presumably the outcomes of these experiments will affect the decision to adopt.

To begin the research agenda one must take a close look at the quality of the data in current use. Scholars, school officials, and policy advocates all make use of the various data sources on school crime—the crime survey data from the NCVS and from the CDC's YRBSS, the principals' reports to the U.S. Department of Education, and the detailed database on crimes known to the police (NIBRS). To an extent the resulting statistics on school crime can be compared across sources, and the results are rather distressing. We found order of magnitude differences in violent crime rates from the NCVS and the YRBSS, for example; even more important, perhaps, is that the NCVS reveals a dramatic reduction in crime rates since 1993, whereas the YRBSS does not show any trend during this time. Despite these problems, it is too often true that users do not investigate the quality of the data or check one source against another. It would be a useful service to all users if there were a comprehensive investigation of the differences in crime rates and patterns across these data sets, together with an investigation of the sources of disagreement. One thing that is clear is that survey results with adolescent subjects are exquisitely sensitive to where and how the questions are administered.

We have several recommendations to guide evaluation research on interventions. The first recommendation is to actually do such research, as suggested above. Given the tens of millions that are being spent on school resource officers, it seems criminal that we do not have good evidence on the effects on how infractions are dealt with, whether crime is suppressed, and more generally whether there is a positive or negative effect on attitudes of students toward school. An impediment to learning about the effects of many school reforms is that the reforms tend to be implemented in all schools in the affected jurisdiction at once. This hinders rigorous evaluation because it leaves no schools in which to measure what would happen in the absence of the reform. A smarter approach would be to randomly assign schools to different phase-in periods, allowing for comparison during the first few years of the schools that implement the reform early and those that will implement it in the future.

Second, and relatedly, when evaluations are conducted of interventions intended to improve academic performance, crime and other forms of misbehavior should be included as outcome measures. We expect that most interventions that are successful in improving academic performance will have salutary effects on behavior, but speculation needs to be documented and is not necessarily the case. Given the strong focus on pushing up academic standards, it is surely important to know what the trade-offs may be.

Third, when misbehavior is included in the list of outcomes, the list of indicators should include those that capture the most serious forms of crime. In a review of 178 studies of school-based prevention, only 18 (10 percent) measured serious violent crime, and 39 (22 percent) measured serious property crime (D. Gottfredson, Wilson, and Najaka 2002). The bulk of the studies measure effects on gateway substance use, rebelliousness, defiant behavior, and related measures but do not include specific crimes or arrests.

Fourth, we note that most of the evaluations of policies that affect the mix of students—truancy and dropout prevention, alternative schools, tracking, grade retention of failing students, and so forth—consider only the effect on the students who are targeted and fail to consider the ecological effects. The exceptions, reviewed in Sections III and IV, suggest that secondary effects on other students may be quite important and should be included when it is possible to implement a comprehensive study.

Fifth, although the Gates Foundation has stopped promoting the idea of smaller high schools, it is still important to identify programs to create more cohesive, communal, personalized environments. From what we know already, the "schools within schools" approach appears promising. At the other end of the ideological and theoretical spectrum, but also interesting, is the idea of offering immediate tangible rewards for good behavior. Old experiments with token economies worked well, and the experiments with cash payments now under way in three cities should yield useful additional information. If either the communal approach or the individual incentive approach appears successful, the challenge will be to design cost-effective programs, the next desirable line of research.

Finally, there is a missing chapter from the literature on schools and crime, which should be filled in. The literature we have reviewed is concerned with the question of how school climate affects crime. The reverse question of how crime affects school climate is also important but is almost entirely neglected by social scientists. It is plausible that crime-ridden schools are going to have difficulty in recruiting the best teachers and administrators, and students from families that have choices will go elsewhere. Any sense of community or legitimacy is going to be lost in a high-crime school where students are fearful of each other and see that the adults do not have adequate control. Documenting the strength and magnitude of such causal links is important in setting priorities for crime control and prevention in schools.

TABLE A1

Studies of School Climate and Problem Behavior, 1980–2008: School-Level Studies

Citation	# Schools	Sample Characteristics	Time Point	Measures of Problem Behavior				Measures of School Climate				
				Substance Use	Crime/ Delin- quency	Victim- ization	Other	Ecology	Milieu	Organizational Structure	Administration/ Management	Culture
Bryk and Driscoll (1988)	357	High School and Beyond: nationally representative samples of high schools	1				x	x	x			x
Chen (2008)	712	School Survey on Crime and Safety: nationally representative sample of secondary public schools	1		x			x	x		x	x
Eitle and Eitle (2004)[a]	740	Middle and high schools from 40 counties in Florida (after excluding 27 rural counties)	1	x				x	x			x
Gottfredson and Gottfredson (1985)	623	Safe School Study: nationally representative sample of 7th–12th graders in public schools	1			x		x	x	x	x	x

Study	N	Sample								
Gottfredson et al. (2005)	254	National Study of Delinquency Prevention in Schools: nationally representative sample of secondary schools	1	x	x		x	x	x	x
O'Neill and McGloin (2007)	2,270	School Survey on Crime and Safety: nationally representative sample of public schools	1	x		x	x	x	x	
Payne, Gottfredson, and Gottfredson (2003)	254	National Study of Delinquency Prevention in Schools: nationally representative sample of secondary schools	1	x		x	x	x	x	x
Roski et al. (1997)	30	Schools that reported significant substance use problem in northeastern Minnesota	1		x					x
Weishew and Peng (1993)	1,051	National Education Longitudinal Study: nationally representative sample of 8th graders	1	x	x		x	x	x	x
Welsh, Stokes, and Greene (2000)	43	Convenient sample of middle school students in Philadelphia	1	x			x		x	x

[a] This is actually a multilevel study of schools nested in counties. It is included with the school-level studies because it does not analyze student-level variability.

TABLE A2

Studies of Problem Behavior and School Climate Dimension—Ecology, 1980–2008: School-Level Studies

Citation	Indicator of School Ecology	Outcome[a]				Control Variables	School Climate Controlled	Comments
		Substance Use	Delin- quency	Victim- ization	Other			
Bryk and Driscoll (1988)	School size				+*		Milieu	Other = classroom disorder
	School selectivity				–			
	Parental cooperation (a resource)				–*			
Chen (2008)	School size		+*			Community crime rate, school urbanicity	Milieu, administration/ management, culture	
Eitle and Eitle (2004)	School organizational structure	+*				Index of dissimilarity, population density, household poverty rate, index crime rate	Milieu, culture	School organiza- tional structure = school size, class size, per-pupil expenditures
Gottfredson and Gottfredson (1985)[b]	Student/teacher ratio			0/0	–/0	Poverty and disorganization, afflu- ence and education, affluent mo- bility, rural (vs. urban) location, distance from business district, population of area, community crime, desegregation	Milieu	Other = teacher victimization
	Teaching resources			–/–	–*/–*			
	Total enrollment			0/0	+*/+			Outcome = junior/ senior high school

396

Study	School characteristic				School ecology characteristic	Construct	Other/Outcome
Gottfredson et al. (2005)	School size and urbanicity	–*	–*	0	Concentrated poverty/African American, residential crowding	Milieu, administration/management, culture	Other = teacher victimization
O'Neill and McGloin (2007)	Total number of students	+*/+*			Crime level, school location	Milieu, organizational structure	Outcome = property/violent crime
	Student/teacher ratio	+/+					
Payne, Gottfredson, and Gottfredson (2003)	School size and urbanicity	–*	–*	0	Concentrated poverty/African American, residential crowding	Milieu, culture	Other = teacher victimization
Weishew and Peng (1993)	School enrollment	+		+*	Parental involvement, time spent alone, self-perception, achievement, educational expectation, participation, % disadvantaged, urbanicity	Milieu, organizational structure, administration/management, culture	Other = misbehavior
	Student/teacher ratio	–		+			
Welsh, Stokes, and Greene (2000)	School size	–			Community poverty, community stability, community crime	Culture	

+* = statistically significant effect in positive direction (i.e., high value on school ecology characteristic is associated with more problem behavior).

+ = statistically nonsignificant effect in positive direction (i.e., high value on school ecology characteristic is associated with more problem behavior).

0 = statistically nonsignificant effect whose direction is unknown.

– = statistically nonsignificant effect in negative direction (i.e., high value on school ecology characteristic is associated with less problem behavior).

–* = statistically significant effect in negative direction (i.e., high value on school ecology characteristic is associated with less problem behavior).

[a] When more than one measure of the school climate or outcome variable is included in the study, the largest association is recorded. When different measures of the same construct result in associations with differing signs, this is noted in the "comments" section.

[b] This is actually a multilevel study of schools nested in counties. It is included with the school-level studies because it does not analyze student-level variability.

397

TABLE A3

Studies of Problem Behavior and School Climate Dimension—Milieu, 1980–2008: School-Level Studies

Citation	Indicator of School Milieu	Outcome[a]				Control Variables	School Climate Controlled	Comments
		Substance Use	Delin-quency	Victim-ization	Other			
Bryk and Driscoll (1988)	Average academic background				−*		Ecology	Other = classroom disorder
	School social class				−*			
	School minority concentration				+			
	School social class diversity				+			
	School ethnic diversity				+*			
Chen (2008)	School transience		+*			Community crime rate, school urbanicity	Ecology, administration/management, culture	School transience = number of students transferred
	Student SES		−					
Eitle and Eitle (2004)	% nonwhite	−*				Index of dissimilarity, population density, household poverty rate, index crime rate	Ecology, culture	Teacher social milieu = % master's degree, average teaching experience
	Teacher social milieu	−*						
	High school (vs. junior school)	+*						
Gottfredson and Gottfredson (1985)[b]	% student female	0/−*			0/0	Poverty and disorganization, affluence and education, affluent mobility, rural (vs. urban) location, distance from business district, population of area, community crime, desegregation	Ecology	Other = teacher victimization Outcome = junior/senior high school

398

Study	Characteristic	mean grade level / % teachers white	0/−* 0/0	+/0	Constructs measured	Comments	Other
	mean grade level	0/−*	0/0				
	% teachers white			+/0			
Gottfredson et al. (2005)	% student male	+*	+*	0	Concentrated poverty/African American, residential crowding	Ecology, administration/management, culture	Other = teacher victimization
	Grade level	−*	−*				
O'Neill and McGloin (2007)	% minority	+/+			Crime level, school location	Ecology, organizational structure	Outcome = property/violent crime
	High (vs. middle) school	+*/−					
	% male	−/−*					
	% free lunch	+/+					
Payne, Gottfredson, and Gottfredson (2003)	% student male	+*	+*	0	Concentrated poverty/African American, residential crowding	Ecology, culture	Other = teacher victimization
	Grade level	−*	−*				
Weishew and Peng (1993)	% male	−	+	+	Parental involvement, time spent alone, self-perception, achievement, educational expectation, participation, % disadvantaged, urbanicity	Ecology, organizational structure, administration/management, culture	Other = misbehavior
	Grade span	+*	−	+			
	Private (vs. public) school	−	+	−*			

+* = statistically significant effect in positive direction (i.e., high value on school milieu characteristic is associated with more problem behavior).

+ = statistically nonsignificant effect in positive direction (i.e., high value on school milieu characteristic is associated with more problem behavior).

0 = statistically nonsignificant effect whose direction is unknown.

− = statistically nonsignificant effect in negative direction (i.e., high value on school milieu characteristic is associated with less problem behavior).

−* = statistically significant effect in negative direction (i.e., high value on school milieu characteristic is associated with less problem behavior).

[a] When more than one measure of the school climate or outcome variable is included in the study, the largest association is recorded. When different measures of the same construct result in associations with differing signs, this is noted in the "comments" section.

[b] This study reported correlations of hundreds of school characteristics with two different measures of school disorder. Only selected associations are summarized here.

TABLE A4

Studies of Problem Behavior and School Climate Dimension—Organizational Structure, 1980–2008: School-Level Studies

| Citation | Indicator of School Organizational Structure | Outcome[a] | | | | Control Variables | School Climate Controlled | Comments |
		Substance Use	Delin-quency	Victim-ization	Other			
Gottfredson and Gott-fredson (1985)[b]	No. different students taught			0/+	0/+*	Poverty and disorganization, affluence and education, affluent mobility, rural (vs. urban) location, distance from business district, population of area, community crime, desegregation	Ecology, milieu, administration/management, culture	Other = teacher victimization Outcome = junior/ senior high school

O'Neill and McGloin (2007)	Classroom change	+*/+*	Crime level, school location	Ecology, milieu	Outcome = property/violent crime

+* = statistically significant effect in positive direction (i.e., high value on school organizational structure characteristic is associated with more problem behavior).

+ = statistically nonsignificant effect in positive direction (i.e., high value on school organizational structure characteristic is associated with more problem behavior).

0 = statistically nonsignificant effect whose direction is unknown.

− = statistically nonsignificant effect in negative direction (i.e., high value on school organizational structure characteristic is associated with less problem behavior).

−* = statistically significant effect in negative direction (i.e., high value on school organizational structure characteristic is associated with less problem behavior).

[a] When more than one measure of the school climate or outcome variable is included in the study, the largest association is recorded. When different measures of the same construct result in associations with differing signs, this is noted in the "comments" section.

[b] This study reported correlations of hundreds of school characteristics with two different measures of school disorder. Only selected associations are summarized here.

TABLE A5

Studies of Problem Behavior and School Climate Dimension—Administration/Management, 1980–2008: School-Level Studies

Citation	Indicator of School Administration/ Management	Outcome[a]				Control Variables	School Climate Controlled	Comments
		Substance Use	Delinq- uency	Victim- ization	Other			
Chen (2008)	Security measures		−			Community crime rate, school urbanicity	Ecology, milieu, culture	Security measures = controls to campus access, monitors stu- dent activities Serious penalties = use of punitive measures for disciplinary problems
	Serious penalties		+*					

Study	Variable			Predictors	Domains	Notes
Gottfredson and Gottfredson (1985)[b]	Teacher-administration cooperation	−/−	−/−*	Poverty and disorganization, affluence and education, affluent mobility, rural (vs. urban) location, distance from business district, population of area, community crime, desegregation	Ecology, milieu, organizational structure, culture	Other = teacher victimization; Outcome = junior/senior high
	Policy confusion	+*/0	+/0			
	Ambiguous sanction	0/0	+*/+*			
	Firm and clear enforcement	0/0	−*/−			
	Fairness and clarity of rules	−*/−*	−/−			
	Student influence	0/−	+/0			
Gottfredson et al. (2005)	Psychosocial climate	0	−*	Concentrated poverty/African American, residential crowding	Ecology, milieu, culture	Other = teacher victimization; Psychosocial climate = organizational focus, planning, administrative leadership
	Discipline management	−*	0			
Weishew and Peng (1993)	Fairness of discipline	−	−*	Parental involvement, time spent alone, self-perception, achievement, educational expectation, participation, % disadvantaged, urbanicity	Ecology, milieu, organizational structure, culture	Other = misbehavior
	Disciplined student environment	−*	−			

TABLE A5 (Continued)

Citation	Indicator of School Adminstration/ Management	Outcome[a]				Control Variables	School Climate Controlled	Comments
		Substance Use	Delinq- uency	Victim- ization	Other			
	Flexibility of school environment	−*	−		−	·		

+* = statistically significant effect in positive direction (i.e., high value on school administration/management characteristic is associated with more problem behavior).

+ = statistically nonsignificant effect in positive direction (i.e., high value on school administration/management characteristic is associated with more problem behavior).

0 = statistically nonsignificant effect whose direction is unknown.

− = statistically nonsignificant effect in negative direction (i.e., high value on school administration/management characteristic is associated with less problem behavior).

−* = statistically significant effect in negative direction (i.e., high value on school administration/management characteristic is associated with less problem behavior).

[a] When more than one measure of the school climate or outcome variable is included in the study, the largest association is recorded. When different measures of the same construct result in associations with differing signs, this is noted in the "comments" section.

[b] This study reported correlations of hundreds of school characteristics with two different measures of school disorder. Only selected associations are summarized here.

TABLE A6

Studies of Problem Behavior and School Climate Dimension— Culture, 1980–2008: School-Level Studies

Citation	Indicator of School Culture	Outcome[a]				School Climate Controlled	Control Variables	Comments
		Substance Use	Delinquency	Victimization	Other			
Bryk and Driscoll (1988)	Communal social organization				−*	Ecology, milieu		Other = classroom disorder
Chen (2008)	School misbehavior		+*			Ecology, milieu, administration/management	Community crime rate, school urbanicity	School misbehavior = frequency of bullying and disorder in the classroom
Eitle and Eitle (2004)	School culture	+*				Ecology, milieu	Index of dissimilarity, population density, household poverty rate, index crime rate	School culture = school absenteeism and dropout rate, % low school achievement
Gottfredson and Gottfredson (1985)[b]	Delinquent youth culture			+/0	+/0	Ecology, milieu, organizational structure, administration/management	Poverty and disorganization, affluence and education, affluent mobility, rural (vs. urban) location, distance from business district, population of area, community crime, desegregation	Other = teacher victimization; Outcome = junior/senior high school
	Belief in conventional rules			+/+	−/−*			
Gottfredson et al. (2005)	Psychosocial climate		0	0	−*	Ecology, milieu, administration/management,	Concentrated poverty/African American, residential crowding	Other = teacher victimization; Psychosocial climate = teacher morale
Payne, Gottfredson, and Gottfredson (2003)	Communal school organization		−*	0	−*	Ecology, milieu	Concentrated poverty/African American, residential crowding	Other = teacher victimization
	Student bonding		−*	−*	0			

405

TABLE A6 (Continued)

Citation	Indicator of School Culture	Outcome[a] Substance Use	Outcome[a] Delinquency	Outcome[a] Victimization	Outcome[a] Other	School Climate Controlled	Control Variables	Comments
Roski et al. (1997)	School norms	−*					Opportunities for alcohol and drug nonuse, community population, community % white, community average family income, community annual average unemployment	Substance use is measured by four different levels of alcohol and marijuana use and only preponderant outcome is coded here. School role model = prevalence/perceived non-use of tobacco and drug by peers and adults
	School role models	−*						
Weishew and Peng (1993)	School climate	−	−		−*	Ecology, milieu, organizational structure, administration/management,	Parental involvement, time spent alone, self-perception, achievement, educational expectation, participation, % disadvantaged, urbanicity	Other = misbehavior. School climate = composite of teacher-administrator relation, priority students place on learning, teacher morale, teachers' attitudes about students, teacher response to individual needs. "Substance abuse problem" was not entered for predicting "substance use"
	Student perception of school	+	−		−*			
	Student perception of teacher	−	+		+			
	Substance abuse problem	0	+*		+*			
Welsh, Stokes, and Greene (2000)	School stability		−*			Ecology	Community poverty, community stability, community crime	School stability = average student attendance and % student turnover

+* = statistically significant effect in positive direction (i.e., high value on school culture characteristic is associated with more problem behavior).
+ = statistically nonsignificant effect in positive direction (i.e., high value on school culture characteristic is associated with more problem behavior).
0 = statistically nonsignificant effect whose direction is unknown.
− = statistically nonsignificant effect in negative direction (i.e., high value on school culture characteristic is associated with less problem behavior).
−* = statistically significant effect in negative direction (i.e., high value on school culture characteristic is associated with less problem behavior).

[a] When more than one measure of the school climate or outcome variable is included in the study, the largest association is recorded. When different measures of the same construct result in associations with differing signs, this is noted in the "comments" section.

[b] This study reported correlations of hundreds of school characteristics with two different measures of school disorder. Only selected associations are summarized here.

TABLE A7

Studies of School Climate and Problem Behavior, 1980–2008: Multilevel Studies

Citation	No. Schools/Individuals	Sample Characteristics	Time Point	Substance Use	Crime/Delinquency	Victimization	Other	Ecology	Milieu	Organizational Structure	Administration/Management	Culture
				Measures of Problem Behavior				Measures of School Climate				
Birnbaum et al. (2003)	16/2,941	Convenient sample of middle schools in Minneapolis	2 (6 mos.)				x		x			
Bisset, Markham, and Aveyard (2007)	166/257,801	7th, 9th, 11th graders from 15 West Midlands district in U.K.	1	x								x
Boardman et al. (2008)	84/1,198	National Longitudinal Study of Adolescent Health: nationally representative sample of 7th–12th graders	1	x					x		x	x
Felson et al. (1994)	87/2,213	Youth in Transition: nationally representative sample of high school boys	2 (18 mos.)		x		x	x	x			x
Gottfredson and DiPietro (forthcoming)	253/13,597	National Study of Delinquency Prevention in Schools: nationally representative sample of secondary schools	1			x		x	x	x	x	x
Henry and Slater (2007)	32/4,216	Students in 16 communities across U.S. who participated in prevention trial	1	x				x	x			x
Hoffmann and Dufur (2008)	883/11,477 (NELS) 142/7,991 (Add Health)	NELS: nationally representative sample of 10th graders Add Health: nationally representative sample of 9th–12th graders	1				x	x	x			x

TABLE A7 (*Continued*)

Citation	No. Schools/ Individuals	Sample Characteristics	Time Point	Measures of Problem Behavior				Measures of School Climate				
				Substance Use	Crime/ Delin- quency	Victim- ization	Other	Ecology	Milieu	Organizational Structure	Administration/ Management	Culture
Hoffmann and Ireland (2004)	883/12,420	NELS: nationally representative sample of 10th and 12th graders	2 (2 yrs.)		x							x
Johnson and Hoffmann (2000)	1,012/16,454 (8th graders) 1,397/13,840 (10th graders)	NELS: nationally representative sample of 8th and 10th graders	2 (2 yrs.)	x				x	x			x
Khoury-Kassabri, Astor, and Benbenishty (2007)	162/10,400	Nationally (Israel) representative sample of 7th–11th graders	1		x			x	x			
Khoury-Kassabri, Benbenishty, and Astor (2005)	162/10,400	Nationally (Israel) representative sample of 7th–11th graders	1			x		x	x		x	x
Khoury-Kassabri et al. (2004)	162/10,400	Nationally (Israel) representative sample of 7th–11th graders	1			x		x	x		x	x
Kumar et al. (2002)	150/16,051 (8th graders) 140/13,251 (10th graders) 142/8,797 (12th graders)	Monitoring the Future: nationally representative sample of 8th, 10th, and 12th graders	1	x				x	x			x
Kumar, O'Malley, and Johnston (2008)	244/27,462 (8th graders) 211/21,920 (10th graders) 200/21,510 (12th graders)	Monitoring the Future: nationally representative sample of 8th, 10th, and 12th graders	1	x				x	x			
Ma (2002)	148/6,883 (6th graders) 92/6,868 (8th graders)	New Brunswick School Climate Study: all 6th and 8th graders in Brunswick, Canada	1			x	x	x	x		x	x
Novak and Clayton (2001)	38/25,368	Annual cross-sectional survey of middle and high schools in Kentucky	1	x					x		x	

Study	Sample	Description										
Payne (2008)	253/13,597	National Study of Delinquency Prevention in Schools: nationally representative sample of secondary schools	1		x			x	x		x	x
Pokorny, Jason, and Schoeny (2004)	14/5399	Representative sample of 6th–8th graders in northern and central Illinois	1	x					x			x
Reis, Trockel, and Mulhall (2007)	198/111,662	Statewide middle school students with diverse background in Illinois	1			x				x		x
Stewart (2003)	528/10,578	NELS: nationally representative sample of 10th graders	1			x	x	x	x		x	x
Welsh (2000)	11/4,640	Middle schools in Philadelphia	1		x	x			x			x
Welsh (2001)	11/4,640	Middle schools in Philadelphia	1		x	x			x			x
Welsh (2003)	11/5,203	Middle schools in Philadelphia	1		x		x			x		x
Welsh, Greene, and Jenkins (1999)	11/7583	Middle schools in Philadelphia	1			x	x			x		x
Wilcox and Clayton (2001)	21/6,169	Kentucky Youth Survey: census-based survey of 6th–12th graders in Kentucky	1	x				x				x

TABLE A8

Studies of Problem Behavior and School Climate Dimension—Ecology, 1980–2008: Multilevel Studies

Citation	Indicator of School Ecology	Outcome[a] Substance Use	Delinquency	Victimization	Other	Control Variables[b]	School Climate Controlled	Comments
Felson et al. (1994)	School size	—	—		—	1. Approval of aggression, academic values, SES, race, family stability, residential stability 2. Urbanicity	Milieu, culture	Other = violence, less serious delinquency
Gottfredson and Di-Pietro (forthcoming)	Student enrollment			−/−*		1. Gender, age, overage for grade, ethnic minority, bonding 2. Community disadvantage, urbanicity	Milieu, organizational structure, administration/management	Outcome = personal/property victimization
	Student/teacher ratio			+*/+				
Henry and Slater (2007)	No. students in the grade	—				1. Sex, age, race, school attachment	Milieu, culture	
Hoffmann and Dufur (2008)	School size				−/+	1. Family structure, parental attachment/ supervision/involvement, academic values/achievement, male, family SES, grade level, race/ethnicity, family moves, student work hours, peer drop out 2. Urbanicity	Milieu, culture	Other = composite of drug and alcohol use, arrested, fighting, suspension from school, and running away from house Outcome = NELS/Add Health sample
Johnson and Hoffmann (2000)	School size	+/+				1. Gender, race, college plans, works 10+ hours a week, GPA, self-esteem, school misconduct, positive school attitude, school dropout, negative peer association, two parents, parental support, parents' education, family income 2. Western region, urban place	Milieu, culture	Outcome = 8th graders/10th graders
	Students per teacher	−/−						

410

Study	Variable	Effect	Controls	Category	Measurement
Khoury-Kassabri, Astor, and Benbenishty (2007)	School size	—	1. Gender, grade level, victimization, fear to attend school, perceived safety, teacher support, school policy, student participation	Milieu	
	Class size	—			
Khoury-Kassabri, Benbenishty, and Astor (2005)	School size	—	1. Gender 2. % unemployment, % working part-time job, % high income, % low income, % low education, % high education, house overcrowding	Milieu, administration/management, culture	For both studies, victimization is measured five different types (serious physical, threats, moderate physical, verbal-social, and property damage) and preponderant outcome is coded here
	Class size	+*			
Khoury-Kassabri et al. (2004)	School size	+	1. Gender, grade, perceived school climate 2. % unemployment, overall crimes, low income, low education	Milieu, administration/management, culture	
	Class size	+*			
Kumar et al. (2002)	School size	−/−/+	1. No. parents, parental education, race, gender, student disapproval of substance use 2. Urbanicity	Milieu, culture	Substance use is measured three different types (cigarettes, heavy drinking, marijuana) and preponderant outcome is coded here. Outcome = 8th/10th/12th graders
Kumar, O'Malley, and Johnston (2008)	Attractive physical environment	−/+*/−*	1. Gender, race/ethnicity, parental education, no. parents 2. Neighborhood drug and alcohol problem, urbanicity	Milieu	Substance use is measured six different types of cigarettes, alcohol, drug use; only preponderant outcome is coded here. Outcome = 8th/10th/12th graders
	Negative physical environment	0			
	No. unobserved areas	0/+*/+*			
	School size	0			

411

TABLE A8 (*Continued*)

Citation	Indicator of School Ecology	Outcome[a] Substance Use	Delinquency	Victimization	Other	Control Variables[b]	School Climate Controlled	Comments
Ma (2002)	School size			0/-	-*/-	1. Gender, SES, no. parents, no. siblings, academic/affective/physical condition 2. Parental involvement	Milieu	Other = bullying Outcome = 6th graders/8th graders
Payne (2008)	Student enrollment		-			1. Gender, age, race 2. Urbanicity, poverty and disorganization	Milieu, organizational structure	
Stewart (2003)	School size				+*	1. School attachment/commitment/belief/ involvement, positive peers, parental school involvement, GPA, family structure, family income, gender, ethnicity 2. Urbanicity	Milieu, culture	Other = misbehavior
Welsh (2003)	School size		+		+	1. Age, race, sex, school effort, school reward, positive peer associations, involvement, belief in rules	Administration/management, culture	Other = misconduct
Welsh, Greene, and Jenkins (1999)	School enrollment				+	1. School effort, school reward, positive peer association, school involvement/ belief, age, race, sex 2. Community poverty, community stability	Culture	Other = misconduct

+* = statistically significant effect in positive direction (i.e., high value on school ecology characteristic is associated with more problem behavior).
+ = statistically nonsignificant effect in positive direction (i.e., high value on school ecology characteristic is associated with more problem behavior).
0 = statistically nonsignificant effect whose direction is unknown.
− = statistically significant effect in negative direction (i.e., high value on school ecology characteristic is associated with less problem behavior).
−* = statistically significant effect in negative direction (i.e., high value on school ecology characteristic is associated with less problem behavior).
[a] When more than one measure of the school climate or outcome variable is included in the study, the largest association is recorded. When different measures of the same construct result in associations with differing signs, this is noted in the "comments" section.
[b] 1 = individual level; 2 = school or community level.

412

TABLE A9

Studies of Problem Behavior and School Climate Dimension—Milieu, 1980–2008: Multilevel Studies

Citation	Indicator of School Milieu	Outcome[a]				Control Variables	School Climate Controlled	Comments
		Substance Use	Delin- quency	Victim- ization	Other			
Birnbaum et al. (2003)	School Functioning Index				−*	1. Sex, race, family structure, free lunch, past 30 days use of alcohol/ marijuana/inhalants, age		Other = violent behavior School Functioning Index = average attendance, student mobility, % staffs less than 3 years, % staffs left midyear, % students passed basic standards reading test, % free lunch, % limited English proficiency
Boardman et al. (2008)	% non-Hispanic and white	−*				1. Gender, age, race/ethnicity, friends/parents are smokers, % friends in common, sibling smoking status, genetic similarity, evidence of heritability 2. % college-educated mothers	Administration/man- agement, culture	Substance use is measured by herita- bility of daily smoking
Felson et al. (1994)	% black		+		+*	1. Approval of aggression, academic values, SES, race, family stability, residential stability 2. Urbanicity	Ecology, culture	Other = violence, less serious delinquency
	Family stability		−		−			
	Residential stability		+		+			
	SES		−		−*			

413

TABLE A9 (*Continued*)

Citation	Indicator of School Milieu	Outcome[a]				Control Variables	School Climate Controlled	Comments
		Substance Use	Delin- quency	Victim- ization	Other			
Gottfredson and DiPietro (forthcoming)	% African American			0/0		1. Gender, age, over age for grade, ethnic minority, bonding 2. Community disadvantage, urbanicity	Ecology, organizational structure, administration/management	Outcome = personal/property victimization
	% Hispanic			0/+				
	% Asian			0/−*				
	Average age			−/−				
	% male			−/+				
Henry and Slater (2007)	% minority	−				1. Sex, age, race, school attachment	Ecology, culture	
	% free lunch	+						
	Average age	−						
Hoffmann and Dufur (2008)	% free lunch				−/0	1. Family structure, parental attachment/supervision/involvement, academic values/achievement, male, family SES, grade level, race/ethnicity, family moves, student work hours, peer drop out 2. Urbanicity	Ecology, culture	Other = composite of drug and alcohol use, arrested, fighting, suspension from school, running away from house Outcome = NELS/Add Health sample
	% minority				−/+*			
	Private school				+/−			
Johnson and Hoffmann (2000)	Catholic school	+*/+				1. Gender, race, college plans, works 10+ hours a week, GPA, self-esteem, school misconduct, positive school attitude, school dropout, negative peer association, two parents, parental support, parents' education, family income 2. Western region, urban place	Ecology, culture	Outcome = 8th graders/10th graders
	% minority	+/+						

414

Study	Variable	Effect	Controls/Other predictors	Theoretical framework	Notes
Khoury-Kassabri, Astor, and Benbenishty (2007)	Social Deprivation Index	+*	1. Gender, grade level, victimization, fear to attend school, perceived safety, teacher support, school policy, student participation	Ecology	
	Arab (vs. Jewish) school	+*			
	High (vs. junior) school	+			
Khoury-Kassabri, Benbenishty, and Astor (2005)	Family poverty	+*	1. Gender 2. % unemployment, % working part-time job, % high income, % low income, % low education, % high education, house overcrowding	Ecology; administration/management, culture	For both studies, victimization is measured five different types (serious physical, threats, moderate physical, verbal-social, and property damage) and preponderant outcome is coded here
	Family low education	+			
	Large families	+*			
	Social Deprivation Index	+*			
	High (vs. junior) school	–*			
Khoury-Kassabri et al. (2004)	Family poverty	+*	1. Gender, grade, perceived school climate 2. % unemployment, overall crimes, low income, low education	Ecology; administration/management, culture	
	Family low education	+*			
	Large families	+*			
	Social Deprivation Index	+*			
	% male	+*			
Kumar et al. (2002)	No. parents	–/–/–	1. No. parents, parents' education, race, gender, student disapproval of substance use 2. Urbanicity	Ecology, culture	Substance use is measured three different types (cigarettes, heavy drinking, marijuana) and preponderant outcome is coded here Outcome = 8th/10th/12th graders
	Parents' education	+/+/+			
	Private (vs. public) school	+*/+*/–			

TABLE A9 (Continued)

Citation	Indicator of School Milieu	Outcome[a] Substance Use	Delin-quency	Victim-ization	Other	School Climate Controlled	Control Variables	Comments
Kumar, O'Malley, and Johnston (2008)	No. parents	0				Ecology	1. Gender, race/ethnicity, parents' education, no. parents, 2. Neighborhood drug and alcohol problem, urbanicity	Substance use is measured by six different types of cigarettes, alcohol, drug use; only preponderant outcome is coded here Outcome = 8th/10th/12th graders
	Parents' education	0						
	School type (public vs. private)	0						
	% white, % black, % Hispanic	0						
Ma (2002)	School mean SES		−/+	+/+		Ecology	1. Gender, SES, no. parents, no. siblings, academic/affective/physical condition 2. Parental involvement	Other = bullying Outcome = 6th graders/8th graders
Novak and Clayton (2001)	School mean SES	+*				Administration/ management	1. Self-regulation, gender, age, race, SES	Substance use is measured by four different types of transitions between stages of smoking and only preponderant outcome is coded here
	Racial heterogeneity	−						
	High (vs. middle) school	+*						
Payne (2008)	% black (student)				−*	Ecology, organizational structure	1. Gender, age, race 2. urbanicity, poverty and disorganization	
	% black (teacher)	0						
	% male	+						
	Grade level	+*						

Study	Characteristic	Sign	Controls	Comments
Pokorny, Jason, and Schoeny (2004)	Mean age	0	1. Grade, race, age, race, sex, parents' education, attitude about tobacco possession law, prevalence of adult/peer tobacco users 2. Mean attitudes toward tobacco possession law, % adult tobacco users	Culture
	% white, black, and Latino	0		
	% male	0		
	Parents' education	0		
Stewart (2003)	% nonwhite	+	1. School attachment/commitment/belief/involvement, positive peers, parental school involvement, GPA, family structure, family income, gender, ethnicity 2. urbanicity	Ecology, culture Other = misbehavior
	% free lunch	+		
Wilcox and Clayton (2001)	% nonwhite	−	1. Sex, age, race, SES, problem behavior, parental gun ownership/use, peer weapon carrying to school, family dysfunction, school attachment, religious ties, threatened at school, property stolen at school, afraid at school	Ecology, culture
	% male	−		
	% free lunch	+		
	Middle (vs. high) school	−		

+* = statistically significant effect in positive direction (i.e., high value on school milieu characteristic is associated with more problem behavior).
+ = statistically nonsignificant effect in positive direction (i.e., high value on school milieu characteristic is associated with more problem behavior).
0 = statistically nonsignificant effect whose direction is unknown.
− = statistically nonsignificant effect in negative direction (i.e., high value on school milieu characteristic is associated with less problem behavior).
−* = statistically significant effect in negative direction (i.e., high value on school milieu characteristic is associated with less problem behavior).
[a] When more than one measure of the school climate or outcome variable is included in the study, the largest association is recorded. When different measures of the same construct result in associations with differing signs, this is noted in the "comments" section.

TABLE A10

Studies of Problem Behavior and School Climate Dimension—Organizational Structure, 1980–2008: Multilevel Studies

| Citation | Indicator of School Organizational Structure | Outcome[a] | | | | Control Variables | School Climate Controlled | Comments |
		Substance Use	Delin-quency	Victim-ization	Other			
Payne (2008)	No. different students taught		–			1. Gender, age, race 2. Urbanicity, poverty and disorganization	Ecology, milieu	
Gottfredson and DiPietro (forthcoming)	No. different students taught			0/+*		1. Gender, age, over age for grade, ethnic minority, bonding 2. Community disadvantage, urbanicity	Ecology, milieu, adminis-tration/management	Outcome = personal/prop-erty victimization

+* = statistically significant effect in positive direction (i.e., high value on school organizational structure characteristic is associated with more problem behavior).
+ = statistically nonsignificant effect in positive direction (i.e., high value on school organizational structure characteristic is associated with more problem behavior).
0 = statistically nonsignificant effect whose direction is unknown.
– = statistically nonsignificant effect in negative direction (i.e., high value on school organizational structure characteristic is associated with less problem behavior).
–* = statistically significant effect in negative direction (i.e., high value on school organizational structure characteristic is associated with less problem behavior).
[a] When more than one measure of the school climate or outcome variable is included in the study, the largest association is recorded. When different measures of the same construct result in associations with differing signs, this is noted in the "comments" section.

TABLE A11

Studies of Problem Behavior and School Climate Dimension—Administration/Management, 1980–2008: Multilevel Studies

Citation	Indicator of School Administration/ Management	Outcome[a] Substance Use	Delin-quency	Victim-ization	Other	Control Variables	School Climate Controlled	Comments
Boardman et al. (2008)	School smoking policy	–				1. Gender, age, race/ethnicity, friends/parents are smokers, % friends in common, sibling smoking status, genetic similarity, evidence of heritability 2. % college-educated mothers	Milieu, culture	School smoking policy = no. disciplinary responses per smoking on school grounds Substance use is measured by heritability of daily smoking
Gottfredson and DiPietro (forthcoming)	School discipline practices			–*/–		1. Gender, age, over age for grade, ethnic minority, bonding 2. community disadvantage, urbanicity	Ecology, milieu, organizational structure	Outcome = personal/property victimization
Khoury-Kassabri, Benbenishty, and Astor (2005)	School policy			–*		1. Gender 2. % unemployment, % working part-time job, % high income, % low income, % low education, % high education, house overcrowding	Ecology, milieu, culture	School policy = students' judgments concerning school policies or procedures to reduce violence Student participation = students' role in addressing school violence issues
	Student participation			–*				
Khoury-Kassabri et al. (2004)	School policy			–*		1. Gender, grade, perceived school climate 2. % unemployment, overall crimes, low income, low education	Ecology, milieu, culture	For both studies, victimization is measured five different types (serious physical, threats, moderate physical, verbal-social, and property damage) and preponderant outcome is coded here
	Student participation			–*				

TABLE A11 (*Continued*)

Citation	Indicator of School Administration/ Management	Outcome[a] Substance Use	Delin-quency	Victim-ization	Other	Control Variables	School Climate Controlled	Comments
Ma (2002)	Discipline climate			−/−*	−/−*	1. Gender, SES, no. parents, no. siblings, academic/affective/physical condition 2. Parental involvement	Ecology, milieu, culture	Other = bullying Outcome = 6th graders/8th graders Discipline climate = the extent to which students internalize the rules, norms, and values of the school, and conform to them
Novak and Clayton (2001)	Involvement	−*				1. Self-regulation, gender, age, race, SES	Milieu	Substance use is measured by four different types of transitions between stages of smoking and only preponderant outcome is coded here Involvement = student involvement in school management Discipline = the degree to which discipline was present in the school
	Discipline	−*						
Reis, Trockel, and Mulhall (2007)	Clear and consistent discipline				0	1. Teacher support, problem-solving skills, problem-coping strategy, friend support, family support, quality of school life, hassle at school, rejection from peer hassles, race, ethnicity, free lunch, male, grade, no. parents, parents' education, religious participation	Culture	Other = aggression
	Student inclusion in policy/ rule process				−*			

420

Study	Management characteristic			Control variables	Theoretical framework	Comments
Welsh (2000)	Planning and action	+	−	1. Age, race, sex, school involvement, positive peer association, belief in school rules, school effort, school rewards	Culture	Other = misconduct Planning and action = the degree to which the school undertakes efforts to plan and implement school improvement
	Fairness of rules	−*	−*			
	Clarity of rules	−*	+			
	Student influence	−*	+			
Welsh (2001)	Planning and action	+	−	1. Age, race, sex, school involvement, positive peer association, belief in school rules, school effort, school rewards 2. Poverty rate	Culture	Student influence = the degree to which students can influence school practices
	Fairness of rules	−*	−*			
	Clarity of rules	−*	+			
	Student influence	−*	+			
Welsh (2003)	Planning and action	+	+	1. Age, race, sex, school effort, school reward, positive peer associations, involvement, belief in rules	Ecology; culture	Other = misconduct
	Fairness of rules	−	−			
	Clarity of rules	+	−			
	Student influence	−	−			

+* = statistically significant effect in positive direction (i.e., high value on school administration/management characteristic is associated with more problem behavior).

+ = statistically nonsignificant effect in positive direction (i.e., high value on school administration/management characteristic is associated with more problem behavior).

0 = statistically nonsignificant effect whose direction is unknown.

− = statistically nonsignificant effect in negative direction (i.e., high value on school administration/management characteristic is associated with less problem behavior).

−* = statistically significant effect in negative direction (i.e., high value on school administration/management characteristic is associated with less problem behavior).

[a]When more than one measure of the school climate or outcome variable is included in the study, the largest association is recorded. When different measures of the same construct result in associations with differing signs, this is noted in the "comments" section.

421

TABLE A12

Studies of Problem Behavior and School Climate Dimension—Culture, 1980–2008: Multilevel Studies

Citation	Indicator of School Culture	Outcome[a]				Control Variables	School Climate Controlled	Comments
		Substance Use	Delin-quency	Victim-ization	Other			
Bisset, Markham, and Ave-yard (2007)	Value-added education	–*				1. Gender, grade, ethnicity, housing tenure, free lunch, drinking with parents 2. Neighborhood deprivation		Value-added education = school support/control
Boardman et al. (2008)	Smoking norms	+*				1. Gender, age, race/ethnicity, friends/parents are smokers, % friends in common, sibling smoking status, genetic similarity, evidence of heritability 2. % college-educated mothers	Milieu, administration/management	Smoking norms = popular students are also smokers Substance use is measured by herita-bility of daily smoking
	Smoking prevalence	–						
Felson et al. (1994)	Subculture of violence		+*		+*	1. Approval of aggression, academic val-ues, SES, race, family stability, residen-tial stability 2. Urbanicity	Ecology, milieu	Other = violence, less serious delinquency
	Academic values		+*		+*			
Gottfredson and DiPietro (forthcoming)	Bonding			–*/+		1. Gender, age, over age for grade, ethnic minority, bonding 2. Community disadvantage, urbanicity	Ecology, milieu, organiza-tional structure, adminis-tration/management	Outcome = personal/property victimization
Henry and Slater (2007)	School attachment	–*				1. Sex, age, race, school attachment	Ecology, milieu	

422

Study	Variable	Sign	Predictors	Theory	Notes
Hoffmann and Dufur (2008)	School quality	−*/−*	1. Family structure, parental attachment/supervision/involvement, academic values/achievement, male, family SES, grade level, race/ethnicity, family moves, student work hours, peer dropout 2. Urbanicity	Ecology, milieu	Other = composite of drug and alcohol use, arrested, fighting, suspension from school, running away from house Outcome = NELS/Add Health sample School quality = support from school administrators and faculty
	Academic emphasis	+*/+			
	School safety	−/−*			
Hoffmann and Ireland (2004)	School quality	−*	1. Self-concept, stressful life events change score, strain, two bio-parents, race/ethnicity 2. Rural/suburban/urban school		School quality = support from school administrators and faculty School problem = the extent to which school has problems with crime, violence, etc.
	Aggregate delinquency	+			
	School problem	+			
	Delinquent values	+*			
Johnson and Hoffmann (2000)	Competitive climate	+*/+*	1. Gender, race, college plans, works 10+ hours a week, GPA, self-esteem, school misconduct, positive school attitude, school dropout, negative peer association, two parents, parental support, parents' education, family income 2. Western region, urban place	Ecology, milieu	Outcome = 8th graders/10th graders
Khoury-Kassabri, Benbenishty, and Astor (2005)	Teachers' support	−*	1. Gender 2. % unemployment, % working part-time job, % high income, % low income, % low education, % high education, house overcrowding	Ecology, milieu, administration/management	For both studies, victimization is measured five different types (serious physical, threats, moderate physical, verbal-social, and property damage) and preponderant outcome is coded here

TABLE A12 (Continued)

Citation	Indicator of School Culture	Outcome[a] Substance Use	Delinquency	Victimization	Other	Control Variables	School Climate Controlled	Comments
Khoury-Kassabri et al. (2004)	Teachers' support			−*		1. Gender, grade, perceived school climate 2. % unemployment, overall crimes, low income, low education	Ecology, milieu, administration/management	
Kumar et al. (2002)	Disapproval of substance use	−*/−*/−*				1. No. parents, parents' education, race, gender, student disapproval of substance use 2. Urbanicity	Ecology, milieu	Substance use is measured three different types (cigarettes, heavy drinking, marijuana) and preponderant outcome is coded here; Outcome = 8th/10th/12th graders
Ma (2002)	Academic press		+/+		−/−*	1. Gender, SES, no. parents, no. siblings, academic/affective/physical condition 2. Parental involvement	Ecology, milieu, administration/management	Other = bullying; Outcome = 6th graders/8th graders
Payne (2008)	Supportive/collaborative relation Common norms and goals		−* −*			1. Gender, age, race 2. Urbanicity, poverty and disorganization	Ecology, milieu, organizational structure	
Pokorny, Jason, and Schoeny (2004)	Perceived peer tobacco use	+				1. Grade, race, age, race, sex, parents' education, attitude about tobacco possession law, prevalence of adult/peer tobacco users 2. Mean attitudes toward tobacco possession law, % adult tobacco users	Milieu	

Study	Variable			Predictors / controls	Category	Notes
Reis, Trockel, and Mulhall (2007)	Teacher support		0	1. Teacher support, problem-solving skills, problem-coping strategy, friend support, family support, quality of school life, hassle at school, rejection from peer hassles, race, ethnicity, free lunch, male, grade, no. parents, parents' education, religious participation	Administration/ management	Other = aggression
	Teacher recognition		0			
	Emphasis on understanding over memorization		−*			
Stewart (2003)	School social problem		+	1. School attachment/commitment/belief/ involvement, positive peers, parental school involvement, GPA, family structure, family income, gender, ethnicity 2. Urbanicity	Ecology, milieu	Other = misbehavior School social problem = the extent to which school is experiencing a range of behavioral problems among students
	School cohesion		−			
Welsh (2000)	Respect for students	−*	−*	1. Age, race, sex, school involvement, positive peer association, belief in school rules, school effort, school rewards	Administration/ management	Other = misconduct
Welsh (2001)	Respect for students	−*	−*	1. Age, race, sex, school involvement, positive peer association, belief in school rules, school effort, school rewards 2. Poverty rate	Administration/ management	Other = misconduct
Welsh (2003)	Respect for students	+	0	1. Age, race, sex, school effort, school reward, positive peer associations, involvement, belief in rules	Ecology, administration/ management	Other = misconduct

TABLE A12 (*Continued*)

Citation	Indicator of School Culture	Outcome[a]				School Climate Controlled	Comments
		Substance Use	Delin- quency	Victim- ization	Other		
Welsh, Greene, and Jenkins (1999)	School attachment				+	Ecology	Other = misconduct
							1. School effort, school reward, positive peer association, school involvement/ belief, age, race, sex
							2. Community poverty, community stability
Wilcox and Clayton (2001)	School deficit		−			Milieu	School deficit = % afraid at school, % property victims, % threatened, problem behavior, family disruption, gun ownership, parental gun ownership, peers carrying weapon
	School capital		−				School capital = school attachment, church attendance, religious commitment

Note on control variables (Wilcox and Clayton): Sex, age, race, SES, problem behavior, parental gun ownership/use, peer weapon carrying to school, family dysfunction, school attachment, religious ties, threatened at school, property stolen at school, afraid at school.

+* = statistically significant effect in positive direction (i.e., high value on school culture characteristic is associated with more problem behavior).
+ = statistically nonsignificant effect in positive direction (i.e., high value on school culture characteristic is associated with more problem behavior).
0 = statistically nonsignificant effect whose direction is unknown.
− = statistically nonsignificant effect in negative direction (i.e., high value on school culture characteristic is associated with less problem behavior).
−* = statistically significant effect in negative direction (i.e., high value on school culture characteristic is associated with less problem behavior).
[a] When more than one measure of the school climate or outcome variable is included in the study, the largest association is recorded. When different measures of the same construct result in associations with differing signs, this is noted in the "comments" section.

426

REFERENCES

Alexander, Karl L., Doris R. Entwisle, and Carrie S. Horsey. 1997. "From First Grade Forward: Early Foundations of High School Dropout." *Sociology of Education* 70:87–107.

American Psychological Association. 1993. *Violence and Youth: Psychology's Response*. Washington, DC: American Psychological Association.

Anderson, Carolyn S. 1982. "The Search for School Climate: A Review of the Research." *Review of Educational Research* 52:368–420.

Bachman, Jerald G., Patrick M. O'Malley, and Jerome Johnston. 1978. *Youth in Transition*. Vol. 6, *Adolescence to Adulthood—Change and Stability in the Lives of Young Men*. Ann Arbor: University of Michigan, Institute for Social Research.

Bayer, Patrick J., Randi Hjalmarsson, and David E. Pozen. 2009. "Building Criminal Capital behind Bars: Peer Effects in Juvenile Corrections." *Quarterly Journal of Economics* 124:105–47.

Bazemore, Gordon, Jeanne Stinchcomb, and Leslie Leip. 2004. "Scared Smart or Bored Straight? Testing a Deterrence Logic in an Evaluation of Police-Led Truancy Intervention." *Justice Quarterly* 21:269–98.

Birnbaum, Amanda S., Leslie A. Lytle, Peter J. Hannan, David M. Murray, Cheryl L. Perry, and Jean L. Foster. 2003. "School Functioning and Violent Behavior among Young Adolescents: A Contextual Analysis." *Health Education Research: Theory and Practice* 18:389–403.

Bisset, Sherri, Wolfgang A. Markham, and Paul Aveyard. 2007. "School Culture as an Influencing Factor on Youth Substance Use." *Journal of Epidemiology and Community Health* 61:485–90.

Boardman, Jason D., Jarron M. Saint Onge, Brett C. Haberstick, David S. Timberlake, and John K. Hewitt. 2008. "Do Schools Moderate the Genetic Determinants of Smoking?" *Behavior Genetics* 38:234–46.

Brooks-Gunn, Jeanne, Greg J. Duncan, Pamela K. Klebanov, and Naomi Sealand. 1993. "Do Neighborhoods Influence Child and Adolescent Development?" *American Journal of Sociology* 99:353–95.

Bry, Brenna H. 1982. "Reducing the Incidence of Adolescent Problems through Preventive Intervention: One- and Five-Year Follow-up." *American Journal of Community Psychology* 10:265–76.

———. 2003. *Achievement Monitoring: Bry's Behavior Monitoring and Reinforcement Program*. New Brunswick, NJ: Rutgers University.

Bry, Brenna H., and F. E. George. 1979. "Evaluating and Improving Prevention Programs: A Strategy from Drug Abuse." *Evaluation and Program Planning* 2:127–36.

———. 1980. "The Preventive Effects of Early Intervention on the Attendance and Grades of Urban Adolescents." *Professional Psychology* 11:252–60.

Bryant, Alison L., John E. Schulenberg, Patrick M. O'Malley, Jerald G. Bachman, and Lloyd D. Johnston. 2003. "How Academic Achievement, Attitudes, and Behaviors Relate to the Course of Substance Use during Adolescence: A 6-Year, Multiwave National Longitudinal Study." *Journal of Research on Adolescence* 13:361–97.

Bryk, Anthony S., and Mary E. Driscoll. 1988. *The High School as Community:*

Contextual Influences and Consequences for Students and Teachers. Madison: University of Wisconsin, National Center on Effective Secondary Schools.

Carrell, Scott E., and Mark L. Hoekstra. 2008. "Externalities in the Classroom: How Children Exposed to Domestic Violence Affect Everyone's Kids." Working Paper no. 14246. Cambridge, MA: National Bureau of Economic Research, http://www.nber.org.

Catalano, Richard F., Michael W. Arthur, J. David Hawkins, Lisa Berglund, and Jeffrey J. Olson. 1998. "Comprehensive Community- and School-Based Interventions to Prevent Antisocial Behavior." In *Serious and Violent Juvenile Offenders: Risk Factors and Successful Interventions,* edited by Rolf Loeber and David P. Farrington. Thousand Oaks, CA: Sage.

Centers for Disease Control and Prevention. 2008. "Youth Risk Behavior Surveillance—United States, 2007." *Morbidity and Mortality Weekly Report Surveillance Summaries* 57, no. SS04 (June 6): 1–131.

Chen, Greg. 2008. "Communities, Students, Schools, and School Crime: A Confirmatory Study of Crime in U.S. High Schools." *Urban Education* 43: 301–18.

Cho, Hyunsan, Denise D. Hallfors, and Victoria Sánchez. 2005. "Evaluation of a High School Peer Group Intervention for At-Risk Youth." *Journal of Abnormal Child Psychology* 33:363–74.

Conduct Problems Prevention Research Group. 1999. "Initial Impact of the Fast Track Prevention Trial for Conduct Problems: The High-Risk Sample." *Journal of Consulting and Clinical Psychology* 67:631–47.

———. 2002. "Evaluation of the First Three Years of the Fast Track Prevention Trial with Children at High Risk for Adolescent Conduct Problems." *Journal of Abnormal Child Psychology* 30:319–57.

———. 2007. "The Fast Track Randomized Controlled Trial to Prevent Externalizing Psychiatric Disorders: Findings from Grades 3 to 9." *Journal of American Academy of Child and Adolescent Psychiatry* 46:1250–62.

———. 2009. "The Effects of the Fast Track Preventive Intervention on the Development of Conduct Disorder across Childhood." Unpublished manuscript. Durham, NC: Duke University.

———. Forthcoming. "Fast Track Intervention Effects on Youth Arrest and Delinquency." *Journal of Experimental Criminology.*

Cook, Philip J. 1980. "Research in Criminal Deterrence: Laying the Groundwork for the Second Decade." In *Crime and Justice: An Annual Review of Research,* vol. 2, edited by Norval Morris and Michael Tonry. Chicago: University of Chicago Press.

———. 1987. "Robbery Violence." *Journal of Criminal Law and Criminology* 70:357–76.

Cook, Philip J., and Rebecca Hutchinson. 2007. "Smoke Signals: Adolescent Smoking and School Continuation." In *Advances in Austrian Economics,* vol. 10, *The Evolution of Consumption: Theories and Practices,* edited by Marina Bianchi. Bingley, UK: Emerald.

Cook, Philip J., and Jens Ludwig. 1997. "Weighing the 'Burden of "Acting

White"': Are There Race Differences in Attitudes towards Education?" *Journal of Policy Analysis and Management* 16:256–78.

———. 1998. "The Burden of 'Acting White': Do Black Adolescents Disparage Academic Achievement?" In *The Black-White Test Score Gap*, edited by Christopher Jencks and Meredith Phillips. Washington, DC: Brookings Institution Press.

———. 2006. "Assigning Youths to Minimize Total Harm." In *Deviant Peer Influences in Programs for Youth: Problems and Solutions*, edited by Kenneth A. Dodge, Thomas J. Dishion, and Jennifer E. Lansford. New York: Guildford.

Cook, Philip J., Robert MacCoun, Clara Muschkin, and Jacob Vigdor. 2008. "The Negative Impact of Starting Middle School in Sixth Grade." *Journal of Policy Analysis and Management* 27:104–21.

Cox, Diane D. 2005. "Evidence-Based Intervention Using Home-School Collaboration." *School of Psychology Quarterly* 20:473–97.

Cullen, Julie Berry, Brian A. Jacob, and Steven Levitt. 2006. "The Effect of School Choice on Participants: Evidence from Randomized Lotteries." *Econometrica* 74:1191–30.

Deming, David. 2009. "Better Schools, Less Crime?" Unpublished manuscript. Cambridge, MA: Harvard University, http://www.people.fas.harvard.edu/~deming/papers/papers.html.

Devoe, Jill F., Katharin Peter, Phillip Kaufman, Sally A. Ruddy, Amanda K. Miller, Mike Planty, Thomas D. Snyder, and Michael R. Rand. 2003. *Indicators of School Crime and Safety: 2003*. NCES 2004-004/NCJ 201257. Washington, DC: National Center for Education Statistics, Institute of Education Sciences, U.S. Department of Education, and Bureau of Justice Statistics, Office of Justice Programs, U.S. Department of Justice.

Devoe, Jill F., Katharin Peter, Margaret Noonan, Thomas D. Snyder, and Katrina Baum. 2005. *Indicators of School Crime and Safety: 2005*. NCES 2006-001/NCJ 210697. Washington, DC: National Center for Education Statistics, Institute of Education Sciences, U.S. Department of Education, and Bureau of Justice Statistics, Office of Justice Programs, U.S. Department of Justice.

Dinkes, Rachel, Emily Forrest Cataldi, and Wendy Lin-Kelly. 2007. *Indicators of School Crime and Safety: 2007*. NCES 2008-021/NCJ 219553. Washington, DC: National Center for Education Statistics, Institute of Education Sciences, U.S. Department of Education, and Bureau of Justice Statistics, Office of Justice Programs, U.S. Department of Justice, http://nces.ed.gov/programs/crimeindicators/crimeindicators2007/ind_05.asp.

Dinkes, Rachel, Jana Kemp, and Katrina Baum. 2009. *Indicators of School Crime and Safety: 2008*. NCES 2009-022/NCJ 226343. Washington, DC: National Center for Education Statistics, Institute of Education Sciences, U.S. Department of Education, and Bureau of Justice Statistics, Office of Justice Programs, U.S. Department of Justice.

Dishion, Thomas J., and Kenneth A. Dodge. 2006. "Deviant Peer Contagion in Interventions and Programs: An Ecological Framework for Understanding Influence Mechanisms." In *Deviant Peer Influences in Programs for Youth:*

Problems and Solutions, edited by Kenneth A. Dodge, Thomas J. Dishion, and Jennifer E. Lansford. New York: Guilford.

Dodge, Kenneth A., John E. Bates, and Gregory S. Pettit. 1990. "Mechanisms in the Cycle of Violence." *Science* 250:1678–83.

Dolan, Lawrence J., Sheppard G. Kellam, C. Hendricks Brown, Lisa Werthamer-Larsson, George W. Rebok, Lawrence S. Mayer, Jolene Laudolff, Jaylan S. Turkkan, Carla Ford, and Leonard Wheeler. 1993. "The Short-Term Impact of Two Classroom-Based Preventive Interventions on Aggressive and Shy Behaviors and Poor Achievement." *Journal of Applied Developmental Psychology* 14:317–45.

Dryfoos, Joy G. 1990. *Adolescents at Risk: Prevalence and Prevention.* New York: Oxford University Press.

Durlak, Joseph A. 1995. *School-Based Prevention Programs for Children and Adolescents.* Thousand Oaks, CA: Sage.

Dynarski, Mark, Philip Gleason, Anu Rangarajan, and Robert Wood. 1998. "Impacts of Dropout Prevention Programs: Final Report. A Research from the School Dropout Demonstration Assistance Program Evaluation (New Jersey Study)." Princeton, NJ: Mathematica Policy Research.

Eby, Lillian T., Tammy D. Allen, Sarah C. Evans, Thomas Ng, and David L. DuBois. 2007. "Does Mentoring Matter? A Multidisciplinary Meta-analysis Comparing Mentored and Non-mentored Individuals." *Journal of Vocational Behavior* 72:254–67.

Eitle, David J., and Tamela M. Eitle. 2004. "School and County Characteristics as Predictors of School Rates of Drug, Alcohol, and Tobacco Offenses." *Journal of Health and Social Behavior* 45:408–21.

Entwisle, Doris R., Karl L. Alexander, and Linda S. Olson. 1997. *Children, Schools, and Inequality.* Boulder, CO: Westview.

Farrington, David P., Bernard Gallagher, Lynda Morley, Raymond J. St. Ledger, and Donald J. West. 1986. "Unemployment, School Leaving, and Crime." *British Journal of Criminology* 26:335–56.

Farrington, David P., and Maria M. Ttofi. 2009. "Reducing School Bullying: Evidence-Based Implications for Policy." In *Crime and Justice: A Review of Research*, vol. 38, edited by Michael Tonry. Chicago: University of Chicago Press.

Felner, Robert D., and Angela M. Adan. 1988. "The School Transitional Environment Project: An Ecological Intervention and Evaluation." In *14 Ounces of Prevention: A Casebook for Practitioners*, edited by R. H. Price, E. L. Cowen, R. P. Lorion, and J. Ramos-McKay. Washington, DC: American Psychological Association.

Felson, Richard B., Allen E. Liska, Scott J. South, and Thomas L. McNulty. 1994. "The Subculture of Violence and Delinquency: Individual vs. School Context Effects." *Social Forces* 73:155–73.

Felson, Richard B., and Jeremy Staff. 2006. "Explaining the Academic Performance–Delinquency Relationship." *Criminology* 44:299–319.

Finn, Jeremy D., Susan B. Gerber, and Jayne Boyd-Zaharias. 2005. "Small

Classes in the Early Grades, Academic Achievement, and Graduating from High School." *Journal of Educational Psychology* 97:214–23.

Finn, Jeremy D., Gina M. Pannozzo, and Charles M. Achilles. 2003. "The 'Why's' of Class Size: Student Behavior in Small Classes." *Review of Educational Research* 73:321–68.

Firestone, William A., and Sheila Rosenblum. 1988. "Building Commitment in Urban High Schools." *Educational Evaluation and Policy Analysis* 10: 285–99.

Flay, Brian R., Anthony Biglan, Robert F. Boruch, Felipe G. Castro, Denise C. Gottfredson, Sheppard G. Kellam, Eve K. Mościcki, Steven Schinke, Jeffrey C. Valentine, and Peter Ji. 2005. "Standards of Evidence: Criteria for Efficacy, Effectiveness and Dissemination." *Prevention Science* 6:151–76.

Fordham, Signithia, and John U. Ogbu. 1986. "Black Students' School Success: Coping with the 'Burden of Acting White.'" *Urban Review* 18:176–206.

Foshee, Vangie A., Karl E. Bauman, Ximena B. Arriaga, Russell W. Helms, Gary G. Koch, and George F. Linder. 1998. "An Evaluation of Safe Dates, an Adolescent Dating Violence Prevention Program." *American Journal of Public Health* 88:45–50.

Foshee, Vangie A., G. F Linder, K. E. Bauman, S. A. Langwick, X. B. Arriaga, J. L. Heath, et al. 1996. "The Safe Dates Project: Theoretical Basis, Evaluation Design, and Selected Baseline Findings." *American Journal of Preventive Medicine* 12:39–47.

Garnier, Helen E., Judith A. Stein, and Jennifer K. Jacobs. 1997. "The Process of Dropping Out of High School: A 19-Year Perspective." *American Educational Research Journal* 34:395–419.

Gates, Bill. 2008. "A Forum on Education in America." Remarks to the Forum on Education, November 11, http://www.gatesfoundation.org/speeches-commentary/Pages/bill-gates-2008-education-forum-speech.aspx.

Ginsberg, C., and L. Loffredo. 1993. "Violence-Related Attitudes and Behaviors of High School Students—New York City 1992." *Journal of School Health* 63:438–40.

Gottfredson, Denise C. 1986. "An Empirical Test of School-Based Environmental and Individual Interventions to Reduce the Risk of Delinquent Behavior." *Criminology* 24:705–31.

———. 1987. "An Evaluation of an Organization Development Approach to Reducing School Disorder." *Evaluation Review* 11:739–63.

———. 1990. "Changing School Structures to Benefit High Risk Youths." In *Understanding Troubled and Troubling Youth: Multidisciplinary Perspectives*, edited by P. E. Leone. Newbury Park, CA: Sage.

———. 1997. "School-Based Crime Prevention." In *Preventing Crime: What Works, What Doesn't, What's Promising: A Report to the United States Congress*, edited by Lawrence W. Sherman, Denise C. Gottfredson, Doris L. Mac-Kenzie, John Eck, Peter Reuter, and Shawn D. Bushway. Washington, DC: U.S. Department of Justice, Office of Justice Programs.

———. 2001. *Schools and Delinquency*. New York: Cambridge University Press.

Gottfredson, Denise C., and Stephanie M. DiPietro. Forthcoming. "School Size, Social Bonding, and Student Victimization." *Sociology of Education*.

Gottfredson, Denise C., Carolyn M. Fink, and Nanette Graham. 1994. "Grade Retention and Problem Behavior." *American Educational Research Journal* 31: 761–84.

Gottfredson, Denise C., David B. Wilson, and Stacy S. Najaka. 2002. "School-Based Crime Prevention." In *Evidence-Based Crime Prevention*, edited by Lawrence W. Sherman, David P. Farrington, Brandon C. Welsh, and Doris L. MacKenzie. London: Routledge.

Gottfredson, Gary D. 1987. "Peer Group Interventions to Reduce the Risk of Delinquent Behavior: A Selective Review and a New Evaluation." *Criminology* 25:671–714.

Gottfredson, Gary D., and Denise C. Gottfredson. 1985. *Victimization in Schools*. New York: Plenum.

———. 2001. "What Schools Do to Prevent Problem Behavior and Promote Safe Environments." *Journal of Educational and Psychological Consultation* 12: 313–44.

———. 2005. "Gang Problems and Gang Programs in a National Sample of Schools." In *The Modern Gang Reader*, edited by Arlen Egley, Cheryl L. Maxson, Jody Miller, and Malcolm W. Klein. Los Angeles: Roxbury.

Gottfredson, Gary D., Denise C. Gottfredson, Ellen R. Czeh, David Cantor, Scott B. Crosse, and Irene Hantman. 2000. "National Study of Delinquency Prevention in Schools. Final Report." Ellicott City, MD: Gottfredson Associates.

Gottfredson, Gary D., Denise C. Gottfredson, Allison A. Payne, and Nisha C. Gottfredson. 2005. "School Climate Predictors of School Disorder: Results from a National Study of Delinquency Prevention in Schools." *Journal of Research in Crime and Delinquency* 42:412–44.

Greenberg, Mark T., and Carol A. Kushé. 1993. *Promoting Social and Emotional Development in Deaf Children: The PATHS Project*. Seattle: University of Washington Press.

———. 1996. "The PATHS Project: Preventive Intervention for Children: Final Report to the National Institute of Mental Health (Grant Number R01MH42131)." Seattle: University of Washington.

Greenberg, Mark T., Carol A. Kushé, Elizabeth T. Cook, and Julie P. Quamma. 1995. "Promoting Emotional Competence in School-Aged Children: The Effects of the PATHS Curriculum." *Development and Psychopathology* 7:117–36.

Gregory, James F. 1995. "The Crime of Punishment: Racial and Gender Disparities in the Use of Corporal Punishment in U.S. Public Schools." *Journal of Negro Education* 64:454–62.

Guerino, Paul, Michael D. Hurwitz, Margaret E. Noonan, and Sarah M. Kaffenberger. 2006. *Crime, Violence, Discipline, and Safety in U.S. Public Schools: Findings from the School Survey on Crime and Safety: 2003–04*. NCES 2009-302rev. Washington, DC: National Center for Education Statistics, Institute of Education Sciences, U.S. Department of Education.

Guryan, Jonathan. 2004. "Desegregation and Black Dropout Rates." *American Economic Review* 94:919–43.

Hahn, Robert A., et al. 2007. "A Review of the Effectiveness of Universal School-Based Programs for the Prevention of Violence." *American Journal of Preventive Medicine* 33:S114–S129.

Hawkins, J. David, David P. Farrington, and Richard F. Catalano. 1998. "Reducing Violence through the Schools." In *Violence in American Schools*, edited by Delbert S. Elliott, Beatrix A. Hamburg, and Kirk R. Williams. New York: Cambridge University Press.

Haynes, V. Dion, and Michael Birnbaum. 2008. "D.C. Tries Cash as a Motivator in School." *Washington Post*, August 22, http://www.washingtonpost.com/wp-dyn/content/article/2008/08/21/AR2008082103874.html.

Henry, Kimberly L., and Michael D. Slater. 2007. "The Contextual Effect of School Attachment on Young Adolescents' Alcohol Use." *Journal of School Health* 77:67–74.

Hernandez, Nelson. 2007 "'No Child' Data on Violence Skewed: Each State Defines 'Dangerous School.'" *Washington Post*, November 18.

Herrera, Carla, Jean B. Grossman, Tina J. Kauh, Amy F. Feldman, Jennifer McMaken, and Linda Z. Jucovy. 2007. *Making a Difference in Schools: The Big Brothers Big Sisters School-Based Mentoring Impact Study*. Philadelphia: Public/Private Ventures.

Hirschfield, Alex. 2008. "Preparing for Prison? The Criminalization of School Discipline in the USA." *Theoretical Criminology* 12:79–101.

Hirschi, Travis. 1969. *Causes of Delinquency*. Berkeley: University of California Press.

Hjalmarsson, Randi. 2009. "Juvenile Jails: A Path to the Straight and Narrow or Hardened Criminality?" *Journal of Law and Economics* 52:779–809.

Hoffmann, John P., and Mikaela J. Dufur. 2008. "Family and School Capital Effects on Delinquency: Substitutes or Complements?" *Sociological Perspectives* 51:29–62.

Hoffmann, John P., and Timothy O. Ireland. 2004. "Strain and Opportunity Structures." *Journal of Quantitative Criminology* 20:263–92.

Ingersoll, Richard M. 2001. "Teacher Turnover and Teacher Shortages: An Organizational Analysis." *American Educational Research Journal* 38:499–534.

Institute of Medicine. 1994. *Reducing Risks for Mental Disorders: Frontiers for Preventive Intervention Research*. Washington, DC: National Academy Press.

Jacob, Brian A., and Lars Lefgren. 2003. "Are Idle Hands the Devil's Workshop? Incapacitation, Concentration, and Juvenile Crime." *American Economic Review* 93:1560–77.

Jang, Sung Joon. 1999. "Age-Varying Effects of Family, School, and Peers on Delinquency: A Multilevel Modeling Test of Interactional Theory." *Criminology* 37:643–85.

Jarjoura, G. Roger. 1993. "Does Dropping Out of School Enhance Delinquent Involvement? Results from a Large-Scale National Probability Sample." *Criminology* 31:149–72.

Jekielek, Susan, Brett Brown, Pilar Marin, and Laura Lippman. 2007. *Public*

School Practices for Violence Prevention and Reduction: 2003–04. NCES-2007-010. Washington, DC: U.S. Department of Education, National Center for Education Statistics.

Jimerson, Shane R. 2001. "Meta-analysis of Grade Retention Research: Implications for Practice in the 21st Century." *School Psychology Review* 30: 420–37.

Jimerson, Shane R., and Phillip Ferguson. 2007. "A Longitudinal Study of Grade Retention: Academic and Behavioral Outcomes of Retained Students through Adolescence." *School Psychology Quarterly* 22:314–39.

Jimerson, Shane R., Sarah M. W. Pletcher, Kelly Graydon, Britton L. Schnurr, Amanda B. Nickerson, and Deborah K. Kundert. 2006. "Beyond Grade Retention and Social Promotion: Promoting the Social and Academic Competence of Students." *Psychology in the Schools* 43:85–97.

Johnson, Robert A., and John P. Hoffmann. 2000. "Adolescent Cigarette Smoking in U.S. Racial/Ethnic Subgroups: Findings from the National Education Longitudinal Study." *Journal of Health and Social Behavior* 41: 392–407.

Karcher, Michael J. 2005. "The Effect of Developmental Mentoring and High School Mentors' Attendance on Their Younger Mentees' Self-Esteem, Social Skills, and Connectedness." *Psychology in the Schools* 42:65–77.

———. 2008. "The Study of Mentoring in the Learning Environment (SMILE): A Randomized Evaluation of the Effectiveness of School-Based Mentoring." *Prevention Science* 9:99–113.

Kellam, Sheppard G., C. Hendricks Brown, Jeanne Poduska, Nick Ialongo, Wei Wang, Peter Toyinbo, Hanno Petras, Carla Ford, Amy Windham, and Holly C. Wilcox. 2008. "Effects of a Universal Classroom Behavior Management Program in First and Second Grades on Young Adult Behavioral, Psychiatric, and Social Outcomes." *Drug and Alcohol Dependence* 95:S5–S28.

Kellam, Sheppard G., George W. Rebok, Nick Ialongo, and Lawrence S. Mayer. 1994. "The Course and Malleability of Aggressive Behavior from Early First Grade into Middle School: Results of a Developmental Epidemiologically-Based Preventive Trial." *Journal of Child Psychology and Psychiatry* 35:259–81.

Kemple, James J., and Cynthia J. Willner. 2008. *Career Academies: Long-Term Impacts on Labor Market Outcomes, Educational Attainment, and Transitions to Adulthood.* New York: MDRC.

Khoury-Kassabri, Mona, Ron A. Astor, and Rami Benbenishty. 2007. "Weapon Carrying in Israeli School: The Contribution of Individual and School Factors." *Health Education and Behavior* 34:453–70.

Khoury-Kassabri, Mona, Rami Benbenishty, and Ron A. Astor. 2005. "The Effects of School Climate, Socioeconomics, and Cultural Factors on Student Victimization in Israel." *Social Work Research* 29:165–80.

Khoury-Kassabri, Mona, Rami Benbenishty, Ron A. Astor, and Anat Zeira. 2004. "The Contributions of Community, Family, and School Variables to Student Victimization." *American Journal of Community Psychology* 34: 187–204.

Kinsler, Josh. 2009. "Suspending the Right to an Education or Preserving It? A Dynamic Equilibrium Model of Student Behavior, Achievement, and Suspension" Working paper. Rochester, NY: Department of Economics, University of Rochester.

Kleiner, Brian, Rebecca Porch, and Elizabeth Farris. 2002. *Public Alternative Schools and Programs for Students at Risk of Education Failure: 2000–01.* NCES 2002-004. Washington, DC: U.S. Department of Education, National Center for Education Statistics.

Kochel, Tammy R., Anna T. Laszlo, and Laura B. Nickles. 2004. "Outcome-Oriented SRO Performance Measures: Learning from a Pilot Study." Washington, DC: U.S. Department of Justice, Office of Community Oriented Policing Services.

Kumar, Revathy, Patrick M. O'Malley, and Lloyd D. Johnston. 2008. "Association between Physical Environment of Secondary Schools and Student Problem Behavior." *Environment and Behavior* 40:455–86.

Kumar, Revathy, Patrick M. O'Malley, Lloyd D. Johnston, John E. Schulenberg, and Jerald G. Bachman. 2002. "Effects of School-Level Norms on Student Substance Use." *Prevention Science* 3:105–24.

LaFree, Gary, and Richard Arum. 2006. "The Impact of Racially Segregated Schooling on the Risk of Adult Incarceration Rates among U.S. Cohorts of African-Americans and Whites since 1930." *Criminology* 44:73–103.

Lavy, Victor, M. Daniele Paserman, and Analia Schlosser. 2008. "Inside the Black Box of Ability Peer Effects: Evidence from Variation in Low Achievers in the Classroom." Working Paper no. 14415. Cambridge, MA: National Bureau of Economic Research, http://www.nber.org.

LeBlanc, Marc, Évelyne Vallières, and Pierre McDuff. 1993. "The Prediction on Males' Adolescent and Adult Offending from School Experience." *Canadian Journal of Criminology* 35:459–78.

Lee, Valerie E., Anthony S. Bryk, and Julia B. Smith. 1993. "The Organization of Effective Secondary Schools." In *Review of Research in Education*, edited by Linda Darling-Hammond. Washington, DC: American Educational Research Association.

Lee, Valerie E., and David T. Burkam. 2003. "Dropping Out of High School: The Role of School Organization and Structure." *American Educational Research Journal* 40:353–93.

Lee, Valerie E., and Douglas D. Ready. 2007. *Schools within Schools: Possibilities and Pitfalls of High School Reform.* New York: Teachers College Press.

Lee, Valerie E., Becky A. Smerdon, Corinne Alfred-Liro, and Shelly L. Brown. 2000. "Inside Large and Small High Schools: Curriculum and Social Relations." *Educational Evaluation and Policy Analysis* 22:147–71.

Lee, Valerie E., and Julia B. Smith. 1995. "Effects of High School Restructuring and Size on Early Gains in Achievement and Engagement." *Sociology of Education* 68:241–70.

Lipsey, Mark W. 1992. "Juvenile Delinquency Treatment: A Meta-analytic Inquiry into the Variability of Effects." In *Meta-analysis for Explanation*, edited by Thomas D. Cook, Harris Cooper, David S. Cordray, Heidi Hartman,

Larry V. Hedges, Richard J. Light, Thomas A. Louis, and Fredrick Mosteller. New York: Russell Sage Foundation.

Lipsey, Mark W., and David B. Wilson. 1993. "The Efficacy of Psychological, Educational, and Behavioral Treatment: Confirmation from Meta-analysis." *American Psychologist* 48:1181–1209.

Lochner, Lance, and Enrico Moretti. 2004. "The Effect of Education on Crime: Evidence from Prison Inmates, Arrests, and Self-Reports." *American Economic Review* 94:155–89.

Luallen, Jeremy. 2006. "School's Out . . . Forever: A Study of Juvenile Crime, At-Risk Youths and Teacher Strikes." *Journal of Urban Economics* 59:75–103.

Lutz, Byron F. 2005. "Post Brown vs. the Board of Education: The Effects of the End of Court-Ordered Desegregation." Finance and Economics Discussion Series Working Paper no. 2005-64. Washington, DC: Board of Governors of the Federal Reserve System.

Ma, Xin. 2002. "Bullying in Middle School: Individual and School Characteristics of Victims and Offenders." *School Effectiveness and School Improvement* 13:63–89.

Maguin, Eugene, and Rolf Loeber. 1995. "Academic Performance and Delinquency." In *Crime and Justice: A Review of Research*, vol. 20, edited by Michael Tonry. Chicago: University of Chicago Press.

McCluskey, Cynthia P., Timothy S. Bynum, and Justin W. Patchin. 2004. "Reducing Chronic Absenteeism: An Assessment of an Early Truancy Initiative." *Crime and Delinquency* 50:214–34.

McFadden, Anna C., and George E. Marsh. 1992. "A Study of Racial and Gender Bias in the Punishment of School Children." *Education and Treatment of Children* 15:140–46.

Mensch, Barbara S., and Denise B. Kandel. 1988. "Dropping Out of High School and Drug Involvement." *Sociology of Education* 61:95–113.

Mosteller, Frederick, Richard J. Light, and Jason A. Sachs. 1996. "Sustained Inquiry in Education: Lessons from Skill Grouping and Class Size." *Harvard Educational Review* 66:797–842.

Multisite Violence Prevention Project. 2008. "The Multisite Violence Prevention Project: Impact of a Universal School-Based Violence Prevention Program on Social-Cognitive Outcomes." *Prevention Science* 9:231–44.

———. 2009. "The Ecological Effects of Universal and Selective Violence Prevention Programs for Middle School Students: A Randomized Trial." *Journal of Consulting and Clinical Psychology* 77:526–42.

Muschkin, Clara, Beth Glennie, and Audrey Beck. 2008. "Effects of School Peers on Student Behavior: Age, Grade Retention, and Disciplinary Infractions in Middle School." *Journal of Policy Analysis and Management* 27:104–21.

Nagin, Daniel S. 1998. "Criminal Deterrence Research at the Outset of the Twenty-first Century." In *Crime and Justice: A Review of Research*, vol. 23, edited by Michael Tonry. Chicago: University of Chicago Press.

Nagin, Daniel S., Linda Pagani, Richard E. Tremblay, and Frank Vitaro. 2003.

"Life Course Turning Points: The Effect of Grade Retention on Physical Aggression." *Development and Psychopathology* 15:343–61.

Najaka, Stacy S., Denise C. Gottfredson, and David B. Wilson. 2001. "A Meta-analytic Inquiry into the Relationship between Selected Risk Factors and Problem Behavior." *Prevention Science* 2:257–71.

National Incident-Based Reporting System. 2006. Extract Files [Computer file]. ICPSR23541-v2. Ann Arbor, MI: Inter-university Consortium for Political and Social Research [distributor], 2009-09-10. doi:10.3886/ICPSR23541.

National Institute of Education. 1978. "Violent Schools–Safe Schools: The Safe School Study Report to Congress." Washington, DC: National Institute of Education.

National Research Council. 2003. *Deadly Lessons: Understanding Lethal School Violence*. Washington, DC: National Academy Press.

Neiman, Samantha, and Jill F. DeVoe. 2009. *Crime, Violence, Discipline, and Safety in U.S. Public Schools: Findings from the School Survey on Crime and Safety: 2007–08.* NCES 2009-326. Washington, DC: National Center for Education Statistics, Institute of Education Sciences, U.S. Department of Education.

New York Times. 2009. "The Principal's Office First." Editorial, January 4, http://www.nytimes.com/2009/01/05/opinion/05mon3.html.

Nolle, Kacey L., Paul Guerino, and Rachel Dinkes. 2007. *Crime, Violence, Discipline, and Safety in US Public Schools: Findings from the School Survey on Crime and Safety: 2005–6.* NCES 2007-361. Washington, DC: National Center for Education Statistics, Institute of Education Sciences, U.S. Department of Education, http://nces.ed.gov/pubs2007/2007361.pdf.

Novak, Scott P., and Richard R. Clayton. 2001. "The Influence of School Environment and Self-Regulation on Transitions between Stages of Cigarette Smoking: A Multilevel Analysis." *Health Psychology* 20:196–207.

Olweus, Dan, Sue Limber, and Sharon Mihalic. 1999. *Blueprints for Violence Prevention: Bullying Prevention Program*. Boulder, CO: Center for the Study and Prevention of Violence.

O'Neill, Lauren, and Jean M. McGloin. 2007. "Considering the Efficacy of Situational Crime Prevention in Schools." *Journal of Criminal Justice* 35: 511–23.

Pagani, Linda, Richard E. Tremblay, Frank Vitaro, Bernard Boulerice, and Pierre McDuff. 2001. "Effects of Grade Retention on Academic Performance and Behavioral Development." *Development and Psychopathology* 13: 297–315.

Payne, Allison A. 2008. "A Multilevel Analysis of the Relationships among Communal School Organization, Student, Bonding, and Delinquency." *Journal of Research in Crime and Delinquency* 45:429–55.

Payne, Allison A., Denise C. Gottfredson, and Gary D. Gottfredson. 2003. "Schools as Communities: The Relationships among Communal School Organization, Student Bonding, and School Disorder." *Criminology* 41:749–77.

Pokorny, Steven B., Leonard A. Jason, and M. E. Schoeny. 2004. "Current

438   Philip J. Cook, Denise C. Gottfredson, and Chongmin Na

Smoking among Young Adolescents: Assessing School Based Contextual Norms." *Tobacco Control* 13:301–7.

Purkey, Stewart C., and Marshall S. Smith. 1983. "Effective Schools: A Review." *Elementary School Journal* 83:427–52.

Reid, John B., Gerald R. Patterson, and James J. Snyder. 2002. *Antisocial Behavior in Children and Adolescents: A Developmental Analysis and the Oregon Model for Intervention.* Washington, DC: American Psychological Association.

Reinke, Wendy M., and Hill M. Walker. 2006. "Deviant Peer Effects in Education." In *Deviant Peer Influences in Programs for Youth: Problems and Solutions,* edited by Kenneth A. Dodge, Thomas J. Dishion, and Jennifer E. Lansford. New York: Guildford.

Reis, Janet, Mickey Trockel, and Peter Mulhall. 2007. "Individual and School Predictors of Middle School Aggression." *Youth and Society* 38:322–47.

Roski, Joachim, Cheryl L. Perry, Paul G. McGovern, Carolyn L. Williams, Kian Farbakhsh, and Sara Veblen-Mortenson. 1997. "School and Community Influence on Adolescent Alcohol and Drug Use." *Health Education Research: Theory and Practice* 12:255–66.

Rutter, Michael, and Barbara Maughan. 2002. "School Effectiveness Findings 1979–2002." *Journal of School Psychology* 40:451–75.

Rutter, Michael, Barbara Maughan, Peter Mortimore, Janet Ouston, and Alan Smith. 1979. *Fifteen Thousand Hours: Secondary Schools and Their Effects on Children.* Cambridge, MA: Harvard University Press.

Samples, Faith, and J. Lawrence Aber. 1998. "Evaluations of School-Based Violence Prevention Programs." In *Violence in American Schools,* edited by Delbert S. Elliott, Beatrix A. Hamburg, and Kirk R. Williams. New York: Cambridge University Press.

Schumaker, Jean B., Melbourne F. Hovell, and James A. Sherman. 1977. "An Analysis of Daily Report Cards and Parent-Managed Privileges in the Improvement of Adolescents' Classroom Performance." *Journal of Applied Behavioral Analysis* 10:449–64.

Simon, Jonathan. 2006. *Governing through Crime: How the War on Crime Transformed American Democracy and Created a Culture of Fear.* New York: Oxford University Press.

Sinclair, Mary F., Sandra L. Christenson, David L. Evelo, and Christine M. Hurley. 1998. "Dropout Prevention for Youth with Disabilities: Efficacy of a Sustained School Engagement Procedure." *Exceptional Children* 65:7–21.

Skiba, Russell J. 2000. "Zero Tolerance, Zero Evidence: An Analysis of School Disciplinary Practices." Policy Research Report. Bloomington: Indiana Education Policy Center.

Solomon, Daniel, Victor Battistich, Dong-il Kim, and Marilyn Watson. 1997. "Teacher Practices Associated with Students' Sense of the Classroom as a Community." *Social Psychology of Education* 1:235–67.

Soulé, David A., Denise C. Gottfredson, and Erin Bauer. 2008. "It's 3 P.M. Do You Know Where Your Child Is? A Study on the Timing of Juvenile Victimization and Delinquency." *Justice Quarterly* 25:623–46.

Sprague, Jeffrey, Hill Walker, Annemieke Golly, Kathy White, Dale Myers, and Tad Shannon. 2001. "Translating Research into Effective Practice: The Effects of a Universal Staff and Student Intervention on Key Indicators of School Safety and Discipline." *Education and Treatment of Children* 24: 495–511.

Stage, Scott A., and David R. Quiroz. 1997. "A Meta-analysis of Interventions to Decrease Disruptive Classroom Behavior in Public Education Settings." *School Psychology Review* 26:333–68.

Stewart, Eric A. 2003. "School Social Bonds, School Climate, and School Misbehavior: A Multilevel Analysis." *Justice Quarterly* 20:575–604.

Sugai, George, and Robert H. Horner. 2008. "What We Know and Need to Know about Preventing Problem Behavior in Schools." *Exceptionality* 16: 67–77.

Sweeten, Gary, Shawn D. Bushway, and Raymond Paternoster. 2009. "Does Dropping Out of School Mean Dropping into Delinquency?" *Criminology* 47:47–91.

Tagiuri, Renato. 1968. "The Concept of Organizational Climate." In *Organizational Climate*, edited by Renato Tagiuri and George H. Litwin. Boston: Graduate School of Business, Harvard University.

Thornberry, Terence P., Melanie Moore, and R. L. Christenson. 1985. "The Effect of Dropping Out of High School on Subsequent Criminal Behavior." *Criminology* 23:3–18.

Thornton, Timothy N., Carole A. Craft, Linda L. Dahlberg, Barbara S. Lynch, and Katie Baer. 2000. *Best Practices of Youth Violence Prevention: A Sourcebook for Community Action*. Atlanta: Centers for Disease Control and Prevention, National Center for Injury Prevention and Control.

Tierney, Joseph P., Jean B. Grossman, and Nancy L. Resch. 1995. *Making a Difference: An Impact Study of Big Brothers Big Sisters*. Philadelphia: Public/Private Ventures.

Tremblay, Richard E. 2006. "Prevention of Violence: Why Not Start at the Beginning?" *Journal of Abnormal Child Psychology* 34:481–87.

Tremblay, Richard E., and Wendy M. Craig. 1995. "Developmental Crime Prevention." In *Building a Safer Society: Strategic Approaches to Crime Prevention*, edited by Michael Tonry and David P. Farrington. Vol. 19 of *Crime and Justice: A Review of Research*, edited by Michael Tonry. Chicago: University of Chicago Press.

Tyson, Karolyn, William Darity, and Domini R. Castellino. 2005. "It's Not 'a Black Thing': Understanding the Burden of Acting White and Other Dilemmas of High Achievement." *American Sociological Review* 70:582–605.

Van Acker, Richard. 2007. "Antisocial, Aggressive, and Violent Behavior in Children and Adolescents within Alternative Education Settings: Prevention and Intervention." *Preventing School Failure* 51:5–12.

Warr, Mark. 1993. "Age, Peers, and Delinquency." *Criminology* 31:17–40.

Washington Times. 2008. "Students Raise Truancy Rate." January 24, http://www.washingtontimes.com/news/2008/jan/24/dc-students-raise-truancy-rate/.

Weiner, David A., Byron F. Lutz, and Jens Ludwig. 2009. "The Effects of School Desegregation on Crime." Working Paper no. 15380. Cambridge, MA: National Bureau of Economic Research, http://www.nber.org.

Weishew, Nancy L., and Samuel S. Peng. 1993. "Variables Predicting Students' Problem Behaviors." *Journal of Educational Research* 87:5–17.

Welsh, Wayne N. 2000. "The Effects of School Climate on School Disorder." *Annals of the American Academy of Political and Social Science* 567:88–107.

———. 2001. "Effects of Student and School Factors on Five Measures of School Disorder." *Justice Quarterly* 18:911–47.

———. 2003. "Individual and Institutional Predictors of School Disorder." *Youth Violence and Juvenile Justice* 1:346–68.

Welsh, Wayne N., Jack R. Greene, and Patricia H. Jenkins. 1999. "School Disorder: The Influence of Individual, Institutional, and Community Factors." *Criminology* 37:73–116.

Welsh, Wayne N., Robert Stokes, and Jack R. Greene. 2000. "A Macro-Level Model of School Disorder." *Journal of Research in Crime and Delinquency* 37: 243–83.

Whitaker, Catherine J., and Linda D. Bastian. 1991. *Teenage Victims: A National Crime Survey Report.* NCJ-128129. Washington, DC: U.S. Department of Justice, Bureau of Justice Statistics.

Wiatrowski, Michael D., Stephen Hansell, Charles R. Massey, and David L. Wilson. 1982. "Curriculum Tracking and Delinquency." *American Sociological Review* 47:151–60.

Wilcox, Pamela, and Richard R. Clayton. 2001. "A Multilevel Analysis of School-Based Weapon Possession." *Justice Quarterly* 18:509–41.

Wilson, David B., Denise C. Gottfredson, and Stacy S. Najaka. 2001. "School-Based Prevention of Problem Behaviors: A Meta-analysis." *Journal of Quantitative Criminology* 17:247–72.

Wilson, Sandra J., and Mark W. Lipsey. 2007. "School-Based Interventions for Aggressive and Disruptive Behavior: Update of a Meta-analysis." *American Journal of Preventive Medicine* 33:S130–S143.

David S. Kirk and John H. Laub

Neighborhood Change and Crime in the Modern Metropolis

ABSTRACT

Few empirical studies of crime have treated neighborhoods as dynamic entities, by examining how processes of growth, change, and decline affect neighborhood rates of crime. From a small yet burgeoning collection of dynamic research related to population migration—including population loss, gentrification, development and demolition of public housing, home ownership and home foreclosure, and immigration—we know that neighborhood change, even when it leads to socioeconomic improvements, tends to have a destabilizing influence that results in increases in crime in the short term. This occurs, in part, because residential turnover undermines informal social control. There is evidence across a variety of neighborhood changes, including population loss from central cities and gentrification, that population migration is a cause and consequence of crime. However, too few studies pay adequate attention to how methodological choices affect inferences about the effects of neighborhoods on crime, and not much is known about the relationship between neighborhood change and crime, especially regarding causal mechanisms. Longitudinal data on neighborhood social and cultural processes and population migration are needed to advance our understanding of neighborhood change and crime.

The outstanding fact of modern society is the growth of
great cities. . . . Yet the processes of expansion, and
especially the rate of expansion, may be studied not only
in the physical growth and business development, but also

David S. Kirk is assistant professor of sociology and faculty research associate of the Population Research Center at the University of Texas at Austin. John H. Laub is Distinguished University Professor of Criminology and Criminal Justice at the University of Maryland at College Park. We thank the editor and anonymous readers for helpful comments on an earlier draft, and we are grateful to Bianca Bersani and Maggie Pendzich-Hardy for research assistance.

441

in the consequent changes in social organization and in
personality types. (Burgess [1925] 1967, pp. 47, 53)

Recent work on communities and crime has turned to the
observation that Shaw and McKay neglected: not only do
communities change their structures over time but so
often do their crime rates. (Reiss 1986, p. 19)

One of the more intriguing puzzles emanating from the past century
of research and scholarship on cities, neighborhoods, and crime is the
lack of serious attention to the idea of change. Given significant
changes in urban dynamics and crime rates since Albert Reiss wrote
the words quoted above for a volume of *Crime and Justice* published
more than two decades ago, we believe that it is time for a focused
review of the state of research on neighborhood change and crime in
the modern metropolis. Whereas neighborhoods may change in a multitude of ways—both physically and socially—we examine social
changes to neighborhoods related to sociodemographics and population migration—in-migration, out-migration, and internal redistribution.

Since the pioneering work of Shaw and McKay (1942) and Quetelet
([1831] 1984), Guerry (1833), Rawson (1839), Mayhew (1862), and
Burgess (1916) before them, a vast assortment of studies have sought
to explain the spatial distribution of crime by examining the differences
across neighborhoods in population characteristics, such as the poverty
rate, and differences in associated neighborhood social processes, such
as informal social control. However, relatively few researchers have
treated neighborhoods dynamically, by examining how processes of
growth, change, and decline affect neighborhood rates of crime.[1] Yet,
a primary intent of the research program of Shaw and McKay (1942;
also Burgess [1925] 1967; Shaw et al. 1929) was to examine the repercussions of the growth of the city for the social organization of neighborhoods and for area rates of delinquency. However, it is not possible
to study growth, or decline, through static research designs. Rather, to

---

[1] By "dynamic" we mean an analytic strategy that allows for an assessment of within-
and between-neighborhood change over time. The variation over time in a characteristic
of a neighborhood such as the crime rate can be decomposed into differences between
neighborhoods and differences over time within each given neighborhood. The average
within-neighborhood crime rate may change over time, while at the same time there
may be little between-neighborhood change.

advance a research program like Shaw and McKay's, it is necessary to allow for the study of neighborhood change.

Unfortunately, during the post–World War II era, criminology turned to individual-level explanations for crime and away from eco-logical explanations advanced by Shaw and McKay (1942) and others prior to the war. This shift occurred, in part, because ecological the-ories of crime such as social disorganization theory poorly predicted individual-level behavior (Robinson 1950; see also Bursik [1988] for a discussion). As but one example of this disciplinary shift, research on criminal deterrence became prominent during the 1970s as numerous scholars came to view criminal behavior as the outcome of individual decision making, although constrained by imperfect information (Nagin 1978; Cook 1980). Yet, the appeal of ecological theories did not lay dormant for long.

The 1980s were marked by a resurgence of interest in ecological change and the ramifications for crime. This resurgence was embodied in a volume of *Crime and Justice* dedicated to communities and crime (Reiss and Tonry 1986). This volume presented the state of the art in ecological studies of crime and included essays related to community careers in crime, housing policies, fear of crime, informal social con-trol, the neighborhood context of police behavior, and gentrification. Many of the studies in this 1986 volume examined the effects of eco-logical changes prior to the mid-1970s. Therefore, it is now time to take stock of the effects of neighborhood migration and sociodemographic changes occurring over the past four decades. Several pertinent questions guide such a review.

One of the most fundamental ways in which neighborhoods change is through shifts in the number and composition of its inhabitants. Importantly, these shifts also affect social networks and, in turn, may influence neighborhood processes such as informal social control. Wes-ley Skogan (1986, p. 207) has stated that "the engine of neighborhood change is selective out-migration from the neighborhood" (see also Frey 1980). What does research reveal about the relationship between population loss and crime? We know that populations change as a re-sult of processes such as middle-class flight (both black and white) to the suburbs, but populations also change as a result of in-migration, especially through immigration. How do changes to the population composition of neighborhoods due to immigration affect crime rates?

Neighborhoods also experience changes in housing stock, which in turn affects the composition of the population. For example, many high-rise public housing developments in U.S. metropolitan areas have been razed in recent years. What are the implications for the distribution of crime and criminals? As a second example, neighborhoods change as a result of gentrification, defined by many as the restoration by the middle class of urban property in poor or working-class neighborhoods. A key question is, what is known about the relation between patterns of gentrification and rates of crime? Economic booms can increase home ownership, which is believed to facilitate neighborhood cohesiveness and residential stability (see Skogan and Maxfield 1981). Does crime decline in neighborhoods that experience an increase in home ownership? In contrast, neighborhoods can change as a result of economic downturns and associated ramifications such as home foreclosures. What does research reveal about the relationship between property foreclosures and crime?

Our principal findings and conclusions are as follows: too few studies of neighborhoods and crime pay adequate attention to how methodological choices such as the operationalization of neighborhood size and boundaries influence inferences about the effect of neighborhoods on crime; many studies do not conceptualize or define what they mean by "neighborhood effects" even as they purport to test for them; population change is both a cause and consequence of crime at the neighborhood level; gentrification leads to short-term increases and long-term declines for both property and violent crime; the siting of public housing has minimal direct effects on crime, and the demolition of public housing may displace crime and may escalate violent crime in the short run; as home ownership increases, crime declines, and, in turn, as home foreclosures increase, crime increases; concentrations of immigrants promote reductions in crime and violence; and few data repositories exist that can be used to examine the association between neighborhood change and crime. In particular, virtually no quantitative data exist that measure changes in neighborhood social and cultural processes over time (e.g., informal social control, fear of crime and disorder, perceptions of the law). Thus, there are many remaining questions to be answered about the relation between neighborhood change and crime, especially regarding the causal mechanisms underlying various types of neighborhood change.

To determine what current empirical research reveals about the relation between neighborhood change and crime, we employed the following selection criteria for studies to examine: research from the 1970s to the present, use of a dynamic longitudinal research design, a neighborhood unit of analysis, a focus on some aspect of population migration and sociodemographic change, and a focus on crime. An abundance of cross-sectional ecological research is suggestive of relationships we might find in a study of neighborhood change (e.g., see Pratt and Cullen 2005), but with few exceptions we decided not to review the cross-sectional literature.

Here is how this essay is organized. Section I discusses the foremost conceptual, definitional, and measurement issues related to the association between neighborhood change and criminal outcomes. Key issues reviewed include defining neighborhoods and units of analysis; defining and conceptualizing the different ways neighborhoods affect behavior, that is, "neighborhood effects"; measuring neighborhood characteristics and change; and selection bias (i.e., residents selecting into neighborhoods). Section II summarizes research related to the association between in-migration, out-migration, population redistribution, and criminal outcomes. Section III outlines a research agenda for examining a number of themes related to neighborhood change and crime, including a call for greater attention to the causal mechanisms underlying neighborhood effects as well as a focus on the role of neighborhood change for explaining trends in crime.

We do not exhaustively cover all the potential ways that neighborhoods change. In the interest of depth of coverage on population migration and sociodemographic change, we have omitted discussions of physical changes to neighborhoods (e.g., economic development and transportation infrastructure) and neighborhood change from criminal justice interventions. Thorough reviews of these subject areas arguably require their own separate essays. Several such overviews have been published in previous volumes of *Crime and Justice* (e.g., Clarke 1995; Ekblom and Pease 1995). In order to give fuller treatment to the topic of neighborhood migration and crime, we excluded discussion of these other important aspects of neighborhood change. Additionally, because our focus is on proximal neighborhood conditions (e.g., gentrification) and their relation to crime, we have chosen to deemphasize the distal forces (e.g., economic conditions and globalization) that bear on neighborhood population change. Certainly macro-level conditions such as economic recession and globalization affect neighborhoods, yet our intent is to review the import of proximate changes to neighborhoods.

I. Conceptual, Definitional, and Measurement Issues

We present here a brief overview of essential technical and conceptual issues that are necessary to consider when examining the literature on the relation between neighborhood change and crime.

A. Defining Neighborhoods and Units of Analysis

What is a neighborhood? How is it conceptually and operationally defined? How researchers define neighborhoods, both conceptually and operationally, may influence inferences about the relation between neighborhood change and crime.

There has been a tendency in the social sciences to use the terms *community* and *neighborhood* interchangeably (Wellman and Leighton 1979). Yet, there is an important distinction between these concepts. Community does not necessarily require locality or territory. Definitions of community tend to emphasize the importance of interpersonal ties, which are vital for sociability, solidarity, and social support (Wellman and Leighton 1979). Many definitions also tend to incorporate residence in a common locality as a basis for defining community. Yet, as Tilly (1973) argues, proximity is not a necessary condition of community; rather, accessibility is necessary. Thus, in the absence of restraints on accessibility (i.e., because of transportation and communication advances), community can thrive without place. We can speak of local communities, but the term *community* encompasses a broader domain than proximate, territorially based ties and sentiments.

Neighborhoods, by contrast, may be conceived as spatial constructions that are defined ecologically, with reference to a geographic area. For instance, Bursik and Grasmick (1993, p. 6) define a neighborhood as, "a small physical area embedded within a larger area in which people inhabit dwellings." Prevailing research suggests that most residents perceive their neighborhoods territorially (Guest and Lee 1984; Lee and Campbell 1997).[2] In neighborhoods, residents share proximity and the circumstances that come with it (Bursik and Grasmick 1993; Chaskin 1997). They may also share common values, sentiment, and social solidarity (i.e., local community), but this is not necessarily the case.

Operationalizing Neighborhood. A number of different methodolog-

---

[2] In an open-ended survey of Nashville residents asking them to define the word *neighborhood*, Lee and Campbell (1997) found that 87 percent of respondents define a neighborhood as a spatial-territorial unit, with some respondents also employing definitions more aligned with our notion of community.

ical approaches have been used to operationalize neighborhoods. Of importance is that the operational definition of neighborhood used in any given study may influence inferences about the causes and consequences of crime (Bursik and Grasmick 1993; Sampson, Morenoff, and Gannon-Rowley 2002; Hipp 2007).[3] Most researchers use administrative definitions of neighborhoods in their assessment of neighborhood effects. Such administrative boundaries include census tracts, face blocks, police districts, and voting districts or political wards. While there are exceptions, the use of administrative units of analysis in neighborhood-based research is often done out of convenience (i.e., data availability). Yet, as stated by Elliott and colleagues, "theory, not convenience should drive our definitions of what constitutes a neighborhood" (2006, p. 298). For instance, if a study of neighborhood change is designed to examine the repercussions of a police intervention implemented at the police beat level, then the unit of analysis should be the beat. If a study is designed to investigate the role of cohesiveness among neighbors, then use of a unit of analysis such as the face block will be useful for capturing the localized nature of social interaction among neighbors.

One recent approach to defining neighborhoods employed by the Project on Human Development in Chicago Neighborhoods (PHDCN) is to follow a spatial definition of neighborhoods that recognizes major geographic boundaries (e.g., expressways, parks, and railroad tracks) but also ensures that neighborhoods are internally homogeneous with respect to various demographic characteristics of residents (e.g., socioeconomic status, race, ethnicity, housing density, and family structure). Based on these criteria and local knowledge, 343 geographically contiguous neighborhood clusters were defined in the city of Chicago with approximately 8,000 residents per cluster (Sampson, Raudenbush, and Earls 1997).

Spatial Scale. The choice between micro- (e.g., blocks or hot spots),

---

[3] This issue is not isolated to studies of crime. Much attention in the discipline of geography has been directed toward the subjects of spatial scale and aggregation (Openshaw 1984). Scale refers to the size or resolution of an areal unit of analysis, and the so-called scale problem refers to the fact that research results may change when the same areal data are combined into larger units of analysis (Openshaw and Taylor 1979, p. 128). The aggregation problem refers to "variation in results due to the use of alternative units of analysis when the number of units is held constant" (Openshaw 1984, p. 8). Given that there are numerous ways to aggregate individual or incident data to a higher unit of analysis, statistical inferences from a given analysis may be dependent upon scale and aggregation.

meso- (e.g., census tracts), or macro-level (e.g., community areas) units of analysis is not merely a methodological issue but also a theoretical one. For instance, situational action theory asserts that criminal behavior is the outcome of the interaction between individuals and their immediate social environment (Wikström 2004, 2006). Wikström (2006, p. 61) argues, "people are moved to action (including acts of crime) by how they *see their action alternatives and make their choices when confronted with the particularities of a setting.*" To understand the etiology of behavior, Wikström asserts that we must understand the import of the behavior settings to which individuals actually take part (Wikström 2006; also Oberwittler and Wikström 2008). These influential behavior settings are not expansive but, rather, are geographically small.

In contrast to this micro-level perspective, social disorganization theory asserts that the relation among neighborhood institutions (e.g., families and schools) is consequential for behavior (Shaw and McKay 1942; Kornhauser 1978). For instance, if schools are isolated from the larger neighborhood community and do not respond to the needs of its residents, then neighborhoods lack a key mechanism of informal social control of youth. Recent research in the social disorganization tradition finds that social control processes among neighborhood institutions are interdependent, with the level of informal social control produced by families and schools dependent on the extent of control in the wider neighborhood (Kirk 2009*b*). The implication is that the informal social control of behavior does not simply reflect social processes occurring on a street block; rather, it is a product of a more expansive web of relations among neighborhood residents, parents, and local institutions.

In general, there are nested levels of geographic areas, and each level may have some effect on criminal behavior (although through differing theoretical mechanisms). Hunter and Suttles (1972) provide a framework for understanding the multiple layers of mechanisms that influence social behavior. They describe four nested levels of residential groupings, each with an ecological basis (from most to least inclusive): First, Local Networks and the Face Block refers to a network of acquaintances based on shared residence on the same block, where residents are recognizable to each other.[4] Second, Defended Neighbor-

---

[4] Related to this nesting, Hunter and Suttles (1972, p. 55) argue, "such a loose network does not constitute a neighborhood nor is it likely to have any residential identity." This

hood refers to the smallest area that possesses a distinct identity, recognizable to both the residents and outsiders. Third, Community of Limited Liability refers to a geographic locality that is recognized and even defined by commercial and government entities that are external to the area (e.g., Hyde Park). Fourth, Expanded Community of Limited Liability refers to an even larger geographic area defined as such out of necessity for groups to gain a larger voice with government or business influences (e.g., the South Side of Chicago).

Numerous studies have concluded that statistical inferences about the size and direction of associations between neighborhood characteristics and outcome variables are dependent on the choice of scale used in an analysis and that the theoretical meaning of neighborhood constructs may vary across different scales (Hannan 1971; Brooks-Gunn et al. 1993; Wooldredge 2002; Hipp 2007).

B. Conceptualizing "Neighborhood Effects"

What exactly is a neighborhood effect? Does a neighborhood effect measure the potential individual-level outcome (e.g., criminal behavior) if an individual moves to a different neighborhood? This is the conceptual approach to neighborhood effects employed in the Moving to Opportunity (MTO) housing mobility studies as well as a recent study by Kirk (2009*a*), which examines the repercussions of induced residential mobility because of Hurricane Katrina on recidivism. Kirk finds that moving away from former neighborhoods substantially lowers a parolee's likelihood of reincarceration and posits that it is because mobility provides an opportunity for parolees to separate from their criminal past and from their former criminal peers. MTO is a program sponsored by the U.S. Department of Housing and Urban Development that was started in 1994 in five cities: Baltimore, Boston, Chicago, Los Angeles, and New York (Katz, Kling, and Liebman 2001; Kling, Liebman, and Katz 2007). The question driving the MTO studies is whether an individual would behave any differently, in terms of crime and a host of other individual outcomes, if he or she lived in a nonpoor neighborhood instead of a poor neighborhood. To answer this question, MTO researchers used an experimental design and random assignment to create the counterfactual scenario of what would have hap-

---

has implications for the study of hot spots of crime. Per Hunter and Suttles's formulation, microplaces such as hot spots do not represent neighborhoods.

pened if a given individual did not live in poverty (or in less poverty). MTO families were randomly assigned to one of three groups: an experimental group, whose members received a housing voucher that had to be used in areas with under 10 percent poverty and who also received counseling assistance from relocation advisors; a Section 8 comparison group, whose members received a geographically unrestricted housing voucher but did not receive relocation assistance; and a control group that received no change in housing assistance. MTO researchers then used a comparison of individual-level behaviors across these three groups to make claims about neighborhood effects. As Sampson (2006b) observes, however, such a research strategy may provide useful information about whether there is an effect of neighborhoods (or moving) but not why. When a given individual moves from one neighborhood to another, "entire bundles of variables change at once, making it difficult to disentangle the change in neighborhood poverty from simultaneous changes in social processes" (Sampson 2006b, p. 48).

An alternative conceptualization of a neighborhood effect, which allows for a consideration of the mechanisms that explain why neighborhoods matter, is to explain neighborhood variation in rates of behavior. In this case, researchers want to examine the effect of a neighborhood change or intervention on crime rates. For example, we could examine how the neighborhood rate of crime changed following the implementation of a community policing strategy in a given neighborhood. Therefore, we can assess neighborhood effects by either moving individuals to different neighborhoods or by changing neighborhoods.[5]

In sum, there are different ways to conceptualize whether and why a neighborhood may affect an outcome such as crime. In the case of the MTO and Katrina studies (Kling, Liebman, and Katz 2007; Kirk 2009a), the neighborhood effect involved a comparison of criminal outcomes between otherwise equivalent individuals where the experimental group moved to a new neighborhood while the control group did not. An alternative conceptualization of a neighborhood effect is to assess the repercussions of an actual change to a given neighborhood (as opposed to mobility). In this essay, we are specifically interested in the effect of neighborhood change but not the effect of individuals changing neighborhoods. Therefore, we do not provide a review of the

[5] See Sobel (2006) and Sampson (2008a) for further discussion of these alternative conceptualizations of "neighborhood effects."

MTO studies or other research that focuses on the effects of mobility at the individual level (for such reviews, see Goering and Feins [2003], Orr et al. [2003], and Ludwig et al. [2008]).

C. Measuring Neighborhood Characteristics

There have been many ecological studies of crime that examine the link between neighborhood structural characteristics (e.g., poverty) and criminal outcomes (see Elmer [1933], Byrne and Sampson [1986], Reiss [1986], and Wikström [1998] for extensive reviews). We focus our attention in this subsection on the measurement of social processes at the neighborhood level (e.g., social organization and local culture). A focus on social processes allows researchers to explore the exact mechanisms by which neighborhood structures influence outcomes such as crime and violence. For example, dating back to the work of Shaw and McKay (1942), a common finding in studies of crime and delinquency is that high poverty and residential instability are associated with high levels of crime. The key question is why. A number of research design considerations must be taken into account in order to measure reliably and validly neighborhood mechanisms that explain why neighborhoods affect criminal outcomes.

First, neighborhood effects may be biased if characteristics of the neighborhood are simply aggregated up from the respondents that are the focal point of analyses. In other words, if measures of neighborhood social organization are obtained by aggregating responses from individual survey participants and used as predictors of the criminal behavior or victimization of those same survey respondents, then same-source bias may result (Duncan and Raudenbush 1999; 2001). In this case, measurement errors in the aggregated neighborhood measures are likely correlated with measurement errors in the outcome variable. For example, those respondents who have been victimized in their neighborhood may rate the neighborhood as more dangerous than respondents who have not been victimized. To avoid same-source bias, characteristics of neighborhoods should be gathered from an independent sample of respondents.

Second, in the interest of measurement, Raudenbush and Sampson (1999) have proposed ecometrics—the science of ecological assessment—with procedures for measuring emergent neighborhood processes as well as methods for assessing the reliability and validity of measurements of neighborhood social processes (see also Wikström

2007). Regarding this notion of emergence, Sampson argues, "neighborhood processes can and should be treated as ecological or collective phenomena rather than as stand-ins for individual-level traits" (2006*b*, p. 36). Relatedly, Sampson and colleagues advocate the use of systematic social observation to assess the physical and observational characteristics of neighborhoods that are not reliably measured in census data or local surveys (Sampson and Raudenbush 1999; Sampson, Morenoff, and Gannon-Rowley 2002; also Reiss 1971). Along similar lines, Wikström (2007) has argued that much ecological research is flawed because residences (e.g., of the offender, victim) are used to capture "their environment," and this strategy does not take into account the different environments that individuals are exposed to. Wikström advocates using "space-time budgets" to study individuals' interactions with varying environments. The fundamental point is that the testing of neighborhood effects requires proper measurement of neighborhood structures and mechanisms.

Third, there is a severe dearth of criminological research that has examined the dynamic nature of neighborhood social processes.[6] There are few social science data repositories with neighborhood-level social process information across an adequate sample of neighborhoods, and most of these data repositories do not have multiple time points. One exception is the Project on Human Development in Chicago Neighborhoods, which conducted a repeated cross-sectional community survey of neighborhood residents in 1995 and in 2002. While studies of changes in neighborhood social processes using the PHDCN data are still in development, early findings from the two waves of data collection suggest that neighborhood collective efficacy remained relatively stable from 1995 to 2002 (Sampson 2006*a*). To explore the association between neighborhood change and crime, it is vital to collect multiple time points of data on neighborhood social processes.

---

[6] In contrast to criminology, much has been written in the political science and sociological literatures about neighborhood change and social processes such as neighborhood activism and political mobilization (for recent discussions, see Pattillo 2007; Hyra 2008). As a penetrating example, Gould (1995) describes how urban transformations in mid-nineteenth-century Paris produced the foundations for neighborhood mobilization during the Paris Commune of 1871. With the advent of the Second Empire in 1852, Napoleon III enlisted Georges Haussmann to transform Paris into an imperial capital. The effect on the population was to disperse many residents, formerly residing in neighborhoods defined by occupation, to peripheral areas of the central city. Here, neighborhood communities formed and solidarity flourished, with these networks and ties ultimately proving to be the foundation of mobilization in 1870 and 1871.

D. Selection Bias and Causality

One significant challenge in ecological research is to determine if an observed difference in some outcome of interest across neighborhoods is in fact caused by contextual characteristics of neighborhoods. The question is, do neighborhood differences in crime result from emergent neighborhood-level factors, or are they simply due to the differential sorting of crime-prone individuals into certain neighborhoods? (see Farrington 1993). While individuals are often constrained in decisions of where they live (or where children go to school), they do have at least a minor influence on those decisions (Manski 1993). Selection bias occurs when an unobserved or unmeasured characteristic of an individual or family influences both where they live and the outcome under study and may therefore account for any relation between neighborhood characteristics and outcomes. Because of these unmeasured characteristics, the effect of neighborhoods on the outcome can potentially be biased (upward or downward).

While it is beyond the scope of this essay to give full consideration to the issue of selection and various solutions, we do highlight a number of approaches social scientists use to address selection (see Manski [1993] and Sobel [2006] for relevant discussions). One common approach is to introduce individual and family characteristics as control variables in statistical models, which may account for differential sorting and the nonrandom process of neighborhood selection. A second approach to address selection is the use of instrumental variables. With an instrumental variables approach, a variable (or variables) that is unrelated to unmeasured characteristics is used as an independent variable to predict neighborhood context, and then the outcome variable is regressed on the predicted neighborhood context. Conceptually, this approach removes the spurious correlation between neighborhood context and unobserved family or individual characteristics (see, e.g., Duncan, Connell, and Klebanov 1997; Kirk 2009a). A third method for accounting for selection is sibling models. Sibling models offer a solution by eliminating the selection bias due to omitted family or parent characteristics. Presumably observed and unobserved family characteristics are equal for each sibling, so that the difference in outcomes across siblings is simply a function of differences in context (e.g., neighborhood or school). If families move, then it is possible to determine how changing contexts influence one sibling at a given age relative to how a previous context influenced an older sibling (see, e.g.,

Duncan, Boisjoly, and Harris 2001). A fourth approach to selection is the use of propensity score matching (or stratification), coupled with sensitivity analysis. With this approach, control and treatment cases are matched according to a propensity score. In this case, the "treatment" refers to some kind of neighborhood condition (e.g., Harding [2003] used neighborhood poverty as a treatment in an analysis of school dropout and teen pregnancy). If control and treatment groups are equivalent prior to treatment, the difference between the two groups after treatment will be attributable to the treatment. Fifth, with longitudinal research, one can assess how neighborhood change is related to change in outcomes or how change of residence leads to changes in outcomes. Finally, one of the more promising approaches to addressing the issues of causality and selection is experimentation.

E. Concluding Remarks

Numerous conceptual and research design considerations need to be understood and addressed when conducting research on neighborhood change and when evaluating the literature on neighborhood change. These considerations include defining, operationalizing, and measuring neighborhoods, as well as the challenge of causally relating changes in neighborhoods to changes in crime. One reason for the relative lack of studies of neighborhood change and crime is that there are relatively few data repositories with combined measures of neighborhood structures, processes, and crime rates across multiple time points. Despite these challenges, the study of neighborhood change is beneficial for our understanding of the nature and distribution of criminal behavior.

II. Population Migration and Sociodemographic Change

The 1980s were marked by a resurging interest in ecological explanations for crime. Two noteworthy studies during this period, by Bursik and Webb (1982) and Schuerman and Kobrin (1986), were at the forefront of the recent expansion of dynamic studies of neighborhoods and crime. These two studies explicitly address the relation between ecological change and the changing spatial distribution of delinquency in Chicago and Los Angeles respectively. In this section, we highlight prevailing research with respect to five different types of population changes: central city population loss, gentrification, the development and demolition of public housing, home ownership and foreclosure, and immigration. First, however, we briefly discuss the work of Bursik and Webb (1982) and Schuerman and Kobrin (1986) in order to provide a bridge between the early Chicago School work on the growth of the city (Burgess [1925] 1967; Shaw and McKay 1942) and contemporary investigations of ecological change.

Bursik and Webb (1982) provide a critical test of Shaw and McKay's (1942) thesis about the stability of the relative distribution of delinquency. Shaw and McKay observed that the relative geographic concentration of delinquency persisted in the same geographic areas of Chicago from 1900 to 1940 and thus concluded that regardless of changes in the racial and ethnic composition of Chicago neighborhoods, the relative distribution of delinquency throughout the city would remain stable over time. Bursik and Webb confirm that temporal changes in neighborhood composition (i.e., population size, percentage of foreign-born white, percentage of nonwhite, and household density) had little influence on changes in male delinquency rates during the 1940s. Yet, a number of ecological changes occurred in Chicago following World War II, including substantial demographic shifts in the population. Bursik and Webb found that these shifts in the population distribution were related to changes in the relative distribution of delinquency from 1950 to 1970, thus countering Shaw and McKay's arguments about the stability of the relative distribution of delinquency.

Schuerman and Kobrin (1986) examined how high-crime neighborhoods in Los Angeles developed. To do so, they used a developmental model to investigate the 20-year histories of Los Angeles neighborhoods and characterized three different stages in the development of neighborhood crime rates. First, "emerging" neighborhoods were those areas with lower levels of crime in 1950 that became high-crime areas by 1970. Second, "transitional" neighborhoods already had moderately high crime rates as of 1950, which became even higher by 1970. Third, "enduring" neighborhoods had high crime rates in 1950 that persisted at least until the last observation period of 1970. In describing the progression, or development, of crime changes, Schuerman and Kobrin found that initial crime changes were due to changes in land use (i.e., residential vs. commercial or industrial) as well as demographic changes (i.e., population size, residential mobility, and divorce). Later changes in crime rates were due to social factors such as socioeconomic status and subcultural influences.

What we learn from Bursik and Webb (1982) and Schuerman and

Kobrin (1986) is that neighborhoods are best treated as dynamic entities. In contrast to the early-twentieth-century observations of Shaw and McKay (1942), Bursik and Webb and Schuerman and Kobrin show that the distribution of crime across space is not altogether stable and does vary as a function of ecological change. While these two studies examined the effects of ecological changes prior to 1970, to follow we take stock of population migration and sociodemographic changes primarily occurring over the past four decades.

A. Central City Population Loss and Middle-Class Flight

Much has been written about the processes of suburbanization and middle-class flight among all races that fundamentally transformed U.S. metropolitan areas during the twentieth century. While considerable media attention and popular discussion today has been directed toward trends in gentrification and suburb-to-city moves, it is still true today that city-to-suburban moves are most common. For instance, data from the 2008 Current Population Survey reveal that nearly 6.4 million households moved in the United States from 2007 to 2008 (U.S. Census Bureau 2009a). Of these households, 4.2 million moved within the same metropolitan area, 790,000 moved between metropolitan areas, and the remainder consisted of metro-to-nonmetro, nonmetro-to-metro, and nonmetro-to-nonmetro moves, as well as movers from abroad. Of the 4.2 million moves within the same metropolitan area, 618,000 moved from the city to the suburbs while 259,000 moved from the suburbs to the city (the remainder consisted of within-city or within-suburb moves). Of the 790,000 households who moved between metropolitan areas, 238,000 moved from the city to the suburbs while 152,000 moved from the suburbs to the city. Thus, despite the allure of gentrifying cities, it is still far more common for households to move from the city to the suburbs than the reverse.

Given these trends, we consider the relation between crime and central city population loss and out-migration flows. More specifically, we provide an overview of studies that implicate crime as a cause or consequence of central city population changes. We focus first on the study of central city population loss during the middle of the twentieth century in order to set the stage for more recent changes.

Frey (1979) addresses the causes of "white flight" to the suburbs during the middle part of the twentieth century and specifically examines two contrasting views: that the exodus of white residents from central cities was racially motivated or that the declining economic and ecological conditions of central cities spurred white flight. Frey suggests that white flight during the 1940s and 1950s was relatively more racially motivated than in later decades, particularly in northern cities that saw an influx of southern black migrants during the 1940s (see also Taeuber and Taeuber 1965). In contrast, he hypothesizes that white flight from cities during the 1960s was due to deteriorating economic and environmental conditions within central cities (e.g., declining tax base and services from prior suburbanization, job migration to the suburbs, and crime).[7] With respect to crime, Frey found that central city crime rates affect both the decision to move somewhere and the choice of a particular destination (within the city or to the suburbs). However, the effect of crime is relatively greater on the choice of destination than on the decision to move. In other words, while high crime rates to some extent do "push" households out of their current places of residence, the salience of crime as a factor in residential migration decisions is most prevalent in choices of where specifically to live.

More recently, in an examination of the crime-population migration relation from 1970 to 1990, Cullen and Levitt (1999) found that for each additional reported index crime in a central city area, there is a net decline in population of approximately one resident. Moreover, findings reveal that a 10 percent rise in crime corresponds to a 1 percent decline in central city population. They also found that more educated households and households with children are more sensitive to crime changes and are therefore more likely to move out of central cities should crime increase.

A number of studies have explored not only the effects of crime change on population flows but also whether population out-migration due to crime is race specific. In an analysis of crime changes and population migration from 1970 to 1980 in all 55 cities in the United States with a population size greater than 250,000, Sampson and Wooldredge (1986) found that crime had an adverse impact on net migration and population size. This was true for both white and nonwhite pop-

---

[7] Taub, Taylor, and Dunham (1984) investigate a similar question in their case studies of neighborhood change in Chicago. They seek to identify the sources of the racial tipping of neighborhoods and turn to crime as an explanation. Perceptions of the seriousness of the neighborhood crime problem influence residents' intentions to move from a neighborhood. They suggest that the impact is variable by race, such that the black-white demand ratio for housing in a given neighborhood increases with increases in crime. In other words, neighborhood crime deflates white demand for housing in a given neighborhood, and the end result may appear to be the racial tipping of a neighborhood.

ulation groups. Thus, high crime rates encourage out-migration from central cities across a variety of racial groups.

Liska and Bellair (1995), using a sample of cities with populations over 50,000, found evidence of a reciprocal relation between the percentage of the nonwhite population of cities and robbery rates. Findings reveal that racial composition affected robbery rates during the 1980s and that robbery rates led to an increase in the percentage of the nonwhite city population in all decades investigated (1950–90). Given that robbery leads to an increase in the percentage of nonwhite residents in a city, Liska and Bellair examine whether this change is due to an increase in the absolute size of the nonwhite population or a decline in the absolute size of the white population. They found support for a thesis of "white flight." Robbery rates have no effect on the size of the nonwhite population but do negatively affect the size of the white population.

A reciprocal finding of the relation between robbery and racial composition is not isolated to central city neighborhoods. In a longitudinal study of suburban dynamics, Liska, Logan, and Bellair (1998) found a significant reciprocal relation between robbery rates and the percentage of the nonwhite population in a suburb and that the relative size of the effect of robbery on future increases in the percentage of the nonwhite population is greater than the effect of suburban racial composition on future rates of robbery. Moreover, they also found that of all predictors of racial change in their model, including a measure of the percentage of the nonwhite population in the previous decade, robbery exerts the greatest influence.

While findings of the relation between crime and population change at the city and suburban level are relatively abundant, evidence of the effect of crime on population loss at the neighborhood level is limited. Yet, it may be the case that increases in crime in urban neighborhoods lead to mobility to lower-crime urban neighborhoods or flight to the suburbs and that out-migration to the suburbs occurs from select urban neighborhoods. Of the studies that have examined population loss at the neighborhood level, Morenoff and Sampson (1997) found a significant negative relationship between neighborhood homicide rates at the beginning of a decade (i.e., initial homicide levels) and the change in neighborhood population over the ensuing decade (1970–80 and 1980–90)—that is, high levels of homicide were followed by population loss. This relationship between homicide and population loss holds when disaggregated by both black and white populations. Interestingly, while initial levels of homicide predict similar population changes for blacks and whites, interdecade changes in the neighborhood level of homicide had differing effects on blacks and whites. Neighborhoods experiencing an increase in homicide over a decade had a decline in the absolute size of the white population yet an increase in the absolute size of the black population. Morenoff and Sampson suggest that forces of segregation (e.g., housing discrimination) constrain the mobility of the black population (see also Massey and Denton 1993). Thus, black residents flee core central city neighborhoods because of high levels of violence, yet they are less likely to move outside of the city than the white population. Rather, black residents move into peripheral neighborhoods still within the city because of segregation. It is in these peripheral areas that homicide increased over the decade.[8]

One question implied by the aforementioned findings is this: while increases in crime push residents, particularly white residents, out of central cities, do declines in crime in central cities pull them back? If so, then the substantial declines in crime and violence that characterized many central cities in the United States during the 1990s should be one explanation for the rise of in-migration and gentrification of central cities in the 1990s and 2000s.

B. Gentrification

Gentrification in many ways represents a reversal of trends associated with earlier periods of middle-class exodus from central cities. Hoover and Vernon's (1959) life cycle model of neighborhood change predicts such a progression. In this model, neighborhoods undergo a process of change characterized by five stages: development, transition, downgrading, thinning out, and renewal. During the first stage, single-family homes are developed, which then leads to increasing density and higher socioeconomic status during the transition stage. Downgrading and thinning out (i.e., population loss) then occur for a variety of reasons, such as changing economic conditions or white flight. Fi-

---

[8] In contrast, Katzman (1980) found that crime does not so much influence out-migration from neighborhoods as it does the selection of particular neighborhoods for in-migration. While factors such as changes in jobs and transition to different stages of the life cycle (e.g., parenthood) influence decisions to move, the choice of particular destination neighborhoods for where to move is partly a function of their crime rates and other locational amenities, such as quality schools (see also Rossi 1955). Moreover, Katzman found that middle-income families are more sensitive to property crime than lower-income families are when deciding where to move, and families with children are more sensitive as well.

nally, renewal and gentrification occur, as middle-income residents are drawn to relatively cheaper housing prices.

While middle-income residents may be drawn to gentrifying neighborhoods in central cities, it is worth reiterating that the modal migration pattern for U.S. residents is still to the suburbs, not a return to the city (Kennedy and Leonard 2001; U.S. Census Bureau 2009*a*). Some scholars even suggest that gentrification does not entail a return of middle-class residents from the suburbs to the central city; rather, gentrification marks a spatial redistribution of residents already residing in the central city (e.g., Covington and Taylor 1989). However, quantifiable evidence of the original locations of gentrifiers is lacking.[9]

The origination of the term "gentrification" has often been credited to Ruth Glass (1964, pp. xviii–xix), who in her study of urban change in London observed, "working class quarters of London have been invaded by the middle classes. . . . Shabby, modest mews and cottages—two rooms up and two down—have been taken over, when their leases have expired, and have become elegant, expensive residences. Larger Victorian houses, downgraded in an earlier or recent period—which were used as lodging houses or were otherwise in multiple occupation—have been upgraded once again. . . . Once this process of 'gentrification' starts in a district, it goes on rapidly until all or most of the original working class occupiers are displaced, and the whole social character of the district is changed." In this definition, there are three key dimensions of gentrification: first, a period of downgrading and disinvestment of central city neighborhoods; second, working-class residents are displaced by middle-class residents; third, the housing stock is transformed, and housing values rise. Recent theorists and researchers have employed definitions similar to the original usage coined by Glass.[10] Smith (1996, p. 32) suggests, "Gentrification is the

---

[9] Much of the discussion of residential mobility in the gentrification literature concerns the extent of displacement and out-migration of former residents. Much less attention has been given to the characteristics of in-movers (for an exception, see Freeman [2005]).

[10] However, not all scholars agree that gentrification is synonymous with the displacement of lower-income residents. Freeman and Braconi (2004) found little evidence of displacement following gentrification in New York City and even show that impoverished residents and those without a college education are less likely to move out of gentrifying neighborhoods than nongentrifying neighborhoods (see also Vigdor 2002). In response, Newman and Wyly (2006) note a number of methodological issues with the Freeman and Braconi study (2004), including the fact that Freeman and Braconi examined the prevalence of displacement well after gentrification had already begun, thereby suggesting that displacement had already occurred and their data (the New York City Housing and Vacancy Survey) were simply not capturing the multitude of displacements from past

process . . . by which poor and working-class neighborhoods in the inner city are refurbished via an influx of private capital and middle-class homebuyers and renters—neighborhoods that had previously experienced disinvestment and a middle-class exodus." Kennedy and Leonard define gentrification as "the process of neighborhood change that results in the replacement of lower income residents with higher income ones" (2001, p. 1).[11] They also emphasize that gentrification tends to occur in cities with tight housing markets and that demand for housing by middle-income residents induces reinvestment into deteriorating neighborhoods. In all these definitions, the emphasis is upon class transformation of neighborhoods, not racial transformation. While many gentrifying areas have undergone changes in racial composition in addition to social class (Smith 1996; Kennedy and Leonard 2001), that is not always the case. For instance, Hyra (2008) observes that the revitalization and gentrification of two historic black communities during the 1990s and 2000s—Harlem in New York and Bronzeville in Chicago—were characterized by an influx of middle-class black residents, not middle-class whites or other races and ethnicities.

In a volume of *Crime and Justice* published more than two decades ago, McDonald (1986) suggested that there may be two contrasting consequences of gentrification for neighborhood crime. First, crime rates may increase with gentrification because of increased opportunity for property crimes and a disruption of social networks and social control processes. A second, alternative hypothesis is that crime declines because relatively more crime-prone individuals are displaced from gentrifying neighborhoods (i.e., a selective migration argument). Outside of these two suggestions by McDonald, a third plausible hypothesis is that gentrifying neighborhoods suffer a short-term rise in crime due to a rapid influx of population and subsequent social instability and

---

time points. Even so, Newman and Wyly found substantially higher rates of displacement than Freeman and Braconi using the same data.

[11] Kennedy and Leonard (2001) draw a distinction between "gentrification" and "revitalization." They define the latter as "the process of enhancing the physical, commercial and social components of neighborhoods and the future prospects of its residents through private sector and/or public sector efforts. Physical components include upgrading of housing stock and streetscapes. Commercial components include the creation of viable businesses and services in the community. Social components include increasing employment and reductions in crime. Gentrification sometimes occurs in the midst of the revitalization process" (Kennedy and Leonard 2001, p. 6). The distinction lies in the fact that gentrification directly implies a displacement of lower-income residents, while revitalization does not necessarily result in such a displacement.

population heterogeneity. Yet, as neighborhoods stabilize in the long term, crime should decline. What does the prevailing research reveal about these hypotheses?

McDonald (1986) provides a descriptive analysis of 14 different gentrifying neighborhoods across Boston, New York City, San Francisco, Seattle, and Washington, DC. In accordance with his second hypothesis, McDonald found a negative relation between gentrification and personal crimes (i.e., homicide, rape, robbery, and aggravated assault) though no effect of gentrification on property crime.

Taylor and Covington (1988) found support for McDonald's first hypothesis, that crime increases in gentrifying neighborhoods. Taylor and Covington conceptualize gentrifying areas as those neighborhoods that experience "dramatic increases in relative house value" and "increasing managerial-professional work forces and increasing educational levels" among residents (1988, p. 559). They operationalize this conception by identifying those Baltimore neighborhoods that initially had low status (i.e., low education levels, low relative house values, high poverty rate, and vacant housing) and low levels of stability (i.e., low percentages of owner-occupied homes and married-couple households) in 1970, which transformed into high-status and high-stability neighborhoods over the course of the 1970s. They found that gentrifying neighborhoods had marked increases in murder and aggravated assault from 1970 to 1980. Taylor and Covington interpret this finding by drawing upon the social disorganization tradition. Changing neighborhoods, whether downgrading or upgrading in status and stability, are characterized by population turnover and, at least initially, heterogeneity in resident characteristics. The repercussions of neighborhood downgrading and upgrading are perhaps best summarized by Bursik and Webb: "When the existing community changes almost completely within a short period of time, the social institutions and social networks may disappear altogether, or existing institutions may persevere in the changed neighborhood but be very resistant to the inclusion of new residents" (1982, pp. 39–40).

In a follow-up study, Covington and Taylor (1989) draw attention to the repercussions of rapid change in neighborhoods in contrast to steady change and define gentrifying neighborhoods as those neighborhoods that demonstrated the most rapid rise in relative home values over the course of the 1970s. They suggest that rapid neighborhood change is a destabilizing force, which undermines neighborhood social networks and informal social control to a much greater extent than in neighborhoods that change more slowly.[12] They found a positive association between gentrification and changes in crime, in this case robbery and larceny. Gentrifying neighborhoods, with rapidly appreciating home values, had relatively greater changes in robbery and larceny in comparison to slowly appreciating neighborhoods. Such a finding accords with Durkheim's (1951) analysis of suicide. In describing the repercussions of sudden declines in societal regulation, Durkheim argues, "when society is disturbed by some painful crisis or by beneficent but abrupt transitions, it is momentarily incapable of exercising this influence [regulation]; thence come the sudden rises in the curve of suicides we have pointed out" (1951, p. 252).

A number of European studies have similarly found that residential turnover in gentrifying areas leads to increases in crime. For instance, in a qualitative investigation of gentrification and displacement in central London during the 1980s, Atkinson (2000, p. 321) found evidence that gentrification leads to the breakdown of close-knit communities because of the turnover of neighborhood residents. This breakdown in community then results in rising crime.

In a study of neighborhood change and victimization in the Netherlands during the 1990s, Van Wilsem, Wittebrood, and De Graaf (2006) found that the likelihood of victimization (property or violence) is greater in neighborhoods characterized by socioeconomic improvements relative to neighborhoods with little change in socioeconomic status. They also found that residential instability substantially mediates the association between neighborhood socioeconomic improvement and victimization. While they do not directly measure social control, they suggest that their findings reveal that the inflow of new residents into a neighborhood undermines cohesion among neighborhood residents and therefore hinders the process of informal social control.

Available evidence thus suggests that gentrification leads to an increase in crime. Yet, recall the third hypothesis, that gentrifying neighborhoods suffer a short-term rise in crime due to population turnover and subsequent social instability and population heterogeneity, but crime declines long term as neighborhoods stabilize and informal social

---

[12] Schuerman and Kobrin (1986) similarly argue that it is the "velocity" of neighborhood change that is consequential to subsequent increases in neighborhood crime rates rather than the mere presence of change.

controls increase. A recent study by Kreager, Lyons, and Hays (2007) found support for this hypothesis. In an investigation of the raw change in violent and property crime in Seattle from 1980 to 2000, they found a positive association between property crime and gentrification in the 1980s during the early stages of gentrification. In other words, in the short-run gentrification leads to an increase in property crime (though they found no effect on violent crime). However, in the long run, both property and violent crime decreased more in gentrifying neighborhoods relative to nongentrifying neighborhoods.[13]

Kreager, Lyons, and Hays interpret their findings as follows: "Our study thus points to the importance of viewing gentrification as a temporal process with varying consequences for urban crime rates: early stages of incomplete gentrification may facilitate greater crime and disorganization whereas later stages, characterized by 'corporatized' urban renewal of the 90's, may transform neighborhoods more completely into relatively organized areas capable of controlling criminal elements" (2007, p. 25). Such a nuanced view of the complexity of gentrification is instructive. Gentrification is not an event but a process. Its effects on crime depend upon the stage of the process. Early stages are often characterized by population turnover as well as income, racial, and ethnic heterogeneity. Later stages are more likely to be characterized by stability and social organization. Thus, just as Schuerman and Kobrin (1986) argued more than 20 years ago, it is best to think of neighborhood change as a temporal process of development (see also Berry 1985).

Thus far we have addressed the effects of gentrification on crime within the gentrifying neighborhood. A few key puzzles remain, however. First, recall that one dimension of Glass's (1964) definition of gentrification is displacement. Working-class residents are displaced by middle-income residents (though see Freeman and Braconi 2004).

---

[13] To operationalize "gentrification," Kreager and colleagues (2007) utilize a database developed by Wyly and Hammel (1999; see also Hammel and Wyly 1996), who classified census tracts in Seattle and other major U.S. cities as (a) gentrifying, (b) nongentrifying poor, and (c) previously high income or appreciating. This classification scheme is based upon an assortment of publicly available data and survey data. Based on median income indicators from the 1960 Census, Wyly and Hammel (1999) identified areas of decay and disinvestment in central cities. To determine which of these decaying areas gentrified, Wyly and Hammel (1999, p. 727) conducted a "block-by-block field survey of tracts" in order to identify "visible evidence of housing reinvestment and class turnover." To further refine their classification of gentrifying neighborhoods, Wyly and Hammel rely upon Home Mortgage Disclosure Act (HMDA) data to confirm the extent of housing investment in those neighborhoods they classified as gentrifying per the survey data.

Does this imply that crime is displaced as well? Unfortunately, investigations of the displacement of crime from gentrification are sorely lacking, yet research by Curtis (1998, 2003) is instructive on this point. In these two studies, Curtis recounts 10 years of ethnographic research in Brooklyn during the 1980s and 1990s, a period during which Puerto Rican, and then later Dominican-controlled drug markets quickly diminished. Curtis (2003) describes the evolution of the Williamsburg neighborhood of Brooklyn, from a mixed industrial-residential area with more than 50 operational breweries prior to the 1960s to an area decimated by the decline in manufacturing that affected so many central cities in the oldest sections of the United States during the last decades of the twentieth century (see, e.g., Wilson 1987). Williamsburg is connected directly to lower Manhattan by the Williamsburg Bridge, and is easily accessible by public transportation. Such ecological advantages made it a prime location as a drug market in the 1960s, 1970s, and 1980s. Yet, this accessibility contributed to gentrification in the 1980s. As Curtis (2003) observes, residents displaced from Manhattan in the mid-1980s because of rising rents flocked to nearby Williamsburg. Many boarded-up buildings and abandoned industrial areas, some of which were used as "shooting galleries" and drug stashes, were transformed into lofts and condos for gentrifiers. With respect to the Williamsburg drug market, Curtis (1998) notes that the effect of gentrification as well as policing interventions was to displace the drug trade to Bushwick, an adjacent neighborhood located to the southeast of Williamsburg. In our view, the story of the relation between gentrification and crime is not complete without such an understanding of the potential for the displacement of crime.

A second remaining puzzle is the reverse causal story—that is, whether declines in property and violent crime during the 1990s spurred the revitalization of central city neighborhoods as well as the movement of middle-class households into gentrifying neighborhoods. In other words, gentrification appears to lower crime, especially in the long run, but did the drop in crime in the United States during the 1990s spur gentrification?[14] We take up this issue in greater detail in

---

[14] In a provocative case study of the gentrification of Los Angeles's Skid Row, Harcourt (2005) questions whether eliminating disorder through order-maintenance policing and other strategies initiates urban renewal and gentrification or whether high-end real estate development in decaying areas leads to reductions in crime and disorder. Interestingly, he observes that real estate developers and would-be gentrifiers actually seek to retain some of the crime, disorder, homelessness, and rampant drug use that characterize Skid

Section III in a discussion of future research agendas, but we indirectly address such questions here by exploring the impact of crime on subsequent property values.[15]

In a metropolitan-level analysis of the change in home values, Manning (1986) found that the initial level of crime in a metropolitan area in 1970 as well as the change in crime from 1970 to 1980 had no bearing on the change in home prices over the same decade. In contrast, an assortment of longitudinal studies pitched at the neighborhood unit of analysis found an inverse relationship between crime and housing values. In an analysis of the residual change in housing values and vacancy rates across Baltimore neighborhoods from 1970 to 1980, Taylor (1995) found that declines in aggravated assault and murder led to a rise in housing values. Similarly, using a hedonic model of home sales prices in Columbus, Ohio, from 1995 to 1998, Tita, Petras, and Greenbaum (2006) found an inverse relationship between violent crime in a given year and home sales price the next year. However, they found no relation between increases in property crime and sales price. Hipp, Tita, and Greenbaum (2009) replicate this finding in an analysis of property values in Los Angeles for the years 1992–97. They found that violent crime negatively affects subsequent property values, yet there is no relationship between property crime and property values. Schwartz, Susin, and Voicu (2003) examine whether the decline in crime in New York City in the early 1990s led to the real estate boom during the latter part of the decade. They found that property sales values increased an average of 17.5 percent from 1994 to 1998, and declines in crime account for one-third (i.e., 6 percent) of this increase. Similar to Tita and colleagues (2006), they found that violent crime affected property values but not property crime.

Thus, dynamic research suggests that there is an inverse relation between crime and property values but that the effect is limited to violent crime, not property crime.[16] This suggests that residential and

---

Row. Harcourt (2005, p. 8) suggests, "it is precisely that juxtaposition of high-end lofts and homeless beggars that gives L.A.'s Skid Row a trendy, urban, edgy, *noir* flavor that is so marketable." In other words, crime sells (within limits).

[15] The relation between crime and housing values is a heavily researched topic across a variety of disciplines. We focus our discussion on dynamic studies that address the relation between change in crime and change in housing values.

[16] While not focused on crime declines, Linden and Rockoff (2008) too found an inverse relation between crime and home sales prices. They use longitudinal data on property sales in Mecklenburg County, NC—which includes the city of Charlotte—to examine within-neighborhood variation in home values in the period just before to right after a

housing decisions are most responsive to changes in violence. While fear of violent victimization adversely affects residents' attachment to their neighborhoods and decreases their willingness to engage collectively in informal social control (Skogan 1986, 1990; Taylor 1995), declines in violence may trigger a reduction in fear that then encourages residents to invest in neighborhoods formerly characterized by violence. Thus, one intervening mechanism between changes in violence and rising property values may be fear of violent victimization.

In sum, results suggest that gentrification initially leads to an increase in crime, as neighborhood change destabilizes processes of regulation and social control.[17] Yet, in the long run, gentrification leads to neighborhood reductions in crime, as social networks form and social control becomes more readily possible. Findings, particularly research by Schwartz, Susin, and Voicu (2003), also suggest that declines in crime likely spurred gentrification through the appearance of safer central city neighborhoods.

C. Public Housing

The effects of public housing in the United States on neighborhood crime rates have received scant attention in the criminological literature, though more consideration has been given to the subject in the urban studies and housing policy literature. Yet, few researchers in any discipline have systematically explored the effects of the initial development of public housing in the United States on crime, and even fewer have examined the repercussions of recent changes in public housing policies for crime.[18] Yet, changes that lead to a redistribution

---

sex offender moved to a given neighborhood. They found that the sale prices of homes fall considerably after a sex offender moves into a neighborhood, though only in close proximity to where the offender is living. Specifically, they found that home prices adjacent to sex offender residences declined 12 percent, but homes one-tenth of a mile away or more did not have an appreciable change in value.

[17] Studies of "boomtowns" and areas of rapid population growth in rural and semirural areas have similarly shown immediate increases in crime following ecological change (see Freudenburg and Jones [1991] for a review). Thus, this Durkheimian dynamic of declining informal social control in the face of rapid social change is not isolated to urban neighborhoods.

[18] Most research of public housing and crime in the United States has gravitated toward tests of the propositions of Oscar Newman's (1972) *Defensible Space* thesis. What we know about the association between public housing and crime in the United States is largely related to the architectural characteristics of housing structures, not the siting of those structures in particular neighborhoods. In the interest of scope, we focus our attention on the implications of public housing on neighborhood rates of crime (a meso-level perspective) as opposed to a focus on which design features of public housing influence why crime occurs in one place rather than another (a micro-level perspective).

of the population, such as the demolition of public housing, may alter the spatial distribution of motivated offenders and may undermine neighborhood informal social control because of residential instability.

The development of public housing in the United States began on a large scale with the U.S. Housing Act of 1937 (Holzman 1996).[19] Much of the early use of public housing was to shelter families temporarily following the Depression and World War II, not to provide permanent residences. In particular, many war veterans resided in public housing for short periods following World War II, before moving to other accommodations (Holzman 1996). It was not until the 1950s that public housing came to be a more enduring form of subsidized residence for low-income families. Much of the public housing stock in the United States was built during this midcentury period (Fagan et al. 1998). Federal policies enacted during this period, as well as local decision making, led to the concentration of public housing developments in areas generally characterized by disadvantage, disorganization, and large proportions of minority residents (Hyra 2008).

One of the most significant changes in recent decades to impoverished urban neighborhoods has been the razing of many high-density public housing developments. Along with these demolitions has come a shift in federal and local strategies from providing housing assistance through high-rise public housing to low-density, scattered-site housing and vouchers (i.e., Section 8 vouchers), which can be used to subsidize housing found in the private rental market.[20] The impetus for these changes has been the well-documented consequences of the concentration of poverty and the concentration of public housing in central city neighborhoods (Wilson 1987; Galster and Zobel 1998). Thus, scattered-site housing as well as the use of housing vouchers is designed to deconcentrate impoverished public housing residents, to integrate

[19] The main focus of this section is on public housing in the United States. For an examination of the link between public housing and crime in Great Britain, see Bottoms and Wiles (1986) and Foster and Hope (1993); for the investigation of public housing and crime in Australia and Canada, respectively, see DeKeseredy et al. (2003) and Weatherburn, Lind, and Ku (1999).

[20] Scattered-site public housing residences are small-scale rental developments typically built or purchased with the help of federal funds and managed by local public housing authorities (Galster and Zobel 1998). Developments generally range in size from single family homes to apartment complexes. Section 8 vouchers are a form of rent subsidy for low-income households provided by the U.S. Department of Housing and Urban Development through local public housing authorities. Subsidies are distributed to landlords directly, with tenants covering the remaining rent. Per the Section 8 program, tenants must contribute at least 30 percent of their monthly adjusted family income to the rent.

public housing residents into middle-class neighborhoods, and to provide residents with increased employment and educational opportunities (Galster and Zobel 1998).

Trends in the allocation of housing vouchers provide clear evidence of the marked shift in housing assistance strategies. In 1996, 1.34 million housing vouchers were issued to households in the United States, and approximately 1.32 million public housing units were available, 90 percent of which were occupied (U.S. Department of Housing and Urban Development 1996). In contrast, by the year 2000, 1.82 million households were issued vouchers while 1.28 million public housing units were available in the United States, 93 percent of which were occupied (U.S. Department of Housing and Urban Development 2000). By 2005, 1.9 million households were receiving housing assistance through vouchers while 1.1 million households were residing in public housing units (Haley 2005). Thus, the ratio of households living in public housing units versus private housing subsidized through vouchers has declined dramatically over time.

One key shift in assisted housing dynamics has been the demolition of a substantial number of distressed public housing units over the past two decades in the United States. In 1989, the U.S. Congress established the National Commission on Severely Distressed Public Housing, which was tasked with identifying severely distressed public housing and with crafting an action plan for remedying the problem (Popkin et al. 2004). This commission ultimately identified 86,000 public housing units (out of the 1.3 million nationwide) as severely distressed, and Congress enacted the Housing Opportunities for People Everywhere (HOPE VI) program in 1992 to fund the replacement and renovation of distressed units. To date, $6 billion has been spent through HOPE VI, with over 78,100 public housing units demolished and another 10,400 units to be redeveloped (Turner et al. 2007).

Another related legislative mandate leading to the recent decline in public housing units is the Omnibus Consolidated Rescissions and Appropriations Act of 1996 (sec. 202). This legislation requires public housing authorities to assess the condition of their public housing developments and the viability of rehabilitating distressed units (Jacob 2004, p. 233). If the cost to rehabilitate and maintain a given distressed housing unit is greater than the estimated cost to provide the residents a housing voucher for use in the private housing market for a period of 20 years, then the housing authority must vacate the unit and remove the unit from its stock of housing. Jacob (2004) reports that roughly 91,000 units across 35 different public housing authorities were scheduled to be demolished because the cost of rehabilitation exceeds that of housing vouchers.

With the changing neighborhood context of public housing in mind, in this subsection we ask two related questions: how does the siting of a public housing development in a given neighborhood influence crime rates in that neighborhood and in proximate neighborhoods, and how has the demolition of public housing units over the past two decades affected neighborhood crime rates?[21] Public housing, and the demolition thereof, may affect neighborhood crime by a number of mechanisms. First, the development of public housing in a given neighborhood may instigate a process of selective migration. That is, different types of families may migrate to a given neighborhood (e.g., more impoverished) relative to current residents. Second, both the development and demolition of public housing may undermine informal social control because of residential turnover and instability.

Question 1: The Effects of Public Housing Development on Crime. There is a long history of resident resentment and opposition to the siting of public housing in their neighborhood (see, e.g., Meyerson and Banfield 1964; Cuomo 1974; Hirsch 1983). Much of this history of opposition is based on the contention that the placement of public housing in a given neighborhood adversely affects property values and increases crime (Freeman and Botein 2002). Opponents assume that public housing influences neighborhood crime because of the migration of relatively more crime-prone residents into the neighborhood and through the increased concentration of poverty, social disorganization, and criminal opportunities (McNulty and Holloway 2000; Freeman and Botein 2002; Santiago, Galster, and Pettit 2003). Despite numerous presumed pathways by which public housing is said to lead to

---

[21] A third line of inquiry would assess the effects of the residential mobility of former residents of razed housing on their criminal behavior. As noted in Sec. I, "neighborhood effects" can be categorized as either (*a*) the effect of moving individuals to different neighborhoods or (*b*) changing neighborhoods. Generally, our interest in this review is the latter. Given our focus on neighborhood change as opposed to residential mobility, we exclude discussion of this third line of inquiry. For readers interested in such investigations of mobility effects from public housing shifts, see Galster and Zobel (1998) and Goetz (2003) for reviews of research. Additionally, see Jacob (2004) for a novel approach (i.e., natural experiment) for examining the impact of forced migration from public housing demolitions on youth outcomes.

increased crime, little research has actually tested these notions, particularly using dynamic research designs.

Of the static studies of U.S. public housing, Roncek and colleagues (1981) examined the relation between subsidized housing and neighborhood crime in Cleveland and found a significant, though substantively small, positive association between proximity to subsidized housing and violent crime. Ultimately they conclude that adjacency to public housing sites is one of the least important predictors of violent crime relative to socioeconomic factors. McNulty and Holloway (2000) found that proximity to public housing developments has a positive effect on neighborhood crime rates, though a substantial amount of the association is mediated by neighborhood disadvantage. Fagan and Davies (2000) found evidence of a diffusion process in that violence within public housing is significantly associated with violence in the surrounding census tract. They explain the diffusion process by suggesting that motivated offenders from within public housing commit violent crimes in the surrounding area because of opportunities or a lack of informal social controls. In contrast, Griffiths and Tita (2009) found no evidence that public housing is a generator of violence in the surrounding area. Rather than spilling over into adjacent areas, homicide involving public housing residents is local. When public housing residents engage in lethal violence, it tends to occur within the public housing development and the immediate neighborhood.

Yet, the limitation of these four studies and others of public housing is the failure to establish causal directionality for the relation between public housing and crime (Santiago, Galster, and Pettit 2003). We still do not know if the development of public housing in a given neighborhood causally leads to an increase in crime (whether in the immediate neighborhood or adjacent neighborhoods) or whether public housing units are simply developed in areas with already high crime rates. To sort out directionality, dynamic research on neighborhood change is essential. Here, we draw upon two illustrative dynamic studies to address causal directionality. First, Bursik (1989) examines whether the change in male delinquency in particular community areas of Chicago from 1970 to 1980 was influenced by the development of new public housing constructions. He found that the presence of new public housing has no direct effect on the residual change in delinquency, yet public housing development does indirectly affect delinquency through residential instability. Bursik also found that public housing in Chicago has typically been sited in those neighborhoods that offered the least resistance to the placement of public housing in the neighborhood. In other words, public housing was developed in certain areas because they were least able to engage in collective opposition. This point about community opposition becomes relevant when addressing the potential for selection bias.

As a second example of a dynamic research design, Santiago, Galster, and Pettit (2003) examine whether proximity to 38 new scattered-site public housing developments in Denver is associated with an increase in neighborhood crime. To do so, they compare the actual postdevelopment neighborhood crime rate in a given area with a hypothetical rate based on the predevelopment crime trend in the neighborhood as well as an adjustment for metrowide crime trends. In other words, they set up a counterfactual scenario that represents the hypothetical rate of neighborhood crime if a scattered-site public housing development had never been built in the neighborhood. They found that proximity to scattered-site public housing is not associated with any postdevelopment increase in crime (whether the total crime rate or violent, property, disorderly conduct, or criminal mischief rates). To the contrary, they found that neighborhood crime decreased after development of scattered-site housing.

In sum, results, whether from static or dynamic research designs, suggest that the effect of the siting of public housing in given areas on neighborhood crime rates is minimal at most (after accounting for preexisting neighborhood conditions). Longitudinal designs, which are better suited for establishing causal directionality, reveal that there is little to no direct effect of public housing on neighborhood crime. Effects, if any, are likely indirect, through residential instability and neighborhood disadvantage. As Bursik (1989) illustrates, the co-occurrence of public housing sites and high crime in a given geographic area may occur simply because neighborhood residents are not sufficiently organized to resist the siting of public housing or to control crime.

Question 2: The Effect of the Recent Shift in Housing Assistance in the United States. United States housing authorities in recent decades have shifted strategies away from high-density housing and toward scattered-site housing and increased use of housing vouchers. Thus, it is pertinent to assess the repercussions for neighborhood crime from the demolition of high-density housing as well as the development of scattered-site housing.

One means to uncover the implications of trends away from high-rise public housing is to compare crime rates in neighborhoods characterized by high-rise developments versus otherwise similar neighborhoods characterized by scattered-site or other lower-density housing configurations. However, as Holzman (1996) observes, most criminological research on public housing in the United States has been limited to a focus on high-rise, high-density public housing developments typically located in older cities in the Midwest and Northeast. Of the very few comparative undertakings, a study by Holzman, Kudrick, and Voytek (1996) is suggestive of possible changes to neighborhood crime from shifts from high-rise to scattered-site housing developments. They compare crime and disorder outcomes across a range of public housing types (high-rise, low-rise, town homes, and scattered-site) and number of units. They found, similar to Newman (1972), that building size is positively related to crime. As for building type, burglary is more likely in scattered-site housing than others and least likely in high rises. Holzman et al. suggest that scattered-site units are more accessible than units in other building types and therefore provide more opportunities for burglary. Fear of crime is less likely in scattered-site housing relative to other types, as are gunshots and drug dealing. Thus, outside of burglary, this research suggests that trends toward scattered-site housing may lead to a decrease in crime.

The Holzman, Kudrick, and Voytek (1996) study does not directly address the effects of public housing demolitions. Up to this point, one may conclude that the siting of high-rise public housing developments may contribute to a slight increase in neighborhood crime, because of an impact on social disorganization and related factors (Roncek, Bell, and Francik 1981; Bursik 1989; McNulty and Holloway 2000). Thus, we may see an increase in social organization and a relative decline in neighborhood crime in neighborhoods where high-density housing has been recently demolished. Findings presented by Suresh and Vito (2007) provide some partial support for such an assertion. They found that hot spots of aggravated assault shifted abruptly in Louisville in the mid-1990s, from the Park DuValle neighborhood to nearby areas. They implicate public housing demolition as an explanation. The Cotter Homes and Lang Homes public housing developments in Park DuValle were both demolished during 1996 and 1997, and former residents were dispersed to a number of developments in different neighborhoods throughout the city. While speculative, Suresh and Vito suggest that the substantial decline in assaults in the Park DuValle neighborhood, as well as the rise in assaults in nearby neighborhoods, could be attributed to the demolition of the two housing projects and the dispersal of residents to other sections of the city.[22]

Declines in crime following public housing demolition may not be immediate and may result in the displacement of crime instead of a net reduction. In a comparison of homicide trends in Chicago, New York, and Los Angeles, Hagedorn and Rauch (2007) implicate variation in housing policy as an explanation for why homicide rates declined much less dramatically in Chicago than in the other two cities, particularly New York. They note that housing policies in South Bronx resulted in much less displacement of residents than occurred on the South Side of Chicago. On the basis of interviews with gang members in Chicago who were displaced from public housing, or who resided in receiving neighborhoods of displaced public housing residents, Hagedorn and Rauch assert that the demolition of public housing forced gang members to relocate to new geographic areas, many of which were already controlled by rival gangs. The result was an escalation of gang conflict over the control of turf and drug markets. Popkin and colleagues (1999) observe the same repercussions of displacement in Chicago following the demolition of buildings in the Henry Horner Homes and the Robert Taylor Homes. They conclude that in the short run, public housing closings and demolitions may escalate violence in adjacent buildings or nearby public housing developments because of the disruption of existing gang territories.

At this point, there is limited research on the effects of public housing demolitions on neighborhood crime. A pre-/postresearch design, particularly an interrupted time series, of neighborhoods where public housing has been demolished is certainly warranted. Likewise, further investigation of receiving neighborhoods of displaced populations is necessary. Initial evidence from the United States suggests that resident displacement because of demolitions may displace crime and may lead to an escalation of violence in the short run as gang territories shift into contested spaces.

The issue of selection plagues much of the research of public hous-

---

[22] Suresh and Vito (2007) examine the decline in the number of aggravated assaults in Park DuValle, but it is unclear whether the rate also declined. There is no discussion of how many residents resided in the two public housing complexes or how much the population count changed in the neighborhood. Thus, the aggravated assault rate may have remained the same following demolition even as the number declined.

ing. The question is whether neighborhood crime is higher in neighborhoods where public housing is located because of the presence of these housing facilities or if public housing was simply built in those areas with already high crime rates. While previous authors have recognized this issue (e.g., Roncek, Bell, and Francik 1981), few have directly addressed it. Bursik (1989) observes that public housing in Chicago has typically been located in neighborhoods lacking in social organization and consequently offered the least opposition to the siting of public housing. Factors such as cheaper rents and real estate prices as well as minimal public resistance weigh heavily on the placement of housing sites (Freeman and Botein 2002). Thus, in order to make valid inferences about the impacts of public housing, accounting for such selection processes is necessary.

D. Home Ownership and Home Foreclosure

Home ownership is a ubiquitous goal in the United States and is symbolic of the path to upward mobility. Some have likened home ownership to citizenship and characterized it as a political right (Perin 1977; Shlay 2006). Home ownership rates in the United States presently stand at approximately 68 percent of households (Joint Center for Housing Studies 2009). Over the past century, there have been two substantial increases, from 1940 to 1960 and from the mid-1990s to 2004 (Shiller 2007; Joint Center for Housing Studies 2008). In the former period, rates increased from 44 percent to 62 percent, largely due to government efforts to spur home ownership following the Great Depression (U.S. Census Bureau 2004; Shiller 2007, 2008).[23] In the latter period, from 1994 to 2004, home ownership increased from 64 percent to 69 percent, due in part to low interest rates, flat home prices following the economic recession of 1990–91, and adoption of automated underwriting tools (Joint Center for Housing Studies 2008). This increase was not substantially fueled by the rise of subprime mortgage loans, as home ownership rates had peaked by the time subprime financial products had become widespread (Joint Center for Housing Studies 2008).

Home ownership has numerous social benefits. Regarding individual effects, evidence suggests that homeowners have greater life satisfaction

---

[23] For instance, the Federal Housing Administration and Fannie Mae were created in the 1930s along with the Federal Deposit Insurance Corporation and the Securities and Exchange Commission.

and self-esteem and that there are health benefits to home ownership, at least for individuals not in default on their loans (see Rohe, Van Zandt, and McCarthy [2000] for a discussion). With respect to social effects, homeowners tend to be more committed to their neighborhoods and are more active in civic and community organizations relative to renters (DiPasquale and Glaeser 1999; Rohe, Van Zandt, and McCarthy 2000; Squires and Kubrin 2006). As for crime, because home ownership furthers neighborhood participation as well as residential stability, it may also be a key determinant of the neighborhood informal social control of crime (Squires and Kubrin 2006). Residential instability hinders the development of cohesive and efficacious neighborhood social networks and thereby undermines a neighborhood's capacity for informal social control (Bursik and Grasmick 1993; Sampson, Raudenbush, and Earls 1997). In accord with these arguments, Alba, Logan, and Bellair (1994) found that homeowners tend to reside in neighborhoods with significantly lower violent crime rates than renters. This finding holds across a variety of racial and ethnic groups. Thus, policies directed at furthering home ownership bear upon neighborhood social control and crime.

One central stimulus to increase home ownership is access to mortgages. Squires and Kubrin (2006) found that the extent of mortgage lending in a neighborhood, as measured by the average loan amount per home buyer, is negatively related to neighborhood rates of violence. This finding holds net of neighborhood disadvantage, residential mobility, and a host of other neighborhood correlates of crime.

Squires and Kubrin note, however, that home ownership "is not a universal elixir for urban ills. . . . Families trapped in a high-priced predatory loan from which they cannot escape or in a declining neighborhood where they are unable to sell their home do not benefit" (2006, p. 115). Per this observation, one timely topic vitally important to neighborhood change is home foreclosure. Foreclosure rates in the United States have risen dramatically since the 1970s. Data reported by the Mortgage Bankers Association reveal that the percentage of all mortgages (conventional, nonconventional, prime, and subprime) entering foreclosure increased from roughly 0.2 percent in 1980 to 0.3 percent in 1990 and then to 0.4 percent by 2000. Foreclosure rates rose to 0.5 percent by 2006, to 0.6 percent by 2007, and to 1.37 percent by the first quarter of 2009 (U.S. Government Accountability Office

2007; Mortgage Bankers Association 2009).[24] In 2008 alone, roughly 2.2 million residential properties entered foreclosure (Mortgage Bankers Association 2008).

The causes of this recent increase are many. Common explanations include rising unemployment, consumer debt, an oversupply of new home constructions, falling home values, limited home refinancing options, and the growth of the secondary mortgage market where individual mortgages are packaged and sold as securities.[25] In addition to these causes, much has been made of the rise and subsequent collapse of the subprime mortgage market as an explanation for both the rise of home foreclosures and the global recession more generally.

Subprime loans are typically directed toward individuals with weak or limited credit histories, low incomes, and high levels of debt relative to income and savings. That said, it is certainly true that many borrowers who could qualify for prime mortgage loans nonetheless took out subprime loans or were steered toward such loans (Schloemer et al. 2006). Relative to prime loans, subprime mortgages have higher interest rates and fees and are more likely to include prepayment penalties. Over a short period, subprime mortgages grew from nonexistence to one-quarter of the mortgage market. In the mid-1990s, subprime loans accounted for 0–1 percent of loan originations (Schloemer et al. 2006). In 2003, subprime loans accounted for 10 percent of the market and then ballooned to nearly a quarter of the market just 3 years later.

Subprime loans account for a substantial share of the loans in default. The foreclosure rate (i.e., homes at any point in the foreclosure pro-

[24] Definitions of "foreclosure rates" vary across data sources. The foreclosure process begins when a borrower defaults on a loan and the lender initiates legal action. There are two stages of the process. Stage 1 entails the initiation of legal action against the borrower, but the borrower is still the owner of the property. During this stage, a borrower may still avert foreclosure of the property by paying past-due payments or making other arrangements with the lender. During stage 2 of the foreclosure process, the property is repossessed and sold. Of the leading industry groups and information services, Realty Trac.com reports foreclosure rates based on the number of properties entering stage 1 or 2 of the process during a given time period. The Mortgage Bankers Association of America reports foreclosure rates based on the number of properties entering stage 1 only. Foreclosures.com reports rates based on the number of properties entering stage 2 only (Chen 2008). Thus, foreclosure rates are not comparable across these sources. We report data from the Mortgage Bankers Association of America in this review.

[25] One common critique of the secondary mortgage market is that loan originators have less incentive to assess the capacity of a potential homeowner to make payments when that mortgage can be bundled with other mortgages and subsequently sold as securities (Shiller 2008). In theory, the bundling of loans spreads risk but not if this bundling of mortgages promotes ill-advised lending practices (e.g., failure to check or verify borrowers' incomes).

cess) on subprime loans equaled 4.5 percent in the fourth quarter of 2006 but 8.7 percent by the fourth quarter of 2007 (Joint Center for Housing Studies 2008). In contrast, the foreclosure rate on prime loans was less than 1 percent in 2007. The Center for Responsible Lending estimated that, as of the end of 2008, 1.5 million subprime loans had already been foreclosed, and another 2 million subprime loans were at least 60 days delinquent on payments and at risk of foreclosure (Garrison, Rogers, and Moore 2009).

Despite the current mortgage crisis in the United States, few scholars have investigated the effects of subprime lending practices or foreclosures on neighborhood rates of crime, and none have done so with a dynamic, longitudinal design. Yet, there are several reasons to expect that foreclosures will adversely affect neighborhood crime rates, especially if there is a concentration of foreclosures in a given neighborhood. First, foreclosures may increase the supply of available targets for a property crime and available locations for prostitutes and drug users to congregate (Spelman 1993). Unoccupied properties are particularly ripe for vandalism and burglary. Second, the repossession of a property leads to residential turnover and potentially the fragmentation of neighborhood social networks. Per the systemic model of social disorganization, social ties among neighborhood residents facilitate the informal social control of crime (Bursik and Grasmick 1993; Sampson, Raudenbush, and Earls 1997). While the exit of a few members of a neighborhood social network because of foreclosure may not undermine social control to a great extent, home foreclosures can easily snowball in a given neighborhood and lead to substantial turnover of the population. Research has shown that home foreclosures depress housing values in the vicinity of the foreclosed property (Immergluck and Smith 2006a), particularly if there is a concentration of foreclosures (Schuetz, Been, and Ellen 2008). Declining property values then lead to an increased risk of mortgage default for the remaining homeowners. Thus, a given neighborhood may reach a tipping point of foreclosures whereby early home repossessions create a tidal wave of subsequent foreclosures and devastate neighborhood social networks.

Of the limited cross-sectional research examining the effect of home foreclosures on crime, Immergluck and Smith (2006b) found that the rate of foreclosures in a given census tract in Chicago in 2001 was significantly predictive of violent crime in the same year, though not property crime. A 1-percentage-point increase in the foreclosure rate corresponds to a 2.33 percent increase in violent crime. While these authors lack data to test intervening mechanisms, they suggest that foreclosures lead to more vacant and abandoned properties, which create opportunities for crime and may weaken resident commitment to the neighborhood.

Of course, it may be the case that rising neighborhood crime rates adversely affect foreclosure rates. In other words, the causal relation between crime and foreclosure may be reciprocal. Given the inverse relation between crime and property values (Taylor 1995; Schwartz, Susin, and Voicu 2003; Tita, Petras, and Greenbaum 2006; Hipp, Tita, and Greenbaum 2009) and that declining property values make mortgage default more likely, it is likely that rising crime at least indirectly leads to higher foreclosure rates. We are unaware of any studies to test this relationship at the neighborhood level, though in a state-level analysis, Feinberg and Nickerson (2002) found that prior crime rates, particularly for violent crime, significantly increase the likelihood of mortgage default.

In sum, research on home ownership, mortgages, foreclosures, and crime, while very limited, suggests that home ownership leads to reductions in crime while foreclosures lead to increases in crime. The causal relation is likely reciprocal, with increases in crime subsequently leading to greater foreclosure rates and declines in home ownership.

E. Immigration

From 2000 to 2008, the U.S. population grew by over 22 million individuals, 8.1 million of whom are accounted for by international migration (U.S. Census Bureau 2008). Over this same period, the foreign-born population in the United States increased by over 22 percent while the native-born population increased 5.3 percent (Pew Hispanic Center 2009). At the time of the 2000 Census, the foreign-born population equaled 11 percent of the total U.S. population. By 2007, this had increased to nearly 13 percent.

While New Jersey, Illinois, Florida, Texas, New York, and especially California had the most sizable foreign-born populations in 2000, which have continued to grow, the largest percentage increases in the size of the foreign-born population from 2000 to 2007 occurred in Alabama, Arizona, Arkansas, Nevada, South Carolina, and Tennessee. The foreign-born population increased by over 50 percent in each of these states in just an 8-year span (Pew Hispanic Center 2009). Immigration represents one significant factor in neighborhood population change. Are there any repercussions for neighborhood rates of crime?

Before proceeding, it is important to make a distinction between two research questions: whether immigrants are any more or less criminal than native-born population groups and whether the process of immigration to metropolitan areas and neighborhoods affects rates of crime for both immigrant and native-born groups. With respect to the first question, Thomas and Znaniecki's (1918) contribution to the theory of social disorganization was based on a study of Polish immigrants in the United States at the beginning of the twentieth century. They viewed social disorganization as the consequence of the breakdown of the isolation of peasant communities. Immigrants to the United States had to manage the change associated with moving to a foreign, industrializing, urban environment and adapt to a new language and a new set of customs very different from where they had come from. Thomas and Znaniecki argued that the older immigrants were more effective at coping with change, whereas their children were more likely to fall into crime and deviance. The youth were still in the process of being socialized and more susceptible to the influence of new attitudes and value systems.

Research from the early part of the twentieth century found that immigrants were less criminally involved than native-born individuals and that immigration had little effect on the volume of crime in the United States (U.S. Immigration Commission 1911; Wickersham Commission 1931). Successive generations displayed higher rates of criminality than their immigrant parents or grandparents, though still generally lower than native-born groups (U.S. Immigration Commission 1911; Wickersham Commission 1931; Sutherland 1934). Recent studies, in an era characterized by immigration from Latin America, Asia, and the Caribbean (as opposed to Europe), have uncovered similar findings. For example, Sampson, Morenoff, and Raudenbush (2005) found that first- and second-generation immigrants are far less likely to commit acts of violence than third-generation immigrants.[26] This is true for Latino immigrant groups as well as non-Latino white and black immigrants (see also Morenoff and Astor 2006; Sampson 2008b). Similarly, Kirk (2008) found that first- and second-generation

---

[26] First generation refers to individuals born outside of the United States, second generation refers to individuals with at least one parent born abroad, and third generation refers to individuals with at least one grandparent born abroad.

immigrants are significantly less likely to be arrested for a crime than third-generation immigrants. Such findings counter the assertions of classic assimilation theory (Warner and Srole 1945; Gordon 1964), which assumes that full assimilation into American society is integral for upward mobility. Rather, in accordance with the findings presented above, some scholars suggest that because assimilation and acculturation have apparent negative consequences for some immigrants, it may be advantageous for immigrants to avoid assimilation into those "segments" of American society characterized by a subculture of crime and violence (Gans 1992; Portes and Zhou 1993; Portes and Rumbaut 1996).

Whether immigrants are more or less criminal than natives is important for understanding the immigration-crime nexus, yet, our interest in this essay is primarily with the effects of the process of immigration.[27] Specifically, we are interested in whether neighborhood population changes due to immigration affect neighborhood crime rates. Since the pioneering work of Shaw and McKay, much attention has focused on the effect of the concentration of immigration into certain neighborhoods. In contrast to Shaw and McKay's early-twentieth-century observation that delinquency rates and the percentage of foreign population correlate positively, numerous studies have found that immigrant concentration and violence are either not related or negatively related (e.g., Butcher and Piehl 1998; Hagan and Palloni 1998; Lee, Martinez, and Rosenfeld 2001; Krueger et al. 2004; Nielsen, Lee, and Martinez 2005; Sampson, Morenoff, and Raudenbush 2005; Stowell and Martinez 2007). A variety of explanations have been used to explain such findings. First, while immigrants often reside in disadvantaged neighborhoods, such areas may not be characterized by the social isolation and disorganization common to so many central city neighborhoods (see Wilson 1987). Rather, immigrants frequently concentrate into ethnic enclaves characterized by familiar cultural traditions and supportive social networks.[28] These social networks, and the social capital derived

---

[27] While our emphasis is on immigration and neighborhood changes in crime, interested readers are encouraged to consult Tonry (1997), Hagan and Palloni (1998), and Martinez and Valenzuela (2006) for a broader treatment of the nexus between immigration and crime.

[28] Of course, ethnic enclaves are not merely a recent phenomenon (see, e.g., Lieberson 1980). One hundred years ago, Chicago School sociologists too observed areas characterized by ethnic enclaves. In the process of the growth of the city, neighborhoods undergo periods of both social organization and social disorganization (Burgess [1925] 1967). The excess of actual city growth (in terms of population) over natural growth disturbs neighborhood equilibrium and leads to social disorganization. Yet, disorganization does even-

from them, facilitate the control of crime and aid the process of assimilation for new arrivals (Portes and Rumbaut 2001). Second, immigration may have spurred the growth and revitalization of many U.S. cities previously depopulated through deindustrialization and suburbanization, thereby indirectly leading to lower levels of central city violence (Waldinger 1989). Third, Sampson provocatively asserts that the "American culture [of violence] is being diluted" through immigration (2008*b*, p. 33). The penetration of immigrants from less violent societies into the United States may be diluting the American culture of many central city neighborhoods that stresses the use of violence to display dominance and social status.

Much of this recent work on immigration and crime is static, correlating neighborhood composition with neighborhood rates of crime at a single time point. Shaw and McKay, however, were especially interested in the growth of the city—a dynamic process. One source of growth is immigration, and one potential outcome of growth is ethnic heterogeneity. In the social disorganization explanation for crime, ethnic heterogeneity impedes communication and interaction among neighborhood residents, thereby undermining processes of informal social control and increasing the likelihood of crime (Shaw and McKay 1942; Sampson and Groves 1989; Bursik and Grasmick 1993). The core argument is not so much that a concentration of immigrants leads to higher crime but, rather, that a heterogeneity of population does. This implies a dynamic process. As the population composition of a neighborhood becomes relatively more heterogeneous than in previous time periods, then crime should rise relative to those previous time periods. Yet, if immigrants move to ethnic enclaves characterized by homogeneous population groups, then informal social control should be unaffected, and crime rates should be stable. Additionally, if a previously heterogeneous neighborhood becomes more homogeneous through a rapid influx of one ethnic group, then social control processes may be enhanced. Does research support such views?

In a city-level analysis of the impact of growth in immigrant population, Butcher and Piehl (1998) found in a cross-sectional analysis that

---

tually lead to reorganization through a natural process of adjustment (Burgess [1925] 1967). With respect to immigration, ethnic enclaves often became destabilized as U.S. cities grew through successive waves of immigration. New immigrant groups, from different countries and regions of Europe, invaded the residential spaces of older groups, and older groups eventually moved to outlying areas. These periods of social disorganization were marked by ethnic heterogeneity and led to elevated crime levels.

immigration and crime rates are positively correlated, yet the association disappears once accounting for citywide demographic and socioeconomic characteristics. Additionally, in a longitudinal analysis, Butcher and Piehl found that increases in recent immigration, defined as the fraction of the metropolitan area who had been living abroad 1 year prior, have no significant effect on changes in crime. That is, immigrant inflows have no consequence for metropolitan area crime rates. This is true for a combined measure of violent and property crime, as well as separately for violent crime.

Using U.S. census data and homicide records from the Chicago Police Department, Chavez and Griffiths (2009) examine the association between homicide trends from 1980 to 1995 and neighborhood changes in the proportion of recent immigrants. They found that neighborhoods with low and temporally stable rates of homicide were the ones most likely to be destination neighborhoods of recent immigrants. Neighborhoods with moderate rates of homicide and those with high, fluctuating rates had declining proportions of recent immigrants over the course of the 1970s and 1980s. These descriptive results suggest that the growth of recent immigrants in a neighborhood is not associated with increases in lethal violence.

MacDonald, Hipp, and Gill (2009) examine whether increases in the concentration of immigrants in Los Angeles neighborhoods during the 1990s led to changes in neighborhood crime counts. Using an instrumental variables framework to minimize the endogeneity between immigrant residential patterns and crime, MacDonald and colleagues found that neighborhoods undergoing a rise in immigrant concentration had greater than expected reductions in total crime and violence, net of the effects of neighborhood poverty, residential stability, population density, and the age structure of the neighborhood. In particular, they found that a 1-standard-deviation increase in the concentration of immigrants leads to a 27 percent reduction in total neighborhood crime and a 50 percent reduction in violent crime.

Much scholarly attention during the early part of the twentieth century was given to the implications of immigration for neighborhood change and crime. Yet, for a variety of reasons, including the drastic decline in immigration following passage of the 1924 Immigration Act, as well as the paradigmatic shift in criminology to a focus on individual-level explanations for criminal behavior, research on the nexus of immigration and crime has not figured anywhere near as prominently since World War II as it did during the early part of the twentieth century. Even since the passage of the 1965 Immigration Act, which has prompted massive influxes of Latin American and Asian immigrants into the United States, there has been relatively little criminological attention given to the issue of immigration. While important research advances have been made in the past decade for understanding the implications of concentrated immigration for crime, very few studies have taken a dynamic approach to the topic. Additionally, sorely unexplored is the potential for contrasting effects of legal versus illegal immigration on neighborhood change and crime. In an era marked by drastic population shifts to urban areas because of immigration, the dearth of criminological research on change is puzzling. From the limited research available, it appears that the concentration of immigration indirectly promotes reductions in crime and violence. While speculative, the intervening mechanism underlying this association may be that the concentration of immigrants facilitates shared goals and values among neighborhood residents and therefore promotes informal social control. An examination of intervening mechanisms is needed.

F. Concluding Remarks

Neighborhoods follow a developmental or life cycle model and undergo patterns of deterioration and revitalization over time. Many central city areas, which deteriorated in the 1960s, 1970s, and 1980s from population loss and economic restructuring, have been revitalized in recent decades. Interestingly, while within-neighborhood poverty rates and concentrated disadvantage changed over this period, the between-neighborhood distribution of poverty and disadvantage was remarkably stable in many U.S. cities (Sampson 2009). In other words, neighborhoods may change internally while at the same time the economic stratification of neighborhoods within a metropolitan area stays the same.[29]

With gentrification, crime declines are not immediate, but research does suggest long-run declines in crime occur as neighborhood social

[29] For instance, Sampson and Morenoff (2006) report a correlation of 0.87 between neighborhood poverty rates in Chicago in 1970 and rates for 1990, thus implying considerable between-neighborhood stability. Yet, the average neighborhood poverty rate increased during this period from 11 percent to 20 percent, and the number of neighborhoods characterized by extreme poverty (over 40 percent poor) increased from 2 percent of neighborhoods in 1970 to over 12 percent by 1990. Thus, poverty became increasingly concentrated, yet the spatial distribution remained durable over time.

networks coalesce to control crime. Yet, relatively unexplored is whether there is a net reduction in crime throughout a metropolitan area from gentrification or just a shift in the relative spatial distribution of crime across neighborhoods as some neighborhoods gentrify while others do not. Similarly, there is some evidence that recent demolitions of high-rise public housing developments have led to reductions in crime in focal neighborhoods, yet they have also produced increases in violence in nearby neighborhoods because resident displacement has disrupted existing gang territories. As for immigration, results reveal that the increasing concentration of immigration in central city neighborhoods has led to reductions in crime. A variety of theoretical rationales have been proposed to explain this finding, yet tests of intervening mechanisms are largely missing from the research literature.

Of course, neighborhoods that have experienced reductions in crime due to gentrification, public housing demolitions, increasing concentrations of immigration, and other forms of migration are not immune from further change. One recent trend that will surely affect the vitality of central city neighborhoods as well as crime rates is the rise in home foreclosures. Moreover, to the extent that foreclosures are spatially concentrated in certain neighborhoods, socioeconomic deterioration and rising crime may also concentrate.

In addition to the cyclical nature of neighborhood development, it is the case that crime is both a cause and a consequence of population migration and sociodemographic change. For instance, in the long run, gentrification appears to lead to declines in neighborhood crime, which then feeds back into neighborhood change by reducing fear and making neighborhoods a more attractive place for residence and investment.

III. Directions for Future Research

In this essay, we examined five facets of neighborhood change related to population migration—population loss, gentrification, public housing development and demolition, home ownership and foreclosure, and immigration. Although there is a developing body of research on neighborhood change and crime, there is much that is not known. Here we offer a research agenda organized around targeted themes that we believe are most promising.[30] We see these five themes—causal

[30] We conclude that it is premature to discuss any policy implications from our review

mechanisms, velocity of change, spatial dependence and political economy, displacement, and crime trends and forecasting—as applicable not only for the particular facets of neighborhood change we examined but also as central to a broader array of neighborhood changes such as economic development, physical changes to neighborhoods, and criminal justice interventions.

A. Causal Mechanisms

Wikström and Sampson suggest that a mechanism explains "*why* a putative cause brings about an effect" (2006, p. 2). Additionally, Sampson argues that a social mechanism is "a theoretically plausible (albeit typically unobservable) contextual process that accounts for or explains a given phenomenon" (2006*b*, p. 32). We know that neighborhoods change and that this change is correlated with changes to both the temporal trend in crime rates within neighborhoods and the relative distribution of crime between neighborhoods. Yet, the key question is, why? For instance, we know that population turnover from gentrification is positively correlated with changes in neighborhood crime (in the short term) and that the concentration of immigration is negatively correlated with crime, but we have less understanding as to why this is the case. One answer appears to be informal social control; instability in neighborhood social networks due to gentrification can undermine informal social control while homogeneous ethnic enclaves of immigrant groups can facilitate social control. Therefore, informal social control is one intervening mechanism that may explain why neighborhood change affects crime. Yet, without repeated measures of informal social control, this causal path remains an untested hypothesis. Examination of the mechanisms that explain why population migration and other neighborhood changes are associated with neighborhood crime needs to be a focus of future research.

B. The Velocity of Change

Early-twentieth-century Chicago School of Sociology researchers argued that social change is a natural, continuous process that involves both adaptation and disruption (Thomas and Znaniecki 1918). In this

---

given the limited base of dynamic longitudinal research to draw on. Moreover, questions about what a neighborhood is, how it is measured, how neighborhood structure and process are measured, and the effects of selection on causality, to name but a few key issues, loom large in any research on neighborhoods and crime.

process, social organization is followed by disorganization, but this eventually gives way to reorganization (Burgess [1925] 1967). In this sense, Burgess argued that neighborhoods metabolize social change. Decades later, Schuerman and Kobrin (1986) argued that it is the "velocity" of neighborhood change that is consequential to subsequent increases in neighborhood crime rates rather than the mere presence of change. Gradual neighborhood change may have little influence on neighborhood crime, yet rapid change may be difficult to metabolize, thus leading to escalations in crime. We found evidence of this pattern. In their study of gentrification, Covington and Taylor (1989) found that gentrifying neighborhoods with rapidly appreciating home values had relatively greater increases in robbery and larceny relative to slowly appreciating neighborhoods. Despite the apparent influence of the velocity of neighborhood change on behavior, virtually no studies of neighborhoods and crime have examined the importance of the pace of change. While conceptualizing and measuring the velocity of neighborhood change will not be easy, we believe this is an important topic for future research.

C. Spatial Dependence and Political Economy

Neighborhoods are interdependent ecological units. Conditions in one neighborhood are influenced by the conditions of spatially proximate neighborhoods as well as the larger urban and global environment. We need a better understanding of how city-level (and county) political and economic decision making influences neighborhood crime (e.g., through zoning, tax incentives to businesses, and tax incentives to homeowners). Recall that Bursik (1989) found that public housing in Chicago has typically been sited in those neighborhoods that offered the least resistance to the placement of public housing in the neighborhood. To the extent that the siting of public housing and neighborhood crime are associated, this means that explanations for neighborhood crime require an understanding of city-level political processes as well as the social relations between neighborhood residents and political decision makers. Prior research suggests that ignoring spatial dependence may lead to biased parameter estimates and erroneous conclusions about the causes of crime (e.g., Messner et al. 1999; Baller et al. 2001). Yet, this issue is not merely methodological, which could be circumvented through spatial regression models. Rather, the substantive reasons for the spatial dependence of crime, such as political economy, need to be a focus of future research (see Logan and Molotch 1987).

D. Displacement

Many argue that gentrification necessarily results in the displacement of low-income groups from central city neighborhoods by middle- and upper-income groups (but see Freeman and Braconi 2004). Similarly, the demolition of public housing units leads to displacement. Yet, the repercussions of resident displacement on the crime rates of sending and receiving neighborhoods are largely unexplored.[31] The challenges are twofold: first, to collect multiple time points of crime data on sending and receiving neighborhoods and, second, to track the movement of displaced individuals. Addressing these challenges is necessary to determine whether (and to what extent) displacement of residents influences neighborhood crime rates and to assess the impact of urban policies designed to deconcentrate poverty.

E. Crime Trends and Forecasting

Explaining the facts of crime is fundamental to criminological research. A bevy of explanations have been offered to explain the crime drop in the 1990s, including economic prosperity, demographic shifts, mass incarceration, and the decline in the crack cocaine market (see, e.g., Rosenfeld 2004; Blumstein and Wallman 2005). Underexplored are the implications of neighborhood change. Fagan (2008) asks what proportion of the change in crime rates is attributable to neighborhood factors, relative to secular trends and unobserved exogenous factors. Additionally, is it possible to anticipate future crime trends from current metropolitan changes? For instance, what does the dramatic increase in home foreclosures in recent years (2007–9) spell for neighborhood crime rates and overall crime trends? What is the effect of the relatively large

---

[31] The media has offered speculative accounts of the repercussions of displacement. For instance, a recent article in the *Atlantic* (Rosin 2008) suggests that violence migrates with those residents displaced from demolished public housing. However, Rosin conflates correlation with causation. While violent crime and displaced residents may be located in the same area, the capacity to make a causal connection depends upon having multiple time points of data (i.e., what was the extent of neighborhood crime prior to the arrival of displaced residents?) and some idea about whether it was actually the new residents that were engaging in violent crime. Rosin's journalistic account of displacement and mobility fails to meet this burden of proof (see Briggs and Dreier [2008] for a discussion) but nonetheless underscores several important research questions regarding the effects of closing public housing units.

inflow of returning exprisoners on neighborhood crime rates? The U.S. Census Bureau (2009*b*) recently reported that just 11.9 percent of U.S. households moved in 2008, the lowest rate since the bureau began tracking such figures in 1948. Given that residential stability is conducive to the informal social control of crime, do these trends in mobility foretell stability or even a reduction in neighborhood crime? To these questions about the sources of crime trends we add an interest in the opposite causal direction: what proportion of changes in neighborhood population and sociodemographics are attributable to crime? Did the crime drop in the 1990s spur gentrification?

Despite over a century of ecological studies of neighborhoods and crime, knowledge about the underlying mechanisms of stability and change at the neighborhood level is limited. Despite massive social changes in cities and beyond throughout the twentieth century, the field of criminology has not kept pace and, as a result, neighborhood change and crime has not been a primary focus of empirical research. In part this is due to the data requirements needed to study neighborhood change and its subsequent effects on crime and vice versa. Years ago, Albert Reiss (1986) bemoaned the lack of longitudinal data on communities and crime. The situation today remains woeful. Important research questions abound, yet few studies contain the requisite repeated observations over time that allow answers to these questions, particularly with respect to the dynamics of change in neighborhood social processes. Thus, building better data sets remains a number 1 priority, as does greater attention to the conceptual and methodological challenges to conducting research on neighborhood change.

REFERENCES

Alba, Richard D., John R. Logan, and Paul E. Bellair. 1994. "Living with Crime: The Implications of Racial/Ethnic Differences in Suburban Location." *Social Forces* 73:395–434.

Atkinson, Rowland. 2000. "The Hidden Cost of Gentrification: Displacement in Central London." *Journal of Housing and the Built Environment* 15:307–26.

Baller, Robert D., Luc Anselin, Steven F. Messner, Glenn Deane, and Darnell F. Hawkins. 2001. "Structural Covariates of U.S. County Homicide Rates: Incorporating Spatial Effects." *Criminology* 39:561–90.

Berry, Brian J. L. 1985. "Islands of Decay in Seas of Renewal." In *The New*

Urban Reality, edited by Paul J. Peterson. Washington, DC: Brookings Institution Press.

Blumstein, Alfred, and Joel Wallman, eds. 2005. *The Crime Drop in America.* 2nd ed. Cambridge: Cambridge University Press.

Bottoms, Anthony E., and Paul Wiles. 1986. "Housing Tenure and Residential Community Crime Careers in Britain." In *Communities and Crime*, edited by Albert J. Reiss Jr. and Michael Tonry. Vol. 8 of *Crime and Justice: A Review of Research*, edited by Michael Tonry and Norval Morris. Chicago: University of Chicago Press.

Briggs, Xavier de Souza, and Peter Dreier. 2008. "Memphis Murder Mystery? No, Just Mistaken Identity." *Shelterforce: The Journal of Affordable Housing and Community Building*, July 22. http://www.shelterforce.org/article/special/1043.

Brooks-Gunn, Jeanne, Greg J. Duncan, Pamela K. Klebanov, and Naomi Sealand. 1993. "Do Neighborhoods Influence Child and Adolescent Development?" *American Journal of Sociology* 99:353–95.

Burgess, Ernest W. 1916. "Juvenile Delinquency in a Small City." *Journal of the American Institute of Criminal Law and Criminology* 6:724–28.

———. 1967. "The Growth of the City: An Introduction to a Research Project." In *The City*, edited by Robert E. Park, Ernest W. Burgess, and Roderick D. McKenzie. Chicago: University Chicago of Press. (Originally published 1925.)

Bursik, Robert J., Jr. 1988. "Social Disorganization and Theories of Crime and Delinquency: Problems and Prospects." *Criminology* 26:519–51.

———. 1989. "Political Decisionmaking and Ecological Models of Delinquency: Conflict and Consensus." In *Theoretical Integration in the Study of Deviance and Crime: Problems and Prospects*, edited by Steven F. Messner, Marvin D. Krohn, and Allen E. Liska. Albany: State University of New York Press.

Bursik, Robert J., Jr., and Harold G. Grasmick. 1993. *Neighborhoods and Crime: The Dimensions of Effective Community Control.* New York: Lexington Books.

Bursik, Robert J., Jr., and Jim Webb. 1982. "Community Change and Patterns of Delinquency." *American Journal of Sociology* 88:24–42.

Butcher, Kristin F., and Anne M. Piehl. 1998. "Cross-City Evidence on the Relationship between Immigration and Crime." *Journal of Policy Analysis and Management* 17:457–93.

Byrne, James M., and Robert J. Sampson. 1986. "Key Issues in the Social Ecology of Crime." In *The Social Ecology of Crime*, edited by James M. Byrne and Robert J. Sampson. New York: Springer.

Chaskin, Robert J. 1997. "Perspectives on Neighborhood and Community: A Review of the Literature." *Social Service Review* 71:521–47.

Chavez, Jorge M., and Elizabeth Griffiths. 2009. "Neighborhood Dynamics of Urban Violence: Understanding the Immigration Connection." *Homicide Studies* 13:261–73.

Chen, Celia. 2008. "Mortgage Foreclosure Data." Presented at the Housing Statistics User Group, June 3, Washington, DC. http://groups.google.com/group/housing-statistics-users-group/files?hl=en.

Clarke, Ronald V. 1995. "Situational Crime Prevention." In *Building a Safer Society: Strategic Approaches to Crime Prevention*, edited by Michael Tonry and David Farrington. Vol. 19 of *Crime and Justice: A Review of Research*, edited by Michael Tonry. Chicago: University of Chicago Press.

Cook, Philip J. 1980. "Research in Criminal Deterrence: Laying the Groundwork for the Second Decade." In *Crime and Justice: A Review of Research*, vol. 2, edited by Norval Morris and Michael Tonry. Chicago: University of Chicago Press.

Covington, Jeanette, and Ralph B. Taylor. 1989. "Gentrification and Crime: Robbery and Larceny Changes in Appreciating Baltimore Neighborhoods during the 1970s." *Urban Affairs Quarterly* 25:142–72.

Cullen, Julie B., and Steven D. Levitt. 1999. "Crime, Urban Flight, and the Consequences for Cities." *Review of Economics and Statistics* 81:159–69.

Cuomo, Mario M. 1974. *Forest Hills Diary: The Crisis in Low-Income Housing*. New York: Random House.

Curtis, Ric. 2003. "Crack, Cocaine and Heroin: Drug Eras in Williamsburg, Brooklyn, 1960–2000." *Addiction Research and Theory* 11:47–63.

Curtis, Richard. 1998. "The Improbable Transformation of Inner-City Neighborhoods: Crime, Violence, Drugs, and Youth in the 1990's." *Journal of Criminal Law and Criminology* 88:1233–76.

DeKeseredy, Walter S., Shahid Alvi, Martin S. Schwartz, and Andreas Tomaszewski. 2003. *Under Siege: Poverty and Crime in a Public Housing Community*. Lanham, MD: Lexington Books.

DiPasquale, Denise, and Edward L. Glaeser. 1999. "Incentives and Social Capital: Are Homeowners Better Citizens?" *Journal of Urban Economics* 34:354–84.

Duncan, Greg J., Johanne Boisjoly, and Kathleen Mullan Harris. 2001. "Sibling, Peer, Neighbor, and Schoolmate Correlations as Indicators of the Importance of Context for Adolescent Development." *Demography* 38:437–47.

Duncan, Greg J., James P. Connell, and Pamela K. Klebanov. 1997. "Conceptual and Methodological Issues in Estimating Causal Effects of Neighborhoods and Family Condition on Individual Development." In *Neighborhood Poverty*, vol. 1, edited by Jeanne Brooks-Gunn, Greg J. Duncan, and J. Lawrence Aber. New York: Sage.

Duncan, Greg J., and Stephen W. Raudenbush. 1999. "Assessing the Effects of Context in Studies of Child and Youth Development." *Educational Psychologist* 34:29–41.

———. 2001. "Neighborhoods and Adolescent Development: How Can We Determine the Links?" In *Does It Take a Village? Community Effects on Children, Adolescents, and Families*, edited by Alan Booth and Ann C. Crouter. Mahwah, NJ: Erlbaum.

Durkheim, Émile. 1951. *Suicide*. New York: Free Press.

Ekblom, Paul, and Ken Pease. 1995. "Evaluating Crime Prevention." In *Building a Safer Society: Strategic Approaches to Crime Prevention*, edited by Michael

Tonry and David Farrington. Vol. 19 of *Crime and Justice: A Review of Research*, edited by Michael Tonry. Chicago: University of Chicago Press.

Elliott, Delbert S., Scott Menard, Bruce Rankin, Amanda Elliott, William J. Wilson, and David Huizinga. 2006. *Good Kids from Bad Neighborhoods: Successful Development in Social Context*. Cambridge: Cambridge University Press.

Elmer, M. C. 1933. "Century-Old Ecological Studies in France." *American Journal of Sociology* 39:63–70.

Fagan, Jeffrey. 2008. "Crime and Neighborhood Change." In *Understanding Crime Trends: Workshop Report*, edited by National Research Council. Committee on Understanding Crime Trends, Committee on Law and Justice, Division of Behavioral and Social Sciences and Education. Washington, DC: National Academies Press.

Fagan, Jeffrey, and Garth Davies. 2000. "Crime in Public Housing: Two-Way Diffusion Effects in Surrounding Neighborhoods." In *Analyzing Crime Patterns: Frontiers of Practice*, edited by Victor Goldsmith, Philip G. McGuire, John H. Mollenkopf, and Timothy A. Ross. Thousand Oaks, CA: Sage.

Fagan, Jeffrey, Tamara Dumanovsky, J. Phillip Thompson, and Garth Davies. 1998. "Crime in Public Housing: Clarifying Research Issues." *National Institute of Justice Journal* 235:2–9.

Farrington, David P. 1993. "Have Any Individual, Family or Neighbourhood Influences on Offending Been Demonstrated Conclusively?" In *Integrating Individual and Ecological Aspects of Crime*, edited by David Farrington, Robert Sampson, and Per-Olof Wikström. Stockholm: National Council on Crime Prevention.

Feinberg, Robert M., and David Nickerson. 2002. "Crime and Residential Mortgage Default: An Empirical Analysis." *Applied Economics Letters* 9: 217–20.

Foster, Janet, and Timothy Hope. 1993. *Housing, Community and Crime: The Impact of the Priority Estate Project*. London: HMSO.

Freeman, Lance. 2005. "Displacement or Succession? Residential Mobility in Gentrifying Neighborhoods." *Urban Affairs Review* 40:463–91.

Freeman, Lance, and Hilary Botein. 2002. "Subsidized Housing and Neighborhood Impacts: A Theoretical Discussion and Review of the Evidence." *Journal of Planning Literature* 16:359–78.

Freeman, Lance, and Frank Braconi. 2004. "Gentrification and Displacement: New York City in the 1990s." *Journal of the American Planning Association* 70:39–52.

Freudenburg, William R., and Robert Emmett Jones. 1991. "Criminal Behavior and Rapid Community Growth: Examining the Evidence." *Rural Sociology* 56:619–45.

Frey, William H. 1979. "Central City White Flight: Racial and Nonracial Causes." *American Sociological Review* 44:425–48.

———. 1980. "Black In-Migration, White Flight, and the Changing Economic Base of the Central City." *American Journal of Sociology* 85:1396–1417.

Galster, George, and Anne Zobel. 1998. "Will Dispersed Housing Programmes Reduce Social Problems in the US?" *Housing Studies* 13:605–22.

Gans, Herbert J. 1992. "Second-Generation Decline: Scenarios for the Economic and Ethnic Futures of the Post-1965 American Immigrants." *Ethnic and Racial Studies* 15:173–92.

Garrison, Sonia, Sam Rogers, and Mary L. Moore. 2009. *Continued Decay and Shaky Repairs: The State of Subprime Loans Today.* Durham, NC: Center for Responsible Lending.

Glass, Ruth. 1964. "Introduction: Aspects of Change." In *London: Aspects of Change*, edited by Centre for Urban Studies. London: MacGibbon & Kee.

Goering, John, and Judith Feins, eds. 2003. *Choosing a Better Life? Evaluating the Moving to Opportunity Social Experiment.* Washington, DC: Urban Institute Press.

Goetz, Edward G. 2003. "Housing Dispersal Programs." *Journal of Planning Literature* 18:3–16.

Gordon, Milton. 1964. *Assimilation in American Life: The Role of Race, Religion, and National Origins.* New York: Oxford University Press.

Gould, Roger V. 1995. *Insurgent Identities: Class, Community, and Protest in Paris from 1848 to the Commune.* Chicago: University of Chicago Press.

Griffiths, Elizabeth, and George Tita. 2009. "Homicide in and around Public Housing: Is Public Housing a Hotbed, a Magnet, or a Generator of Violence for the Surrounding Community?" *Social Problems* 56:474–93.

Guerry, André Michel. 1833. *Essai sur la statistique morale de la France.* Paris: Crochard.

Guest, Avery M., and Barrett A. Lee. 1984. "How Urbanites Define Their Neighborhoods." *Population and Environment* 7:32–56.

Hagan, John, and Alberto Palloni. 1998. "Immigration and Crime in the United States." In *The Immigration Debate: Studies on the Economic, Demographic, and Fiscal Effects of Immigration*, edited by James P. Smith and Barry Edmonston. Washington, DC: National Academy Press.

Hagedorn, John, and Brigid Rauch. 2007. "Housing, Gangs, and Homicide: What We Can Learn from Chicago." *Urban Affairs Review* 42:435–56.

Haley, Barbara A. 2005. "Guest Editor's Introduction." *Cityscape: A Journal of Policy Development and Research* 8:1–4.

Hammel, Daniel J., and Elvin K. Wyly. 1996. "A Model for Identifying Gentrified Areas with Census Data." *Urban Geography* 17:248–68.

Hannan, Michael T. 1971. *Aggregation and Disaggregation in Sociology.* Lexington, MA: Lexington Books.

Harcourt, Bernard E. 2005. "Policing L.A.'s Skid Row: Crime and Real Estate Development in Downtown Los Angeles (An Experiment in Real Time)." *University of Chicago Legal Forum.* http://ssrn.com/abstract=739130.

Harding, David J. 2003. "Counterfactual Models of Neighborhood Effects: The Effect of Neighborhood Poverty on High School Dropout and Teenage Pregnancy." *American Journal of Sociology* 109:676–719.

Hipp, John R. 2007. "Block, Tract, and Levels of Aggregation: Neighborhood Structure and Crime and Disorder as a Case in Point." *American Sociological Review* 72:659–80.

Hipp, John R., George E. Tita, and Robert T. Greenbaum. 2009. "Drive-Bys and Trade-Ups: Examining the Directionality of the Crime and Residential Instability Relationship." *Social Forces* 87:1777–1812.

Hirsch, Arnold R. 1983. *Making the Second Ghetto: Race and Housing in Chicago, 1940–1960*. New York: Cambridge University Press.

Holzman, Harold R. 1996. "Criminological Research on Public Housing: Toward a Better Understanding of People, Places, and Spaces." *Crime and Delinquency* 42:361–78.

Holzman, Harold R., Tari R. Kudrick, and Kenneth P. Voytek. 1996. "Revisiting the Relationship between Crime and Architectural Design: An Analysis of Data from HUD's 1994 Survey of Public Housing Residents." *Cityscape: A Journal of Policy Development and Research* 2:107–26.

Hoover, Edgar M., and Raymond Vernon. 1959. *Anatomy of a Metropolis*. Cambridge, MA: Harvard University Press.

Hunter, Albert, and Gerald D. Suttles. 1972. "The Expanding Community of Limited Liability." In *The Social Construction of Communities*, by Gerald D. Suttles. Chicago: University of Chicago Press.

Hyra, Derek S. 2008. *The New Urban Renewal: The Economic Transformation of Harlem and Bronzeville*. Chicago: University of Chicago Press.

Immergluck, Dan, and Geoff Smith. 2006a. "The External Costs of Foreclosure: The Impact of Single-Family Mortgage Foreclosures on Property Values." *Housing Policy Debate* 17:57–79.

———. 2006b. "The Impact of Single-Family Mortgage Foreclosures on Neighborhood Crime." *Housing Studies* 21:851–66.

Jacob, Brian A. 2004. "Public Housing, Housing Vouchers, and Student Achievement: Evidence from Public Housing Demolitions in Chicago." *American Economic Review* 94:233–58.

Joint Center for Housing Studies. 2008. *The State of the Nation's Housing: 2008*. Cambridge, MA: Joint Center for Housing Studies of Harvard University.

———. 2009. *The State of the Nation's Housing: 2009*. Cambridge, MA: Joint Center for Housing Studies of Harvard University.

Katz, Lawrence F., Jeffrey R. Kling, and Jeffrey B. Liebman. 2001. "Moving to Opportunity in Boston: Early Results of a Randomized Mobility Experiment." *Quarterly Journal of Economics* 116:607–54.

Katzman, Martin T. 1980. "The Contribution of Crime to Urban Decline." *Urban Studies* 17:277–86.

Kennedy, Maureen, and Paul Leonard. 2001. *Dealing with Neighborhood Change: A Primer on Gentrification and Policy Choices*. Washington, DC: Brookings Institution.

Kirk, David S. 2008. "The Neighborhood Context of Racial and Ethnic Disparities in Arrest." *Demography* 45:55–77.

———. 2009a. "A Natural Experiment on Residential Change and Recidivism: Lessons from Hurricane Katrina." *American Sociological Review* 74:484–505.

———. 2009b. "Unraveling the Contextual Effects on Student Suspension and Juvenile Arrest: The Independent and Interdependent Influences of School, Neighborhood, and Family Controls." *Criminology* 47:479–520.

Kling, Jeffrey R., Jeffrey B. Liebman, and Lawrence F. Katz. 2007. "Experimental Analysis of Neighborhood Effects." *Econometrica* 75:83–119.

Kornhauser, Ruth R. 1978. *Social Sources of Delinquency*. Chicago: University of Chicago Press.

Kreager, Derek A., Christopher Lyons, and Zachary Hays. 2007. "Condos, Coffeeshops, and Crime: 1990's Urban Revitalization and Seattle Crime Trends." Paper presented at the 2007 American Society of Criminology annual conference, Atlanta.

Krueger, P. M., S. A. Bond Huie, R. G. Rogers, and R. A. Hummer. 2004. "Neighborhoods and Homicide Mortality: An Analysis of Race/Ethnic Differences." *Journal of Epidemiology and Community Health* 58:223–30.

Lee, Barrett A., and Karen E. Campbell. 1997. "Common Ground? Urban Neighborhoods as Survey Respondents See Them." *Social Science Quarterly* 78:922–36.

Lee, Matthew T., Ramiro Martinez Jr., and Richard Rosenfeld. 2001. "Does Immigration Increase Homicide? Negative Evidence from Three Border Cities." *Sociological Quarterly* 42:559–80.

Lieberson, Stanley. 1980. *A Piece of the Pie: Black and White Immigrants since 1880*. Berkeley: University of California Press.

Linden, Leigh, and Jonah E. Rockoff. 2008. "Estimate of the Impact of Crime Risk on Property Values from Megan's Laws." *American Economic Review* 98: 1103–27.

Liska, Allen E., and Paul E. Bellair. 1995. "Violent-Crime Rates and Racial Composition: Convergence over Time." *American Journal of Sociology* 101: 578–610.

Liska, Allen E., John R. Logan, and Paul E. Bellair. 1998. "Race and Violent Crime in the Suburbs." *American Sociological Review* 63:27–38.

Logan, John R., and Harvey L. Molotch. 1987. *Urban Fortunes: The Political Economy of Place*. Berkeley: University of California Press.

Ludwig, Jens, Jeffrey B. Liebman, Jeffrey R. Kling, Greg J. Duncan, Lawrence F. Katz, Ronald C. Kessler, and Lisa Sanbonmatsu. 2008. "What Can We Learn about Neighborhood Effects from the Moving to Opportunity Experiment? A Comment on Clampet-Lundquist and Massey." *American Journal of Sociology* 114:144–88.

MacDonald, John M., John R. Hipp, and Charlotte Gill. 2009. "Neighborhood Effects of Immigrant Concentration on Crime: Do Immigrants Make Communities Safer?" Working paper, August 6. Philadelphia: University of Pennsylvania, Department of Criminology.

Manning, Christopher A. 1986. "Intercity Differences in Home Price Appreciation." *Journal of Real Estate Research* 1:45–66.

Manski, Charles F. 1993. "Identification of Endogenous Social Effects: The Reflection Problem." *Review of Economic Studies* 60:531–42.

Martinez, Ramiro, Jr., and Abel Valenzuela Jr., eds. 2006. *Immigration and Crime: Race, Ethnicity, and Violence*. New York: New York University Press.

Massey, Douglas S., and Nancy A. Denton. 1993. *American Apartheid: Segre-*

gation and the Making of the Underclass. Cambridge, MA: Harvard University Press.

Mayhew, Henry. 1862. *London Labour and the London Poor.* Vol. 4. London: Charles Griffin.

McDonald, Scott C. 1986. "Does Gentrification Affect Crime Rates?" In *Communities and Crime,* edited by Albert J. Reiss Jr. and Michael Tonry. Vol. 8 of *Crime and Justice: A Review of Research,* edited by Michael Tonry and Norval Morris. Chicago: University of Chicago Press.

McNulty, Thomas L., and Steven R. Holloway. 2000. "Race, Crime, and Public Housing in Atlanta: Testing a Conditional Effect Hypothesis." *Social Forces* 79:707–29.

Messner, Steven F., Luc Anselin, Robert D. Baller, Darnell F. Hawkins, Glenn Deane, and Stewart E. Tolnay. 1999. "The Spatial Patterning of County Homicide Rates: An Application of Exploratory Spatial Data Analysis." *Journal of Quantitative Criminology* 15:423–50.

Meyerson, Martin, and Edward C. Banfield. 1964. *Politics, Planning and the Public Interest: The Case of Public Housing in Chicago.* Glencoe, IL: Free Press.

Morenoff, Jeffrey D., and Avraham Astor. 2006. "Immigrant Assimilation and Crime: Generational Differences in Youth Violence in Chicago." In *Immigration and Crime: Race, Ethnicity, and Violence,* edited by Ramiro Martinez Jr. and Abel Valenzuela Jr. New York: New York University Press.

Morenoff, Jeffrey D., and Robert J. Sampson. 1997. "Violent Crime and the Spatial Dynamics of Neighborhood Transition: Chicago, 1970–1990." *Social Forces* 76:31–64.

Mortgage Bankers Association. 2008. "Delinquencies Increase, Foreclosure Starts Flat in Latest MBA National Delinquency Survey." Press release, December 5. http://www.mortgagebankers.org/NewsandMedia/PressCenter/66626.htm.

———. 2009. "Delinquencies and Foreclosures Continue to Climb in Latest MBA National Delinquency Survey." Press release, May 28. http://www.mortgagebankers.org/NewsandMedia/PressCenter/69031.htm.

Nagin, Daniel. 1978. "General Deterrence: A Review of the Empirical Evidence." In *Deterrence and Incapacitation: Estimating the Effects of Criminal Sanctions on Crime Rates,* edited by Alfred Blumstein, Jacqueline Cohen, and Daniel Nagin. Washington, DC: National Academy Press.

Newman, Kathe, and Elvin K. Wyly. 2006. "The Right to Stay Put, Revisited: Gentrification and Resistance to Displacement in New York City." *Urban Studies* 43:23–57.

Newman, Oscar. 1972. *Defensible Space: Crime Prevention through Urban Design.* New York: Macmillan.

Nielsen, Amie L., Matthew T. Lee, and Ramiro Martinez Jr. 2005. "Integrating Race, Place and Motive in Social Disorganization Theory: Lessons from a Comparison of Black and Latino Homicide Types in Two Immigrant Destination Cities." *Criminology* 43:837–72.

Oberwittler, Dietrich, and Per-Olof H. Wikström. 2008. "Why Small Is Better: Advancing the Study of the Role of Behavioral Contexts in Crime Causation." In *Putting Crime in Its Place: Units of Analysis in Geographic Criminology*, edited by David Weisburd, Wim Bernasco, and Gerben Bruinsma. New York: Springer.

Openshaw, Stan. 1984. *The Modifiable Areal Unit Problem*. Norwich: Geo Books.

Openshaw, Stan, and P. J. Taylor 1979. "A Million or So Correlation Coefficients: Three Experiments on the Modifiable Areal Unit Problem." In *Statistical Applications in the Spatial Sciences*, edited by N. Wrigley. London: Pion.

Orr, Larry, Judith D. Feins, Robin Jacob, Erik Beecroft, Lisa Sanbonmatsu, Lawrence F. Katz, Jeffrey B. Liebman, and Jeffrey R. Kling. 2003. *Moving to Opportunity Interim Impacts Evaluation*. Washington, DC: U.S. Department of Housing and Urban Development.

Pattillo, Mary E. 2007. *Black on the Block: The Politics of Race and Class in the City*. Chicago: University of Chicago Press.

Perin, Constance. 1977. *Everything in Its Place: Social Order and Land Use in America*. Princeton, NJ: Princeton University Press.

Pew Hispanic Center. 2009. *Statistical Portrait of the Foreign-Born Population in the United States, 2007*. Washington, DC: Pew Hispanic Center.

Popkin, Susan J., Victoria E. Gwiasda, Dennis P. Rosenbaum, Jean M. Amendolia, Wendell A. Johnson, and Lynn M. Olson. 1999. "Combating Crime in Public Housing: A Qualitative and Quantitative Longitudinal Analysis of the Chicago Housing Authority's Anti-drug Initiative." *Justice Quarterly* 16: 519–57.

Popkin, Susan J., Bruce Katz, Mary K. Cunningham, Karen D. Brown, Jeremy Gustafson, and Margery A. Turner. 2004. *A Decade of HOPE VI: Research Findings and Policy Challenges*. Washington, DC: Urban Institute.

Portes, Alejandro, and Rubén G. Rumbaut. 1996. *Immigrant America: A Portrait*. 2nd ed. Berkeley: University of California Press.

———. 2001. *Legacies: The Story of the Immigrant Second Generation*. Berkeley: University of California Press.

Portes, Alejandro, and Min Zhou. 1993. "The New Second Generation: Segmented Assimilation and Its Variants." *Annals of the American Academy of Political and Social Science* 530:74–96.

Pratt, Travis C., and Francis T. Cullen. 2005. "Assessing Macro-Level Predictors and Theories of Crime: A Meta-Analysis." In *Crime and Justice: A Review of Research*, vol. 32, edited by Michael Tonry. Chicago: University of Chicago Press.

Quetelet, Adolphe. 1984. *Research on the Propensity for Crime at Different Ages*. Translated and introduced by Sawyer F. Sylvester. Cincinnati: Anderson. (Originally published 1831.)

Raudenbush, Stephen W., and Robert J. Sampson. 1999. "'Ecometrics': Toward a Science of Assessing Ecological Settings, with Application to the Systematic Social Observation of Neighborhoods." *Sociological Methodology* 29:1–41.

Rawson, Rawson W. 1839. "An Inquiry into the Statistics of Crime in England and Wales." *Journal of the Statistical Society of London* 2:316–44.

Reiss, Albert J., Jr. 1971. "Systematic Observations of Natural Social Phenomena." *Sociological Methodology* 3:3–33.

————. 1986. "Why Are Communities Important in Understanding Crime?" In *Communities and Crime*, edited by Albert J. Reiss Jr. and Michael Tonry. Vol. 8 of *Crime and Justice: A Review of Research*, edited by Michael Tonry and Norval Morris. Chicago: University of Chicago Press.

Reiss, Albert J., Jr., and Michael Tonry, eds. 1986. *Communities and Crime*. Vol. 8 of *Crime and Justice: A Review of Research*, edited by Michael Tonry and Norval Morris. Chicago: University of Chicago Press.

Robinson, W. S. 1950. "Ecological Correlation and the Behavior of Individuals." *American Sociological Review* 15:351–57.

Rohe, William M., Shannon Van Zandt, and George McCarthy. 2000. *The Social Benefits and Costs of Homeownership: A Critical Assessment of the Research*. Chapel Hill: Center for Urban and Regional Studies, University of North Carolina.

Roncek, Dennis W., Ralph Bell, and Jeffrey M. A. Francik. 1981. "Housing Projects and Crime: Testing a Proximity Hypothesis." *Social Problems* 29: 151–66.

Rosenfeld, Richard. 2004. "The Case of the Unsolved Crime Decline." *Scientific American* (February):82–89.

Rosin, Hanna. 2008. "American Murder Mystery." *Atlantic* 301(July/August): 40–54.

Rossi, Peter H. 1955. *Why Families Move*. Beverly Hills, CA: Sage.

Sampson, Robert J. 2006a. "Collective Efficacy Theory: Lessons Learned and Directions for Future Inquiry." In *Taking Stock: The Status of Criminological Theory*. Advances in Criminological Theory, vol. 15, edited by Francis T. Cullen, John Paul Wright, and Kristie R. Blevins. New Brunswick, NJ: Transaction Publishers.

————. 2006b. "How Does Community Context Matter? Social Mechanisms and the Explanation of Crime." In *The Explanation of Crime: Context, Mechanisms, and Development*, edited by Per-Olof H. Wikström and Robert J. Sampson. New York: Cambridge University Press.

————. 2008a. "Moving to Inequality: Neighborhood Effects and Experiments Meet Social Structure." *American Journal of Sociology* 114:189–231.

————. 2008b. "Rethinking Crime and Immigration." *Contexts* 7:28–33.

————. 2009. "Racial Stratification and the Durable Tangle of Neighborhood Inequality." *Annals of the American Academy of Political and Social Science* 621: 260–80.

Sampson, Robert J., and W. Byron Groves. 1989. "Community Structure and Crime: Testing Social Disorganization Theory." *American Journal of Sociology* 94:744–802.

Sampson, Robert J., and Jeffrey D. Morenoff. 2006. "Durable Inequality: Spatial Dynamics, Social Processes, and the Persistence of Poverty in Chicago Neighborhoods." In *Poverty Traps*, edited by Samuel Bowles, Steven N. Durlauf, and Karla Hoff. Princeton, NJ: Princeton University Press.

Sampson, Robert J., Jeffrey D. Morenoff, and Thomas P. Gannon-Rowley. 2002. "Assessing 'Neighborhood Effects': Social Processes and New Directions in Research." *Annual Review of Sociology* 28:443–78.

Sampson, Robert J., Jeffrey D. Morenoff, and Stephen W. Raudenbush. 2005. "Social Anatomy of Racial and Ethnic Disparities in Violence." *American Journal of Public Health* 95:224–32.

Sampson, Robert J., and Stephen W. Raudenbush. 1999. "Systematic Social Observation of Public Spaces: A New Look at Disorder in Urban Neighborhoods." *American Journal of Sociology* 105:603–51.

Sampson, Robert J., Stephen W. Raudenbush, and Felton Earls. 1997. "Neighborhoods and Violent Crime: A Multilevel Study of Collective Efficacy." *Science* 227:918–24.

Sampson, Robert J., and John D. Wooldredge. 1986. "Evidence That High Crime Rates Encourage Migration Away from Central Cities." *Sociology and Social Research* 90:310–14.

Santiago, Anna M., George C. Galster, and Kathryn L. S. Pettit. 2003. "Neighborhood Crime and Scattered-Site Public Housing." *Urban Studies* 40: 2147–63.

Schloemer, Ellen, Wei Li, Keith Ernst, and Kathleen Keest. 2006. *Losing Ground: Foreclosures in the Subprime Market and Their Cost to Homeowners*. Durham, NC: Center for Responsible Lending.

Schuerman, Leo, and Solomon Kobrin. 1986. "Community Careers in Crime." In *Communities and Crime*, edited by Albert J. Reiss Jr. and Michael Tonry. Vol. 8 of *Crime and Justice: A Review of Research*, edited by Michael Tonry and Norval Morris. Chicago: University of Chicago Press.

Schuetz, Jenny, Vicki Been, and Ingrid Gould Ellen. 2008. "Neighborhood Effects of Concentrated Mortgage Foreclosures." *Journal of Housing Economics* 17:306–19.

Schwartz, Amy E., Scott Susin, and Ioan Voicu. 2003. "Has Falling Crime Driven New York City's Real Estate Boom?" *Journal of Housing Research* 14: 101–35.

Shaw, Clifford R., with collaboration of Frederick M. Zorbaugh, Henry D. McKay, and Leonard S. Cottrell. 1929. *Delinquency Areas: A Study of the Geographic Distribution of School Truants, Juvenile Delinquents, and Adult Offenders in Chicago*. Chicago: University of Chicago Press.

Shaw, Clifford R., and Henry D. McKay. 1942. *Juvenile Delinquency and Urban Areas*. Chicago: University of Chicago Press.

Shiller, Robert J. 2007. "Understanding Recent Trends in House Prices and Home Ownership." Working Paper no. W13553. Cambridge, MA: National Bureau of Economic Research.

———. 2008. *The Subprime Solution: How Today's Global Financial Crisis Happened, and What to Do about It*. Princeton, NJ: Princeton University Press.

Shlay, Anne B. 2006. "Low-Income Homeownership: American Dream or Delusion?" *Urban Studies* 43:511–31.

Skogan, Wesley G. 1986. "Fear of Crime and Neighborhood Change." In *Communities and Crime*, edited by Albert J. Reiss Jr. and Michael Tonry. Vol. 8 of *Crime and Justice: A Review of Research*, edited by Michael Tonry and Norval Morris. Chicago: University of Chicago Press.

————. 1990. *Disorder and Decline: Crime and the Spiral of Decay in American Neighborhoods*. New York: Free Press.

Skogan, Wesley G., and Michael G. Maxfield. 1981. *Coping with Crime: Individual and Neighborhood Reactions*. Beverly Hills, CA: Sage.

Smith, Neil. 1996. *The New Urban Frontier: Gentrification and the Revanchist City*. London: Routledge.

Sobel, Michael E. 2006. "Spatial Concentration and Social Stratification: Does the Clustering of Disadvantage 'Beget' Bad Outcomes?" In *Poverty Traps*, edited by Samuel Bowles, Steven N. Durlauf, and Karla Hoff. Princeton, NJ: Princeton University Press.

Spelman, William. 1993. "Abandoned Buildings: Magnets for Crime?" *Journal of Criminal Justice* 21:481–95.

Squires, Gregory D., and Charis E. Kubrin. 2006. *Privileged Places: Race, Residence, and the Structure of Opportunity*. Boulder, CO: Rienner.

Stowell, Jacob I., and Ramiro Martinez. 2007. "Displaced, Dispossessed, or Lawless? Examining the Link between Ethnicity, Immigration, and Violence." *Aggression and Violent Behavior* 12:564–81.

Suresh, Geetha, and Gennaro F. Vito. 2007. "The Tragedy of Public Housing: Spatial Analysis of Hotspots of Aggravated Assaults in Louisville, KY (1989–1998)." *American Journal of Criminal Justice* 32:99–115.

Sutherland, Edwin H. 1934. *Principles of Criminology*. Philadelphia: Lippincott.

Taeuber, Karl E., and Alma F. Taeuber. 1965. *Negroes in Cities*. Chicago: Aldine.

Taub, Richard P., D. Garth Taylor, and Jan D. Dunham. 1984. *Paths of Neighborhood Change: Race and Crime in Urban America*. Chicago: University of Chicago Press.

Taylor, Ralph B. 1995. "The Impact of Crime on Communities." *Annals of the American Academy of Political and Social Science* 539:28–45.

Taylor, Ralph B., and Jeanette Covington. 1988. "Neighborhood Changes in Ecology and Violence." *Criminology* 26:553–90.

Thomas, William I., and Florian Znaniecki. 1918. *The Polish Peasant in Europe and America*. Vols. 1–2. Chicago: University of Chicago Press.

Tilly, Charles. 1973. "Do Communities Act?" *Sociological Inquiry* 43:209–40.

Tita, George E., Tricia L. Petras, and Robert T. Greenbaum. 2006. "Crime and Residential Choice: A Neighborhood Level Analysis of the Impact of Crime on Housing Prices." *Journal of Quantitative Criminology* 22:299–317.

Tonry, Michael. 1997. "Ethnicity, Crime, and Immigration." In *Ethnicity, Crime, and Immigration: Comparative and Cross-National Perspectives*, edited by Michael Tonry. Vol. 21 of *Crime and Justice: A Review of Research*, edited by Michael Tonry. Chicago: University of Chicago Press.

Turner, Margery A., Mark Woolley, G. Thomas Kingsley, Susan J. Popkin, Diane Levy, and Elizabeth Cove. 2007. *Estimating the Public Costs and Benefits of HOPE VI Investments: Methodological Report*. Washington, DC: Urban Institute.

U.S. Census Bureau. 2004. *Historical Census of Housing Tables: Homeownership*. http://www.census.gov/hhes/www/housing/census/historic/owner.html.

————. 2008. *Cumulative Estimates of the Components of Population Change for the United States, Regions, and States: April 1, 2000 to July 1, 2008.* http://www.census.gov/popest/states/tables/NST-EST2008-04.xls.

————. 2009a. *Current Population Survey: Geographical Mobility; 2007 to 2008.* http://www.census.gov/population/socdemo/migration/cps2008/tab21.xls.

————. 2009b. "Residential Mover Rate in U.S. Is Lowest since Census Bureau Began Tracking in 1948." Press release, April 22. http://www.census.gov/Press-Release/www/releases/archives/mobility_of_the_population/013609.html.

U.S. Department of Housing and Urban Development. 1996. *A Picture of Subsidized Households, December 1996.* Washington, DC: U.S. Department of Housing and Urban Development. http://www.huduser.org/datasets/assthsg/statedata96/us.htm.

————. 2000. *A Picture of Subsidized Households, 2000.* Washington, DC: U.S. Department of Housing and Urban Development. http://www.huduser.org/picture2000/index.html.

U.S. Government Accountability Office. 2007. *Information on Recent Default and Foreclosure Trends for Home Mortgages and Associated Economic and Market Developments.* Report GAO-08-78R. Washington, DC: U.S. Government Accountability Office. http://www.gao.gov/new.items/d0878r.pdf.

U.S. Immigration Commission. 1911. *Immigration and Crime.* Vol. 36. Washington, DC: U.S. Government Printing Office.

Van Wilsem, Johan, Karin Wittebrood, and Nan Dirk De Graaf. 2006. "Socioeconomic Dynamics of Neighborhoods and the Risk of Crime Victimization: A Multilevel Study of Improving, Declining, and Stable Areas in the Netherlands." *Social Problems* 53:226–47.

Vigdor, Jacob L. 2002. "Does Gentrification Harm the Poor?" *Brookings-Wharton Papers on Urban Affairs* 2002:133–73.

Waldinger, Roger. 1989. "Immigration and Urban Change." *Annual Review of Sociology* 15:211–32.

Warner, W. Lloyd, and Leo Srole. 1945. *The Social Systems of American Ethnic Groups.* New Haven, CT: Yale University Press.

Weatherburn, Don, Bronwyn Lind, and Simon Ku. 1999. "'Hotbeds of Crime?' Crime and Public Housing in Urban Sydney." *Crime and Delinquency* 45:256–71.

Wellman, Barry, and Barry Leighton. 1979. "Networks, Neighborhoods, and Communities: Approaches to the Study of the Community Question." *Urban Affairs Quarterly* 14:363–90.

Wickersham Commission. 1931. *National Commission on Law Observance and Enforcement: Report on Crime and the Foreign Born.* Report no. 10. Washington, DC: U.S. Government Printing Office.

Wikström, Per-Olof. 1998. "Communities and Crime." In *Oxford Handbook on Crime and Punishment*, edited by Michael Tonry. Oxford: Oxford University Press.

————. 2004. "Crime as Alternative: Towards a Cross-Level Situational Action Theory of Crime Causation." In *Beyond Empiricism: Institutions and Intentions in the Study of Crime.* Advances in Criminological Theory 13, edited by Joan McCord. New Brunswick, NJ: Transaction Press.

———. 2006. "Individuals, Settings, and Acts of Crime: Situational Mechanisms and the Explanation of Crime." In *The Explanation of Crime: Context, Mechanisms, and Development*, edited by Per-Olof H. Wikström and Robert J. Sampson. Cambridge: Cambridge University Press.

———. 2007. "The Social Ecology of Crime: The Role of the Environment in Crime Causation." In *Internationales Handbuch der Kriminologie*, edited by Hans Joachim Schneider. Berlin: De Gruyter Recht.

Wikström, Per-Olof H., and Robert J. Sampson. 2006. "Introduction: Toward a Unified Approach to Crime and Its Explanation." In *The Explanation of Crime: Context, Mechanisms, and Development*, edited by Per-Olof H. Wikström and Robert J. Sampson. New York: Cambridge University Press.

Wilson, William J. 1987. *The Truly Disadvantaged: The Inner City, the Underclass, and Public Policy*. Chicago: University of Chicago Press.

Wooldredge, John. 2002. "Examining the (Ir)Relevance of Aggregation Bias for Multilevel Studies of Neighborhoods and Crime with an Example Comparing Census Tracts to Official Neighborhoods in Cincinnati." *Criminology* 40:681–709.

Wyly, Elvin K., and Daniel J. Hammel. 1999. "Islands of Decay in Seas of Renewal: Urban Housing Policy and the Resurgence of Gentrification." *Housing Policy Debate* 10:711–71.

Dirk van Zyl Smit

Regulation of Prison Conditions

ABSTRACT

Prisons in modern societies are complex bureaucracies that are subject to regulation through a range of external monitoring and internal inspection mechanisms. Internal inspections are closely connected to the bureaucracies that manage individual prison systems. External monitoring is conducted by international, regional, and national organizations. In theory, international monitoring by organs of the United Nations has a worldwide reach, but its impact in a particular country depends on whether the country has ratified the relevant international instrument and agreed to being monitored. Regional monitoring is particularly prominent in Europe. It is less prominent in other regions. The form that national external monitoring adopts varies greatly between countries. It may be done by a specially created inspectorate, human rights committee, or ombudsman. Local monitoring committees for individual prisons, complaints procedures, and court actions may all serve regulatory functions. These diverse bodies are most effective as monitoring organizations when they are independent, apply clear standards, and have political support. Their efficacy may be increased by international support and the acceptance at the national level of the salience of human rights standards for prison conditions.

Prisons are closed institutions. They are established and funded by governments to hold people against their will. In the case of sentenced prisoners at least, this loss of liberty is a deliberately inflicted punishment. Prisons are supposed to protect society, immediately by keeping their inmates, the prisoners, out of the wider society, and, ideally, by eventually returning them to society as citizens who will lead crime-

Dirk van Zyl Smit is professor of comparative and international penal law in the University of Nottingham and emeritus professor of criminology in the University of Cape Town. He wishes to thank William Parker-Jenkins, Giovanna Frisso, and David Hayes for research assistance and the editor, Michael Tonry, and two anonymous reviewers for helpful comments on an earlier draft.

free lives. In the process of imprisonment the prison authorities exercise direct and enormous power over those who are imprisoned. This power shapes the conditions under which prisoners are held. These conditions not only determine the quality of prisoners' lives but may also literally be a matter of life or death for them. Regulating prison conditions is therefore of prime importance both for prisoners and for society as a whole, which also has a wider interest in the efficacy of prisons.

At its best, concern about prison conditions is motivated by the recognition that prisoners as human beings have a right to dignity that should be recognized notwithstanding their incarceration. Regulation of prisons may seek to determine whether prison conditions are such that prisoners can live in prison in a way that allows them to survive with their dignity and humanity intact and, ideally, improve themselves in the process. However, prison conditions may also be regulated for other reasons: the government may wish, for example, to ensure that the resources that it is putting into prisons are being spent appropriately. It may even want to ensure that prison conditions are not "too soft," so that prisoners are not having "too easy a time." Regulation may also attempt to determine whether conditions in prisons are preventing escapes or providing prisoners with opportunities for "resocialization."

In order to reflect on and compare the regulation of prison conditions around the world it is necessary to have a conceptual framework for describing the very different regulatory techniques that have been developed. One relatively simple framework is to recognize, as the 2006 European Prison Rules (EPR) do,[1] that, broadly speaking, this regulation has taken two primary forms.[2] The first, the internal form, has been one in which prisons are subject to controls similar to those over other institutions by comparable government departments. In this regard, the EPR refer to regular inspection by government agencies in

[1] Recommendation Rec(2006) 2 of the Committee of Ministers to Member States of the Council of Europe on EPR adopted by the Committee of Ministers on January 11, 2006, at the 952nd meeting of the Ministers' Deputies. The rules are available electronically at https://wcd.coe.int/ViewDoc.jsp?id=955747. The EPR are discussed more fully in Sec. I.B below.

[2] The distinction is drawn in Rule 9, one of the basic principles of the EPR, which states simply: "All prisons shall be subject to regular government inspection *and* independent monitoring" (emphasis added). "Governmental inspection" and "independent monitoring" are dealt with in more detail in Rules 92 and 93, respectively. A similar distinction is drawn in the context of Canada by Ivan Zinger (2006).

order to assess whether prisons are administered in accordance with the requirements of national and international law. Second, regulation has taken the form of independent monitoring that is external to, and independent from, the prison or prison system that is to be regulated. Such monitoring could be conducted by both national and international institutions.[3]

Both forms of regulation have several variations.[4] They depend crucially on national administrative and legal systems and their relationship to national, as well as regional and international, forms of oversight. Internal regulation has largely been predicated on fundamental changes in state administration that have taken place in most countries, albeit at very different stages and to different degrees, since the rise of the modern prison system in Western countries two centuries ago. All forms of administration, including prisons, in modern bureaucratic states are subject to internal audits of expenses and performance that amount to far more intensive controls than were historically the case.

External monitoring may take various forms, which may have a great impact on its efficacy. It may be conducted by elements in the state administration that are only partly separated from the bureaucracy that is directly responsible for the prison system. Thus in most countries there are auditors or inspectors of some kind who report on conditions in individual penal institutions and on how they are administered. Typically they are not primarily responsible to a department of prisons or "corrections" but rather to either a minister of state or even directly to an elected parliament.

External monitoring, by contrast, may be conducted by bodies that are fully independent of the national administration. Such fully independent regulation can take several forms. It may be international and thus clearly separate from the national bureaucracy. This is the case if the monitoring is conducted by an agency or "special rapporteur" appointed by the United Nations or by a regional human rights agency that has a basis in international law to do so. However, as will become apparent, such monitoring is not available in all regions of the world

---

[3] Silvia Casale (2009) has proposed a similar, but tripartite, model in which a distinction is drawn between internal, external, and international scrutiny.

[4] Michele Deitch (2006) has developed a model of "non-judicial oversight" that distinguishes six functions—regulation, audit, accreditation, investigation, reporting, and inspection and monitoring—that oversight may have. Many of these functions of oversight are discussed in this essay. However, the terminology I have adopted would include them under the term "regulation," which I give a wider meaning.

and in any event may not be permitted by a particular national government.

A measure of independent and external monitoring may come from nongovernmental organizations that are not elected but nevertheless form an important part of the pluralist fabric of modern democracies. In this regard one must bear in mind the role that is played by both international nongovernmental organizations, such as the International Committee of the Red Cross (ICRC), Amnesty International, and Penal Reform International, and by national nongovernmental organizations, such as the Howard League in both New Zealand and the United Kingdom.[5] Nongovernmental organizations may regulate prisons directly by inspecting them and making policy recommendations on prison conditions. More often, however, they operate as a pressure group or "public conscience" to encourage government or other bodies to perform their regulatory functions.

External monitoring of prisons may also be conducted by the courts, both international and national. It is important to recognize this role, as some sociological literature on prison regulation focuses on (improved) means of administrative control but ignores the important effects that the judicial branch can have directly and indirectly on prison conditions. However, the place of the courts in the regulation of prison conditions can vary considerably, depending on their structural role in prison-related decision making, deeper national constitutional traditions, and, in the case of international and regionally based courts, the degree of recognition their judgments have in national law.

Analysis of techniques of regulation cannot be separated entirely from the question about the substantive conditions that prisons can be expected to meet and that regulation, both internal and external, aims to ensure. Here too, there are variations between countries both in the standards themselves and in the sources from which they are derived. These variations have to be borne in mind when analyzing how techniques of regulation are implemented.

Historically, much of the drive for prison regulation has been mo-

---

[5] The role of the Red Cross in respect of prisons is discussed at http://www.icrc.org/. The role of Amnesty International in respect of prisons is discussed at http://www.amnesty.org.uk/. The role of Penal Reform International in respect of prisons is particularly significant in Eastern Europe and Africa. It is outlined at http://www.penalreform.org/. There are details of the role of the Howard League in New Zealand at http://www.howardleague.co.nz/index.html. The role of the Howard League in England and Wales is discussed at http://www.howardleague.org/. A similar role is performed in Canada by the John Howard Society of Canada: see http://www.johnhoward.ca/jhsmiss.htm.

tivated by concern for the protection of the human dignity of prisoners. Exposés of prison conditions, from John Howard (1792) onward, have been driven by a concern for the humanity of prisoners held under "appalling" conditions and have been followed by calls for establishing mechanisms and forms of regulation that would ensure that such conditions would be outlawed. The idea of substantive standards that prisons should meet has deep roots in the right not to be subject to certain forms of punishment that can be described as "cruel and inhuman" or, latterly, as torture or "inhuman or degrading" punishment or treatment. These ideas were found in the English Bill of Rights of 1688, and the amendments to the Constitution of the United States of America and the French Déclaration des droits de l'homme et du citoyen a century later. However, their emergence into recognizable standards that could be enforced by regulation backed by law is very much a product of the post–Second World War period, in which the recognition of prisoners as bearers of human rights became much more prominent at both the national and international levels.

This essay aims to shed light on how the regulation of prison conditions is achieved in modern prison systems by describing what is known about key aspects of such regulation in a number of countries. The approach adopted is both indirect and selective. It is indirect in the sense that in Section I it outlines the emergence of substantive standards for prison conditions at the international and regional levels and then turns to their international implementation as a means of regulating prison conditions at the national level. The effects of international standards on the regulation of national prison conditions are distinctly mixed, for they are only one element, and not necessarily the most important one, in the regulation of prison conditions.

Section I.*A* focuses strongly on the role of the United Nations in the regulation of prison conditions. It explains that there are two key international instruments of treaty status that contain important general principles applicable to prisoners' rights—the International Covenant on Civil and Political Rights (ICCPR) and the United Nations Convention against Torture and Other Cruel, Inhuman and Degrading Treatment or Punishment (CAT)—and that these instruments are supplemented by other guidelines that do not have treaty status themselves, such as the United Nations Standard Minimum Rules for the Treatment of Prisoners.[6] It also considers the key United Nations or-

---

[6] Full text of the ICCPR is available at http://www2.ohchr.org/english/law/ccpr.htm.

gans that are of particular relevance to applying these principles to the regulation of prison conditions. They include the Human Rights Committee,[7] which is concerned with the implementation of the ICCPR, and a new body, the Subcommittee for the Prevention of Torture (SPT), which must enforce the provisions of Optional Protocol to the Convention against Torture (OPCAT).[8] OPCAT is a newly adopted protocol to the CAT, which commits states that are parties to it to taking active steps to prevent the ill treatment of prisoners (and other detainees).

Section I.*B* conducts a similar analysis of the relevant legal instruments at a regional level. Most attention is devoted to Europe, where the European Convention on Human Rights (ECHR) and particularly the European Convention for the Prevention of Torture and Inhuman or Degrading Treatment or Punishment (ECPT) are the key treaty-level instruments.[9] (They are supplemented by the EPR, which contain more detailed provisions but do not have treaty status.) The application of the primary instruments, together with the EPR, to prisons by the European Court for Human Rights (ECtHR) and the European Committee for the Prevention of Torture (CPT), respectively, is shown to create a relatively effective form of regional monitoring of prison conditions.[10]

This section also considers the regional human rights position in respect of prisons in the Americas and in Africa. In both regions there are treaties and enforcement mechanisms that are similar to those in

---

See http://www2.ohchr.org/english/bodies/cat/ for the full text of the CAT. Standard Minimum Rules for the Treatment of Prisoners (adopted August 30, 1955, by the First United Nations Congress on the Prevention of Crime and the Treatment of Offenders, UN Doc. A/CONF/611, annex I; adopted by the United Nations Economic and Social Council, ESC Res. 663 C [XXIV], July 31, 1957, 24 UN ESSCOR Supp. [No. 1] 11, UN Doc. E/3048 [1957] and 2076 [LXII] [1957]). The rules are available at http://www2.ohchr.org/english/law/pdf/treatmentprisoners.pdf.

[7] See http://www2.ohchr.org/english/bodies/hrc/ for a description of the supervisory role of the Human Rights Committee (HRC).

[8] Optional Protocol to the Convention against Torture and Other Cruel, Inhuman or Degrading Treatment or Punishment, December 18, 2002, GA Res. 57/199, UN Doc. A/RES/57/199. See http://www2.ohchr.org/english/bodies/cat/opcat/index.htm.

[9] The text of the ECHR can be found at http://www.echr.coe.int/nr/rdonlyres/d5cc24a7-dc13-4318-b457-5c9014916d7a/0/englishanglais.pdf. The text of the ECPT is available at http://www.cpt.coe.int/EN/documents/ecpt.htm.

[10] For general information about its activities, see the court's Web site, http://www.echr.coe.int/ECHR/homepage_en. General information about the CPT may be found at http://www.cpt.coe.int/en/about.htm. This includes its founding documents and its country and annual reports, as well as its consolidated standards, which are discussed below.

Europe, but they are apparently not as effective as their European counterparts.

The regulation of prison conditions at the national level is dealt with in Section II. It is selective in that it focuses on developments only in a few countries and does not attempt a systematic overview of all forms of regulation of prison conditions in the world. It is also selective in that it does not seek to describe fully all the regulatory techniques used in the countries to which it does refer. Instead, it focuses on features that illustrate different forms of regulation, which may be a prominent feature of the country concerned and shed some light on the full range of techniques that can be used to regulate prison conditions.

The descriptions of national regulation begin by first examining at a number of instances of regulation in European countries where the effects of international standards may be expected to be the greatest. Particular attention is paid in the first instance to the United Kingdom (and within it to England and Wales[11]), which not only has a complex relationship with attempts at outside monitoring of its prison conditions but also has a large range of regulatory institutions that may serve as comparators for regulation elsewhere. Germany and the Netherlands are considered as examples of Western European states where regulation has developed in diverse ways in response to international pressures that are similar to those facing the United Kingdom but against a background of different legal and administrative traditions. Other Western European states are discussed more briefly, particularly in Scandinavia and the postcommunist states of Eastern Europe. The latter offer examples of states where regulation is influenced by aspects of their governmental history and the more recent changes in their relationship with pan-European institutions at the European center.

I contrast European developments with those in South Africa, and more briefly, in Section II.G, with those in some countries in the Asia-Pacific region, where, although there are not as direct regional pressures as in Europe for intensified regulation of prison conditions, reforms have nevertheless taken place. I consider in particular the role of more indirect transfer of ideas within a wider human rights culture.

I then discuss regulation in the United States, where a large percentage of the world's prisoners are housed and international standards ostensibly have not played a major role, as they are at best ignored, if

---

[11] Scotland and Northern Ireland have separate and slightly different regulatory systems.

not met with outright hostility. In this instance the focus is on the interplay of national forces that have shaped the regulation of prison conditions.

Finally, Section III examines the enormous gaps in the regulation of prison conditions that still exist at both the international and national levels. I consider what could be done about them. A combination of independent oversight at the national level, informed by human rights principles and backed by an international body with similar values, could hold the key to effective regulation. The OPCAT may have a crucial role in this regard, but its widespread implementation faces severe practical problems. In general, more work needs to done toward understanding how prison regulation interacts with the very different social climates found in prison in different societies in order to understand how effective such regulation may be perceived to be by prisoners themselves.

I. The International Dimension

At the international level it was the growing recognition of human rights, including the rights of prisoners, in the period after the Second World War that led eventually to the creation of an international apparatus to regulate prison conditions. There have been several stages in this process, which, arguably, is still far from complete.

A. International Human Rights

The first stage was the rise of international human rights law and in particular the affirmation of the right to be free of torture and of cruel, inhuman, or degrading treatment or punishment, which came to be seen as an element of the right to human dignity, an explicit principle of international human rights law. Thus, as early as 1948, article 1 of the Universal Declaration of Human Rights recognized human dignity,[12] while article 5 outlawed torture and cruel, inhuman, or degrading treatment or punishment. At the international level, human dignity and the prohibition of torture and cruel, inhuman, and degrading treatment or punishment were given significance as concepts underpinning the regulation of prison conditions by the ICCPR and CAT, adopted in 1966 and 1984, respectively. Of these, the former was arguably most important in terms of the recognition of prisoners' rights, which could

[12] The Universal Declaration is available at http://www.un.org/en/documents/udhr/.

only be achieved if adequate prison conditions existed. Not only did it provide that "all persons deprived of their liberty shall be treated with humanity with respect for the inherent dignity of the human person" (art. 10.1) and that "no one should be subjected to torture or to cruel, inhuman or degrading treatment or punishment" (art. 7), but it also contained further provisions that could be interpreted as setting implicit requirements in respect of prison conditions. The most interesting of these is the requirement in article 10.3 that "the penitentiary system shall comprise treatment of prisoners the essential aim of which shall be their social rehabilitation," which can been seen as an overarching requirement according to which the treatment of all sentenced prisoners and the prison conditions to facilitate it should be judged (Nowak 2005). Article 10 also contains references to how unconvicted and juvenile prisoners should be treated.

States that are parties to international treaties of course undertake to uphold them, although how this is done may vary according to their national constitutional relationship to the domestic implementation of treaty obligations. Moreover, both the ICCPR and the CAT provide mechanisms designed to ensure that they are enforced. Key to these is a system of reports by states parties on the steps they were taking to ensure compliance with the treaties. Such reports are made to the treaty bodies composed of independent experts, the Human Rights Committee and the Committee against Torture,[13] respectively. However, as mechanisms for regulating prison conditions, these face two key difficulties. First, the treaties on which they are based do not spell out what prison conditions are required to meet the obligations they create, and second, the powers of the treaty bodies charged with compliance may not be adequate to develop and enforce at the international level regulatory controls of prison conditions.

In practice, the first difficulty has been met largely by relying on the 1955 United Nations Standard Minimum Rules for the Treatment of Prisoners and, to a lesser extent, on the subsequent Body of Principles for the Protection of All Persons under Any Form of Detention or Imprisonment and Basic Principles for the Treatment of Prisoners.[14]

---

[13] See http://www2.ohchr.org/english/bodies/hrc/ for a description of the role of the HRC and the key documents that are the sources of its authority. Details about the work of the Committee against Torture can be found at http://www2.ohchr.org/english/bodies/cat/.

[14] *Body of Principles for the Protection of All Persons under any Form of Detention or Imprisonment*, December 9, 1988, GA Res. 43/173, annex, 43 UN GAOR Supp. (No. 49)

These instruments, particularly the first, contain provisions relating to substantive prison conditions, which, if fully enforced, would go some way toward setting clear standards against which prison systems could be judged. Although these instruments are "soft" international law and therefore, unlike treaties, not directly binding on states, the Human Rights Committee in particular has referred to them when interpreting the ICCPR, which does have treaty status. It has done so in its evaluation of national reports on compliance with the ICCPR, in its general comments on article 10 of the covenant, and in its response to individual petitions by prisoners who claim that their human dignity is being infringed or that they are subject to illegal treatment or punishment under the covenant. The result is that the United Nations Standard Minimum Rules for the Treatment of Prisoners in particular has grown in status to the point where it is recognized that "some of their specific rules may reflect legal obligations" (Rodley and Pollard 2009, p. 383). Thus, for example, the prohibition on placing a prisoner in a dark cell (Rule 31) is seen as a form of treatment that is specifically forbidden and therefore routinely regarded as a form of the cruel, inhuman, or degrading treatment outlawed by article 7 of the ICCPR. Even where this is not the case, Standard Minimum Rules can provide guidance in interpreting the general guidance in applying the ICCPR to prisoners.

That there are secondary legal instruments dealing with prison conditions at the international level, which can be linked to international treaties, does not make them into an effective international regulatory framework with real impact on national prison conditions. The reality is that both the ICCPR and the CAT were adopted during the period of the Cold War, when major states were extraordinarily leery of any form of international regulation that would infringe on their sovereignty or that could make negative findings about them that could be used propagandistically to discredit them (Nowak 2005). The result was that the enforcement mechanisms that they adopted are relatively weak. Both treaties provide for states parties to submit national reports on their enforcement, and procedures for interstate and individual complaints. In both instances, however, the individual complaints pro-

298, UN Doc. A/43/49. See http://www2.ohchr.org/english/law/pdf/bodyprinciples.pdf. *Basic Principles for the Treatment of Prisoners*, December 14, 1990, GA Res. 45/111, annex, 45 UN GAOR Supp. (No. 49A) 200, UN Doc. A/45/49. See http://www2.ohchr.org/english/law/pdf/basicprinciples.pdf.

cedures are optional, in the case of the ICCPR by way of accession to an additional protocol. Many of the states that have acceded are in Europe or the Americas, where there are regional human rights instruments that may take precedence. In the case of the CAT in particular, only a minority of states have provided this facility to their citizens, and the impact on the regulation of prisons has been very limited (Nowak and McArthur 2008).

More states allow their citizens a right of individual complaint to the Human Rights Committee.[15] It has been more active with respect to individual complaints and has dealt more frequently with prison matters, to the extent that it is possible to determine its views on key prison conditions, such as sanitation, light, ventilation, and overcrowding. Serious deficits in this regard have been held to infringe both article 10 requirements that prisoners must be treated with humanity and dignity as well as article 7 prohibitions on ill treatment (Williams 1990; Nowak 2005, pp. 172–75; Conte and Burchill 2009, pp. 124–51; Rodley and Pollard 2009). In some instances the Human Rights Committee has ordered legal or policy changes, and, in findings that closely parallel legal judgments, it has declared that reparation should be made to individuals whose rights have been infringed. However, the difficulty remains that even a finding that a state has breached its obligations, either in a specific case or on the basis of analysis of national reports, is not legally binding. The best that the Human Rights Committee can do in practice is to appoint a special rapporteur to follow up, but, as a majority of states found to be in violation of the committee's views either challenge the findings or simply ignore them, it is relatively powerless. The Human Rights Committee too cannot be regarded as an effective agent for the systematic regulation of prison conditions.

Much the same can be said about the systematic impact of other United Nations regulatory initiatives that relate to prison conditions. The position of Special Rapporteur on Torture was created by the United Nations Commission on Human Rights in 1985.[16] The mandate of the Special Rapporteur, who is appointed directly by resolution

---

[15] The right of individual complaint is granted by the First Optional Protocol to the ICCPR 1966, which may be found at http://www2.ohchr.org/english/law/ccpr-one.htm. A list of states that have signed and/or ratified the protocol may be found at http://treaties.un.org/Pages/ViewDetails.aspx?src = TREATY&mtdsg_no = IV-5&chapter = 4 &lang = en.

[16] Additional information about the role and legal basis of the Special Rapporteur may be found at http://www2.ohchr.org/english/issues/torture/rapporteur/.

of the Human Rights Council (the successor to the Commission on Human Rights) covers all countries, irrespective of whether a state has ratified the CAT. The Special Rapporteur acts by transmitting urgent appeals to states with regard to individuals reported to be at risk of torture, as well as communications on past alleged cases of torture, and by undertaking fact-finding visits to countries. These can and do include visits to prisons. The Special Rapporteur can request invitations to visit countries or invitations might be unsolicited. Not all countries issue invitations on request, but, when they do, they undertake not to place restrictions on the Special Rapporteur's access to persons deprived of their liberty.[17] The current Special Rapporteur, Manfred Nowak, has spoken eloquently of the importance that visits have in influencing prison conditions:

> Preventive visits to places of detention have a double purpose. The very fact that national or international experts have the power to inspect every place of detention at any time without prior announcement, have access to prison registers and other documents, are entitled to speak with every detainee in private and to carry out medical investigations of torture victims has a strong deterrent effect. At the same time, such visits create the opportunity for independent experts to examine, at first hand, the treatment of prisoners and detainees and the general conditions of detention. The manner in which a society treats its prisoners and detainees, including aliens, is a major indicator of the commitment of such a society to human rights in general. Many problems stem from inadequate systems which can easily be improved through regular monitoring. By carrying out regular visits to places of detention, the visiting experts usually establish a constructive dialogue with the authorities concerned in order to help them resolve problems observed.
>
> Based on his experience as head of an expert commission carrying out regular visits to police detention centres in Austria and from fact-finding missions in his capacity as United Nations Special Rapporteur on the question of torture, the Special Rapporteur is deeply convinced that a system of unannounced visits to all places of detention by independent experts is by far the most effective and sustainable mechanism for gradually developing a

---

[17] Details of the work of the Special Rapporteur, including requests for visits that have not been granted (inter alia by the United States, which has had a request pending since 2004), can be found at http://www2.ohchr.org/english/issues/torture/rapporteur/.

prison culture based more on respect for human dignity and personal integrity than on fear, exclusion and contempt.[18]

There are, however, limits on what a single person can do, and the Special Rapporteur therefore seeks to coordinate his work with that of other inspection bodies.

Article 37(c) of the Convention on the Rights of the Child is of direct relevance to the conditions of detention of children as it provides that "Every child deprived of liberty shall be treated with humanity and respect for the inherent dignity of the human person, and in a manner which takes into account the needs of persons of his or her age."[19] The Committee on the Rights of the Child is responsible for the interpretation of the convention.[20] Although it cannot hear individual complaints, it can make general comments. In much the same way as the Human Rights Committee has done with the United Nations Standard Minimum Rules for the Treatment of Prisoners, it has sought in its General Comment 10 in 2007 to apply more detailed United Nations standards,[21] in particular, the "Beijing Rules," that is, the Standard Minimum Rules for the Administration of Juvenile Justice, and the "Havana Rules," that is, the Rules for the Protection of

---

[18] Interim report of the Special Rapporteur of the Commission on Human Rights on *Torture and Other Cruel, Inhuman or Degrading Treatment or Punishment*, submitted in accordance with assembly resolution 60/148, submitted on August 14, 2006, Doc. A/61/259, paras. 72 and 73. Available at http://www.icj.org/IMG/NowakGAReport2006.pdf.

[19] Available at http://www2.ohchr.org/english/law/pdf/crc.pdf.

[20] The committee is a body of 18 independent experts elected by states parties to the convention for a term of 4 years, although a longer term may be achieved through reelection (art. 43). It is responsible for monitoring the implementation of the convention and its two Optional Protocols by states parties, who are obliged to provide reports to the committee within 2 years of ratification of the convention, and subsequently every 5 years. The committee is also empowered to request additional information from a state party (art. 44). (Similar obligations and powers are also found in art. 8 of the Optional Protocol of the Convention on the Rights of the Child on the Involvement of Children in Armed Conflict, which may be of relevance should, for instance, children be detained as prisoners of war or otherwise during a conflict.) Finally, the committee is empowered to recommend areas of study to the General Assembly of the United Nations, as well as to submit general comments and suggestions to it, subject to the commentary of any "concerned" states parties (art. 45). In practice, the committee issues General Comments on themes of international human rights law as they relate to the protection of children's rights, including the rights of those in detention. For more general information about the committee and for an archive of its publications, see its Web site: http://www2.ohchr.org/english/bodies/crc/index.htm.

[21] UN Committee on the Rights of the Child (CRC), *CRC General Comment No. 10 (2007): Children's Rights in Juvenile Justice*, April 25, 2007, CRC/C/GC/10. The *Comment* can be found at http://www2.ohchr.org/english/bodies/crc/docs/CRC.C.GC.10.pdf.

Juveniles Deprived of Their Liberty to imprisoned children, which in this context means persons under the age of 18 years.[22]

Before leaving behind consideration of the international instruments for the control of prison conditions, mention must be made of the most recent initiative, the OPCAT, which came into force in 2006.[23] On the face of it, OPCAT has the potential to overcome many of the shortcomings that exist in other international enforcement apparatuses as a means of regulating prison conditions. The OPCAT does not contain any new substantive provisions but is designed to enforce the prohibition of torture and other forms of ill treatment outlawed by the CAT. The explicit objective of OPCAT is to "establish a system of regular visits undertaken by independent *international and national* bodies to places where people are deprived of their liberty, in order to prevent torture and other cruel, inhuman or degrading treatment or punishment" (art. 1, emphasis added). The emphasis on both national and international dimensions is the outcome of a delicate compromise that took more than a decade to negotiate between states that favored a robust international inspectorate and those that did not want such an inspectorate but sought instead to strengthen international controls (Evans and Haenni-Dale 2004; Nowak and McArthur 2008).

What is unique about OPCAT is that it aims to achieve this objective of regular visits to prisons and other places of detention by creating a new body, the SPT, and by requiring states parties themselves to enforce the CAT through the creation at the national level of what it calls National Preventive Mechanisms (NPMs).[24] Both of these institutions build on existing mechanisms. The former, the SPT, is clearly modeled on the CPT, which, as will become apparent in the next section, is the primary pan-European mechanism for regulating prison

[22] For the Standard Minimum Rules for the Administration of Juvenile Justice ("The Beijing Rules"), November 29, 1985, GA Res. 40/33, annex, 40 UN GAOR Supp. (No. 53) 207, UN Doc. A/40/53, see http://www2.ohchr.org/english/law/pdf/beijingrules.pdf. For the Rules for the Protection of Juveniles Deprived of Their Liberty ("The Havana Rules"), December 14, 1990. GA Res. 45/113, annex, 45 UN GAOR Supp. (No. 49A) 205, UN Doc. A/45/49, see http://www2.ohchr.org/english/law/pdf/res45_113.pdf.
[23] The text of OPCAT and updated information about the states that have become parties, as well as on the implementation of OPCAT, can be found at http://www2.ohchr.org/english/bodies/cat/opcat/index.htm. Much of the work to propagate OPCAT was undertaken by the Geneva-based nongovernmental organization, the Association for the Prevention of Torture (APT). Further information on OPCAT can be found at http://www.apt.ch/.
[24] Article 17 of OPCAT provides that each state party shall establish "one or several independent national preventive mechanisms for the prevention of torture at the domestic level."

conditions. The members of the SPT are elected by the states parties but serve in their individual capacities.[25]

The latter, the NPM, is a new concept. The idea is that states should develop a new independent inspection body or bodies, or designate their existing inspecting body or bodies, if they are sufficiently independent, as NPMs and ensure in this way that requirements of the CAT are met (Steinerte and Murray 2009). States parties undertake to work closely with the SPT both as an inspecting mechanism in its own right and as an international body that will liaise with and guide the NPMs.

In Section III, I consider the potential effects of this new initiative on how prison conditions are regulated throughout the world. For the moment it should simply be recorded that OPCAT has only just begun its work and that it is being done under severely straitened financial circumstances.

B. Regional Initiatives

Regional initiatives to reinforce the recognition of human rights at a level beyond that of the nation-state also emerged, in Europe and elsewhere, in the immediate post–Second World War period. In 1950, article 3 of the ECHR prohibited torture and inhuman or degrading treatment or punishment. In 1969, article 5 of the American Convention on Human Rights too confirmed the importance of treating all persons deprived of liberty with human dignity and prohibited torture and cruel, inhuman, or degrading treatment or punishment. Finally, in 1981, article 5 of the African Charter on Human and Peoples' Rights prohibited all forms of exploitation and degradation, among which it also specifically included torture and cruel, inhuman, or degrading punishment and treatment. An important exception is the Asia-Pacific region, which does not have similar binding regional human rights instruments to prohibit torture and other abuses against prisoners (Pasha 2010).

1. *Europe.* The ECHR was supported by the Council of Europe established in 1949, with a general brief to encourage the recognition of human rights in Europe, and by the European Commission of Hu-

[25] Article 5 of OPCAT provides that initially there should be 10 members until the number states that are parties to the protocol reaches 50, at which stage the number should be increased to 25. By early 2010 there were exactly 50 parties, which means that shortly the number of members will have to be increased.

man Rights and ECtHR,[26] as the mechanism for enforcing the convention among member states. Imprisonment was not initially high on the agenda, and it was not until 1975 that the ECtHR gave its first major decision on prisoners' rights (*Golder v. United Kingdom* [App. No. 4451/70 (1979–1980) 1 EHRR 524 (February 21, 1975)]). Other specifically European initiatives dealing with prison conditions also took time to develop. In 1973, the Committee of Ministers of the Council of Europe adopted a fresh set of specifically European, Standard Minimum Rules for the Treatment of Prisoners and followed this with further resolutions and recommendations dealing with specific aspects of imprisonment.[27] However, these early initiatives could not be regarded as constituting anything like a binding European framework for the regulation of prison conditions.[28]

Much of this changed with the adoption in 1987 of the ECPT. It grew directly out of dissatisfaction with the slow process of adopting an enforceable United Nations Convention against Torture and the desire to ensure that the prohibition against torture and other prohibited forms of treatment could be enforced by an international body that conducted regular inspections. The ECPT did not create any new rights. It simply established the CPT[29] and laid down that it "shall by means of visits, examine the treatment of persons deprived of their liberty with a view to strengthening, if necessary, the protection of such persons from torture and from inhuman or degrading treatment or punishment" (art. 1). The CPT is composed of independent experts elected for a 4-year term by the Committee of Ministers of the Council

---

[26] The ECHR was abolished in 1998 and its work absorbed into that of the ECtHR. For more general information about its activities, see the court's Web site, http://www.echr.coe.int/ECHR/homepage_en.

[27] The committee is composed of the Ministers of Foreign Affairs of every member state of the council or their permanent diplomatic representatives in Strasbourg, and it convenes once a year. Its role combines those of a forum for intergovernmental discussion of human rights challenges within Europe and as a resolver of these challenges. It has been highly active in this latter role and remains instrumental in the creation of the highly advanced European human rights system. For more general information about the committee, see its Web site, http://www.coe.int/t/cm/home_en.asp. Resolution (73) 5 on the Standard Minimum Rules for the Treatment of Prisoners, adopted by the Committee of Ministers of the Council of Europe on January 19, 1973, at the 217th meeting of the ministers' deputies. The rules are available at https://wcd.coe.int/com .instranet.InstraServlet?command = com.instranet.CmdBlobGet&InstranetImage = 588982&SecMode = 1&DocId = 645672&Usage = 2.

[28] For a fuller account of this history, see Van Zyl Smit and Snacken (2009, chap. 1).

[29] General information about the CPT may be found at http://www.cpt.coe.int/en/about.htm. This includes its founding documents and its country and annual reports, as well as its consolidated standards that are discussed below.

of Europe. There is one member for each of the 47 member states of the council. They are chosen from a short list put forward by the states and may be reelected twice.

From the beginning, the CPT interpreted this simple brief widely (Morgan and Evans 2001; Casale 2006). The CPT did not regard itself as bound by the interpretations by the ECtHR of the words "torture" and "inhuman or degrading treatment or punishment," which are contained in identical form in the ECHR. Instead, it felt free to develop its own understanding of how the authorities should act to prevent such outcomes. This led to its making extensive recommendations in its reports on individual countries about what prison[30] conditions should be like to ensure that they did not allow inhuman or degrading treatment. These recommendations refer both to specific requirements, such as the minimum square meters of floor space that should be available per prisoner in certain types of sleeping accommodation,[31] and to more general recommendations about the prison regimes, for example, that all prisoners sentenced to life imprisonment should be given a prison regime that prepares them for release.[32] Aspects of these recommendations have been consolidated in its annual reports, which in turn were extracted and published in the so-called CPT Standards, which can be read as a narrative account of standards that European prisons should meet.

It is worth describing briefly how the CPT functions in its capacity as a multinational prison monitoring body. Article 3 of the ECPT places a reciprocal duty to cooperate on the member states and the CPT. States parties must help the CPT to perform its tasks, by granting access to all places of detention and providing all relevant information. In addition, they must respond to the CPT country visit reports within 6 months, and in a final response after 1 year they must set out how they will take into account its recommendations. The CPT must inform the member states of its visits and is bound by the confidentiality of its findings.

---

[30] The CPT also deals with other forms of detention, e.g., in mental institutions, which are not of direct relevance to this essay.

[31] The CPT requirements in this regard have to be deduced for a number of its report and pronouncements: see Van Zyl Smit and Snacken (2009, p. 132).

[32] CPT, *Report to the Hungarian Government on the Visit to Hungary Carried out by the European Committee for the Prevention of Torture and Inhuman or Degrading Treatment or Punishment (CPT) from 30 January to 1 February 2007* (CPT/Inf [2007] 24), para. 33. The report is available on the CPT Web site, http://www.cpt.coe.int/documents/hun/2007-24-inf-eng.pdf.

The reports on the visits are confidential but can be published at the request or with the consent of the country concerned. If a state does not cooperate with the CPT or systematically does not follow its recommendations, the CPT may publish a statement about its key findings and recommendations without the consent of the state concerned. In practice, as the countries that were first visited all consented to the publication of their reports, the moral pressure to publish is high. As a result, most CPT reports are published together with the responses of the member states (Cassese 1996; Van Zyl Smit and Snacken 2009).

The independence of the CPT follows from the circumstance that its members, one for each state party, do not represent their countries but are experts in one of the fields of the CPT's competence and are not involved in visits in their own country. Its effectiveness results from its ability to receive important information and react quickly to it, both through the procedure it has developed for giving short notice of its visits if necessary and by following up on its recommendations through periodic and ad hoc visits (Snacken 2004). Examples of the latter include a visit to Frankfurt Airport from May 25 to May 28, 1998, to investigate allegations that asylum seekers were being subjected to degrading conditions of detention,[33] and a visit on January 26 and 27, 2010, to the Turkish Island of Imrali, where Abdullah Öcalan, arguably Turkey's most famous political prisoner, is being detained.[34]

The importance of the CPT was greatly increased by the major political events of the early 1990s. After the fall of communism in Eastern Europe, all European countries, with the exception of Belarus, became members of the Council of Europe. As a condition of membership, they had to accede to both the ECHR and the ECPT, and they also had to undertake specifically to bring their prison conditions into line with European human rights norms.

European governments tend to respond in some detail to the reports of the CPT. Usually they comment on the steps that they have taken to implement reforms. Thus, for example, the government of Lithuania informed the CPT that it has amended its legislation to bring it in line

---

[33] See the CPT press release, "Visit by European Committee for the Prevention of Torture to Germany," on its Web site, http://www.cpt.coe.int/documents/deu/1998-06-03-eng.htm).

[34] See the CPT press release, "Council of Europe Anti-Torture Committee Visits Prison on the Island of Imrali (Turkey)," on its Web site, http://www.cpt.coe.int/documents/tur/2010-02-01-eng.htm.

with the requirements of the CPT.[35] Governments are not always this cooperative, however. In rare instances they do not respond at all: the Russian government, for example, has failed to respond to reports of prison conditions in Chechnya, thus eventually provoking a critical statement from the CPT.[36] In other exceptional instances governments have disputed the findings of the CPT directly: in 2009, for example, the Czech government rejected outright the strong condemnation by the CPT of the castration of sex offenders in Czech prison and psychiatric institutions.[37]

The CPT has also been prepared to expand its brief and address wider policy issues. Most notably it has argued that unacceptable prison conditions caused by overcrowding must be met by reducing prison populations, as building programs did not provide long-term solutions (Snacken 2006). While the CPT standards remain an important source of norms applicable to prisons, in the past decade the judgments of the ECtHR and the recommendations of the Committee of Ministers of the Council of Europe, particularly the 2006 EPR, have increased in significance as sources of these norms. In the case of the court, an initial reluctance to give judgments on issues dealing with substantive prison conditions, identified by Stephen Livingstone (2000), has all but disappeared. Although the court still warns that the level of unacceptability of prison conditions must reach a minimum level for it to be regarded as amounting to cruel and unusual treatment, it now routinely finds that overcrowding and other shortcomings in prison conditions infringe article 3 of the ECHR. (See, e.g., *Dougoz v. Greece* [App. No. 40907/98 (2002) 34 EHRR 61, March 6, 2001]; *Kalashnikov v. Russia* [App. No. 47095/99 (2003) 36 EHRR 34, July 15, 2002].) Moreover,

[35] CPT, *Report to the Lithuanian Government on the Visit to Lithuania Carried out by the European Committee for the Prevention of Torture and Inhuman or Degrading Treatment or Punishment (CPT) from 17 to 24 February 2004* (CPT/Inf [2006]), para. 48, available at the CPT Web site, http://www.cpt.coe.int/documents/ltu/2006-09-inf-eng.pdf.

[36] See, e.g., the public statement concerning the Chechen Republic of the Russian Federation (made on March 13, 2007) (CPT/Inf [2007] 17) available at the CPT Web site, http://www.cpt.coe.int/documents/rus/2007-17-inf-eng.pdf.

[37] CPT, *Report to the Czech Government on the Visit to the Czech Republic Carried out by the European Committee for the Prevention of Torture and Inhuman or Degrading Treatment or Punishment (CPT) from 25 March to 2 April 2008* (CPT/Inf [2009] 8) available at the CPT Web site at http://www.cpt.coe.int/documents/cze/2009-08-inf-eng.htm and the response of the Czech government, *Response of the Czech Government to the Report of the European Committee for the Prevention of Torture and Inhuman or Degrading Treatment or Punishment (CPT) on Its Visit to the Czech Republic from 25 March to 2 April 2008* (CPT/Inf [2009] 9) available at the CPT Web site at http://www.cpt.coe.int/documents/cze/2009-09-inf-eng.htm.

the court has made it clear that lack of resources and lack of intention to infringe this right are not acceptable excuses for inhuman or degrading treatment of prisoners (*Poltoratskiy v. Ukraine* [App. No. 38812/97 (2004) 39 EHRR 43, April 29, 2003]; *I.I. v. Bulgaria* [App. No. 44082/98, June 9, 2005]). Other convention rights, including the right to a private and family life, have been developed into substantive prisoners' rights that directly affect prison conditions (see, e.g., *Enea v. Italy* [App. No. 74912/01, September 17, 2009]).

The EPR and related recommendations have been developed too. They are now cast much more explicitly in terms that recognize the rights of all prisoners to certain prison conditions. Indeed, the updated "Basic Principles" at the start of the rules are explicit in this regard, with Rule 1 establishing that "All persons deprived of their liberty *shall* be treated with respect for their human rights" (emphasis added; note the positive, obligatory language). This approach may be contrasted with the EPR published in 1987,[38] Rule 1 of which is formulated as a general obligation on the state rather than as an individual right.[39] In addition, many of the rules of the 2006 EPR facilitate the continued exercise of human rights guaranteed by the ECHR: for example, in article 8 the right to respect for private and family life and for correspondence is facilitated by Rule 24, which requires states to provide a maximum level of contact with the outside world (at least as a general principle). Moreover, they provide specifically that there should be both national governmental inspection (Rule 92) and independent monitoring of prisons (Rule 93). They place a duty on independent monitoring bodies to make their findings public (Rule 93.1) and to cooperate with international agencies that are legally entitled to visit prisons (Rule 93.2).

A feature of the way that the ECtHR, the CPT, and EPR operate in Europe is the extent to which they reinforce each other. Thus the ECtHR relies on the EPR and other recommendations of the Council of Europe (as well as on the ICCPR, to which all European countries are parties) and increasingly cites them in detail as the "European legal instruments" when developing its own conceptions of what prison con-

[38] An electronic copy of these former rules can be found at https://wcd.coe.int/com.instranet.InstraServlet?command = com.instranet.CmdBlobGet&InstranetImage = 607507&SecMode = 1&DocId = 692778&Usage = 2.

[39] Rule 1 reads: "The deprivation of liberty shall be effected in material and moral conditions which ensure respect for human dignity and are in conformity with these rules."

ditions should be like. This has been done explicitly by the Grand Chamber of the ECtHR in recent years (see, e.g., *Dickson v. United Kingdom* 2007 [App. No. 44362/04 (2008) 46 EHRR 41, December 4, 2007, para. 29]). In *Gülmez v. Turkey* (App. No. 16330/02, May 20, 2008, para. 63), the ECtHR went further and ordered the respondent state directly to bring its legislation on prison discipline "in line with the principles set out in articles 57 § 2 (b) and 59 (c) of the European Prison Rules." The ECtHR also often cites the reports of the CPT, both as a source of policy and as a source of factual findings when establishing the background situation of relevance to decisions in individual cases.

The wider question remains whether, considered separately or together, these bodies can be regarded as providing a mechanism for regulating European prison conditions that operates at the European level. In this regard Jim Murdoch (2006, p. 52) has commented: "The European system of the protection of persons deprived of their liberty is thus a complex scheme of interwoven standard-setting and implementation machinery which draws on international expectations and domestic practices and is given practical force through state goodwill and when necessary by the threat of judicial condemnation." However, the fact that such a system can be identified (De Jonge 2007; Van Zyl Smit and Snacken 2009) does not necessarily mean that it is recognized throughout Europe as a key element in the regulation of national prison conditions. An evaluation of the impact of the European system as a whole has not been undertaken, and the best one can do is to comment on the impact of its constituent parts, as is done to some extent when individual countries are discussed below.

As far as the ECtHR is concerned, one would do well to distinguish between legal technicalities and practical outcomes. The ECtHR is not a European supreme court, and the enforcement of its judgments is dependent on a political process involving the Committee of Ministers of the Council of Europe. In practice, though, its decisions, including those to do with prisons, are, unlike those of the Human Rights Committee at the international level, rarely flouted directly by European states. Instead, also in the area of prison law, they are regarded as binding and, allowing for the very different constitutional and legal traditions of European states, as very strong precedents, if not formally binding in all cases. What does happen, however, is that national governments interpret, as restrictively as possible, judgments of the ECtHR of which they disapprove.

2. *The Americas.*   Although the European system may have evolved most fully, developments in human rights law in other regions also affect prison conditions. One such development is to be found in the Americas, where the American Convention on Human Rights and the Inter-American Convention to Prevent and Punish Torture[40] closely parallel the ICCPR and the CAT in their prohibitions on torture and inhuman or degrading treatment and punishment (Rodley and Pollard 2009, p. 51). Both are enforceable through the Inter-American Commission on Human Rights. The commission, a body established under a mandate in terms of Chapter VII of the American Convention on Human Rights, consists of seven independent experts from different member states of the Organization of American States (OAS).[41] They are elected for a term of 4 years from a short list composed of three candidates proposed by each of the member states of the OAS by that organization's general assembly. Since 2000, the commission has considered cases involving prison conditions in a significant number of countries: Argentina, Brazil, Colombia, Peru, Paraguay, Mexico, Cuba, Jamaica, Guatemala, Ecuador, Surinam, Honduras, Venezuela, El Salvador, and the United States.[42] In all these cases, the commission ordered the adoption of provisional measures to avoid serious and irreparable harm to the human rights of individuals deprived of liberty.

Some of these cases were later submitted by the commission to the Inter-American Court of Human Rights,[43] a regional judicial body established in 1979 by the OAS to enforce and uphold the American Convention on Human Rights. The court's adjudicatory jurisdiction extends only to cases referred by states or by the commission,[44] and it requires the member state's voluntary consent, which may be granted

[40] The text of the convention is available at http://www.oas.org/juridico/English/treaties/b-32.html. For the Inter-American Convention to Prevent and Punish Torture, see http://www.oas.org/JURIDICO/ENGLISH/Treaties/a-51.html.

[41] General information on this regional organization may be found at http://www.oas.org/en/default.asp.

[42] For more general information about the commission, see its Web site, http://www.cidh.oas.org/DefaultE.htm.

[43] For general information about the court, see http://www.corteidh.or.cr/index.cfm. Note that certain information on the court's Web site is available only in Spanish.

[44] Set out in its statute, which was produced by the Ninth Session of the General Assembly of the OAS and set out in Resolution 448–0/79. The statute may be viewed at http://www.oas.org/xxxivga/english/reference_docs/Estatuto_CorteIDH.pdf.

either for individual cases or absolutely.[45] The court has also used its powers in terms of the American Convention on Human Rights to order the adoption of provisional measures to deal with major human rights abuses, such as the occurrence of multiple killings in prison as a result of prisoner riots.[46]

By and large the general compliance with the provisional measures ordered by the commission and the court has not been satisfactory. It is common to find a statement by the commission or the court in which, even though the measures adopted by the state are welcomed, they are often not considered sufficient to guarantee the right to life and to safety of the detainees or are found to be ineffective. In *Persons Imprisoned in the "Dr. Sebastião Martins Silveira" Penitentiary in Araraquara' São Paulo v. Brazil* (Inter-Am. C. H. R. [Ser. E] [2006], Order of the Court of September 30, 2006, p. 13[47]), the court quoted the commission as commenting:

> that even after the Order of the President dated July 28, 2006, and while they were at the Araraquara Penitentiary, the beneficiaries remained in an open yard without the presence of any State officers to keep order. Many of them suffered from serious illnesses and medical conditions such as hepatitis B and C, ulcers, HIV/AIDS, umbilical hernia, auricular infections, eye infections and severe hemorrhoids and were not receiving adequate medical assistance. They further stated that food provided was not enough or adequate since the inmates themselves had to prepare it and that the water available might be contaminated by the presence of glass pieces and roaches wings. The minimum conditions for a decent life were not being protected, there were no appropriate places for the inmates to sleep and there were not enough products for their personal hygiene. The beneficiaries were not allowed to contact their next of kin or their attorneys. No administrative or judicial investigation was conducted in order to determine those responsi-

---

[45] Articles 61–63 of the American Convention. Currently 21 states have acceded to the jurisdiction of the court in all cases arising; see http://www.cidh.org/Basicos/English/Basic4.Amer.Conv.Ratif.htm.

[46] See, e.g., *Capital El Rodeo I & El Rodeo II Judicial Confinement Center v. Venezuela* (2008 Inter-Am. C. H. R. [Ser. E] 865, Order of the Court of February 8, 2008). Other examples are *Yare I and Yare II Capital Region Penitentiary Center v. Venezuela* (2008 Inter-Am. C. H. R. [Ser. E] 864, Order of the Court of March 30, 2006); *Penitentiary Centre of the Central Occidental Region (Uribana Prison) v. Venezuela,* (2007 Inter-Am. C. H. R. [Ser. E] 721, Order of the Court of February 2, 2007). These judgments can be found at the Web site of the court, http://www.corteidh.or.cr/index.cfm?&CFID=342502&CFTOKEN=40287078.

[47] Available online at http://www.corteidh.or.cr/docs/medidas/araraquara_se_02_ing.pdf.

ble for the generation and maintenance of the detention conditions that the beneficiaries had to endure. There was only an administrative investigation commenced in order to identify and punish those detainees that had been involved in the riot of June 16, 2006.

In this instance the court reiterated its previous order but could do little more, as it does not possess any more obligatory powers with which to enforce its decisions. It remains largely at the mercy of the political will of the member states over which it adjudicates, a fact that has led to the prevalence of the commission within this region as a standard setter. In general, full compliance with the final judgments of the court has also been problematic (Cavallaro and Brewer 2008, p. 786).

Another measure adopted to guarantee that persons subjected to imprisonment in the states that are members of the OAS have their rights respected was the creation of the position of Special Rapporteur on the Rights of Persons Deprived of Liberty in the Inter-American Commission of Human Rights, a commission member appointed pursuant to article 15 of the Rules of Procedure of the Commission by the Commission,[48] with a maximum 3-year term that can be renewed by a fresh commission vote indefinitely. The functions of the Special Rapporteur include visiting places of detention, including places of detention of minors; preparing reports on the prison situation in detention centers in a country, region, or subregion; making recommendations to member states on the conditions of detention or imprisonment and monitoring compliance with them, and promoting the protection of fundamental rights and guarantees of the detained persons and their families, with special attention to the duties of the prison authorities and international rules on the use of force and firearms by officials responsible for enforcing the law (Escobar 2007, p. 62).[49]

Since 2004 the Rapporteur has visited penitentiaries in Guatemala, Argentina, Brazil, Honduras, Colombia, Dominican Republic, Argentina, Haiti, Bolivia, Chile, and Uruguay (Dulitzky 2008 p. 105). However, there appears to have been little by way of independent evaluation of the efficacy of these visits. The most recent achievement of the

[48] The rules are available at http://www.cidh.oas.org/Basicos/English/Basic18.Rules OfProcedureIACHR.htm.
[49] The Mandate of the Rapporteur may be found, in Spanish, at http://www.cidh.oas .org/PRIVADAS/mandato.htm.

Rapporteur was the adoption, by the Inter-American Commission of Human Rights, of the Principles and Best Practices on the Protection of Persons Deprived of Liberty in the Americas,[50] as part of the process of drafting an Inter-American Declaration on the rights, duties, and care of persons under any form of detention or imprisonment. This may serve to reinforce structures that regulate prison conditions, as Principle XXIV provides: "In accordance with national legislation and international law, regular visits and inspections of places of deprivation of liberty shall be conducted by national and international institutions and organizations, in order to ascertain, at any time and under any circumstance, the conditions of deprivation of liberty and the respect for human rights."

3. *Africa.*   In the African context too there have been attempts to develop a system that could regulate prison conditions from the basis of the primary human rights institutions. Not only has the African Commission of Human and Peoples' Rights, the body charged with the enforcement of the African Charter on Human and Peoples' Rights,[51] commented that the provision of the charter prohibiting torture and cruel, inhuman, and degrading treatment and punishment (art. 5) requires that prison conditions should meet minimum standards, but the commission has appointed a Special Rapporteur for Prisons from the ranks of the commissioners to report on prison conditions in Africa and on occasion has heard individual complaints on conditions of detention. A recent example of such a complaint that led to the commission making a finding on the shortcomings of substantive prison conditions was the matter of *Institute for Human Rights and Development in Africa v. Republic of Angola* (May 22, 2008, reported in the 24th Action Report of the Africommission of Human Rights [2007–8], pp. 86–107).[52] For substantive standards, the judgments of the African Commission rely mostly on international instruments, such as the United Nations Standard Minimum Rules for the Treatment of Prisoners and the United Nations Body of Principles for the Protection

[50] *The Principles and Best Practices on the Protection of Persons Deprived of Liberty in the Americas*, adopted by the Inter-American Commission of Human Rights on March 13, 2008, at the 121st regular meeting, OEA/Ser/L/V/II.131 doc. 26. They are online at   http://www.cidh.oas.org/Basicos/English/Basic21.a.Principles%20and%20Best%20 Practices%20PDL.htm.

[51] The charter is available from http://www.achpr.org/english/_info/charter_en.html.

[52] A copy of this report, annexed to Document EX.CL/446 (XIII) (2008) of the African Union, is available at http://www.achpr.org/english/activity_reports/23rd%20and %2024th%20Activity%20Reports.pdf. For a discussion of this case, see Bekker (2009).

of All Persons under Any Form of Detention or Imprisonment (Murray 2008, p. 211). However, the commission has acknowledged the 1996 Kampala Declaration on Prison Conditions in Africa and the 2002 Ouagadougou Declaration and Plan of Action on Accelerating Prison Reform in Africa, as well as the 2002 Robben Island Guidelines (Niyizurugero and Lessène 2010),[53] documents that were to a greater or lesser extent developed by international and regional nongovernmental organizations as reflective of best practices that should be adopted in the African context. All these documents include references to substantive conditions that need to be met in prisons to ensure that they do not end up subjecting their inmates to ill treatment that contravenes the charter (Murray 2008, pp. 214–15).

In 1997, the African Commission of Human Rights appointed a Special Rapporteur on Prisons and Conditions of Detention in Africa. Between 1997 and 2004, the Special Rapporteur on Prisons visited prisons in 13 countries and published reports on them (Viljoen 2007). The Special Rapporteur empowered by the African Commission (acting under art. 45 of the charter) to examine and make recommendations on the state of prisons in Africa, encourage states to comply with the charter and other international human rights law, and, when requested by the commission, advise it on matters arising before it. The commission appoints the Special Rapporteur from within its own membership for a period of 2 years and may renew this mandate any number of times.[54]

The African process has been compared unfavorably, however, with that of the CPT (Murray 2008; see also Viljoen 2005) on several grounds. First, the visits depend on the permission of the country concerned, which means that the Special Rapporteur on Prisons was unable to react to complaints or to develop a program of visits that would cover the whole continent in the way that the CPT does in Europe. Second, the reports have been criticized for not making clear the basis on which their findings were made and for not relating them to standards set by the African Charter on Human and Peoples' Rights or to

[53] See http://cicr.org/web/eng/siteeng0.nsf/html/57JNPL for a full copy of the Kampala Declaration. The Ouagadougou Declaration and Action Plan can be found at http://www.achpr.org/english/declarations/declaration_ouagadougou_en.html. The guidelines are also available at http://www.achpr.org/english/declarations/declaration_robben islands_en.html.

[54] More information on the Special Rapporteur on Prisons may be found at http://www.achpr.org/english/_info/index_prison_en.html (see also Viljoen 2007, pp. 393–97; Sarkin 2008, pp. 32–34).

other international instruments. It is also suggested that they did not pay enough critical attention to the legal grounds for the detention of unconvicted prisoners who were often held for very long periods before trial.

Although there is evidence that in some cases improvements in prison conditions did follow from recommendations made in individual reports of the Special Rapporteur (Viljoen 2005), this was not generally the case. The overall conclusion on developments in Africa is largely negative. The sporadic visits of the Special Rapporteur and the inadequate and relatively unmethodical reports that have followed from them, together with delays in the African Commission in pronouncing on serious abuses in prison, make it clear that one cannot speak of an effective system for the regulation of prison conditions having emerged at the African regional level. This said, over the years the Special Rapporteurs on Prisons have played an important role in highlighting major issues of African human rights, such as capital and corporate punishment (Sarkin 2008, p. 34), although on narrower questions of prison regulation they have remained largely constrained by political and budgetary limitations.

II. National Regulation

The initial focus on international regulation of prison conditions should not distract our attention from the fact that most of the immediate regulation is done at a national or even local level. How such regulation is practiced is best studied by focusing in the first instance on the functioning of individual national prison systems rather than on regulatory mechanisms that may appear to be similar but have different roles and highly varied impact in different societies.

A. England and Wales

The prison system in England and Wales is an example of a system in which substantive standards that prison conditions must meet are relatively poorly developed in legislation (Livingstone, Owen, and MacDonald 2008). The primary law, the Prison Act, dates back to 1952,[55] and, although it has been amended many times, it does not deal with prison conditions in any detail. More detail is contained in the

---

[55] The text of the Prison Act 1952 is available at http://www.opsi.gov.uk/Revised Statutes/Acts/ukpga/1952/cukpga_19520052_en_1.

Prison Rules,[56] which are regulations made in terms of the act. Historically they have not been regarded as a source of enforceable rights of prisoners to specific prison conditions, although, as explained below, this position has changed somewhat as the courts have gradually come to rely more heavily on them when questions of prisoners' rights arise. Standing orders and instructions issued by the prison service contain fuller information, but, although they have been public in recent years, they cannot be regarded as creating legally binding criteria for prison conditions.

The overall result of this relatively weak statutory position is that internal regulation of prison conditions in England and Wales is primarily focused on the implementation of self-generated standards. A good point of departure on these internal procedures of regulation is the work of Alison Liebling (2004), who has described in some detail how, in England and Wales, the national authorities seek to measure internal performance and thus regulate prison conditions. According to Liebling, the key internal techniques of regulation applied by the central prison administration in England and Wales are key performance indicators (KPIs) and target and standards audits.

Key performance indicators are techniques for measuring specific organizational goals: for example, it may be a goal of the prison system as a whole to ensure that prison regimes provide purposeful activity for prisoners and that prison life is conducted in a relatively drug-free environment. Indicators of whether this is being done are then created in ways that can be measured: for example, a percentage of prisoners who are out of their cells for more than a certain number of hours each week, or the requirement that in regular drug tests no more than a certain percentage of prisoners should test positive. Such indicators can be applied in a sophisticated way to individual prisons, by setting goals for them to achieve that can be varied by setting specific key performance targets (KPTs) according to the challenges that a prison with a particular type of population or function faces.

The use of KPIs and KPTs is complemented by standards audits conducted by the Prison Service Audit Unit, that is, a body internal to the Prison Service (Bennett 2007). Its function is to ensure that staff apply all policies, financial and other, and procedures contained in the Prison Act, rules, standing orders, and instructions in a consistent way.

---

[56] The Prison Rules may be found at http://www.hmprisonservice.gov.uk/assets/documents/1000499Fprison_rules_1999_consolidated_jan_2010.pdf.

The auditing process depends on staff in prisons keeping accurate records. In practice, a large part of the process is concerned with checking these records rather than ensuring that substantive standards of relevance to prison conditions are met.

External regulation, as identified by Liebling (2004), comes primarily from the national prison inspectorate and local independent monitoring boards (IMBs). In contrast to the process-driven internal forms of regulation in England and Wales, Her Majesty's Inspectorate of Prisons (HMIP) is concerned much more with the substance of prison conditions.[57] What the HMIP has done is to design its notion of what a healthy prison is, quite independently of the standards adopted by the prison service itself (Owers 2006). The HMIP is concerned with identifying what it describes as a healthy prison. The "Expectations" that healthy prisons are supposed to meet are set out in an official document of that name (HMIP 2006, p. 3), which specifies the "criteria for assessing conditions in prison and the treatment of prisoners." These criteria have been developed directly from international and regional prison standards rather than from the standards adopted by the prison service itself (Owers 2006). Close examination shows that this has been done in considerable detail. Every individual recommendation is cross-referenced to the relevant international or regional instrument. It is striking just how comprehensive the list is. It includes all the international and regional treaty obligations that the UK government has in this area, as well as the secondary standards of international and regional bodies of which the United Kingdom is a member. The 2006 EPR, in particular, are cited repeatedly to justify the most detailed "expectations." Reference is also made to key judgments of ECtHR, which has set expectations in specific areas.

Structurally, the HMIP is a government-appointed body. However, it is independent of the Prison Service. Her Majesty's Chief Inspector of Prisons reports directly to the Secretary of State for Justice on the treatment of prisoners and conditions in prison, and the reports are tabled in Parliament (sec. 5A of the Prison Act 1952). The Chief Inspector of Prisons is not someone with a prison service background, although members of her staff may be. The work is done by a mixture of scheduled and unscheduled inspections of individual prisons and thematic reports on particular issues, such as health care, that cut across

[57] For more general information on HMIP, see http://www.justice.gov.uk/inspectorates/hmi-prisons/aboutus.htm.

the system as a whole.[58] In practice, Her Majesty's Chief Inspectors of Prisons have proved to be fiercely independent.[59] Although chief inspectors have no direct policy-making function and merely report to the secretary of state, their reports are routinely published and contribute strongly to the public debate about prisons. The reports have been widely praised as providing independent and reliable accounts of prison conditions in England and Wales. They have changed prison practice in crucial ways: for example, by exposing the unhygienic and degrading practice of "slopping out" and eventually having it abolished,[60] they have contributed directly to improving prison conditions. Their influence is so pervasive that the HMIP can be said indirectly to regulate prison conditions.

The second most important form of external monitoring of prison activity in England and Wales is that provided by the IMBs, formerly known as Boards of Visitors. Such boards, composed of volunteer lay citizens, have been established for each prison in the country. The function of the IMB is to "act as watchdog of the daily life and regime in an individual prison" (Livingstone, Owen, and MacDonald 2008, p. 11). The IMBs have access to all prisoners, who can complain to them about prison conditions, and to all parts of the prison for which they are appointed. The IMBs act by calling the attention of the governor of the prison to any matter that requires his attention and to inform the secretary of state (the minister) of any abuse. It is not entirely clear how effective this has been as a form of regulating prison regimes, but it is a component of the democratic oversight of prison conditions.[61]

The four institutions that have been discussed are not the sole regulators of prison conditions in England and Wales. In their overview of the regulatory structure of the English prison system, Hood et al. (1999) have pointed to several other relevant regulators. They include the Treasury (finance ministry) and National Audit Office, whose stric-

---

[58] The Annual Reports of the Chief Inspector may be found at http://www.justice .gov.uk/inspectorates/hmi-prisons/annual-reports.htm. Unscheduled reports may be found at http://www.justice.gov.uk/inspectorates/hmi-prisons/inspectorate-reports.htm. A database of thematic reports of HMIP is available at http://www.justice.gov.uk/inspectorates/hmi-prisons/thematic-reports-and-research.htm.

[59] For autobiographical accounts of the travails of Chief Inspectors of Prisons in establishing and protecting their independence, see Tumim (1992) and Ramsbottom (2003).

[60] "Slopping out" is the process whereby prisoners who do not have access to a lavatory when they are locked up during the night have to use a bucket, which is then emptied in the morning.

[61] See more generally http://www.imb.gov.uk/.

tures may exercise important indirect influence on prison conditions. In other instances, food hygiene, for example, local authority inspectors, such as environmental health officials, may have an important regulatory influence in a specific area.

Privately run prisons are a feature of the prison system in England and Wales, and these may be thought to pose special problems of regulation. However, in practice, these prisons are subject to the same regulation as public sector prisons, including visits by the HMIP. (The EPR also provide that private prisons shall be subject to the same regulations as public prisons.) In addition, there is one important additional regulatory figure. In each such prison there is a government official, called the controller, whose function it is to ensure that the terms of the contract between the government and the private contractors are met.[62] In practice, the contract terms are very similar to the KPIs by which prisons in the public sector are judged. Ensuring that they are met thus has a direct impact on prison conditions that can be measured effectively in this way.

Other regulatory institutions that are recognized by Hood et al. (1999) include the prison (and probation) ombudsman to whom prisoners may complain about any aspects of their life in prison.[63] The ombudsman, however, has no statutory powers and is appointed by and reports to the Secretary of State for Justice. The scope of his work is subject to numerous restrictions (Livingstone, Owen, and MacDonald 2008). Nevertheless, his recommendations that relate to prison conditions, particularly with regard to deaths in prison, in respect of which he has additional investigatory functions, are taken seriously and usually implemented (Owers 2006; Harding 2007).

Other institutions intervene only sporadically in a regulatory role. Prisoners may approach a member of Parliament who can raise issues on their behalf. From time to time the government may also appoint ad hoc investigatory commissions that inquire into specific incidents or problems. Of these, the investigation into the riots at Strangeways Prison (Woolf 1991) had the greatest impact on prison conditions in

[62] Until recently, the controller also performed some disciplinary functions, but these were abolished by the Offender Management Act 2007. This is an unfortunate change, as it reduces the role of the state in overseeing prisoners in an aspect of prison life where they are particularly vulnerable to abuse of power by the private contractors who control the prison.

[63] For general information about the ombudsman, see http://www.ppo.gov.uk/.

modern times, not least because it recommended a new approach to the maintenance of order in prison (Sparks, Bottoms, and Hay 1996).

Finally, Hood et al. (1999) note the role of the major European inspecting body, the CPT, in regulating British prisons through its inspection and reporting functions. They also mention the "private oversight by groups outside government such as the Howard League and the Prison Reform Trust," which help "to shape the activity of bureaucratic regulators" (p. 118).

To this already long list of regulatory institutions in England and Wales must be added the role of the ordinary courts. Historically, English courts tended to keep out of the regulation of prisons and routinely deferred to the authorities when it came to challenges from prisoners to the conditions that were provided for them in prison (Van Zyl Smit 2007). Perhaps for this reason, from the 1970s onward, several of the most important court decisions that directly affected English prison practices were taken by the ECtHR in Strasbourg rather than by the courts in London. However, that has gradually changed: prisoners' rights generally are being recognized more freely by English courts, and both the common law and ECHR, which has been incorporated indirectly into English law (via Schedule 1 of the Human Rights Act 1998), are being applied to this end. However, as Lazarus (2004, 2006) has pointed out, the process is inherently flawed, as English law has no clear understanding of the purpose of imprisonment against which to judge the administrative actions of the authorities. In this regard the absence of modern prison legislation, which sets out a clear purpose of imprisonment and defines prisoners' rights to acceptable prison conditions in a way that would meet the legal certainty requirements of the rule of law, is highly problematic.

Perhaps the best example of where legal intervention has had a direct and positive influence on prison conditions in the United Kingdom in a way that can be regarded as regulating prison conditions comes from Scotland rather than from England and Wales. In Scotland the practice of slopping out persisted longer than it did in England. It was heavily criticized by the CPT.[64] Promises were made by the UK government to change the practice, and money was voted for the building of suf-

---

[64] CPT, *Report to the United Kingdom Government on the Visit to the United Kingdom Carried out by the European Committee for the Prevention of Torture and Inhuman or Degrading Treatment or Punishment (CPT) from 15 to 31 May 1994*, 1994[CPT/Inf (96) 11] paras. 349–51. The report is available from the CPT Web site, http://www.cpt.coe.int/documents/gbr/1996-11-inf-eng.pdf.

ficient in-cell lavatories, but nothing was done about it. Finally, a Scottish prisoner sued the authorities on the grounds that his human rights had been breached as he was suffering from severe eczema because of the conditions in which he had been forced to live (*Napier v. Scottish Ministers* [2004] SLT 555 [2004] UKHRR 881). The Scottish court ruled in his favor, arguing that holding him under these conditions breached his right not to be subject to inhuman or degrading treatment—a right recognized in Scots law under both the Scotland Act and the UK-wide Human Rights Act. Napier was awarded damages. The practical effect on prison conditions was that the authorities had to move smartly to abolish the practice of slopping out while fighting the claims of many other prisoners who had suffered similarly. The judgment in this case also highlights how different regulatory standards forces can work together, for the court referred to both the ECHR and the EPR. It placed considerable weight on the reports of the CPT that had condemned the practice of slopping out and noted the failure of the Scottish executive to abide by earlier government undertakings to rectify the problem.

This degree of perceived fit between various national and international regulatory activities in the United Kingdom is fairly rare, however. It seems fair to say that, at the internal level, attempts at outside regulation are treated with some distrust. An illustration of the thinking of the government in this regard can be found in its response to the question of the Council of Europe on what it was trying to do to implement the 2006 EPR. While most governments attempted to demonstrate what they were doing positively, the UK government replied as follows:

> The position of the EPR within England and Wales is different to the position in other nations as the EPR are mirrored by internal prison rules which are included in staff training whereas EPR are not. It has never been the position that the European Prison Rules, UN Minimum Standard Rules or any of its international obligations are identified within its own domestic legislation or included in its staff training, but rather that its own domestic legislation covers all its international obligations. It is therefore, not intended that a major launch is undertaken of the EPR. However, the policy leads for the Prison Service are aware of the need to ensure that their policies conform to international standards and the responsibility to insure Prison Rules continue to reflect its obligations. (Council of Europe 2007, p. 3)

This arrogant assumption that the United Kingdom's (minimal) legislation and limited prisoners' rights jurisprudence is somehow in step with, if not ahead of, international standards, while that of "other nations" is not, explains to a large extent why the United Kingdom has so often been found to be in breach of the ECHR on prison matters. These breaches range from early cases dealing with access to lawyers and the courts (*Golder v. United Kingdom*, App. No. 4451/70 [1979–80] 1 EHRR 524, February 21, 1975) and to correspondence (*Silver v. United Kingdom* (App. Nos. 5947/72 *et al.* [1983] 5 EHRR 347, March 25, 1983), to the more recent decisions finding that some prison disciplinary procedures did not meet the required due process standards (*Ezeh and Connors v. United Kingdom* [App. Nos. 39665/98 and 40086/ 98 (2004) 39 EHRR 1, October 9, 2003]) and that some visitors to prison were being searched in a way that amounted to degrading treatment in contravention of the ECHR (*Wainright v. United Kingdom*, App. No. 12350/04 [2007] 44 EHRR 40, September 26, 2006). It also underlies the delays and avoiding tactics that have characterized the reluctant implementation by the United Kingdom of the latest decisions of the Grand Chamber of the ECtHR against it on prisoners' rights, such as the requirement that their right to vote be extended (*Hirst v. United Kingdom [No. 2]* App. No. 74025/01 [2006] 42 EHRR 41, October 6, 2001) or that their right to found a family by artificial insemination be respected (*Dickson v. United Kingdom* App. No. 44362/ 04 [2008] 46 EHRR 41, December 4, 2007; see Van Zyl Smit and Snacken, forthcoming).

In all, the regulatory position in England and Wales was well summarized by Hood et al. (1999, p. 116): "Prisons in England and Wales are subject to one of the densest patterns of oversight of any public sector activity. There has been a tendency to add new layers of regulation at various times without taking anything away, creating considerable overlap and duplication. Regulators who lacked formal powers were nevertheless observed to develop less formal mechanisms for seeking modification of behaviour." For all the success of some forms of regulation, such as the HMIP, this still seems to be true of England and Wales today. The question remains whether the position is different in other countries, both in Europe and further afield.

B. Germany

Modern Germany is subject to the same network of international and regional treaty obligations and related recommendations, standards, and guidelines as the United Kingdom. Some of the national regulatory institutions are very similar too: the so-called *Anstaltsbeiräte*, for example, perform locally based regulatory and liaison functions for individual prisons, a great deal like those of the IMBs in England and Wales, although arguably their powers are even more limited (Koeppel 1999; Dünkel 2001). At the other end of the spectrum, parliamentary supervision through the occasional intervention of members of Parliament who take up the cause of individual prisoners or question practices at specific prisons occurs in Germany too.

The legal basis for recognition and protection of prisoners' rights to humane prison conditions, however, has developed quite differently in Germany and the United Kingdom. The motor force for this development was not in the first instance the recognition of international human rights but the full application of German constitutional doctrine to prison matters. In a remarkable series of judgments in the early 1970s, the German Federal Constitutional Court rejected the idea that prisoners stood under a particular authority relationship to the state, which meant that the authorities had a wide discretion to decide how they should be treated (1972 BVerfGE 33, 1, 2BvR 41/71 [March 14, 1972]). Instead, prisoners had all the rights of ordinary citizens except those that were limited, as the constitution required, by primary legislation. As Germany did not have any primary legislation dealing with prisoners at the time, this meant that all existing prison regimes were technically unconstitutional. The court, however, gave the state time to introduce new prison legislation that would set out clearly the rights that prisoners had and implicitly the conditions that prisons would have to meet to hold prisoners under conditions of human dignity as required by the constitution. Moreover, the court held that such law would have to recognize that, because of their inherent, constitutionally protected, human dignity, prisoners would have to have an opportunity to resocialize themselves, and that the German state, since it was a *Socialstaat* (social welfare state), had the constitutional duty to provide them with prison conditions that gave them the opportunity to do so (*Lebach* 1973 BVerfGE 35, 203, 1 BvR 635/73 [June 5, 1973]). The result was that in 1976 a federal prison act (*Strafvollzugsgesetz*) was passed, which spelled out the rights of prisoners in considerable detail and made them enforceable through the courts.

The substantive recognition in the 1976 act of prisoners' rights to prison conditions in which they could live with dignity has been complemented by a highly developed system of legal regulation. At the most basic level the prisons, known formally as *Justizvollzuganstalten*, literally institutions for the implementation of justice, are characterized by a highly legalized culture: most heads of prisons are legally qualified and tend to make their decisions in a way that closely follows legal forms. Prisoners have a constitutional right to challenge any decision that affects their legal rights before a court. In practice, the courts of first instance are the special state courts known as *Strafvollstreckungskammern*. These courts not only hear prisoners' appeals about decisions that affect their rights to humane prison conditions but also have a wide range of functions in respect of the operation of the prison system generally, including temporary and conditional release. They specialize in prison matters, and the idea is that their judges should have a background in criminology and knowledge of prisons that enable them to make expert judgments on penological matters (Kaiser, Kerner, and Schöch 1991, p. 214). From these specialist chambers prisoners have rights of appeal to higher regional courts and, in matters where their constitutional rights are affected, to the Federal Constitutional Court.

Some scholars are critical of the system of judicial control. They point out that some concepts in the 1976 Act are vague and allow the authorities considerable discretion (Dünkel 2001); they note that relatively few appeals to the courts are successful (Feest and Selling 1988); and they are critical that most decisions are taken solely on the basis of written submissions, which removes even the specialist chambers from day-to-day operation of the prison. Moreover, German law has no mechanism for ensuring that court orders are obeyed: it is assumed that officials always follow the rule of law, something that is not always empirically true where prisons are involved (Dünkel 1997).

While these points are well taken, they should be placed in perspective. The *Strafvollstreckungskammern* make thousands of decisions on prison matters each year, and many of these are appealed to higher courts. While German law does not have a formal system of precedent, a higher regional court that wishes to make a decision that differs from that of another court of the same status must refer the case to the federal court. This, together with an extensive system of reporting decisions, also those of *Strafvollstreckungskammern*, in specialist journals and commentaries, means that a very comprehensive system of informal precedent has developed to shape the regulation of prison conditions. Add to this that the specialist courts proceed inquisitorially and relatively expeditiously, the reality, to an outside observer at least, is of a system where regulatory power is exercised to an extraordinary degree by specialist judges.

Finally, it is significant that the German constitutional law has continued to develop in ways that directly affect prison conditions. The Federal Constitutional Court has widened the constitutional rights of prisoners in this regard even further. Thus it has ruled that they have a right to adequate compensation for their labor (1988 BVerfG 98, 169, 2 BvR 441/90 [July 1, 1988]) and to be housed in single cells (2002 BVerfG, 2 BvR 553/01 [February 27, 2002]). The latter ruling in particular affects prison conditions profoundly. It is noteworthy that in its major decisions on prisoners' rights the Federal Constitutional Court has relied mostly on interpreting the constitution and applying it, while urging the legislature to do the same when designing new laws. Recently, however, it has cast its net wider. In 2006, it required the legislature to produce a new law on youth detention that would ensure that their rights were clearly defined and restricted only in primary legislation as required by the constitution (Dünkel and Van Zyl Smit 2007). It warned the legislature that in developing a new law it had to take into account current penological knowledge and the best interests of the detained youths. It then gave the legislature a clear indication of how it should proceed:

> It could be an indication that insufficient attention has been paid to the constitutional requirements of taking into account current knowledge and giving appropriate weight to the interests of the inmates if the requirements of international law or of international standards with human rights implications, such as the guidelines or recommendations adopted by the organs of the United Nations or the Council of Europe are not taken into account or if the legislation falls below these requirements. (BVerfG, Decision of May 31, 2006, para. 63, author's translation)[65]

[65] A similar approach has long been adopted in Switzerland, where the federal court has also noted that, while rights and duties cannot be deduced directly from the recommendations of the Council of Europe, they are still of considerable significance (BGE, 118 Ia 64 [February 12, 1992], p. 70). The Swiss Federal Court explained that for the

The practical effect of this passage is that the legislature must pay much closer attention to recommendations such as the EPR, which contain detailed guidelines on prison conditions, when developing new legislation. This is significant, as an amendment to the German constitution in 2007, introduced as part of a wider reorganization of federal and state powers, means that individual *Länder* (states that make up the federation) are free to adopt their own prison legislation. However, given the entrenched federal constitutional jurisprudence on prisoners' rights and the extensive system of regulation by the courts, it is unlikely that they will be able to make prison conditions much more restrictive than they currently are (Müller-Dietz 2008). The highly legalized forms of regulation of prison conditions are likely to remain in force throughout Germany.

C. The Netherlands

The Netherlands is a Western European country whose mechanisms for regulating prison conditions can be compared to those of the United Kingdom and of Germany in some aspects but not others. It too has a similar set of treaty obligations and commitments to international standards and guidelines. The substantive prison law of the Netherlands is more developed than that of England and Wales, as its major legislation, the Penitentiary Principles Acts of both 1953 and 1998, deal more clearly with prison conditions than does the 1952 English Prison Act. However, there is perhaps more ambiguity about the status of the application of resocialization as the purpose of imprisonment for all prisoners than there is in the German Prison Act. The bureaucratic controls of prison operations in mainland Netherlands (if not in the territories such as the Netherlands Antilles, which technically form part of the Kingdom of the Netherlands and are therefore subject to the jurisdiction of the ECtHR[66]) perform largely similar functions to those in England and Wales.

---

legislator and prison authorities they were guidelines as to how prisons should be administered appropriately. The Swiss court itself would also take them into account in the concretization of the constitutional guarantees of the Federal Swiss Constitution as well as the European Convention on Human Rights. These European instruments contained, the court continued, important guidelines for a modern practice of implementing criminal punishment that would guarantee the fundamental right of recognition of their human dignity and the freedoms that the Swiss Constitution allowed prisoners to continue to enjoy.

[66] The ECtHR has made a number of findings against the government of the Netherlands for complaints arising from the Netherlands Antilles. See, e.g., *Mathew v. the*

A minor difference is that the Dutch prison inspectorate does not have the independence of its English counterpart and therefore must be seen as internal to the prison system in a way that is akin to the English audit system. Expressed differently, the Dutch inspectorate performs an internal inspection rather than an external monitoring function.

Dutch prisoners have access to the courts as the Dutch prison legislation can be tested in terms of the normal principles of administrative law as well as in terms of article 15(4) of the Constitution of the Netherlands, which provides that the basic right of incarcerated people can be limited only to the extent that incarceration necessarily restricts the exercise of these rights (Kelk 2008). However, recourse to the ordinary courts is not as widespread as in Germany because of the highly developed complaints procedure.

The Dutch complaints procedure is significantly different from those in England or Germany in that it combines the functions of internal and external regulatory institutions found in a number of other countries in a unique and effective way (Serrarens 2007; Kelk 2008). The procedure emerged out of the work of the Supervision Committees (*Commissisies van Toezicht*), which were established in individual prisons by the 1953 Act. Initially, they strongly resembled the English IMBs and the German *Anstaltsbeiräte* in that they were supposedly lay representatives of the local community who heard the complaints of prisoners and facilitated the relationship between the prisoners and the head of the prison, while ensuring that prisoners were correctly treated. However, the complaints aspect of their work developed into a formal procedure that is now regulated by the 1998 Penitentiary Principles Act.

The procedure, in brief, is that prisoners can complain about prison conditions and treatment to which they are subject to a complaints committee, which is a subcommittee of the supervision committee. Its chair is usually a lawyer and its findings are made in writing, usually after an oral hearing at which the prisoner may be legally represented. The written judgments of a complaints committee may and do rely on a range of sources of law, not only the Dutch prison legislation but

---

Netherlands (App. No. 24919/03 [2006]) 43 EHRR 23 [September 29, 2005]), where conditions in which a disabled, but extremely aggressive, prisoner was housed were held to be degrading treatment in breach of art. 3 of the European Convention on Human Rights.

also the ECHR and the ICCPR as interpreted by the ECtHR and the Human Rights Committee, respectively. They are legally binding in the sense that the complaints committee can instruct the governor to follow them directly or to make a decision in the light of them. A prisoner may even be compensated for a decision wrongly to deprive him of something to which he is entitled. There is also the possibility of an appeal to the appeals committee of the Central Council for the Enforcement of Criminal Law. The result of this elaborate process is an extensive body of "jurisprudence," which is reported and has provided a valuable source of precedent on prisoners' rights and on the prison conditions to which they are reasonably entitled (Kelk 2008).

Dutch scholars have reflected on the extent to which Dutch penal policy in general and the treatment and conditions in particular are shaped by international and regional instruments (De Jonge 2007; Lange 2008). The consensus is that considerable attention is paid to the decisions of the ECtHR that interpret and apply the ECHR, particularly where they relate directly to the Netherlands. Decisions of the ECtHR are routinely cited and quoted by the Dutch courts and complaints commissions dealing with prison matters. Specific findings of the CPT that have condemned a particular prison regime, relating to prisoners in maximum security institutions, for example, have been followed too. This is true especially where the ECtHR has relied on a report of the CPT to make a finding against the Netherlands: for example, in *Van der Ven v. the Netherlands* (App. No. 50901/99 [2004] 38 EHRR 46 [February 4, 2003]), where excessive searches were held to be a form of degrading treatment that contravened article 3 of the ECHR. However, Lange (2008) is critical that the wider preventive recommendations of the CPT are not used more in the development of Dutch policy toward prisoners. De Jonge (2007) too is skeptical of the very limited use made of the EPR and the tendency of Dutch politicians to rely only on some rules and not others when developing new policies. Rules that do not suit them are all too easily dismissed as mere "soft law."

D. Other Western European Countries

The description of aspects of national mechanisms regulating prison conditions in three European countries illustrates well just how much they vary and how careful one must be not to categorize them or to make assumptions about the significance and influence of particular bodies in ostensibly similar systems. Nevertheless, one can highlight certain patterns in regulatory mechanisms.[67]

One of these is the replication of the direct, structurally determined, involvement of the judiciary in prison matters. For example, the German *Strafvollstreckungkammern* with their specialist judges have close equivalents in the offices of the *juge de l'application de peines* in France (Poncela 2001), *magistrato di sorveglianza* in Italy (Gualazzi and Mancuso 2010), and the *juez de vigilancia* in Spain (De la Cuesta and Blanco 2007). Although there are important variations between them, they have in common that they involve specialist members of the judiciary, sometimes sitting as a specialist chamber of a court, who have a function both in deciding on release of prisoners and, at the same time, safeguarding their rights and ensuring that prison conditions meet minimum standards. National critics, who often tend to be harsher than outsiders, recognize the value of their expertise. However, they often doubt their independence, sometimes for structural reasons that do not give them the independence from prison administrators that one would expect of the office of a judge (Dünkel 1997). Moreover, in France, for example, they cannot give binding instructions to the authorities in respect of prison conditions (Herzog-Evans 1997). Critics also argue on the more sociological grounds that their constant involvement in prison matters leads to their being "captured" by the priorities of penal administrators, on whom they may be dependent for information and access.

A second office that needs further consideration in the context of regulating prisons is the role of the ombudsman. What an ombudsman is and does may vary enormously from country to country. Thus in England and Wales a specialized ombudsman deals with prisoner complaints but appears to have only limited influence on the overall regulation of prison conditions. In the Netherlands, complaints are dealt with differently, but the national ombudsman has jurisdiction over prison matters as well as over other matters of state administration. However, the prison complaints system covers the area so comprehensively that the national ombudsman deals with only a handful of such matters a year (Kelk 2008).

This position must be contrasted with that in Sweden and other Scandinavian countries, where the national ombudsman is a key actor in the regulation of prison conditions. Thus, for example, the Swedish

[67] For an earlier attempt at such generalization in respect of England and Wales, France, and West Germany, see Vagg (1994).

parliamentary ombudsman hears about a thousand complaints from prisoners a year. The ombudsman has wide powers of investigation and a powerfully entrenched position in the national constitutional order. It would be "unthinkable" to deny the ombudsman information (Nordenfelt 2007, p. 47). In practice the ombudsman can enforce her decisions, not only by making recommendations to government on practices that should be changed to improve prison conditions, but by taking disciplinary steps against officials and, if necessary, prosecuting them.

To outsiders the powerful oversight of prison conditions provided by an ombudsman who enjoys extensive legitimacy may seem ideal. Domestic critics are not so easily impressed, however. Recently, for example, Greve and Snare (2009) have documented moves away from the protections that the *Rechtsstaat* guarantees in the prisons systems of both Denmark and Sweden and point out that in several ways prison conditions have become materially harsher and the existing guarantees harder to enforce. This change of climate will inevitably affect the efficacy of the work of the ombudsman inasmuch as she relies on established legal rules in the prison context, for even in the Scandinavian context, the ombudsman may be restricted by legislatively imposed policies on prison conditions.

E. Eastern Europe

These shortcomings are, however, minor relative to those faced by countries of Eastern Europe after the collapse of communism. When those countries sought to join the Council of Europe, they were required to reorganize their prison systems. This reorganization included both the clear articulation of prisoners' rights in their laws and the creation of regulatory mechanisms to ensure that prison conditions met their standards. The first, substantive, requirement was easiest to meet. There was widespread enactment of primary legislation in countries such as Russia (Oleinik 2007), Poland (Stando-Kawecka 2001), and others (Walmsley 2003) to create the substantive legal framework for prisoners' rights.

On the level of regulatory mechanisms the changes demanded by the Western Europeans were surprisingly explicit. First, prisons should be moved out of the direct bureaucratic control of the Ministry of the Interior and placed under the control of the Ministry of Justice. Second, the lines of oversight should be changed. Historically, in many

Eastern European countries, the public prosecuting authority had responsibility for the oversight over prisons. The conflict of interest here is obvious too. It is in this regard that several Western European models have been added to the mechanisms for regulating prison conditions in Eastern Europe. Specialist judges have not proved popular, but both complaints commissions and ombudsmen have become the overseers of choice of prison conditions, with the latter enthusiastically endorsed in both Poland (Paprzycki 2008) and Hungary (Gönczöl 1997). All these national mechanisms have been reinforced at the European level by the CPT, which has focused much of its energies on visits to Eastern European countries, and the ECtHR, which in the last decade has heard many cases originating in Eastern Europe on questions relating to the rights of prisoners.

In practice difficulties remain. These range, in Russia as in other Eastern European countries, from lack of capacity in justice ministries to manage prisons and to enforce inspections that should regulate prison conditions, to the high legal costs for prisoners seeking redress for the infringement of their rights (Oleinik 2007; Rieckhof 2008). In Russia in particular there is a danger that the human rights–driven idealism of the postcommunist period, which led to the active development of new ways of regulating prison conditions, will dissipate in the face of a resurgent Russian nationalism and renewed hostility to European ideas (Piacentini 2006; Van Zyl Smit and Snacken 2009).

F. South Africa

While most countries in Europe have increasingly been drawn into a regulatory framework that is reinforced by European policies and to a growing extent enforced directly by European institutions, in other parts of the world regulation of prison conditions has been reformed, and new forms of regulations established, without the same powerful regional forces being at work. In these instances more attention has been paid to comparative examples of what is perceived to be national best practice.

South Africa is an interesting example of a country that underwent a dramatic change in its political structure with the abolition of apartheid and the establishment of a constitutional democracy. As in Eastern Europe, doing something about its repressive prisons and the limited mechanisms regulating prison conditions was a priority. However, unlike the Eastern Europeans, the South Africans faced little pressure from the region or the international community. They were largely free to choose their own reformist models. The legal solutions that South Africa adopted began explicitly with the new constitution. Both the so-called interim Constitution of 1993 and the "final" Constitution of 1996 contained a prohibition on torture and cruel, inhuman, or degrading treatment or punishment, which closely followed the established international pattern for a modern a bill of rights (Bassiouni 1993).[68] In addition, reflecting the role of the prison in the repressive old South African regime, the new constitutions contained an explicit provision that "everyone who is detained, including every sentenced prisoner, has the right . . . to conditions of detention that are consistent with human dignity, including at least exercise and the provision, at state expense, of adequate accommodation, nutrition, reading material and medical treatment" (sec. 35 [2] of the Constitution of the Republic of South Africa, No. 108 of 1996). These core conditions of imprisonment are enforceable through the courts and the so-called Institutions Supporting Constitutional Democracy, including a Public Protector (ombudsman) and a Human Rights Commission (chap. 9 of the Constitution of the Republic of South Africa, No. 108 of 1996).

In due course the constitutional protections were complemented by new prison legislation, the Correctional Services Act of 1998,[69] which specified prisoners' rights to adequate prison conditions more comprehensively. At the same time the act created a range of new oversight measures over the recently demilitarized prisons' service. Internal oversight was strengthened by providing for internal service evaluation through internal audits, inspections, and investigations.

External safeguards included a National Council of Correctional Services headed by a high court judge to advise on policy and, most important, a dual system of monitoring consisting of a national judicial inspectorate and independent prison visitors appointed for each prison.[70] The system was designed to operate from the bottom up. Independent prison visitors, private citizens especially appointed to the task by the inspecting judge, would perform the function of a com-

[68] The "final" 1996 Constitution may be found at http://www.info.gov.za/documents/constitution/1996/a108-96.pdf. For the "interim" 1993 Constitution, see http://www.info.gov.za/documents/constitution/93cons.htm.
[69] The text of the act, in English and Afrikaans, is available at http://www.info.gov.za/view/DownloadFileAction?id=70646.
[70] The national courts, backed by national constitutions that guaranteed substantive rights, also began to play an increasing role in regulating prison conditions in South Africa and other states in the region, such as Namibia (Bukurura 2002).

plaints body and would hear and attempt to resolve complaints at the level of the individual prison. Cases that could not be resolved would eventually be referred to the inspecting judge. The idea was that the independent prison visitors would provide a steady flow of information about prison conditions to the inspecting judge. At the same time, it would obviate the need for a separate complaints system.

The South African judicial inspectorate was closely modeled on HMIP in England, with the important difference that the South African inspector had to be a high court judge.[71] This "Inspecting Judge" is appointed by the president and is responsible for recruiting assistants and an inspectorate (secs. 86–87, 89 of the Correctional Services Act, No. 111 of 1998). The inspecting judge was to conduct inspections in the same way and with similar powers to HMIP, although this would be combined with the function of dealing with complaints. Underneath the inspecting judge are the "Independent Prison Visitors," one of whom is assigned to each prison by the judge, primarily as a means of evidence gathering for the judge's annual (and extraordinary) reports to the executive (pursuant to sec. 90.4 of the 1998 Act), mainly by way of regular visits to the assigned prison. The visitors need not have any specific qualifications (see generally chap. 10 of the 1998 Act).

In 2004 both the judicial inspectorate (Jagwanth 2004; see also Woods 2009) and the independent prison visitors (Gallinetti 2004) were themselves subject to independent evaluation. The conclusion was that, generally speaking, both systems operated effectively within their own parameters. However, although the inspecting judge has made major efforts to persuade the authorities to reduce prison overcrowding and was instrumental in introducing several reforms in that regard, there was little evidence that either body had succeeded in monitoring, and thus indirectly regulating, prison conditions generally, or in improving them substantially. Nevertheless, the influence of these bodies has been significantly stronger than the constitutionally mandated Institutions Supporting Constitutional Democracy, whose wider remit has led to their paying relatively little attention to prison conditions.

The gaps in oversight have not been filled by regional monitoring either. Although the Special Rapporteur on prisons of the African Commission on Human and Peoples' Rights has produced a report on

[71] For more information about the inspectorate, see http://judicialinsp.pwv.gov.za/Default.asp.

South Africa,[72] it is not comparable to the detailed reports of the CPT. There is a dearth of the proactive dialogue between the regional inspecting body and the national state of the kind that the CPT has followed with the states it inspects in Europe. There is little reason to believe that either pan-African or international institutions have played a significant part in the regulation of prison conditions in South Africa. To some extent this is simply a function of the relative weakness of regional institutions in the area.

G. Countries of the Asia-Pacific Region

In the large Asia-Pacific region, where regional prison regulation has yet to emerge, it is hard to discern an overall trend in prison regulation at the national level. There is some indication that national human rights institutions have become increasingly involved in the prevention of torture in a number of countries and therefore also in prison matters (Pasha 2010), but China, a major local state, is not included in this analysis.

In other instances regulatory models from elsewhere that are directed specifically at prisons have been adopted, but on a somewhat piecemeal basis. In some Australian states, particularly in Western Australia where there is a system of prison inspections similar to that employed by HMIP in England (Harding 2007), independent mechanisms for the regulation of imprisonment have gradually emerged.

Also in Japan, following a series of prison scandals, prison-visiting committees were introduced in 2005 (Kuwayama 2010). These committees were specifically modeled on the English IMBs and the German *Anstaltsbeiräte*, but have been criticized by the Human Rights Committee of the United Nations for lacking independence.[73] Moreover, they operate only at the level of local prisons and are not combined into any national monitoring structure.

New Zealand is an exception in this region. Not only is it one of only three Asian Pacific countries to have ratified OPCAT,[74] but it also

---

[72] The report, "Republic of South Africa: First Periodic Report on the African Charter on Human and Peoples' Rights: 2001 Page," is available at http://www.achpr.org/english/Archives/State%20reports/eng/South%20Africa/RSA%20report_2_eng.pdf.

[73] The Concluding Observation of the Human Rights Committee (UN Doc. CCPR/C/JPN/CO/5, December 18, 2008). The document can be found at http://www.mofa.go.jp/POLICY/human/civil_ccpr2.pdf.

[74] The other two are Cambodia and the Maldives. See Global Status of OPCAT Ratification, http://www.apt.ch/index.php?option = com_k2&view = item&layout = item&id = 662&Itemid = 252&lang = en.

has a strong domestic human rights tradition that has been developed into a network of institutions that regulate its prisons (Harding and Morgan 2010). These include an independent national ombudsman who has statutory powers to act as a prison monitor and who is recognized as a National Preventive Mechanism for prisons for purposes of OPCAT. There is also a "quasi-independent" Inspector of Corrections, who performs similar functions (Harding and Morgan 2010, p. 111.)

H. The United States of America

When it comes to international instruments concerning prison standards, the United States is in a different position from the other countries described. For both political and constitutional reasons, it is reluctant to ratify human rights treaties, and when it has, it has sought to do so in a way that will not affect existing U.S. law or practice (Henkin 1995). This reluctance is even clearer where any form of international monitoring is involved. The United States is not a signatory to the Convention on the Rights of the Child. It has acceded to the ICCPR, but with a key reservation declaring that it "considers itself bound by article 7 to the extent that 'cruel, inhuman or degrading treatment or punishment' means the cruel and unusual punishment and treatment prohibited by the Fifth, Eighth and/or Fourteenth Amendments to the Constitution of the United States" (Nowak 2005, p. 964). Several countries objected to this reservation on the basis that such an attempt to limit a nonderogable right cast doubt on the commitment of the United States to the fundamental principles of the ICCPR (Nowak 2005, p. xxi). The HRC also expressed this view in a General Comment.[75] In addition, the United States declared that it "understands that paragraph 3 of article 10 does not diminish the goals of punishment, deterrence and incapacitation as additional legitimate purposes for a penitentiary system" (Nowak 2005, p. 964). As the United States has not ratified the First Protocol to the ICCPR, U.S. citizens cannot approach the Human Rights Committee directly. Similarly, the United States has not ratified the American Convention of Human Rights and the Inter-American Convention to Prevent and Punish Tor-

---

[75] *Human Rights Committee, General Comment 24 (52), General Comment on Issues Relating to Reservations Made upon Ratification or Accession to the Covenant or the Optional Protocols Thereto, or in Relation to Declarations under Article 41 of the Covenant*, November 2, 1994, UN Doc. CCPR/C/21/Rev.1/Add. The *Comment* is available at http://www.unhcr.org/refworld/pdfid/453883fc11.pdf.

ture. Add to that the extraordinary diversity of prison systems and forms of prison governance at federal, national, and local levels, and one may conclude too readily that few generalizations can be made about regulation of prison conditions in the United States generally, except that it is patchy and uneven.

Such pessimism would ignore two important features of the regulation of prison conditions in the United States, namely the role of the standard setting and accreditation by professional bodies, particularly by the American Correctional Association (ACA),[76] and the "hands-on" role of the courts. Both require further elaboration.

The ACA is a professional association of North American "correctional practitioners," which has developed a detailed set of standards for prisons that it describes as "the national benchmark for the effective operation of correctional systems throughout the United States [that] are necessary to ensure that correctional facilities are operated professionally."[77] These standards contain very precise requirements relating both to physical standards, for accommodation for example, and to processes that have to be followed by the prison administration (Morgan 2000). More recently, the accreditation process has included some consideration of the quality of life in prison. Institutions that wish to be accredited by the ACA must submit themselves, and pay for, an evaluation conducted by an interdisciplinary expert team. The accreditation process is in the view of David Bogard, an ACA commissioner, "the closest approximation of a national external oversight mechanism in the U.S." Bogard notes that the process is voluntary, and most penal institutions in the United States are not accredited: more state prisons than local jails are accredited. This latter comment is particularly interesting as it points again to the diversity of types of institutions that can exist within one country and the differing degrees of control that is exercised over them.[78] In Texas, for example, although ACA accreditation is voluntary, the state requires private prisons to be accredited as a condition of its contractual relationship with them. However, local jails that are privatized are not subject to the same requirement (Bogard

---

[76] See generally http://www.aca.org/standards/.

[77] American Correctional Association, Standards and Accreditation: Frequently Asked Questions: http://www.aca.org/standards/faq.asp#standards.

[78] In this essay the term "prison" is used, also in the context of the United States, to refer to penal institutions of all kinds, except where, as in this instance, distinctions are drawn between federal penitentiaries, state prisons, and local jails.

2007). Indeed, external monitoring of local jails may be almost exclusively in the hands of elected officials.

The ACA accreditation process must be seen in tandem with the widespread intervention of the courts in the regulation of prison conditions in the United States. Viewed from an international perspective, what is unusual is not that prisoners approach the courts to enforce their rights to appropriate prison conditions but that in the majority of states the courts have intervened by becoming involved in the day-to-day administration of the prisons and thus directly in the regulation of prison conditions. Special masters have been appointed that have run regulated prison conditions in individual prisons or even whole prison systems for decades (Feeley and Rubin 1998).

American scholars have sought to understand why this form of regulation of prison conditions has been so influential (Jacobs 1983; DiIulio 1990; Deitch 1991; Feeley and Rubin 1998; Feeley and Swearingen 2004). Their conclusion is that it grew out of the wider civil rights movement in the 1960s, which had demonstrated that large-scale legal intervention could have significant effects. Although more restrictive interpretations of prisoners' rights by the U.S. Supreme Court and attempts by Congress to limit prisoners' rights litigation, most notably by the 1996 Prison Litigation Reform Act, have reduced prison litigation (Collins 2004), such litigation has continued to be a factor in the regulation of prison conditions in the United States (Feeley and Swearingen 2004), albeit one that is less effective than before (Schlanger and Shay 2008). In part this was because it chimed with attempts that were simultaneously also being made at other levels to reshape prisons into modern rational bureaucracies. Feeley and Swearingen (2004, p. 438), for example, comment that the modernizing efforts of the ACA found an echo in the courts, which embraced the ACA's "bible," the *Manual of Correctional Standards*, to guide their own reform efforts, and which have continued to do so. The interrelationship between the courts and the ACA, however, is not necessarily positive. Morgan (2000) has noted that the ACA does not tend to set standards in areas where the courts have not done so. In his words: "In this sense the ACA is essentially a *reactive* mechanism representing the interests of penal providers" (Morgan 2000, p. 339).

A general reason for the courts to intervene, to an extent that would perhaps not be considered necessary or appropriate elsewhere, has to do with the paralysis of other political avenues for reshaping prison policy in order to produce acceptable prison conditions (Sterngold 2008). In August 2009 this came to a head dramatically in California. A federal court, confronted by persistent evidence that, because of gross overcrowding over many years, the Californian prison system had not provided prisoners with a minimum standard of health care, ordered the state to produce for its approval a scheme for the release of 46,000 prisoners within 2 years, so that it would be able to provide adequate health care for the remainder (*Coleman v. Schwarzenegger* 2009, LEXIS 67943, No. CIV S-90-0520 LKK JFM P, slip op. [E.D.CA & N.D.CA, August 4, 2009] [three-judge panel]). The court explained that it had been driven to this extreme step by the consistent failure of the state government to provide sufficient resources to produce prison conditions that were constitutionally acceptable for the many additional prisoners that its "tough on crime" policies had incarcerated and had kept incarcerated for long periods. In the view of the court, the current economic crisis made any other solution impracticable; as the political process had demonstrated that it was incapable of taking the necessary steps, judicial compulsion was required to ensure that they were.[79]

Litigation, however, has limits as a tool for regulating prisons. As Schlanger (2006, p. 622) has pointed out:

> In some ways . . . prisons [in the United States] are worse today—more idle, more dehumanizing—but Eighth Amendment law is extremely limited: It exempts from constitutional analysis many of the issues that matter most to prisoners, such as educational programming, work and other activities, and the custody level. So even though today's paradigmatic prison failings are deeply troubling, they do not violate our current understanding of the Constitution. While today's inmates do more time and there are more of them (which magnifies the importance of whatever failings our prisons have), there is little question that most American prisons stay more comfortably above the low constitutional floor today than they did in the past. (2006, p. 622)

---

[79] On September 11, 2009, the California legislature responded by reducing the reform that would go some way to meet the cuts in prison population required by the court (Goldmacher and McGreevy 2009). Whether this will settle the matter remains doubtful.

III. Paths to the Future

As modern governments have become increasingly sophisticated, they have developed more complex lines of authority and bureaucratic controls within the state sector to regulate state pressures. In turn, this has created the possibility of microregulation of individual prisons and the conditions in them by the higher management echelons of larger prison systems (Jacobs 1977). Added to this is the emergence of techniques of public administration that use new bureaucratic techniques, such as key performance indicators and the more extensive use of auditing tools, which were initially more common in the private sector, to facilitate further the regulation of prison management (Liebling 2004).

The structural similarities of modern prison bureaucracies should not mask the reality that there are subtle differences in what regulators are asked to examine. Emerging most clearly in the context of England and Wales, there is a tension between the tools of bureaucratic measurement applied internally by the Prison Service and the more humanistic standards developed by HMIP, for example. A further tension exists between human rights–based claims for improved prison conditions, which have been largely the preserve of lawyers, and the preoccupation with minimization of the risks posed by prisoners, which increasingly has been defined as an area of bureaucratic expertise not easily open to outside challenge (Murphy and Whitty 2007).

Within a broadly human rights approach to imprisonment there are differences too, which relate to the substance of what may be claimed on behalf of prisoners, through the courts and otherwise, in order to "regulate" prison conditions. It seems that in countries such as Germany, where there is a clear idea not only that prisoners must be protected against abuse but that their human dignity must be recognized in other ways, including giving them a right to resocialize themselves, rights-based protection through the courts is more successful.

A clear understanding of the basis of prisoners' rights also makes it easier for the courts to intervene on their behalf and thus to affect their overall conditions of detention. In England, for example, where there is a limited and conceptually underdeveloped notion of prisoners' rights, courts have declined to intervene in disputes relating to prisoners' rights to vote, declaring a philosophical dispute beyond their competence.[80] In contrast, courts in other jurisdictions—Canada, South

[80] In R (Pearson and Martinez) v. Secretary of State for the Home Department [2001] HRLR

Africa, and the ECtHR, for example[81]—where there are more fully developed notions of prisoners' rights, have all found the issue clearly justiciable and dismissed claims that loss of the right to vote could be justified as an additional implicit punishment or even that it could somehow have a reformative influence.

The use of different legal standards and different regulatory techniques may make the regulatory process more complex than the evolution of clearer lines of bureaucratic authority may suggest, particularly where different elements of the bureaucracy seek to regulate prisons in different ways. This is complicated enough when purely internal regulation is concerned. However, the picture is further complicated where regulation is external to the prison bureaucracy. Moreover, the distinction between internal inspection and external monitoring is not always as clear in practice as is sometimes assumed.

It is also clear that a degree of independence of the organs of external oversight from the prison bureaucracy does not necessarily determine their influence on prison conditions. Equally important is the information that they gather and the power that they have to influence the actual prison conditions. However, regulatory agencies, such as prison inspectorates and ombudsmen, do gain some of their authority by their independence being recognized. Independent regulatory agencies may also play an important part in shaping wider policies that affect prison conditions. For example, the strictures of the CPT or of the federal court in California against overcrowding that causes unacceptable prison conditions may directly affect fundamental decisions about how many people should be imprisoned in a particular system.

Where there is a large degree of respect for international and regional institutions, as is, broadly speaking, the case in Europe, regulation by such institutions can add the authority of independent monitoring conducted by such institutions. However, even this effect is

---

39, Judge Kennedy found that there was more to punishment than forcible detention and noted loss of the "privilege" to vote could be a further, albeit unarticulated, element of punishment. The judge was quite happy to leave it to the state to decide what the purpose of the restriction on the right to vote was, remarking rather weakly that the aim of the restriction "may not be easy to articulate" and suggesting that the "true nature of disenfranchisement" should be left to the philosophers to decide (at para. 39). What this attitude reveals is a fundamental disregard by the court of the need to regulate the way in which the state curtails prisoners' rights and thus determines prison conditions.

[81] Canada: *Sauvé v. Canada (Chief Electoral Officer)* 2002 SCC 68; South Africa: *Minister of Home Affairs v. National Institute for Crime Prevention and the Reintegration of Offenders (NICRO) and Others*, 2005 (3) SA 280 (CC); ECtHR: *Hirst v. United Kingdom (No. 2)* (App. No. 74025/01 [2006] 42 EHRR 41, October 6, 2001).

uneven as it depends both on the significance attached to such "outside" monitoring in individual countries and on the very diverse regulatory systems that continue to operate at the national level in spite of the overall trend to bureaucratic regularity. Moreover, there is inbuilt tension between human rights–led institutions, such as the CPT and the ECtHR in the European context, which are gradually developing standards driven by wider concepts of human dignity, and the desire for "neat" bureaucratic measures at the national level. In this regard Morgan (2000) has drawn an insightful comparison between the standards developed by the CPT in Europe and those of the ACA in the United States. He notes that both sets of standards contain considerable detail and provide a benchmark against which physical conditions in particular can be judged objectively. However, the proactive human rights orientation of the CPT makes it much more effective in developing standards that deal with regimes, in maximum security institutions, for example, that might be unnecessarily repressive, even where meeting technical standards of the kind set by the ACA.

In many parts of the world, however, the problem is not so much a clash of different regulatory standards but their almost total absence. Thus, in Africa regional regulation is weak and in the Asia-Pacific region it does not exist. The states that have their own relatively effective regulatory mechanisms in these regions are the exception rather than the rule.

Viewed globally, the regulation of prison conditions faces the challenge of applying internationally recognized human rights values to the regulatory process. This challenge manifests itself differently in different parts of the world. In countries with developed national legal and bureaucratic structures, the question is how best to ensure that the existing structures conform to the wider norms. In less developed countries, national regulatory mechanisms need to be established and their compliance with international standards ensured at the same time. At the conceptual level, the structure put forward by OPCAT, with its flexible combination of an international inspectorate, in the form of the SPT, applying international human rights standards, combined with NPMs, has the potential to address both issues.

At a strategic level this has been recognized too. A country such as the United Kingdom has been able to recognize several of its existing oversight bodies as NPMs, while coordinating them under the leadership of HMIP, which has a track record of principle-driven and independent external regulation. In other instances, states have developed, with the assistance of the SPT and the international nongovernmental organization, the APT,[82] new NPMs that meet the criteria of independence while applying human rights–based standards of regulation effectively. France, for example, has chosen to establish a new NPM, the General Inspector for Places of Deprivation of Liberty (Law no. 2007–1545 of October 30, 2007, *instituant un Contrôleur general des lieux de privation de liberté*). Several other countries have chosen to designate an existing national human rights body as their NPM and to make special provision for it to perform this work (Steinerte and Murray 2009).

In a perfect world, a sophisticated central OPCAT operation should be able to influence national strategies through the NPMs to develop optimal national regulatory systems that are sensitive to different national regulatory traditions, while at the same time using its direct powers of inspection strategically to advance human rights standards. There are considerable challenges, however, in persuading states to ratify OPCAT and create the necessary national mechanisms for its enforcement (Olivier and Narvaez 2009). Only a minority of states have yet ratified OPCAT, and China and the United States of America, both countries with large prison populations, show no sign of doing so. There is a real risk that the SPT, which is the functional heart of OPCAT, will remain a relatively insignificant organization within the larger United Nations human rights framework.

Globalization can, however, hasten the establishment of internationally recognized standards for regimes and mechanisms for their enforcement in other ways. Thus, for example, the various international criminal tribunals and courts, such as the International Criminal Tribunal for the former Yugoslavia, the International Criminal Tribunal for Rwanda, and the International Criminal Court, have had to think about conditions in their detention facilities and about ways of ensuring that prisoners held there or in national systems when serving their internationally imposed sentences have adequate prison conditions (Van Zyl Smit 2005). They too have turned to international standards to help them prescribe conditions and to international organizations such as the ICRC and the CPT to assist in monitoring whether they are being applied in practice. Although the regulations developed by

---

[82] The worldwide program of the APT is discussed on its Web site, http://www.apt.ch/.

the tribunals and the courts for their own detention facilities may be criticized as insufficiently detailed, and the monitoring methods as not allowing sufficient publicity about prison conditions (Mulgrew 2009), their very existence is recognition of the importance of the regulation of clearly defined prison conditions.[83]

Finally, it must be recognized that, while there have been several studies of different methods of the regulation of prison conditions, and much, sometimes polemical, debate about them, not nearly as much has been written about the substance of the standards they apply or their relative efficacy. Little or no work has been done, for example, on comparing homicide or suicide rates in prisons to which different regulatory systems are applied.

More work also needs to be done on the more subtle differences between systems that may influence what form of regulation will be most effective and also on the substantive standards to be applied to them. While a form of regulation may demonstrably be effective in its own terms, there is much less agreement about what constitute desirable prison conditions. In this regard scholars who have sought to develop measures that are independent of those generated by inspecting and monitoring bodies have much to offer. It would be very interesting, for example, to see how Alison Liebling's (2004) concept of the moral performance of prisons could be applied across prison systems operating in different cultures. Anton Oleinik's study, which compares the prison social climates in Russia and former Soviet bloc countries with those in France and Canada, is a step in this direction (Oleinik 2006), for he argues that cultural factors rather than material conditions alone are key determinants of how prison conditions are experienced by prisoners. However, extended studies of this kind need to be combined with careful efforts to disentangle the effects of regulation from wider social forces that may shape prison conditions. What this essay has shown is the complexity of the relationship between prison regulatory agencies and wider social formations.

---

[83] In the context of dealing with international terrorism there have been attempts to avoid the application of all national and international standards to conditions of detention. However, even such a powerful a country as the United States has not been able to achieve this fully. When it sought to avoid such standards and forms of inspection by holding prisoners in Guantanamo Bay, and thus outside the reach of both internal U.S. regulation and international monitoring, the demand for the recognition of some minimum standards and for international monitoring was so strong that the United States has been forced to compromise and gradually modify the standards it applies and the access it allows to bodies, such as the ICRC.

REFERENCES

Bassiouni, M. C. 1993. "Human Rights in the Context of Criminal Justice: Identifying International Procedural Protections and the Equivalent Protection in National Constitutions." *Duke Journal of Comparative and International Law* 3:235–97.

Bekker, G. 2009. "Mass Expulsion of Foreign Nationals: A 'Special Violation of Human Rights'—Communication 292/2004 Institute for Human Rights and Development in Africa v. Republic of Angola." *African Human Rights Law Journal* 9:262–73.

Bennett, J. 2007. "Measuring Order and Control in the Prison Service." In *Handbook on Prisons*, edited by Y. Jewkes. Cullompton: Willan.

Bogard, D. 2007. "American Correctional Association Standards and Accreditation." In *Opening up a Closed World: What Constitutes Effective Prison Oversight?* vol. 1, *Conference Proceedings*, edited by M. Deitch. Austin: Lyndon B. Johnson School of Public Affairs, University of Texas at Austin.

Bukurura, S. 2002. "Emerging Trends in the Protection of Prisoners' Rights in Southern Africa." *African Human Rights Law Journal* 2:92–109.

Casale, S. 2006. "Mechanisms for Custodial Oversight." *Journal of Law and Policy* 22:217–29.

———. 2009 "A System of Preventive Oversight." *Essex Human Rights Review* 6(1):6–14.

Cassese, A. 1996. *Inhuman States: Imprisonment, Detention and Torture in Europe Today*. Cambridge: Polity Press.

Cavallaro, J., and S. Brewer. 2008. "Reevaluating Regional Human Rights Litigation in the Twenty-first Century: The Case of the Inter-American Court." *American Journal of International Law* 102(4):768–827.

Collins, W. 2004. "Bumps in the Road to the Courthouse: The Supreme Court and the Prison Litigation Reform Act." *Pace Law Review* 24:651–74.

Conte, A., and R. Burchill. 2009. *Defining Civil and Political Rights: The Jurisprudence of the United Nations Human Rights Committee*. 2nd ed. Farnham: Ashgate.

Council of Europe. 2007. *European Committee on Crime Problems (CDPC): Replies Received from the CDPC Delegations Following the Council of Europe Secretariat's Request for Information Regarding the Translation and Implementation of the European Prison Rules*, June 19, 2007. cdpc/docs 2007/cdpc (2007) 14rev2-e. Strasbourg: Council of Europe.

Deitch, M. 1991. "Rights, Remedies, and Restrained Reform." *Texas Law Review* 70:521–35.

———. 2006. "Effective Prison Oversight." Prepared for the Commission on Safety and Abuse in America's Prisons, 4th Hearing, Los Angeles, February 8. http://www.prisoncommission.org/statements/deitch_michele.pdf.

De Jonge, G. 2007. "European Detention Standards." In *Dutch Prisons*, edited by M. Moerings and M. Boone. The Hague: BJU Legal Publishers.

De la Cuesta, J. L., and I. Blanco. 2007. "Le système pénitentiaire espagnol." In *Les systèmes pénitentiaires dans le monde*, edited by J. P. Céré and C. Japiassú. Paris: Dalloz.

DiIulio, J. 1990. *Courts, Corrections, and the Constitution: The Impact of Judicial Intervention on Prison and Jails.* New York: Oxford University Press.

Dulitzky, A. E. 2008. "La OEA y los derechos humanos: Nuevos perfiles para el sistema interamericano." *Diálogo Político* 4:69–109.

Dünkel, F. 1997. "Judicial Control and Supervision." In *Monitoring Prison Conditions in Europe*, edited by Penal Reform International. Paris: Penal Reform International.

———. 2001. "Germany." In *Imprisonment Today and Tomorrow: International Perspectives on Prisoners' Rights and Prison Conditions*, edited by D. van Zyl Smit and F. Dünkel. 2nd ed. The Hague: Kluwer Law International.

Dünkel, F., and D. van Zyl Smit. 2007. "The Implementation of Youth Imprisonment and Constitutional Law in Germany." *Punishment and Society* 9: 347–69.

Escobar, G. 2007. *Informe sobre derechos humanos sistema penitenciario.* Madrid: Trama Editorial.

Evans, M., and C. Haenni-Dale. 2004. "Preventing Torture? The Development of the Optional Protocol to the UN Convention against Torture." *Human Rights Law Review* 4:19–55.

Feeley, M., and E. Rubin. 1998. *Judicial Policy Making and the Modern State: How the Courts Reformed America's Prisons.* Cambridge: Cambridge University Press.

Feeley, M., and V. Swearingen. 2004. "The Prison Conditions Cases and the Bureaucratization of American Corrections: Influences, Impacts and Implications." *Pace Law Review* 24:433–76.

Feest, J., and P. Selling. 1988. "Rechtstatsachen über Rechtsbeschwerden." In *Kriminologische Forschung der 80er Jahren*, edited by G. Kaiser, H. Kury, and H.-J. Albrecht. Freiburg: Max Planck Institut für ausländisches und internationales Recht.

Gallinetti, J. 2004. *Report on the Evaluation of the Independent Prison Visitors System.* CSPRI Research Paper Series 5. Cape Town: CSPRI.

Goldmacher, S., and P. McGreevy. 2009. "California Legislature OKs State Prison Cuts." *Los Angeles Times*, September 12. http://articles.latimes.com/2009/sep/12/local/me-legis12.

Gonçzöl, K. 1997. "Protecting Prisoners' Rights in the New Democracies." In *Monitoring Prison Conditions in Europe*, edited by Penal Reform International. Paris: Penal Reform International.

Greve, V., and A. Snare. 2009. "Ideologies and Realities in Prison Law: Some Trends." In *Criminal Law, Scandinavian Studies in Law*, vol. 54, edited by P. Wahlgren. Stockholm: Stockholm Institute for Scandinavian Law.

Gualazzi, A., and C. Mancuso. 2010. "Italy." In *Release for Prison: European Policy and Practice*, edited by N. Padfield, D. van Zyl Smit, and F. Dünkel. Cullompton: Willan.

Harding, R. 2007. "Inspecting Prisons." In *Handbook on Prisons*, edited by Y. Jewkes. Collumpton: Willan.

Harding, R., and N. Morgan. 2010. "OPCAT in the Asia-Pacific and Australasia." *Essex Human Rights Review* 6(2):99–123.

Henkin, L. 1995. "U.S. Ratification of Human Rights Conventions: The Ghost of Senator Bricker." *American Journal of International Law* 89:341–50.

Herzog-Evans, M. 1997."Judicial Oversight on Prison Sentences." In *Monitoring Prison Conditions in Europe*, edited by Penal Reform International. Paris: Penal Reform International.

HMIP (Her Majesty's Inspectorate of Prisons). 2006. *Expectations: Criteria for Assessing the Conditions in Prisons and the Treatment of Prisoners.* London: Her Majesty's Inspectorate of Prisons.

Hood, C., O. James, G. Jones, C. Scott, and T. Travers. 1999. *Regulation Inside Government: Waste-Watchers, Quality Police, and Sleazebusters.* Oxford: Oxford University Press.

Howard, J. 1792. *The State of the Prisons in England and Wales, with Preliminary Observations, and an Account of Some Foreign Prisons and Hospitals.* London: Johnson, Dilly & Cadell.

Jacobs, J. 1977. *Stateville: The Penitentiary in Mass Society.* Chicago: University of Chicago Press.

———. 1983. "The Prisoners' Rights Movement and Its Impact." In *New Perspectives on Prisons and Imprisonment*, edited by J. Jacobs. Ithaca, NY: Cornell University Press.

Jagwanth, S. 2004. *A Review of the Judicial Inspectorate of Prison of South Africa.* CSPRI Research Paper Series 7. Cape Town: CSPRI.

Kaiser, G., H. J. Kerner, and H. Schöch. 1991. *Strafvollzug.* 4th ed. Heidelberg: C. F. Müller.

Kelk, C. 2008. *Nederlands detentierecht.* Deventer: Kluwer.

Koeppel, K. 1999. *Kontrolle des Strafvollzugs: Individueller Rechtsschutz und generelle Aufsicht; ein Rechtsvergleich.* Mönchengladbach: Forum Verlag.

Kuwayama, A. 2010. "Exploring the Possibility of Designating a National Preventive Mechanism in Japan." *Essex Human Rights Review* 6(2):125–62.

Lange, J. 2008. *Detentie genormeerd: Een onderzoek naar de betekenis van het CPT voor de inrichting van vrijheidsbeneming in Nederland.* Nijmegen: WLP.

Lazarus, L. 2004. *Contrasting Prisoners' Rights: A Comparative Examination of England and Germany.* Oxford: Oxford University Press.

———. 2006. "Conceptions of Liberty Deprivation." *Modern Law Review* 69: 738–69.

Liebling, A. 2004. *Prisons and Their Moral Performance: A Study of Values, Quality, and Prison Life.* Oxford: Oxford University Press.

Livingstone, S. 2000. "Prisoners' Rights in the Context of the European Convention on Human Rights." *Punishment and Society* 2:309–24.

Livingstone, S., T. Owen, and A. MacDonald. 2008. *Prison Law.* 4th ed. Oxford: Oxford University Press.

Morgan. R. 2000. "Developing Prison Standards Compared." *Punishment and Society* 2:325–42.

Morgan, R., and M. Evans. 2001. *Combating Torture in Europe.* Strasbourg: Council of Europe.

Mulgrew, R. 2009. "On the Enforcement of Sentences Imposed by International Courts: Challenges Faced by the Special Court for Sierra Leone." *Journal of International Criminal Justice* 7:373–96.

Müller-Dietz, H. 2008. "Strafvollzug und Verfassungsrecht." In *Humanisierung des Strafvollzugs: Konzepte und Praxismodelle*, edited by F. Dünkel, K. Drenkhahn, and C. Morgenstern. Mönchengladbach: Forum Verlag.

Murdoch, J. 2006. *The Treatment of Prisoners: European Standards*. Strasbourg: Council of Europe.

Murphy, T., and N. Whitty. 2007. "Risk and Human Rights in UK Prison Governance." *British Journal of Criminology* 47:798–816.

Murray, R. 2008. "The African Commission's Approach to Prisons." In *Human Rights in African Prisons*, edited by J. Sarkin. Pretoria: HRSC Press; Athens: Ohio University Press.

Niyizurugero, J. B., and G. Lessène. 2010. "The Robben Island Guidelines: An Essential Tool for the Prevention of Torture in Africa." *Essex Human Rights Review* 6(2):91–114.

Nordenfelt, C. 2007. "The Swedish Parliamentary Ombudsman for Penal Matters." In *Opening up a Closed World: What Constitutes Effective Prison Oversight?* vol. 1, *Conference Proceedings*, edited by M. Deitch. Austin: University of Texas.

Nowak, M. 2005, *U.N. Covenant on Civil and Political Rights: CCPR Commentary*. Kehl and Strasbourg: N. P. Engel.

Nowak, M., and E. McArthur. 2008. *The United States Convention against Torture: A Commentary*. Oxford: Oxford University Press.

Oleinik, A. 2006. "A Plurality of Total Institutions: Towards a Comparative Penology." *Crime Law and Social Change* 46:161–80.

———. 2007. "Le système pénitentiaire russe." In *Les systèmes pénitentiaires dans le monde*, edited by J. P. Céré and C. Japiassú. Paris: Dalloz.

Olivier, A., and M. Narvaez. 2009. "OPCAT Challenges and the Way Forwards: The Ratification and Implementation of the Optional Protocol to the UN Convention against Torture." *Essex Human Rights Review* 6(1):6–14.

Owers, A. 2006. "The Protection of Prisoners' Rights in England and Wales." *European Journal on Criminal Policy and Research* 12:85–91.

Paprzycki, L. 2008. "The Ombudsman's Role in Ensuring the Protection of the Rights of Detainees in Poland." In *Prison Policy and Prisoners' Rights: Proceedings of the Colloquium of the IPPF*, Stavern, Norway, June 25–28, edited by the IPPF. Nijmegen: Wolf Legal Publishers.

Pasha, S. 2010. "National Human Rights Institutions and Their Role in the Struggle against Torture in the Asia-Pacific Region." *Essex Human Rights Review* 6(2):115–36.

Piacentini, L. 2006. "Prisons during Transition: Promoting a Common Penal Identity through International Norms." In *Perspectives on Punishment: The Contours of Control*, edited by S. Armstrong and L. McAra. Oxford: Oxford University Press.

Poncela, P. 2001. *Droit de la peine*. 2nd ed. Paris: Presses Universitaires de France.

Ramsbottom, D. 2003. *Prisongate: The Shocking State of Britain's Prisons and the Need for Visionary Change.* London: Free Press.

Rieckhof, S. 2008. *Strafvollzug in Russland.* Mönchengladbach: Forum Verlag.

Rodley, N., and M. Pollard. 2009. *The Treatment of Prisoners under International Law.* 3rd ed. Oxford: Oxford University Press.

Sarkin, J. 2008. *Human Rights in African Prisons.* Athens: Ohio University Press.

Schlanger, M. 2006. "Civil Rights Injunctions over Time: A Case Study of Jail and Prison Court Orders." *New York University Law Review* 81:550–630.

Schlanger, M., and G. Shay. 2008. "Preserving the Rule of Law in America's Jails and Prisons: The Case for Amending the Prison Litigation Reform Act." *University of Pennsylvania Journal of Constitutional Law* 11:139–54.

Serrarens, J. 2007. "Complaints Procedures." In *Dutch Prisons*, edited by M. Moerings and M. Boone. The Hague: BJU Legal Publishers.

Snacken, S. 2004. "Het Europees Comité voor de Preventie van Foltering en Onmenselijke of Vernederende Behandeling of Bestraffing." In *Ceci n'est pas un juriste . . . , Liber Amicorum Bart De Schutter*, edited by M. Cools, C. Eliaerts, S. Gutwirth, T. Joris, and B. Spruyt. Brussels: VUB Press.

———. 2006. "A Reductionist Penal Policy and European Human Rights Standards." *European Journal on Criminal Policy and Research* 12:143–64.

Sparks, R., A. E. Bottoms, and W. Hay. 1996. *Prisons and the Problem of Order.* Oxford: Clarendon.

Stando-Kawecka, B. 2001. "Poland." In *Imprisonment Today and Tomorrow: International Perspectives on Prisoners' Rights and Prison Conditions*, edited by D. van Zyl Smit and F. Dünkel. 2nd ed. The Hague: Kluwer Law International.

Steinerte, E., and R. Murray. 2009. "Same but Different? National Human Rights Commissions and Ombudsman Institutions as National Preventive Mechanisms under the Optional Protocol to the UN Torture Convention." *Essex Human Rights Review* 6(1):54–72.

Sterngold, J. 2008. "Worst of the Worst: California's Hard Lessons in How Not to Run a Prison System." *Mother Jones*, July/August, 48–53.

Tumim, S. 1992. "The Inspector as Critic: The Job of HM Chief Inspector of Prisons." *Political Quarterly* 63:5–11.

Vagg, J. 1994. *Grievance and Disciplinary Processes: A Review of the Situation in England and Wales, France, and West Germany.* Oxford: Oxford University Press.

Van Zyl Smit, D. 2005. "International Imprisonment." *International and Comparative Law Quarterly* 54:357–86.

———. 2007. "Prisoners' Rights." In *Handbook on Prisons*, edited by Y. Jewkes. Cullompton: Willan.

Van Zyl Smit, D., and S. Snacken. 2009. *Principles of European Prison Law and Policy: Penology and Human Rights.* Oxford: Oxford University Press.

———. Forthcoming. "Shaping Penal Policy from Above? The Role of the Grand Chamber of the European Court of Human Rights." In *International and Comparative Criminal Justice and Urban Governance*, edited by A. Crawford. Cambridge: Cambridge University Press.

Viljoen, F. 2007. *International Human Rights Law in Africa*. Oxford: Oxford University Press.

———. 2005. "The Special Rapporteur on Prison (SRP) and Conditions of Detention in Africa: Achievements and Possibilities." *Human Rights Quarterly* 27:125–71.

Walmsley, R. 2003. *Further Developments in the Penal Systems of Central and Eastern Europe*. Helsinki: HEUNI.

Williams, P. 1990. *Treatment of Detainees: Examination of Issues Relevant to Detention by the United Nations Human Rights Committee*. Geneva: Henri Dunant Institute.

Woods, S. 2009. "'Capture' and the South African Judicial Inspectorate of Prisons: A Micro-level Analysis." *International Criminal Justice Review* 19: 46–63.

Woolf, Lord Justice. 1991. *Prison Disturbances April 1990*. London: Home Office.

Zinger, Ivan. 2006. "Human Rights Compliance and the Role of External Prison Oversight." *Canadian Journal of Criminology and Criminal Justice* 48: 127–40.

Kathleen Daly and Brigitte Bouhours

Rape and Attrition in the Legal Process: A Comparative Analysis of Five Countries

ABSTRACT

Despite legal reforms, there has been little improvement in police, prosecutor, and court handling of rape and sexual assault. In the past 15 years in Australia, Canada, England and Wales, Scotland, and the United States, victimization surveys show that 14 percent of sexual violence victims report the offense to the police. Of these, 30 percent proceed to prosecution, 20 percent are adjudicated in court, 12.5 percent are convicted of any sexual offense, and 6.5 percent are convicted of the original offense charged. In the past 35 years, average conviction rates have declined from 18 percent to 12.5 percent, although they have not fallen in all countries. Significant country differences are evident in how cases are handled and where in the legal process attrition is most likely. There is some good news: a victim's "good" character and credibility and stranger relations are less important than they once were in police or court outcomes. However, evidence of nonconsent (witness evidence, physical injuries to the victim, suspect's use of a weapon) continues to be important.

In 1978, the first studies written in English of police and court responses to rape were published. As of September 2007, over 90 attrition studies had reported findings for Australia, Canada, England and

Kathleen Daly is professor of criminology and criminal justice at Griffith University (Brisbane). Brigitte Bouhours is research officer in the Centre of Excellence in Policing and Security, Australian National University (Canberra), formerly, senior research assistant, Griffith University, working with Daly for 9 years to October 2009. We are grateful to Michael Tonry and the reviewers for their extended and helpful comments on an earlier draft.

565

Wales, Scotland, and the United States from 1970 to 2005.[1] Some analyze the same data set, and the findings from others can be combined; thus, the unique set of cases reduces to 75. In this essay, we analyze this body of research from five countries[2] to identify patterns in police, prosecutor, and court handling of rape and sexual assault cases. It is contextualized by victimization surveys, police statistics, and court data from the countries examined. We also explore the factors associated with conviction and attrition such as the victim's character and credibility, prompt reporting of the offense, victim-offender relations, and evidence of nonconsent.

The project began with a more simple aim: to summarize English-language studies of rape case handling by the police and courts. However, we soon discovered that there were widely varying estimates of attrition and conviction in the literature. Authors cited different studies or selected findings or focused on some jurisdictions or countries. Conviction rates were given, but often it was not clear if they pertained to any offense or to the original offense charged, and researchers calculated estimates and defined outcomes in different ways.

Research on the prevalence of rape and its legal handling is highly politicized and contested. Victim advocates are criticized for providing "widely inflated estimates" of sexual victimization (Gilbert 1997, p. 101), and skeptics can be criticized for not understanding sexual violence in more fluid terms, as a continuum (Kelly 1988). Legal definitions of rape have changed in the last three decades, but the more consequential change is social and political. This was encapsulated in early feminist challenges to the "real rape" construct, that rape is carried out by a stranger, using a weapon, and with serious victim injury (Estrich 1987), when the more typical rape is by a known person, without a weapon, and without physical evidence of nonconsent. As legal

---

[1] Since September 2007, New Zealand has completed a rape attrition study (Triggs et al. 2009). Other studies that are planned or under way include the Irish Rape Attrition Project (2010), a rape attrition study of 11 U.K. and European countries (Lovett and Kelly 2009), the Understanding Attrition in Rape Cases Project in Sussex (McMillan and Thomas 2008), and a rape attrition study planned for South Africa (Gender, Health and Justice Research Unit 2008). Johnson, Ollus, and Nevala (2008) report estimates from the International Violence Against Women Survey that we cite when relevant.

[2] We initially combined England and Wales and Scotland but then decided to treat them separately because their rape law and criminal procedures differ, as do their attrition rates over time. In Scotland, unlike England and Wales, the definition of rape is still gender specific, although this is changing. The Scottish criminal justice system includes an additional stage, that of the procurator fiscal, who takes on some duties of the police and the prosecution (personal communication with Michele Burman, January 24, 2008).

definitions and sociopolitical understandings of rape widened and as advocacy for victims grew from the 1970s onward, research on rape has been caught up in a politics of rape. Debates initially focused on rape prevalence (e.g., was it an epidemic or not?). In the past decade, debates have matured, but governments have been called on to do more. Low or declining conviction rates, faulty or questionable police investigations, and poor treatment of rape victims have put pressure on governments to review rape laws and legal procedure, not for the first time, but yet again.

As our research progressed, the need to create an authoritative and comprehensive record of what is known about rape and its handling in the legal process became clear. Reviews by Bryden and Lengwick (1997), Kelly (2001), Lievore (2004), Koss (2006), and Du Mont and White (2007) consider the prevalence and contexts of sexual victimization, victims' reporting patterns, and justice system responses. However, ours is the first study to assemble and harmonize the relevant body of research to estimate rates of conviction and of case attrition at different stages of the legal process and to identify factors associated with case attrition or retention. To provide a comparative context and understanding of the patterns that may emerge, we also review rape law reform and compare police statistics and court outcomes in the five countries studied.

A note on definitions. Rape is "unwanted oral, anal, or vaginal penetration against consent through force, threat of force, or when incapacitated" (Koss 2006, p. 208). It includes sexual intercourse with children (typically at law, under 16). "Rape" differs from "sexual assault" and "all sexual offenses." Sexual assault refers to a wider set of offenses, including penetrative (i.e., rape) and nonpenetrative (e.g., indecent assault) offenses that touch the body sexually. "All sexual offenses" include rape, sexual assault, and "no touch" offenses (e.g., indecent behavior or sexual exposure). Although most attrition research is concerned with the sociolegal response to rape (i.e., forced penetrative sex), victimization surveys, attrition studies, and official police and court data may include a broader set of offenses and victims of varied age groups.[3] For simplicity of expression, we use victim and offender throughout the essay, without the "alleged" preface, and we use victim rather than survivor or victim-survivor.

---

[3] Because the composition of offenses varies, depending on the study or official data source, we use the more generic terms "sexual victimization" or "sexual offenses."

Here are our major findings. Of sexual offenses reported to the police during the past 35 years, the overall rate of conviction to any sexual offense is 15 percent.[4] When an early period (1970–89) is compared with a later period (1990–2005), this rate has declined significantly[5] from 18 to 12.5 percent. Significant decreases have occurred in England and Wales, Canada, and to a lesser degree in Australia, but not in the United States or Scotland. Across the three decades, the overall rate of conviction to any sexual offense is a bit higher in samples of child or youth victims than those of mixed age or adults only. Significant decreases in conviction rates over time are evident in samples of mixed age and child or youth victims and across all types of sexual offenses.

With regard to where attrition occurs in the legal process, the following are averages across countries for the more recent period. Of sexual offenses reported to the police, 30 percent proceed past the police to prosecution, 20 percent are adjudicated in court, 12.5 percent are convicted of any sexual offense, and 6.5 percent are convicted of the original offense charged. Few cases go to trial (8 percent) and are convicted at trial (4.5 percent). Attrition is greatest at the start of the sociolegal process: from victimization surveys, an average 14 percent of victims report the offense to the police. Once reported, a minority of cases proceed past the police to the prosecutor's office, and this occurs for a variety of reasons. Suspects cannot be identified or located, victims withdraw complaints, and the police believe that there is insufficient evidence to charge a suspect or the victim's story lacks credibility. Attrition averages do not tell the whole story and can be misleading because there are significant differences by country and time period in the police and court handling of cases.

One explanation for decreasing conviction rates is that as more sexual offenses are reported to the police, they contain a higher share of known relations and rape contexts that do not accord with the real rape construct. At the same time, police, prosecutorial, and court decisions continue to operate with the real rape construct in mind. We find that this explanation applies best to England and Wales but is less evident in other countries. Of the four countries with sufficient re-

---

[4] The terms "overall rate of conviction" and "overall conviction rate" refer to the proportion of cases reported to the police that are convicted of any sexual offense.

[5] When we say "significantly" here and elsewhere in discussing the results, the reference is to statistically significant differences.

search, the United States is an anomaly with no change in conviction rates over time. There is no one pattern of conviction and attrition in the countries studied.

We recognize that legal reforms of the past several decades may have helped some victims, but all commentators agree that the gains have been modest. We call for a shift in the priorities of legal reform—away from the trial and toward mechanisms of encouraging admissions to offending, which includes pursuing alternative pathways of participation and support for victims, offenders, and others affected by sexual offenses.

This essay has six sections. Section I reviews research and survey data on the prevalence of rape, on reporting to the police, and on case processing in the prosecutorial and judicial systems. It also discusses charges in rape law in the five countries. Section II sets out questions and related hypotheses examined in later sections. Section III describes the scope of the analysis, our strategy for locating relevant studies, problems of data comparability, and how estimates of conviction and attrition were calculated (app. B discusses these matters in more detail). Section IV presents and discusses the main findings. In Section V we examine our findings in relation to the questions and hypotheses set out in Section II. The final section puts forward ideas for more innovative and effective responses to rape and sexual assault, including cases that are not reported to the police and those that are reported, but subsequently withdrawn in the criminal process.

I. Attrition Research in Comparative Context

To understand patterns of rape case attrition over time and across different jurisdictions requires attention to a wider social and legal context. Since the 1960s and 1970s, with the rise of second-wave feminism, the legal definitions and social meanings of rape began to change. Major challenges were raised by feminist scholars about the veracity of official data and the harsh treatment of victims in the legal process.

A. Was It Rape? Reporting Rape to the Police and Legal Responses

Estrich's (1987) review of the literature up to the mid-1980s analyzed the interrelationships among victims' experiences of rape, sample survey estimates of victimization, victims' reports to the police, and how cases were handled by the police and courts. She coined the term "real rape," drawing from Kalven and Zeisel's (1966, p. 252) term "aggravated rape." Real rape has one or more of these elements: stranger relations, multiple assailants, weapon use, and evidence of serious physical injury. Or as Estrich says, the real rape image is of an "armed man jumping from the bushes" (p. 8). By contrast "not real" rape (also termed "simple" rape) has none of these aggravating elements: the offender is a lone man, whom the woman knows (a neighbor, an acquaintance, a date), using no weapon, and leaving no physical injuries or bruises on a victim.[6] Estrich argued that in simple rape contexts, questions about a woman's character, credibility, and believability were especially likely to be raised. Although real rape was reported to the police by victims and treated seriously by the criminal justice system, simple rape was "far more common, vastly underreported, and dramatically ignored" by the police and courts (p. 10).

From early victimization surveys in the United States (the National Crime Surveys [NCS] conducted during 1973–82), the Bureau of Justice Statistics (1985) estimated that 52 percent of rapes (both attempted and completed) were reported to the police. It soon became apparent that the NCS had grossly underestimated the prevalence of rape and overestimated the likelihood of victim reports to the police because of the way in which the survey questions were asked. Other studies in the United States appeared at the time (e.g., Russell 1975; Williams 1984; see Estrich 1987, pp. 11–14) showing that women who were sexually assaulted by persons they knew (acquaintances, friends, neighbors, or relatives) were far less likely to report the offense to the police and to victim survey interviewers compared to women who were assaulted by strangers.

The Sexual Experiences Survey, developed by Koss and colleagues in the mid-1980s (Koss and Gidycz 1985; Koss, Gidycz, and Wisniewski 1987), broadened the behaviors associated with rape. Using this instrument, the authors found that the rate of rape was at least 10 times greater than that estimated from the NCS (see Johnson, Ollus, and Nevala 2008, pp. 10–14).[7] In 1992, the NCS sexual and domestic

---

[6] Although Estrich (1987) draws from Kalven and Zeisel's (1966) work in defining real rape, her analysis focuses mainly on different responses to stranger and known relationship cases.

[7] Although Koss and colleagues were criticized by Gilbert (1997) for overestimating prevalence, a more recent study of victimization on U.S. college campuses vindicates Koss's point that estimates change dramatically, by 10 times, when questions are asked differently (see Fisher, Cullen, and Turner 2000, pp. 11–14).

violence victimization questions were redesigned, and special modules were introduced in the British Crime Survey in 1994 to elicit respondents' experiences with rape and sexual assault. Both led to significant increases in the estimated rates of sexual victimization. In 1993, Statistics Canada fielded the first national survey of women's experiences of sexual and physical victimization, which used more sensitive approaches to elicit information and conduct the interviews (see a review of methods used in Johnson and Sacco [1995] and Johnson [1996]); their approach was adopted in other countries during the 1990s. The International Crime Victim Survey (ICVS) began to gather victimization data in 1989 from 60 countries (now numbering 70 countries), but it was not designed to elicit an understanding of female experiences of sexual or physical victimization. To address this problem, the International Violence Against Women Survey (IVAWS) project was established as an international comparative survey of women's experience of sexual and physical violence and of criminal justice responses. After pilot studies in 2001 and 2002, the first survey was carried out during 2003–5 in 11 countries of the developed and developing world. Publications are now emerging (see, e.g., Mouzos and Makkai [2004] for Australia and Johnson, Ollus, and Nevala [2008] for the entire sample) that present a complex picture of victimization and reporting patterns, with an analytical emphasis on partner and nonpartner violence.[8]

Several observations can be made. Reliable estimates of female sexual victimization and associated estimates of reports to the police are recent. Such estimates depend on how the questions are asked and the degree to which the interview context is supportive of participants. As methodologies improve to elicit the frequency, types, and contexts of rape and sexual assault and the estimated incidence of sexual victimization increases, the rate at which women tell survey researchers that they reported the offense to the police decreases. Thus, when victimization surveys capture a larger share of "nontraditional" rapes (simple rapes and those involving known relations), the rate at which victims say to interviewers that they reported the offense to the police goes down. Likewise, the composition of reports received by the police may have an increasingly larger share of nontraditional rapes over time because there are more supports and services for victims, coupled with a

---

[8] Where relevant, we draw on the IVAWS findings. However, just one of the five countries in our study (Australia) participated in the IVAWS.

changed consciousness about rape, to bring these incidents to police attention.

Table 1 itemizes the major surveys of sexual victimization conducted since 1992 in four countries that are the subject of this study. It shows that across all the surveys, the rates of report to the police range from 6 percent (the first victim-friendly survey in Canada) to a high of 32 percent (a standard victimization survey in the United States, albeit with redesigned questions). When the latter unusually high estimate is excluded, the average rate of victim report is 14 percent.[9] By country, rates of report are 15–19 percent (United States), 14–18 percent (England and Wales), 12–20 percent (Australia), 6–19 percent (Canada), and 12 percent (New Zealand).

For age, surveyed victims are typically 16 or older, and the youngest age group (16–24 years) has the highest rate of sexual victimization. Where data are available, however, the highest rate of sexual victimization is found for those 10–14 years (Snyder 2000; AIC 2008). In research on child and youth victims (those 12–17 years), the rate of reporting sexual victimization to the police ranges from a high of 30 percent for "violent sexual assault" from the National Crime Victimization Survey (NCVS; Finkelhor and Ormrod 1999) to 13 percent for "sexual assault" (Kilpatrick and Saunders 1997) and to a low of 3 percent for "sexual victimization" (Finkelhor and Dziuba-Leatherman 1994; cited in Finkelhor, Wolak, and Berliner 2001, p. 18). Although the number of studies is small (and all are from the United States), they suggest a somewhat lower likelihood that child and youth victims report sexual victimization to the police than adult victims.

Why, on average, do 86 percent of victims not report rape and sexual assault to the police? The reasons given by victims, often in combination, are not viewing the assault as rape or not thinking that others will view it as rape; fearing that others will disbelieve or blame her, including family members or friends; fearing or distrusting the police and court processes; fearing threats or further attacks by the offender or his family and friends; and having divided loyalties when reporting a family member or ex-partner (Kelly 2001, pp. 9–10; Lievore 2003). Because many victims are unsure about what to do or may blame them-

[9] By comparison, estimates of reports to the police for nonpartner sexual violence, drawing from the IVAWS project, are somewhat lower: ranging from 4 percent (Poland), to 6–8 percent (Costa Rica, Denmark, Australia, and the Czech Republic), to 13 percent (Mozambique; Johnson, Ollus, and Nevala 2008, fig. 6.12, p. 147; table III.12, p. 210).

selves, they may delay their report to the police. The police, in turn, may interpret delay as a sign that the assault was not serious or that a victim is not being fully truthful. Young women's potential for victimization is high in social occasions in which alcohol or illegal drugs are used. These contexts heighten a risk of what is termed "acquaintance" rape, although the assaults may be viewed by victims, general members of society, and legal authorities as nontraditional forms, not as real rape.

B. Real Rape and Victim-Offender Relations

An important question for attrition research is whether the relative composition of aggravated and simple rapes, or of stranger rapes, reported to the police has changed over time. In England and Wales, attention has been drawn to the growing gap between women's reports to the police and a diminished rate of court convictions (Kelly, Lovett, and Regan 2005, p. 25). One explanation is that an increasing share of nontraditional rapes, which are more difficult to prove in court, are being reported to the police.

Evidence from varied jurisdictions over time is lacking on victim-offender relations and reporting patterns, but two studies are relevant. Baumer's (2004) analysis of the NCS for 1973–91 finds that of the 51 percent of rapes that victims said they reported to the police, half involved known persons. Data from the redesigned NCVS for 1992–2002 show that of the 30 percent of rapes that victims said they reported to the police, 84 percent involved known persons. From multivariate analyses, Baumer finds that in the 1970s and 1980s, women were less likely to report being raped by a known person than by a stranger, but by the early 1990s, victim-offender relationships had no effect on the likelihood that victims reported rape offenses to the police. He suggests that increases in victims' reports of nonstranger rapes can be attributed to changing perceptions of and broadened definitions of rape that include acquaintances and intimates. The second study, by Harris and Grace (1999), compares British Home Office data for 1985 and 1996 on the stranger share of cases reported to the police. They find a drop in the stranger share from 30 percent to 12 percent (see also Grace, Lloyd, and Smith 1992).

To pursue this question further, we identified a subsample of cases from our attrition sample that examined victim-offender relations as an attrition factor and then reread each to determine the stranger re-

TABLE 1
Rates of Reporting Sexual Assault Victimization to Police

Source and Citation	Rate of Report to Police (%)	Country	Survey Year	Age of Victim
National Crime Victimization Survey (NCVS) 2000 (Rennison 2002, p. 1)	32	United States	1992–2000	12+
Crime and Safety Australia 2002 (ABS 2003, pp. 28–29)	20	Australia	2002	18+
National Violence Against Women Survey (NVAWS) 1995–96 (Tjaden and Thoennes 2006, pp. 7, 33–34)	19	United States	1995–96	18+
International Crime Victims Survey (ICVS) (van Kesteren et al. 2000, pp. 188, 194)	19	Canada	2000	16+
British Crime Survey (BCS) (Myhill and Allen 2002, p. 1)	18	England and Wales	1998, 2000[a]	16+
International Crime Victims Survey (ICVS) (van Kesteren et al. 2000, pp. 189, 195)	15	United States	2000	16+

Women's Safety Survey (ABS 1996, pp. 4, 32)	15	Australia	1996	18+
International Crime Victims Survey (ICVS) (van Kesteren et al. 2000, pp. 188, 194)	15	Australia	2000	16+
International Crime Victims Survey (ICVS) (van Kesteren et al. 2000, pp. 188, 194)	14	England and Wales	2000	16+
International Violence Against Women Survey (IVAWS) (Mouzos and Makkai 2004, pp. 2, 102)	12[b]	Australia	2002–3	18+
New Zealand National Survey of Crime Victims 2001 (Morris and Reilly 2003, para. 3.2)	12	New Zealand	2000–2001	15+
General Social Survey on Victimization (Kong et al. 2003, p. 6)	8	Canada	1999	15+
Violence Against Women Survey 1993 (WAVAW 2005)	6	Canada	1993	18+
Mean rate of reporting to police[c]	14			

[a] Because of the small number of females reporting sexual victimization, responses on sexual victimization for two waves of the BCS (1998 and 2000) were combined.

[b] This is the rate for sexual assault by nonpartners; sexual assault by partners is 15 percent.

[c] Excludes the U.S. rate of 32 percent, which is an outlier.

lationship share of offenses reported to the police. A data set of 27 studies was initially assembled, but the number was reduced to 13; these clearly specified the stranger share of cases reported to police.[10] The 13 studies were mainly from the United States and England and Wales, with one each from Australia and Canada. Our ministudy found that stranger relations were a significantly higher share of cases reported to the police in the 1970s and 1980s (48 percent) than in the 1990s forward (26 percent). Although the sample size is small, the findings confirm that the stranger relations share of rapes reported to the police has decreased over time.

C. Legal Reform and Its Impact

When one compares rape case handling by country, a key element is variation in legal reform. There are several dimensions to consider: first, country differences in the timing and scope of rape law reform; second, the elements that are typically part of rape law reform; and, third, research on the effects of rape law reform on police and court handling of cases. A complicating factor is that rape law reform likely affects victims' reporting patterns to the police. As our discussion above suggests, one consequence of rape law reform is that a higher share of reported rapes involve known relations, and this may result in decreased convictions.

Country differences exist in the timing and scope of rape law reform. Reform emerged in the mid-1970s in the United States and Australia, soon followed by Canada in the early 1980s. Legal change came much later to England and Wales and Scotland. Some amendments were made to English law during the 1970s and 1990s, but no comprehensive legislative change occurred until 2003, with the passage of the Sexual Offences Act 2003. In Scotland, some reform was introduced in the mid-1980s and again in 2002, but comprehensive reform has not yet been introduced.[11]

Before rape law reform, a victim's character, behavior, and sexual history were relevant and lawful factors in decisions; there needed to

[10] The excluded studies were those that began with police "founded" or "crimed" cases, offenses cleared by arrest, cases referred to prosecution, or defendants in court. All of these are affected by victim-offender relations, and especially the latter three, in the profile of suspects who can be identified.

[11] We schematize developments in rape law reform. Evidence for and definitions of "consent" (or nonconsent) in rape law are complex and have been evolving in the past decade; they are not addressed in detail here.

be witness corroboration of a victim's statement and substantial evidence of victim resistance and injury. Rape was defined as forced vaginal intercourse only, and husbands were exempt from prosecution. When legal reforms were introduced, the aim was to shift attention away from a victim's character and sexual history to an offender's behavior, to eliminate the witness corroboration rule and other stringent physical evidence requirements to prove nonconsent, and to expand the definition of rape.

In the United States, all the states enacted rape law reforms by the mid-1980s (Futter and Mebane 2001), although these varied in scope and comprehensiveness. They include rape shield laws that restricted using evidence at trial about a victim's sexual history, elimination of the corroboration rule, and in some states, elimination of evidence of physical resistance. The definition of rape expanded from the single offense of rape (vaginal intercourse with the penis) to a series of graded offenses that were associated with aggravating circumstances and acts. Sexual intercourse was broadened to include oral and anal penetration and male victims. By 1993, marital rape was criminalized in all states (Bergen 2006).

Frohmann and Mertz (1994, p. 831) suggest that legal reform had dual goals of efficacy (i.e., increasing the likelihood of conviction) and process (i.e., "attention to women's perceptions and experience of the process itself"), but these goals did "not always coincide." For example, a prosecution may result in conviction, "but also devastation for the victim." Drawing from Spohn and Horney's (1992) key work, they concluded that with some exceptions, legal reforms had little or no effect on rates of reporting rape, prosecution, and conviction. Despite the good intentions of professionals, organizational or professional priorities often trumped victims' needs (Frohmann and Mertz 1994, pp. 832–35). Reviewing the effects of legal reform in the United States 15 years later, Koss (2006, p. 217) said that although feminist and victim movements "achieved spectacular success by the standards of social change," reforms had positively affected only a small number of women, drawing from Bryden (2000), Seidman and Vickers (2005), and Bublick (2006) (see also Schulhofer 1998, chap. 2).

In Australia, as in the United States, major legal reforms were introduced in all the states, beginning in the mid-1970s, although they varied in scope and intensity (Bargen and Fishwick 1995; Heath 2005). Legal reform addressed key areas of a victim's sexual history, witness corroboration, physical resistance (and associated definitions of consent), and definitions of rape and sexual intercourse. As in the United States, several Australian studies on the impact of legal reform (Brereton 1994; NSW Department for Women 1996) found that older practices continued, despite legal change. During the early 2000s, major reviews of rape law and procedure were undertaken in most states, including Victoria, New South Wales, South Australia, and Western Australia.

In Canada, comprehensive legislative change was introduced in 1983, with reforms aimed at encouraging victims to report rape to the police and limiting the introduction of evidence on a woman's sexual history. Rape was redefined as a type of assault with varying degrees of seriousness, and it included marital rape and male victims. Roberts (1996) reports that between 1983 and 1994, rape reporting to the police increased by 130 percent, with much of the increase occurring in the years immediately following the introduction of legal reform. However, Tang (1998, p. 263) suggests that for Canada, "sexual assault is still under-reported; victims fear the system is biased against them. Founding, charging, and conviction rates remained low." Gunn and Linden (1997) attempted, but were not able, to confidently estimate conviction rates in the pre- and postreform years.

In England and Wales, several amendments were made to the Sexual Offences Act 1956 to redefine rape. In 1976, a shift was made from "against her will," with evidence of physical resistance required, to "without her consent"; in 1994, rape definitions were broadened to include male and marital rape (see Temkin 2002). The Sexual Offences Act 2003 consolidated what had been piecemeal changes up to that time, and it introduced two major areas of change: widening the definition and scope of rape and sexual offenses and changing the definition of consent. As in Australia and Canada, the recent legislation in England and Wales provides a statutory definition of consent, including a list of circumstances when consent is not possible (see Temkin and Krahé 2008, pp. 26–27).

Legal reform came last to Scotland. Changes to the rape shield laws were first introduced in 1986 and extended in 1995 and 2002. Brown, Burman, and Jamieson (1993) and Burman et al. (2007, p. 8) conclude that the 1986 and 1995 legislation was "largely ineffective"; indeed, after the 2002 act, Burman et al. find that "*more* sexual history and character evidence [was being introduced than before]" (p. 7). Scotland's rape law includes only female victims, and its corroboration rule is still in place, although it applies to all offenses, not just rape (personal communication with Michele Burman, January 24, 2008).

Of the 75 cases analyzed in our study, just 12 (or 16 percent) were carried out before any legal reform in that jurisdiction, and an additional 11 percent were conducted in jurisdictions after some reform. Of the 12 prereform cases, most (nine) are from U.S. jurisdictions, two from Canada, and one from Scotland. Thus, studies of the police and court response to rape are largely of practices after the introduction of reforms in specific jurisdictions or countries.

Rape law reform is a long-term process of efforts to change legal culture, organizational and professional practices, and attitudes toward and beliefs about men's and women's sexualities, culpabilities, and responsibilities for sexual victimization. There is a long line of actions and interactions between the passage of a law and changes in people's attitudes and behaviors that give effect to that law; and as Smart (1989) suggests, the law is itself resistant to change. Although virtually all commentators suggest that there has been little or no significant impact of legal reform, we hypothesize that countries initiating reform earlier (the United States, Australia, and Canada) would show different conviction patterns than England and Wales and Scotland, which initiated reform much later. At the same time, we recognize that legal reform, coupled with research infrastructure and support services to victims, has likely affected victims more than criminal justice officials or legal practices. This is evident from several studies of victim reporting patterns (Harris and Grace 1999; Baumer 2004), including our ministudy. To explore this matter further, we turn to an analysis of crimes reported to the police over time by country.

D. Rape and Sexual Assault Recorded by Police

In reviewing official police data, we have three aims: to determine if there is a relationship between the emergence and consolidation of legal reform and rates of reported rape and sexual assault to the police, to identify country differences or patterns, and to consider how official police data may inform our analysis of attrition research.

It is widely recognized that official police data do not accurately reflect the true incidence of rape or sexual assault or increases and decreases over time. However, our aim is to glean general patterns from the data (see fig. 1). An immediate problem in attempting to make

Year	US Rape only[b]	Australia Rape only then sexual assault[c]	Canada Sexual assault[d]	England & Wales Sexual assault[e]	Scotland Sexual assault[f]
1971	20.5				
1975	increase	5.6			
1980	36.8	8.8		37.0	
1981	36.0	10.2		34.2	
1982					
1983			54.7	slight	
1984		rape only		increase	
1985	little		up and down,		
1986	variation	rates trebled	but general	39.9	
1987		in the 1990s	increase	43.9	
1988	↓		108.3		
1989	38.1				63.5
1990	41.2				
1991	42.3	↓		further	little
1992	peak 42.8	29.7	121.1	increase	variation
1993	41.1	71.1	peak 121.1		
1994	39.3	71.3	109.2	↓	↓
1995	37.1	70.9	96.0	53.5	63.2
1996	36.3	78.9	90.4	57.5	63.2
1997		sexual assault			
1998					
1999					up and down,
2000	rate of	rate of	rate of	rate of	but slow
2001	decline	increase	decline	increase	increase
2002	15 percent	16 percent	25 percent	53 percent	
2003		↓			
2004		91.4			
2005	↓	89.0	↓	↓	↓
2006	30.9	88.0	68.0	87.8	76.4

FIG. 1.—Rates of rape and sexual assault recorded by police (per 100,000 population).[a]
[a]Population includes males and females of all ages. For all countries except the United States, data include male and female victims. [b]Data include only forcible rape of females and are from Bureau of Justice Statistics Data Online (http://bjsdata.ojp.usdoj.gov/dataonline). [c]Data for 1974–92 include only rape and are from Walker (1994, pp. 6–7). Data for 1996–2006 include penetrative offenses (rape and USI) and nonpenetrative offenses (indecent assault). Rates for 1993–95 are from ABS (1994, p. 5; 1996, pp. 13–14). Data for 1996–2006 are from AIC (2008, p. 9) and were calculated using population data from ABS (2002, table 5.1 for 1996–2000; 2008, table 7.1 for 2000–2005). [d]Data include penetrative offenses (rape) and nonpenetrative offenses (indecent assault), and sexual offenses against children (level 1, 2, and 3 sexual assault). Data for 1983–88 are from Roberts and Gebotys (1992, p. 563); for 1992–96, from Kong (1997, p. 15); for 1997–2001, from Savoie (2002, p. 14); and for 2002–6, from Silver (2007, p. 9). Rates for 1983–96 were calculated using population data from Sustainability Report (2008). [e]Data include penetrative offenses (rape and USI) and nonpenetrative offenses (indecent assault). Data for 1979–89 are from Home Office (1989, p. 41); for 1990–95, from Home Office (1996, p. 58); for 1996, from Walker et al. (2006, p. 27); and for 1997–2006, from Sian et al. (2007, p. 37). Rates for 1979–95 were calculated using population data from Office for National Statistics (1997, p. 51); for 1996–2006, from National Statistics Online (2008, table 1.2). [f]Data include penetrative offenses (rape and USI) and nonpenetrative offenses (indecent assault). Data for 1988–96 are from Scottish Executive (1998, online table) and for 1997–2006, from Scottish Executive (2007b, p. 12). Rates for 1979–95 were calculated using population data from Office for National Statistics (1997, p. 51); for 1996–2006, from National Statistics Online (2008, table 1.2).

comparisons is that countries count different types of sexual offenses. As detailed in the figure notes, the United States counts rape only; Australia counted rape in the 1980s but then shifted to the broader category of sexual assault in the 1990s; and Canada, England and Wales, and Scotland count sexual assault. To compare recent patterns, we focus on rates of increase or decrease from 1996 to 2006.

In the United States, rates of reported rape to the police remained steady in the 1980s (after major increases in the 1970s); they peaked in the early 1990s and began to decline, with a 15 percent rate of decline from 1996 to the present. For Canada, rates of reported sexual assault increased during the 1980s. As in the United States, they peaked in the early 1990s and began to decline in 1994–95 and have declined since then (25 percent rate of decline from 1996 to the present). For Australia, rates of reported rape increased substantially in the 1980s. In contrast to the United States or Canada, rates of reported sexual assault in Australia increased somewhat from 1996 to 2004 (16 percent rate of increase), with a suggestive decreasing trend to 2006. The picture for England and Wales differs markedly. During the 1980s and to the mid-1990s, there were small but steady increases each year in reported sexual assault, but from 1996 to 2006, the rate of increase grew substantially (a 53 percent rate of increase).[12] Available data for Scotland show up-and-down fluctuations of reported sexual assault from 1996 to the present, with a suggestive upward trend.

These data suggest a relationship between rates of reported rape or sexual assault and the rise and consolidation of significant legal reform. Early reform countries (the United States, Australia, and Canada) do show substantial increases coinciding with legal reform, although these occurred earlier in the United States (in the 1970s) than in Australia and Canada (in the 1980s). By comparison, in England and Wales, a later reform country, rates of reported sexual assault did not begin to rise substantially until the late 1980s and have since shown a high rate of increase. In Scotland, where legal reform is still under way, rates of reported sexual assault were not counted until 1989; from then to 2006, there is a small increase.

There are also notable country differences. In the United States and Canada, after peaking in the early 1990s, rates have since declined. In Australia, rates increased slightly from the mid-1990s to 2004 but have

[12] Although England and Wales experienced a large rate of increase from 1996 to 2006, its rate of reported sexual assault in 2006 was about the same as Australia's.

since stabilized or declined somewhat. By contrast, England and Wales is exceptional in its large rate of increase in reported sexual assault from 1996 to 2006.

On the basis of these data, we would expect to see distinctive patterns in attrition research for England and Wales. With strong increases in reported sexual assault, there would be significant pressure on police organizational resources and routines to process cases, with one result being higher rates of attrition at the police stage. Making inferences from a country's police data to the findings from its attrition research is, of course, tenuous. Police data are gathered for an entire country (and three of the five countries are very large and geographically dispersed), whereas attrition studies come from selected cities or states, which may vary greatly in police and court practices.

E. Published Court Data

Attrition is smaller at the court stage, but it is at this stage when victims are most visibly subject to a second victimization by the trial process (NSW Department for Women 1996; Temkin and Krahé 2008). There are problems comparing countries' court data, but the statistics may offer broad clues about court culture and organizational practices.[13]

Three problems arise in comparing the court data. First, the published statistics for England and Wales do not show the number or percentage of "other outcomes" (i.e., cases that are dismissed, withdrawn, or not proceeded with); data from all the other countries do. With these cases excluded, the conviction rate for England and Wales is inflated and not comparable to that of other countries.[14] Second, with "other outcomes" excluded in the British data, the trial rate also cannot be compared with that of other countries. Third, Canada and Scotland do not report the number of cases that go to trial or trial outcomes.

Table 2 presents the available court data on conviction rates, trial

[13] Some have asked if attrition for rape is any different from that for murder or robbery (see, e.g., Myers and LaFree 1982; Galvin and Polk 1983). The answer is that we do not know when the base is crimes reported to the police. We analyzed the countries' court data for 2001–6 and found that once cases are in court, conviction for rape is ranked third or tied in second place with homicide/murder or robbery. In no country is conviction for rape ranked in first place. Garner and Maxwell's (2009) analysis of attrition for intimate partner violence finds an overall average conviction rate of 16.4 percent. Their paper can be read as a companion piece to ours.

[14] The same approach is taken by the Australian Bureau of Statistics (2007) in its compilation of Australia-wide court data; for that reason, we do not rely on that source but use more complete data from South Australia.

rates, and conviction at trial. Column 1, outcome % of total cases, shows that in the United States and South Australia, 31 percent of cases are not proceeded with, dismissed, or withdrawn. However, the share of guilty pleas is much higher in the United States (61 percent) than in South Australia (37 percent). In column 2, the trial rate is calculated in two ways. First, the trial rate is the percentage of all cases in court (including "other outcomes") that go to trial;[15] and then the comparison trial rate, in parentheses, is calculated as N of cases going to trial/(N of guilty pleas + N of cases going to trial). We can use this second figure in comparing the British trial rate with that in other countries. Column 4 presents the conviction rate for trial cases and for total cases (i.e., the denominator includes "other outcomes").

Table 2 suggests that court processes vary by country. First, the conviction rate of total rape cases (rape or rape and unlawful sexual intercourse [USI]) is higher in the United States (67 percent) than in South Australia, Canada, and Scotland, where it ranges from 47 to 52 percent. Second, the trial rate for the United States is lower than that for South Australia (respectively, 8 percent and 32 percent), but the rate of conviction at trial is higher (respectively, 74 percent and 47 percent). In the Scottish data, the conviction rate for indecent assaults (nonpenetrative offenses) is higher than it is for rape (78 percent and 47 percent, respectively). Offense and age-based differences in conviction rates are explored further in the next table.

Table 3 assembles data from New South Wales and Victoria to determine if trial rates and rates of conviction vary by the age of victims and type of offense. In New South Wales, for offenses against children (defined as under 18 years), the trial rate is 33 percent, the rate of conviction at trial is 45 percent, and the conviction rate for the total cases charged is 62 percent. However, for offenses against adults, the trial rate is higher (42 percent) and the rate of conviction at trial is lower (35 percent), as is the conviction rate for total cases (43 percent). A similar age-based pattern is evident when comparing rape and USI. The latter offense is relevant only to younger-aged victims, whereas rape can include victims of all ages.[16] For rape, the trial rate is 46

---

[15] This definition of the trial rate is also used in our analysis of attrition research; see app. table B1.

[16] The precise victim age for USI varies by jurisdiction, but typically, it is less than 16 years. Further legal distinctions are made for USI with victims under 12 or 13 years, which is legally more serious. The key legal point is that nonconsent is not relevant in USI cases. Cases may initially be charged with rape, but a defendant may be permitted to plead to USI when the state's evidence of nonconsent is weak.

TABLE 2
Court Cases and Conviction Rates for Rape

Charged Offense and Outcome	Outcome % of Total Cases (1)	Trial Rate (Comparison Trial Rate)[a] (2)	N Guilty (3)	Conviction Rate (4)
		A. United States, 2002		
Rape and attempted rape (N = 760):				
Guilty plea (N = 464)	61%	...	464	
Trial (N = 61)	8%	8% (12%)	45	74% (at trial)
Other outcomes (N = 235)[b]	31%	...	...	
Total N cases	760		509	67% (all cases)
		B. South Australia, 2001–5		
Rape, attempted rape, and unlawful sexual intercourse (N = 463):				
Guilty plea (N = 170)	37%	...	170	
Trial (N = 149)	32%	32% (47%)	70	47% (at trial)
Other outcomes (N = 144)[b]	31%	...	...	
Total N cases	463		240	52% (all cases)
		C. Canada, 2005–6		
Rape and attempted rape (N = 3,145):				
Total N cases	3,145	No trial information	1,583	50% (all cases)
		D. England and Wales, 2005[c]		
Rape and unlawful sexual intercourse (N = 2,577):				
Guilty plea (N = 802)	31%	...	802	
Trial (N = 1,775)	69%	Unknown (69%)	515	29% (at trial)
Other outcomes[b]	Not shown	...	...	
Total N cases	2,577		509	Cannot determine accurately

TABLE 2 (*Continued*)

Charged Offense and Outcome	Outcome % of Total Cases (1)	Trial Rate (Comparison Trial Rate)ᵃ (2)	N Guilty (3)	Conviction Rate (4)
		E. Scotland, 2005–6		
Rape and attempted rape (N = 126): Total N cases	126	No trial information	59	47% (all cases)
Indecent assault (N = 108): Total N cases	108	No trial information	84	78% (all cases)

SOURCE.—For the United States, data are from Cohen and Reaves (2006, p. 24); for South Australia, the Office of Crime Statistics and Research (2002–6); for Canada, Statistics Canada (2007); for England and Wales, Office for Criminal Justice Reform (2006); for Scotland, Scottish Executive (2007a). N's were calculated or adapted from percentages given in the sourced material.

ᵃ The comparison trial rate is calculated as N cases going to trial/(N guilty pleas + cases going to trial).

ᵇ Depending on the jurisdiction, other outcomes are not proceeded with, dismissed, diverted, deferred, or withdrawn cases, or defendant failed to appear or died.

ᶜ Published data show a conviction rate of 51 percent, but this excludes cases dismissed or withdrawn, is inflated, and cannot be compared to the other countries.

percent, the rate of conviction at trial is 48 percent, and the conviction rate for all cases charged is 65 percent. By comparison, for USI, the trial rate is lower (34 percent) and conviction at trial is higher (58 percent), as is the conviction rate for total cases (74 percent). These data suggest that cases involving adult victims and charges of rape face more hurdles in the legal process than those involving younger-aged victims and charges of USI. The results for age confirm patterns noted by Harris and Grace (1999, p. 32) for England and Wales: the highest rates of conviction are for younger-aged victims (under 13 years) and the lowest for women over 25.

For the comparison trial rates for rape and rape and USI (table 2), England and Wales has a most unusual pattern of a high trial rate (69 percent) and a very low conviction rate at trial (29 percent). The comparison trial rate for the United States is 12 percent; for South Australia, 47 percent; and for Victoria, 52 percent (rape) and 39 percent (USI); all have a much higher rate of conviction at trial than England and Wales.

TABLE 3

Court Cases and Conviction Rates for Sexual Assault by Age of Victim (NSW) and Type of Offense (Victoria)

Charged Offense and Outcome	Outcome % of Total Cases (1)	Trial Rate (Comparison Trial Rate)[a] (2)	N Guilty (3)	Conviction Rate (4)
	A. New South Wales, 2004–6			
Sexual assault and related offenses against children (N = 827):[b]				
Guilty plea (N = 390)	47%	...	390	
Trial (N = 272)	33%	33% (41%)	122	45% (at trial)
Other outcomes (N = 165)[c]	20%	...	...	
Total N cases	827		509	62% (all cases)
Sexual assault and related offenses against adults (N = 793):[d]				
Guilty plea (N = 223)	28%	...	223	
Trial (N = 331)	42%	42% (60%)	116	35% (at trial)
Other outcomes (N = 239)[c]	30%	...	...	
Total N cases	793		339	43% (all cases)
	B. Victoria, 1997–99			
Rape (N = 282):[e]				
Guilty plea (N = 119)	42%	...	119	
Trial (N = 130)	46%	46% (52%)	63	48% (at trial)
Other outcomes (N = 33)[c]	12%	...	...	
Total N cases	282		182	65% (all cases)
Unlawful sexual intercourse (N = 224):[e]				
Guilty plea (N = 121)	54%	...	121	
Trial (N = 77)	34%	34% (39%)	45	58% (at trial)
Other outcomes (N = 26)[c]	12%	...	...	
Total N cases	224		166	74% (all cases)

SOURCE.—Data for New South Wales are from the NSW Bureau of Crime Statistics and Research (2007, p. 2). Data for Victoria on rape are from Victorian Law Reform Commission (2001, pp. 42, 194) and on USI from Victorian Law Reform Commission (2003, pp. 89, 94–95). N's were calculated or adapted from percentages given in the sourced material.

[a] The comparison trial rate is calculated as N cases going to trial/(N guilty pleas + cases going to trial).

[b] Children are those under 18 years. Data include all penetrative offenses (rape, attempted rape, USI) and nonpenetrative offenses (indecent assault and indecency).

[c] Other outcomes include not proceeded with, dismissed, withdrawn, or defendant failed to appear or died.

[d] Includes the same offenses as n. b (above) except USI, which applies only to cases with a victim younger than 16 years.

[e] Victims in rape cases are of all ages, but in USI cases, they are younger than 16 years.

F. Which Victims Are More Credible?

A contentious area of rape case handling in law and legal practice is that inferences are drawn about a suspect's culpability, or a defendant's guilt or innocence, that are based on victim-offender relationships, along with a victim's "character," "credibility," and "conduct." Estrich's (1987) analysis of nineteenth- and twentieth-century rape cases (up to the mid-1970s) in the United States shows a general "distrust" toward women victims, particularly those who knew an offender. Such distrust continued, she argued, in the 1970s and 1980s after the introduction of rape law reform.

In a classic early work, Kalven and Zeisel (1966, pp. 249–57) pointed out that in rape trials, a jury does not focus solely on the question of consent. Rather, "it closely, and often harshly, scrutinizes the female complainant and is moved to leniency . . . when there are suggestions of contributory behavior on her part" (p. 249). Such contributory behavior or a victim's "assumptions of risk" include drinking or going home from a bar with the defendant or having been in a previous relationship with the defendant.[17]

Thus, according to these authors, attention to a victim's character and credibility will emerge more often in some cases (simple rape) than in others (aggravated rape). With some exceptions (e.g., Horney and Spohn 1996), few researchers have directly tested this proposition. Rather, they identify elements that distinguish "genuine" from other victims (Spears and Spohn 1996, p. 192) or "traditional" from "non-traditional" rape victims (La Free 1989). Genuine victims are those having a "good" moral character (e.g., no history of drug or alcohol abuse, of previous offending, or of working in the sex industry); who did not engage in risk-taking behavior before the offense (walking alone at night, hitchhiking, at a bar alone, going home with an offender); who screamed and physically resisted an assault; and who reported the offense right away. LaFree distinguishes traditional women who conform to traditional gender roles from those who do not (p. 51). Like Spears and Spohn (1996), he considers two dimensions of a woman's character and behavior in rape cases: general "lifestyle" and reputation and what occurred just before the offense. Traditional rape

---

[17] Kalven and Zeisel (1966) also say that although a jury is likely to acquit a defendant when there is perceived "contributory fault" by the victim, if it has the option of convicting on a lesser offense, it will do so: "The jury's stance is not so much that involuntary intercourse under these circumstances is no crime at all, but rather that it does not have the gravity of rape" (p. 250).

victims dress modestly, are not sexually active outside marriage, and do not work in "disreputable" occupations; and leading up to the offense, they do not engage in risk-taking behaviors (of the sort already noted).[18]

There is an age base to constructions of genuine and traditional victims and "aggravated" and "simple" rape: they apply to adults, not children. As Spears and Spohn (1996) find in analyzing prosecutors' charging decisions, elements of a child's moral character and reputation, or of risk taking, are not relevant. Few child victim cases can be classified as aggravated since most involve a lone person the child knows, without a weapon or serious physical injury. On the basis of their research, the child victims who are believed are those for whom there is a witness to the offense.

However, in adult victim cases, a woman's character and risk taking do affect police, prosecutor, court, and jury decisions (see citations to studies up to the mid-1990s by Horney and Spohn [1996, pp. 135–36]). Believable and credible adult victims have a good moral character and sexual reputation, and they have not engaged in perceived risk-taking behavior before the incident. Credibility is enhanced when the offense is reported right away rather than some time later and when the accused is someone the victim has never met. In addition to these elements are case and evidence factors, which reinforce (or undermine) a complainant's credibility (as well as the ability to positively identify a suspect). They include witness and forensic evidence, physical injury to the victim, and use of force or a weapon.

II. Questions, Hypotheses, and Doubts

Our study raises questions about conviction rates and their variability, attrition (or retention) rates at different stages in the legal process, and the factors associated with police and court decisions. They are as follows:

QUESTION 1.   With victims' reports to the police as the base, what is the overall rate of conviction (by plea or trial) to any sexual offense and to the original offense?

---

[18] LaFree's terminology of "traditional" and "nontraditional" rape victims differs from how others distinguish traditional and nontraditional rape, with the latter referring to victim-offender relations and offense elements.

QUESTION 2.   Do overall conviction rates vary over time, by country, by age of victim, or by type of offense?

QUESTION 3.   What are the attrition rates at each stage of the legal process?

QUESTION 4.   What is the trial rate and the conviction rate at trial?

QUESTION 5.   For those pleading guilty or found guilty, what percentage receive a detention sentence?

QUESTION 6.   What factors are associated with police and court decisions at different stages of the legal process?

We examine victims' age, character and credibility, and promptness in reporting the offense; victim-offender relationships; the suspect's criminal history; physical/forensic evidence; victim injury; and use of force or weapon.

In addition, we test claims about the changing nature of rape cases reported to the police and the implications this may have for changes in conviction rates. Our review shows that countries vary as to when legal reform began, in trends of reported rape and sexual assault to the police, and in how courts handle cases. We test relationships that flow logically from these dimensions of law and the legal process. Finally, we test the strength and durability of the factors associated with the real rape construct, as we define it, in adult victim cases. Specifically, we test the degree to which stranger relations, victim character and credibility, and evidence factors are related to police and court decisions. Although we expect these factors to play little or no role in child victim cases, we are interested to determine what factors do play a role. We put forward the following hypotheses.

HYPOTHESIS 1.   The overall rate of conviction has decreased over time.

HYPOTHESIS 2.   Countries that initiated legal reform earlier (the United States, Australia, and Canada) have higher overall conviction rates than England and Wales and Scotland, which initiated reform later.

HYPOTHESIS 3.   Attrition is greatest in England and Wales, where rates of report to the police have steadily increased over time, comparison trial rates are highest, and conviction at trial is low.

HYPOTHESIS 4.   The real rape construct is relevant to police and court decisions in adult cases but not in child victim cases.

Hypothesis 1 is derived, in part, from research in England and

Wales, which suggests that rising rates of reported sexual assault to the police, which likely contain more nontraditional cases (known relations and simple rape), have led to reductions in the conviction rate (Harris and Grace 1999; Kelly 2001). It is supplemented by our ministudy, for which we found a higher share of stranger relations in study samples from the 1970s and 1980s than in those from the 1990s onward.

For hypothesis 2, most commentators say that legal reform has had little or no effect on increasing rates of conviction. However, we might expect some organizational change to have occurred in countries where comprehensive legal reform has been in place for some time, which may facilitate higher conviction rates. It is also possible that just the opposite is occurring. Early reform countries may have increasing rates of victims' reports to the police that are not adequately responded to, which result in lower conviction rates.

Hypothesis 3 is generated from police reports and published court data on trial rates and conviction at trial. In contrast to other countries, England and Wales has seen a sharp increase in reports of sexual assault to the police during the 1990s and continuing into the early 2000s. Such increases have likely put pressure on organizational routines and resources in police departments, which have resulted in greater attrition at this stage of the legal process. In addition, British court data suggest a high trial rate but a low conviction rate at trial. In other countries and especially the United States, a greater share of cases are settled by guilty plea, with a lower trial rate and a higher rate of conviction at trial. For hypothesis 4, we have every reason to suspect that the real rape construct remains relevant in police and court decisions in adult victim cases.

Doubts may be raised by the ambitiousness and scale of this research. Virtually all rape case attrition studies focus on one jurisdiction (a city, state, or country) or perhaps several cities or states. None has examined multiple countries or periods as long as 35 years. None has attempted to relate attrition research findings to trends in published police or court data. Few compare findings from adult and child victim samples or, more generally, explore the role of victims' ages in police and court decisions. There are good reasons why researchers have taken their course of action and not ours. They are better able to specify the legal contexts, organizational constraints, and work group practices in the jurisdictions studied. They are better able to separate samples or exclude cases by victims' ages or offense types (although as we shall see, such precision is often lacking in attrition studies). They can be more precise and may have fewer doubts about what they are finding.

In our study, many interpretive doubts flow from using a country level of aggregation, broad time frames, and country- or state-level police and court data that are not strictly comparable. Countries' data may count different things (e.g., rape, USI, both rape and USI, sexual assault), and they may exclude vital clues about legal culture and organizational processes (e.g., the trial rate, conviction at trial, other court outcomes). The attrition studies themselves are not a representative sample of jurisdictions from the five countries but are likely to reflect biases of place (more often urban areas) and researchers' access.

Conviction and attrition rates in rape and sexual assault cases are created from a complex mix of victims' decisions to report certain kinds of cases; police decisions and abilities to locate suspects and proceed with certain cases; and prosecutorial decisions to adjudicate or withdraw certain cases, take pleas, or go to trial. This complexity is occurring within a changing and charged political and social environment in which it is likely that a more heterogeneous set of rape and sexual assault cases are being reported to the police in the last decade or so compared with three decades ago. Comprehensive legal reform may be associated with increasing or decreasing conviction rates, depending on the level of resources, enlightenment, and readiness required for justice officials and members of society to change. Finally, as Frohmann and Mertz (1994) suggest, improving conviction rates is one goal of legal reform; another is changing processes to achieve a more respectful treatment and better understanding of rape victims. Despite these complexities and interpretive doubts, there is much to be gained by exploring broad trends and taking a comparative perspective in understanding the legal response to rape.

III. Study Methods

Our search began by identifying all English-language journal articles, book chapters, reports, and books that investigated the police and court handling of sexual offenses in the legal process. The main countries were the United States, Australia, Canada, England and Wales, and Scotland. We would have wanted to include studies from continental Europe written in English, but only two from Scandinavian countries (Helweg-Larsen 1985; Pentillä and Karhumen 1990) turned up in the search process. As the research progressed, we decided for comparative purposes to examine only common-law countries; thus, these two studies were dropped. Ultimately, the body of work we are describing is limited to practices in common-law, English-speaking countries of the developed world. The findings may provide a platform for future comparative work on common-law and civil-law countries and in nations of the developing world.

A. Inclusion Criteria and Search Strategies

Our search considered all published work up to September 1, 2007, with an open start time because we wanted to include the earliest studies. We discovered two types of studies. One is the *flow study*, which tracks cases through all the stages of the criminal justice system, that is, police, prosecution, and court stages, and presents an overall rate of conviction from report to the police to final court outcome. A second is the *snapshot study*, which analyzes attrition at one or more stages of the legal process and provides the proportion or number of cases that proceeded past the police or past prosecution or resulted in conviction in court. Most flow studies also examined attrition at each stage of the legal process. We used both to estimate overall rates of conviction and attrition at each stage of the legal process and to identify the factors associated with attrition. Four search strategies were used.

First, we consulted major academic sources (e.g., Bryden and Lengwick 1997; Kelly 2000, 2001; Lievore 2003; Koss 2006; Du Mont and White 2007), government sources and reviews (e.g., HM Crown Prosecution Service Inspectorate 2002; NSW Legislative Council 2002; Queensland Crime and Misconduct Commission 2003; NSW Criminal Justice Sexual Offences Taskforce 2005; South Australia Legislative Review Committee 2005), and bibliographies on legal responses to rape and sexual assault.

Second, we searched online databases for study content and well-known authors. Databases that covered a range of disciplinary areas were searched, including criminology, law, social science, and health in English-speaking jurisdictions.

Third, we searched government, research center, and victim advocacy Web sites. For each country, Web sites of justice and health departments, leading criminology research organizations (e.g., Australian Institute of Criminology), and victim advocacy Web sites (e.g., National Center for Victims of Crime) were searched.

Fourth, we reviewed early works on rape and the criminal justice system for citations to other early studies that did not surface in electronic searches.

B. Cases in the Study

Over 90 published and unpublished studies met our criteria. Upon closer inspection, we found that authors sometimes published the results of the same data set in two or more outlets or that two published studies could be combined as one case in our data set. Thus, the initial number of studies reduced to 75 unique cases.[19] These are sorted alphabetically by author surname in appendix A (table A1), which lists the study context, offenses analyzed, data collection period, sample size, and type of attrition and conviction data.

Several studies and reports were considered but dropped. Kelly and Regan (2001; see also Regan and Kelly 2003) provided attrition figures supplied by European government departments, but some figures were doubtful or it was unclear how they were generated. Other studies considered but not included are those by Heenan and Murray (2006) and Brown, Hamilton, and O'Neill (2007), who tracked cases from police reports to charging or court proceedings but did not give court outcomes, and Hanly (2007), who focused solely on jury trials.[20]

C. Assembling the Data Set and Making Estimates

There were many technical challenges in assembling the data set and estimating conviction and attrition rates. We highlight what we did, but a more detailed explanation is contained in appendix B.

1. *Coding the Studies.*   We developed a coding schedule with qualitative and numerical information. The variables included the study's aim, date and length of data collection, jurisdiction, sample size and selection, offense types studied, age and sex of victims and offenders (when given), the number and percentage of cases at each legal stage (police, prosecution, court, trial), overall conviction rate, factors linked

---

[19] The original list of studies and finalized set are available for those interested. We thought we had identified all the studies meeting our criteria but recently learned that we had overlooked an early U.S. attrition study (McCahill, Meyer, and Fischman 1979). That study's overall conviction rate, reported below, is within 1 percentage point of our estimate for the United States in the early period.

[20] Studies that examined factors associated with police or court outcomes but did not examine conviction or attrition rates were not included (e.g., a well-known study by Kerstetter [1990]).

to police and court decisions, study quality score, and a summary of the major findings.

Study samples were gathered in different ways. Most flow studies drew their samples from cases reported to the police. However, the entry points for some studies of child sexual assault were cases reported to a children's hospital or child protection unit; for adult victims, some drew samples from hospital emergency rooms or sexual assault crisis centers. Problems in sample selection bias, if any, were noted.

Studies varied in clarity and precision. At times, it was not clear what the initial base of cases was (e.g., all reports to the police or a smaller subset) nor at what exact stage of the legal process the official file was obtained. This posed problems in estimating conviction and attrition rates accurately, but each problem was resolved by using a consistent set of rules for including or excluding cases. The character and composition of sexual offenses studied varied, and at times, it was not clear which offenses were studied. This was important to code as accurately as possible because as offense categories move from rape and penetrative offenses to broader categories of sexual assault and all sexual offenses, we can expect to see an increasing rate of conviction. This is apparent in countries' court data (tables 2 and 3) and research on youth sex offenses (Daly 2006).

The most frequent flaw in the studies was a lack of detail on victims' ages and inconsistency in defining age ranges. As a result, we could not create discrete age categories. Some studies had victims of all ages, but the authors did not specify the range of ages; in others, the youngest victim age was given, but it ranged from 10 to 18. We ultimately decided on three categories: "adult only" has victims 16 years and older, "mixed age" has victims of all ages, and "child and youth victim only" has victims under 18. Although the adult only and child/youth categories overlap a bit (which reflects distinctions at law for age of consent and offender age classifications), this is of less concern than the omnibus mixed age group. There was nothing we could do about this problem: it reflects how researchers have carried out their studies.

2. *Estimating Attrition and Conviction.*   Once a case is reported to the police, there are four major sites of attrition: whether it moves past the police to prosecution (i.e., an arrest is made and charges are laid), whether it moves past prosecution to court (i.e., the case is listed for adjudication in court), whether it remains in court or is dismissed or withdrawn, and whether or not the defendant pleads guilty or is found

guilty at trial. More detail on the stages of attrition and how each was calculated is shown in appendix B.

A key feature of our study is harmonizing conviction and attrition estimates across studies that have employed differing counting and estimation rules. Appendix B shows how this was accomplished and the rules we used; it describes how we pooled estimates from the flow and snapshot studies to achieve a more stable overall conviction rate and how statistical tests of significance were carried out. We highlight several points. The attrition estimates for the police and prosecutorial stages are somewhat rubbery because administrative practices can vary across and within countries, particularly when there are specialized rape and sexual assault units. We estimate conviction rates in two ways: to any sexual offense and to the original sexual offense. Although some argue that attrition occurs when a conviction is to a less serious sexual offense than that charged (e.g., Kelly 2001, p. 31), we do not define attrition this way. Charge or sentence bargaining is an inevitable feature of the criminal court process, although it may be practiced to a greater degree in some countries than in others.

3. *Assessing Study Quality.*   Studies varied in quality and precision; for this reason, we spent considerable time determining whether they should be weighted differently. Although the literature on study quality focuses mainly on meta-analysis and randomized experiments (e.g., Farrington 2003), this was not applicable to our review. Rather, drawing from Khan et al. (2001, p. 5), we are analyzing a set of "case studies." Appendix B describes a study quality score and conviction and attrition results with an unweighted sample and two types of weighted samples. There were nil or negligible differences between the three samples; thus, we use the unweighted sample.

IV. Findings on Conviction, Attrition, and Factors
Affecting Outcomes

Of the 75 study cases, about half (48 percent) are from the United States (see table 4, col. 1). Over half (53 percent) analyze penetrative offenses only (rape, attempted rape, and USI); the rest analyze a broader array of sexual offenses. Over half (54 percent) have victims of mixed ages; 17 percent, adults only; and 29 percent, child and youth victims only. In an analysis not shown in the table, we found that a much higher share of child or youth victim cases were associated with

TABLE 4

Description of the Rape Attrition Study Sample

	All Cases: Percent (N) (1)		Cases with an Overall Conviction Rate:[a] Percent (N) (2)	
Country:				
United States	48	(36)	41	(27)
Australia	23	(17)	25	(16)
Canada	13	(10)	15	(10)
England and Wales	12	(9)	14	(9)
Scotland	4	(3)	5	(3)
Total	100	(75)	100	(65)
Data period:				
Early period: 1970–89	51	(38)	52	(34)
Later period: 1990–2005	49	(37)	48	(31)
Victims:				
Adult only (16+)	17	(13)	14	(9)
Mixed age	54	(40)	58	(38)
Child/youth victims only (<18)	29	(22)	28	(18)
Type of offense:				
Rape and penetrative offenses	53	(40)	52	(34)
All sexual offenses[b]	47	(35)	48	(31)
Stages of attrition in the criminal justice system:[c]				
Police	49	(36)		
Prosecution	54	(40)		
Court	81	(60)		
Trial	49	(37)		
Sentencing	28	(21)		

[a] Pooled sample estimates come from the flow studies (N = 38) and a portion of the snapshot studies (N = 27) (excludes outlier case 59).

[b] Includes penetrative, touch, and no touch sexual offenses.

[c] The percentages add to greater than 100 because a study may look at several stages of the criminal process (excludes outlier case 59).

a broader set of sexual offenses (94 percent) compared to mixed age victim (32 percent) or adult only victim (22 percent) cases.

The year of data gathering ranges from 1970 to 2005. Estimates cluster in two phases: earlier (1970–89 data) and later (1990–2005 data). These two phases also correspond to older and newer ways of researching sexual victimization. Thus, it seemed logical to use these indicators to draw a temporal line in our analysis. These earlier and later phases do not coincide with pre- and postlegal reform because all five countries had some type of legal reform by the end of the 1980s, although some had gone substantially further than others. Rather, the more recent period (1990 forward) can be viewed as a time when legal reform matured, when there was a more developed consciousness by victims (and victim support groups) of expanding definitions of rape, and when more research attention was given to sample surveys of physical and sexual victimization, using more sensitive methods. Studies from the earlier period are mainly from the United States (63 percent), whereas those from the later period have a better mix (United States, 32.5 percent; Australia, 35 percent; Canada, 11 percent; England and Wales, 16 percent; and Scotland, 5.5 percent).

Other descriptors, not shown in the table, are as follows. Data gathering ranged from 2 months to 12 years; in most cases, there is a 12–24-month time frame. Australia and the United States are governed by state-level legislation. Most of the Australian cases are from New South Wales (47 percent) or Victoria (29 percent); for the United States, the jurisdictions are more dispersed, often with multiple states or cities studied.[21] Canadian criminal law is the same across the provinces, although most attrition studies are from Manitoba (40 percent) and British Columbia (30 percent).

A. Overall Conviction Rates

Table 5 displays the overall rates of conviction for any sexual offense and for the original sexual offense, based on estimates generated from the flow and snapshot studies.[22] For the averages across all countries (top rows), it can be seen that across three decades, the average (mean) overall conviction rate is 15 percent, and conviction to the original offense charged by the police is 9 percent.[23] When we disaggregate by time period, the overall rate of conviction for any sexual offense in the early period is 18 percent but reduces significantly to 12.5 percent in

---

[21] For the United States, the majority of the studies were conducted in states in the Northeast, Midwest, Southwest, and West. No studies were from states in the South.

[22] For all estimates of conviction and stage attrition, the decision was made to exclude case 59 (Patterson 2005) because it tested a special emergency room program (the SANE program) that produced unusually high rates of conviction; however, this study is included in the analysis of factors associated with attrition.

[23] Here and in all tables, we report all conviction and stage attrition rates to 0.5 percent. Results that were xx.3 percent or less were rounded down; results that ranged from xx.4 to xx.6 percent were reported as xx.5 percent; and results that were xx.7 percent or up were rounded up.

TABLE 5

Combined Overall Rates of Conviction from Flow and Snapshot Studies by Country

	1970–2005 (1)	1970–2005 (2)	1970–89 (3)	1990–2005 (4)	Difference (%) (5)
		Conviction to			
	Any Sexual Offense	Original Sexual Offense	Any Sexual Offense		
All countries	$N=65$	$N=22$	$N=34$	$N=31$	
Range (%)	7–35	5–19	11–35	7–19	
Mean (%)	15	9	18	12.5	-5.5[a]
			Original Sexual Offense		
All countries			$N=11$	$N=11$	
Range (%)			6–19	5–10	
Mean (%)			11	6.5	-4.5[b]
	Any Sexual Offense	Original Sexual Offense	Any Sexual Offense		
United States	$N=27$	$N=6$	$N=20$	$N=7$	
Range (%)	7–18	6–13	7–17	11–18	
Mean (%)	13	8	13[c]	14	$+1.0$
Australia	$N=16$	$N=7$	$N=4$	$N=12$	
Range (%)	7–20	6–12	14–20	7–17	
Mean (%)	13	10.5	17	11.5	-5.5[a]
Canada	$N=10$	$N=1$	$N=6$	$N=4$	
Range (%)	11–32	9	19–32	11–17	
Mean (%)	21	...	26.5	14	-12.5[a]
England and Wales	$N=9$	$N=6$	$N=3$	$N=6$	
Range (%)	7–35	5–19	11–35	7–12	
Mean (%)	15	8.5	24	10	-14.0[a]
Scotland[d]	$N=3$	$N=2$	$N=1$	$N=2$	
Range (%)	13–19	10–15	18	13–19	
Mean (%)	17.5	14	...	17.5	...
Four-country[e]	$N=38$	$N=16$	$N=14$	$N=24$	
Range (%)	7–35	5–19	11–35	7–19	
Mean (%)	16.5	9.5	23	12	-11.0[a]

[a] Significant drop in convictions from the early to the later period, $p < .01$.
[b] Significant drop in convictions from the early to the later period, $p < .05$.
[c] The U.S. conviction rate is significantly lower than the four-country rate, $p < .05$.
[d] Like all the estimates, the Scottish estimates are based on an average of the snapshot and flow studies that gives more weight to the flow studies. See app. table B2.
[e] Australia, Canada, England and Wales, and Scotland.

the later period. The corresponding figures for conviction to the original sexual offense are 11 percent and 6.5 percent, respectively.

For conviction rates by country across time (cols. 1 and 2), the mean rates are somewhat lower for the United States (13 percent), Australia (13 percent), and England and Wales (15 percent) compared with Scotland (17.5 percent, an estimate based on only three studies)[24] and Canada (21 percent). These averages belie a more complex story of variability by country and time period, which is shown in table 7 below. This is visualized in two ways. Figure 2 shows overall conviction rates for all studies as a scatter plot. Figure 3 gives the best-fitting line by country (excluding Scotland, which has too few cases). For the United States, the overall conviction rates are nearly identical in the earlier and later time periods (13 and 14 percent, respectively). By contrast, the rates for Australia, Canada, England and Wales, and Scotland (a four-country average) decreased significantly: from 23 to 12 percent.[25] The generally low rate of conviction for the United States, although unusual in the earlier period, is typical of the rates for England and Wales, Canada, and Australia in the later period. From 1990 onward, there is less dispersion in conviction rates for the five countries.

Drawing from Kelly's (2001) analysis, several commentators have noted a large drop in conviction rates in England and Wales (e.g., Lievore 2004; Koss 2006). On the basis of our analysis, there is a considerable drop, but how much of a drop depends on which studies are used and what is defined as the "conviction rate" (i.e., conviction to any sexual offense or to the original sexual offense). Some may rely only on the inflated statistic initially reported by Grace, Lloyd, and Smith (1992) of 34 percent (since corrected by the authors to 27 percent; see Harris and Grace 1999) and San Lazaro, Steele, and Donaldson's (1996) estimate of 35 percent. However, another British study, which is on the cusp of the early and later period as we define it (Gregory and Lees 1996; data period midpoint 1989), found an 11 percent conviction rate. For the earlier period, then, we calculate the average attrition rate from three British studies to be 24 percent. Because the United States and Canada have more studies from the earlier

---

[24] The Scottish estimate of 17.5 percent is an average of one snapshot and two flow studies that gives more weight to the flow studies; it is not a straight arithmetic average. See app. table B2.

[25] We include Scotland in this average, although its pattern of conviction differs from that of the other three countries. If Scotland is excluded, a three-country average is nearly the same: 23.5 percent and 11.5 percent in the early and later period, respectively.

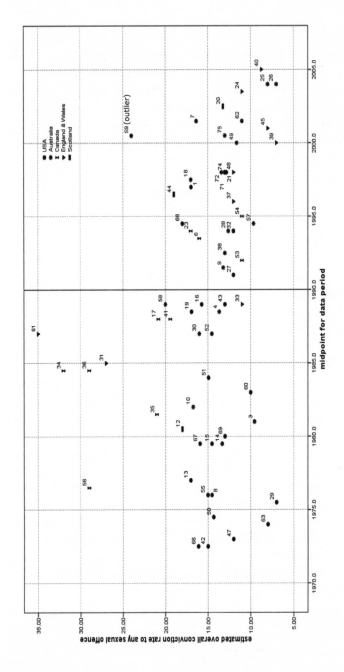

FIG. 2.—Estimated overall conviction rate to any sexual offense: each study's outcome

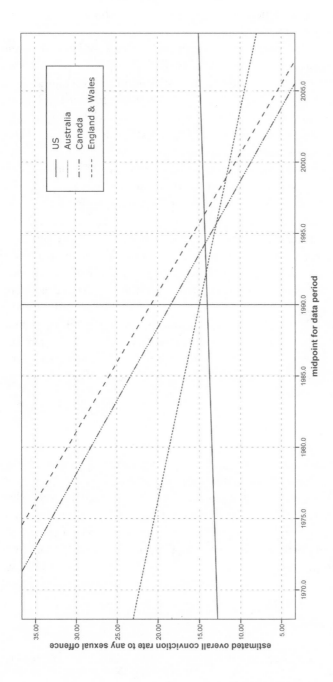

FIG. 3.—Estimated overall conviction rate to any sexual offense: best-fitting line by country

period, we can be somewhat more confident of temporal trends from these two countries.

In summary, overall rates of conviction for rape and sexual assault have remained the same in the United States (13–14 percent over time).[26] Studies from Canada show a significant decrease in rates of conviction from the early and later periods (from 26.5 to 14 percent). Those from Australia also show a significant decline (from 17 to 11.5 percent),[27] although not as large as Canada's. For England and Wales, overall conviction rates have dropped significantly, from 24 to 10 percent. Averages for Scotland remain stable over time (18 and 17.5 percent), but there are just three estimates. Countries' average conviction rates are more dispersed in the earlier period (ranging from 13 to 26.5 percent) than in the later period (10–14 percent, excluding Scotland).

For victim's age and types of offense (table 6), across the three decades, overall rates of conviction are somewhat higher in samples of child or youth victims (18.5 percent) than those of mixed age (15 percent) or adults only (12 percent). Over time, there is a significant drop in conviction for mixed age (16.5 to 13 percent) and child or youth victim cases (22 to 13 percent). Significant differences in conviction are evident by type of offense, both across time and in the more recent time period, with an expectably lower rate for rape and penetrative offenses (13 percent), compared to a broader range of sexual offenses (17 percent).

B. Attrition by Stage of the Legal Process

Data from the flow and snapshot studies were joined to estimate attrition at each stage of the criminal process (table 7). Across all time periods and five countries, after cases are reported to the police, 65 percent are dropped; in other words, 35 percent proceed past the police to the prosecution. From the prosecutor's desk, 66 percent proceed to court. Once in court, 66 percent of cases are convicted of any sexual offense and 42 percent are convicted of the original sexual offense. On average, 38 percent of cases go to trial, and 58.5 percent are found guilty at trial. Of those convicted, 60 percent are sentenced to incarceration, but we do not know what percentage actually served time

---

[26] The overall rate of conviction in McCahill, Meyer, and Fischman (1979) was 12 percent.

[27] In Triggs et al.'s (2009) study of adult victim "sexual violation" cases in 2005–7 for New Zealand, the overall rate of conviction to any sexual offense was 14 percent, which falls within the 10–14 percent range found in our study.

TABLE 6

Combined Overall Rates of Conviction from Flow and Snapshot
Studies by Victim Age and Offense Type

	1970–2005	1970–2005	1970–89	1990–2005	Difference (%)
			Conviction to		
	Any Sexual Offense (N = 65)	Original Sexual Offense (N = 22)	Any Sexual Offense (N = 65)		
By age of victims:					
Adult (16+)	N=9	N=6	N=3	N=6	
Range (%)	8–18	6–15	11–18	8–13	
Mean (%)	12	9.5	14	11	−3.0
Mixed age	N=38	N=14	N=20	N=18	
Range (%)	7–29	5–19	7–29	7–19	
Mean (%)	15	9	16.5	13	−3.5[a]
Child/youth (<18)	N=18	N=2	N=11	N=7	
Range (%)	7–35	9–12	10–35	7–18	
Mean (%)	18.5	11	22	13	−9.0[a]
By type of offense:					
Rape and penetrative	N=34	N=20	N=16	N=18	
Range (%)	7–29	5–19	7–29	7–17	
Mean (%)	13[c]	9	15.5	11	−4.5[a]
All sexual offenses[b]	N=31	N=2	N=18	N=13	
Range (%)	7–35	11–12	10–35	7–19	
Mean (%)	17	12	20.5	14	−6.5[a]

[a] Significant drop in convictions from the early to the later period, $p < .05$.

[b] Includes penetrative offenses, touch, and no touch sexual offenses.

[c] The conviction rate for rape and penetrative offenses is significantly lower than for all sexual offenses, $p < .05$.

because studies do not report suspended or partially suspended sentences. The average across time and countries for our measure of "case flow into court" (the product of police and prosecutor decisions) is 23 percent.

Table 8 gives selected findings by age of victim and offense type across time. Case flow into court is higher for child or youth cases (26 percent) than for mixed age (23 percent) or adult cases (21 percent).[28] Of cases in court, conviction is significantly less likely in samples of

[28] We use "case flow into court" here and in table 9 because, in part, the police and prosecutor figures are variably measured and in part to simplify presentation of the data.

TABLE 7

Proportion of Cases That Proceed Past the Different Stages
of the Criminal Justice Process across All Countries and Time
Periods

	Cases That Proceed	
Criminal Justice System Stage[a]	Range (%)	Mean (%)
Of cases reported to police, those referred for prosecution (N = 36)	15–56	35[b]
Of cases referred for prosecution, those referred to court (N = 40)	33–87	66
Of cases in court, those convicted of any sex offense (N = 60)[c]	35–88	66
Of cases in court, those convicted of original sex offense (N = 21)[c]	25–67	42
Of cases in court, those going to trial (N = 33)	11–75	38
Of trial cases, those found guilty at trial of any sex offense (N = 37)	27–94	58.5
Of cases sentenced,[c] those with incarceration imposed (N = 21)[d]	22–97	60

[a] The N's in parentheses refer to the number of studies that provided information at each stage considered.
[b] Case flow into court: 23 percent (35 percent × 66 percent).
[c] Includes those found guilty at trial and those who pleaded guilty.
[d] Incarceration imposed includes both suspended and nonsuspended sentences.

adults only (53 percent) compared to those of mixed ages (67 percent) or children or youths (70.5 percent). Trial rates are significantly lower in child or youth cases than in mixed age or adult cases, but conviction at trial is similar across age groups. The likelihood of an incarceration penalty is significantly lower in child or youth cases (49.5 percent) than in adult cases (73 percent). The findings for age are linked to the types of offenses analyzed. Rape and penetrative offenses have a significantly higher rate of cases going to trial (43 percent) than the broader category of all sexual offenses (29 percent), and they attract a higher rate of detention. The trial and detention rates for adult and mixed age victims are based largely on analyses of rape and penetrative offenses only, whereas those for child or youth victims are based on a wider set of sexual offenses. We acknowledge that these analyses by victim's age and offense type are not entirely satisfactory: except for adult only and rape and penetrative offenses only, the age and offense categories are not discrete but overlapping. Future research needs to take better care in coding and analyzing victims' ages and types of offenses.

TABLE 8

Rates of Case Flow into Court, Court Conviction, and Sentencing Outcome by Victim Age and Offense Type (%)

	Flow into Court	Court Conviction to Any Sex Offense	Cases Going to Trial	Trial Conviction to Any Sex Offense	Incarceration Imposed
By age of victim:					
Adult (16+)		$N=9$	$N=7$	$N=8$	$N=5$
Range		35–76	18–74	27–94	46–97
Mean	21	53[a]	46.5[b]	55	73
Mixed age		$N=34$	$N=14$	$N=15$	$N=5$
Range		43–88	15–75	38–89	48–88
Mean	23	67	43	59	69.5
Child/youth (<18)		$N=17$	$N=12$	$N=15$	$N=11$
Range		44–85	11–48	36–87	22–69
Mean	26	70.5	28	60	49.5[c]
By type of offense:					
Rape and penetrative		$N=32$	$N=21$	$N=22$	$N=6$
Range		35–88	15–75	31–94	48–97
Mean	21	64	43[d]	59	73
All sexual offenses[e]		$N=28$	$N=12$	$N=15$	$N=15$
Range		42–87	11–48	27–87	22–89
Mean	25	68	29	57.5	55

[a] Rate for adult cases is significantly lower than that for mixed age and child/youth cases, $p < .05$.
[b] Rate for adult cases is significantly higher than that for child/youth cases, $p < .05$.
[c] Rate for child/youth cases is significantly lower than that for mixed age and adult cases, $p < .05$.
[d] Rate for penetrative offenses is significantly higher than that for all sexual offenses, $p < .05$.
[e] Includes penetrative offenses, touch, and no touch sexual offenses.

C. Attrition at Police and Court Stages by Country and over Time

Table 9 arrays the stage outcomes by time and country, and it shows that the story of attrition is again more complex than one average across one time period or place. We reiterate that these estimates are averages derived from the available body of research studies, not from a sample of jurisdictions. For all countries combined, there is a reduction in case flow into court from the early to the later period (from 26 to 20 percent); this arises from significant reductions in the rate at which cases proceed past the police and prosecution into court. This average masks important country differences.

For the United States, there is no change over time in the case flow

TABLE 9
Rates of Case Flow into Court, Court Conviction, and Sentencing Outcome by Time and Country (%)

	Flow into Court		Court Conviction to Any Sex Offense		Cases Going to Trial		Trial Conviction to Any Sex Offense		Incarceration Imposed	
	1970–89	1990–2005	1970–89	1990–2005	1970–89	1990–2005	1970–89	1990–2005	1970–89	1990–2005
All countries										
Mean	26	20	N=32 69.5	N=28 62[b]	N=14 34	N=19 41	N=15 64	N=22 54.5	N=11 63	N=10 57
Countries:[a]										
United States										
Mean	20	19	N=18 69	N=5 82[b]	N=8 32.5	N=4 20	N=9 68.5	N=6 82[b]	N=7 62.5	N=3 77
Australia										
Mean	20.5	20	N=4 74	N=12 61[c]	N=3 36	N=9 45	N=3 60	N=10 41[c]	N=2 52	N=5 41
Canada										
Mean	35	26[c]	N=6 72	N=4 53[c]	N=2 31.5	N=0 ...	N=2 62	N=0 ...	N=2 74.5	N=2 65.5
England and Wales										
Mean	34	17[c]	N=3 68	N=6 57	N=0 ...	N=5 51	N=0 ...	N=5 46	N=0 ...	N=0 ...

[a] Rates for Scotland are not shown because there are too few cases for each time period. Range of conviction rates is shown in table 5.
[b] Rates for the later period are significantly higher than those for the early period; $p < .05$ for court; $p < .10$ for trial.
[c] Rates for the later period are significantly lower than those for the early period, $p < .05$.

into court (about 20 percent in both periods) but a significant increase in conviction to any sexual offense once cases are in court (from 69 to 82 percent). The rate at which cases go to trial has declined from the early to the later period (32.5 to 20 percent), and the rate of conviction at trial has increased significantly (68.5 to 82 percent). Canada evinces a different pattern: a significant decrease in case flow into court, although it remains relatively high (from 35 to 26 percent), and a significant drop in conviction once cases are in court (from 72 to 53 percent). (There are too few studies to calculate trial rates or convictions at trial for Canada.) The pattern is different, yet again, for Australia. In the earlier period, the flow into court, court conviction, and trial rates and outcomes are comparable to those of the United States. Yet, in the later period, there is a significant decrease in conviction once cases are in court (from 74 to 61 percent). The rate of cases going to trial increases somewhat (from 36 to 45 percent), but the rate of conviction at trial drops significantly (60 to 41 percent).[29]

The pattern for England and Wales is similar to Canada's, although its reduction in case flow into court is more dramatic, dropping significantly from 34 to 17 percent. Data not shown in the table show that this drop is caused mainly by a significant reduction in cases proceeding past the police (from 45 to 27 percent), more so than a reduction in cases proceeding past prosecution into court (from 75 to 63 percent). Once cases are in court, the rate of conviction declines from the early to the later period (68 to 57 percent). For the later period, the trial rate and conviction at trial are similar to Australia's.[30]

In summary, studies from the United States and Australia show a stable pattern of high rates of attrition at the police and prosecution stages over two time periods (80 percent of cases dropped). However, rates of court conviction have increased significantly in the United States but decreased significantly in Australia. Canada has a relatively high case flow into court; however, this has decreased significantly over time, and court conviction has dropped sharply. For England and Wales, case flow into court has decreased significantly, and as in Aus-

[29] The figures for Australia are nearly identical to those reported in Johnson, Ollus, and Nevala (2008, p. 148) for Australia from the IVAWS project: of nonpartner sexual and physical violence cases reported to the police, 23 percent resulted in charges laid (case flow into court); once in court, 63 percent resulted in conviction. The findings are based on what victims recalled during an interview.

[30] For England and Wales, the later period estimate of conviction at trial from our attrition study (46 percent) is considerably better than that given in British court data for 2005 (29 percent; see table 2 above).

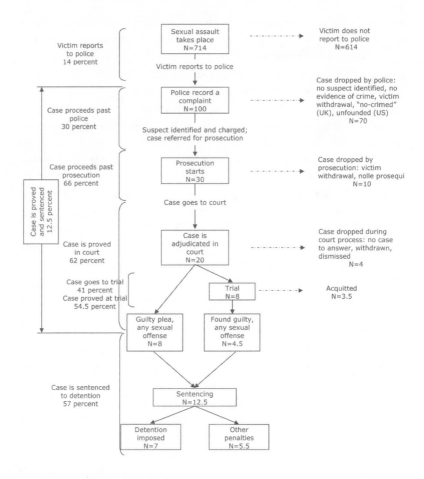

FIG. 4.—The journey of 100 cases reported to police, five countries, 1990–2005

tralia and Canada, court conviction has declined, although not as sharply.

D. The Journey of 100 Cases Reported to the Police

A staple item in the rape attrition literature is a chart displaying the journey of 100 cases reported to the police. This is constructed from a selected set of studies, typically from one country, and often with little attention to the years of data gathering. Now that we are aware of country and temporal variation, it will be difficult to construct just one journey. Figure 4 illustrates the attrition process for the five countries combined in the later period.

The largest source of attrition is a victim's decision to report the assault to the police or not, with 14 percent on average reporting offenses. For every 100 sexual offenses reported, there are over 600 instances of sexual victimizations not reported. Of 100 reported cases, 70 do not go further than the police stage. The reasons are many: the inability to identify or locate a suspect, victims' withdrawing complaints, and police judgments that the case will be difficult to prosecute for a range of reasons. Once the case has been referred to the prosecutor's office, the rate of attrition decreases. About one-third of cases are dropped before reaching court because prosecutors have doubts of securing a conviction at trial, or a victim is unwilling or unable to continue as a witness, among other reasons. Of the 100 reported cases, 20 are adjudicated in court. Of cases in court, eight go to trial, eight are settled by guilty plea to the same or less serious offense, and four are withdrawn or dismissed. Just over half the trial cases are convicted of a sexual offense. Of 100 cases reported to the police, 12.5 percent are convicted of a sexual offense.

E. Factors in Police, Prosecutorial, and Court Outcomes

Of the 75 studies, 43 (57 percent) analyzed one or more factors associated with police or prosecutorial or court decisions to drop cases or proceed with them, and 10 of the 43 were of child or youth victims only. Typically, the studies coded information in police, prosecution, and court files. It is unlikely that any factor was used in arguments in open court, although this was not explicitly mentioned. We sought to determine if the set of 75 studies differed along key variables from the 43 that analyzed factors. Our analyses revealed no differences in conviction and attrition rates; thus, we are satisfied that our results can be generalized.

1. *Coding the Factors.*   The nine factors studied were constructions of the victim and the offense (age, sex, character and credibility, promptness in reporting, and victim-offender relations); the suspect's background (criminal history); and strength of evidence (forensic and witness evidence, victim injury, suspect's use of force or weapon).[31] Table 10 lists the factors, their definition and content, and coding de-

---

[31] We did not analyze the impact of racial and ethnic classifications of victims or offenders on outcomes. Eleven studies (all from the United States) presented data about the race/ethnicity of a victim or offender, but the effects on outcomes were not recorded in a comparable manner. Sex is relevant to studies of child or youth victims but not to other age groups.

TABLE 10

Factors Related to Police and Prosecution/Court Decisions: Definitions, Coding, and Distributions

Factor	Definition	Percent of Studies with Factor[a]		Coding
Factors relating to the victim and the construction of the offense:				
Victim's age	Age of victims to compare outcome for younger or older victims	A/MA CY	79 100	All studies: age or age range in years as reported in study Adult and mixed age: not studied
Victim's sex	Victim's sex (child/youth only) to determine if this matters	A/MA CY	0 60	Child/youth only: sex of victim as reported in studies
Victim's good character and credibility	Characteristics that legal officials interpret as showing the victim's "good" moral character and credibility	A/MA CY	58 20	All studies: elements include the victim did not engage in risky behavior before the rape, did not use alcohol or drugs before the rape, never had consensual intercourse with the suspect before the rape; has little sexual experience, no criminal record, and story is consistent Child/youth only: relevant for adolescent victims only
Victim's promptness in reporting	Time between the sexual assault and the victim's report to the police; delay in reporting may give rise to a suspicion that the victim made up the story; relates also to victim credibility	A/MA CY	42 50	All studies: hours between the assault and report to police or indication of promptness as reported in studies Child/youth only: relevant for adolescent victims only

Suspect is stranger	Relationship between victim and suspect; stranger relation is the main focus for adult victims; literature suggests that stranger cases are more likely to proceed and result in conviction	A/MA CY	88 90	All studies: stranger vs. known suspect (e.g., friend, acquaintance, work colleague, family member) At police stage, suspect is stranger was coded as + or − related to laying charges only when, as far as could be determined, the relationship was not linked to the ability to identify a suspect, but to police decision making to drop or proceed; for comparability, all studies were coded in the same way, regardless of victim age
Factors relating to the suspect: Suspect has criminal history	Suspect's history of arrests or convictions; suspects known to the police may more likely be arrested or prosecuted	A/MA CY	33 20	All studies: previous conviction for sexual or nonsexual offense; or the suspect is known to police, with a previous arrest or having been questioned
Factors relating to evidence: Forensic or witness evidence	Elements or persons that corroborate or confirm the victim's story and identify a suspect	A/MA CY	67	Adult and mixed age: elements such as forensic evidence of the offender's presence, the presence of semen in the victim's vagina, or a third party witnessing the sexual assault Child/youth only: see below

611

TABLE 10 (*Continued*)

Factor	Definition	Percent of Studies with Factor[a]		Coding
Victim's injury/victim resistance	Evidence such as injury or marks on the victim's body or verbal expression (screaming) seen as evidence of victim's nonconsent	A/MA CY	88 70	Adult and mixed age: physical injuries to the victim, evidence of physical resistance, or verbal expression of nonconsent Child/youth only: forensic or witness evidence and victim's injury coded as a single factor incorporating all elements because few studies examined these factors
Suspect's use of force/weapon	Evidence that the suspect forced or threatened the victim into sexual activity, seen as evidence of victim's nonconsent	A/MA CY	67 0	Adult and mixed age: suspect used or threatened to use force or a weapon against the victim Child/youth only: factor not studied

[a] A/MA = adult and mixed age victims (*N* = 33); CY = child/youth victims (*N* = 10).

cisions made. Initially, we had intended to investigate three decision contexts of police, prosecution, and court. However, most studies did not make precise distinctions between prosecution and court decisions; thus, we combined them as one outcome context. The coding notes on table 10 (col. 3) show decisions made in the analysis and, where relevant, coding decisions in child or youth victim cases.

For the 33 studies of adult and mixed age victims, the most frequently investigated factors are victim-offender relations, victim injury, and victim age (about 80–88 percent); next is witness or physical evidence, weapon/use of force, and victim character and credibility (about 60–67 percent), followed by promptness in reporting (42 percent) and suspect's criminal history (33 percent; see table 10, col. 2). About half the studies each are from the early and later period. About half are from the United States; Canada and England and Wales each contribute nearly 20 percent and Australia the rest.

2. *From Studies to Observations.*   Because the studies analyze police or prosecution and court decisions, and often both, it is important to distinguish these and to see each as an "observation" from the study. The 33 studies produced a total of 281 observations of positive, negative, or no relationship to the factor: 38 percent from the police stage and 62 percent from prosecution and court. With an analysis of observations as the focus, the number of findings for each factor can be increased. Thus we are better able to examine similarities and differences in the strength and direction of the factors for police and prosecution and court decision making. Each observation was coded according to the direction of the effect: positively, negatively, or no association, with the case proceeding past the police to the prosecutor or convicted in court. Appendix C displays the outcomes of the factors for the 43 studies, with table C1 for the adult and mixed age studies and table C2 for child or youth studies. A plus (+) indicates a positive correlation; a minus (−), a negative correlation; ellipses (…), no relation; and a dash (--), that the factor was not considered in the study.

3. *Effects of Factors on Case Outcomes for Adult and Mixed Age Cases.* Table 11 shows the effects of seven factors for the early and later periods for adult and mixed age victim cases (the victim's age is discussed below, and the victim's sex is considered only in the child/youth studies). In the results for the early period and with both stages combined, the factor evincing the most consistent effect on police and court de-

TABLE 11

Impact of Each Factor on Police and Court Outcome, by Time Period: Adult and Mixed Age Victims

Stage	Victim's Good Character and Credibility (%)	Victim's Promptness in Reporting (%)	Suspect Is Stranger (%)	Suspect's Criminal History (%)	Forensic/Witness Evidence (%)	Victim's Injury/Resistance (%)	Use of Force/Weapon (%)
			Early Period 1970–89				
All stages	$N=18$	$N=9$	$N=21$	$N=12$	$N=20$	$N=24$	$N=15$
(+) effect	89	33	48	58	45	67	47
Police	$N=7$	$N=3$	$N=8$	$N=5$	$N=8$	$N=10$	$N=6$
(+) effect	100	33	38	80	13	70	50
Prosecution/court	$N=11$	$N=6$	$N=13$	$N=7$	$N=12$	$N=14$	$N=9$
(+) effect	82	33	54	43	67[a]	64	44
			Later Period, 1990–2005				
All stages	$N=13$	$N=12$	$N=28$	$N=3$	$N=16$	$N=25$	$N=22$
(+) effect	38[b]	33	25[c]	67	50	76	55
Police	$N=5$	$N=4$	$N=12$	$N=3$	$N=6$	$N=10$	$N=9$
(+) effect	40[d]	25	41	0	50	80	67
Prosecution/court	$N=8$	$N=8$	$N=16$	$N=3$	$N=10$	$N=15$	$N=13$
(+) effect	38[c]	38	13[d,e]	67	50	73	46

[a] Significantly stronger impact on prosecution/court than on police outcome, $p < .05$.

[b] Significant drop in later period, $p < .01$.

[c] Significant drop in later period, $p < .10$.

[d] Significant drop in later period, $p < .05$.

[e] Significantly stronger impact on prosecution/court than on police outcome, $p < .10$.

cisions is the victim's character and credibility (89 percent). Next is the presence of injuries (67 percent) and the suspect's criminal history (58 percent). Close to half of the observations show that stranger relations (48 percent), use of force or weapon (47 percent), and forensic or witness evidence (45 percent) affected legal outcomes. On the basis of the research literature, we might have expected to see an even greater influence of stranger relations in the earlier period, but this dichotomy may fail to capture a range of relationships that affect police and court decisions.

In the later period with police and court and prosecution stages combined, the picture changes significantly for two factors: the influence of victim character and credibility decreases significantly (from 89 to 38 percent), as does stranger relations (from 48 to 25 percent).[32] Forensic or witness evidence, injury, and weapon factors increase somewhat (by 5–9 percentage points), although the increase is not statistically significant. There are too few studies to analyze country and temporal variation, but we combined Australia, Canada, and England and Wales and then compared their combined results with those for the United States for each time period. The pattern of results is the same for the two groups.

A similar temporal pattern appears when the data are disaggregated by police and court/prosecution decisions. The effect of the victim's character and credibility is strong in the early period for police (100 percent) and prosecution and court (82 percent) decisions but drops significantly in the later period for both. The drop in the effects of stranger relations is significant for prosecution and court decisions, but not for police decisions. Just one factor had differential effects for the police compared to prosecution or court: forensic or witness evidence differentiated prosecution and court outcomes, but not those for the police, and only in the early period. In the later period, this factor had a similar influence on police and prosecution/court outcomes. Although not statistically significant, the effect of the forensic or witness evidence at the police stage increases by over 35 percentage points from the early to the later period.

The 33 studies suggest that the real rape construct, as we define it, is more strongly evinced in the earlier period but attenuates somewhat in the later period, with a significant reduction in the effect of a victim's

[32] With small N sizes, we consider relationships significant at the $p < .10$ level.

Kathleen Daly and Brigitte Bouhours

character and credibility and stranger relationships on police and prosecution and court decisions. At the same time, the continued strength of the three evidence factors suggests that independent evidence of nonconsent (e.g., a third-party witness, physical injuries, weapon present) and specific kinds of evidence (i.e., marks on the victim's body) are required. Whereas socially constructed notions of "good" and "bad" victims may have relatively less influence in decision making in the more recent period, the legal requirement for physical evidence of nonconsent remains. Across the two time periods, a victim's prompt reporting affects one-third of cases; there are no police/court differences and no change over time. This aspect of victim credibility plays some role in officials' decision making, but not as strongly as other factors. Across the two time periods, the suspect's having a criminal history does affect police and prosecution and court outcomes. This factor receives relatively less attention in the literature, but our study suggests that constructions of "good" and "bad" offenders are also relevant in understanding attrition, with the latter group more likely to be retained in the criminal process or convicted.

Of the 33 studies, 26 analyze the victim's age, and there are 43 observations from police and court decisions. Age is a difficult factor to assess because studies contain victims of varied age ranges, results are reported imprecisely, and the age relationship is itself complex. Of the 43 observations, a substantial minority (42 percent) show a positive relationship between younger-aged victims and police proceeding or prosecution and court outcomes. "Younger-aged" includes victims termed simply "younger," "teenagers," and under the ages of 18, 16, and 13. However, in about half the cases ($N = 22$), the victim's age did not differentiate decisions, and for three, the direction of the relationship appeared to be opposite what we expected.[33]

4. *Effects of Factors on Case Outcomes for Child or Youth Victims.* For the 10 child or youth victim studies, the typical factors analyzed are the age of victim, stranger victim-offender relations, physical evidence, and the victim's sex (see table 10 and app. table C2). Of 13 observations for age, an age threshold can be discerned in five: cases with victims aged 5–10 years are more likely to proceed past the police or be pros-

[33] Cases 41 and 43 have positive court outcomes for victims over 6 and 13 years of age. For case 47, a negative sign for police outcomes (not proceeding with the case) is explained by the fact that both victims were under 18 and the offense occurred between peers.

ecuted or convicted than those with younger victims. In two, prosecution or court conviction is more likely when victims are younger (with no age cutoff given), but in six, there is no effect of age. The 10 observations for the victim's sex show no consistent pattern of cases proceeding: there is no effect in five, three show effects for female victims, and two show effects for male victims. Of 12 observations for stranger relations, just one had an effect, with nonstranger cases more likely to be convicted (this is explained by a higher guilty plea rate for intrafamilial offenses). Of 10 observations for forensic or witness evidence, just three were related positively to police and prosecution/court decisions.

Several points can be drawn. First, it is important to distinguish the handling of cases by victim's age. As we expected, for younger victims, the real rape construct is irrelevant: neither the victim's character or credibility nor stranger relations bear on legal outcomes, and the role of forensic or witness evidence is relatively less influential. Second, when there is an effect of victim's age, it is complex. Across all 43 studies, most observations (about 55–60 percent) show no or contrary effects of age; for adult and mixed age samples, effects are evident for those cases with younger victims or younger than 13–18; for child or youth victims, cases with victims older than 5–10 years are more likely to proceed or be convicted. Future research can be improved in these ways: by analyzing the age gap between victim and offender, not just the absolute age of victims and offenders; being mindful of an "age threshold" below which victims may be considered "too young" for police or prosecutors to proceed; and being more precise in describing victims' ages. Third, for adult and mixed age samples, there appears to be a positive development in the more recent period with a reduction in the effect of a victim's character and credibility and stranger victim-offender relations on police and prosecution and court decisions. It is not clear how this finding relates to the significant decline in overall conviction in three countries but stability in two others. The continuing (and increasing) importance of the evidence factors for adult and mixed age samples suggests that independent proof of nonconsent (injuries, another witness, use of weapon) remains important for successful prosecution and conviction of cases.

V. Taking Stock of Attrition Research: Questions and Hypotheses Reprised

This study is the first to review and assess in a systematic fashion three dimensions of rape case attrition in the legal process: estimates of the overall conviction rate, estimates of case attrition at different stages of the legal process, and the factors associated with conviction and attrition. We assembled, analyzed, and harmonized the findings of 75 studies from five common-law countries over three decades. To contextualize and understand variation in conviction and attrition rates by country and over time, we introduced comparative material on the emergence and consolidation of legal reform, victims' reporting patterns from victimization surveys, police statistics on reported rape, and published court data on rape and sexual assault.

Our review is comprehensive and synthetic, but it is prudent to note its limitations. The estimates of conviction and attrition, along with the factors associated with attrition, are not derived from a representative sample of jurisdictions from the five countries. Rather, they come from places that permitted researcher investigation, perhaps places that were proximate to researchers' universities or government departments; and they describe the police and court handling of rape in largely, although not exclusively, urban areas. Thus, our claims about the temporal and country variation in rape case attrition are made from the information available, and the number of cases is not large. The range in the percentages for overall conviction rates and attrition rates at different stages of the legal process should also alert readers that in many jurisdictions, outcomes often stray from the averages. Variation by region, state or province, or local area within countries, including remote and reserve areas of Indigenous and Native peoples (Amnesty International 2007), especially in the United States, Canada, and Australia, is likely to be considerable, but until there are more studies and data available, we are unable to say more than this.

The initial impetus behind this study—to identify the "average rate of conviction" to sexual offenses of those reported to the police—was, in hindsight, naive. As our investigations progressed, we learned why. Conviction estimates and rates of attrition depend on when and where research is conducted, types of offenses, and the age of victims. Average rates may tell us something, but they mask temporal, country, and other sources of variability.

Our study had six questions and four hypotheses. Questions 1–5 were about the overall rate of conviction for sexual offenses reported to the police and attrition at particular stages of the criminal justice system. Across three decades in five countries, the average overall rate of conviction to any sexual offense is 15 percent and to the original offense, 9 percent. Conviction and attrition rate averages can be misleading, however, because they vary over time and by country.

The overall conviction rate in the earlier period (1970–89) is 18 percent but drops to 12.5 percent in the later period (1990–2005). The United States and Scotland are unique among the five countries in showing no decline, although the number of Scottish cases is small. Of all countries, England and Wales and Canada have the largest decline in conviction rates (14 and 12.5 percentage points, respectively). In Australia, the decline is less dramatic (5.5 percentage points). Changes in countries' overall conviction rates reflect different patterns of case attrition. For England and Wales, there is a large drop in the case flow into court, coupled with a relatively high trial rate; for Canada, there is a slight drop in case flow into court but a large drop in court conviction; and for Australia, there is a decline in court conviction only. In the later period, England and Wales and Australia show a similar pattern of high trial rates (45–51 percent) but low conviction rates at trial (41–46 percent; unfortunately, trial data are lacking for Canada and Scotland). By comparison, in the later period, the United States has a low trial rate, higher conviction at trial, and overall a higher court conviction rate.

Conviction rates are also sensitive to the ages of victims and offense types. Averages across time and country show that child or youth victim cases are more likely to result in conviction than adult victim cases (18.5 percent compared to 12 percent, respectively) and that rape and penetrative offenses are less likely to be convicted than a broader set of sexual offenses (13 percent and 17 percent, respectively).

Hypothesis 1, that there is a decline in conviction rates over time, is confirmed when using aggregated conviction rates, but it does not hold when disaggregated by country. Rates of conviction decreased in England and Wales and Canada and, to a lesser degree, in Australia, but not in the United States. Compared to the earlier period, overall conviction rates are more similar in the later period, ranging from 10 to 14 percent, for four countries (excluding Scotland).

Hypothesis 2, that the early reform countries would have higher overall rates of conviction than the later reform countries, is not confirmed because no consistent pattern emerges. Overall conviction rates for the later period are somewhat higher for two of three early reform countries (the United States and Canada at 14 percent) and lower for one of two later reform countries (England and Wales at 10 percent). However, the hypothesis is not supported with conviction rates for Australia and Scotland.

Hypothesis 3, that England and Wales would show the highest degree of attrition over time, is supported. Unlike other countries, England and Wales has seen an unusually high rate of increase in reported sexual assault to the police from 1996 to the present. We cannot be sure why such increases are occurring, but among other reasons, we suspect that recent, more comprehensive legal reform and victim supports have contributed to more victims coming forward with complaints. The flow into court percentage has dropped from the earlier to the later period (34 to 17 percent), the largest of any country. This may reflect, in part, increased caseload pressure on police resources and organizational routines and, in part, a changing composition of sexual assaults reported to the police in England and Wales.

Of the five jurisdictions studied, just one—England and Wales— evinces a clear pattern between increases in the rate of reporting sexual assault to the police, decreases in the flow of cases into court, and decreases in the overall rate of conviction. In Australia, there were increases in rates of reporting sexual assault, with a decrease in the overall conviction rate but no change in the flow of cases into court. The other countries do not evince any of these relationships. In Canada, the reported rate of sexual assault has decreased, and so too has the flow of cases into court and the overall conviction rate. In the United States, the reported rate of rape has decreased, but the overall conviction rate has stayed about the same. In Scotland, which has just three studies, there are some increases in reported sexual assault but no change in conviction rates.

One problem in making sense of these complex relationships is that we are drawing from different levels of aggregation and sources of information, particularly for Canada, Australia, and the United States, for which trends in national rates of reported rape and sexual assault are being compared with those in the specific jurisdictions where attrition studies have been carried out, not a representative sample of jurisdictions by state or province.

Although victimization surveys in the United States, studies in England and Wales, and our ministudy show that more "nontraditional" types of rape and sexual assault (i.e., those involving known relations) are being reported to the police from the early 1990s to 2005, a factor that may be associated with decreasing rates of conviction in the later period, our study does not have adequate information to tease out the complexities of this relationship across all countries with certainty. The relationship is not evident for Canada or the United States, where there is a clear decline in reported rape or sexual assault. It is possible, of course, that rates of reported rape and sexual assault can be decreasing while at the same time nontraditional rapes reported to the police are increasing.

For question 6, on the continued relevance of the real rape construct for adult and mixed age victim studies, there is mixed support. The main factors associated with cases proceeding past the police and prosecution and court outcomes in both time periods were evidence related (forensic or witness evidence, victim injury, and weapon present). However, whereas the victim's character and credibility had a strong influence on police and court decisions in the early period, this reduced significantly in the later period. Both this factor and stranger victim-offender relations had relatively less impact on outcomes in the later period. Evidence factors remain important over time; and from this, we may infer that the state's burden of proving nonconsent remains a constant. In both time periods, the suspect's criminal history affected police and prosecutorial and court decisions, but a victim's promptness in reporting the offense was relatively less important.

As expected, the real rape construct has little relevance for child or youth victim cases. It appears that the standard factors used in attrition studies do not adequately differentiate police, prosecutorial, and court decisions in child or youth victim cases. Even factors that might differentiate outcomes (e.g., sex of the victim) were not associated in any consistent way. Future research needs to explore what does matter in police and prosecutor or court decisions in these cases.

We have answered questions about rape case attrition in the criminal justice system, but many more have been raised. We consider just two. Why do patterns of prosecution and conviction in U.S. courts differ from those in England and Wales, Canada, and, to a lesser degree, Australia? What explains decreases in conviction rates in some countries but not in others?

The United States has a longstanding practice of plea bargaining.

Published court data and our analysis of attrition studies show that U.S. trial rates are lower, conviction rates at trial are higher, and most convictions are secured by guilty pleas; this is especially evident in the more recent period. Some decades ago, Polk (1985) showed that California court practices differed from those in England and Wales in having a lower case flow into court but higher court conviction rates. This approach to prosecution in the United States (which is likely applicable to many offenses, not just to rape) has been a standard organizational practice for as long as courts have been studied in that country. By comparison, England and Wales, Australia, and Canada came to plea bargaining later, as an officially recognized practice.

From the early to the later period in the United States, case flow into court rates did not change, and conviction by plea bargaining increased. There was a drop in the trial rate and an increase in the rate of conviction at trial. By comparison, in England and Wales, case flow into court dropped greatly over time to levels at and below that of the United States, but prosecutorial practices did not adjust. Rather, the standard organizational practice of going to trial continued, despite moderate levels of conviction at trial. Offense composition, in particular, an increasing share of nontraditional rapes, coupled with an increased press of cases on police and court resources, have likely played a role in reducing overall conviction rates in England and Wales. But in addition, compared to the United States, the greater emphasis in British court culture on adjudication and conviction by trial, rather than disposition by plea and sentence bargaining, has likely affected outcomes.

Rather than asking, why did the conviction rate in the United States not decrease over time, we may wonder why it was lower in the 1970s and 1980s compared to other countries. This is difficult to know. The pattern for the United States in the early period is quite similar to that of Australia: a low flow into court rate, a similar rate of court conviction, and a similar rate of cases going to trial and convicted at trial. However, Australia's overall conviction rate is a bit higher in the early period; differences are more apparent in the later period in the court and trial conviction patterns of the two countries.

VI. What Should Be Done?

In 2008 we began presenting these findings on conviction and attrition to many people at seminars and conferences. They ask us, what should be done? No one answer satisfies them. For some time, we have been conducting research on innovative justice responses to rape and sexual assault, comparing court and conference (restorative justice) responses to youth sex offending in Australia (e.g., Daly 2006, 2008; Daly and Curtis-Fawley 2006; Bouhours and Daly 2007). We are now examining other contexts of sexual violence (e.g., in postconflict societies). It is clear that an individualized model of prosecution and trial is not relevant or workable in these contexts and that other social mechanisms must be identified. A global perspective is required that considers widely varying contexts of rape and sexual assault; for now, we consider any city in North America, Australia, or the United Kingdom.

First, in working largely within the legal system, the focus of legal reform must shift away from the rape trial and its evidentiary hurdles and toward mechanisms that encourage admissions by offenders (only those who are factually guilty, of course) at a very early stage. This includes, but is not limited to, more sophisticated police interviewing and better plea-bargaining skills of prosecutors and defense attorneys; there may also be a range of positive reasons to make very early admissions (such as no conviction recorded). Legal practitioners must reassess their sources of professional status and success: rather than adversarial trial heroics, greater emphasis could be placed on negotiating skills and acumen (Daly 2008; see also Freiberg 2007). Many people do not like this component because they think it will result in coerced admissions, increasing criminalization, and rising incarceration. That is not what we envisage. Rather, a changed societal context is required in which "sex offenders" are less stigmatized and demonized and in which sexual offending is recognized as being varied in seriousness and not necessarily requiring a criminal law response. Rather than negative and punitive legal mechanisms upon conviction (such as offender registries), more socially inclusive and integrative approaches should be used. Many people do not like this component either, but for other reasons: they believe it may send the "wrong message" that sexual violence is not being taken seriously. Both components are required, however, if a more innovative justice response to sexual violence is to succeed.

Second, and again working within the legal system, victims, offend-

ers, and others affected by sexual offenses could have greater participation and voice. A variety of sentencing and plea-taking alternatives
is possible, but these can be set in motion only after an admission to
offending. Restorative justice conferences as a supplement to court sentencing or as a presentence activity, post–guilty plea (Sherman et al.
2005), or part of a guilty plea (Combs 2007) could give victims a
greater opportunity to describe the effects of an offense, for offenders
to understand that what they did was wrong and harmful, and for others to check and challenge denials of wrongdoing (Daly and Curtis-
Fawley 2006). Again, many people do not like this idea (see, e.g., Cossins 2008). Indeed, with the exception of New Zealand, a pilot project
in Arizona, and some jurisdictions in Australia, Belgium, and the
United Kingdom, restorative justice conferencing for sexual offenses is
not permitted as a sentencing option. When it is used, it is almost
exclusively for youth sex offending.

Frohmann and Mertz (1994) identified dual goals of legal reform:
"efficacy" (increasing convictions) and "process" (better treatment and
understanding of victims). We have proposed ways to improve efficacy
(although with an emphasis on admissions more than convictions) and
to improve the process with greater victim participation. The third set
of proposals considers ways to improve processes for victims outside
the criminal justice system or when reported cases are subsequently
withdrawn from court adjudication. Less is written about these contexts, which is ironic because it is what the vast majority of victims
experience.

There are a variety of circumstances to consider, among them: a
victim may want to *disclose* an offense to someone but not *report* it to
the police; a victim may report a case and there is strong evidence, but
the police are unable to locate a suspect; a victim's case may not be
strong legally, although the police and prosecutor believe her story.
There are many groups in civil society (e.g., rape crisis centers and
faith groups) that already facilitate disclosure and assist victims. Their
work could be widened to include informal justice activities. For reported cases that are subsequently withdrawn, informal justice activities
could be used, such as restorative justice conferences without offenders
or other types of meetings that can validate and vindicate a victim's
story. Victim advocates now recognize that because "the wishes and
needs of victims are often diametrically opposed to the requirements
of legal proceedings" (Herman 2005, p. 574), more effective mecha-

nisms of "social acknowledgment, support, validation from the community, and vindication" (pp. 574, 585) are needed. These may operate as informal justice processes within civil society or within criminal or civil justice, or as formal justice processes that do not rely on a standard criminal justice model of prosecution and trial.

The way forward, then, is identifying a menu of options for victims and offenders within and outside the legal system; having a more inclusive and less demonizing response to sex offending; giving greater attention to the earliest stages of the legal process (or even prior to a legal process) before a suspect's denials harden; allowing greater participation of victims and offenders during plea taking and presentence; and reducing an emphasis on trial heroics and adversarialism by members of the legal profession. We acknowledge Temkin and Krahé's (2008) proposal for further rape law reform and educational campaigns to change attitudes about sexual behavior. Their ideas have merit, but a more radical change agenda is required, with a focus on greater participation, social support, and societal inclusion of offenders, victims, and others affected by sexual offending and victimization. Incremental legal reform will not get us there.

TABLE A1

Studies in the Review, Overall Conviction Rates, and Stages of the Legal System Examined

ID	Authors	Study Features[a]	Place	Data Period	Length of Study (Mos.)	N[b]	Offense[c]	V's Age[d]	Overall Convic. Orig. (%)	Overall Convic. Any %	Proc. Pol. (%)	Proc. Pros. (%)	Convic. Court Orig. (%)	Convic. Court Any (%)	% Going to Trial (%)	Of Trials, Guilty (%)	Incarc. Impd.
1	Beichner and Spohn 2005	Factors	U.S., KS, FL	1996–98	24	399	Rape, penetrative offenses	12+	...	17	x	x	...	x	x	x	...
2	Bouffard 2000	Factors	U.S., urban district not specified	1995	12	326	Felony sexual assault	16+	...	...	x	...	...	...	...	...	...
3	Bradshaw and Marks 1990	Factors, CY	U.S., TX	1975–87	144	350	Felony sexual offense	<18	...	9.5	...	x	...	x	x	x	...
4	Brereton 1993		Aus., VIC	1988–89	24	319	Rape and attempted rape	Mixed	9	14	...	x	x	x	x	...	...
5	Brewer et al. 1997	Factors, CY	U.S., SW	1989–90	18	200	Sexual offenses against children	<18	...	...	...	x	...	...	...	...	...
6	BC Ministry of Attorney General 1997	Flow	Canada, BC	1993–94	24	1,709	Penetrative offenses and indecent assault	Mixed	...	16	x	x	...	x	...	...	x
7	Cahill 2004	CY	U.S., OR	2001–2	24	65	Sexual assault against youths	12–17	...	16	...	...	...	x	x	x	...
8	Caringella-MacDonald 1985b		U.S., MI	1975–77	36	135	Rape and attempted rape	Mixed	...	14.5	x	x	...	x	...	...	...
9	Cashmore 1995	Factors, CY	Aus., NSW	1991–92	12	263	Child sexual assault	<18	...	13	...	...	...	x	x	x	x
10	Cashmore and Horsky 1987, 1988	Factors, CY	Aus., NSW	1982	12	235	Indictable offenses	<18	...	17	...	...	...	x	x	x	x
11	Cashmore and Trimboli 2005	CY	Aus., NSW	2004	10	50	Child sexual assault	<18	...	...	...	...	...	...	...	x	...
12	Chambers and Millar 1983, 1986	Flow, Factors	Scotland, Edinburgh, Glasgow	1980–81	15	196	Rape and attempted rape	18+	15	18	x	x	x	x	x	x	...
13	Chandler and Torney 1981	Flow, Factors	U.S., HI	1976–78	24	260	Rape	Mixed	...	17	x	x	...	x	x	x	x
14	Chapman and Smith 1987		U.S., VA, NJ, CA	1978–81	48	123	Felony sexual assault	18+	...	13	...	...	...	x	...	...	x
15	Chapman and Smith 1987	CY	U.S., CA, NJ, VA	1978–81	48	154	Felony sexual offense	<18	...	14.5	...	...	...	x	x	x	x
16	Cheit and Goldschmidt 1997	CY	U.S., RI	1985–93	108	1,138	Felony sexual offense	<18	...	16	...	...	...	x	x	x	x
17	Clark and Hepworth 1994	Flow	Canada	1988	12	29,111	Rape and sexual assault	Mixed	...	21	x	x	...	x	x	...	...
18	CMC 2003[b]		Aus., QLD	1994–2001	Varies by stage	27,349/ 12,451	All sexual offenses	Mixed	...	17	x	x	...	x	...	...	...
19	Cross et al. 1995	CY	U.S., CA, IA, MN, NY	1988–89	12	552	Child sexual assault	<18	...	17	...	x	...	x	x	x	x
20	Crown Office and Procurator Fiscal 2006[e]		Scotland	2002–3	12	610/ 228	Rape	18+	10	13	...	x	x	x	x	x	x

21	Daly 2006[f]		Aus., SA	1995–2001	78	344	All sexual offenses	Mixed	11	13	...	...	x	x	...	...	...
22	De Jong and Rose 1991	Factors, CY	U.S., Philadelphia	1987–88	12	115	Felony sexual offense	<18	...	...	...	...	...	...	...	x	...
23	Du Mont and Myhr 2000	Flow, Factors	Canada, ONT	1994	12	187	Sexual assault	15+	...	17	x	x	...	x	...	...	...
24	Feist et al. 2007	Flow, Factors	England and Wales	2003–4	12	676	Rape and attempted rape	Mixed	5	11	x	x	x	x	x	x	...
25	Fitzgerald 2006	Flow, Factors	Aus., NSW	2004	12	4,132	Sexual assault, indecent assault, acts of indecency	16+	...	8	x	...	...	x	...	...	x
26	Fitzgerald 2006	Flow, Factors, CY	Aus., NSW	2004	12	3,752	Sexual assaults, indecent assault, acts of indecency	<16	...	7	x	...	...	x	...	...	x
27	Frazier and Haney 1996	Flow, Factors	U.S., MW	1991	12	569	Rape and attempted rape	16+	...	12	x	...	...	x	...	...	...
28	Gallagher et al. 1997	CY	Aus., NSW	1994	12	501	Child sexual assault	<16	...	12.5	...	...	...	x	x	x	x
29	Galvin and Polk 1983	Flow	U.S., CA	1974–77	48	11,249	Rape	Mixed	...	7	x	x	...	x	x	x	x
30	Goddard and Hiller 1992	Flow, CY	Aus., VIC	1987	10	64	Child sexual assault	<15	...	16	x	x	...	x	...	...	...
31	Grace et al. 1992	Flow, Factors	England and Wales	1985	3	464	Rape and attempted rape	Mixed	19	27	x	x	x	x	...	...	...
32	Gray-Eurom et al. 2002	Flow, Factors	U.S., FL	1993–95	24	774	Sexual assault	12+	...	12	x	x	...	x	...	...	...
33	Gregory and Lees 1996	Flow, Factors	England and Wales, London	1988–90	24	109	Rape and attempted rape	16+	8	11	x	x	x	x	...	...	...
34	Gunn and Linden 1994	Flow, Factors, CY	Canada, Winnipeg	1984–85	24	340	Child sexual abuse	<17	...	32	x	x	...	x	x	x	x
35	Gunn and Linden 1997	Flow, Factors	Canada, Winnipeg	1981–82	24	315	Penetrative offenses and indecent assault	Mixed	...	21	x	x	...	x	...	...	...
36	Gunn and Linden 1997	Flow, Factors	Canada, Winnipeg	1984–85	24	523	Penetrative offenses and indecent assault	Mixed	...	29	x	x	...	x	...	...	...
37	Harris and Grace 1999	Flow, Factors	England and Wales	1996	12	483	Rape	Mixed	6	12	x	x	x	x	...	...	...
38	Heenan and McKelvie 1997		Aus., VIC	1992–93	24	251	Rape, penetrative offenses	Mixed	7	13	...	...	x	x	x	x	...
39	HMCPSI 2002[e]	Factors	England and Wales	2000	12	1,741/230	Rape	Mixed	6.5	7	x	x	x	x	x	x	...
40	HMCPSI 2007[e]		England and Wales	2005	12	752/75	Rape	Mixed	...	9	x	...	...	x	x	x	...
41	Hobson 2002	Factors	Canada, Halifax	1983–93	132	328	Sexual assault	Mixed	...	19.5	...	...	...	x	...	...	x
42	Holmstrom and Burgess 1978	Flow, Factors	U.S., Boston	1972–73	12	110	Rape	Mixed	7	15	x	x	x	x	x	x	...
43	Horney and Spohn 1996	Flow, Factors	U.S., Detroit	1989	12	653	Rape	16+	6	13	x	x	x	...	...	...	...
44	Jamieson 2001	Flow	Scotland	1996–97	15	78	Rape and attempted rape, indecent assault	Mixed	...	19	x	x	x	x	...	...	...
45	Kelly et al. 2005	Flow, Factors	England	2000–2002	24	2,284	Rape	Mixed	...	8	x	x	...	x	x	x	...
46	Kingsnorth et al. 1998	Factors	U.S., CA	1992–94	36	365	Rape and attempted rape	14+	...	...	...	...	...	...	...	x	x
47	LaFree 1989	Flow, Factors	U.S., IN	1970–76	36	881	Forcible sex offenses	Mixed	...	12	x	x	...	x	x	x	x
48	Lea et al. 2003	Flow, Factors	England, SW	1996–2000	60	341	Rape and attempted rape	16+	6	12	...	...	...	...	...	...	...
49	Lievore 2004	Factors	Aus., NSW, ACT, NT, WA, TAS	1999–2001	24	141	Rape	16+	8	11.5	...	x	x	x	x	x	...
50	Loh 1980	Factors	U.S., Seattle	1972–77	72	445	Forcible sex offenses	Mixed	9.5	14	...	x	x	x	...	...	...
51	Mac Murray 1989, 1991	Factors, CY	U.S., Boston	1983–85	24	144	Child sexual assault	<18	...	15	...	x	...	x	...	...	x
52	Martone et al. 1996	CY	U.S., Chicago	1986–88	24	66	Felony sexual offenses against children	<17	...	14.5	...	...	...	x	x	x	...
53	McGregor et al. 1999	Flow, Factors	Canada, Vancouver	1992	12	95	Sexual assault	10+	...	11	x	x	...	x	...	...	...
54	McGregor et al. 2002	Flow, Factors	Canada, BC	1993–97	60	462	Sexual assault	Mixed	...	11	x	x	...	x	...	...	x
55	McNickle Rose and Randall 1978	Flow	U.S., SW	1976	2	129	Sexual assault	Mixed	...	15	x	x	...	x	...	...	...
56	Minch et al. 1987	Flow, Factors	Canada, Winnipeg	1976–77	24	211	Rape and attempted rape	Mixed	9	29	x	x	x	x	x	x	...
57	NSW Department for Women 1996		Aus., NSW	1994–95	12	150	Sexual assault excluding indecent assault	16+	...	10	...	...	...	x	x	x	...

TABLE A1 (*Continued*)

ID	Authors	Study Features[a]	Place	Data Period	Length of Study (Mos.)	N[b]	Offense[c]	V's Age[d]	Overall Convic. Orig. (%)	Overall Convic. Any %	Proc. Pol. (%)	Proc. Pros. (%)	Convic. Court Orig. (%)	Convic. Court Any (%)	% Going to Trial	% Of Trials, Guilty (%)	Incarc. Impd.
58	Parkinson et al. 2002	CY	Aus., Sydney	1988–90	24	163	Child sexual assault	5–15	12	20	…	…	x	x	x	x	x
59	Patterson 2005[a]	Factors	U.S., MI	1999–2002	39	185	Rape	18+		24	x	x	x	x	x	x	x
60	Rambow et al. 1992	Flow, Factors	U.S., Minneapolis	1983	12	182	Sexual assault	16+	…	10	x	x	…	x	…	…	…
61	San Lazaro et al. 1996	Flow, CY	England, North	1986–88	24	154	Child sexual assault	<16	…	35	x	x	x	x	…	…	…
62	Snodgrass 2006	Flow	U.S., AK	2000–2003	36	1,032	Rape and sexual assault	Mixed	…	11	x	x	x	x	…	…	…
63	Soules et al. 1978	Flow	U.S., Denver	1974	5	99	Rape	9+	5	8	…	…	…	x	…	…	…
64	Spears and Spohn 1997	Factors, CY	U.S., Detroit	1989	12	132	Child sexual assault	<13	…	…	…	x	…	x	…	…	…
65	Spohn and Holleran 2001	Factors	U.S., Kansas City, Philadelphia	1996–98	36	526	Rape and sexual assault	12+	…	…	…	x	x	x	…	…	x
66	Spohn and Horney 1993	Factors	U.S., Detroit	1970–75	60	279	Rape and sexual assault	Mixed	13	16	…	…	x	x	…	…	…
67	Spohn and Horney 1993	Factors	U.S., Detroit	1975–84	120	533	Rape and sexual assault	Mixed	12.5	16	…	…	x	x	…	…	…
68	Stroud et al. 2000	Flow, Factors, CY	U.S., NM	1993–96	48	957	Child sexual assault	<18	…	18	x	…	…	x	x	…	…
69	Tintinalli and Hoelzer 1985	Flow, Factors	U.S., Detroit	1980	6	372	Rape	13+	9	13	…	…	x	x	…	…	x
70	U.S. Senate Committee 1993	Flow, Factors	U.S., 10 states	1990	12	7,530	Rape	16+	…	…	…	…	…	…	…	…	…
71	Victorian Law Review Commission 2001		Aus., VIC	1997–99	24	357	Rape	Mixed	6	13	…	x	x	x	x	x	…
72	Victorian Law Review Commission 2003	CY	Aus., VIC	1997–99	24	258	USI	<16	9	13.5	…	x	x	x	x	x	…
73	Weninger 1978	Factors	U.S., TX	1970–76	72	201	Rape and attempted rape	Mixed	…	…	x	…	…	x	…	x	…
74	Wiley et al. 2003	Flow	U.S., urban district not specified	1997–99	33	888	Sexual assault	15+	…	13	…	…	…	x	x	x	…
75	Wundersitz 2003	Flow, CY	Aus., SA	2000–2001	12	952	All sexual offenses against children	<18	…	13	x	x	x	x	…	…	x

[a] This variable lists selected elements of the studies: "flow" indicates that the study reported on overall conviction rate; "factors" that the study examined one or more factors and is listed in app. B; "CY" that the study focuses on child/youth victims (under 18 years) only; if it also includes factors, it is listed in app. table B2.

[b] Number of cases in the attrition analysis. If the analysis covers the whole legal process, it is the number of cases reported to the police; otherwise, it is the number of cases at the first stage considered.

[c] This classification is based on the seriousness of the legal charges as reported by the study author(s).

[d] When the victim's age was not given in the study, we classified victim ages as mixed.

[e] Study is based on snapshots of the criminal justice system. Figures in the N column are N in police sample/N in court sample.

[f] This is the only study that focuses on youth offenders (<18 years) who were dealt with in the Youth Court and by conference.

[g] This study is not included in the rate analysis because it is an outlier, but it is included in the analysis of factors linked to conviction.

APPENDIX B
Estimating Attrition and Conviction

A. Youth Suspects

For the flow studies, the cases reported to the police included all suspects, regardless of age. In most of these studies, the authors then dropped any youths from subsequent analyses, and appropriately so, because they would be handled in other court jurisdictions. Of the flow studies, 11 reported the number of youths dropped, and we were able to correct the number of suspects at the police stage accordingly. For 19 flow and snapshot studies, however, it was not clear if youth suspects were included or not in the sample; this is a possible source of "false attrition." On the basis of the 11 flow studies with sufficient information, we estimate that the proportion of youth suspects in samples of sexual assault cases reported to the police ranges from 11 to 22 percent (mean, 16 percent). This proportion varies according to the offenses considered: more youth suspects are in studies of child victims than of adult victims.

B. Stages of Attrition and Calculations

When a victim reports a rape or sexual assault to the police, they may record the complaint but then classify the case as "unfounded" (United States and Canada) or "no crimed" (England and Wales and Scotland) because it is deemed not to be a crime. Attrition at the police stage also occurs when no suspect can be identified, the victim withdraws the complaint, or there is not enough evidence to charge a suspect. After a suspect is arrested and charged, prosecutors may drop the case if they think a conviction is unlikely; or the victim may withdraw because she does not want to go through a trial. Once in court, cases may be dismissed or withdrawn by officials. If the case goes to trial, a judge or jury may find the defendant not guilty. Table B1 shows how attrition and conviction are calculated in this study.

C. Harmonization

Harmonization required that we apply our counting and estimation rules systematically across the studies. At times, this meant that we needed to correct estimates made by the study author(s) to ensure that our estimates were accurate and comparable. Here we consider three points about the estimates: police base rates, sites of attrition, and defining conviction.

Police base rates are a crucial starting point in any study because they form the basis for all subsequent calculations of attrition and conviction. Some authors included, but others excluded, cases that the police classified as unfounded or no crimed. When possible, we recalculated a study's conviction rates to include unfounded and no crimed cases in the police base rates. This is conventional practice in attrition research today and for good reason: there is significant temporal and jurisdictional variation in the degree to which cases are deemed unfounded or no crimed (in 1973, 1 percent of rape complaints to the police were deemed unfounded in Detroit and 54

TABLE B1
Method of Calculating Key Variables

Percentage of Cases That	Rate
Proceed past police[a]	N cases referred for prosecution $\div$ N cases reported to police
Proceed past prosecution	N cases in court $\div$ N cases referred for prosecution
Are convicted of any sex offense[b]	N convicted of at least one sex offense $\div$ N cases in court
Are convicted of original sex offense	N convicted of original sex offense $\div$ N cases in court
Go to trial	N cases going to trial $\div$ N cases in court
Are convicted at trial of any sex offense	N convicted at trial of at least one sex offense $\div$ N cases going to trial
Are sentenced to incarceration[c]	N cases with incarceration imposed $\div$ N cases convicted of any offense
For 38 flow studies:	
M_{flow} = mean overall rate of conviction to any sex offense	N convicted of at least one sex offense $\div$ N cases reported to police
$M_{flow/orig}$ = mean overall rate of conviction to original sex offense	N convicted of original sex offense $\div$ N cases reported to police

[a] Denominator includes "no crimed" or "unfounded" cases.

[b] In studies with little detail provided, the convicted offense could be a nonsexual offense.

[c] No study specified whether the incarceration was to serve or was wholly or partially suspended.

percent in Chicago; see Estrich 1987, pp. 15–16). Part of what is occurring is attrition based on police judgments of a complaint's credibility and character.

Attrition at different stages of the legal process is an important point of our investigation, but decision-making sites are not always precise or clear. For example, comparing two U.S. jurisdictions, Spohn and Holleran (2001) noted that in Kansas City, the decision to charge a suspect with sexual assault was made by a specialized prosecution unit, whereas in Philadelphia, the decision was made by the police before the case reached the specialized prosecution unit. Thus, attrition (or retention) in the charging decision occurred in the prosecutor stage in Kansas City but in the police stage in Philadelphia. The attrition estimates for the police and prosecutorial stages, in particular, should be viewed as somewhat rubbery.

D. Estimating Overall Conviction Rates

The 38 flow studies provide the most accurate estimate of the overall rate of conviction. However, we augmented the pool of studies by computing

TABLE B2
Four Steps in Estimating Overall Conviction Rates from 65 Studies

Step 1: flow into court
Flow into court = mean % of cases that are referred to court:[a]
$$P_{police} \times P_{prosec}$$
P_{police} = mean % cases that proceed past police[b]
P_{prosec} = mean % cases that proceed past prosecution[b]

Step 2: estimating overall rates of conviction for 27 snapshot studies
We applied the flow into court measure for the relevant country and time period to each of the 27 snapshot studies:
$$\text{Flow into court} \times \text{\% convicted of at least one sex offense}$$

Step 3: estimate from pooled flow and snapshot studies[c]
Mean overall rates of conviction from 38 flow studies and estimates from 27 snapshot studies:
$$M_{pooled} = \frac{\Sigma \text{overall rates of conviction from flow studies} + \text{estimates from snapshot studies}}{65}$$

Step 4: harmonizing rates from flow studies and estimates from snapshot studies
Final overall rate of conviction reported:
$$(M_{flow} + M_{pooled})/2$$
M_{flow}: mean overall conviction rate from flow studies only ($N = 38$; see table 4)
M_{pooled}: mean overall rate of conviction from pooled flow and snapshot studies ($N = 65$; see step 3)

NOTE.—Calculations are shown for conviction to any sexual offense; where possible, we calculated conviction to original sexual offense using the same principle and relevant data.

[a] Each mean is computed from both flow and snapshot studies.

[b] We calculated the flow into court by country and time period by multiplying P_{police} and P_{prosec} for each relevant country and/or time period. Results were as follows: early period: United States, 19.9 percent; Australia, 20.4 percent; Canada, 34.7 percent; England and Wales, 34.1 percent; Scotland, 38 percent; later period: United States, 19.2 percent; Australia, 19.7 percent; Canada, 26.3 percent; England and Wales, 16.8 percent; Scotland, 38 percent.

[c] The N of studies in the nominator and denominator will reduce by country and time period.

estimates of conviction from the 27 snapshot studies that had a rate of court conviction. We did this in four stages as shown in table B2.

In step 1, we constructed a measure of the flow into court, that is, the proportion of cases reported to the police that were referred to court for adjudication. The flow into court measure is the product of two estimates: the mean rate of cases that proceeded past the police and the mean rate of cases that proceeded past prosecution. Drawing from data in the flow and snapshot studies, we calculated the flow into court by country and early or later time period. In step 2, we estimated an overall rate of conviction for each relevant snapshot study by multiplying the flow into court measure with the rate of court conviction. Where possible, we also calculated a rate of conviction to the original sexual offense. In step 3, we pooled our total of 65 overall rates of conviction to any sexual offense (38 from flow studies and 27 estimated from snapshot studies) and 22 overall rates of conviction to the original sexual offense (11 from flow studies and 11 estimated from snapshot studies).

In step 4, we compared the mean overall rate of conviction from the flow studies only ($N = 38$) with the mean overall rate of conviction obtained by pooling results from flow studies and estimates from snapshot studies ($N = 65$). There was a negligible difference between these two means. However, some discrepancies of less than 2 percentage points arose when we disaggregated the results in smaller groups, such as rates by country and time period. For example, from the flow studies only ($N = 9$), the overall conviction rate for the United States in the early period was 12.2 percent; with the estimate from the pooled flow and snapshot studies ($N = 20$), it was 13.5 percent (a difference of 1.3 percentage points). To solve such discrepancies, the two rates were then averaged to produce the final rates reported in the essay. The rates from the flow studies contribute 75 percent to the final rate average because the flow study rates are more accurate than the estimated snapshot study rates.

We were interested to test the significance of any differences in conviction rates between countries, time periods, age of victims, and types of offense. However, because our final estimated rates of conviction were means of two rates, tests of statistical significance could not be directly computed. We resolved the problem in the following way. First, using analysis of variance, we tested the mean differences for each set of estimates: (*a*) the rate obtained from 38 flow studies only and (*b*) the rate obtained from pooling the 65 flow studies and estimates from snapshot studies. We then applied the following rules:

1. If the test was not significant for estimates *a* and *b*, the difference between the final estimated means was not significant.
2. If the test was significant for both estimates *a* and *b*, we inferred that the difference between the final estimated means was also significant.

We ran about 50 tests using the two sets of estimates. In almost all cases, there was no discrepancy between estimates *a* and *b*. However, in four cases, the test was significant at $p < .05$ for estimate *a* or *b* but not for both. In these cases, we assessed three factors associated with significance (sample size, size of the effect, and standard deviation) to make a final determination of statistical significance.

E. Study Quality

Adapting from criteria proposed by Khan et al. (2001), together with an overall quality judgment (Daly and Bordt 1995, p. 174), we created a study quality score with these elements: the study is based on a representative sample, criteria for inclusion are explicit, outcomes are precise and clearly reported, and an overall attrition rate is calculated. Quality scores ranged from 1 to 6 (mean 3.63, standard deviation 1.3); they had a similar distribution across flow and snapshot studies, countries, types of victims, types of offense, and time periods.

We considered whether additional weights should be applied on the basis of a study's sample size. Samples varied greatly, ranging from 50 to over 29,000 cases. The mean was 426, the median was 335, and 85 percent of the studies had samples of fewer than 1,000 cases. Diagnostics showed a curvilinear relationship between study quality and sample size. Lowest-quality studies (scores of 1 and 2) had both high and low sample sizes; highest-quality studies (a score of 6) had lower sample sizes than the median. Therefore, we could not weight cases on the basis of sample size alone. Khan et al. (2001) suggest applying greater weight to studies with a sample size above the mean sample size. We explored a contingent size-quality weighting approach in which studies meeting a certain threshold (quality score of 4 or higher, sample size greater than 426 cases) were given an additional weight.

Analyses were carried out with the unweighted sample, quality score weighted, and contingent size-quality weighted for the overall conviction rate and estimates at each stage of the legal process. There were nil or negligible differences between the three samples: the mean overall conviction rate was the same, and the percentages proceeding past stages of the justice system differed by no more than 1 percentage point. These results suggest that despite variability in study quality, conviction and attrition rates are robust and stable. Because the quality score added little useful correction to our estimates, we use the unweighted sample in all the analyses.

APPENDIX C

TABLE C1

Factors Related to Case Outcomes: Adult and Mixed Ages Victims

ID	Authors	Stages of Criminal Justice System Analyzed	Victim's Age	Victim's Good Character and Credibility	Victim's Promptness in Reporting	Suspect Is Stranger[a]	Suspect Has Criminal History	Forensic/Witness Evidence	Victim's Injury/Resistance	Suspect's Use of Force/Weapon
1	Beichner and Spohn 2005	Prosecution Court	+ court V younger	+ court	+ court	... court	- -	+ court	+ court	+ court
2	Bouffard 2000	Police Prosecution	... police ... court	- -	- -	+ police ... court	- -	- -	- -	+ police ... court
12	Chambers and Millar 1983, 1986	All	- -	+ police + court	- -	- -	+ police ... court	... police + court	+ police + court	- -
13	Chandler and Torney 1981	All	+ police + court V teen	+ police + court	- -	+ police + court	+ police + court	- -	+ police + court	+ police + court
23	Du Mont and Myhr 2000	All	+ police V teen ... court	... police ... court	... police ... court	- police ... court	- -	+ police ... court	+ police + court	+ police + court
24	Feist et al. 2007	All	+ police + court V < 16	... police ... court V > 16	+ police + court V > 16	... police ... court	- -	+ police + court V > 16	+ police + court V > 16	- -

634

#	Study	Sample								
25	Fitzgerald 2006[b]	All	... police / ... court / + court / V < 16	– –	.* police / court	– –	– –	– –	+ police / ... court	+ police / ... court
27	Frazier and Haney 1996	All	– –	... police / court	+ police / ... court	– –	+ police / court	+ police / ... court	+ police / court	... police / ... court
31	Grace et al. 1992	All	+police / + court / V < 16	– –	+ police / + court	– –	+ police / + court	– –	+ police / + court	+ police / + court
32	Gray-Eurom et al. 2002	All	+police / + court / V < 18	– –	... police / ... court	– –	... police / ... court	... police / ... court	+ police / + court	+ police / + court
33	Gregory and Lees 1996	All	– –	– –	+ police / + court	– –	– –	– –	– –	– –
35	Gunn and Linden 1997	All	+ police / V < 18 / ... court	– –	.* police / court	– –	... police / + court	... police / + court	+ police / + court	... police / ... court
36	Gunn and Linden 1997	All	... police / ... court	– –	.* police / court	– –	... police / + court	... police / + court	+ police / + court	... police / ... court
37	Harris and Grace 1999	All	+ police / + court / V < 16 / V < 13	– –	+ police / court	– –	+ police / court	+ police / ... court	– –	+ police / ... court
39	HMCPSI 2002	All	+ court / V < 16	– –	– –	– –	– –	– –	... court	– –
41	Hobson 2002	Court	+ court / V > 6	– –	+ court / ... court	– –	– –	– –	– –	– –
42	Holmstrom and Burgess 1978[c]	All	+ court / V younger	+ court	+ court	– –	+ court	+ court	+ court	– –

TABLE C1 (*Continued*)

ID	Authors	Stages of Criminal Justice System Analyzed	Victim's Age	Victim's Good Character and Credibility	Victim's Promptness in Reporting	Suspect Is Stranger[a]	Suspect Has Criminal History	Forensic/Witness Evidence	Victim's Injury/Resistance	Suspect's Use of Force/Weapon
43	Horney and Spohn 1996	All	... police + court + court V > 13	... police ... court	... police ... court	... police ... court	+ police + court	+ police + court	+ police ... court	... police ... court
45	Kelly et al. 2005	All	+ court V < 16	+ police + court	- -	+ police + court	- -	- -	... police + court	... police + court
46	Kingsnorth et al. 1998	Prosecution Court	+ court V younger	- -	+ court	... court	+ court	+ court	+ court	... court
47	LaFree 1989[d]	All	- police V < 18	+ police + court	+ police + court	... police ... court	... police + court	... police + court	... police ... court	+ police ... court
48	Lea et al. 2003	All	... police ... court	- -	... police ... court	+ police -court	- -	- -	... police ... court	... police ... court
49	Lievore 2004	Prosecution Court	... court	... court	... court	+ court	... court	+ court	+ court	+ court
50	Loh 1980	Prosecution Court	... court	+ court	... court	... court	- -	+ court	... court	+ court
53	McGregor et al. 1999	All	... police ... court	- -	- -	* police ... court	- -	... police ... court	+ police ... court	+ police ... court
54	McGregor et al. 2002	All	... police ... court	- -	- -	- police ... court	- -	... police ... court	+ police + court	- -
56	Minch et al. 1987	All	- -	+ police ... court	... police ... court	- -	- -	... police ... court	... police ... court	- -

59	Patterson 2005	All	... police ... court	+ police ... court	... police ... court	... police ... court	- -	- -	+ police + court
60	Rambow et al. 1992	All	- -	- -	- -	... police ... court	- -	... police ... court	- -
65	Spohn and Holleran 2001[e]	Prosecution	... court	+ court	... court	... court	+ court	+ court	+ court
66	Spohn and Horney 1993	Court	... court	+ court	... court	... court	... court	... court	... court
69	Tintinalli and Hoelzer 1985	All	- -	- -	... police + court	... police + court	- -	... police ... court	- -
73	Weninger 1978	Prosecution	- -	- -	- -	+ court	+ court	+ court	+ court

NOTE.—Dash (- -): factor was not examined in the study. Ellipses (. . .): factor was examined but had no impact on outcome. Police: factor positively (+) or negatively (−) related to police charging and referring case for prosecution. Court: factor positively (+) or negatively (−) related to case being prosecuted and/or convicted in court.

[a] Stranger relations was coded positively or negatively for police only for police decision-making process, not for whether a suspect could be identified. When the study reported a negative effect for stranger relations and police laying charges, but this was due to not being able to identify a suspect, the results are coded as "no effect" and flagged with an asterisk.

[b] This study analyzed the impact of aggravating factors, which were defined as injuries to the victim, use of force or threats, and/ or presence of weapon.

[c] This study did not report the specific stage of the legal process when the factors had an impact.

[d] In this study police were less likely to lay charges when the victim was under 18 and reported being raped by a male peer.

[e] Presence of victim's injury was related to charging in partner violence cases; the presence of a weapon was related to prosecutorial charging in stranger cases.

637

TABLE C2

Factors Related to Case Outcomes: Child/Youth Victims (under 18 Years)

ID	Authors	Stages of Criminal Justice System Analyzed	Victim's Age	Victim's Sex	Victim's Good Character and Credibility	Victim's Promptness in Reporting	Suspect Is Stranger[a]	Suspect's Criminal History	Forensic/Witness Evidence
3	Bradshaw and Marks 1990	Prosecution Court	... court	- -	- -	... court	... court	- -	+ court
5	Brewer et al. 1997	Prosecution	+ court V > 8	... court	- -	+ court	... court	- -	- -
9	Cashmore 1995	Court	+ court V younger	- -	- -	- -	... court	- -	- -
10	Cashmore and Horsky 1987, 1988	Court	+ court V younger	+ court V female	- -	- -	... court	... court	... court
22	De Jong and Rose 1991	Court	+ court V > 7	... court	- -	... court	... court	- -	... court

26	Fitzgerald 2006	All	+ police V > 10 ... court	+ police V female ... court	- -	- -	...* police ... court	- -	+ police ... court
34	Gunn and Linden 1994	All	... police ... court	... police + court V male	+ police + court	+ police ... court	... police ... court	- -	- police - court
51	MacMurray 1989, 1991	Prosecution Court	+ court V > 5	+ court V male	- -	- -	- -	- -	- -
64	Spears and Spohn 1997	Prosecution	... court	- -	... court	... court	... court	+ court	+ court
68	Stroud et al. 2000	All	+ police V > 8 ... court	+ police V female ... court	- -	- -	... police ... court	- -	... police ... court

---

[a] Victim and offender were stranger was coded as positively or negatively related to police laying charges only in relation to the police decision-making process, not in relation to the possibility of identifying a suspect or not. When the study reported a negative effect of stranger relations and police laying charges, but this was due to not being able to identify a suspect, the results are coded as "no effect" and flagged with an asterisk.

REFERENCES

ABS (Australian Bureau of Statistics). 1994–96. *National Crime Statistics, 1993–95*. Catalogue no. 4510.0. Canberra: Commonwealth of Australia.

———. 1996. *Women's Safety Survey 1996*. Catalogue no. 4128.0. Canberra: Commonwealth of Australia.

———. 2002. *Year Book Australia, 2002*. Catalogue no. 1301.0. Canberra: Australian Bureau of Statistics.

———. 2003. *Crime and Safety Australia, 2002*. Catalogue no. 4509.0. Canberra: Commonwealth of Australia.

———. 2007. *Criminal Courts, 2005–06*. Catalogue no. 4513.0. Canberra: Australian Bureau of Statistics.

———. 2008. *Year Book Australia, 2008*. Catalogue no. 1301.0. Canberra: Australian Bureau of Statistics.

AIC (Australian Institute of Criminology). 2008. *Australian Crime: Facts and Figures, 2007*. Canberra: Australian Institute of Criminology.

Amnesty International. 2007. *Maze of Injustice: The Failure to Protect Indigenous Women from Sexual Violence in the USA*. New York: Amnesty International USA.

Bargen, Jenny, and Elaine Fishwick. 1995. *Sexual Assault Law Reform: A National Perspective*. Canberra: Office of the Status of Women.

Baumer, Eric. 2004. *Temporal Variation in the Likelihood of Police Notification by Victims of Rapes, 1973–2000*. Washington, DC: U.S. Department of Justice, Bureau of Justice Statistics.

Beichner, Dawn, and Cassia Spohn. 2005. "Prosecutorial Charging Decisions in Sexual Assault Cases: Examining the Impact of a Specialized Prosecution Unit." *Criminal Justice Policy Review* 16:461–98.

Bergen, Raquel K. 2006. *Marital Rape: New Research and Directions*. Harrisburg, PA: National Online Resource Center on Violence against Women. http://new.vawnet.org/Assoc_Files_VAWnet/AR_MaritalRapeRevised.pdf.

Bouffard, Jeffrey. 2000. "Predicting Type of Sexual Assault Case Closure from Victim, Suspect, and Case Characteristics." *Journal of Criminal Justice* 28:527–42.

Bouhours, Brigitte, and Kathleen Daly. 2007. "Youth Sex Offenders in Court: An Analysis of Judicial Sentencing Remarks." *Punishment and Society* 9:371–94.

Bradshaw, Tausha, and Alan E. Marks. 1990. "Beyond a Reasonable Doubt: Factors That Influence the Legal Disposition of Child Sexual Abuse Cases." *Crime and Delinquency* 36:276–85.

Brereton, David. 1993. "Rape Prosecutions in Victoria." In *Women and the Law*, Conference Proceedings no. 16, edited by Patricia Easteal and Sandra McKillop. Canberra: Australian Institute of Criminology.

———. 1994. "'Real Rape,' Law Reform and the Role of Research: The Evolution of the Victorian Crimes (Rape) Act 1991." *Australian and New Zealand Journal of Criminology* 27:74–94.

Brewer, Kathleen, Daryl Rowe, and Devon Brewer. 1997. "Factors Related to Prosecution of Child Sexual Abuse Cases." *Journal of Child Sexual Abuse* 6:91–111.

British Columbia Ministry of Attorney General. 1997. *Survey of Sexual Assaults Reported to Police in British Columbia, 1993–1994*. Vancouver: Police Services Division, BC Ministry of Attorney General.

Brown, Beverley, Michelle Burman, and Lynn Jamieson. 1993. *Sex Crimes on Trial: Sexual History and Sexual Character Evidence in Scottish Sexual Offense Trials*. Edinburgh: Edinburgh University Press.

Brown, Jennifer, Carys Hamilton, and Darragh O'Neill. 2007. "Characteristics Associated with Rape Attrition and the Role Played by Skepticism or Legal Rationality by Investigators and Prosecutors." *Psychology, Crime and Law* 13: 355–70.

Bryden, David. 2000. "Redefining Rape." *Buffalo Criminal Law Review* 3: 317–512.

Bryden, David, and Sonja Lengwick. 1997. "Rape in the Criminal Justice System." *Journal of Criminal Law and Criminology* 87:1194–1384.

Bublick, Ellen M. 2006. "Tort Suits Filed by Rape and Sexual Assault Victims in Civil Courts: Lessons for Courts, Classrooms, and Constituencies." *Southern Methodist University Law Review* 59:55–122.

Bureau of Justice Statistics. 1985. *National Crime Surveys: National Sample of Rape Victims, 1973–1982*. Washington, DC: U.S. Department of Justice, Bureau of Justice Statistics.

Burman, Michele, Lynn Jamieson, Jan Nicholson, and Oona Brooks. 2007. *Impact of Aspects of the Law of Evidence in Sexual Offense Trials: An Evaluation Study*. Edinburgh: Scottish Government Social Research.

Cahill, Lesa L. 2004. "Adolescent Sexual Assault: Timing of Physical Exam, Exam Findings, Prior Sexual History, and Legal Outcome." MS thesis, Gonzaga University, Department of Nursing.

Caringella-MacDonald, Susan. 1985. "Sexual Assault Prosecution: An Examination of Model Rape Legislation in Michigan." In *Criminal Justice, Politics, and Women: The Aftermath of Legally Mandated Change*, edited by Claudine Schweber and Clarice Feinman. New York: Haworth.

Cashmore, Judy. 1995. "The Prosecution of Child Sexual Assault: A Survey of NSW DPP Solicitors." *Australian and New Zealand Journal of Criminology* 28:32–54.

Cashmore, Judy, and Marion Horsky. 1987. *Child Sexual Assault: The Court Response*. Sydney: NSW Bureau of Crime Statistics and Research, Attorney General's Department.

———. 1988. "The Prosecution of Child Sexual Assault." *Australian and New Zealand Journal of Criminology* 21:241–52.

Cashmore, Judy, and Lily Trimboli. 2005. *An Evaluation of the NSW Child Sexual Assault Specialist Jurisdiction Pilot*. Sydney: NSW Bureau of Crime Statistics and Research.

Chambers, Gerry, and Ann Millar. 1983. *Investigating Sexual Assault*. Edinburgh: Scottish Office, Central Research Unit.

———. 1986. *Prosecuting Sexual Assault*. Edinburgh: Scottish Office, Central Research Unit.

Chandler, Susan, and Martha Torney. 1981. "The Decision and the Processing of Rape Victims through the Criminal Justice System." *California Sociologist* 4:155–69.

Chapman, Jane, and Barbara Smith. 1987. "Are Sexual Abusers of Children Treated Differently than Those Who Abuse Adults?" *Response* 10:17–21.

Cheit, Ross, and Erica Goldschmidt. 1997. "Child Molesters in the Criminal Justice System: A Comprehensive Case-Flow Analysis of the Rhode Island Docket (1985–1993)." *New England Journal on Criminal and Civil Confinement* 23:267–302.

Clark, Scott, and Dorothy Hepworth. 1994. "Effects of Reform Legislation on the Processing of Sexual Assault Cases." In *Confronting Sexual Assault: A Decade of Legal and Social Change*, edited by Julian Roberts and Renate Mohr. Toronto: University of Toronto Press.

Cohen, Thomas, and Brian Reaves. 2006. *Felony Defendants in Large Urban Counties, 2002*. Washington, DC: U.S. Department of Justice, Bureau of Justice Statistics.

Combs, Nancy. 2007. *Guilty Pleas in International Criminal Law: Constructing a Restorative Justice Approach*. Stanford, CA: Stanford University Press.

Cossins, Annie. 2008. "Restorative Justice and Child Sex Offences: The Theory and the Practice." *British Journal of Criminology* 48(3):359–78.

Cross, Theodore, Debra Whitcomb, and Edward De Vos. 1995. "Criminal Justice Outcomes of Prosecution of Child Sexual Abuse: A Case Flow Analysis." *Child Abuse and Neglect* 19:1431–42.

Crown Office and Procurator Fiscal Service (Scotland). 2006. *Review of the Investigation and Prosecution of Sexual Offense in Scotland*. Edinburgh: Crown Office and Procurator Fiscal Service.

Daly, Kathleen. 2006. "Restorative Justice and Sexual Assault: An Archival Study of Court and Conference Cases." *British Journal of Criminology* 46: 334–56.

———. 2008. "Setting the Record Straight and a Call for Radical Change: A Reply to Annie Cossins on 'Restorative Justice and Child Sex Offenses.'" *British Journal of Criminology* 48:557–66.

Daly, Kathleen, and Rebecca Bordt. 1995. "Sex Effects and Sentencing: An Analysis of the Statistical Literature." *Justice Quarterly* 12:143–77.

Daly, Kathleen, and Sarah Curtis-Fawley. 2006. "Restorative Justice for Victims of Sexual Assault." In *Gender and Crime: Patterns of Victimization and Offending*, edited by Karen Heimer and Candace Kruttschnitt. New York: New York University Press.

De Jong, Allan, and Mimi Rose. 1991. "Legal Proof of Child Sexual Abuse in the Absence of Physical Evidence." *Pediatrics* 88:506–11.

Du Mont, Janice, and Terri L. Myhr. 2000. "So Few Convictions: The Role of Client-Related Characteristics in the Legal Process of Sexual Assaults." *Violence against Women* 6:1109–36.

Du Mont, Janice, and Deborah White. 2007. *The Uses and Impacts of Medicolegal Evidence in Sexual Assault Cases: A Global Review*. Geneva: World Health Organization.

Estrich, Susan. 1987. *Real Rape*. Cambridge, MA: Harvard University Press.

Farrington, David. 2003. "Methodological Quality Standards for Evaluation Research." *Annals of the American Academy of Political and Social Science* 587: 49–68.

Feist, Andy, Jane Ashe, Jane Lawrence, Duncan McPhee, and Rachel Wilson. 2007. *Investigating and Detecting Recorded Offenses of Rape*. London: Home Office.

Finkelhor, David, and Jennifer Dziuba-Leatherman. 1994. "Children as Victims of Violence: A National Survey." *Pediatrics* 94:413–20.

Finkelhor, David, and Richard Ormrod. 1999. "Reporting Crime against Juveniles." *Juvenile Justice Bulletin* (November):1–7.

Finkelhor, David, Janis Wolak, and Lucy Berliner. 2001. "Police Reporting and Professional Help Seeking for Child Crime Victims: A Review." *Child Maltreatment* 6:17–30.

Fisher, Bonnie, Francis Cullen, and Michael Turner. 2000. *The Sexual Victimization of College Women*. Washington, DC: U.S. Department of Justice, Office of Justice Programs.

Fitzgerald, Jacqueline. 2006. *The Attrition of Sexual Offenses from the New South Wales Criminal Justice System*. Crime and Justice Bulletin no. 92. Sydney: NSW Bureau of Crime Statistics and Research.

Frazier, Patricia, and Beth Haney. 1996. "Sexual Assault Cases in the Legal System: Police, Prosecutor, and Victim Perspectives." *Law and Human Behavior* 20:607–28.

Freiberg, Arie. 2007. "Non-adversarial Approaches to Criminal Justice." *Journal of Justice Administration* 16:205–22.

Frohmann, Lisa, and Elizabeth Mertz. 1994. "Legal Reform and Social Construction: Violence, Gender, and the Law." *Law and Social Inquiry* 19:829–51.

Futter, Stacy, and Walter Mebane. 2001. "The Effects of Rape Law Reform on Rape Case Processing." *Berkeley Women's Law Journal* 16:72–139.

Gallagher, Patricia, Jennifer Hickey, and David Ash. 1997. *Child Sexual Assault: An Analysis of Matters Determined in the District Court of New South Wales during 1994*. Sydney: Judicial Commission of NSW.

Galvin, Jim, and Kenneth Polk. 1983. "Attrition in Case Processing: Is Rape Unique?" *Journal of Research in Crime and Delinquency* 20:126–54.

Garner, Joel, and Christopher Maxwell. 2009. "Prosecution and Conviction Rates for Intimate Partner Violence." *Criminal Justice Review* 34:44–79.

Gender, Health, and Justice Research Unit. 2008. "Rape Attrition: Understanding Case Withdrawals." http://www.ghjru.uct.ac.za/projects.htm.

Gilbert, Neil. 1997. "Advocacy Research and Social Policy." In *Crime and Justice: A Review of Research*, vol. 22, edited by Michael Tonry. Chicago: University of Chicago Press.

Goddard, Chris, and Patricia Hiller. 1992. *Tracking Physical and Sexual Abuse Cases from a Hospital Setting into Victoria's Criminal Justice and Child Protection System*, vol. 1. Melbourne: Department of Social Work, Monash University.

Grace, Sharon, Charles Lloyd, and Lorna Smith. 1992. *Rape: From Recording to Conviction*. London: Home Office.

Gray-Eurom, Kelly, David Seaberg, and Robert Wears. 2002. "The Prosecution of Sexual Assault Cases: Correlation with Forensic Evidence." *Annals of Emergency Medicine* 39:39–46.

Gregory, Jeanne, and Sue Lees. 1996. "Attrition in Rape and Sexual Assault Cases." *British Journal of Criminology* 36:1–17.

Gunn, Rita, and Rick Linden. 1994. "The Processing of Child Sexual Abuse Cases." In *Confronting Sexual Assault: A Decade of Legal and Social Change*, edited by Julian Roberts and Renate Mohr. Toronto: University of Toronto Press.

———. 1997. "The Impact of Law Reform on the Processing of Sexual Assault Cases." *Canadian Review of Sociology and Anthropology* 34:155–73.

Hanly, Conor. 2007. "Jury Composition in Rape Cases: Results from the Rape Attrition Project." Paper presented at the Irish Criminology Conference, Dublin, September 5–6.

Harris, Jessica, and Sharon Grace. 1999. *A Question of Evidence? Investigating and Prosecuting Rape in the 1990s*. London: Home Office.

Heath, Mary. 2005. *The Law and Sexual Offenses against Adults in Australia*. ACSSA Issues no. 4. Melbourne: Australian Centre for the Study of Sexual Assault, Australian Institute of Family Studies.

Heenan, Melanie, and Helen McKelvie. 1997. *The Crimes (Rape) Act 1991: An Evaluation Report*. Rape Law Reform Evaluation Project Report no. 2. Melbourne: Attorney-General's Legislation and Policy Branch, Department of Justice.

Heenan, Melanie, and Suellen Murray. 2006. *Study of Reported Rapes in Victoria, 2000–2003*. Melbourne: Office of Women's Policy, Department for Victorian Communities.

Helweg-Larsen, Karin. 1985. "The Value of the Medico-legal Examination in Sexual Offenses." *Forensic Science International* 27:145–55.

Herman, Judith. 2005. "Justice from the Victim's Perspective." *Violence against Women* 11:571–602.

HMCPSI (Her Majesty's Crown Prosecution Service Inspectorate). 2002. *A Report on the Joint Inspection into the Investigation and Prosecution of Cases Involving Allegations of Rape*. London: Home Office.

———. 2007. *Without Consent: A Report on the Joint Review of the Investigation and Prosecution of Rape Offenses*. London: Home Office.

Hobson, Heather. 2002. *Second Victimization? The Criminal Justice System's Response to Complainants for Sexual Assault*. Halifax, NS: Dalhousie University.

Holmstrom, Lynda, and Ann Burgess. 1978. *The Victim of Rape: Institutional Reactions*. New York: Wiley.

Home Office. 1989. *Criminal Statistics, England and Wales, 1989*. London: Home Office.

———. 1996. *Criminal Statistics, England and Wales, 1996*. London: Home Office.

Horney, Julie, and Cassia Spohn. 1996. "The Influence of Blame and Believability Factors on the Processing of Simple versus Aggravated Rape Cases." *Criminology* 34:135–62.

Irish Rape Attrition Project. 2010. Conor Hanly staff page. http://www
.nuigalway.ie/law/staff/conor_hanly.html.

Jamieson, Lynn. 2001. "The Treatment of Women Reporting Sexual Assault
by the Scottish Criminal Justice System." *Scottish Journal of Criminal Justice
Studies* 7:70–86.

Johnson, Holly. 1996. *Dangerous Domains: Violence against Women in Canada.*
Toronto: Nelson.

Johnson, Holly, Natalia Ollus, and Sami Nevala. 2008. *Violence against Women:
An International Perspective.* New York: Springer.

Johnson, Holly, and Vincent Sacco. 1995. "Researching Violence against
Women: Statistics Canada's National Survey." *Canadian Journal of Criminology* 37:281–304.

Kalven, Harry, and Hans Zeisel. 1966. *The American Jury.* Boston: Little,
Brown.

Kelly, Liz. 1988. *Surviving Sexual Violence.* Minneapolis: University of Minnesota Press.

———. 2000. "A War of Attrition." *Trouble and Strife* 40:9–16.

———. 2001. *Routes to (In)justice: A Research Review on the Reporting, Investigation and Prosecution of Rape Cases.* London: Home Office. http://www
.hmcpsi.gov.uk/documents/services/reports/THM/Rapelitrev.pdf.

Kelly, Liz, Jo Lovett, and Linda Regan. 2005. *A Gap or a Chasm? Attrition in
Reported Rape Cases.* London: Home Office.

Kelly, Liz, and Linda Regan. 2001. *Rape: The Forgotten Issue?* London: Child
and Women Abuse Studies Unit.

Kerstetter, Wayne. 1990. "Gateway to Justice: Police and Prosecutorial Response to Sexual Assaults against Women." *Journal of Criminal Law and
Criminology* 81:267–313.

Khan, Khalid, Gerben ter Riet, Jennie Popay, John Nixon, and Jos Kleijnen.
2001. "Stage II Conducting the Review: Phase 5 Study Quality Assessment."
In *Undertaking Systematic Reviews of Research on Effectiveness*, edited by Khalid
Khan, Gerben ter Riet, Julie Glanville, Amanda Sowden, and Jos Kleijnen.
York: Centre for Reviews and Dissemination.

Kilpatrick, Dean, and Benjamin Saunders. 1997. *Prevalence and Consequences of
Child Victimization: Results from the National Survey of Adolescents.* Washington, DC: U.S. Department of Justice, Bureau of Justice Statistics.

Kingsnorth, Rodney, John Lopez, Jennifer Wentworth, and Debra Cummings.
1998. "Adult Sexual Assault: The Role of Racial/Ethnic Composition in
Prosecution and Sentencing." *Journal of Criminal Justice* 26:359–71.

Kong, Rebecca. 1997. "Canadian Crime Statistics, 1996." *Juristat* 17:1–22.

Kong, Rebecca, Holly Johnson, Sara Beattie, and Andrea Cardillo. 2003. "Sexual Offences in Canada." *Juristat* 23:1–22.

Koss, Mary. 2006. "Restoring Rape Survivors: Justice, Advocacy, and a Call to
Action." *Annals of the New York Academy of Sciences* 1087:206–34.

Koss, Mary, and Christine Gidycz. 1985. "The Sexual Experiences Survey:
Reliability and Validity." *Journal of Consulting and Clinical Psychology* 53:
442–43.

Koss, Mary, Christine Gidycz, and Nadine Wisniewski. 1987. "The Scope of Rape: Incidence and Prevalence of Sexual Aggression and Victimization in a National Sample of Higher Education Students." *Journal of Counseling and Clinical Psychology* 55:162–70.

LaFree, Gary. 1989. *Rape and Criminal Justice: The Social Construction of Rape.* Belmont, CA: Wadsworth.

Lea, Susan, Ursula Lanvers, and Steve Shaw. 2003. "Attrition in Rape Cases: Developing a Profile and Identifying Relevant Factors." *British Journal of Criminology* 43:583–99.

Lievore, Denise. 2003. *Non-reporting and Hidden Recording of Sexual Assault: An International Literature Review.* Canberra: Office of the Status of Women, Commonwealth of Australia.

———. 2004. *Prosecutorial Decisions in Adult Sexual Assault Cases: An Australian Study.* Canberra: Office of the Status of Women, Commonwealth of Australia.

Loh, Wallace. 1980. "The Impact of Common Law and Reform Rape Statutes on Prosecution: An Empirical Study." *Washington Law Review* 55:543–62.

Lovett, Jo, and Liz Kelly. 2009. *Different Systems, Similar Outcomes? Tracking Attrition in Reported Rape Cases across Europe.* Final Research Report. London: Child and Woman Abuse Studies Unit, London Metropolitan University.

MacMurray, Bruce. 1989. "Criminal Determination for Child Sexual Abuse: Prosecutor Case-Screening Judgments." *Journal of Interpersonal Violence* 4: 233–44.

———. 1991. "Legal Responses of Prosecutors to Child Sexual Assault: A Case Comparison of Two Counties." In *Abused and Battered: Social and Legal Responses to Family Violence,* edited by Dean Knudsen and JoAnn Miller. New York: Aldine de Gruyter.

Martone, Mary, Paula Jaudes, and Mark Cavins. 1996. "Criminal Prosecution of Child Sexual Abuse Cases." *Child Abuse and Neglect* 20:457–64.

McCahill, Thomas, Linda Meyer, and Arthur Fischman. 1979. *The Aftermath of Rape.* Lexington, MA: Lexington.

McGregor, Margaret, Janice Du Mont, and Terri Myhr. 2002. "Sexual Assault Forensic Medical Examination: Is Evidence Related to Successful Prosecution?" *Annals of Emergency Medicine* 39(6):639–47.

McGregor, Margaret, Grace Le, Stephen Marion, and Ellen Weibe. 1999. "Examination for Sexual Assault: Is the Documentation of Physical Injury Associated with the Laying of Charges? A Retrospective Cohort Study." *Canadian Medical Association Journal* 160:1565–69.

McMillan, Lesley, and Michelle Thomas. 2008. "Understanding Attrition in Rape Cases: Overview and Preliminary Findings." Paper presented at the eighth annual conference of the European Society of Criminology, Edinburgh, September 4.

McNickle Rose, Vicki, and Susan Randall. 1978. "Where Have All the Rapists Gone? An Illustration of the Attrition-of-Justice Phenomenon." In *Violent Crime: Historical and Contemporary Issues,* edited by James Inciardi and Anne Pottieger. Beverly Hills, CA: Sage.

Minch, Candice, Rick Linden, and Stuart Johnson. 1987. "Attrition in the Processing of Rape." *Canadian Journal of Criminology* 29:389–404.

Morris, Allison, and James Reilly. 2003. *The New Zealand National Survey of Crime Victims, 2001*. Wellington: Ministry of Justice.

Mouzos, Jenny, and Toni Makkai. 2004. *Women's Experiences of Male Violence: Findings from the Australian Component of the International Violence against Women Survey (IVAWS)*. Canberra: Australian Institute of Criminology.

Myers, Martha, and Gary LaFree. 1982. "Sexual Assault and Its Prosecution: A Comparison with Other Crimes." *Journal of Criminal Law and Criminology* 73:1282–1305.

Myhill, Andy, and Jonathan Allen. 2002. *Rape and Sexual Assault of Women: Findings from the British Crime Survey*. London: Research, Development and Statistics Directorate, Home Office.

National Statistics Online (UK). 2008. *Population: National, 1971 Onwards*. London: Office for National Statistics. http://www.statistics.gov.uk/statbase/ssdataset.asp?vlnk=9542&More=Y.

NSW Bureau of Crime Statistics and Research. 2007. *Sexual Violence Information Sheet*. Sydney: Attorney-General's Department of NSW.

NSW Criminal Justice Sexual Offences Taskforce. 2005. *Responding to Sexual Assault: The Way Forward*. Sydney: Attorney General's Department of NSW.

NSW Department for Women. 1996. *Heroines of Fortitude: The Experiences of Women in Court as Victims of Sexual Assault*. Woolloomooloom, NSW: Department for Women.

NSW Legislative Council, Standing Committee on Law and Justice, ed. 2002. *Report on Child Sexual Assault Prosecutions*. Sydney: NSW Parliament.

Office for Criminal Justice Reform. 2006. *Criminal Statistics 2005, England and Wales*. London: Home Office.

Office for National Statistics. 1997. "Population: National." *Population Trends* 90:51.

Office of Crime Statistics and Research. 2002–6. *Crime and Justice in South Australia, Adult Courts and Corrections*. Adelaide: South Australian Attorney-General's Department.

Parkinson, Patrick, Sandra Shrimpton, Heather Swanston, Brian O'Toole, and Kim Oates. 2002. "The Process of Attrition in Child Sexual Assault Cases: A Case Flow Analysis of Criminal Investigations and Prosecutions." *Australian and New Zealand Journal of Criminology* 35:347–62.

Patterson, Debra. 2005. "The Legal Prosecution of Adult Rape Cases Processed by a Sexual Assault Nurse Examiner Program." MA thesis, Michigan State University, Department of Psychology.

Pentillä, A., and P. J. Karhumen. 1990. "Medicolegal Findings among Rape Victims." *Medical Law* 9:725–37.

Polk, Kenneth. 1985. "A Comparative Analysis of Attrition of Rape Cases." *British Journal of Criminology* 25:280–84.

Queensland Crime and Misconduct Commission. 2003. *Seeking Justice: An Inquiry into the Handling of Sexual Offenses by the Criminal Justice System*. Brisbane: Crime and Misconduct Commission.

Rambow, Beth, Cher Adkinson, Thomas H. Frost, and Garry F. Peterson. 1992. "Female Sexual Assault: Medical and Legal Implications." *Annals of Emergency Medicine* 21:727–31.

Regan, Linda, and Liz Kelly. 2003. *Rape: Still a Forgotten Issue.* London: Child and Woman Abuse Studies Unit.

Rennison, Callie. 2002. *Rape and Sexual Assault: Reporting to Police and Medical Attention, 1992–2000.* Washington, DC: U.S. Department of Justice, Bureau of Justice Statistics.

Roberts, Julian. 1996. "Sexual Assault in Canada: Recent Statistical Trends." *Queen's Law Journal* 21:395–421.

Roberts, Julian, and Robert Gebotys. 1992. "Reforming Rape Laws: Effect of Legislative Change in Canada." *Law and Human Behavior* 16:555–73.

Russell, Diana. 1975. *The Politics of Rape: The Victim's Perspective.* New York: Stein & Day.

San Lazaro, Camille, Alison M. Steele, and Liam J. Donaldson. 1996. "Outcome of Criminal Investigation into Allegations of Sexual Abuse." *Archives of Disease in Childhood* 75:149–52.

Savoie, Jose. 2002. "Crime Statistics in Canada, 2001." *Juristat* 22:1–22.

Schulhofer, Stephen. 1998. *Unwanted Sex: The Culture of Intimidation and the Failure of the Law.* Cambridge, MA: Harvard University Press.

Scottish Executive. 1998. *Recorded Crime in Scotland, 1997.* Edinburgh: Scottish Executive.

———. 2007*a*. *Criminal Proceedings in Scottish Courts, 2005/06.* Edinburgh: Scottish Executive.

———. 2007*b*. *Recorded Crime in Scotland, 2006–07.* Edinburgh: Scottish Executive.

Seidman, Ilene, and Susan Vickers. 2005. "The Second Wave: An Agenda for the Next Thirty Years of Rape Law Reform." *Suffolk University Law Review* 38:457–90.

Sherman, Lawrence, Heather Strang, Caroline Angel, Daniel Woods, Geoffrey Barnes, Sarah Bennett, and Nova Inkpen. 2005. "Effects of Face-to-Face Restorative Justice on Victims of Crime in Four Randomized, Controlled Trials." *Journal of Experimental Criminology* 1:367–95.

Sian, Nicholas, Chris Kershaw, and Allison Walker, eds. 2007. *Crime in England and Wales, 2006/07.* London: Home Office.

Silver, Warren. 2007. "Canadian Crime Statistics, 1996." *Juristat* 27:1–15.

Smart, Carol. 1989. *Feminism and the Power of Law.* London: Routledge.

Snodgrass, Matthew. 2006. "Sexual Assault Case Processing: A Descriptive Model of Attrition and Decision Making." *Alaska Justice Forum* 23:4–8.

Snyder, Howard. 2000. *Sexual Assault of Young Children as Reported to Law Enforcement: Victim, Incident, and Offender Characteristics.* Washington, DC: U.S. Department of Justice, Bureau of Justice Statistics.

Soules, Michael, Stephen Stewart, K. M. Brown, and Albert Pollard. 1978. "The Spectrum of Alleged Rape." *Journal of Reproductive Medicine* 20:33–39.

South Australian Legislative Review Committee. 2005. *Inquiry into Sexual Assault Conviction Rates.* Adelaide: South Australia Parliament.

Spears, Jeffrey, and Cassia Spohn. 1996. "The Genuine Victim and Prosecutors' Charging Decisions in Sexual Assault Cases." *American Journal of Criminal Justice* 20:183–206.
———. 1997. "The Effect of Evidence Factors and Victim Characteristics on
Prosecutors' Charging Decisions in Sexual Assault Cases." *Justice Quarterly*
14:501–24.
Spohn, Cassia, and David Holleran. 2001. "Prosecuting Sexual Assault: A
Comparison of Charging Decisions in Sexual Assault Cases Involving
Strangers, Acquaintances, and Intimate Partners." *Justice Quarterly* 18:
651–88.
Spohn, Cassia, and Julie Horney. 1992. *Rape Law Reform: A Grassroots Revo-
lution and Its Impact.* New York: Plenum.
———. 1993. "Rape Law Reform and the Effect of Victim Characteristics on
Case Processing." *Journal of Quantitative Criminology* 9:383–409.
Statistics Canada. 2007. *Cases in Adult Criminal Court, by Province and Territory.*
Ottawa: Statistics Canada.
Stroud, Delores, Sonja Martens, and Julia Barker. 2000. "Criminal Investigation of Child Sexual Abuse: A Comparison of Cases Referred to the Pros-
ecutor to Those Not Referred." *Child Abuse and Neglect* 24:689–700.
Sustainability Report. 2008. "Canada's Population, 1861–2050." York: Institute
for Research and Innovation in Sustainability. http://www.sustreport.org/
signals/Cdn_population.xls.
Tang, Kwong-leung. 1998. "Rape Law Reform in Canada: The Success and
Limits of Legislation." *International Journal of Offender Therapy and Compar-
ative Criminology* 42(3):258–70.
Temkin, Jennifer. 2002. *Rape and the Legal Process.* Oxford: Oxford University
Press.
Temkin, Jennifer, and Barbara Krahé. 2008. *Sexual Assault and the Justice Gap:
A Question of Attitude.* Oxford: Hart.
Tintinalli, Judith, and Marion Hoelzer. 1985. "Clinical Findings and Legal
Resolution in Sexual Assault." *Annals of Emergency Medicine* 14:447–53.
Tjaden, Patricia, and Nancy Thoennes. 2006. *Extent, Nature, and Consequences
of Rape Victimization: Findings from the National Violence against Women Sur-
vey.* Washington, DC: U.S. Department of Justice, Office of Justice
Programs.
Triggs, Sue, Elaine Mossman, Jan Jordan, and Venezia Kingi. 2009. *Responding
to Sexual Violence: Attrition in the New Zealand Criminal Justice System.* Wel-
lington: Ministry of Women's Affairs.
U.S. Senate Judiciary Committee. 1993. *The Response to Rape: Detours on the
Road to Equal Justice.* Washington, DC: U.S. Senate.
Van Kesteren, John, Pat Mayhew, and Paul Nieuwbeerta. 2000. *Criminal Vic-
timisation in Seventeen Industrialised Countries: Key Findings from the 2000 In-
ternational Crime Victims Survey.* The Hague: Ministry of Justice, WODC.
Victorian Law Reform Commission. 2001. "Sexual Offences: Law and Procedure." Discussion paper. Melbourne: Victorian Law Reform Commission.

————. 2003. *Sexual Offences: Interim Report*. Melbourne: Victorian Law Reform Commission.

Walker, Allison, Chris Kershaw, and Nicholas Sian, eds. 2006. *Crime in England and Wales, 2005/06*. London: Home Office.

Walker, John. 1994. Trends in Crime and Criminal Justice. In *The Australian Criminal Justice System: The Mid-1990s*, edited by Duncan Chappell and Paul Wilson. Melbourne: Butterworths.

WAVAW (Women Against Violence Against Women). 2005. "Rape Statistics." http://www.wavaw.ca/informed_stats.php.

Weninger, Robert A. 1978. "Factors Affecting the Prosecution of Rape: A Case Study of Travis County, Texas." *Virginia Law Review* 64:357–97.

Wiley, Jennifer, Naomi Sugar, David Fine, and Linda Eckert. 2003. "Legal Outcomes of Sexual Assault." *American Journal of Obstetrics and Gynecology* 188:1638–41.

Williams, Joyce. 1984. "Secondary Victimization: Confronting Public Attitudes about Rape." *Victimology* 9:66–81.

Wundersitz, Joyce. 2003. *Child Victims of Sexual Offences: Tracking from Police Incident Report to Finalisation in Court*. Briefing paper. Adelaide: Office of Crime Statistics and Research.